The Brand and Its History

T0371915

This book delves into the origins and evolution of trademark and branding practices in a wide range of geographical areas and periods, providing key knowledge for academics, professionals, and general audiences on the complex world of brands.

The volume compiles the work of twenty-five prominent scholars worldwide, who are studying trademarks and branding practices from medieval times to the present, and from specific European countries to the United States, New Zealand, Canada, Latin America, and the Soviet Union. The first part of the book provides new insights on pre-modern craft marks, on the emergence of trademark legal regimes during the nineteenth century, and on trademark and business strategies in specific regions of the world, and in distinct economic sectors and cultural contexts. As industrialisation and globalisation spread during the twentieth century, trademarking led to modern branding and international marketing, a process driven by new economic and also cultural factors. The second part of the book explores the cultural side of the brand and offers challenging studies on how luxury, fashion, culture associations, and the consolidation of national identities played key roles in the evolution of modern branding.

This edited volume will not only be of great value to scholars, students, and policymakers interested in trademark/branding research, but to marketing and legal practitioners as well, aiming to delve into the origins of modern brand strategies.

The chapters in this book were originally published as two special issues of the journal, *Business History*.

Patricio Sáiz is Professor of Economic History in Madrid, where he conducts research on the economic effects of intellectual property rights. During the last twenty years he has overseen a significant project at the Spanish Patent and Trademark Office to analyse and study its historical documentation.

Rafael Castro is Associate Professor of Economic History in Madrid. His research includes extensive work—in historical perspective—on foreign direct investments, intellectual property rights, international relations, political economy of the enterprise, and public economics.

The Brand and Its History

Trademarks, Branding and National Identity

Edited by
Patricio Sáiz and Rafael Castro

Routledge
Taylor & Francis Group

LONDON AND NEW YORK

First published 2022
by Routledge
4 Park Square, Milton Park, Abingdon, Oxon OX14 4RN

and by Routledge
605 Third Avenue, New York, NY 10158

Routledge is an imprint of the Taylor & Francis Group, an informa business

© 2022 Taylor & Francis

All rights reserved. No part of this book may be reprinted or reproduced or utilised in any form
or by any electronic, mechanical, or other means, now known or hereafter invented, including
photocopying and recording, or in any information storage or retrieval system, without
permission in writing from the publishers.

Trademark notice: Product or corporate names may be trademarks or registered trademarks, and
are used only for identification and explanation without intent to infringe.

British Library Cataloguing in Publication Data
A catalogue record for this book is available from the British Library

ISBN: 978-1-032-18733-4 (hbk)
ISBN: 978-1-032-18735-8 (pbk)
ISBN: 978-1-003-25597-0 (ebk)

DOI: 10.4324/9781003255970

Typeset in Myriad Pro
by Newgen Publishing UK

Publisher's Note
The publisher accepts responsibility for any inconsistencies that may have arisen during the
conversion of this book from journal articles to book chapters, namely the inclusion of journal
terminology.

Disclaimer
Every effort has been made to contact copyright holders for their permission to reprint material
in this book. The publishers would be grateful to hear from any copyright holder who is not here
acknowledged and will undertake to rectify any errors or omissions in future editions of this book.

Contents

Part II
Branding, Culture, and National Identity

Citation Information

The following chapters were originally published in the journal, *Business History*, volume 60, issue 8 (2018) and volume 62, issue 1 (2020). When citing this material, please use the original page numbering for each article, as follows:

Chapter 15

The emergence of Italy as a fashion country: Nation branding and collective meaning creation at Florence's fashion shows (1951–1965)
Valeria Pinchera and Diego Rinallo
Business History, volume 62, issue 1 (2020), pp. 151–178

Chapter 16

Dreaming of the West: The power of the brand in Soviet Lithuania, 1960s–1980s
Brigita Tranavičiūtė
Business History, volume 62, issue 1 (2020), pp. 179–195

For any permission-related enquiries please visit:
www.tandfonline.com/page/help/permissions

Notes on Contributors

Felicity Barnes is Senior Lecturer in the Department of History, University of Auckland, specialising in New Zealand and imperial history.

Carlo Marco Belfanti is Professor of Economic History at the University of Brescia, Italy.

Matthew J. Bellamy is Associate Professor of History at Carleton University in Ottawa. He specializes in Canadian business history.

Jose Bellido is Senior Lecturer in Law at the University of Kent, Canterbury, United Kingdom.

Claudio Besana is Professor of Economic History and Business History at 'Mario romani' Department of Economic and Social History and Geographical sciences, Università Cattolica del Sacro Cuore, Milan.

Kathy Bowrey is Professor in the Faculty of Law at the University of New South Wales, Sydney, Australia.

Rafael Castro is Associate Professor of Economic History in Madrid. His research includes extensive work – in historical perspective – on foreign direct investments, intellectual property rights, international relations, political economy of the enterprise, and public economics.

Pierre-Yves Donzé is Professor of Business History at Osaka University, Japan, and a visiting professor at the University of Fribourg, Switzerland. His research interests include history of international business, business history of luxury and fashion, and history of medical technology.

Paul Duguid is Adjunct Full Professor in the School of Information at the University of California, Berkeley, USA.

Igor Goñi-Mendizabal is Lecturer at the School of Economics of the University of the Basque Country (Bilbao, Spain). He holds a PhD in Geography and History from the University of the Basque Country. He is specialised in the economic history of the Basque gun making industry.

Carlos Gabriel Guimarães is Professor of Economic History at Universidade Federal Fluminense in Niteroi/Rio de Janeiro, and former president of the Brazilian Association of Researchers in Economic History (ABPHE). His interests include banking and financial history and the impact of foreign investment in Brazil.

David M. Higgins is Professor in the Accounting and Finance division at Newcastle University Business School. He has published widely in modern business history, with particular reference to the protection of intellectual property and corporate governance.

Andrea Maria Locatelli, PhD in Economic and Social History (Bocconi University, Milan) and Professor of Economic History at 'Mario Romani' Department of Economic and Social History and Geographical sciences, Università Cattolica del Sacro Cuore, Milan.

Elisabetta Merlo is Associate Professor of Economic History at Bocconi University. She has published extensively on the history of Italian fashion business.

Thomas Mollanger, Ph.D. in Economic History (Bordeaux University - 2018), Member of Fiduciae project, and Finalist of EBHA Best Dissertation Prize.

Mario Perugini is Research Fellow at Bocconi University (Milan, Italy), where he teaches economic history and business history. His principal fields of research are the history of Italian chemical industry, history of cartels and history of international business.

Valeria Pinchera is Associate Professor of Economic History at the University of Pisa. Her research interests include Italian fashion history and the history of consumption.

Ramon Ramon-Muñoz is Associate Professor in Economic History at the Department of Economic History, Institutions, Politics and World Economy, University of Barcelona.

Diego Rinallo is Associate Professor of Marketing at EM Lyon Business School. His research interests include trade shows and other collective marketing events, fashion and consumer culture theory.

Alexandre Saes is Professor of Economic History in the Department of Economics at the University of São Paulo, Brazil and President of the Brazilian Association of Economic History (ABPHE). His interests include the history of electric power in Brazil.

Patricio Sáiz is Professor of Economic History in Madrid, where he conducts research on the economic effects of intellectual property rights. During the last twenty years he has overseen a significant project at the Spanish Patent and Trademark Office to analyse and study its historical documentation.

Luiz Fernando Saraiva is Professor of Economic History at Universidade Federal Fluminense and Director of the Research Centre POLIS, Niteroi/Rio de Janeiro. His research interests include this history of intellectual property rights.

Teresa da Silva Lopes is Professor of International Business and Business History, and Director of the Centre for Evolution of Global Business and Institutions at the University of York, UK. Her interests include the history of global business and the use of trademark data to help explain firm and industry growth, and economic development.

Ilaria Suffia, PhD in Business History and Management (University of Milan, Milan) and Research Fellow at 'Mario romani' Department of Economic and Social History and Geographical sciences, Università Cattolica del Sacro Cuore, Milan.

Brigita Tranavičiūtė, Kaunas University of Technology, Institute of Architecture and Construction, Kaunas, Lithuania.

Preface

Since the 1990s, the weight and importance of intangible assets in economies and businesses have increased substantially. Companies, governments, and people have become increasingly conscious of the key roles of knowledge and innovation to competition, employment, education, and, broadly, to twenty-first century society.

In this so-called 'society of knowledge', technology, creativity, and their legal counterparts—including patent and copyright issues—flood daily through administration councils, international institutions, and digital newspapers. Likewise, the revolution of information and globalisation has led to new forms of commercial innovation and the omnipresence of names and logos, in a few decades building a worldwide 'branded society'. Correspondingly, brands (and trademarks, their counterparts) have gained relevance and turned into strategic economic assets. Now, branding is a significant consideration for companies, local or multinational, and also for governmental and non-governmental agencies and institutions, as well as for all kinds of professionals, from doctors and teachers to lawyers and real-estate agents to unconventional occupations such as YouTubers and TikTokers.

At a recent conference on the global impact of brands,[1] Teresa da Silva Lopes suggested in her keynote speech that branding impacts even global vaccination drives during this strange pandemic era. Generally, people associate vaccine effectiveness with the name of one or another pharmaceutical company—over medical technology or scientific knowledge—and thereby establish their preferences. Without a doubt, we are living in a 'society of brands'.

However, contrary to what occurred with invention activity and patents, it took a long time to introduce trademarks and brands into social scientists' and humanities research agendas. In fact, although there is a growing interest in brand research from economics, law, sociology, and business studies, there is still a general lack of knowledge about this key intangible asset's origins and evolution throughout the centuries. Indeed, the purpose of the present book is twofold. First, to review and build upon previous research on trademarks and branding carried out in distinct academic fields; second, to offer contributions based on current investigation of the history of trademarks and brands—investigations that also aim to show the path for further studies.

Thus, this book compiles the work of prominent scholars worldwide, who are studying the origins and evolution of trademarks and branding practices from medieval times to the present, and from specific European countries to the United States, New Zealand, Canada, Latin America, and the Soviet Union.

Trademarks and brands are broadly used as synonyms in non-specialized media but, although complementary to each other, they have distinct characteristics. Trademarks are more concrete and measurable, as the legal part of the brand, while branding is a more complex issue aimed at connecting a firm's values to the consumer's emotions. That is why this book is organized in two main parts (with eight chapters each) focused first, on trademark legal issues and commercial practices and, second, on cross-cultural factors in international branding. These are, indeed, the titles of the first chapters of each part, which serve as introductions to the state of the art and to the work of the authors.

The first part of the book provides new insights into pre-modern craft marks, the emergence of trademark legal regimes in nineteenth-century United States, and the evolution of trademark and business strategies in specific regions of the world, and in distinct economic sectors and cultural contexts (from cognac brandy business in France to the cheese industry in Italy, to Disney's entrepreneurial expansion in Spain and to how trademarks were used to hide the origin of Basque gun-making workshops or to disguise British investors in Brazil). As industrialisation and globalisation spread during the twentieth century, these and other trademark and business practices led to modern branding and international marketing, a process driven by new economic and also cultural factors. Thus, the second part of the book more deeply involves the cultural side of brands and offers challenging studies on how luxury, fashion, culture associations, and the consolidation of national identities played key roles in the evolution of modern branding. The distinct chapters of this section investigate branding in Swiss watch companies, in Italian fashion businesses, and in cultural associations based on the British Empire (New Zealand and Canada), as well as the expansion of marketing practices in international olive oil trade, and the political significance of brands in Soviet Lithuania.

The reasons for the book having two parts with introductory/editorial chapters is that they were originally published as independent special issues in the journal *Business History* in 2018 and 2020.[2] However, all these chapters were part of the same project. This book compiles and makes available all the contributions in a single volume, recouping the project's original spirit and concept. The studies that the reader presently holds in their hands developed mainly between 2014 and 2018. A kick-off multidisciplinary research seminar and an international conference session titled 'The Brand and Its History: Economic, Business, and Social Value', both held in Madrid in 2014,[3] led to a successful call for papers for the aforementioned special issues. Many of the contributions were also presented and discussed in distinct seminars and conferences, where trademark and brand research produced mounting results during those years.

Furthermore, since 2018 the interest in these topics from multiple disciplines is likewise growing. For instance, new historical studies on trademarks and brands led to the International Congress on Brands and Designations of Origins in Porto (2021)[4] and to several sessions in the Second World Congress of Business History (2021),[5] in recent Business History Conferences (2018–2021),[6] and in the last face-to-face European Business History Association meeting (2019) before the pandemic.[7]

With respect to trademarks, there were also specialised sessions in innovation studies or economic geography international meetings, such as the Fifth Geography of Innovation Conference (2020),[8] or in the European Policy for Intellectual Property conferences, such as the last one held in Madrid (2021).[9] Indeed, top international journals in those fields recently published special issues focused on trademark empirical research, including also historical perspectives,[10] and have other trademark issues in preparation. That is the case of the journal *Regional Studies* that, during 2020, collected contributions (finally published in 2021) for the special issue 'Regions and Trademarks',[11] or *Industry and Innovation* that in 2020 published a double special issue called 'Trademarks and their Role in Innovation, Entrepreneurship and Industrial Organization'.[12]

With respect to branding, marketing scholars made a clean sweep in the field. To stay current is not an easy task due to the huge quantity of papers, special issues, and conferences in the myriad subfields. However, we can grasp where the discipline is going through the activity of top journals. For example, facing the process of deglobalization, in 2020 the *Journal of International Marketing* published a special issue, 'Marketing in a Globalized World: Challenges and Opportunities', which included new brand perspectives.[13] Due to changes in technology, media, and the consumer, the *Journal of Consumer Research* delves into 'The Future of Brands in a Changing Consumer Marketplace', with a special issue under preparation.[14] Since the 2008 financial crisis and, of course, with the COVID crisis, it seems that a lively field is on fashion: the Critical Marketing, a new approach that yields an enriched understanding of marketing theory and practice, its role in society, and its relationship with consumers themselves. Special issue projects such as 'Brands & Activism' in the *Journal of Brand Management*,[15] or recently published books such as *The Routledge Companion to Critical Marketing*, synthesise the state of the art and offer historical perspectives.[16] During the last few years, brand topics expanded also in business studies, with a significant increase in the number of manuscripts, especially in the field of family business. The *Journal of Business Research*, for instance, is preparing a special issue on 'Marketing and Consumer Research in Family Business'.[17] Finally, cross-disciplinary brand research arose in topics such as climate change (the journal *Sustainability* has a special issue on 'Cultural Branding for Sustainability'),[18] nation branding (with interdisciplinary research projects such as 'Nordic Branding' at the University of Oslo),[19] or regional science (where the aforementioned *Regional Studies* has another special issue in preparation titled 'Places as Brands: Emerging Strategies and the Challenges of Leveraging Place-Based Intangibles').[20]

Definitively, trademarks and brands are on the map, which, along with current investigations, will open new and promising research lines and produce increasing opportunities for historical and evolutionary approaches. This book proves it. The effort from the participating scholars provides interesting case studies and contributes to a better understanding of the origins of trademark and branding practices in the past and, therefore, improves our present and future comprehension of the complex world of brands.

To close the Preface, we thank all the authors who contributed to this book, for their availability, kindness, support, and patience.

Madrid, Autumn 2021
Patricio Sáiz and Rafael Castro

Notes

1. "The Impacts of Brands on Firms, Industries and Nations", *International Congress on Brands and Designations of Origin. History and Identity*, Universidade do Porto, CITCEM, May 13–14, 2021.
2. *Business History*, 2018, 60(8) and 2020, 62(1).
3. *The Brand and Its History: Economic, Business, and Social Value* (multidisciplinary research seminar), Universidad Autónoma de Madrid, 22–23 May 2014 (see https://ibcnetwork.org/gestion/uploads/news_events/document_9.pdf), and *XI International Congress of the Spanish Economic*

History Association, CUNEF, Madrid, 4–5 September 2014 (see https://ibcnetwork.org/gestion/uploads/news_events/document_6.pdf).

4. See note 1.

5. "Brands, Marketing and Identity", *Second World Congress on Business History*, University of Nagoya, Nagoya, 9–11 September 2021.

6. "Brands and Trademarks in the Evolution of Industries" and "Advertising, Branding, and Merchandizing: European, U.S., and Trans-Atlantic", *Business History Conference Annual Meeting*, Baltimore, Maryland, 5–7 April 2018; "Market Strategies for Local Brands in Global Contexts", *Business History Conference Annual Meeting*, Cartagena de Indias, 14–16 March 2019; and "Branding and Image-Building in the United States, c.1830-1910", *Business History Conference Virtual Meeting*, 11–13 March 2021.

7. "Beware of Brands" and "Branding for Success", *23rd European Business History Conference,* Erasmus University, Rotterdam, 29–31 August 2019.

8. "Trademarks in Space", *Fifth Geography of Innovation Conference*, University of Stavanger, RUNIN, SCIR, 29–31 January 2020.

9. "Frontiers in Empirical Trademark Research", *Annual Conference of EPIP* (European Policy for Intellectual Property), CSIC, Madrid, 8–10 September 2021.

10. See, for instance, Sáiz, Patricio and Zofío, José Luis (2021): "The Making and Consolidation of the First National Trademark System: Diffusion of Trademarks across Spanish Regions (1850–1920)", *Regional Studies* (forthcoming) DOI: 10.1080/00343404.2021.1887472.

11. See the editorial: Castaldi, Carolina and Mendonça, Sandro (2021): "Regions and Trademarks: Research Opportunities and Policy Insights from Leveraging Trademarks in Regional Innovation Studies", *Regional Studies* (forthcoming).

12. See the editorial: Castaldi, Carolina; Block, Joern; and Flikkema, Meindert J. (2020): "Why and When Do Firms Trademark? Bridging Perspectives from Industrial Organisation, Innovation and Entrepreneurship", *Industry and Innovation*, 27(1–2), 1–10.

13. See the editorial: Hewett, Kelly (2020): "Introduction to the Special Issue on Marketing in a Globalized World: Challenges and Opportunities", *Journal of International Marketing*, 28(3) 1–2.

14. See the call for papers at https://academic.oup.com/jcr/article/46/4/i1/5618713.

15. See the call for papers at www.palgrave.com/gp/journal/41262/authors/call-for-papers.

16. Tadajewski, Mark; Higgins, Matthew; Denegri-Knott, Janice; and Varman, Rohit (Eds.), (2019): *The Routledge Companion to Critical Marketing*, Routledge, New York.

17. See the call for papers at www.journals.elsevier.com/journal-of-business-research/call-for-papers/marketing-and-consumer-research-in-family-business.

18. See the call for papers at www.mdpi.com/journal/sustainability/special_issues/cultural_branding.

19. See the project webpage at www.uio.no/english/research/strategic-research-areas/nordic/research/research-groups/nordic-branding/index.html.

20. See the call for papers at www.regionalstudies.org/publications/special-issues/?journal=418#!

Part I
Trademarks and Branding

Trademarks in branding: Legal issues and commercial practices

Patricio Sáiz and Rafael Castro

ABSTRACT
The call for a special symposium on 'The Brand and Its History' has led to two journal issues that focus on trademarks and brands, respectively. This issue is devoted to trademarks, the more concrete, well-documented, and measurable aspect of brands. This editorial introduces trademark studies; summarises previous contributions from economic, legal, business, and historical literature; provides a short overview of the topics and findings of the seven articles included in this issue; and reflects on further research.

'The history of modern brands is to a significant degree dependent on the history of trademarks.'[1]

Introduction

After a multidisciplinary research seminar and an international conference session, titled 'The Brand and Its History: Economic, Business, and Social Value', held in Madrid in 2014,[2] our proposition for a *Business History* special issue was approved by the editorial board in June 2015, and the call for papers was published in September.[3] Over the next 10 months, nearly 30 proposals in various stages of completion poured into our in-boxes, exceeding our expectations and demonstrating the growing interest in brands and trademarks from business historians and other field-related scholars. Several proposals were not fully developed or were only laterally linked to the project, but 20 of these papers made the first-round adjudication before June 2016. Thorough peer reviews took place over the course of a year, after which 14 papers made the final selection. Our call had grown into a two-issue symposium. We thank all the scholars who submitted papers and showed such interest in this topic.

From the variety of topics received, two distinct but clearly related research lines emerged, leading to these two special issues: this one, focused on brand's legal and practical issues; that is, the trademark; and the other, on cross-cultural factors in international branding. Although trademarks and brands are usually studied jointly and may certainly have blurred borders, they also carry distinct phenomena. Indeed, trademarks are the more concrete, well-documented, and measurable aspect of brands. Historically, trademarks emerged before modern branding as a way of connecting goods to their producers; signalling origins, quality, or related properties; and differentiating similar products on the market. Thus, trademarks were usually registered and authorised, first locally and then nationally or internationally, in case of legal actions and the need to defend rights. Brands are more complex phenomena that may be built from registered trademarks or firms' names, but they can also emerge from unregistered symbols; firm practices; or distinct processes that emotionally connect producers' values and reputations to consumers' feelings, creating symbiotic, usually enduring, and—nowadays—transnational relationships. In such a process, advertising, marketing, fashion, and socio-cultural factors may play crucial roles.[4]

This first special issue is devoted to trademarks, and comprises seven articles related to legal issues and commercial practices in distinct periods and countries. The following sections summarise trademark-related research topics, highlight contributors' findings, and suggest further research paths.

An overview of academic research on trademarks

Trademarks and brands can be studied together as related entrepreneurial processes and, therefore, there are key works and common literature in both fields. Notwithstanding this, the purpose of this special issue is to highlight specific research on trademarks as the more tangible aspect of the brand. In fact, trademarks have been mainly studied in four fields: economics, legal research, business studies, and business history.

Economics, law, and business studies

As with many aspects related to intellectual property rights (IPRs), with very few exceptions, trademarks did not capture economists' attention until the late 1980s and early 1990s. The earliest attention was by Andreas Papandreou in 1956, who, in a simple manner, inquired into the economic effects of trademarks and their monopolistic character.[5] Two decades later, an interesting but largely unnoticed work by Surendra Patel appeared on the political economy of trademarks from the field of development economics. In 1979, Patel, an economist and director of the Technology division of the United Nations Conference on Trade and Development, edited a remarkable special issue of *World Development* that focused on the trademark system in developing countries.[6] Especially concerned with the hundreds of thousands of foreign-owned trademarks of all classes of consumer goods, including pharmaceutical products, contributors to that special issue provided analyses and discussions on the role of trademarks in international economics, their use by corporations, their distinct economic effects on First and Third Worlds, and on related legal issues.[7]

Despite these interesting analyses, trademarks as a field was not established for eight more years, until 1987, by the Chicago school of economics, not least owing to the influential work of William Landes and Richard Posner.[8] George Akerlof had previously written on trademark/brands' relevant roles in counteracting the effects of quality uncertainty in the markets,[9] and Landes and Posner continued from that point. The theory was that trademarks are informational for consumers and markets, and, therefore, trademark laws would promote economic efficiency. However, in a certain sense, economic theory has traditionally considered trademarks as the ugly duckling of IPRs. From economics of information and signalling to property rights and transaction cost theories, trademarks have been always analysed as private goods or as idiosyncratic investments and quality indicators, hardly related to innovation or creation processes and far from public goods theory. Therefore, trademarks have held little interest in comparison to patents and copyright.[10] Few theoretical developments have occurred since 1987, and those that have generally are within the same framework.[11] Even revisionists who swim against the tide on the economics of IPRs, such as Michele Boldrin and David Levine, exclude trademarks because they are 'different in nature than patents and copyrights'.[12]

Only recently have a few scholars who are specialists both in economics and law, such as David Barnes, claimed that trademarks can be analysed as impure public goods with simultaneous rivalrous and nonrivalrous uses by suppliers and consumers. Such 'referential use' of trademarks by consumers means that there could be market failures and nonoptimal production/use of trademarks that related laws usually do not address. This means that, as with patents and copyright issues, more government intervention may be required to provide an optimal amount of information about products and their sources.[13] Although this newer approach has links with the economics of IPRs, the neoclassical view of trademarks has nevertheless prevailed.[14] Trademarks are normally treated as private goods that reduce search costs and ensure quality, although the growth of branding has also led to new economic functions, such as the protection of intangible outputs (meanings, identity, or status),[15] which may introduce other theoretical frameworks and perspectives, such as those from behavioural economics.[16]

Private property rights have also been a guideline for a key field in trademark studies: legal research. In fact, IPR practitioners and law scholars were among the first to be interested in trademarking, for two obvious reasons: (1) the analysis of legislation and its evolution can shed light on its effects on business and commercial practices; and (2) there are few better ways to understand the actual work of an institution than through case laws and court precedents. An understanding of these two can lead to new legal proposals that can improve, modify, or even abolish laws or parts of them under certain circumstances.[17] These reasons are behind the first contributions of trademark practitioners, attorneys, and law scholars published in specialised periodicals (such as the *Journal of the Patent Office Society* and the *Trademark Reporter*) as well as in academic law journals between the 1960s and 1980s.[18]

The influence of economics, and especially of the Chicago school, on trademark research was rapidly extended in studies by legal scholars. Certainly, the search-costs, procompetitive use, and economic-efficiency theories of trademarks have impacted law doctrines and still have strong advocates.[19] Nevertheless, starting in the mid-1990s, legal scholars began to question, qualify, and criticise such dominant accounts; to highlight trademarks' monopolistic side,[20] and enforcement costs[21]; and to note other trademark uses and abuses that influenced trademark doctrines.[22] Moreover, certain scholars claim that trademark laws were never specifically designed to protect consumers or encourage information availability in the markets, but were to protect producers from illegitimate copies of their products.[23] These scholars consider that the dominant economic approach to trademarks is overrated, and call for new theories.[24] This criticism has led to scholars exploring new aspects of trademarks, especially as related to their actual use in the twenty-first century; to the limits of their enforceability; and to challenges in the global era, which have been conducted from legal as well as interdisciplinary perspectives: anthropology, philosophy, linguistics, sociology, and business history. These challenges have produced remarkable discussions and contributions to the field, especially through edited volumes.[25]

Starting in the 1980s, trademarks also captured the growing interest of business studies, especially in the fields of marketing, finance, and management. In fact, the first works appeared in the *Journal of Marketing* in an attempt to draw managers' attention to trademark-related legal issues, business implications, and importance of advanced trademark strategies. The first piece, published in 1981 by Meir Statman and Tyzoon Tyebjee, was an outstanding analysis on how pharmaceutical firms used trademarks to maintain monopolies after patent drug extinction and how trademark loyalty was a barrier to price competition. The authors proposed to weaken trademark rights by passing them into public domain at the same time that their related patents ended, especially in critical businesses such as the drug industry.[26] Unfortunately, and curiously, business scholars have seldom followed this business approach to trademarks, corporate IPRs, and public policy, obviously deciding to focus more on managerial and strategic issues.[27] It was not by chance that Professor of Business Dorothy Cohen titled her two influential articles 'Trademark Strategy', published in 1986 and 1991. Cohen first offered thorough information on trademark characteristics—registering, franchising, licensing, and counterfeiting possibilities—and then claimed that firm and marketing managers should be well aware of changes in trademark laws and of court cases in order to design appropriate corporate tactics 'for implementing this tool'.[28]

Such corporate tactics should aim mainly at promoting a firm's trademark, which hints at what has been the main concern of business studies: branding. This was especially true after the guiding work of David Aaker, author of *Managing Brand Equity* (1991), who really opened the door on the complexity of brands and the necessity of analysing brand equity as a function of other issues, such as brand loyalty, awareness, perception, associations, extensions, and globalisation.[29] As a result, brands and branding rapidly replaced trademarks in the business scholars' research agenda, and related publications expanded exponentially. Starting in 1991, hundreds of works on different aspects of branding have crowded marketing and management journals, steering away from the original interest: the legal side of brands.

Nonetheless, several business scholars have addressed trademarks and produced academic studies and offered strategic advice for managers on legal issues such as trademark protection of product characteristics;[30] the consequences for businesses and marketing when laws change, for example, as with trademark dilution,[31] or parallel importation of trademarked products and grey markets;[32] and the effects of significant court cases regarding trademarks and brands.[33] One line of business research has scrutinised, and used increasingly available, trademark data and firms' trademark portfolios in order to assess the financial impact of branding;[34] firms' market value;[35] and specific trademark strategies, such as to build reputations through opposition to others' trademark applications.[36] Trademark data has recently been correlated with different businesses' statistics in an attempt to build new (and sometimes contrived) comprehensive models. These models can include, for example, the analyses of trademarks and firms' investments in information technologies in order to explore product variety;[37] the relationship between start-up firms' trademarks and venture capitalist valuations;[38] and the predicting capacity of firm-specific variables (e.g. company age and size, level of human capital, geographical proximity to competitors, etc.) on trademarking.[39]

Business history

The academic fields of economics, law, and business have provided intriguing research on trademarks, although these fields are not generally characterised by their interest in history. Nonetheless, legal experts were among the first to be concerned about the origins of trademarks, a tradition inaugurated in 1925 by Frank Schechter[40] that, to a certain extent, has continued over time.[41] Many of the legal studies already mentioned, which were published during the second half of the twentieth century, have introductory sections with brief historical accounts on trademarks' birth and evolution. However, legal scholars such as Lionel Bently have recently provided significant contributions focused on the systematic use of history as an analytical tool to explore trademark doctrines and to provide empirical evidence of the evolution of trademark law and court practices.[42] Similarly, although there is mention of trademark history in some business studies, marketing and management scholars such as Ross Petty have recently begun to show serious interest in the history of trademarks and brands.[43] Interest in marketing history led to the creation of the *Journal of Historical Research in Marketing* in 2009, in which it is possible to find works that explore trademark-related issues, such as how design patents and copyrights were used to protect labels before US trademark acts.[44] However, marketing scholars are more often interested in the origins of adverts and branding than in trademarks.[45]

The most relevant effort into trademarks' historical role has come from the field of business history. Although it might be possible to quote several references from general historians of the 1970s and 1980s who dealt with marks in classical antiquity—think Greek vases or Roman bricks[46]—or to produce exhaustive catalogues on trademark symbols in certain industries,[47] the pivotal launch was the celebrated 1992 article by Mira Wilkins on the 'neglected intangible asset', published in this same journal.[48] This seminal work drew the attention of business historians and scholars to the significant role of trademarks (and branding practices) in the rise of the modern corporation during the late nineteenth and early twentieth centuries. Wilkins used the terms trademark, brand name, trade name, and company name as equivalents, although her work dealt mainly with the legal and commercial sides of distinctive signs. A couple of years later, Geoffrey Jones and Nicholas Morgan edited *Adding Value*,[49] a book mainly focused on brands and marketing in food and beverages, in which Jones[50] introduced Wilkins's and Mark Casson's chapters[51] as opposing, or with opposite findings, when in reality they were complementary works on two sides of the issue: trademarking as a legal tool and branding as a cultural and ideological phenomenon.

The trademark baton was quickly passed to David Higgins and Geoffrey Tweedale, who in 1995 extended historical research to Europe through a significant British case study: the Sheffield cutlery and tool industries.[52] The work analysed marketing practices from seventeenth-century crafts guilds to the nineteenth-century modern trademark system,[53] and showed how trademarks emerged initially to combat counterfeiting and signal geographic origin, which influenced trademark legislation. While Wilkins highlighted the role of corporations and globalisation in the United States, Higgins and Tweedale gave prominence to British traditional industrial districts and small firms in which modern trademarks played a decreasing role in global markets over the long term. This early dichotomy between Chandlerian accounts and evolutionary explanations on how trademarks and brands emerged remained in subsequent works, and is still ongoing.

During the twenty-first century, trademark (and branding) historical research gathered speed. Early on, business historians were more concerned with branding than trademarks, which was in line with Casson's findings and suggestions, and they were also more interested in corporations' marketing strategies in consumer goods than in other field of production, which was in line with Wilkins's thesis on the role of modern firms in consumer societies. Thus, several key branding historical cases—related to processed food,[54] household goods,[55] cosmetics,[56] and, predominantly, alcoholic beverages[57]—were soon published in the main journals of the field. Other studies, such as those by Teresa da Silva Lopes and Casson,[58] challenged theoretical developments on entrepreneurship, marketing innovation, and brands.

Trademark research remained active through debates on the origin of trademarking practices and analyses of legislation, business conflicts, and court cases. Paul Duguid, for instance, wrote that discrete and older uses of trademarks in the British alcoholic beverage sector reflected tensions among small producers, distributors, and consumers long before the rise of the modern corporation.[59] Through the analysis of disaggregated alcohol supply chains, first adverts, and court cases, Duguid refuted, or at least convincingly qualified, Chandlerian accounts on trademarks origin, functions, and evolution. Business historians' efforts to disentangle trademark institutions have extended to collaborating with legal scholars. Along with Bently's work on the origin of British trademark laws,[60] Higgins and Duguid have also deepened understandings of legal issues. Higgins, for example, has reflected on the business consequences of the evolution of British law;[61] and Duguid has demonstrated the pioneering role of France in establishing trademark legislation and a national registry,[62] as well as the legal activity carried out by several US states before federal legislation.[63]

Higgins offered for the first time a general approach to trademark statistics when he conducted a time-series and sectoral analysis of the evolution of trademark registrations in the United Kingdom between 1882 and 1914.[64] Meanwhile, Duguid called for expanding trademark research in order to understand modern branding: 'While business historians have given the history of brands a good deal of attention, they have generally given less to the history of trademarks and trademark law'.[65] In fact, 2008–2010 were critical years in establishing additional lines of trademark research. Parallel exhaustive efforts to quantify trademarks registries were carried out not only by Higgins but also by Duguid, Lopes, and John Mercer, who analysed more than a 100 years of trademark data in France, the United Kingdom, and the United States (1857–1870 to 1970). After summing up law evolution in the three countries, the authors studied annual trademark registrations and showed, among other things, France's numerical dominance—or consumer goods prevalence—throughout the period.[66] They thus established fertile ground for further research and encouraged scholars to pursue it.

These endeavours were channelled through several meetings and workshops that focussed on trademarks and brands, such as those at the University of York in 2009: 'A New Kind of Property: An Old Perspective on Trademarks' and 'Branding at the Periphery: An International Comparative Perspective'. This led to a key collective book, *Trademarks, Brands and Competitiveness* as well as a *Business History Review* special issue: 'Behind the Brand', both edited by Lopes and Duguid.[67] These publications gathered scholars from diverse fields, many of whom were working on the analyses of trademark registries. This included Christian Helmers and Mark Rogers, who used recent trademark data for the United Kingdom

(1996–2000) to measure firms' performances;[68] Patricio Sáiz and Paloma Fernández-Pérez, who analysed trademarks registered in Spain between 1850 and 1946 by sector and highlighted the role of Catalonia and the textile industry;[69] Lopes and Casson, who studied how British multinationals protected and managed their trademarks internationally between 1870 and 1929 to reveal firms' strategies to combat counterfeiting abroad;[70] and Higgins, who deepened knowledge about British trademark registration intensity by sector between 1876 and 1914 and provided new perspectives on the role of durable goods such as metals and textiles.[71] Trademark quantitative data were also used in related works published later, such as the analysis by Montserrat Llonch-Casanovas of the Catalan knitwear industry's performance over the long-term,[72] and the study by Lopes and Paulo Guimaraes on the prominent role of light consumer goods industries and their product and marketing innovation during British industrial decline (1876–1914).[73]

Trademark history: transversal topics

Other trademark topics of interest have emerged over the last 10–15 years, in many cases from the aforementioned workshops, discussions, publications, and scholars. These topics cover three main issues: (1) trademark practices in territories outside of Europe and the United States; (2) analyses of how trademarks evolved into brands; and (3) the origins of special trademark modalities such as geographical indications or certification marks. With respect to the first topic, several studies have provided initial insights into Latin America by investigating how global firms handle trademark extensions in different countries. Julio Moreno demonstrated in 2009 how Coca-Cola rejected direct investments when local institutions did not guarantee full trademark property rights, and he also provided comparative results of this strategy in Argentina, Uruguay, and Brazil.[74] Argentina was also the target of Andrea LLuch's work on how legislation emerged and evolved and how trademarks gradually extended through rural areas between 1900 and 1930, a process that established new consumption patterns.[75] Finally, Christine Farley has contributed from the field of legal history to better understand the still poorly known Pan-American Trademark Convention of 1929, which had already convened six times starting in 1889. The United States tried to strongly influence the agreement that came out of this 1929 convention, in a clear defence of corporate interests, by promoting that previous trademark rights in one country (obviously the United States) could block new applicants in other countries simply by demonstrating that the petitioner knew of the original trademark's existence and use. However, the rule of international reciprocity had an unintended consequence: it broke the previously unshakeable US principle of territoriality. The 1929 agreement is still in force today.[76]

Regarding the second topic—how trademarks evolved into powerful brands—it is possible to find case studies that analyse successful companies and their brands by providing accounts on how these firms legally protected, strategically managed, or commercially promoted their trademarks. Nevertheless, there remains a lack of historical reflection on how trademark systems worked in the past, what of their elements influenced branding success or failure, and what factors actually determined trademarks' endurance and empowerment over time. Systematic analyses of trademark registries and related data could enlarge our understanding of those processes. This was the purpose of Mercer in his 2010 work on the origin and evolution of 'brand names'. By looking for nondescriptive word-based trademarks in the British registry between 1876 and 1926 and then cross-checking data from other sources (contemporaneous journals, advertising agencies, and selected firms), Mercer showed a progressive shift in the registry 'from marks as descriptions of origin to brands as items of artifice.'[77] Thus, his work demonstrated a gradual change from classical trademark functions towards the introduction of brand properties such as emotional associations. Similarly, Stefan Schwarzkopf analysed how advertising agencies were key agents in the process of turning trademarks into brands from 1890 to 1930, and how their role evolved during the 1920s from simply using registered trademarks in advertising to conceptualising and developing modern branding.[78] Patricia Van Den Eeckhout and Peter Scholliers turned the issue inside-out when they studied products' price lists from two Belgium retailing firms from 1890 to 1940 in order to explore the actual quantity and evolution of branded and unbranded goods. The results demonstrated how trademarked products increased throughout the period, especially for certain food and beverage goods; how the range of trademarks for the same good widened; and how the two firms followed distinct sale strategies concerning, for instance, own marked products or private labels.[79]

For the third topic, trademark research has dealt with the historical origins and development of special-mark modalities such as collective marks, certification marks, protected designations of origin (PDO), or protected geographical indications (PGIs). In fact, signalling the geographical origins of a product or its quality was implicit in trademarks because initial legislation in many countries only allowed manufacturers with working factories or retailers with open establishments to register their trademarks. As Alessandro Stanziani highlighted in order to explain the genesis of French *appçelations d'origine controlee* in the wine industry in the 1930s, such modalities had an old tradition in France because guild marks functioned as collective-certification marks and indicated origins in the *ancien régime*. Even though such marks were eventually abolished with liberal revolutions, nineteenth-century trademark systems recovered similar regulations when markets and general trademarking did not generate enough or efficient information.[80] Collective marks were protected in Germany starting in 1872, in France from 1873, and in Great Britain from 1883. Likewise, Duguid has shown that several US states developed collective, service, and certification marks during the nineteenth century, although it was not possible to find regulations in US federal law until 1946. Collective and certification marks in the United States were primarily used by trade unions,[81] which to a certain point highlights Stanziani's ideas on trademark collective action as a sociological phenomenon.

PDOs mix geographical indications with characteristics of collective marks and, sometimes, with production standards or certifications. They appeared in the wine industry in the first half of the twentieth century, and were generalised to other food and beverages and even to textiles and other products during the second half of the century.[82] Currently there are hundreds of PDOs and PGIs in Europe and other parts of the world because of an increasingly linked global market, in which geographical origin might be decreasingly significant, as Bronwyn Parry reported in recent works.[83] The demand for famous branded goods strongly exceeds supply capacity from original places of production. What once were essential quality indicators able to push producers' reputations forward from certain delimited areas, as occurred with Porto[84] and Champagne, [85] today function as real global brands[86] with a market call difficult to cover. For some scholars, such as Dev Gangjee and Higgins, original administrative boundaries were not only the fruit of regional conditions but also of political and power struggles amongst producers.[87] Some of these battles were over specific geographical indications becoming diluted and carrying generic terms, especially desired by other regions or countries that produce similar items.[88] Undoubtedly, PDOs and PGIs make interesting topics to discuss that surpass the possibilities of this summary, although a forthcoming book on 'Brands, Geographic Origin and the Global Economy' by Higgins—which we are eager to read—promises to shed new light and data on geographical indications, country of origin, and 'made in' cases.[89]

Contributions in this special issue

All the articles included in this special issue deepen several of the topics discussed above. Carlo Belfanti deals with European preindustrial economies and reflects on the nature and function of masters' marks and collective marks from the Middle Ages to the eighteenth century. His findings challenge the idea of the existence of a progressive path from guild marks to modern trademarks or brands. In a context in which counterfeiting and imitation were generalised practices, masters' and collective marks were not always a way to guarantee quality or origin. Indeed, such marking practices could have had specific functions according to certain territories and centuries: from socio-economic conventions concerning a good's quality based on a guild's mark in the Middle Age to how conventions developed on product taxonomies based on place of origin indications. Thus, Belfanti suggests that in the early modern period (the sixteenth to eighteenth centuries), masters' marks lost ground in favour of other ways of signalisation. Furthermore, Belfanti offers new explanations of the origin of modern trademarking by looking at eighteenth-century Venetian producers' (and especially traders') practices that led to registering logos in order to identify and protect original manufacturers in common but rival trades. Finally, Belfanti offers evidence on how these early forms of trademarks in several countries may have led to early forms of branding (including innovative packaging and adverts) during the late eighteenth century.

Duguid calls again into question Chandlerian accounts on the role of corporations in the development of modern trademarks, and expands his previous findings of early legislation in the United States. Specifically, Duguid delves into the genesis of the 1863 California trademark law to disentangle its precedents and political and commercial ins and outs. At the heart of the California law was preventing adulteration of alcoholic beverages and the necessity of organising a registry for previously operating marks. Duguid's challenging thesis is that the ultimate origins of legal changes were agricultural and retail interests, not manufacturer or industrialist interests. Commodification then was the driving force in Californian trademark dispositions. Moreover, evidence from the first trademark registrations suggests, first, a strong association with place and type of production and, second, a significant presence of associations and, especially, unions, in order to signal the labour characteristics involved in production. All of this highlights 'old' functions of marks in contrast to industrialist accounts. Finally, Duguid stresses how US federal laws reversed these initial paths during the late nineteenth and early twentieth centuries, which reinforced conventional narratives.

Lopes, Guimaraes, Alexandre Saes, and Luiz Saraiva offer fresh insights into the role of trademark systems and British expatriate entrepreneurs in developing economies, including Brazil from 1875 to 1914. Their article extend trademark research to new regions and how marketing, managerial, and entrepreneurial knowledge can be transferred from pioneers to latecomers, as occurred with technological advances. After detailing the origins and evolution of Brazilian trademark laws from 1875 onwards, they discuss trademark registrations before World War I. They found a strong presence of foreign activity and a concentration of trademarks in the textile sector, especially where British interests and investments were higher. In fact, their analysis of textile firms with more registered trademarks shows that those with British expatriates acting as local managers or even shareholders were more active in trademarking. The authors link this to superior strategic and managerial expertise and, thus, to undervaluing Britain's international role as these processes cannot be accounted for as part of foreign investments. The analysis of Brazil's first registered trademarks demonstrates a higher presence of importers, brokers, retailers, and distributors instead of manufacturers, which is in line with Duguid's findings on California.

Similarly, Igor Goñi provides exciting trademark research on new sectors and regions, in this case, gun making in the Basque Country. Starting with a gunsmith tradition in early modern Spain, an entire industrial district that specialised in handguns emerged around the town of Eibar during the nineteenth and early twentieth centuries. It was formed by numerous small- and medium-sized firms that cooperated yet also competed in the same international markets, using registered and unregistered trademarks extensively in order to differentiate their products and achieve an extraordinary performance in marketing and branding. By 1905 the district's production was only surpassed by one European centre: Liège, in Belgium. Notwithstanding the district's success, Goñi shows how Eibar mainly manufactured poor-quality firearms copied from abroad. This lack of technological capacities was substituted with marketing and managerial knowledge—a powerful tool, as Lopes and colleagues also highlight—and was the reason behind the trademark activity of the district. For instance, it was common to use words in English or other foreign languages for a non-usual purpose: to conceal the origins of the product and its bad reputation, which may be also the reason for the existence of nonregistered trademarks. Eibar firms wanted to sell guns, not build brands and reputation. This is one of the more interesting examples of how trademarking can be developed for particular aims in specific contexts. Moreover, as Duguid showed with wines and other products in California, Goñi shows how unions registered trademarks defensively to certify the production of certain parts of the guns. The article ends with a case study to disentangle the marketing strategies driven by a significant firm in the district—ASTRA-Unceta & Cia—which eventually developed an enduring brand of its own.

A new long-term trademark dataset is also the basis for the work of Ilaria Suffia, Andrea Locatelli, and Claudio Besana, who analysed trademark registrations from three main Italian cheese manufacturers—Galbani, Invernizzi, and Locatelli—from 1890 to 2015. First, the authors draw out the general framework of the Italian dairy industry and the origins and evolution of those three cheese companies. They then discuss registration trends of the two main periods of trademarking activity that they found: 1930s to 1950s, and 1980s onwards. They suggest these two periods were responses to adverse economic shocks and the anticipation of market changes during recovery periods. This data allowed for a full study of the particular behaviours of each firm, decade by decade, as well as the types of trademarks they registered, related not only to product names and images but also to logos, packaging, and slogans. The authors linked these data to the marketing strategies followed by the firms in Italy and abroad. Finally, they analysed trademark first registrations and subsequent renewals to demonstrate, for instance, that from the 1980s onwards, these companies looked to the past and to tradition to sell in today's global markets.

Thomas Mollanger explores a classical sector in trademark studies: alcoholic beverages and the supply chain of cognac production and distribution in France and the United Kingdom. Mollanger shows how intermediaries and retailers controlled the final product during the first half of the nineteenth century. They prepared the final mixtures, stamped their own marks for local and regional markets, and developed reputations among consumers. Mollanger's thesis is that the development of trademark legislation in France in the late 1850s and the signature of bilateral agreements with the United Kingdom and other countries during the 1860s were key to reversing this situation. Using the new legal tool, producers were able to progressively integrate distribution and marketing practices in order to transfer trust from final retailers to original manufacturers. Studying one of the main firms in the sector—Hennenssy—Mollanger shows how producers took a multipronged approach by increasing investments in legal defence and adverts and pressuring for control in bottling and labelling in order to offer a homogenised final product. This article builds on Duguid's classical research on alcohol supply chains and demonstrates how the process worked in French cognac.

The final article in this special issue is by Jose Bellido and Kathy Bowrey, who investigate how Disney spread to Europe, and particularly to Spain, during the 1930s. In so doing, they challenge the traditional vision of the key role of IPRs for multinational expansion. They show how Disney neither owned any significant trademark or design in Spain nor enforced any copyright protection during the period studied. Moreover, when Disney arrived, there were local entrepreneurs using the already famous Mickey Mouse name and likeness in drawings that they even registered at the Spanish Patent and Trademark Office. Despite this, Disney succeeded in turning its brand into long-term, powerful, international assets. Bellido and Bowrey carefully disentangled the strategies followed by Disney, which surprisingly began a license policy even without possessing any legal rights in Spain by negotiating with those who were using its designs. Step-by-step, and linked to profuse adverts and merchandising activities, Disney's scheme accomplished expected results. Contrary to what Coca-Cola did—conditioning their investments to the possibilities of trademark enforcement,[90]—Disney adopted a flexible strategy that was both smart and effective. It took advantage of piracy activities to engage with local cultures, negotiate with domestic commercial agents, and build a network of relationships and licenses that eventually helped it first to thrive and then to gain traction on legal grounds. Bellido and Bowrey's article and case study provide new clues on multinationals' expansion and their IPR strategies, especially in the service sector.

Further research on trademarks history

Along with the interesting work on trademarks already being carried out in business history and other fields, there are additional opportunities to expand historical research on related issues. This ranges from the remote origins of trademarks to the development of modern laws and trademark systems around the world, and from the collection and analysis of new trademark datasets to the study of distinct trademark modalities, sectors, and users. Business historians can provide—as the contributors to this special issue demonstrate—compelling theoretical discussions and empirical evidence on the role of distinctive signs in the evolution of businesses' and firms' management strategies.

In this final section, we would like to highlight a specific key issue for further research: the collection, construction, and exploitation of trademark historical databases. As the more measurable aspect of branding, trademark data are available locally, regionally, nationally, and internationally, and business and economic historians have just began to scratch this enormous mine of information. Research on patent history, for instance, has been widely expanded over the last few decades through the growing availability of historical databases. In the age of big-data, new methodologies and perspectives, such as social network analysis, are increasingly used with historical data. Expanding historical trademark datasets will lead to new research possibilities and the opportunity to focus on still poorly addressed issues, such as what role trademarks had in national and international trade or how they were related to innovation processes.

Over the last 15 years, the increasing accessibility to contemporary trademark records generated by current IPR institutions—such as the World Intellectual Property Organization (WIPO) and the European Union Intellectual Property Office (EUIPO)—has led to economic and business analyses using trademark evidence, statistics, and surveys to investigate these two significant topics: trade and innovation. Regarding trade, several works have explored the relationship between worldwide trademark registrations and international trading patterns during the 1990s. The research has shown how asymmetric ownership of trademarks between high-income and low-income countries is linked to export–import structures;[91] how quality and brand differentiation positively affects exports among high-income economies;[92] and how developing countries can use discrimination measures against foreign trademark applicants as 'behind-the-border' barriers to trade.[93] Trade and trademarks have also been tackled through comparative legal studies on, for instance, the problem of parallel imports.[94] Obviously, all these issues can be explored from an historical perspective to answer: How did such links between trademarking and commerce function in the past?

The relationship between trademarks and innovation has attracted even more interest. Traditionally, innovation has been studied from patent and research and development (R&D) perspectives, and only recently have scholars discovered and discussed the potential of trademark data. First works have drawn attention on how pharmaceutical and biotechnological innovative firms use and manage trademarks,[95] and more generally, on how they are a good innovation proxy in the service sector, especially in knowledge-based services.[96] Moreover, based on an exhaustive analysis of 'community trademark' data from 15 countries between 1996 and 2002, and of Portuguese domestic data from 1980 to 2001, the seminal 2004 article by Sandro Mendonça, Tiago Pereira, and Manuel Godinho shows that trademarks can capture relevant aspects of innovation and industrial change phenomena, from product innovation to links between technological and marketing innovation.[97] Since that article, several scholars have explored trademarks and innovation in recent periods and generally agree on their usefulness. Scholars have investigated trademark's links to innovative behaviour and firm performance;[98] their links with patent and commercial monopolies;[99] and their links to innovative start-up valuation by venture capitalists.[100] Other studies have investigated trademarking at the firm level and have provided empirical evidence on why innovative companies register trademarks[101] and what factors, such as size or R&D engagement, influence their propensity to use this intangible asset.[102] Although in 2016 Philipp Schautschick and Christine Greenhalgh claimed that not all innovative firms use trademarks,[103] there is only one paper, by Benedikt Herz and Malwina Mejer, that argues that the observed increase in trademarking over the last few decades that scholars link to product, marketing, and service innovations may essentially be distorted, and that there is a much simpler explanation: the evolution of trademark fees.[104]

Although business historians have begun to stress the relationship between branding and entrepreneurial innovation and have provided first views on longitudinal trademark datasets, as well as case studies on trademarks use in commerce, there is a clear opportunity to expand studies on trademark, international trade, and innovation processes from the past, especially using newly released data. The United States Patent and Trademark Office has even recently released an outstanding and complete relational dataset on trademark case files from 1870 to the present. From the collection of seven million trademarks, approximately 650,000 are from the 1870s to 1960s, which puts incredibly useful data into the hands of business and economic historians.[105] Other important historical large trademark databases are being released for other countries, including Spain (1850–1920),[106] and there are outstanding efforts to collect and systematise historical records in other European and Latin American countries, generally driven by business history scholars or research groups. Thus, all of these initiatives indicate that trademark history has a promising and challenging future and that business historians have a demanding task ahead.

Notes

1. Duguid, "French Connections," 4.
2. The Brand and Its History: Economic, Business, and Social Value (multidisciplinary research seminar), Universidad Autónoma de Madrid, 22–23 May 2014 (see http://ibcnetwork.org/gestion/uploads/news_events/document_9.pdf), and XI International Congress of the Spanish Economic History Association, CUNEF, Madrid, 4–5 September 2014 (see http://ibcnetwork.org/gestion/uploads/news_events/document_6.pdf).
3. See Business History, call for papers, http://ibcnetwork.org/gestion/uploads/news_events/document_23.pdf
4. On the differences between trademarks and brands, see Aaker, *Managing Brand Equity*, chap. 1; Bently, "The Making of Modern Trade Mark Law," 3–7; Davis, "Between a Sign"; Lopes and Duguid, "Introduction," 2010, 1; Schwarzkopf, "Turning Trademarks into Brands"; Mercer, "A Mark of Distinction," 18; Davis and Maniatis, "Trademarks, Brands, and Competition," 120–121; Lopes and Guimaraes, "Trademarks and British Dominance," 795; Barnes and Higgins, "Brand Image," 6.
5. Papandreou, "The Economic Effect."
6. Patel, "Editor's Introduction."
7. Patel, "Trademarks"; Chudnovsky, "Foreign Trademarks"; Correa, "Main Issues"; Greer, "The Economic Benefits"; Alvarez Soberanis, "The Need to Establish"; Venkatasubramanian, "The Law of Trademarks"; Eze, "Trademarks in Nigeria." See also the previous work of another United Nations Conference on Trade and Development staff member: O'Brien, "Trademarks in Developing Countries."
8. Landes and Posner, "Trademark Law."
9. Akerlof, "The Market for 'Lemons,'" 499–500.
10. Landes and Posner, "Trademark Law"; Economides, "The Economics of Trademarks"; Landes and Posner, *The Economic Structure*, chap. 7.
11. For instance, contract theory suggested that along with a quality-assurance function, trademarks also contribute to 'specific performance', that is, fulfilment of specific terms of contracts among firms and customers. See De Alessi and Staaf, "What Does Reputation Really Assure?"
12. Boldrin and Levine, *Against Intellectual Monopoly*, 8.
13. Barnes, "A New Economics of Trademarks," 25–26, 50.
14. See, for instance, Ramello, "What's in a Sign?"

15. Griffiths, "A Law-and-Economics Perspective."
16. Aldred, "The Economic Rationale," 273–277.
17. See, for instance, Burgunder, "An Economic-Approach," 416. For a recent proposal for an international registry of famous global trademarks (brands), see Lee, "The Global Trade Mark."
18. Dam, "Trademarks, Price Discrimination"; Deller, "The Role of Trademarks"; Boguslavsky, "Legal Protection"; Diamond, "The Public Interest"; Fletcher, "Joint Registration of Trademarks"; Burgunder, "Trademark Protection"; Coolley, "Transfer of Trademarks."
19. Lemley, "Ex Ante versus Ex Post"; Dogan and Lemley, "A Search-Cost Theory."
20. McClure, "Trademarks and Competition"; Davis and Maniatis, "Trademarks, Brands, and Competition."
21. Bone, "Enforcement Costs."
22. Beebe, "The Semiotic Analysis"; Beebe, "Search and Persuasion."
23. McKenna, "The Normative Foundations."
24. McKenna, "A Consumer Decision-Making."
25. Phillips, *Trade Marks at the Limit*; Bently, Davis, and Ginsburg, *Trade Marks and Brands*; Dinwoodie and Janis, *Trademark Law and Theory*; Fhima, *Trade Mark Law*; Calboli and Lee, *Trademark Protection*.
26. Statman and Tyebjee, "Trademarks, Patents."
27. Only from the history of science (medicine) has this topic recently been resumed; see Greene, "The Materiality of the Brand."
28. Cohen, "Trademark Strategy," 73; see also Cohen, "Trademark Strategy Revisited"; on the same theme, see Coolley, "Transfer of Trademarks", who offered information to managers concerning trademark transfers, etc.
29. Aaker, *Managing Brand Equity*.
30. Burgunder, "Trademark Protection."
31. Peterson, Smith, and Zerrillo, "Trademark Dilution."
32. Clarke and Owens, "Trademark Rights."
33. Magid, Cox, and Cox, "Quantifying Brand Image."
34. Krasnikov, Mishra, and Orozco, "Evaluating the Financial Impact."
35. Sandner, *The Valuation*, chap. 4; Sandner and Block, "The Market Value."
36. Von Graevenitz, "Which Reputations Does a Brand Owner Need?"
37. Gao and Hitt, "Information Technology and Trademarks."
38. Block et al., "Trademarks and Venture Capital."
39. Mamede, Fernandes, and Godinho, "Patterns and Determinants."
40. Schechter, *Historical Foundations*.
41. Diamond, "The Historical Development."
42. Dawson and Firth, *Trade Marks Retrospective*; Dawson, "English Trade Mark Law"; McKenna, "The Normative Foundations"; Bently, "From Communication to Thing"; Bently, "The Making of Modern Trade Mark Law"; Morris, "Trademarks as Sources"; Bently, "Day v Day."
43. Petty, "The Codevelopment of Trademark Law."
44. Petty, "From Label to Trademark."
45. See, for instance, the contributions compiled by Jones and Tadajewski, *The Routledge Companion*.
46. Johnston, "Trademarks on Greek Vases"; Helen, *Organization of Roman*; Roller, *The Nonverbal Graffiti*; see also Diamond, "The Historical Development."
47. Woodhead, *Trademarks on Base-Metal Tableware*.
48. Wilkins, "The Neglected Intangible Asset."
49. Jones and Morgan, *Adding Value*.
50. Jones, "Brands and Marketing."
51. Wilkins, "When and Why"; Casson, "Economic Ideology."
52. Higgins and Tweedale, "Asset or Liability?"
53. On preindustrial marking practices see Richardson, "Brand Names"; Maitte, "Labels, Brands"; De Munck, "The Agency of Branding."
54. Koehn, "Henry Heinz."

55. Church and Clark, "Product Development."
56. Miskell, "Cavity Protection or Cosmetic Perfection?"
57. Lopes, "Brands and the Evolution"; Jones, "Brand Building"; Lopes, *Global Brands*; Fernandez, "Unsuccessful Response."
58. Lopes and Casson, "Entrepreneurship."
59. Duguid, "Developing the Brand."
60. Bently, "From Communication to Thing"; Bently, "The Making of Modern Trade Mark Law."
61. Higgins, "The Making of Modern Trade Mark Law"; see also Higgins, "Trademarks and Infringement."
62. Duguid, "French Connections."
63. Duguid, "Establishing the Mark"; see also Duguid, "An Anniversary to Mark."
64. Higgins, "The Making of Modern Trade Mark Law," 49–55.
65. Duguid, "French Connections," 4.
66. Duguid, Mercer, and Lopes, "Transactions and Interactions"; Duguid, Mercer, and Lopes, "Reading Registrations."
67. See Lopes and Duguid, "Introduction," 2010; and Lopes and Duguid, "Introduction," 2012.
68. Helmers and Rogers, "Trademarks and Performance."
69. Sáiz and Fernández-Pérez, "Catalonian Trademarks."
70. Lopes and Casson, "Brand Protection."
71. Higgins, "Forgotten Heroes."
72. Llonch-Casanovas, "Trademarks, Product Differentiation."
73. Lopes and Guimaraes, "Trademarks and British Dominance."
74. Moreno, "Trademarks, Institutions."
75. Lluch, "Marca registrada."
76. Farley, "The Forgotten Pan-American."
77. Mercer, "A Mark of Distinction," 35.
78. Schwarzkopf, "Turning Trademarks into Brands."
79. Van Den Eeckhout and Scholliers, "The Proliferation of Brands."
80. Stanziani, "Wine Reputation and Quality Controls"; Stanziani, "Les Signes de Qualité."
81. Duguid, "Establishing the Mark"; Duguid, "A Case of Prejudice?"
82. See, for instance, Câmara, "Madeira Embroidery."
83. See, for instance, Parry, "Geographical Indications."
84. Duguid, "Networks and Knowledge," 523–524; Simpson, "Selling to Reluctant Drinkers."
85. Duguid, "Developing the Brand"; Stanziani, "Wine Reputation and Quality Controls"; Simpson, "Selling to Reluctant Drinkers"; Parry, "Geographical Indications"; Gangjee, "(Re)Locating Geographical Indications."
86. Hull, "Cultural Branding," 3.
87. Gangjee, "(Re)Locating Geographical Indications."
88. Higgins, "The Making of Modern Trade Mark Law," 55–60.
89. Higgins, *Brands, Geographic Origin*.
90. See Moreno, "Trademarks, Institutions."
91. Baroncelli, Fink, and Javorcik, "The Global Distribution of Trademarks."
92. Fink, Javorcik, and Spatareanu, "Income-Related Biases"; see also similar conclusions using Community Trademark applications for the year 2003: Mangàni, "Measuring Variety."
93. Baroncelli, Krivonos, and Olarreaga, "Trademark Protection or Protectionism?"
94. Grigoriadis, *Trade Marks and Free Trade*.
95. Perry and McHugh, "Trademarks."
96. Schmoch, "Service Marks"; Schmoch and Gauch, "Service Marks"; Gotsch and Hipp, "Measurement of Innovation"; see also Flikkema, De Man, and Castaldi, "Are Trademark Counts…?"
97. Mendonça, Pereira, and Godinho, "Trademarks as an Indicator."
98. Especially, again, in the service sector; see Helmers and Rogers, "Trademarks and Performance"; Greenhalgh and Rogers, "Trade Marks and Performance."
99. Davis and Maniatis, "Trademarks, Brands, and Competition," 127–130.

100. Block et al., "Trademarks and Venture Capital"; Zhou et al., "Patents, Trademarks."
101. Block et al., "Why Do SMEs File Trademarks?"
102. Crass, "Which Firms Use Trademarks and Why?"
103. Schautschick and Greenhalgh, "Empirical Studies on Trade Marks," 364–366.
104. Herz and Mejer, "On the Fee Elasticity."
105. Graham et al., "The USPTO Trademark Case Files Dataset"; Graham, Marco, and Myers, "Monetizing Marks."
106. See IBC Network, 'Database on Trademark Applications, Spain (1850–1914)', http://ibcnetwork. org/e_research_resource.php?id=5

Acknowledgements

We want to sincerely acknowledge: (1) the *Business History* editorial board, and especially Ray Stokes and Andrea Colli for their constant support in the preparation of this two-issue symposium; (2) attendees of 'The Brand and Its History: Economic, Business, and Social Value', at the UAM Multidisciplinary Research Seminar (Madrid, 22–23 May 2014) and of our session at the International Congress of the Spanish Economic History Association (Madrid, 4–5 September 2014); and (3) the selfless professional collaboration of dozens of scholars who acted as reviewers for this two-issue symposium: Glyn Atwal, John Balmer, María Inés Barbero, Patrizia Battilani, Lionel Bently, Stephen Brown, Andrea Caracausi, Catherine Carstairs, Montserrat Casanovas, Jordi Catalan, Samir Chargui, Howard Cox, Jennifer Davis, Bert De Munck, Stephanie Decker, Timothy Dewhirst, María Fernández Moya, Gabriel Galvez-Behar, Xavier García, Francesca Golfetto, Andrew Griffiths, Tristan Jacques, Kai Lamertz, Manuel Llorca-Jaña, Laura Macchion, Maria Eugénia Mata, Peter Miskell, Philippe Moati, Mads Mordhorst, Jonathan Morris, Simon Mowatt, Margrit Müller, Juan Luis Pan Montojo, Eugenia Paulicelli, Yovanna Pineda, Jordi Planas, John Potvin, Veronique Pouillard, David Rolph, Jeremy David Rowan, Peter Scott, Marina Shereshева, Fredrik Tell, Nebahat Tokatli, Jesús-María Valdaliso, Michelangelo Vasta, Terence Witkowski, and Sergei Zhuk.

Disclosure statement

No potential conflict of interest was reported by the author.

References:

Aaker, David A. *Managing Brand Equity: Capitalizing on the Value of a Brand Name.* New York: The Free Press, 1991.

Akerlof, George A. "The Market for 'Lemons': Quality Uncertainty and the Market Mechanism." *The Quaterly Journal of Economics* 84, no. 3 (1970): 488–500.

Aldred, Jonathan. "The Economic Rationale of Trade Marks: An Economist's Critique." In *Trade Marks and Brands. An Interdisciplinary Critique*, edited by Lionel Bently, Jennifer Davis, and Jane C. Ginsburg, 267–282. Cambridge: Cambridge University Press, 2008.

Alvarez Soberanis, Jaime. "The Need to Establish a Policy Restricting the Use of Foreign Trademarks in Developing Countries: The Case of Mexico." *World Development* 7, no. 7 (1979): 713–726.

Barnes, David W. "A New Economics of Trademarks." *Northwestern Journal of Technology and Intellectual Property* 5, no. 1 (2006): 23–27.

Barnes, Felicity, and David M. Higgins. "Brand Image, Cultural Association and Marketing: 'New Zealand' Butter and Lamb Exports to Britain, c. 1920–1938." *Business History* (2017) (on-line advance: 10.1080/00076791.2017.1344223).

Baroncelli, Eugenia, Carsten Fink, and Beata Smarzynska Javorcik. "The Global Distribution of Trademarks: Some Stylised Facts." *The World Economy* 28, no. 6 (2005): 765–782.

Baroncelli, Eugenia, Ekaterina Krivonos, and Marcelo Olarreaga. "Trademark Protection or Protectionism?" *Review of International Economics* 15, no. 1 (2007): 126–145.

Beebe, Barton. "Search and Persuasion in Trade Mark Law." *Michigan Law Review* 103, no. 8 (2005): 2020–2072.

Beebe, Barton. "The Semiotic Analysis of Trademark Law." *Ucla Law Review* 51, no. 3 (2004): 621–704.

Bently, Lionel. "Day v Day, Day and Martin (1816)." In *Landmark Cases in Intellectual Property Law*, edited by Jose Bellido. Portland, Oregon: Hart Publishing, 2017.

Bently, Lionel. "From Communication to Thing: Historical Aspects of the Conceptualisation of Trade Marks as Property." In *Trademark Law and Theory: A Handbook of Contemporary Research*, edited by Graeme B. Dinwoodie and Mark D. Janis, 3–41. Cheltenham, UK: Edward Elgar, 2008.

Bently, Lionel. "The Making of Modern Trade Mark Law: The Construction of the Legal Concept of Trade Mark (1860–1880)." In *Trade Marks and Brands. An Interdisciplinary Critique*, edited by Lionel Bently, Jennifer Davis, and Jane C. Ginsburg, 3–41. Cambridge: Cambridge University Press, 2008.

Bently, Lionel, Jennifer Davis, and Jane C. Ginsburg, eds. *Trade Marks and Brands: An Interdisciplinary Critique*. Cambridge, U.K.: Cambridge University Press, 2008.

Block, Joern H., Geertjan De Vries, Jan H. Schumann, and Philipp Sandner. "Trademarks and Venture Capital Valuation." *Journal of Business Venturing* 29, no. 4 (2014): 525–542.

Block, Joern H., Christian O. Fisch, Alexander Hahn, and Philipp G. Sandner. "Why Do SMEs File Trademarks? Insights from Firms in Innovative Industries." *Research Policy* 44, no. 10 (2015): 1915–1930.

Boguslavsky, Mark. "Legal Protection of Trademarks in USSR." *Journal of the Patent Office Society* 52, no. 1 (1970): 44–53.

Boldrin, Michele, and David K. Levine. *Against Intellectual Monopoly*. Cambridge: Cambridge University Press, 2008.

Bone, Robert G. "Enforcement Costs and Trademark Puzzles." *Virginia Law Review* 90, no. 8 (2004): 2099–2185.

Burgunder, Lee B. "An Economic-Approach to Trademark Genericism." *American Business Law Journal* 23, no. 3 (1985): 391–416.

Burgunder, Lee B. "Trademark Protection of Product Characteristics: A Predictive Model." *Journal of Public Policy & Marketing* 16, no. 2 (1997): 277–288.

Calboli, Irene, and Edward Lee, eds. *Trademark Protection and Territoriality Challenges in a Global Economy*. Cheltenham: Edward Elgar, 2014.

Câmara, Maria Benedita Almada. "Madeira Embroidery: A Failed Collective Brand (1935-59)." *Business History* 53, no. 4 (2011): 583–599.

Casson, Mark. "Economic Ideology and Consumer Society." In *Adding Value: Brands and Marketing in Food and Drink*, edited by Geoffrey Jones and Nicholas J. Morgan, 41–58. London: Routledge, 1994.

Chudnovsky, Daniel. "Foreign Trademarks in Developing-Countries." *World Development* 7, no. 7 (1979): 663–682.

Church, Roy, and Christine Clark. "Product Development of Branded, Packaged Household Goods in Britain, 1870–1914: Colman's, Reckitt's, and Lever Brothers." *Enterprise & Society* 2, no. 3 (2001): 503–542.

Clarke, Irvine, and Margaret Owens. "Trademark Rights in Gray Markets." *International Marketing Review* 17, no. 3 (2000): 272–286.

Cohen, Dorothy. "Trademark Strategy." *Journal of Marketing* 50, no. 1 (1986): 61–74.

Cohen, Dorothy. "Trademark Strategy Revisited." *Journal of Marketing* 55, no. 3 (1991): 46–59.

Coolley, Ronald B. "Transfer of Trademarks in Acquisitions, Mergers and Bankruptcies." *Journal of the Patent and Trademark Office Society* 68, no. 3 (1986): 115–126.

Correa, Carlos. "Main Issues in the Regulation of Licence Arrangements on Foreign Trademarks: The Latin American Experience." *World Development* 7, no. 7 (1979): 705–711.

Crass, Dirk. "Which Firms Use Trademarks and Why? Representative Firm-Level Evidence from Germany." *Working Paper*. Centre for European Economic Research, 2014. http://ftp.zew.de/pub/zew-docs/dp/dp14118.pdf.

Dam, Kenneth W. "Trademarks, Price Discrimination and the Bureau of Customs." *Journal of Law & Economics* 7, no. 1 (1964): 45–60.

Davis, Jennifer. "Between a Sign and a Brand: Mapping the Boundaries of a Registered Trade Mark in European Union Trade Mark Law." In *Trade Marks and Brands. An Interdisciplinary Critique*, edited by Lionel Bently, Jennifer Davis, and Jane C. Ginsburg, 65–91. Cambridge: Cambridge University Press, 2008.

Davis, Jennifer, and Spyros Maniatis. "Trademarks, Brands, and Competition." In *Trademarks, Brands, and Competitiveness*, edited by Teresa da Silva Lopes and Paul Duguid, 119–137. New York, NY: Routledge, 2010.

Dawson, Norma. "English Trade Mark Law in the Eighteenth Century: Blanchard v Hill Revisited. Another 'Case of Monopolies'?" *The Journal of Legal History* 24, no. 2 (2003): 111–142.

Dawson, Norma, and Alison Firth, eds. *Trade Marks Retrospective*. London: Sweet & Maxwell, 2000.

De Alessi, Louis, and Robert J. Staaf. "What Does Reputation Really Assure? The Relationship of Trademarks to Expectations and Legal Remedies." *Economic Inquiry* 32, no. 3 (1994): 477–485.

De Munck, Bert. "The Agency of Branding and the Location of Value. Hallmarks and Monograms in Early Modern Tableware Industries." *Business History* 54, no. 7 (2012): 1055–1076.

Deller, Anthony William. "The Role of Trademarks in Our Modern Economy." *Journal of the Patent Office Society* 47, no. 3 (1965): 182–203.

Diamond, Sidney A. "The Historical Development of Trademarks." *Trademark Reporter* 65 (1975): 265–290.

Diamond, Sidney A. "The Public Interest and the Trademark System." *Journal of the Patent Office Society* 62, no. 9 (1980): 528–545.

Dinwoodie, Graeme B., and Mark D. Janis. *Trademark Law and Theory: A Handbook of Contemporary Research*. Cheltenham, UK: Edward Elgar, 2008.

Dogan, Stacey L., and Mark A. Lemley. "A Search-Costs Theory of Limiting Doctrines in Trademark Law." In *Trademark Law and Theory: A Handbook of Contemporary Research*, edited by Graeme B. Dinwoodie and Mark D. Janis, 65–94. Cheltenham, UK: Edward Elgar, 2008.

Duguid, Paul. "A Case of Prejudice? The Uncertain Development of Collective and Certification Marks." *Business History Review* 86, no. 2 (2012): 311–333.

Duguid, Paul. "An Anniversary to Mark: The Who, What, When, and Why of California's Trademark Registration Law of 1863." *Working Paper. Munich Personal RePEc Archive*. Munich, 2013. http://mpra.ub.uni-muenchen.de/51854/.

Duguid, Paul. "Developing the Brand: The Case of Alcohol, 1800–1880." *Enterprise & Society* 4, no. 3 (2003): 405–441.

Duguid, Paul. "Establishing the Mark. A Partial History." *Presented at the Workshop: A New Kind of Property. An Old Perspective on Trademarks*, University of York (UK), November 2009.

Duguid, Paul. "French Connections: The International Propagation of Trademarks in the Nineteenth Century." *Enterprise & Society* 10, no. 1 (2009): 3–37.

Duguid, Paul. "Networks and Knowledge: The Beginning and End of the Port Commodity Chain, 1703–1860." *Business History Review* 79, no. 3 (2005): 493–526.

Duguid, Paul, John Mercer, and Teresa da Silva Lopes. "Reading Registrations. An Overview of 100 Years of Trademark Registrations in France, the United Kingdom, and the United States." In *Trademarks, Brands, and Competitiveness*, edited by Paul Duguid and Teresa da Silva Lopes, 9–30. New York, NY: Routledge, 2010.

Duguid, Paul, John Mercer, and Teresa da Silva Lopes. "Transactions and Interactions. Preliminary Reflections on a Hundred Years of Trade Mark Registration Data." In *EHBA 12th Annual Congress*. Bergen, Norway, 2008. http://www.ebha.org/ebha2008/papers/Duguid-Mercer-Lopes_ebha_2008.pdf.

Economides, Nicholas S. "The Economics of Trademarks." *Trademark Reporter* 78 (1988): 523–539.

Eze, Osita C. "Trademarks in Nigeria." *World Development* 7, no. 7 (1979): 727–736.

Farley, Christine Haight. "The Forgotten Pan-American Trademark Convention of 1929: A Bold Vision of Extraterritorial Meets Current Realities." *Working Paper*. American University Washington College Law, 2013.

Fernandez, Eva. "Unsuccessful Responses to Quality Uncertainty: Brands in Spain's Sherry Industry, 1920-1990." *Business History* 52, no. 1 (2010): 100–119.

Fhima, Ilanah Simon, ed. *Trade Mark Law and Sharing Names: Exploring Use of the Same Mark by Multiple Undertakings*. Cheltenham, UK: Edward Elgar, 2009.

Fink, Carsten, Beata Smarzynska Javorcik, and Mariana Spatareanu. "Income-Related Biases in International Trade: What Do Trademark Registration Data Tell Us?" *Review of World Economics* 141, no. 1 (2005): 79–103.

Fletcher, Patricia Kimball. "Joint Registration of Trademarks and the Economic Value of a Trademark System." *University of Miami Law Review* 36 (1982): 297–335.

Flikkema, Meindert, Ard-Pieter De Man, and Carolina Castaldi. "Are Trademark Counts a Valid Indicator of Innovation? Results of an in-Depth Study of New Benelux Trademarks Filed by SMEs." *Industry and Innovation* 21, no. 4 (2014): 310–331.

Gangjee, Dev. "(Re)Locating Geographical Indications: A Response to Bronwyn Parry." In *Trade Marks and Brands. An Interdisciplinary Critique*, edited by Lionel Bently, Jennifer Davis, and Jane C. Ginsburg, 381–397. Cambridge: Cambridge University Press, 2008.

Gao, Guodong, and Lorin M. Hitt. "Information Technology and Trademarks: Implications for Product Variety." *Management Science* 58, no. 6 (2012): 1211–1226.

Gotsch, Matthias, and Christiane Hipp. "Measurement of Innovation Activities in the Knowledge-Intensive Services Industry: A Trademark Approach." *Service Industries Journal* 32, no. 13 (2012): 2167–2184.

Graham, Stuart J. H., Galen Hancock, Alan C. Marco, and Amanda Fila Myers. "The USPTO Trademark Case Files Dataset: Descriptions, Lessons, and Insights." *Journal of Economics & Management Strategy* 22, no. 4 (2013): 669–705.

Graham, Stuart J. H., Alan C. Marco, and Amanda Fila Myers. "Monetizing Marks: Insights from the USPTO Trademark Assignment Dataset." *Scholarly Paper*. Rochester, NY: Social Science Research Network, 2015. https://papers.ssrn.com/abstract=2430962.

Greene, Jeremy A. "The Materiality of the Brand: Form, Function, and the Pharmaceutical Trademark." *History and Technology* 29, no. 2 (2013): 210–226.

Greenhalgh, Christine, and Mark Rogers. "Trade Marks and Performance in Services and Manufacturing Firms: Evidence of Schumpeterian Competition through Innovation." *Australian Economic Review* 45, no. 1 (2012): 50–76.

Greer, Douglas F. "The Economic Benefits and Costs of Trademarks: Lessons for the Developing Countries." *World Development* 7, no. 7 (1979): 683–704.

Griffiths, Andrew. "A Law-and-Economics Perspective on Trade Marks." In *Trade Marks and Brands. An Interdisciplinary Critique*, edited by Lionel Bently, Jennifer Davis, and Jane C. Ginsburg, 241–266. Cambridge: Cambridge University Press, 2008.

Grigoriadis, Lazaros G. *Trade Marks and Free Trade: A Global Analysis*. Heidelberg: Springer International Publishing, 2014.

Helen, Tapio. *Organization of Roman Brick Production in the First and Second Centuries A. D.: An Interpretation of Roman Brick Stamps*. Helsinki: Institutum Romanum Finlandiae, 1975.

Helmers, Christian, and Mark Rogers. "Trademarks and Performance in UK Firms." In *Trademarks, Brands, and Competitiveness*, edited by Teresa da Silva Lopes and Paul Duguid, 55–76. New York, NY: Routledge, 2010.

Herz, Benedikt, and Malwina Mejer. "On the Fee Elasticity of the Demand for Trademarks in Europe." *Oxford Economic Papers* 68, no. 4 (2016): 1039–1061.

Higgins, David M. *Brands, Geographic Origin, and the Global Economy: A History from the Nineteenth Century to the Present*. Cambridge: Cambridge University Press, 2018.

Higgins, David M. "'Forgotten Heroes and Forgotten Issues': Business and Trademark History during the Nineteenth Century." *Business History Review* 86, no. 2 (2012): 261–285.

Higgins, David M. "The Making of Modern Trade Mark Law: The UK, 1860–1914. A Business History Perspective." In *Trade Marks and Brands. An Interdisciplinary Critique*, edited by Lionel Bently, Jennifer Davis, and Jane C. Ginsburg, 42–62. Cambridge: Cambridge University Press, 2008.

Higgins, David M. "Trademarks and Infringement in Britain, c.1875-c.1900." In *Trademarks, Brands, and Competitiveness*, edited by Teresa da Silva Lopes and Paul Duguid, 102–118. New York, NY: Routledge, 2010.

Higgins, David M., and Geoffrey Tweedale. "Asset or Liability? Trade Marks in the Sheffield Cutlery and Tool Trades." *Business History* 37, no 3 (1995): 1–27.

Hull, Gordon. "Cultural Branding, Geographic Source Indicators and Commodification." *Theory, Culture & Society* 33, no. 2 (2016): 125–145.

Johnston, A. W. "Trademarks on Greek Vases." *Greece & Rome* 21, no. 2 (1974): 138–152.

Jones, D. G. Brian, and Mark Tadajewski, eds. *The Routledge Companion to Marketing History*. London: Routledge, 2016.

Jones, Geoffrey. "Brands and Marketing." In *Adding Value: Brands and Marketing in Food and Drink*, edited by Geoffrey Jones and Nicholas J. Morgan, 1–12. London: Routledge, 1994.

Jones, Geoffrey, and Nicholas J. Morgan, eds. *Adding Value: Brands and Marketing in Food and Drink*. London: Routledge, 1994.

Jones, Stephen R. H. "Brand Building and Structural Change in the Scotch Whisky Industry since 1975." *Business History* 45, no. 3 (2003): 72–89.

Koehn, Nancy F. "Henry Heinz and Brand Creation in the Late Nineteenth Century: Making Markets for Processed Food." *Business History Review* 73, no. 3 (1999): 349–393.

Krasnikov, Alexander, Saurabh Mishra, and David Orozco. "Evaluating the Financial Impact of Branding Using Trademarks: A Framework and Empirical Evidence." *Journal of Marketing* 73, no. 6 (2009): 154–166.

Landes, William M., and Richard A. Posner. *The Economic Structure of Intellectual Property Law*. Cambridge, MA: Harvard University Press, 2003.

Landes, William M., and Richard A. Posner. "Trademark Law: An Economic Perspective." *Journal of Law and Economics* 30, no. 2 (1987): 265–309.

Lee, Edward. "The Global Trade Mark." *University of Pennsylvania Journal of International Law* 35, no. 4 (2014): 917–967.

Lemley, Mark A. "Ex Ante versus Ex Post Justifications for Intellectual Property." *The University of Chicago Law Review* 71, no. 1 (2004): 129–149.

Llonch-Casanovas, Montserrat. "Trademarks, Product Differentiation and Competitiveness in the Catalan Knitwear Districts during the Twentieth Century." *Business History* 54, no. 2 (2012): 179–200.

Lluch, Andrea. "Marca registrada… Reflexiones sobre el uso de las marcas comerciales, el consumo y la comercialización de bienes en el mundo rural argentino (1900-1930)." *Mundo Agrario* 13, no. 26 (2013): 1–25.

Lopes, Teresa da Silva. "Brands and the Evolution of Multinationals in Alcoholic Beverages." *Business History* 44, no. 3 (2002): 1–30.

Lopes, Teresa da Silva. *Global Brands: The Evolution of Multinationals in Alcoholic Beverages*. Cambridge: Cambridge University Press, 2007.

Lopes, Teresa da Silva, and Mark Casson. "Brand Protection and the Globalization of British Business." *Business History Review* 86, no. 2 (2012): 287–310.

Lopes, Teresa da Silva, and Mark Casson. "Entrepreneurship and the Development of Global Brands." *Business History Review* 81, no. 4 (2007): 651–680.

Lopes, Teresa da Silva, and Paul Duguid. "Introduction: Behind the Brand." *Business History Review* 86, no. 2 (2012): 235–238.

Lopes, Teresa da Silva, and Paul Duguid. "Introduction: Brands and Competitiveness." In *Trademarks, Brands, and Competitiveness*, edited by Teresa da Silva Lopes and Paul Duguid, 1–8. New York, NY: Routledge, 2010.

Lopes, Teresa da Silva, and Paulo Guimaraes. "Trademarks and British Dominance in Consumer Goods, 1876–1914." *Economic History Review* 67, no. 3 (2014): 793–817.

Magid, Julie Manning, Anthony D. Cox, and Dena S. Cox. "Quantifying Brand Image: Empirical Evidence of Trademark Dilution." *American Business Law Journal* 43, no. 1 (2006): 1–42.

Maitte, Corine. "Labels, Brands, and Market Integration in the Modern Era." *Business and Economic History On-Line* 7 (2009): 1–16.

Mamede, Ricardo P., Teresa F. Fernandes, and Manuel M. Godinho. "Patterns and Determinants of Trademark Use in Portugal." In *Knowledge-Intensive Entrepreneurship in Low-Tech Industries*, edited by Hartmut Hirsch-Kreinsen and Isabel Schwinge, 95–116. Cheltenham, UK: Edward Elgar, 2014.

Mangàni, Andrea. "Measuring Variety and Quality of Products with Trademarks." *International Economic Journal* 21, no. 4 (2007): 613–631.

McClure, Daniel M. "Trademarks and Competition: The Recent History." *Law and Contemporary Problems* 59, no. 2 (1996): 13–43.

McKenna, Mark P. "A Consumer Decision-Making Theory of Trademark Law." *Virginia Law Review* 98, no. 1 (2012): 67–141.

McKenna, Mark P. "The Normative Foundations of Trademark Law." *Notre Dame Law Review* 82, no. 5 (2007): 1839–1916.

Mendonça, Sandro, Tiago Santos Pereira, and Manuel Mira Godinho. "Trademarks as an Indicator of Innovation and Industrial Change." *Research Policy* 33, no. 9 (2004): 1385–1404.

Mercer, John. "A Mark of Distinction: Branding and Trade Mark Law in the UK from the 1860s." *Business History* 52, no. 1 (2010): 17–42.

Miskell, Peter. "Cavity Protection or Cosmetic Perfection? Innovation and Marketing of Toothpaste Brands in the United States and Western Europe, 1955–1985." *Business History Review* 78, no. 1 (2004): 29–60.

Moreno, Julio E. "Trademarks, Institutions, and Coca-Cola's Corporate Expansion to South America." *Presented at the Workshop: Branding at the Periphery: An International Comparative Perspective,* University of York (UK), November 2009.

Morris, P. Sean. "Trademarks as Sources of Market Power: Legal and Historical Encounters." *Liverpool Law Review* 38, no. 2 (2017): 159–185.

O'Brien, Peter. "Trademarks in Developing Countries." *Journal of Modern African Studies* 14, no. 2 (1976): 297–309.

Papandreou, Andreas G. "The Economic Effect of Trademarks." *California Law Review* 44, no. 3 (1956): 503–510.

Parry, Bronwyn. "Geographical Indications: Not All 'Champagne and Roses.'" In *Trade Marks and Brands. An Interdisciplinary Critique,* edited by Lionel Bently, Jennifer Davis, and Jane C. Ginsburg, 361–380. Cambridge: Cambridge University Press, 2008.

Patel, Surendra J. "Editor's Introduction." *World Development* 7, no. 7 (1979): 649–651.

Patel, Surendra J. "Trademarks and the Third World." *World Development* 7, no. 7 (1979): 653–662.

Perry, E. Lynn, and Margaret C. McHugh. "Trademarks: The 'Misunderstood' Intellectual Property. There's More to a Company's Intellectual Property than Its Patents and Trade Secrets." *Nature Biotechnology* 20, no. 6 (2002): 627–628.

Peterson, Robert A., Karen H. Smith, and Philip C. Zerrillo. "Trademark Dilution and the Practice of Marketing." *Journal of the Academy of Marketing Science* 27, no. 2 (1999): 255–268.

Petty, Ross D. "From Label to Trademark: The Legal Origins of the Concept of Brand Identity in Nineteenth Century America." *Journal of Historical Research in Marketing* 4, no. 1 (2012): 129–153.

Petty, Ross D. "The Codevelopment of Trademark Law and the Concept of Brand Marketing in the United States before 1946." *Journal of Macromarketing* 31, no. 1 (2011): 85–99.

Phillips, Jeremy, ed. *Trade Marks at the Limit.* Cheltenham, UK: Edward Elgar Publishing, 2006.

Ramello, Giovanni B. "What's in a Sign? Trademark Law and Economic Theory." *Journal of Economic Surveys* 20, no. 4 (2006): 547–565.

Richardson, Gary. "Brand Names before the Industrial Revolution." *Working Paper no. 13930.* National Bureau of Economic Research, 2008. http://www.nber.org/papers/w13930.pdf

Roller, Lynn E. *Gordion Special Studies I: The Nonverbal Graffiti, Dipinti, and Stamps.* Philadelphia, PA: The University Museum - University of Pennsylvania, 1987.

Sáiz, Patricio, and Rafael Castro. "Foreign Direct Investments and Intellectual Property Rights. International Intangible Assets in Spain circa 1820–1939." *Enterprise & Society* 18, no. 4 (2017): 846–892.

Sáiz, Patricio, and Paloma Fernández-Pérez. "Catalonian Trademarks and the Development of Marketing Knowledge in Spain, 1850–1946." *Business History Review* 86, no. 2 (2012): 239–260.

Sandner, Philipp G. *The Valuation of Intangible Assets: An Exploration of Patent and Trademark Portfolios.* Wiesbaden: Springer Gabler, 2009.

Sandner, Philipp G., and Joern Block. "The Market Value of R&D, Patents, and Trademarks." *Research Policy* 40, no. 7 (2011): 969–985.

Schautschick, Philipp, and Christine Greenhalgh. "Empirical Studies of Trade Marks. The Existing Economic Literature." *Economics of Innovation and New Technology* 25, no. 4 (2016): 358–390.

Schechter, Frank I. *Historical Foundations of the Law Relating to Trade-Marks.* New York, NY: Columbia University Press, 1925.

Schmoch, Ulrich. "Service Marks as Novel Innovation Indicator." *Research Evaluation* 12, no. 2 (2003): 149–156.

Schmoch, Ulrich, and Stephan Gauch. "Service Marks as Indicators for Innovation in Knowledge-Based Services." *Research Evaluation* 18, no. 4 (2009): 323–335.

Schwarzkopf, Stefan. "Turning Trademarks into Brands: How Advertising Agencies Practiced and Conceptualized Branding, 1890–1930." In *Trademarks, Brands, and Competitiveness*, edited by Teresa da Silva Lopes and Paul Duguid, 165–193. New York, NY: Routledge, 2010.

Simpson, James. "Selling to Reluctant Drinkers: The British Wine Market, 1860–1914." *Economic History Review* 57, no. 1 (2004): 80–108.

Stanziani, Alessandro. "Les Signes de Qualité. Normes, Réputation et Confiance (XIXe-XXe Siècles)." *Revue de Synthèse* 127, no. 2 (2006): 329–358.

Stanziani, Alessandro. "Wine Reputation and Quality Controls: The Origin of the AOCs in 19th Century France." *European Journal of Law and Economics* 18, no. 2 (2004): 149–167.

Statman, Meir, and Tyzoon T. Tyebjee. "Trademarks, Patents, and Innovation in the Ethical Drug Industry." *Journal of Marketing* 45, no. 3 (1981): 71–81.

Van Den Eeckhout, Patricia, and Peter Scholliers. "The Proliferation of Brands: The Case of Food in Belgium, 1890–1940." *Enterprise & Society* 13, no. 1 (2012): 53–84.

Venkatasubramanian, P. B. "The Law of Trademarks in India." *World Development* 7, no. 7 (1979): 737–746.

Von Graevenitz, Georg. "Which Reputations Does a Brand Owner Need? Evidence from Trade Mark Opposition." *Discussion Paper*. GESY. SBF/TR 15, 2007. http://papers.ssrn.com/sol3/papers.cfm?abstract_id=1443425.

Wilkins, Mira. "The Neglected Intangible Asset: The Influence of the Trade Mark on the Rise of the Modern Corporation." *Business History* 34, no. 1 (1992): 66–95.

Wilkins, Mira. "When and Why Brand Names in Food and Drink?" In *Adding Value: Brands and Marketing in Food and Drink*, edited by Geoffrey Jones and Nicholas J. Morgan, 15–40. London: Routledge, 1994.

Woodhead, Eileen. *Trademarks on Base-Metal Tableware: Late 18th Century to circa 1900 (Including Marks on Britannia Metal, Iron, Steel, Copper Alloys, and Silver-Plated Goods). Studies in Archaeology, Architecture, and History*. Ottawa: National Historic Sites, Parks Service, Environment Canada, 1991.

Zhou, Haibo, Philipp G. Sandner, Simon Luca Martinelli, and Joern H. Block. "Patents, Trademarks, and Their Complementarity in Venture Capital Funding." *Technovation* 47 (2016): 14–22.

Branding before the brand: Marks, imitations and counterfeits in pre-modern Europe

Carlo Marco Belfanti

ABSTRACT

This article aims to analyse the practices of branding adopted in the European pre-modern economy in order to communicate information about the product to the consumer. It examines the nature and function of master's marks and collective marks and their interaction with processes of imitation and counterfeiting, and takes a stance in the debate on the origins of the modern brand, arguing in favour of the thesis that early forms of brand may be found only in the economic context of the eighteenth century and not before.

1. Introduction

Economic and business historians set the analysis of the brand in a context characterised, on the one hand, by the progressive differentiation in the brand itself from the – prevalently legal- sphere of the trademark, and on the other, by the dynamics of competitiveness, where the time frame of reference for this evolution is that of the nineteenth and twentieth centuries.[1] As far as the first aspect is concerned, it is noted however, that diverse authors maintain that the practice of branding is much more antique: from the Middle Ages onwards, single craftsmen and guilds used marks singly and collectively to define a framework of qualitative standards and to furnish the consumer with information about the product, while the literature on the topic regarding the brand includes studies that set its origins in periods as far apart as antiquity and the eighteenth century.[2] Secondly, some of the interaction generated by trademarks and brands as factors of competitiveness in the economy of the nineteenth and twentieth centuries may already be detectable in the markets of the pre-modern age:[3] for this period too, there are cases of imitation or counterfeiting of successful products which were already known to the consumer thanks either to the master's or the guild's or to collective mark.

The practice of branding – in the widest sense of the term – over a long period merits therefore more profound study and raises some important questions: who were those entitled to use the maker's mark and to what ends? Up to what point was the maker's marking an efficient tool? How did it interact with its imitations and counterfeiting? And, above all, when and how did the early forms of brand effectively emerge? This article aims to answer these questions, analysing the practices of branding adopted in the European pre-modern economy with the aim of communicating information about the product to the consumer. Drawing on secondary sources it examines the nature and function of master's marks and collective marks and their interaction with processes of imitation and counterfeiting. Marked goods, imitations and counterfeits were not antithetic or in contraposition to each other, but were instead complementary and an integral part of the process of the formation of a European space of competition, through which shared market standards were shaped. Finally, the article takes a stance in the debate on the origins of the modern brand, arguing in favour of the thesis that early forms of brand may be found only in the economic context of the eighteenth century and not before. In the framework of interpretation proposed by the 'Economics of Conventions' makers' marks, standardised taxonomies of products, trademarks and brands may be considered diverse solutions of 'conventions of quality', but the application of the theory of conventions to history requires caution.[4]

The section 2 of the article examines the variegated reality of the master's marks in use in manufacturing activity in pre-modern Europe, marks which, while being connected by the same general aim – that of giving information on the product – were highly diversified as far as regards who was entitled to confer such a mark – craftsmen, guilds, city magistrates or state officials -, but also as far as concerns the type of information offered: in some cases it was the identity of the craftsman, in others the place of production, in still others the raw material or the respect of requirements governing the production process. The mark appears as an institution which was relatively weak due to the great variability of statutes, of limited territorial validity, and the consequent difficulties of enforcement, but it carried out – indirectly if you wish – a significant role in setting up a path towards the consolidation, application and recognition of quality standards. The imitation of the products with major success on the market generated competition among the actors, as the section 3 of the article illustrates, and the spread of the imitations led, despite paradoxes and contradictions, to a sort of convergence and to the definition of a new system of taxonomies of products – and quality – which in some measure substituted the maker's mark. The section 4 of the article analyses the emergence of the first attempts to elaborate, through patents or privileges, early forms of trademark as the identifying element of a business, which were not only able to transmit information to the consumer but also to become of themselves an instrument of competitiveness, and therefore the beginnings of the process of construction of early forms of brand. The section 5 provides some final remarks.

2. The maker's mark: a protean institution

The first studies on the origins of the practice of branding manufactured items which were identifiable through the placing of seals, bulls, monograms, or hallmarks date back to the first decades of the twentieth century, and were carried out above all through the initiative of legal historians interested in analysing the precedents of modern legislation on modern trademarks.[5] Interest in this subject has been revived in recent times, when historians – probably motivated by the growing attention to the study of the history of consumer culture,[6] but also stimulated by the pervasive presence of the brand in contemporary society – began to dedicate attention to the evolution of the mark, studying its institutional, economic and social implications.[7]

The origins of the maker's mark date back to the Middle Ages with the rise of the urban guilds, within which the need to create a framework of intellectual property that would be the bearer of a series of information relative to the product itself responded to the need to introduce references that would help the consumer to make his own choices in a market system in rapid expansion, but still largely dominated by uncertainties and uneven information. The maker's mark, under the various concrete forms it might take on (seals, bulls, monograms, hallmarks), represented therefore a conventional sign, recognisable within a system of shared regulation. The refining of such regulations was often the fruit of a complex and articulated interaction between the artisans, the guild organisations and the political power operating on a determinate territory. The typology of maker's mark adopted could vary according to the production sector, on the basis of the technical restrictions imposed by the production process and in consideration of the raw materials used, as it the information offered might indeed be differentiated: in some cases, it was possible to identify the individual craftsman, in others to guarantee the quality of the raw materials used, while in still other cases it was the respect for the production regulations established by the guilds that was certified.[8]

One of the first historians of the trademark, Frank Schechter, expressed a negative evaluation of the system hinging on the medieval guilds, considering it a set-up that imposed a series of restrictions on production with the aim of protecting the earnings deriving from the monopolistic position of the guild craftsmen in every single area: 'Consequently, while the modern trade-mark is distinctly an asset to its owner, the medieval craftman's mark was essentially a liability.'[9] Leaving aside the debatable comparative evaluation between the efficiency of the medieval master's mark and the present day trademark, which represent different solutions for totally diverse economic contexts, some scholars doubt that craft guilds were able to solve information asymmetries concerning quality.[10] It is essential to keep in mind that, as we will see, the use of the master's mark underwent considerable evolution between the Middle Ages and the Early Modern period, the fruit of the adaptation of those institutions to changes in the economic context: an evolution which took on diverse connotations both according to the production sector and the economic policy adopted in the various contexts.[11] As a consequence, how effective the master's mark was as an instrument for resolving the information asymmetries about product quality could vary greatly according to the period and the historical context. In fact, much of the evidence that attests to the inadequacy of the master's and guild marks as a guarantee of quality of the product refer to the Early Modern Age, while there is decidedly less knowledge of the medieval period. This is due in part to the lack of sources and in part to the scarcity of in-depth empirical research: it remains therefore unclear whether such inefficiency is an intrinsic limit or, if, instead, it is a weakness that emerged in a given historical context.

The metal working sector is particularly interesting because it is a sphere in which the individual craftsman's mark played a particularly important role. The need to offer information to the consumer, who was not able to verify the quality of the raw materials used, underlay the use of master's marks and punches to stamp on objects made in precious metals which can be found in all European cities, where often a public office for the assaying of gold and silver was also set up.[12] Such a practice was also prevalent among craftsmen who worked common metals too: these materials were not precious but were, however, of notable strategic importance because they were destined for the production of weapons, such as, the well-known Lombard steel of the fifteenth century, which was marked with famed symbols.

Going beyond the production of semi-worked items – like steel – to finished products, the craftsman's mark did not only certify the raw materials used but also the manufacturing quality, which, precisely since we are dealing with weapons, was of decisive importance: this was the case of armour, helmets, swords, spurs and other types of Lombard weapon manufacture, which were highly reputed on the European market in the Late Middle Ages.

Although it found diffuse application in the metal wares sector, the maker's mark was also used in the most important late medieval and early modern manufacture, that of textiles. Bulls and marks served to certify the respect of a production process codified by the guilds that operated in the wool sector.[13] However, diversely from what has been stated in respect of the metal working sector, in which the individual master's mark seems to have long carried out an important role, in the textile sector it was the collective – city or guild – mark that was prevalent at least from the Late Middle Ages. In Milan in the fourteenth century, for example, it was the seal of the city that guaranteed that the woollen cloth had been made according to the guild regulations.[14] Similar situations may be found in Venice, Padua and Verona, as well as in Florence.[15] In Flanders, the other important European wool producing area, the production set up consolidated in the course of the fifteenth century was organised on the same principle: 'The effective industrial unit was not the individual draper ... but rather the urban drapery itself ... and all drapers within that collective produced the same brand or brands of sealed woollens, as prescribed by civic regulations'.[16] In England too in the sixteenth century the textile activity was characterised by the use of a collective mark.[17]

An interesting case of the collective mark for textile products is that instituted in the cities of Osnabruck and Munster in Westphalia. Osnabruck in 1404 and Munster in 1458 introduced the institution called 'Legge', the city agency that had the task of checking that the linen cloth produced on the territory, while not being uniform in character, respected some – summarily defined requirements of quality, such as the thread used or adequate weaving or even the dimensions of the work. The cloth that passed the test was destined for exportation. It was marked and made into rolls, which, in their turn were further marked and distinguished into two separate levels of higher and lower quality.[18]

In France the mercantile economic policy of the chief minister Colbert led to the construction of a truly national system of control over textile production based on different levels of verification. The first check was made at local level, where production originated and, in general, was entrusted to the guilds. This initial check permitted the goods to acquire a mark called 'marque de visite', formed by a lead seal applied to the cloth. A second check was carried out by the merchants at the moment of the sale. The checks were then made even more efficient by the visits of government officials who periodically inspected the workshops spread across the country. The 'public' marks that guaranteed the quality of the product and safeguarded its reputation on the international market could be integrated with 'private' master's marks that were marks that identified the producer.[19]

The spread of the maker's mark as an instrument through which to communicate information about the product to the consumer gave however the opportunity to use false maker's marks as a form of competition. Such a practice was very common in the sphere of wool cloth making, as it was in the sector of the production of fustian, made in Germany but sold under Venetian master's marks.[20] The counterfeiting of individual marks was repeatedly denounced to the authorities by the craftsmen that produced articles in metal. In Milan, during the course of the fifteenth century, numerous court cases were disputed between the armourers concerning the question of the counterfeiting of master's marks that had identified the armour and bladed weapons produced in the workshops of the diverse dynasties of craftsmen for generations.[21]

According to Richard T. Rapp, it was counterfeiting that was precisely one of the fundamental causes of the crisis in Venetian manufacturing in the course of the seventeenth century:

> In the Early 1600's northern manufacturers ... practiced all forms of smuggling. ... Also smuggling enabled counterfeit merchandise to pass undetected into the market place. Many thousands of pseudo-Venetian clothes came onto the selling tables from the most unlikely places of origin. The chief stratagem of cloth smugglers was to imitate typical Venetian signs and marks. ... These signs were supposed to guarantee the quality and origin of the cloth. ... Foreign soap makers used similar tactics: luxury soap from Genoa and Leghorn with fake Venetian trademarks flooded the Mediterranean.[22]

Widespread use of counterfeiting is one of the arguments that cast doubt on the effectiveness of the master's mark as a tool for resolving information asymmetries and guaranteeing quality standards.[23] These doubts find further confirmation in the contrasting relationship between individual mark and collective mark in two European production districts specialised in the making of knives, Thiers in France and Sheffield in England.[24]

The production activity at Thiers was regulated from 1582 at least and the ordinances required that every craftsman stamp his master's mark, which was deposited and registered, on the objects made. The master's mark was the property of the craftsman who could transmit it to his heirs, sell it or even hire it out to others. However, neither the existence of the individual master's marks, nor the control exercised by the guild organizations were able to ensure respect for the qualitative standard through time, as is shown by the fact that, in the eighteenth century, the reputation of the master's marks of craftsmen from Thiers was extremely variable, and, as we will see, such variability fed counterfeiting. There were in fact, on the Thiers territory, producers who sought to reduce the costs of production, even at the expense of quality of the product, and who did not hesitate to reproduce the marks of more highly considered craftsmen on their own products in order to gain a larger market share.[25]

The guild of knife-making artisans in Hallamshire dates to 1624, when it was incorporated under the name of Cutler's Company of Hallamshire. In the course of the eighteenth century, Sheffield became the most important production centre in the country, replacing its old rival London. The constitution of the guild consolidated the formal recognition of the individual master's marks, which had already been registered and deposited from 1614. The high quality of the products made in Sheffield won international prestige for the Hallamshire craftsmen: 'Sheffield marks were therefore held in very high esteem and were an absolute guarantee of quality.'[26] Perhaps precisely for this reason Sheffield cutlery – exactly as had happened in Thiers – became the target for widespread counterfeiting carried out by producers who sold cheaper items on the international market which however carried the better known Sheffield die stamp.

In both cities, the possibility of creating a collective mark was explored, certifying the origin and quality of the product: an umbrella under which all the producers on the territory might gather, thus benefiting from a form of geographical identification to add to the individual mark, intended in some way resolve the problems caused by the unfair competition which made articles of inferior quality with the counterfeited mark. In Thiers, the initiative was taken by central government, which, in 1732, ordered a second obligatory mark naming the product's place of origin. The initiative, however, aroused the fierce opposition of some producers, who saw in the collective mark a limit rather than an advantage, believing it limited their margins of freedom, especially where selling unmarked articles abroad in order to pass them off as local, not imported, products was concerned: a sign that production orientation was decidedly towards satisfying a market for products of a not very high quality and that the 'Thiers' mark did not offer any competitive advantage.[27] In Sheffield, during the nineteenth century, the Cutler's Company tried to defend the mark 'Made in Sheffield' without any great success. In this case too, however, the producers had divergent interests and therefore it was not possible to consolidate any significant cooperation to this end, so much so that the 'Made in Sheffield' brand was neither deposited nor registered by the Cutler's Company until 1924. The only producers to gain an advantage from the idea of a collective mark were those who made articles of inferior quality, who aimed at exploiting the advantage of reference to the district.[28] It seems therefore that in the sphere of the production districts the collective mark to be integrated with that of the individual craftsman, albeit for diverse reasons, did not represent an advantageous solution: in one case indeed – Thiers – the commercial and production strategies seem to have taken a direction that did not find the marker's mark to be a significant asset, while in the other – Sheffield – the factory mark became a more apt instrument to represent a choice of quality.[29]

Summing up the evidence proposed, it could be said that the practice of marking craft products with the aim of transmitting information about the product was widespread in pre-modern Europe, but the devices used, the sources for legitimising and the informative scope could be very different,[30] just as the effectiveness was not homogeneous. As far as the devices employed are concerned, for instance, in the metal wares sector the master's mark was incorporated into the product itself, 'burned', as Wilson Bastos and Sidney Levy have recently written,[31] while in the textile sector the master's mark was 'added' rather than incorporated. Secondly, the sources that made the mark legitimate, or as Bert De Munck put it 'the agencies of branding'[32] were diverse, that is, which institutional figure exercised control over the product and had the faculty of branding, it could differ. The craftsman himself, when and where directly responsible for the finished product, could have the right to apply his own mark, but in other cases it could be the guilds or city authorities or the state which held such power. Thirdly, the mark gave the consumer diverse information according to the specific case, the quality of the raw materials, the identity of the craftsman – also with the aim of discouraging fraud – respect of the prescribed production techniques, the dimensions, the place of production.

The various pieces of the puzzle may be pieced together in the sphere of the interpretation framework of the 'Economics of Convention'.[33] Such a variety of solutions in fact seems to outline a context in which practices, aimed at clarifying diverse ways of qualifying a product and which might find the agreement of the different subjects involved, are tried out. If in the Late Middle Ages that agreement was found in a complex and articulated system of maker's marks, between the sixteenth and eighteenth centuries, instead, the agreement took on another form through a process of the definition of product taxonomies, based on 'impersonal' standards, identified by the place of production rather than by an individual guarantee offered by a master's mark. The literature does not offer proof of the effectiveness of the master's mark as a guarantee of quality in the medieval period, nor, however, is there clear evidence to the contrary: above all, no alternative 'conventions' emerge. In the Early Modern Age the master's mark appears to gradually lose its effectiveness in carrying out the function of transmitting information about the product that it had originally had: the spread of counterfeiting as a form of competition, the political weakening of the craft guilds as 'agencies of branding'[34] and, above all, the rise of other repertoires of evaluation may be identified as the cause.

3. Beyond the maker's mark: a plurality of imitative taxonomies

Giovanni Botero, author of the treatise 'Cause della grandezza delle città' (Causes of the greatness of the cities), published at the end of the sixteenth century, underlined that a 'typical' specialisation was effectively a competitive factor:

> It will be of great advantage, in attracting people to our city, that she should have some important trade in her hands: this may be either wholly due to her rich earth from which all things come, or in part; or due to the capability of her inhabitants. ... There is also an excellence in skill, which either for the quality of the water, or for the subtlety of the inhabitants or for the hidden knowledge of the same, or for other similar reason succeeds better in one place than another, as with weapons in Damascus and in Schiraz, as with tapestries in Arras, woollen cloth in Florence, velvet in Genoa, brocade in Milan and scarlet cloth in Venice.[35]

The commercial manuals of the seventeenth and eighteenth centuries describe the geography of the myriad European specialisations in great detail,[36] a geography of 'production worlds'[37] whose productions took on the character of standardised typologies in a system of conventions:[38] typologies of products that became the object of imitation where imitation was then sustained and incentivised by the states as forms of competition through the concession of privileges.[39] The expressions that summarise this evolution are 'all'uso di ...' or 'façon de ...' or '...-style'. There are numerous examples which involve more or less all the sectors. Starting with the production of edged blade weapons, Luciana Frangioni wrote:

> In the widespread practice of the production of objects that imitated others of more consolidated fame ... Florence made swords in the guise of those of Bordeaux, sword pommels «Magna» [Germany] style, sword points in the Hungarian and «Magna» [Germany] styles, spear shafts and heads in the Spanish style, bowstrings in the Hungarian fashion, picks in the Milan style. ... English style bows. Furthermore, Florence produced knives in the Naples style (with the Neapolitan handles) sword points Pisa-style. ...Milan produced spurs counterfeited in the style of Lyon, arrowheads in the English mode, buckles and straps copying the Catalan fashion, sword points in the Pisan mode, bucklers in the style of Bordeaux, chain mail coifs made in the Naples-style.'[40]

In the Venetian Republic, between the end of the seventeenth and the beginning of the eighteenth centuries, privileges were conceded, first, for the production of fine majolica ware 'Lodi-style', then for those 'Genua-style' and finally 'Delft-style' and 'English-style'.[41] Interesting cases come from the textile sector. From the fifteenth century, for example, in Piacenza woollen cloth was made in the 'Monza fashion'.[42] The results of competition through imitation were at times paradoxical, as in the silk sector, where in Genua, in order to compete with Venice, in the second half of the fifteenth century, they began to produce silk cloth 'ad Venetum modum' (Venice-style), while in the second half of the sixteenth century in Venice they made velvet 'alla Zenoina' (Genua-style). The competition played with technical standards too, such as the width of the cloth which could offer a competitive advantage, so that, for example, in 1489 the Florentine silk merchants requested that the width of cloth made in Florence be made uniform to those which were narrower, but more sought after on the market, known to the consumers as those 'in the Venice fashion', produced in Venice, but also in Lucca. Similarly, in 1542 the Genovese silk makers decided to reduce the width of their own cloth on the model of those produced in Florence and Lucca.[43]

Naturally there was no lack of manipulation that allowed giving the product a more appealing status. According to Jacques Heers, in the course of the fifteenth century the Genovese exported local cloth as English or Florentine cloth – the internal market was more difficult to deceive. [44] Carlo Poni has reconstructed the history of silk velvet woven in Milan, from where it was sent to Holland and then re-sent to Milan, where it was finally sold as Dutch velvet, earning profit for the commission agents. [45] Also significant in this regard is the letter which the *Prévot des Marchands* of Lyon sent to Colbert in 1665 to report on the status of silk manufacture in Lyon, which had by then almost completely substituted the Italian made cloth on the markets in Paris, even if the cloth from Lyon continued to be sold as Italian. The French consumers still preferred Italian products to the point that the Prévot wrote, 'les marchands de Paris … obligent nos ouvriers à mettre sur leur étoffes les planches et les marques des pays étrangers'. In a subsequent letter the Prévot reiterated that 'tout ce qui s'envoie de cette ville à Paris s'y vend sous le nom des fabricants d'Italie'. [46]

In the eighteenth century in Venice French ribbons were called 'Lyon-style', a more famous silk production centre than that of St. Etienne, where the ribbons were effectively made; in Turin the English ribbons were called 'London' or 'from England', but in all probability came from Coventry; in Cadiz and Lisbon the Italian ribbons were labelled 'from Genua'; and finally the ribbons made in Padua were sold in London with the label 'in the Venice fashion'. [47] These selfsame ribbons became a 'conventional' reference whose place of production was susceptible to manipulation; in his *Dictionnaire Universel de Commerce* Savary de Bruslons explains under the entry 'Padoue' that it concerns an *'espèce de ruban'* and adds :

> On fabrique en France des Padoues en divers endroits, mais le meilleurs qui se fassent … sont les Padoues de Lyon, qu'on appelle de la sorte, non qu'ils s'y fabriquent tous, mais parce que c'est de cette ville que le marchands de Paris les tirent, quoique les ouvriers qui les travaillent ayent pour la plupart leur métiers à S. Etienne, petite ville de Forest, et à S. Chaumont, autre petite ville du Lyonnois. [48]

Such geography of 'production worlds' fed a market that was in some measure 'regulated' by taxonomies – which, as has been seen, were not always coherent – of products that inspired and oriented the process of imitation, which also included the imitation of luxury products, which might have been local, but were generally imported from the Orient, made in cheaper material so as to make them accessible to a wider range of consumers. [49] Mercantilist policies that incentivised the starting up of import substitution production activity through the concession of privileges carried out a decisive role in the spread and consolidation of these product taxonomies. This evolution, which may have begun as early as the sixteenth century and was consolidated in the following two centuries, seems therefore oriented towards the sharing of qualitative standards whose reference point was a sort of archetype defined on the basis of a model refined in its place of origin, but which later became a 'convention'. The function of transmitting information on the characteristics of the product which the master's mark or guild mark had carried out in the Late Middle Ages seems to become less effective also because the introduction of products' standards – conforming to recognised taxonomies, a kind of *'convention industrielle'* [50] – combined with a new consumer culture, assigned an increasingly important role to interaction with the consumer. Definition of the quality of the product was no longer an exclusive appanage of the craftsman, who guaranteed the characteristics of the raw materials and the use of consolidated production techniques, but increasingly involved not only the merchant but also the consumer. If it is true that 'The problem of "quality" under asymmetric information is solved

… rather by providing reliable information about quality so they can choose the quality-price combination they prefer,[51] it is equally true that the consumer needed a reference framework as a base on which to make choices in a phase in which 'design appears to have gradually replaced "intrinsic value" (i.e. the value of the raw material used) as the basis of quality.'[52]

4. From the master's mark to the early forms of trademark and brand?

According to a consolidated historiographic tradition the modern trademark, protected by national laws introduced in the course of the nineteenth century, was direct descendant of the master's mark adopted by the medieval guilds:[53] if this were true, then the master's mark, while having lost efficiency in the Early Modern Age as a guarantee of a particular representation of the quality of the product, would, however, have been given renewed value as a legal point of reference. As is known, the history of the trademark is interwoven with that of the brand,[54] but some recent studies dedicated to the history of the brand have argued that the brand might already have been be present, not only from the Middle Ages, but even in Antiquity, in the urbanised societies of the fourth millenium before Christ; another study, in reality rather more dated, claims instead Chinese primacy in the rise of the brand on the basis of a very approximative comparative reconstruction between Europe and China.[55]

Taking the differences existing between the concept of trademark and the concept of brand[56] as given, what answers does the evidence gathered offer on the question of the continuity between master's mark and trademark? And, furthermore, up to what point may we speak of brand before legal recognition of the trademark?

The decline of the master's mark as an effective guarantee of a particular representation of quality is reflected in both in the loss of prestige of the craftsman and in the political weakening of the craft guilds: the task of showing the product to be of valid quality – quality in terms of design and novelty – passed into the hands of the merchants who interacted with the final consumer:[57] it is among these merchant-entrepreneurs that the need to find forms through which to communicate their identity arose. This connection is explicitly recalled in a business commerce handbook published in Genua at the end of the eighteenth century: 'Each workshop has its own *trademark*, through which outsiders may learn to distinguish between good and sorry manufacture. Those who have worked ill will fall into discredit, as perfect manufacturing will never lack for success.'[58]

In the eighteenth century, in Venice the producers of beads and other glass objects deposited and registered the logo that identified the 'trademark' of the diverse manufacturers which was printed onto a card and inserted into the packages that were sent to be sold. The famous Giorgio Barbaria, for example, had deposited his own logo with sayings in Greek and French, while the goods sold by Pietro Sermonti were marked by a drawing that showed six mountains and the caption *'Fabbrica di manifatture a lume di Pietro Sermonti in Venezia – Fabrique de manifacture a lume de Pierre Sermonti à Venise'*.[59] Gian Battista Roan, another producer of glass beads, explained the reasons that led him to register his own 'trademark' which were 'so that others of the trade might not use it and with this *trademark* our manufacture has always a good issue both in the Venetian area and abroad.'[60] Roan, who registered his 'trademark' in 1727 with the logo of the Golden Tree, had begun to receive complaints from his clients concerning unfulfilled orders and the scarce quality of the merchandise from the start of that year. A rapid investigation led to the discovery that the cause of all his problems was a business rival, Francesco Padovan, who had had some hundreds of labels printed that reproduced, even if in slightly smaller dimensions, the logo of the Golden Tree, under which he had sent goods to Germany, generating confusion among Roan's habitual clients and discrediting his business.[61]

In the Venetian Republic these 'early forms of trademark' were also adopted in the sector of earthenware,[62] as well as medicinal products: a famous medicine, the so-called *Triaca*, considered the panacea for all ills, which was a Venetian speciality and whose formula was kept secret, was sold with the label of two well-known Venetian 'trademarks' *Testa d'oro* and *'Madonna'* and was the object of reiterated counterfeiting.[63] Another example is that of Domenico Bettini, a Bolognese merchant, who in 1767 decided to start up a business in the production of silk veils and in his request to the Silk Guild for the necessary authorisation presented the logo of the *'trademark* for the workshop of fine veils by Domenico Bettini' which would represent the new business.[64] Registering the logo – with the magistrates of the *Giustizia Vecchia* in Venice or the Silk Guild in Bologna – did not have the same legal value as that guaranteed by the nineteenth century trademark laws,[65] but its legitimacy was recognised by the courts; moreover, the Venetian Republic, like many states of the *Ancien Régime*, granted privileges to entrepreneurs who introduced innovative production processes, which, in some measure, protected against counterfeiting.[66] It does not, therefore, appear out of place to consider these as 'early forms of trademark'.

In France, as has been seen, a strong, capillary system of public control over production which overlapped eventual local collective or individual marks was in vigour. The regulatory structure created by Colbert had the aim of assuring the market – and, above all, the international market – that French products respected quality standards that had been defined.[67] However, there is no lack of examples of producers who succeeded in eluding the controls and in creating their own identity, such as in the experience of silk manufacture in Nimes in the eighteenth century.[68] If one looks at Paris, the capital testifies to the numerous, articulate strategies used by the merchants-entrepreneurs and shopkeepers to attract consumers through advertisements which presented the logo of the firm through flyers or bill heads,[69] So, in France too, privilege could offer legal protection to innovative business initiatives and therefore, indirectly, to eventual logos or symbols adopted to identify the business.[70]

England, the laboratory of what has been called 'the consumer revolution',[71] shows interesting evidences. From the beginning of the eighteenth century at least the British market began to be a battlefield on which businesses that were active in the various sectors of consumer goods faced each other and contended for success; they fought with the weapons of advertising: exhibitions, auctions, shop window displays, adverts in newspapers, catalogues, and bill heads and above all trade cards. These trade cards were used both to promote commercial activity and to represent production companies.[72] Decorative objects and furnishings in metal, like teapots, cutlery, candelabras, lamps and other plated articles that imitated those in more precious metals, fed an ever increasing demand in England in the eighteenth century and in this sector too ambitious businessmen like Matthew Boulton made wide use of the advertising techniques that have been described to give their own business its own character.[73]

There are at least two cases in which historians use the term brand without any hesitation. John Styles has brilliantly illustrated the debut of branded products on the British market between the seventeenth and the eighteenth centuries reconstructing the pioneering role carried out by proprietary medicines. The precocity with which the brand identity was adopted in this sector was justified by the need to reassure consumers as to the reliability of the product destined to have an impact on their health, distinguishing it from the traditional generic remedies that were sold by the apothecaries and pharmacists. The producers of medicinal products launched massive advertising in the British newspapers to promote their wares, but also had recourse to innovative strategies based on the packaging: little bottles of blown glass of a particular shape were adopted which the brand name had impressed in relief on the glass itself. Perhaps the most famous example is that of Robert Turlington, whose 'Balsam of life' was sold in the characteristic bottle and accompanied by instructions as to its use, as well as by testimony from satisfied customers.[74] According to Patrick Wallis, the precocious impulse to build an early identity of brand for patent medicines could be explained also by the need to resist widespread counterfeiting. Turlington himself, manufacturer of the celebrated *Balsam of Life*, modified the labels of his products with great frequency to dismay his competitors, who had ably reproduced them. Another manufacturer, Richard Stoughton, thus warned his clients:

> That you be not deceived, pray ask for it by my name and mind the stamps on the other side, for the bottles are sealed with the same on the top, viz., my name in a cipher and round it in the words at length, Richard Soughton. If the bottle be not (for the future) always sealed with the same and you have not such paper as this stamp with the same with each bottle, 'tis a counterfeit'.[75]

The second case, that of Josiah Wedgwood, is well known: a successful businessman in the ceramics field thanks also to innovative, articulated marketing techniques. After having obtained patronage from exponents of the Court and among the nobility, who were exploited as testimonials, Wedgwood experimented with methods such as campaigns of 'inertia-selling', diversification of the product, distribution of illustrated catalogues, advertising in the newspapers, discounts and special offers, free transport and delivery, as well as headed bills and invoices with the trademark of the business.[76] The need to create what might be called the brand identity of the business was in fact evident to him, as is shown by a letter from 1773, in which he wrote apropos of his own products: 'It will be absolutely necessary for us to mark them and advertise that mark'.[77] According to Nancy Koehn 'Wedgwood used his knowledge to create not only an excellent product, but also a widely recognised brand name and other significant connections with his customer'.[78]

During the eighteenth century the need arose in a much more evident fashion than in the preceding centuries to represent the business through the adoption of a 'trademark' which could be recognised by the consumer and which would benefit from some form of legal recognition. The literature offers some earlier examples, such as the case of the Veronese merchant Carlo Radice, whose name was known and appreciated on the German market in the second half of the sixteenth century. In 1583 he appointed a solicitor to protect his reputation against other merchants who used his 'trademark'.[79] Yet another example is that of Aldo Manuzio, the famous Venetian printer and editor, who reached such fame and prestige in Europe that the so-called *'aldine'* editions became the object of able counterfeiting: in 1518 he denounced the counterfeiting of the 'trademark' on his books in which the symbol of the dolphin was facing right, while in his original the symbol was facing left.[80] Nonetheless, it was above all in the eighteenth century, that the 'trademark', into which artwork, mottos and other graphics were incorporated, was increasingly adopted as a marketing instrument by firms that worked both in the manufacturing and in the trade sectors, thus neatly distinguishing the trademark from the master's mark. At the same time the widespread use of the privilege or of the patent as a form of legitimisation of the business initiative offered, albeit indirectly, a formal recognition of the 'trademark' that identified the business.[81]

The rise of these 'early forms of trademark' supported the introduction of the 'early forms of brand', as cited above, creating a mode of representing the identity of the firm which had legal recognition. The so-called 'consumer revolution' which took place in England in the eighteenth century, but which also involved, although to a lesser extent, other European states, was marked by the enlarging of the market: to be competitive businesses adopted innovative communication strategies that in their turn constructed a brand identity,[82] not only with the aim of distinguishing themselves from their competitors, but also offering the consumer an exclusive relationship, whether the purchase was of medicinal products or of pottery.

5. Conclusion

In the pre-modern economy the maker's mark was an instrument used to solve information asymmetries between producers and consumers. The maker's mark could take the form of master's mark or collective mark and, in the second case, the actors entitled to brand the goods could be craft guilds, urban magistrates, or state officials: these institutions used the mark for different ends and therefore the information that was incorporated and the effective communication conveyed were diversified. The widest used forms of maker's mark were those of the master's mark and the guild mark: in the debate that developed amongst historians on the role played by the craftsmen and their organisations in the pre-modern economy, some authors have doubted that the craft guilds were effective in guaranteeing quality standards. While there is no relevant evidence that the maker's mark was an inadequate instrument in the Middle Ages for informing the consumer about the characteristics of the product – only further research will confirm or deny this – the situation appears to change in Early Modern Times because of the decline in the political influence of the craft guilds in some countries and of the emergence of other repertoires of evaluating quality. On the one hand, the guarantee offered by the maker's mark – the raw materials, the identity of the craftsman, the respect of codified production techniques – became increasingly less meaningful in the light of the emergence of a different system of 'quality conventions', defined by taxonomies of product that were based on production standards set by convergent systems of imitation – '… -style', 'à la façon de'. On the other hand, the nature itself of the guarantee of quality offered by the maker's mark – that which De Munck has defined as 'intrinsic value' – seems to be less and less decisive in the face of the increasing importance attributed to criteria relative to the aesthetic aspect of the product, or in other words, to its fashion value. Both the dynamics described evoke a transformation in the process of the definition of the qualification of the product, in which the craftsman played an increasingly minor role, while seeing a major involvement of the merchant-entrepreneurs who operated on a market where the demand was increasingly orientated by a consumer culture. In the context characterised by such a consumer culture and, above all, by a growing propensity to consumption – particularly in the course of the eighteenth century and especially in England – the necessity for firms to be identified and represented by a symbol, recognisable by the consumer, whether by an image, a drawing or a motto, seems to assert itself. Such a need did not yet find a formal legal protection, as would happen in the nineteenth century, however, through privilege or patent, the entrepreneur found a form of institutional recognition which, even though indirectly, offered a guarantee to his business as an 'early form of trademark'.[83] There are examples of businesses that went much beyond, experimenting pioneering strategies of marketing that aimed at constructing a kind of brand identity, an 'early form of brand'. In the literature, widely differing stances have been taken on the origin of the brand, but it is in the context described above that the conditions that allow us to glimpse the emergence of the elements that constitute the modern brand may be found. First of all, there was the formation of an ever increasing market fed by a consumer culture ready to perceive the stimulus offered by the first advertising campaigns adopted by businesses; in the second place, marketing strategies were created, which, in a more or less aware fashion, aimed at furnishing a representation of the product able to stimulate new sensibilities; and, last, but not least, if it is true, as John Mercer has written, that the trademark is the indispensable tangible support for the intangible virtues of the brand,[84] then 'early forms of trademark', supported by patent or privilege, were already accessible.

Notes

1. Bently, Davis and Ginsburg, *Trade Marks and Brands*; Da Silva Lopes and Duguid, *Trademarks, Brands and Competitiveness*; Da Silva Lopes and Casson, "Brand Protection"; Da Silva Lopes and Guimaraes, "Trademarks and British Dominance"; Higgins, "Forgotten Heroes and Forgotten Issues"; Mercer, "A Mark of Distinction."
2. Bastos and Levy, "A History of the Concept of Branding"; De Munck, "The Agency of Branding"; Duguid, "Brand in chain"; Epstein, "Craft Guilds in Pre-modern Economy"; Hamilton and Lai, "Consumerism without Capitalism"; Koehn, *Brand New*; Maitte, "Labels, Brands, and Market Integration"; McKendrick, Brewer and Plumb, *The Birth of a Consumer Society*; Moore and Reid, "The Birth of Brand"; Richardson, *Brand Names*; Schwarkopf, "Turning Trademarks into Brands"; Stanziani, "Marques, Marques Collectives"; Wengrow, "Prehistories of Commodity Branding."
3. Da Silva Lopes and Casson, "Brand Protection"; Da Silva Lopes and Guimaraes, "Trademarks and British Dominance"; Greenhalgh and Rogers, "Trade Marks and Performances"; Higgins, "Forgotten Heroes and Forgotten Issues"; Mendonça, Santos Pereira and Mira Godinho, "Trademark as an Indicator"; Mercer, "A Mark of Distinction."
4. See the special issue of *Historical Social Research* on *The Economie des conventions. Transdisciplinary Discussions and Perspectives* and in particular the following articles: Bessy, "Institutions and Conventions of Quality"; Thévenot, "Convening the Company of Historians"; De Munck, "Conventions, the Great Transformation."
5. See Schechter, *The Historical Foundations*.
6. See McKendrick, Brewer and Plumb, *The Birth of a Consumer Society*; Spufford, *The Great Reclothing of Rural England*; Weatherill, *Consumer Behaviour and Material Culture*; Lemire, *Fashion's Favourite*; Brewer and Porter, *Consumption and the World of Goods*; Berg, *Luxury and Pleasure*; De Vries, *The Industrious Revolution*.
7. See, amongst others, Beltran, Chaveau and Galvez-Behar, *Des brevets et des marques*; Stanziani, "Marques, marques collectives," 229–238; Richardson, *Brand Names*; Maitte, "Labels, Brands, and Market Integration," 1–15; De Munck, "The Agency of Branding," 1055–1076.
8. Beltran, Chaveau and Galvez-Behar, *Des brevets et des marques*, 88–90; Stanziani, "Marques, Marque Collectives," 229–230; De Munck, "The Agency of Branding."
9. Schechter, *The Historical Foundations*, 78. On this point see also Hamilton and Lai, "Consumerism Without Capitalism," 253–279; Wengrow, "Prehistory of Commodity Branding," 7–34.
10. The best known is Sheilagh Ogilvie: see Ogilvie, "The Economics of Guilds."
11. See Richardson, "Guilds, Laws and Markets," 20–23.
12. Ibid., 59–60; Rosa, "Appunti per una storia dell'oreficeria milanese," 139–146; Beltran, Chaveau. Galvez-Behar, *Des brevets et des marques*, 88–90; De Munck, "The Agency of Branding," 1061.

13. Cardon, *La draperie au Moyen Age*, 594–600.
14. Mainoni, "Il mercato della lana," 20–43.
15. Lecce, *Vicende dell'industria della lana*; Borgherini, *L'arte della lana in Padova*; Malanima, *La decadenza di un'economia cittadina*; Mozzato, *La mariegola dell'Arte della lana*.
16. Munro, "Medieval Woollens," 247–248.
17. Schechter, *Historical Foundations*, 88–95.
18. Jeggle, *Munsterisches Leinen*; Jeggle, "Pre-industrial Worlds of Production."
19. Grenier, "Une économie de l'identification", 25–53; Minard, "Réputation, normes et qualité", 69–89.
20. Demo, *L'anima della città*, 180 and 276; Frangioni, "Sui modi di produzione," 545.
21. Biscaro, "Due controversie in tema di marchi di fabbrica nel secolo XV," 337–338; Motta, "Armaioli milanesi," 187–232.
22. Rapp, "The Unmaking of the Mediterranean Trade Hegemony," 508 and 510.
23. Caracausi, "Information Asymmetries," 22.
24. Higgins and Tweedale, "Asset or Liability"; Maitte, "Labels, Brands, and Market Integration"; Guenzi, *Cutlery Trade*.
25. Maitte, "Labels, Brands, and Market Integration," 9–11.
26. Higgins and Tweedale, "Asset or Liability," 5.
27. Maitte, "Labels, Brands, and Market Integration," 11.
28. Higgins and Tweedale, "Asset or Liability."
29. According to De Munck at the beginning of the 1500s in the metal wares sector the master's marks of the single craftsmen were subordinate to collective marks in the cities of the Southern Low Countries and in Nuremberg: these situations would therefore be included in the general tendency to substitute individual master's marks with collective marks (city or guild) (De Munck, "The Agency of Branding," 1057–1060).
30. According to De Munck the common feature was the 'intrinsic value' (De Munck, "Product Quality and Intrinsic Value," 110–113).
31. Bastos and Levy, "A History of the Concept of Branding," 350–352.
32. De Munck, "The Agency of Branding."
33. Eymard-Duvernay, "Conventions de qualité." See also Stanziani, *Histoire de la qualité alimentaire*, 23–36; De Munck, "Guilds, Product Quality and Intrinsic Value."
34. De Munck, "The Agency of Branding," 1064–1067; Ogilvie, "The Economics of Guilds," 171; Caracausi, "Information Asymmetries and Craft Guilds."
35. Botero, *Della ragion di stato*, 377–378. On this point see also Richardson, *Brand Names*, 20–27.
36. Grenier, "Une économie de l'identification," 34–35.
37. Salais and Storper, *Les mondes de production*.
38. 'Generally speaking, economics of convention … recognises that beyond institutional codified rules which organise the "markets" there is a place for more informal or implicit rules that we can call "conventions". They facilitate the coordination of economic agents under the conditions of uncertainty and incomplete rules, in particular by stabilising commune designation or qualification of product' (Bessy. "Institutions and Conventions of Quality," 15).
39. Belfanti, "Guilds, Patents and the Circulation of Technical Knowledge," 569–589; Belfanti, "Between Mercantilism and Market," 319–338; Maitte, "Imiitation, copie, contrefaçon." 23–25.
40. Frangioni, "Preposizioni semplici," 614.
41. Favero, "Privilegi d'industria e diritti di proprietà," 2; Favero, "Old and New Ceramics", 306–310.
42. Mainoni, "Il mercato della lana." For more examples see, among others, Panciera, *L'arte matrice*, 98–113.
43. Molà, *The Silk Industry*, 160.
44. Heers, "La mode et les marchés des draps de laine," 199–200.
45. Poni, *La seta in Italia*, 507.
46. Poni, *La seta in Italia*, 536.
47. Caracausi, *Small Innovation, Big Transformation*.
48. Savary de Bruslons, *Dictionnaire universel de commerce*, vol. 4, 3. See also Maitte, "Imitation, copie, contrefaçon, faux," 13–14.

49. Berg, "From Imitation to Invention"; Caracausi, "Information Asymmetries"; Coquery, "The Language of Success"; Maitte, "Imitation, copie, contrefaçon, faux"; Styles, "Product Innovation in Early Modern London."

50. Eymard-Duvernay, "Conventions de qualité," 338–344.

51. Ogilvie, "The Economics of Guilds," 179.

52. De Munck, "The Agency of Branding," 1065. See also De Munck, "Product Quality and Intrinsic Value," 112; Maitte, "Labels, Brands and Market Integration," 3–4. Marsilio Landriani, who visited the most important European manufactures during the second half of the eighteenth century, wrote: 'The fashion ... demands an apparent solidity. For, in fact, what would be the use of real solidity if the instability of fashion condemns as absurd today that which it hailed as excellent yesterday?' (Belfanti, "Guilds, Patents and the Circulation of Technical Knowledge," 589).

53. Bently, "The Making of the Modern Trade Mark Law", 3.

54. Bently, Davis and Ginsburg, Trade Marks and Brands; Da Silva Lopes and Duguid, Trademarks, Brands and Competitiveness.

55. Bastos and Levy, "A History of the Concept of Branding"; Hamilton and Lai, "Consumerism without Capitalism"; Moore and Reid, "The Birth of Brand"; Wengrow, "Prehistories of Commodity Branding."

56. The trademark is a sign, a name, a symbol or a combination of the aforementioned elements, protected by law on intellectual property, where it exists, by which a business represents itself to the consumers. The brand, while basing itself on the trademark for legal protection, incorporates a personality and an identity, inspires the consumer with feelings, memories, behaviour and fidelity. The image of the brand is constructed through, more or less advanced strategies of communication, aimed at defining its identity and character (see Bently, Davis and Ginsburg, Trade Marks and Brands; Da Silva Lopes and Duguid, Trademarks, Brands and Competitiveness; Da Silva Lopes and Guimaraes, "Trademarks and British Dominance"; Mercer, "A Mark of Distinction").

57. De Munck, "The Agency of Branding," 1064–1067; Belfanti, "Guilds, Patents and the Circulation of Technical Knowledge," 586–589.

58. Costantini, Elementi di commerzio, 113, emphasis added.

59. Archivio di Stato di Venezia, Censori, b. 47, Marche delli negozianti dell'arte dei perleri, 1782.

60. Cella, "Storia di un marchio contraffatto," 19–30, emphasis added.

61. Cella, "Storia di un marchio contraffatto," 19–30.

62. Favero, "Old and New Ceramics".

63. Andreozzi, "Per vestiario o per addobbi o per lusso".

64. Giusberti, Impresa e avventura, 80, emphasis added.

65. Trademark laws were duly enacted by the modern state for the whole community of the citizens, while Privileges were an institutional solution provided by the feudal system to meet the needs of an individual.

66. Belfanti, "Guilds, Patents and the Circulation of Technical Knowledge"; Belfanti, "Between Mercantilism and Market"; Favero, "Privilegi d'industria e diritti di proprietà"; Maitte, "Imitation, copie, contrefaçon, faux," 23–25.

67. Minard, "Réputations, normes et qualité, » 79–89; Grenier, "Une économie de l'identification," 28–42.

68. Maitte, "Labels, Brands and Market Integration," 5.

69. Coquery, "The Language of Success."

70. 'The privilege presents a twofold dimension, namely a license to carry out an economic activity and the accompanying advantages. For the entrepreneur, the privilege means a guarantee that covers business risk. Without the assurance that he will benefit some advantages able to reduce an uncertain profitability in an emerging market, he was not inclined to involve his fortune and is reputation. ... From the point of view of the State, the privilege is an incentive as far as the beneficial owner might promote economic growth, enrichment for the nation and public welfare' (Conchon and Lemaigre-Gaffier, The Economic Privilege in Old Regime France). See also: Hilaire-Pérez, L'invention technique; Maitte, "Imitation, copie, contrefaçon, faux," 23–25.

71. McKendrick, Brewer and Plumb, The Birth of a Consumer Society.

72. Walker, "Advertising in London Newspapers," 112–131; McKendrick, "The Commercialization of Fashion," 84–94; Berg, *Luxury and Pleasure*, 271–277.
73. Berg, *Luxury and Pleasure*, 182–188.
74. Styles, "Product Innovation in Early Modern London," 148–158; Wallis, *Commercial Innovation in Early Modern England*. 'However, since in the late-seventeenth and early-eighteenth century the dividing line between medicaments, foodstuffs and beverages was fine, the concept of branded goods sold at fixed prices, often imposed nation-wide, spread into the grocery and confectionary trades' (Cox, *The Complete Tradesman*, 103).
75. Wallis, *Commercial Innovations*.
76. McKendrick, "Josiah Wedgwood," 100–145; Koehn, *Brand New*, 11–42.
77. McKendrick, "Josiah Wedgwood," 124.
78. Koehn, *Brand New*, 4.
79. Demo, "Dall'auge al declino," 279–280.
80. Beltran, Chaveau, Galvez-Behar, *Des brevets des marques*, 89; Pulsoni, "I classici italiani di Aldo Manuzio," 477–487. See also Duguid, "Brands in chain", 141–147.
81. See Garner, *Die Ökonomie des Privilegs*.
82. Koehn, *Brand New*, 5, 326–328.
83. 'Privilege in Modern Europe played the part of an institution which reduced uncertainty and was suited to inspire confidence in the potential partners of those businesses it underpinned. … Privilege at the same time provided security for the property of the inventor or the entrepreneur, encouraged investment, stimulated and regulated competition, and provided an edge in recruiting a workforce or in technical diffusion' (Garner, Hilaire-Pérez, Maitte, Margairaz, *Revisiting Economic Privileges*).
84. '[The trademark] is the tangible item of intellectual property – the logo, name, design or image – on which the brand rests. But brand also incorporates intangibles such as identity, association and personality' (Mercer, "A Mark of Distinction," 18).

Acknowledgments

The author would like to thank Patricio Sàiz, Rafael Castro and two anonymous referees for commenting on and suggesting ideas for this article.

Disclosure statement

No potential conflict of interest was reported by the author.

References

Andreozzi, Daniele. "'Per vestiario o per addobbi o per lusso'. Mercati del lusso, prodotti di imitazione, scambi internazionali e strategie commerciali nella Trieste settecentesca." In *Luxes et internationalisation (XVI-XIX siècles)*, edited by Nadège Sougy, 145–164. Neuchatel: Alphil, 2013.
Bastos, Wilson, and Sidney Levy. "A history of the concept of branding: practice and theory." *Journal of Historical Research in Marketing* 4 (2012): 347–368.
Belfanti, Carlo Marco. "Guilds, Patents and the Circulation of Technical Knowledge. Northern Italy during the Early Modern Age." *Technology and Culture* 45 (2004): 569–589.
Belfanti, Carlo Marco. "Between Mercantilism and Market: Privileges for Invention in Early Modern Europe." *Journal of Institutional Economics* 2 (2006): 319–338.

Belfanti, Carlo Marco. "A Chain of Skills: the Production Cycle of Firearms Manufacture in the Brescia Area from the Sixteenth to the Eighteenth Centuries." In *Guilds, Markets and Work Regulations in Italy, 16th -19th centuries*, edited by Guenzi Alberto, Massa Paola and Piola Caselli Fausto, 266–283. Aldershot: Ashgate, 1998.

Beltran, Alain, Chaveau Sophie, and Galvez-Behar Gabriel. *Des brevets et des marques. Une histoire de la propriété industrielle.* Paris: Fayard, 2001.

Bently, Lionel, Davis Jennifer, and Jane C. Ginsburg, eds. *Trade Marks and Brands.* Cambridge: Cambridge University Press, 2008.

Bently, Lionel. "The making of the modern trade mark law: the conception of the legal cncept of trade mark (1860-1880)." In *Trade Marks and Brands*, edited by Lionel Bently, Davis Jennifer and Jane C. Ginsburg, 3–41. Cambridge: Cambridge University Press, 2008.

Berg, Maxine. "From Imitation to Invention: Creating Commodities in Eighteenth-century Britain." *Economic History Review* 55 (2002): 1–30.

Berg, Maxine. *Luxury and Pleasure in Eighteenth-Century Britain.* Oxford: Oxford University Press, 2005.

Bessy, Christian. "Institutions and Conventions of Quality." *Historical Social Research* 37 (2012): 15–21.

Biscaro, Gerolamo. "Due controversie in tema di marchi di fabbrica nel secolo XV." *Archivio storico lombardo* 39 (1912): 337–338.

Boccia, Lionello G. "L'antica produzione di armi in Lombardia." In *Armi e armature lombarde*, edited by Lionello G. Boccia, Francesco Rossi, and Marco Morin, 5–12. Milan: Electa, 1980.

Borgherini, Maria. *L'arte della lana in Padova durante il governo della Repubblica di Venezia, 1405-1797.* Venice: Deputazione di storia patria, 1964.

Botero, Giovanni. *Della ragion di stato...con tre libri delle cause della grandezza delle città.* Turin: Utet, 1948.

Brewer, John, and Roy Porter, eds. *Consumption and the World of Goods.* New York: Routledge, 1993.

Caracausi, Andrea. "Information Asymmetries and Craft Guilds in Pre-Modern Markets: Evidence from Italian Proto-Industry." *The Economic History Review* (forthcoming), Early view: 1–26.

Caracausi, Andrea. *Small Innovation, Big Transformation: Italian Ribbons between Global and Local Markets.* paper presented at the Pasold Research Fund Conference, *Innovation before the Modern. Cloth and Clothing in Early Modern Europe*, Nordiska Museet, Stockholm, 27-29 September 2012.

Cardon, Dominique. *La draperie au Moyen Age.* Paris: Editions du CNRS, 1991.

Cella, Riccardo. "Storia di un marchio contraffatto a Venezia nel XVIII secolo." *Rivista della Stazione Sperimentale del Vetro* 41 (2011): 19–30.

Christof, Jeggle. "Pre-industrial Worlds of Production: Conventions, Institutions and Organisations." *Historical Social Research* 36 (2011): 125–149.

Conchon, Anne, and Pauline Lemaigre-Gaffier. *The Economic Privilege in Old Regime France: A Source of Advantages?* paper presented at the XVII World Economic History Congress, Session "Privileges and economic development from the 16th to the 19th century: a comparative approach (Europe-Asia), Kyoto, 3-5 August 2015.

Coquery, Natacha. "The Language of Success. Marketing and Distributing Semi-Luxury Goods in Eigheenth-century Paris." *Journal of Design History* 17 (2004): 71–89.

Costantini, Giuseppe Antonio. *Elementi di commerzio, osiano massime generali per coltivarlo...* Genua, 1762.

Cox, Nancy. *The Complete Tradesman. A Study of Retailing, 1550-1820.* Aldershot: Ashgate, 2000.

Da Silva Lopes, Teresa, and Mark Casson. "Brand Protection and the Globalization of the British Business." *Business History Review* 86 (2012): 287–310.

Da Silva Lopes, Teresa, and Paul Duguid, eds. *Trademarks, Brands and Competitiveness.* New York and London: Routledge, 2010.

Da Silva Lopes, Teresa, and Paulo Guimares. "Trademarks and British Dominance in Consumer Goods, 1876-1914." *Economic History Review* 67 (2014): 793–817.

De Munck, Bert. "Guilds, Product Quality and Intrinsic Value: Towards a History of Conventions?" *Historical Social Research* 36 (2011): 103–124.

De Munck, Bert. "The Agency of Branding and the Location of Value. Hallmarks and Monograms in Early Modern Tableware Industries." *Business History* 54 (2012): 1055–1076.

De Munck, Bert. "Conventions, the Great Transformation and Actor Network Theory." *Historical Social Research* 37 (2012): 44–54.

Demo, Edoardo. *L'anima della città. L'industria tessile a Verona e Vicenza (1400-1550)*. Milan: Unicopli, 2001.

Demo, Edoardo. "Dall'auge al declino. Manifattura, commercio locale e traffici internazionali a Cremona in Età Moderna." In *Storia di Cremona*, edited by Giorgio Politi (a cura di), vol. IV, 263–287. Bergamo: Bolis, 2006.

Duguid, Paul. "Brands in chain." In *Trademarks, Brands and Competitiveness*, edited by Teresa Da Silva Lopes and Paul Duguid, 138–164. London and New York: Routledge, 2010

Epstein, Stephen R. "Craft Guilds in Pre-Modern Economy: A Discussion." *The Economic History Review* 61 (2008): 155–174.

Eymard-Duvernay, François. "Conventions de qualité et forms de coordination." *Revue Economique* 40 (1989): 329–360.

Favero, Giovanni. "Privilegi d'industria e diritti di proprietà nella manifatture di ceramica della Repubblica di Venezia (XVII-XVIII secolo)." Quaderni Storici 46 (2011): 185–220.

Favero, Giovanni. "Old and New Ceramics. Manufacturers, Products, and Markets in the Venetian Republic in the Seventeenth and Eighteenth Century." In *At the Center of the Old World*, edited by Paola Lanaro, 271–316. Toronto, 2006.

Frangioni, Luciana. "Sui modi di produzione e sul commercio dei fustagni milanesi alla fine del Trecento. Problemi economici e giuridici." *Nuova rivista storica* 61 (1977): 439–554.

Frangioni, Luciana. "Preposizioni semplici diverse per mercerie milanesi (e fiorentine) del Trecento." *Nuova Rivista Storica* 69 (1985): 611–626.

Garner, Guillaume, ed. *Die Ökonomie des Privilegs, Westeuropa 16.–19. Jahrhundert. L'économie du privilège, Europe occidentale XVIe–XIXe siècles*. Francfort am Main: Klostermann, 2016.

Garner, Guillame, Liliane Hilaire-Pérez, Corine Maitte, and Dominique Margairaz. *Revisiting Economic Privileges in Western Europe (France, Italy, England, The Holy Roman Empire), from the Sixteenth to the Nineteenth century: Beyond National History*. paper presented at the XVII World Economic History Congress, Session "Privileges and economic development from the 16th to the 19th century: a comparative approach (Europe-Asia), Kyoto, 3-5 August 2015.

Giusberti, Fabio. *Impresa e avventura. L'industria del velo di seta a Bologna nel XVIII secolo*. Milan: Franco Angeli, 1989.

Greenhalgh, Christine, and Rogers Mark. "Trade Marks and Performances in Services and Manufacturing Firms: Evidence of Schumpeterian Competition through Innovation." *The Australian Economic Review* 45 (2012): 50–76.

Grenier, Jean-Yves. "Une économie de l'identification." In *La qualité des produits en France (XVIIIe-XXe siècles)*, edited by Alessandro Stanziani (sous la direction de), 25–53. Paris: Belin, 2003.

Guenzi, Alberto. *Cutlery trade. Le origini corporative dei distretti industriali in Europa (secoli XV-XX)*. Turin: Rosenberg e Sellier, 2014.

Hamilton, Gary G., and Chi-Kong Lai. "Consumerism Without Capitalism: Consumption and Brand Names in Late Imperial China." In *The Social Economy of Consumption*, edited by Henry J. Rutz and Benjamin S. Orlove, 253–279. Lanham Md.: University of America Press, 1989.

Heers, Jacques. "La mode et les marchés des draps de laine: Gênes et la montagne à la fin du Moyen." In *Produzione, commercio e consumo dei panni di lana (nei secoli XII-XVIII)*, edited by Marco Spallanzani, 199–220. Florence: Le Monnier, 1976.

Higgins, David. "'Forgotten Heroes and Forgotten Issues'. Business and Trademark History During the Nineteenth Century." *Business History Review* 86 (2012): 261–285.

Higgins, David, and Tweedale Geoffrey. "Asset or Liability? Trade Marks in the Sheffield Cutlery and Tool Trades." *Business History* 37 (1995): 1–27.

Hilaire-Pérez, Liliane. *L'invention technique au siècle de Lumières*. Paris: Albin Michel, 2000.

Jeggle, Christof. *"Munsterisches Leinen": Branding Line in Early Modern Munster/Westphalia (16th-17th centuries."* paper presented at the XVth World Economic History Congress, Utrecht, 2009.

Koehn, Nancy F. *Brand New. How Entrepreneurs Earned Consumers' Trust form Wedgwood to Dell*. Boston: Harvard University Press, 2001.

Lecce, Michele. *Vicende dell'industria della lana e della seta a Verona dalle origini al 16 secolo*. Verona: Ghidini e Fiorini, 1955.

Lemire, Beverly. *Fashion's Favourite: The Cotton Trade and the Consumer in Britain, 1660-1800*. Oxford and New York: Oxford University Press, 1991.

Mainoni, Patrizia. "Il mercato della lana a Milano dal XIV al XV secolo." *Archivio Storico Lombardo* (1984): 20–43.

Maitte, Corine. "Labels, Brands, and Market Integration in the Modern Era." *Business and Economic History On Line* 7 (2009): 1–15.

Maitte, Corine. "Imitation, copie, contrefaçon, faux: définitions et pratiques sous l'Ancien Règime." *Entreprises et histoire* n. 78 (2015): 13–26.

Maitte, Corine. « Voyage d'un Piemontais au coeur des manufactures de draps de l'Europe du Nord. Le tour de l'Europe lainière de Gian Batta Xaverio Mocaffy, 1766-1767 " In *Wool: Products and Markets (13th-20th century)*, edited by Giovanni Luigi Fontana and Gerard Gayot, 627–644. Padua: Cleup, 2004.

Malanima, Paolo. *La decadenza di un'economia cittadina : l'industria di Firenze nei secoli XVI-XVIII*. Bologna: Il Mulino, 1982.

McKendrick, Neil, John Brewer, and J. H. Plumb. *The Birth of a Consumer Society. The Commercialization of Eighteenth-century England*. London: Europa Publications, 1982.

McKendrick, Neil. "Josiah Wedgwood and the Commercialization of the Potteries." In *The Birth of a Consumer Society*, edited by McKendrick, Brewer and Plumb, 100–145. London: Europa Publications, 1982.

McKendrick, Neil. "The Commercialization of Fashion." In *The Birth of a Consumer Society*, edited by McKendrick, Brewer and Plumb, London: Europa Publications, 1982. 84–94.

Mendonça, Sandro, Tiago Santos Pereira, and Mira Godinho Manuel. "Trademarks as an Indicator of Innovation and Industrial Change." *Research policy* 33 (2004): 1385–1404.

Mercer, John. "A mark of distinction: branding and trade mark la in the UK from the 1860s." *Business History* 52 (2010): 17–42.

Minard, Philippe. "Réputations, normes et qualité dans l'industrie textile française au XVIIIème siècle." In *La qualité des produits en France (XVIIIe-XXe siècles)*, edited by Alessandro Stanziani (sous la direction de), 69–89. Paris: Belin, 2003.

Molà, Luca. *The Silk Industry of Renaissance Venice*. Baltimore and London: The Johns Hopkins University Press, 2000.

Moore, Karl, and Susan Reid. The Birth of Brand: 4000 Years of Branding. *Business History* 50 (2008): 419–432.

Moreau, Fabienne. "Le commerce du Champagne au XIXème siècle: sur la piste des bouteilles de champagne Veuve Clicquot découvertes dans un épave de la Mer Baltique en 2010." In *Le commerce du luxe/Le luxe du commerce*, edited by Natacha Coquery et Alain Bonnet (Sous la direction de), 52–63. Paris: Mare & Martin, 2015.

Motta, Enrico. "Armaioli milanesi nel periodo visconteo-sforzesco." *Archivio Storico lombardo* 41 (1914): 187–232.

Mozzato, Andrea. *La mariegola dell'Arte della lana di Venezia, 1244-1595*. Venice: Fonti per la storia di Venezia, 2002.

Munro, John H. "Medieval Woollens: The Western European Woollen Industries and Their Struggles for International Markets." In *The Cambridge History of Western Textiles*, edited by Jenkins David, vol. I. 228–324. Cambridge: Cambridge University Press, 2003.

Ogilvie, Sheilagh. "The Economics of Guilds." *Journal of Economic Perspectives* 28 (2014): 169–192.

Panciera, Walter. *L'arte matrice. I lanifici della Repubblica di Venezia nei secoli XVII e XVIII*. Treviso: Fondazione Benetton, 1996.

Poni, Carlo. *La seta in Italia. Un grande industria prima della rivoluzione industriale*. Bologna: Il Mulino, 2009.

Pulsoni, Carlo. "I classici italiani di Aldo Manuzio e le loro contraffazioni." *Critica del testo* 5 (2002): 477–487.

Rapp, Richard T. "The Unmaking of the Mediterranean Trade Hegemony: International Trade Rivalry and the Commercial Revolution." *The Journal of Economic History* 35 (1975), 499–525.

Rapp, Richard T. *Industry and Economic Decline in Seventeenth-Century Venice*. Cambridge (Mass.) and London: Harvard University Press, 1976.

Richardson, Gary. "Guilds, Laws and Markets for Manufactured Merchandise in Late-Medieval England." *Explorations in Economic History* 41 (2004): 1–25.

Richardson, Gary. *Brand Names Before the Industrial Revolution*. NBER Working Paper Series, WP 13930, April 2008.

Rosa, Gilda. "Appunti per una storia dell'oreficeria milanese." *Archivio storico lombardo* 86 (1959): 139–146.

Salais, Robert et Michael Storper. *Les mondes de production. Enquete sur l'identité économique de la France*. Paris: Editions de l'EHESS, 1993.

Savary de Bruslons, Jacques. *Dictionnaire universel de commerce*. Paris, 1741.

Schechter, Frank I. *The Historical Foundations of the Law Relating to Trade-Marks*. New York: Columbia University Press, 1925.

Schwarkopf, Stefan. "Turning Trademarks into Brands. How Advertising Agencies Practiced and Conceptualized Branding, 1890-1930." In *Trademarks, Brands and Competitiveness*, edited by Teresa Da Silva Lopes and Paul Duguid, 165–193. London and New York: Routledge, 2010.

Spufford, Margaret. *The Great Reclothing of Rural England*. London: Hambledon Press, 1984.

Stanziani, Alessandro. *Histoire de la qualité alimentaire (XIXe-XX siècles)*. Paris: Seuil, 2005.

Stanziani, Alessandro. "Marques, Marques Collectives." In *Dictionnaire historique de l'économie-droit*, edited by Alessandro Stanziani (sous la direction de), 229–238. Paris: L.G.D.J., 2007.

Styles, John. "Product Innovation in Early Modern London." *Past and Present*, n. 168 (2000): 148–158.

Thévenot, Laurent. "Convening the Company of Historians to go into Conventions, Power, Critiques and Engagement." *Historical Social Research* 37 (2012): 22–35.

de Vries, Jan. *The Industrious Revolution*. Cambridge: Cambridge University Press, 2008.

Walker, R. B. "Advertising in London Newspapers, 1650-1750." *Business History* 15 (1973): 112–130.

Wallis, Patrick. *Commercial Innovation in Early Modern England: Proprietary Medicine and the Invention of Branding*, paper presented at the World Economic History Congress, Utrecht, 2009.

Weatherill, Lorna. *Consumer Behaviour and Material Culture in Britain 1660-1760*. London and New York: Routledge, 1988.

Wengrow, David. "Prehistory of Commodity Branding." *Current Anthropology* 49 (2008): 7–34.

Wilkins, Mira. "The Neglected Intangible Asset: The Influence of the Trade Mark on the Rise of the Modern Corporation." *Business History* 34 (1992): 66–94.

Early marks: American trademarks before US trademark law

Paul Duguid

ABSTRACT

Historians identify the process of registration as key to the 'modern mark'. Hence the introduction of trademark registration with the US federal law of 1870 appears as a pivotal event, endorsing Chandlerean accounts of the modern mark as a product of the 'Second Industrial Revolution'. Such accounts overlook the earlier registration laws in places where economic conditions challenge claims for an industrial origin to registration. This article looks at California's registration law, which antedated the US federal law by seven years, asking whether it is merely an exception to prove the Chandlerean rule, or an example that asks us to question Chandlerean assumptions.

Legal historians identify trademark registration as a central component of the 'modern' trademark, while standard business history offers the 'Second Industrial Revolution' as the critical cause of this modernisation. The legal historian Lionel Bently argues that registration finally allowed the mark to be conceptualised as an 'object of property', while the influential business historian Alfred Chandler suggests that this transformation was sought by the makers of 'branded, packaged products' to accommodate the new forms of organisation, production, and distribution that emerged in the 'revolution'. Mira Wilkins's influential work on the trademark and the 'modern corporation' argues that the 'large enterprise in the late nineteenth century coincided with the major change from common law ... to [trademark] statutes' and, by extension, that legal protection of the sort that trademark registration provided 'only became of key importance with the rise of the giant enterprise'. James Beniger makes similar connections, casting brands, with their new legal protection in registered trademarks, as central informational device in the nineteenth-century's corporate-driven 'control revolution'. Looking to the UK, David Higgins sees its novel registration laws as the 'outcome of sustained pressure' from the new sorts of 'commercial and industrial' organisations that Chandler, Wilkins, and Beniger describe. Chandler's 'visible hand' and Beniger's 'control' are, from these perspectives, manifest not only in the emerging forms of corporate organisation, but also in the laws that developed to serve their interests, and trademark registration law is portrayed as one of these. The critical dates of 1870 and 1875, when the US and UK respectively introduced trademark registration law, fit well with these converging legal and business-historical accounts.[1]

The historiography that supports these views, leading from particular moments and causes to particular places, rests on a particular geography. Chandler's purview extends from the US East Coast to the 'Old West', from the industrialists of Philadelphia and the cigarette makers of North Carolina to the grain silos of Minneapolis and the meat packers of Chicago. Wilkins looks at the 'giant American-headquartered corporations' of the late-nineteenth-century, East Coast cities, confident that trademarks emerged there as they had little importance for the growers of 'apples or oranges' of the agricultural US. Beniger stays within this familiar Chandlerean topology, looking at Midvale Steel in Pennsylvania and 'milling, and soap making … cigarette rolling … food canning [and] film processing plants', while on the other side of the Atlantic, Higgins points us to the Marshallian clusters of steel and cloth in industrial England as they reorganised and centralised in the late nineteenth century.[2]

From their geographical vantage point, such histories provide compelling accounts of cause and effect – new corporate structures lobbying for law to meet their needs – and of time and place – industrial clusters and their markets in the late nineteenth century. Nonetheless, such accounts come with curious geographical blind spots, overlooking other parts of Europe, the British colonies, and the Americas. Because such regions were, by standard accounts, late to industrialise and so in no need of the modern law, we might assume developments in them are irrelevant to the story of historical transformation. Yet even Frank Schechter's canonical legal history, while recognising that US '[s]tates noted for [manufacturing] industries may … be credited with the larger proportion' of trademark registrations in the nineteenth century, notes in passing that the US and UK both introduced registration 'not so much for the protection of manufacturers at home, but … to obtain the advantages of reciprocal statutes in foreign countries'. US and UK law, Schechter concedes (via a quotation in a footnote), developed in response to prompting from continental Europe, which it turns out was not the laggard, but significantly in the forefront of the development of trademarks and registration, led by France and Spain and soon followed by other European countries.[3] Pushing against 'long held assumptions about the traditional foundations of trade mark law', Amanda Scardamaglia has shown that Australian legislation anticipated UK registration laws.[4] Relentless focus on US federal law suggests furthermore that historians have not only failed to look outside the North American continent, but also inside. They give primacy to the US federal registration law of 1870, yet when that law was passed, trademark registration was already well established, not only on the European continent and in Australia, but also in Canada and five US states. California, Oregon, Nevada, Kansas and Missouri, in that order, all passed trademark registration law in the 1860s, yet none was the locus of conventional Chandlerean industry, and none gets much attention in legal or Chandlerean accounts.[5]

This article thus looks at California, the first US state to introduce trademark registration, to see what light it can cast on conventional histories of trademark law. In section 1, I consider whether, though early, California's story merely conforms to the conventional, industrially driven accounts or whether it might offer something not found in these. Arguing that it can at least modify some standard assumptions, section 2 then introduces actors and sectors that, implicated in the state's struggle to transition from mining to an economy built around agricultural commodities, contributed both indirectly and directly to the development of marks. Section 3 then turns to the evolution of the California trademark law, noting prior forms of state-controlled marking that throw light on the distinctive development of California law. Sections 4 and 5 trace the way in which apparently parochial interests developed into more general ones as the state and its law developed. Section 6 uses the process of codifying the law to show how the state struggled with questions raised by registration about the relation between common law rights and statutory rights – questions that may well have inhibited others from writing such law. Section 7 then stands back to consider whether, given its distinctive pathway, the resulting law fits with standard definitions of modern trademark law and, if it does not, whether notions of commodification rather than industrialisation might better explain the early development of such law. Highlighting the significance of commodification, I nevertheless suggest that industrialisation did affect subsequent law in ways that led to the suppression of the earlier history by cumulative and Whiggishly triumphalist accounts, even as the path-breaking Lanham Act of 1946 circled federal law back towards the early though unacknowledged California model. Section 8 then briefly addresses the question of why California played such a significant role in the development of trademark registration legislation in the common law countries, while the conclusion then wonders what about business history, which has generally overlooked California's contribution, implicitly favours alternative linear, progressive accounts of the sort told about trademarks and offers some suggestions as to how the allure of such Whiggish narratives might be resisted.

1. Questioning Californian conformity

Though California's law precedes other US trademark registration laws, a cursory glance might suggest that it nonetheless conforms with accounts of new, industrialised corporations pushing for registration. 'Star players' in California business – Borax, Del Monte, Ghirardelli, Martinelli, Levi Strauss, Sperry and others – established marks that endure today.[6] Offering official recognition of a mark when there was no federal equivalent, the state's register, the first in the nation, also drew prominent firms from beyond California – Derringer, the Philadelphia arms manufacturer, for example. And even when there was federal registration, other prominent national businesses – Anheuser beer, for instance – registered simultaneously under both jurisdictions, suggesting that contemporaries saw the California and federal registers as usefully complementary. Similarly, prominent foreign firms were quick to seek protection in California. Among these were the French Champagne firms Clicquot and Heidsieck, influential, as we shall see, in California's marking history as they had been in France's.[7] All these businesses evidently found advantage in California's law. There is little evidence, however, that, beyond the French, any played much part in the law's formation.[8] As we shall see, the emergence of California registration is significantly a local story, yet internally the California of the early 1860s was hardly a site of Chandlerean industrialisation. The state was struggling to extract its economy from mining, the sector closest to 'industrial' within California, but one that played no direct role in the development of the law. As part of that struggle, the state turned to agriculture, the sector of 'apples and oranges' that Wilkins argued had little need for marks.[9] If not to industry, then perhaps we should look to trade as a motivating factor in California's innovation as trademark law is conventionally linked with the growth of trade and the control of distant markets. But here too California does not readily conform: in the 1860s it was still isolated from the rest of the nation by the intransigent Sierra Nevada mountains, though roads began to cross these by the beginning of the 1860s and railways by the end.[10] During this period, outside gold and mining equipment, California's principal products were agricultural and these primarily fed the state, though a limited amount shipped from its ports. During the gestation of the registration law, California wines, for example, which eventually became a major agricultural export for the state, were, according to Thomas Pinney, 'unknown on the Atlantic coast'.[11] Certainly, the desire to trade with the rest of the nation and the world anticipated the law, but the ability to do so came later, suggesting trade may have been as much affect as cause.

Perhaps, then, for all its precedence, relative isolation prevents California's innovation from adding to broader history. California's might be merely a parochial story. Certainly, however innovative, its registrations can seem paltry: in 1870, the first year of federal registration, there are only 40 new entries in the California register. But before dismissing California on these grounds, we should compare California's registrations to those in that new, potentially supersessive federal register. Here, where the pent-up demand of the Eastern industrial sector would be expected to show, we find only 121 registrations. California achieved one third of the national number with fewer than 2% of its population.[12] Moreover, beyond state boundaries and beyond the out-of-state businesses who prudently registered in California, there were others who found significance in California's law. For example, in his *Grand Dictionnaire International de la Propriété*, a seminal text on trademark legislation published in the year of the Madrid international agreement on marks, Comte Maillard de Marafy felt that California's contribution to marking deserved an entry to itself, separate from the US entry.[13] In sum, though the conditions assumed to give rise to trademark registration law – industrialisation, long-distance trade – hardly obtained in California in the 1860s, such a law passed there before it passed in those places where such conditions did prevail. Both local and out-of-state businesses then took advantage of it, while international commentators took note. Thus it seems prudent for modern historians to try to understand how that law came about.

2. The wine rush

In January of 1863, a first-term state senator, Manasseh S. Whiting, introduced a trademarking bill to the California legislature, and in April the state's governor, Leland Stanford, signed the resulting 'Act Concerning Trade-marks and Trade Names' into law.[14] The following month 'Fish's Infallible Hair Restorative' became the first registration under the law, and, not long after that, early litigation arose, including some concerning that registration.[15] Though it could have claimed these as hometown firsts for the US and second only to Canada in the entire realm of common law, Whiting's local paper, San Francisco's *Daily Alta California* initially portrayed the law as a parochial concern, including it in the general category of legislation specifically relating to 'local [i.e. San Francisco] affairs'.[16]

In fact, it was as much his business as his town that drove Whiting's legislation. Whiting was a 'wine and liquor dealer'. He had come to California during the Gold Rush of 1849 but, like many, succeeded not in the mountain mines, but in the coastal city that supplied them, San Francisco.[17] The factors that led to his legislation reveal numerous connections between gold and alcohol. First, with the advent of the Gold Rush, California's wine sector set aside its roots in the vineyards of the religious Missions and reconfigured itself to serve a market rapidly being reshaped by mining.[18] Second, as the 'Rush' of '49 subsided, many Californians looked to wine to replace gold in the state's economy.[19] And third, as we shall see, the wine trade, in good part for strategic, political reasons, shifted from brandy-fortified wines favoured by early clients and tried to develop a reputation for purity. So doing, like the gold trade before it, the sector called on the state government to play a role in certifying quality and punishing adulteration.[20] For all these reasons, both romantic and pragmatic connections between gold, wine, and California developed. Romantically, one wine grower exclaimed, 'Our glorious State is golden for the glitter of its shining ore! Golden, for the beautiful hue of its harvests! Heaven grant it golden for the beautiful color of its Wine!' More pragmatically, an 1861 legislative report on wine predicted that soon 'the annual crop of gold will be second in value to the wine crop'. [21]

The romantic vision came from the vintner Arpad Haraszthy. His father, Colonel Agoston Haraszthy, one of the most influential figures in California wine growing, built some of the more pragmatic links from gold to wine. Haraszthy senior arrived in California from Hungary a year before Whiting. He became a senator a decade before Whiting and subsequently Assayer at the new San Francisco Mint and then its Melter and Refiner, overseeing government purification and certification of ore brought down from mountain mines. While at the Mint, Haraszthy bought land and planted vines, and having established his own vineyard, turned with his son to developing and promoting the California wine trade. In 1861, following recommendations by the legislature's Select Committee on the Vine-Growing Interests of California, the governor appointed the former Assayer to a commission 'to report ... upon the means best adapted to promote the improvement and growth of the vine in California', which sent Haraszthy on a tour of the wine countries of Europe.[22] On his return, Haraszthy published the influential *Grape Culture: Wines, and Wine Making* (1862), which, as it railed against the spurious wines sold as 'Bordeaux' in California, promoted the ideal of pure and unadulterated California wine, telling an eager state that there was no need for falsification because 'California is superior in all the conditions ... to the most favored wine producing regions of Europe'.[23] Whiting too, as we shall see, turned from dealing with miners and legislating to proselytising for pure wine, setting up the *Wine Dealers' Gazette*, the 'acknowledged organ of the Wine and Liquor Trade', the first such periodical, much as his California trademark registration law was the first such law.[24]

3. To your marks

Schechter's canonical history of trademark legislation records that 'in England no parliamentary consideration of a broad and general nature was given to the matter [of trademark protection] until 1862.[25] A look at the 'broad and general' concerns of California's legislature, by contrast, shows that in the decade that stretched from Haraszthy's to Whiting's terms, politicians regularly raised concerns about purity, certification, and registration in ways that built a path towards trademark law. A law to create and regulate the San Francisco Mint was passed in the first session of the California legislature and made the Assayer's position, which Haraszthy was the first to hold, responsible for certifying California's gold, which, if satisfactory, the Mint branded with the mark 'Cal'.[26] In 1855, the legislature passed further law to penalise anyone counterfeiting this mark.[27] These laws worked simultaneously to protect those producing and receiving gold, but in the process also to protect and to project the state's reputation for probity at a time when for many it epitomised the 'Wild West'. As the state sought to temper that reputation, the importance of government oversight in guaranteeing quality and limiting fraud extended beyond gold. In 1852 the legislature established an Inspector of Flour, whose role, not unlike the Assayer's, involved grading and branding flour as 'Superfine' or 'Fine'. Given the limits of the inspector's reach, some of the responsibility for flour grading was delegated to the flour trade itself: uninspected flour was allowed to carry 'private marks' to the same effect as the inspector's, but such marks were to 'be deemed a "Warranty" by such vendor', who would be prosecuted if the mark was misused.[28]

In surveying earlier forms of branding in an agricultural state, it would be unwise to overlook the numerous regulations for cattle marks and brands. For instance, the 'Act Concerning Marks and Brands' of 1849–50 created a register; it insisted that all marks be distinctive; it imposed penalties for unlawfully altering, defacing, or imitating a mark; and it obliged the county recorder to make registrations available for inspection in adjacent counties.[29] Each of these regulations anticipates the trademark law, but should a connection between brands for cattle and for commodities still appear far-fetched, it was directly acknowledged when California codified its law in 1872 (see section 6, below) and united agricultural marks and brands and trademarks in a single chapter.[30]

The sector that most engaged the legislature around questions of marks and purity, however, was the alcohol trade. Although alcohol might appear just another comestible commodity, like flour, beef, and pork, it presented particular challenges that were more directly associated with the state's gold mining identity. First, the gold camps were famous for drunkenness and debauchery and the alcohol trade was seen as fueling such behaviour. And second, as its prime consumers were not highly discriminating, the alcohol trade was regularly accused of adulterating and falsifying what it sold. Moreover, as gold was taken to symbolise the early state, so the miners were taken to represent its citizens, and the state's entire population were thus easily depicted as drunkards by association.[31] In response, and in a major threat to the wine sector, less-debauched citizens became increasingly attracted to the US's thriving temperance movement. In 1846, temperance societies had persuaded the state legislature in Maine to introduce prohibition, and over the next decade several states passed 'Maine Laws' so that, by the 1850s, many Californians hoped that as the state had acquired Maine's reputation for drunkenness, in response it would adopt its prohibition law. Others resisted such laws as undue government intervention, but often in ways that only reaffirmed ideas about California's dissipated citizenry. In 1855, for example, a mining camp gained attention by drunkenly burning in effigy a former assembly member who had favoured a 'prohibitory liquor law' and denouncing such legislation as a restraint on 'Freedom of Liberty!' and 'Freedom of Action!'.[32]

If miners disliked prohibitory liquor laws, so too did the wine trade. But its leaders came to realise that, while they could not embrace the call for temperance, they also could not categorically oppose it. To do so would put a sector that was trying to cultivate a reputation for probity and taste on the same side as the notorious miners. The author Bret Harte would later encapsulate the trade's position in his famous story *The Outcasts of Poker Flat*. Having made its money in the Gold Rush, the town of Poker Flat attempts to vanquish its reputation for drunkenness, gambling, and loose morals by expelling representatives of each vice.[33] In the related political struggles of the day, the wine trade needed to make sure that, though associated with such dissipation, it was nevertheless not among those expelled, but rather allowed to stay. As we shall see, trade organisations like the Wine Association regularly intimated that if a reputation for widespread drunkenness was not in the interest of the state's image, prohibition would not be in the interest of its economy. Directly or implicitly, sector representatives increasingly claimed that those made drunk or ill by alcohol were primarily victims not of alcohol per se, but of impure and adulterated alcoholic beverages, and they petitioned the state, in the spirit of Poker Flat, to banish the wicked adulterators and leave in their place upright vendors of pure, well-supervised alcohol, whose principal value was its restorative and medicinal powers. Where temperance champions called for legislative intervention on behalf of prohibition, their opponents called rather for such intervention on behalf of pure wine.

In fact, as with gold, flour, and cattle, the state had been involved in regulating and certifying alcohol from its earliest days. In 1851 it required retailers of 'spirituous liquors, wines, or liquids' be licensed. The next year it extended that requirement to dealers in alcohol, drugs, and medicine, though, significantly, the 'agricultural production of this state' was excepted from the law's remit.[34] The same year the legislature established the role of Gauger of the Port of San Francisco with the task of inspecting and certifying all 'wines and liquors' arriving in San Francisco and marking them as to quantity and quality.[35] Both these laws ostensibly called on the state to protect its consumers. By focusing on external sources, they simultaneously induced it to protect its home production. As the temperance movement grew, however, the state threatened to become less protective of the alcohol trade, which, as noted above, by 1855 faced prohibition laws. Petitions in support of these laws flooded the state capital, and one law made significant progress until, once again, a clause was added to exclude in-state production. The bill's sponsor withdrew in protest and legislative support collapsed. Defeat of this 'Maine Law' was not a complete triumph for the alcohol sector, however: a state-wide plebiscite calling for temperance replaced it. Eventually that too was defeated, but it pushed the alcohol trade in general to take a position neither wholly opposed to the temperance claims nor wholly with the 'wets', but rather standing in between, alongside an exemplary wine sector, thereby making the villain not all alcohol but only the adulterated kind, while calling on the state to help patrol the boundary between the two by, among other things, providing distinguishing marks for quality as it had with gold and flour. Temperance foes called this invidious partition of the alcohol trade, led by wine producers, 'skulking behind the grape'. Nevertheless, in calling on the state to save the Jekyll of pure wine from the Hyde of adulterated alcohol, the sector and the state moved a little closer towards the trademark law of 1863. [36]

4. From parochial to general concerns

In 1860, the sector's delicate position obliged it to support an anti-adulteration bill ('To Prohibit the Sale and disposal of Adulterated Spirituous or Alcoholic Liquors, Wines, or Cider') introduced by a senator who was also an officer of the Sons of Temperance. Investigations of adulteration by the House of Commons in the UK along with curious rumours in the US suggesting that alcohol was regularly laced with strychnine and lurid reports of the effect of bad alcohol used in embalming helped propel the passage of this bill, and, despite being cautioned by Arpad Haraszthy to 'reflect well before you act', the wine sector found itself obliged to go along, even though the bill no longer carried the standard exclusion for local produce.[37] In what we shall see reflected a growing trend, sectoral limits in the act were soon transcended by second anti-adulteration act in 1862 that broadened the target from specified beverages to food and drink in general. Taking another step towards comprehensive trademark law, this bill turned attention from content alone to include packaging and labelling and the use of false names or descriptions. The Wine Growers Association set up a committee to look into the law and again decided that, whatever its reservations, the Association should prudently voice support in order to affirm its own purity and to distinguish what it called its 'customary … additions' (the brandy it had been used to add to 'fortify' wines, for example) from adulteration.[38]

In 1860, the year of the first anti-adulteration bill, another marking-related bill was intro-duced that was also of interest to anyone selling bottled goods. At that time, the state had so little industry that, despite its burgeoning wine, water, and soft-drink trade, it had no glass manufacturers. The new law sought to 'prevent illegal traffic in soda water bottles', which retailers regularly refilled with what were widely assumed to be counterfeit or con-taminated products. The bill prohibited the resale of bottles bearing a 'private mark', but while the idea of such legislation drew some support, others who acknowledged that the 'private trade-mark ought to be protected', nevertheless held that a sector-specific focus was too narrow and there should instead be 'a general law in relation to trade-marks'. The 1860 'bottle' bill was rejected, but clearly not through antipathy to trademarks.[39]

In these various ways, the path towards trademarks developed out of anxieties over fraud and adulteration, which, from the alcohol sector's point of view, served usefully to distract from temperance indignation. A couple of years before the rejected 1860 'bottle law', the *Daily Alta California* had insisted that:

> [O]ur Legislature should fix the stamp of criminality on all forgery of labels and trademarks, the adulteration of any article bearing a label or trademark, and the sale from a labelled package of an article known to be spurious. A statute making such provisions would be of much value to protect the public and honest and enterprising tradesmen.[40]

The following year, the same paper alerted the state to threats to its reputation in a story about New Yorkers selling bad wine through 'low grog shops' and labelling it as produce of California. While the paper narrowed the focus to the wine trade, it simultaneously broad-ened the implications to embrace the state as a whole and for a solution called for trademark legislation:

> The wine interest is becoming too important to the wealth of our State and the health of our peo-ple for us to allow those frauds to go unnoticed or unpunished. ... We know enough, however, about the evil to perceive that something may be done by statutes to forbid the adulteration of all wines made in this State, the counterfeiting of all labels and trademarks of California wine, and the filling of all labels, and barrels, kegs, bottles, etc., bearing a trademark of one wine with any different liquor for the purposes of deception.[41]

As the press saw common ground among these different issues, it is not surprising that bottling and labelling legislation involving more than soda water soon developed. The first, 'An Act Concerning Certain trade-marks', passed in1861 and sought to protect the health of California citizens and the reputation of its producers by regulating the marks of 'Every person engaged in manufacturing, or bottling of foreign, or native California, wine, cider, porter, ale, beer, soda water, or mineral water'. Principally, it allowed such persons to register their mark with the Secretary of State, who recorded the first mark the day the law passed.[42]

Where the adulteration law was driven by hyperbolic stories of strychnine and embalmed corpses, this version of trademark law drew its support from a well-reported case going through the California courts at the time and of particular interest to the wine trade. In 1861, the San Francisco agent of Veuve Clicquot accused a local importer of selling German Hock under the well-known name of 'Clicquot Champagne'.[43] In France, the champagne sector had carefully cultivated protection for its marks since the 1820s. Veuve Clicquot had regis-tered its marks in the Marne in 1825 and watched carefully over their use ever since to such an extent that when the *Alta* lectured the California wine trade on the importance of culti-vating reputation, it pointed to the 'brand of "Veuve Clicquot"' as a model for 'the guarantee of its quality'.[44]

The court proceedings revealed many of the details of Clicquot's trademarking practices, but more significantly they also underwrote claims for the need to respect marks such as Clicquot's within the state in order to have the state's marks respected without, and the California wine trade, having subdued opposition and increased production within the state was starting see opportunities outside. As Haraszthy's book reported, European wine production had been attacked by disease (principally oidium) since the 1850s, while production in the eastern US had become a victim of the civil war.[45] Moreover, though the end of the infestation and the war could not be seen, West Coast producers, having just been connected by telegraph, might have felt that they could see in the not too distant future the arrival of their Governor's railroad connecting them to the markets and the ports of the East.[46] With such prospects in mind, the wine sector, now represented in the state Senate by Manasseh Whiting, the wine merchant, who won his seat almost as the court ruled in Clicquot's favour, sought to generalise the law once more. As with the succession of anti-adulteration laws before it, the new law went beyond the food-and-drink-focused 'Act Concerning Certain trade-marks' of 1861 (which it repealed) to 'An Act Concerning Trade-marks and Names', without any sectoral limitations.[47] The register, which to this point had only contained the names of bottlers, was now opened for anyone using 'any peculiar name, letters, marks, device, figures, or other trade-mark or name … to designate … an article manufactured or sold by him'. After almost a decade of related if often uncoordinated steps towards this point, the California legislature, responding to myriad local, sectoral, and political interests, but pushed by a wine merchant who seems to have engaged in state politics for this purpose alone, had eventually enacted general trademark registration law, law that as the *Alta* noted, went significantly beyond common law precedent in this area, while helping to keep temperance at bay.[48]

Despite the internal precedents, the state's press saw outside influence. Where earlier laws, particularly the adulteration laws, had primarily protected state producers from foreign competition, the *Alta* saw the law of 1863 as principally protecting foreign products from local misbehavior: 'The object is to prevent imitation of certain foreign liquors, which are bottled abroad, and the bottles after having been emptied are bought up by counterfeiters, who fill them up with fraudulent mixture'[49]. Such protection of foreigners, the paper pointed out, also served local interests as these practices 'injur[ed] the business of the men engaged in importing the genuine article'. Whiting's bill, the *Alta* claimed, 'was drawn up at the request of some importers of San Francisco', the sorts of people with whom Whiting, in his other role as 'wine and liquor merchant' would have had regular interaction. There is no clear evidence of direct influence, but certainly serving the interests of exporters to the state and of importers in the state, the bill also served the state's producers and retailers, who found their own marks and reputations protected simultaneously.[50]

5. Change and constancy

Though broad and general in its eventual form, and despite claims of foreign pressure, this path-breaking trademark law was shaped to a significant degree by relatively narrow local agricultural and retail interests, rather than the industrial interests favoured in standard accounts of early trademark registration legislation. Whiting was undoubtedly instrumental in the procedure. Though brief, his entry into politics helped make sure that his sector's interests were recognised and temperance forestalled. He appears to have left no personal account to help gauge his intentions, but Senate records indicate he was minimally active in other legislation: other acts he worked on were few compared to his those of his colleagues, and those he did take up predominantly addressed the narrow interests of his constituency in contrast to the broad appeal of his trademark law.[51] We get a little more insight into his interests by tracking his life after 1863. His single term over and his trademark law enacted, Whiting, after a brief foray into mining, returned to the retail end of the wine trade, from where, like Haraszthy at the production end, he took up proselytising for the sector, first with a book, *Treatise on Wine, Spirits, and Teas,* written with his business partner, and then with the aforementioned *Wine Dealers' Gazette.*[52] The former is little more than a promotional pamphlet, claiming that Whiting's business specialised in detecting adulterations and selected only pure products, to the benefit of its customers. To emphasise his selectivity, Whiting registered the mark 'Selected Cuvée' for 'foreign and domestic wines and whiskies', reflecting the way retailers rather than producers developed many of the marks at this time.[53] Whiting's *Gazette* also portrayed itself as the enemy of adulteration and the champion of achieving purity through reliable trademarking, noting in 1873 that the 'persistent course of this paper from its existence to the present time is exposing and warring against the violation of trade-marks' and 'hold[ing] the fabricators' of adulterations 'up to deserved contempts' and challeng[ing] their 'bogus brands'.[54]

As with his move into legislation in 1862, Whiting's move into journalism was probably in good part a response to threatening strategies from the temperance movement. In 1870 the Good Templars of California expanded and revamped their publication the *Weekly Rescue.* Whiting's *Gazette* made a fitting opposition.[55]

Another Whiting trademark indicates another shape his opposition took. Defeated in its attempts to win state-wide prohibition, in the 1870s the temperance movement began to support an alternative, the 'local option'. Modeled on an Illinois law, the 'option' was brought to the Senate in a bill framed by the State Temperance Alliance and, curiously, presented by the senator from Napa. The bill sought to allow 'every township, incorporated city or county to vote on the question of granting licenses to sell intoxicating liquors'. For the alcohol trade, the entire bill was a significant challenge, but the most toxic part came in its 'civil liability' clause, which allowed that anyone injured 'in person, property, or in means of support by any intoxicated person, or in consequence of intoxication, may recover damages therefore from the person, who, by selling or otherwise furnishing the liquor, caused the intoxication'.[56] With the wine sector clearly in view, the *Alta* expostulated that such a law would be responsible for 'the destruction of $20,000,000 of property ... throwing nearly 16,000 men out of employment... retarding the prosperity of [San Francisco] a quarter of a century, and of doing an incalculable injury to trade and commerce', including, no doubt, Whiting's business.[57] Though the local option law passed, when it emerged, the liability section had been stripped out, for which Whiting's *Gazette* took credit. The law also included a critical exemption: '[n]othing contained in the provisions of this Act shall prevent the issuing of licenses to druggists for the sale of liquors for medicinal and manufacturing purposes'. If Whiting did not take credit for this, he was certainly in a position to take advantage of it, for in 1870 he had registered a mark for 'Medicinal Whiskey'. This particular mark was one part of a thorough rebranding as his advertising now described Whiting's shop as 'of medicated liquor fame' and repositioned his business as providing 'wines required for medicinal purposes' and 'accommodat[ing] physicians', for whose need of medicine Whiting obligingly kept his store open late on New Year's Eve. Where once he had argued forcefully that pure alcohol did no harm, he now rebranded his product to insist that it did you good and continued to sell it unimpeded by liability or locality while protected by robust law.[58] From making a mark through registration law, Whiting turned to making use of the mark to rebrand a product in ways that innumerable businesses, small, like Whiting's, as well as large, have done since.

6. Codification

In 1870, the US passed its trademark registration law, an occasion that, despite its dismissal a decade later by the Supreme Court (see below), historians will no doubt celebrate as precedent making when its 150th anniversary comes up in 2020. As we have seen, California had well-established law that had been in operation for seven years before the federal law and survived court challenges, yet its anniversary passed in almost complete silence, in good part because historians have generally been unaware of its prior existence. Yet the California law was not entirely isolated within California. In 1872, the trademark law was codified with the rest of California law and it acknowledged its relation to international law by explicitly taking its definition of the mark from the UK Merchandize Marks Act of 1862.[59] While it borrowed, it also lent. Nevada, which passed its own law in 1865, cut its statute unchanged from California's cloth. Oregon, Kansas, and Missouri followed soon after and to different degrees reflected, refined, or rejected aspects of the California law.[60]

Nor, despite its circuitous antecedents, was the California law merely a step in the right direction, as can be said of the Merchandize Marks Act. Bently usefully codifies the key features of modern trademark law: 'the establishment of a central registry'; 'conceptualization of the mark as an object of property'; 'recognition of a dual system of protection: one based on registration, the other based on use in the marketplace'; and the 'development of international arrangements for the protection of marks in foreign territories'.[61] California certainly had the first three. Where Oregon, Kansas, and Missouri originally began with regional registers (as, indeed, did France), California centralised registration with the secretary of state from the bottle law of 1861, continued with the law of 1863, and by the beginning of the following century had some 4000 registrations of state, national, and international marks.

The law of 1863 was also quite clear in the recognition of property, asserting that 'Any person who has first adopted and used a trade-mark or name, whether within or beyond the limit of this state, shall be considered its original owner … ownership may be transferred … [and] entitled to the same protection … as other personal property'. The law also provided Bently's 'dual system of protection', for the opportunity to register did not alter existing common law protections accruing to first users. Courts were repeatedly asked to address the question of whether statutory trademark law compromised common law rights of ownership. And where US federal and UK courts had been reluctant to see marks as property, California courts addressed this issue early and decisively in the case of *Derringer* v. *Plate*, and the court was quite clear in its assertion:

> The right of property does not in any manner depend for its inceptive existence or support upon statutory law, though its enjoyment may be better secured and guarded, and infringements upon the rights of the proprietor may be more effectually prevented or redressed by the aid of the statute than at common law. … It is nowhere declared, either directly or indirectly, that property in a trademark can be acquired only in the mode provided by the act; but, on the contrary, it appears, by collating sections one and 10, that no one is permitted to file his claim with the Secretary of State unless he is the exclusive owner of the trademark.[62]

The only one of Bently's conditions that does not apply so readily concerns the 'international arrangements', for California, as a state, could not enter into international treaties. Nonetheless, as we have seen, it offered its protection to all marks, 'whether within or beyond the limit of this state' and, indeed, here it had certain advantages over the federal register. Where the federal government had difficulty registering UK marks until 1876, when that country's law finally met its treaty obligation to provide reciprocal registration rights, California's registers and courts were open to foreign firms like Clicquot and Heidsieck. In all, the California law was not a vestige of earlier marking practices, but rather a harbinger of future ones.

7. Commodification

While the law of 1863 effectively met Bently's conditions for modern trademark law, as I have argued the making of that law does not fit so readily with the standard account of industrialisation and its Chandlerean companies driving and shaping such law. Rather, this story of trademark innovation comes in a state that, in the wake of the Gold Rush, was primarily agricultural and struggling to emancipate itself from an economy built on the extraction of natural resources. Richard Walker argues, extraction economies often lose control of the wealth they generate as well-established urban centres 'plunder' their output.[63] California, Walker argued, is noteworthy in avoiding that pitfall by supporting not merely the production, but also the commodification of alternative agricultural resources. By extension, I suggest, California's trademark law made a significant contribution to that process in ways that tell us something about both California and trademarking. Walker identifies four 'principal components of California's development by commodification: "capital accumulation, industrialization, state intervention and promotion, and the development of a property regime".[64] Accumulated capital came initially from the mines, whose wealth, as Gray Brechin argues, was significantly 'plundered' by the cities, which in turn provided consumers for the state's agricultural and small commodity producers rather than industrialists, a description that fits both Haraszthy and Whiting.[65] In this case, we should see Walker's second component, industrialisation, not simply, as so often, as an autonomous driver of economic (and legal) change, but rather as to a significant degree, the driven.

Walker's final two criteria help us appreciate how trademark law might have contributed to the driving. As the gold business began to falter, the eyes of government turned towards agriculture and particularly towards California wine as its likely successor in contributing to the state's wealth. Government eyes turning in this direction did not come from within the state alone. From the mid-1850s, the US Patent Office had sponsored reports on the country's potential to develop a productive wine sector and portrayed California as a plausible centre of such a sector. Soon after, the state took an active part in promoting this suggestion.[66] State legislators sponsored various committees to advance the state's capabilities such as the 'Select Committee on the Vine-Growing Interests' of 1859, which led in turn to the 'Committee on the Growth, Culture and Improvement of the Grape Vine', which then sent Haraszthy to Europe and led to later institutions such as the State Board of Viticulture and the University of California.[67] And in 1859, to promote new growers, the legislature freed vineyards of taxation until their vines were four-years-old.[68]

After state intervention, Walker's remaining requirement for the successful transformation into a commodity economy is a robust 'property regime'. While histories of the state focus on such things as the quashing of land grants provided under the Mexican administration, it seems reasonable to put the innovative trademark law in this category, as it became clear that a reliable name was a key indicator of the reliability of wine and, in turn, property rights in that name were thought to promote the reliability of such endorsements. Hence, trademark law and the protection of property in brands represented another intervention by the state to foster the growth of and commodification within this critical, agricultural sector. However, here once again California resists conventional theory in ways that further suggest that practices on the ground differ from the theory that generally tries to account for them.

William Landes and Richard Posner's seminal text on the economic theory of the mark holds that the mark does not indicate a place of production nor the particular producers involved. Rather, it primarily seeks to distinguish the producer's commodity from others of the same type.[69] If this is right, the state of California has little to contribute to the commodification of wine brands. To substantiate their claim, Landes and Posner predict that honest producers will 'create new generic words' for their marks, as their main goal will be to distinguish their mark (as well as their produce) from all others'. Unless we dismiss the registrants as inherently fraudulent, California registrations resist this argument for what Landes and Posner call 'a market of languages', where 'inventing new words' will be rife. Among California registrations, such 'new words' are remarkably rare while marks that seek to associate the marked product with place and production are fairly common. After 'California', 'Golden' on its own and along with 'Gate', 'State', and 'West' are the most common term used, followed by others such as '49', and 'Yosemite'.[70] The reluctance to coin new words suggests that trademark registrants, rather than simply trying to distinguish themselves, as Landes and Posner assume, have to deal with the tension between, on the one hand making a distinction', yet on the other, associating their produce with similar commodities that are, for example, produced in the same place or by the same procedures.[71]

Given the influence of the wine sector, the tradition of *terroire* within that sector, and the state's claim to be a uniquely beneficial wine growing area, it is not surprising that wine companies in particular, encouraged by the success of Champagne, cultivated associations of place and producer that echoed the *appellations* and marks of Europe, which not only invoke a place of origin, but also particular production practices shared by all associated with particular places.[72] But the attraction of shared, located, and collectives identities went far beyond wine: innumerable other products laid claim to California localities, and the register reveals within these many other 'association' marks (as such marks that indicated the endorsement of a group or association were known at the time) from the Point Reyes Ranchers, the Mendocino Hop Growers, to the Newcastle Fruit Growers Shipping and Preserving Association, and beyond.[73] The strongest and most influential associations among these registrants were unions, signalling characteristics of the labour involved in production. To distinguish union-made products from those made by foreign, child, prison, and 'sweated' labour, union 'locals' began to register marks in California in the 1870s and an amendment to the political code passed in 1887 made their right to register explicit.[74] Other state legislatures passed similar laws, and associations, cooperatives, and unions across the country took up the practice. At the end of the century, the US Industrial Commission on Labor Relations acknowledged that '[n]early all the States have now adopted a statute allowing members of a union ... or any other ... association ... to adopt labels or trade-marks'.[75] At around the same time, international treaty partners, US judges, and the Commissioner of Patents all argued that such *appellations* and associations should be allowed in the federal

register. This is not entirely surprising. Information, which is how theorists have long characterised the mark, suffers from an inability to testify on its own behalf. Unchecked in the
producer's hand, it can be used to mislead or conceal as much as to inform and clarify.
Consequently, from the consumer's point of view, a second voice, be it of an association, a
union, or a certifying body, which may endorse or may challenge the first, can contribute a
good deal.[76]

Despite the appeals noted above for such voices and despite accommodating state laws,
led by California, federal legislators resisted. To understand this response, we need to turn briefly
to the strange progress of US federal trademark law. The federal law that was passed in 1870
had been justified under the 'Progress' clause of the US Constitution. In 1879 the US Supreme
Court invalidated that justification and hence the federal law. In 1881, Congress introduced a
replacement justified under the Constitution's 'Treaty' clause.[77] Serving primarily to meet prior
treaty obligations, the law only protected marks 'used in commerce with foreign nations or
with the Indian tribes'. Under this law the US Patent Office continued registration and the courts
offered some protection, but the registrar refused to acknowledge the right of associations to
register. In 1898, under pressure to bring US law into line with its treaty partners, most of which
did allow association marks, President McKinley formed a committee to propose new law.
Evidence was invited from 'commercial and manufacturing organisations' as well as the
Manufacturers Association of America, the Pharmaceutical Association and the Association of
Retail Druggists, but no testimony seems to have been solicited or heard from associations or
unions, nor from individual states. When the new law was finally passed to wide acclaim in
1905, it was quite unlike state law and refused to recognise association marks.[78] It may be here,
rather than in the origins of the mark, that the industrialists championed by Chandlereans
played their major part in law making. The 1905 mark was fashioned at their prompting to
meet their interests and exclude those of other associations. As a result, the law also failed to
fulfill its purpose of bringing US law into line with the country's treaty obligations.[79] If the
resulting federal law had any connection with California, it might be that it took the concept
of commodification to an extreme. As Karl Marx observed, the commodity could serve as a
'fetish' to distract from or obscure the conditions and the relations of its production, and the
new federal law helped meet such fetishisation. The national registers, unlike the states', were
no longer open to protecting or projecting the place of production, the means of production,
the labour involved, or the collectives represented. Indeed, rather than project these, the mark
now "concealed instead of disclosing", effectively making other inputs invisible, other voices
inaudible.[80] Concealing these inputs and voices, the 1905 law also helped to conceal their
contribution to early trademarking development and practice. Consequently, when the
'Lanham Act' was passed in 1946 and finally did recognise forms of collectivity and association,
it was credited with originality and praised for bringing the mark into line with the needs of
modern industry.[81] The US was again portrayed as leading rather than, as it in fact was, abjectly
following. Such celebrations in turn allowed the linear, progressive, and ultimately triumphalist
account of trademark and business history to trump the actual, convoluted history and the
competing interests involved.

8. Why California?

This article questions the conventional accounts of industrialisation leading to trademark
registration law, showing that the laws of the iconic industrial powers, the US and Great

Britain, were preceded not only in California, but also across Europe and in the British colonies of Australia and Canada. This alternative history raises two questions: Why did trademark registration arise in these places and not in the canonical industrial nations? And why has this alternative history been overlooked?

To address the first question, I have argued elsewhere that France, which from the early nineteenth century continually developed its trademark law and in the mid-century turned to international treaties to encourage others to recognise and standardise such laws, was one of the leading forces in the making of modern trademark law.[82] As Schechter's footnote mentioned above acknowledges, the UK laws of 1862 and 1875 and the US law of 1870 can all be seen as responses to French prodding, and thus it is not surprising to see the French contributing to the account of the California law above.[83] Nevertheless, the question of why law came into those countries from outlying colonial territories or states remains.

Bently suggests that in these places 'benefits of such registries outweighed their perceived dangers'.[84] These perceived dangers included concern over whether registration was 'declarative', a recognition of pre-established rights, or 'attributive', necessary to establishing such rights. Wherever registration was introduced, trademark owners worried that their rights would be pre-empted by a competitor beating them to the register, and this concern provoked resistance to registration. This concern was raised, as noted above, in anticipation of the California law, in early case law that followed, and later in the process of the codification of California law. Each time the law was changed, anxious questions on this topic arose.

Such anxiety may have led the industrial states in the common law countries to let others try first. Scardamaglia suggests that Australia probably served as a testing ground, allowing the British Parliament, which revealed profound doubts about registration in the debates that led to the Merchandise Marks Act, to see whether registration was indeed feasible.[85] California offered a similar natural experiment in the US. As federal legislators seem to have studiously ignored that state's contribution, it may be that they did not like all that they saw, and thus California is remarkably omitted from discussions that led to the law of 1905.[86] I have suggested here and elsewhere that part of that antipathy may have arisen from the California law's willingness to countenance union marks confronting increasing anti-union sentiment in the country at the time that the law of 1905 developed.[87]

If all this helps explain why the UK and the US followed rather than led, it does not indicate why, in the US, California led. As I have tried to explain above, the state's efforts to commodify its agricultural production in the aftermath of the Gold Rush contributed significantly. At the heart of this process of commodification lay the wine trade, which allowed an aspect of nature with great potential in the California climate to be bottled and branded in ways that would be highly profitable to both producers and the state as long as those brands were suitably protected by state regulation. That this process of state-supported commodification had been well established by the French no doubt made the legislature in Sacramento more receptive to French influence than the one in Washington. Thus it took until the Lanham Act of 1946 for the federal government to fully comply with treaties signed with France in the nineteenth century and to align its law with the California law.

9. Conclusion

Having addressed why legislation may have ignored the case of California, we are left to consider why business history should also have ignored it. The broader, less Darwinian historical perspective, of the sort I have tried to present here, holds that the Lanham Act, far from the next step in a linear progression, as it is usually presented, was an acute U-turn, finally bringing US law and practice into line not only with foreign treaties, but also with a tradition that California had begun to develop some 80 years before. In many ways the triumph of the linear account is not surprising. In 1941, a little before Lanham, Daniel Boorstin argued that legal historians saw their craft as 'an alchemy for distilling legal principles' so that 'the present forms of institutions seem to be their inevitable forms'.[88] Such a teleological approach understandably leaves aside the incidental; but, like the law reports on which legal history draws, it can produce historical narrative in which the past is used primarily to endorse the present, as if every important step we take inevitably takes us forward and there is no place for U-turns.[89] Similarly, economic history has intermittently configured itself around rather similar assumptions of Darwinian or Spenserian evolution, drawing on legal history for whatever conveniently fitted with its March of progress and leaving out what was less convenient.[90] Of course, all history must leave out far more than it includes. Nevertheless, it is occasionally profitable to turn to what has been left aside to see whether it is merely insignificant or whether, when taken into account, it might productively unsettle rather than merely endorse Whiggish narratives.[91] As business history often relies on legal and economic history, this is an area where honouring others' omissions might also involve unconsciously importing unacknowledged teleological assumptions, another 'trap' for the field that might be added to Philip Scranton and Patrick Fridenson's useful list.[92] Hence, though it always risks leading us down dead ends and engaging with minutiae, an important contribution to our field can be to look at aspects of history that have been overlooked or omitted, despite claims to historical precedence that alone would seem to merit attention, to see whether the omissions might ask us to adjust, rather than merely serve to reinforce, standard accounts.[93] This article suggests that the early development of trademark registration in California, driven by commodification, a topic generally subordinated to industrialisation, might offer plausible alternative narratives and reorder standard accounts as well as telling us something about the field and its methods.

Notes

1. Bently, "Making of Modern Trade Mark Law," 4; Chandler, *Scale and Scope*, 62; Wilkins, "The Neglected Intangible Asset," 69; Beniger, *Control Revolution, passim*; Higgins, "Making of Modern Trade-mark Law," 42; Chandler, *Visible Hand*; "Act to Revise, Consolidate, and Amend the Statutes relating to Patents and Copyrights" 16 Stat. 198 1848–187; "Trade Marks Registration Act, 1875," 38 & 39 Vict. Chap. 91.
2. Chandler, *Scale and Scope*; Wilkins, "Neglected Intangible Asset," 69; Beniger, *Control Revolution*, 294, 264; Higgins, "Making of Modern Trade-mark Law."
3. Schechter, *Historical Foundations*, 446, 140. In 1862, a House of Commons committee noted that trademark registration was already functioning in Austria, Bavaria, Belgium, France, Hanover, the Netherlands, Portugal, Prussia, Russia, Sardinia, Saxony, Spain, Sweden, Norway, and Württemberg. *Report from the Select Committee on Trade Marks Bill*, para. 72. For France's influence, see Duguid, "French Connections"; for Spain, see Sáiz and Fernández Pérez, "Catalonian Trademarks."
4. Scardamaglia, *Colonial Australian Trade Mark Law*, 119. Table 1, p. 22, shows that South Australia passed a registration act in 1863 and was followed by Tasmania, Queensland, and New South Wales in 1865. Registration did not begin in any state, however, until 1865.
5. California passed its registration law in 1863, Oregon, 1864, Nevada, 1865, Kansas and Missouri, 1866. See "Act Containing Trade Marks and Names," *Statutes of California*, 1863, Chap. 129

[hereafter California Statutes are noted by the year and chapter of the *Statutes*]; "Of Trade and Stock Marks and Brands," *Laws of Oregon*, 1874, Chap. 23; "Act Concerning Trade Marks and Names," *Statutes of the State of Nevada*, 1864–5, Chap. 82; "Act to Prevent the Counterfeiting, Changing, or Destroying Trade Marks, Devices and Brands," *Laws of the State of Kansas*, 1866, Chap. 66; "Act to Protect Mechanics, Manufacturers and Others in their Trade Marks," *Laws of the State of Missouri*, 99. Other US states had trademark law, much as the UK had its Merchandise Marks Act (25 & 26 Vict.); none, however, had registration before California. Edward Rogers brief history of trademarks notes that New York (1847), Connecticut (1859), Iowa (1860), Michigan (1863) had trademark law by 1863, but besides omitting California, Rogers fails to note that these states did not offer registration. Rogers, "Some Historical Matters," 42. Rogers's omission suggests that he took his list from the report of the commissioners appointed to examine US trademark law in 1898, whose list of 'all the State statutes on the subject prior to the first national statute approved July 8, 1870' also omits California. US Congress, *Report of the Commissioners*, 91–2. Although New York appears first in both lists, it only introduced registration in 1889, and that just for 'associations or unions'. *Laws of New York*, 1899, Chap. 385. The Province of Canada passed its registration law in 1861 "An Act to Amend the Act Respecting Trade-Marks and to Provide for the Registration of Trade-Marks." See Smart, *The Law of Trade-Marks and Designs in Canada*, Chap. IV. As Bently notes, 'a number of colonies established their own systems in the 1860s'. See Bently, "Extraordinary Multiplicity," 170.

6. 'Star players' comes from Scranton and Fridenson, *Reimagining Business History*, 5. Registration data are drawn from the trademark applications and trademark registers in the California State Archives, Sacramento, the Missouri State Archive, and the annual *Report of the Commissioner of Patents and Trade-Marks*. I am grateful to the state archivists for help with this work. Borax was entered in 1890 as mark number 1874 in the California register. Hereafter entries will be identified by registrant, date, and number. Del Monte Milling, 1884 1194; Ghiradelli, 1880 595; Martinelli, 1875 313; Levi Strauss, 1881 726; Sperry, 1875 321 I. While these businesses would seem to fall into the Chandlerean mould, Ghiradelli initially opposed the idea of trademarks (*Daily Alta California* [hereafter *Alta*], 1861, June 12, 1), while Levi Strauss did not apply for a trademark for his famous riveted jeans until some 10 years after their introduction and eight years after their patent.

7. Derringer, 1863 20; Anheuser, 1877 413; Clicquot, 1864 26; Heidsieck, 1864 27. E. Anheuser also registered a federal mark in 1877, yet curiously it did not register in its own state, Missouri, though registration was available there. See *Annual Report of the Commissioner of Patents for the Year 1877*. For the influence of Champagne firms in the development of French law, see Duguid, "French Connections."

8. For the French contribution (see section 4).

9. On the 'industrialisation', see Jung, "Capitalism Comes to the Diggings."

10. Nash, "A Veritable Revolution."

11. Pinney, *Makers of American Wine*, 68.

12. Decennial census numbers suggest that throughout the nineteenth century, California had a higher per capita rate of registration than the federal government. For another comparison, in the first year of its operation, the Canadian registration law of 1861 registered nine marks. See *Canada Gazette*, XXII No. 11, 14 March 1863, pp. 778–779. At the time, the population of Canada was more than eight times that of California.

13. 'L'importance de l'état de Californie … a grandi considérablement en peu d'années. … Ces considérations nous décident à détacher de la législation des États-Unis celle qui concerne particulièrement la Californie'. Maillard de Marafy, *Grand Dictionnaire*, 2:309.

14. *Journal of the California Senate. Fourteenth Session*, 88 and *passim*. *Statutes* 1863 Chap. 129.

15. Charles Story, 1863 12. (Story's mark was not number 1 because registrations under the bottle law (see section 4) preceded it. *Fish v Redington*, 31 Cal 185 (1866).

16. 'San Francisco Bills', *Alta*, 1863, April 13, 1; Elsewhere the paper took a more cosmopolitan view, puffing the law as 'better than any trade-mark law to be found in any State or country'. 'Trade-mark Bill', *Alta*, 1863, Feb 2, 1.

17. For the city's relation to the mines, see Brechin, *Imperial San Francisco*.

18. Pinney argues that the earliest vines came to California in 1778, but that the main sources of early cultivation were the Missions. *Makers of American Wine*, 58.
19. Scardamaglia puts the Australian 'gold rush' among the 'localised factors' that led to Australian trademark registration law. *Colonial Australian Trade Marks*, 6.
20. Early California wines, known as 'port' and 'Angelica' were often heavily fortified with spirits, causing a New York critic to complain that 'A bottle full of [Angelica] contains I don't know how many headaches'. Pinney, *Makers of American Wine*, 66.
21. Arpad Haraszthy, 'The Vine and Wine in Europe', 1. 'Report of the Assembly Select Committee on the Vine-Growing Interests of California', *Alta*, 1861, Feb 26, 1.
22. Pinney, *History of Wine*, 275.
23. Agoston Haraszthy, *Grape Culture*, xv.
24. Rowell, *Rowell's American Newspaper Directory*, 1006.
25. Schechter, *Historical Foundations*, 139.
26. *Statutes* 1849–50 Chap. 123.
27. *Statutes* 1855 Chap. 143.
28. *Statutes* 1852 Chap. 57. All flour had to be branded. Purchasers of flour branded by the seller could call on the Inspector if the flour seemed substandard. If the Inspector agreed, the seller could be 'deemed guilty of fraud' and fined up to $50. Grades of 'Middling', 'Bad', and 'Condemned' were added in the 'Amendatory' act of the following year, *Statutes* 1853 Chap. 174.
29. *Statutes* 1849–50 Chap. 89. The California trademark law of 1861 (see section 4) along with those of Missouri and Kansas initially required registration by county, suggesting a precedent set by prior cattle brand and mark legislation. By 1863 the legislature had evidently realised that commodities might wander further than cattle.
30. *Political Code of the State of California*, Chap. 7. See also the title of the Oregon law of 1864 (see footnote 5).
31. See, for example, Benton, *The California Pilgrim*, quoted in Ostrander, *Prohibition Movement*, 2.
32. "Disgraceful Conduct," *Sacramento Daily Union*, 1855, May 21, 2.
33. Bret Harte, *The Outcasts of Poker Flat*.
34. *Statutes*, 1851, Chap. 39.
35. *Statutes*, 1851, Chap. 58.
36. Ostrander, *Prohibition Movement*, 14–15, *passim*. "California Legislature," *Sacramento Daily Union*, 1855, March 22, 3.
37. *Statutes*, 1860, Chap. 223. D.W. Welty, an elected officer of the 'Sons of Temperance', introduced the bill. *Sacramento Daily Union*, 1859, Dec 27, 3. "No Strychnine in Whisky," *Sacramento Daily Union*, 1860, Nov 1, 4; "Revolting Charges in San Francisco," *Sacramento Daily Union*, 1858, Sep. 10, 3. *California Farmer and Journal of Useful Sciences*, 1862, 18 July, 1. Pinney, *Wine Makers*, 63.
38. "The Wine Growers' Convention," *Sacramento Daily Union*, 1862, Dec 12, 3. The committee argued that ' Perhaps it would be well to amend the Act so as to define adulterations of wine, so that there may be no mistake. ... These customs and others similar in character reputable among the most honest wine growers, should be carefully distinguished from all mixtures of colouring matter, drugs and diluted alcohol, the use of which is so nearly akin to fraud that no line of separation can be safely drawn'.
39. 'California Legislature', *Sacramento Daily Union*, 1860, Feb 25, 1. The wine sector may have had an interest in rejecting this bill. Pinney notes a report that most of the 12,000 bottles that Kohler and Frohling, a major San Francisco wine merchant and exporter, used annually came recycled from the San Francisco junk dealers. *Wine Makers*, 69.
40. 'Native vs. Imported Wines', *Alta*, 1858, Dec 14, 1.
41. "Frauds in Fabricating and Adulterating Wine," *Alta*, 1859, Oct 8, 2.
42. *Statutes*, 1861, Chap. 478. The law passed on May 18th; on that day Delahanty and Skelly (1861 1) recorded their mark for soda water. By a curious coincidence, the Canadian trademark registration law was assented to on the same day. *Canada Gazette*, XX No. 21 (1861), 1. I found no sign that either law was influenced by (nor its legislators aware of) the other. Revealing other shared interests, Scardamaglia notes that Australia's law was influenced by the concerns of 'the bottlers of aerated waters and cordials, who were especially alarmed about the unauthorised use of their trade marks and embossed bottles'. *Colonial Australian Trade Mark Law*, 10.

43. Haraszthy had described the Clicquot name as 'known all over the world'. *Grape Culture*, 114.
44. "Répertoire de 1825 à 1858. Marques de Fabrique et de Commerce," Archives Départmentales de la Marne. "Californian and Other Wines," *Alta*, 1860, Sept 5, 2.
45. During the oidium outbreak, French production sank from 39 million to 11 million hectoliters. Campbell, *Phylloxera*, 31. Meanwhile, between 1860 and 1863, years of the war, California wine exports to the east increased 100%. Carosso, *California Wine Industry*, 34.
46. Leland Stanford, the governor who signed the 1863 act into law, had set up the Central Pacific Railroad the previous year and begun to build a road across the Sierra Nevada mountains. In future years, he would also own extensive vineyards. See Carosso, *California Wine Industry*; Bethel, "The Golden Skein."
47. *Statutes* 1863 Chap. 129.
48. For the *Alta*, see note 16.
49. "Our Legislative Correspondence," *Alta*, 1863, Jan 18, 1.
50. In the wine trade, the boundary between the native and foreign interests could be hard to draw. In 1862, the French consul noted a large number of foreign winemakers were at work in the state. "Un grand nombre de vignerons Français et Allemands sont employés." "Rapport Commercial pour 1861 [de] Consulat de France à San Francisco," Archives National de France, Fontes Commercial, California, f12/2593. "Californian and Other Wines," *Alta*, 1860, Sept 5, 2. "Our Legislative Correspondence," *Alta*, 1863, Jan 27, 1. As Scardamaglia notes, such interests cast doubt on conventional accounts of trademark law developing to serve consumer interests. *Colonial Australian Trade Mark Law*, passim.
51. If he is compared to fellow members of the Commerce and Navigation Committee, to which his bill was referred, Whiting worked on five bills over the session, the other three worked on six, nine, and 20 respectively. Of the remaining bills Whiting worked on, one addressed the roads and another the fire brigade of San Francisco, Whiting's city. *Journals of the California Senate, Thirteenth Session*.
52. Whiting and Berry, *Treatise on Wines, Spirits, and Teas*.
53. It would be useful to know the number of retailers as opposed to producers in the register, but the data available do not provide them. Of registrations in general and of the wine registrations in particular from the nineteenth century, about 60% of the registrations in general and of the wine registrations in particular come with a San Francisco address. While many of these would have been retailers, several are likely to have been, or been proxies for, producers, and many would have been both producers and retailers. Under 5% came from out of state, and those we can more reasonably assume were not retailers.
54. "Trade-Marks," *Wine Dealers' Gazette*, 1873 No.2: 1.
55. The *Rescue* began in 1864. According to the *Wine Dealer's Gazette*, it portrayed Whiting as a fallen figure, 'formerly a member of your Legislature', but now associating 'with the whisky-makers and drunkard-makers [who] force you to swallow the filthy mixtures … poison which they manufacture', *Gazette*, 1874, 3(4): 1.
56. "A Plea for 'The Civil Damages Act'," *Pacific Rural Press*, 1873, Aug 2, 67.
57. 1874 Chap. 300. *Alta*,1874, June 26, 2.
58. 'Medicinal Whisky', 1870 284; [Advertisements] *Alta*, 1868, March 22, 2; 1868, Dec 25, 2.
59. *Political Code of the State of California*, Chap. 7.
60. For the laws, see note 5.
61. Bently, *Making of Modern Trademark Law*, 3.
62. For reluctance, see Schechter, 141. *Derringer v Plate* 29 Cal 293 (1865). Had other jurisdictions (or, indeed, California itself) paid attention to this ruling, a lot of court time might have been saved.
63. Walker, "California's Golden Road to Riches."
64. Walker, "California's Golden Road to Riches," 168.
65. Brechin, *Imperial San Francisco*.
66. *Annual Report of the Commissioner of Patents* 1858; ibid, 1859.
67. See Carosso, *California Wine Industry*, 55; Sullivan, *A Companion to California Wine*, 374. The University of California, as an agricultural college with particular interests in wine, was one peripheral outgrowth of this enthusiasm.

68. *Statutes* 1859 Chap. 199.
69. Landes and Posner, "Trademark Law."
70. These names contrast with the national register, where in 1877, for example, words like 'imperial' and 'regal' top the chart. Among the almost 4000 California registrations made by 1901, there are some 140 'nonce' words, almost half of these were adaptions that ended in -*ene*, -*ine*, or -*yne* (such as Linsene, Eucolyptine, or Neuralodyne), falling in with attempts of the time to associate medical products with scientific discoveries. In contrast, the register has some 98 marks for this period with 'Golden', 45 with 'sun', 16 with 'sunset', 13 with 'bay', 10 with 'Yosemite', and eight with 'Sierra' and '49'. These counts cannot be returned as simple percentages, as many of the marks registered images rather than words. Though here again, many of these images are of recognisable California landmarks. For the source of the state data, see note 6. For the Federal data, see *Annual Report of the Commissioner of Patents*, 1877.
71. To support their argument, Landes and Posner cite George Zipf's linguistic analysis of brand names. Trade Mark Law, 271. Zipf himself, however, argues to the contrary 'we do not find different brand-names for different producers or for different products'. Instead an 'inverse square relationship … suggests a subtle "balance" between the number of different brand-names and the comparative frequency of their usage by different firms'. Zipf, "Brand Names," 363. The numbers in note 68 suggest something of a Zipf-like 'balance'.
72. While protecting its *appellations*, California has long been willing to appropriate those of others. Sainsevain led the way in this by registering marks for Champagne and Port while the Italian-Swiss Agricultural Society registered 'Tipo Chianti' which Pinney argues was 'the single most important brand name product of the California wine industry'. See Mendelson, *From Demon to Darling*; Pinney, *Makers of American Wine*, 80.
73. In current US law, 'association marks' are called 'collective' or 'certification' marks. Collective marks (such as 'girl scout cookies') may be used by anyone who is part of the organisation owning the mark (i.e., a girl scout). Certification marks (such as 'Fair Trade Coffee') may be used by anyone who meets the standards set by owner of the mark (e.g. Fair Trade U.S.A). See http://www.uspto.gov/learning-and-resources/trademark-faqs; visited July 25, 2016.
74. *Statutes* 1887 Chap. 150.
75. US Industrial Commission, *Report of the Industrial Commission on Labor Legislation*, 129.
76. Duguid, "Information in the Mark and the Marketplace."
77. The 'Progress' clause of the US Constitution (Article 1, Section 8, Clause 8) gave Congress the power to 'promote the Progress of Science and useful Arts, by securing for limited Times to Authors and Inventors the exclusive right to their respective Writings and Discoveries'. The 'Treaty' clause (Article 1, Section 10, Clause 1) reserved the right to make treaties to the federal government. See http://www.archives.gov/exhibits/charters/constitution.html; visited July 25, 2016. For an account of the 'turbulent' legislative and legal struggles, see Rosen, "In Search of the Trade-Mark Cases." Schechter is curiously confused about this progression. See *Historical Foundations*, 140.
78. US Congress, *Report of the Commissioners*. 33 Stat. 724 1897–1907.
79. Duguid, "A Case of Prejudice?"
80. Marx, *Capital* I: 41, 47, *passim*.
81. US 60 Stat. 1943–1946. For praise of Lanham, see Duguid, "A Case of Prejudice?"
82. Duguid, "French Connections."
83. For Schechter's footnote, see note 3.
84. Bently, "Extraordinary Multiplicity," 170.
85. Colonial Australian Trade Mark Law, 116.
86. See, for example, the note on Rogers' omission of California (note 5). If this is indeed the case it may more appropriately be called an act of Commission rather than omission.
87. If that is the case, it produces a curious cycle. The French lead in marking built in part upon the continuous tradition of guilds in that country. These, the precursors of unions, had been outlawed in Britain since the Statute of Monopolies (1623).
88. Boorstin, 'Tradition and Method in Legal History', 426.
89. Writing at a time of crisis for law reports, W.T.S. Daniel argued that these should select cases with an eye to providing 'precedents for future guidance'. Daniel, *The History & Origin of the Law Report*, 88.

90. Harris, "Encounters of Economic History and Legal History."
91. Boorstin echoes Herbert Butterfield's famous argument about Whig historians who 'emphasise certain principles of progress in the past … to produce a story which is a ratification if not the glorification of the present'. *Whig Interpretation of History*, v.
92. Scranton and Fridenson, *Reimagining Business History*.
93. See, for example, Atmore's challenge to teleological and determinist accounts in 'Railway Interests'.

Acknowledgements

I am particularly grateful to Megan Finn and Deven Desai, both of whom read earlier drafts of this paper and offered insightful and helpful comments, to archivists in the US and Europe, and particularly in California, who gave me ready access to the sources drawn upon in the argument, and to the editors of this special issue and its anonymous reviewers, who provided particularly helpful suggestions, which I have tried to follow.

Disclosure statement

No potential conflict of interest was reported by the author.

Funding

Support for research contributing to this paper was provided by the Economic and Social Research Council, U.K., the France-Berkeley Fund, and the Centre de Recherche en Gestion at the École Polytechnique, Paris.

Sources

Archives
California State Archive, Sacramento, California.
Missouri State Archive, Jefferson City, Missouri.
St Louis Municipal Archive, St Louis, Missouri.
Archives Départmentales de la Marne, France.
Archives National de France, Paris.

Government Reports
U.S. Congress, *Annual Report of the Commissioner of Patents*. Washington: U.S. Government Printing Office. Various years.
U. S. Industrial Commission, *Report of the Industrial Commission on Labor Legislation*. Washington DC: Government Printing, Office, 1900.
U.S. Congress, *Report of the Commissioners Appointed to Revise the Statutes Relating to Patents, Trade and other Marks, and Trade and Commercial Names*. Washington DC: US Congress, 1900.
House of Commons, *Report from the Select Committee on Trade Marks Bill, and Merchandize Marks Bill*. London: House of Commons, 1862.

California Senate, *Journals of the California Senate*. Various Years.

California Assembly, *Report of the Assembly Select Committee on the Vine-Growing Interests of California*. 1861 [reported in Daily Alta California 1861 Feb. 26: 1]

Laws
U.K. Law
"Statute of Monopolies, 1623." 21 Ja. 1 Chap. 3
"Trade Marks Registration Act, 1875." 38 & 39 Vict. Chap. 91.

U.S. Federal Laws
"An Act to Revise, Consolidate, and Amend the Statutes relating to Patents and Copyrights" 16 Stat 198 1848-1897

"An Act to Authorize the Registration of Trade-Marks" 33 Stat 724 1897-1907.

"An Act To Provide for the Registration and Protection of Trade-Marks Used in Commerce" 60 Stat 1943-1946. [The "Lanham Act"]

U.S. State Statutes [except California, for which, see below]

The Statutes of the State of Nevada Passed at the Third Regular Session of the Legislative Assembly. Virginia, VA: John Church, 1864.

The Laws of The State of Kansas Passed at the Sixth Session. Lawrence, Kansas: Speer & Ross, 1866.

The Laws of the State of Kansas Passed at the Adjourned Session of the Twenty-Third General Assembly. Jefferson City: Ellwood Kirby, 1868.

The Laws of the State of Missouri Passed at the Adjourned Session of the Twenty-Third General Assembly. Jefferson City: Emory S. Foster, Public Printer, 1866

Laws of New York Passed at the One Hundred and Twelfth Session of the Legislature. Albany: Banks & Brothers, 1889.

The Organic and Other General Laws of Oregon: Together with the National Constitution and Other Public Acts and Statutes of the United States, 1843-1872. [San Francisco]: Eugene Semple, State Printer, 1874

The Statutes of California, various years.

The Political Code of the State of California. San Francisco: Sumner Whitney & Co. 1874."An Act Creating the Office of State Assayer, Melter, and Refiner of Gold and Defining His Duty." 1849-50 Chap. 123.

"An Act Concerning Marks and Brands." 1849-50 Chap. 89.

"An Act Concerning Licenses." 1851 Chap. 39.

"An Act to Provide a Gauger for the Port of San Francisco." 1851 Chap. 58.

"An Act to Provide for the Inspection of Flour." 1852 Chap. 57.

"An Amendatory of an Act Entitled 'Act to Provide for the Inspection of Flour,' Passed May Third, One Thousand Eight Hundred and Fifty-Two." 1853 Chap. 174.

"An Act to Prevent the Counterfeiting of Gold Dust and Other Species of Gold Dust." 1855 Chap. 143.

"An Act to Add Section 24209 to the Business and Professions Code, Relating to Alcoholic Beverages." 1859 Chap. 199.

"An Act to Prohibit the Sale and disposal of Adulterated Spirituous or Alcoholic Liquors, Wines, or Cider." 1860 Chap. 223.

"An Act Containing Trade Marks and Names." 1863 Chap. 129.

An Act to Permit Voters of Every Township or Incorporated City in this State, to Vote on the Question of Granting Licenses to Sell Intoxicating Liquors. 1874 Chap. 300.

"An Act to Add Two New Sections to the Political Code ... Relating to Trademarks." 1887 Chap. 150.

Newspapers

California Farmer and Journal of Useful Sciences
Canada Gazette
Daily Alta California
Pacific Rural Press
Sacramento Daily Union

Weekly Rescue
Wine Dealers' Gazette

Books and articles

Atmore, Henry. "Railway Interests and the 'Rope of Air' 1840–8." *British Journal for the History of Science* 37, no. 3 (2004): 245–279.

Beniger, James R. *The Control Revolution: Technological and Economic Origins of the Information Society.* Cambridge, MA: Harvard University Press, 1986.

Bently, Lionel. "The Making of Modern Trade Mark Law: The Construction of the Legal Concept of Trade Mark." In *Trade Marks and Brands: An Interdisciplinary Critique*, edited by Lionel Bently, Jennifer Davis and Jane Ginsburg, 3–41. Cambridge: Cambridge University Press, 2008.

Bently, Lionel. "From Communication to Thing: Historical Aspects of the Conceptualisation of Trade Marks as Property." In *Trademark Law and Theory: A Handbook of Contemporary Research*, edited by Graeme B. Dinwoodie and Mark D. Janis, 3–41. Cheltenham, UK: Edward Elgar, 2008.

Bently, Lionel. "The 'Extraordinary Multiplicity' of Intellectual Property Laws in the British Colonies in the Nineteenth Century." *Theoretical Inquiries in Law* 12, no. 1 (2011): 161–200.

Bethel, A. C. W. "The Golden Skein: California's Gold-Rush Transportation Network." In *A Golden State: Mining and Economic Development in Gold Rush California*, edited by James J Rawls and Richard J. Orsi, 250–268. Berkeley: University of California Press, 1999.

Boorstin, Daniel J. "Tradition and Method in Legal History." *Harvard Law Review* 54, no. 3 (1941): 424–436.

Brechin, Gray. *Imperial San Francisco: Urban Power, Earthly Ruin.* Berkeley, CA: University of California Press, 1999.

Butterfield, Herbert. *The Whig Interpretation of History.* London: G. Bell & Sons, 1959.

Campbell, Christy. *Phylloxera: How Wine Was Saved for the World.* London: Harper/Collins, 2004.

Carosso, Vincent P. *The California Wine Industry, 1830–1895: A Study of the Formative Years.* Berkeley, CA: University of California Press, 1976.

Chandler, Alfred D. *Scale and Scope: The Dynamics of Industrial Capitalism.* Cambridge, MA: Harvard University Press, 1990.

Chandler, Alfred D. *The Visible Hand: The Managerial Revolution in American Business.* Cambridge, MA: Harvard University Press, 1977.

Daniel, W. T. S. *The History and Origin of the Law Reports: Together with a Compilation of Various Documents Shewing the Progress and Result of Proceedings.* London: W. Clowes & Sons, 1884.

Duguid, Paul. "Information in the Mark and the Marketplace: A Multivocal Account." *Enterprise and Society* 15, no. 1 (2014): 1–30.

Duguid, Paul. "A Case of Prejudice?: The Uncertain Development of Collective and Certification Marks." *Business History Review* 86, no. 2 (2012): 311–333.

Duguid, Paul. "French Connections: The International Propagation of Trademarks in the Nineteenth Century." *Enterprise & Society* 10, no. 1 (2009): 3–37.

Haraszthy, Arpad. "The Vine and Wine in Europe." California Farmer and Journal of Useful Sciences 16 no. 11 (December 1862): 1.

Haraszthy, Arpad. "The Vine and Wine in Europe." *California Farmer and Journal of Useful Sciences* July 18 (1862): 1.

Harris, Ron. "The Encounters of Economic History and Legal History." *Law and History Review* 21, no. 2 (2003): 297–346.

Harte, Bret. "The Outlaws of Poker Flat." Chap. 2 In *The Luck of Roaring Camp, and Other Sketches*, 19–36. New York: Houghton Mifflin, 1869.

Higgins, David. "The Making of Modern Trade Mark Law: The UK, 1860-1914. A Business History Perspective." In *Trade Marks and Brands: An Interdisciplinary Critique*, edited by Lionel Bently, Jennifer Davis, and Jane Ginsburg, 42–61. Cambridge: Cambridge University Press, 2008.

Jung, Maureen A. "Capitalism Comes to the Diggings: From Gold-Rush Adventure to Corporate Enterprise." In *A Golden State: Mining and Economic Development in Gold Rush California*, edited by James J. Rawls and Richard J. Orsi, 52–74. Berkeley: University of California Press, 1999.

Landes, William M., and Richard A. Posner. "Trademark Law: An Economic Perspective." *Journal of Law & Economics* 30, no. 2 (1987): 265–309.

Maillard de Marafy, Comte de. *Grand Dictionnaire International de la Propriété Industrielle au Point de Vue du Nom Commercial des Marques de Fabrique et de Commerce et de la Concurrence Déloyale* [International Dictionary of Industrial Property Concerning Trade Marks, Marks of Fabrication, and Unfair Competition]. 6 vols. Paris: Chevalier-Marescq & Cie, 1890–1892.

Marx, Karl. *Capital: A Critical Analysis of Capitalist Production*. Translated S. Mooreand E. Aveling. Edited by Frederick Engels. 3 vols. New York: International Publishers, 1947.

Meissner, Daniel. "Bridging the Pacific: California and the China Flour Trade," *California History* 76, no. 4 (1997/8): 82–93.

Mendelson, Richard. *From Demon to Darling: A Legal History of Wine in America*. Berkeley: University of California Press, 2009.

Nash, Gerald D. "A Veritable Revolution: The Global Economic Significance of the California Gold Rush." In *A Golden State: Mining and Economic Development in Gold Rush California*, edited by James J. Rawls and Richard J. Orsi, 276–289. Berkeley: University of California Press, 1999.

Ostrander, Gilman M. *The Prohibition Movement in California, 1848–1933*. Berkeley: University of California Press, 1957.

Pinney, Thomas. *The Makers of American Wine: A Record of Two Hundred Years*. Berkeley: University of California Press, 2012.

Pinney, Thomas. *A History of Wine America: From the Beginnings to Prohibition*. Berkeley: University of California Press, 1998.

Rogers, Edward S. "Some Historical Matters Concerning Trade Marks." *Michigan Law Review* 9 (1910-11): 29–42.

Rosen, Zvi S. "In Search of the *Trade-Mark Cases*: The Nascent Treaty Power and the Turbulent Origins of Federal Trademark Law." *St John's Law Review* 83, no. 3 (2009): 827–904.

Rowell, Geo. P. *Rowell's American Newspaper Directory*. New York: Geo. P. Rowell & Co, 1880.

Sáiz, Patricio and Paloma Fernández Pérez "Catalonian Trademarks and the Development of Marketing Knowledge in Spain, 1850-1946." *Business History Review* 86, no. 2 (2012): 239–260.

Scardamaglia, Amanda. *Colonial Australian Trade Mark Law: Narratives in Lawmaking, People, Power, and Place*. Melbourne: Australian Scholarly Publishing, 2015.

Schechter, Frank I. *The Historical Foundations of the Law Relating to Trade Marks*. New York: Columbia University Press, 1925.

Scranton, Philip, and Patrick Fridenson. *Reimagining Business History*. Baltimore, MD: Johns Hopkins, 2013.

Smart, Russel S. *The Law of Trade-Marks and Designs in Canada*. Toronto: Canada Law Book Co, 1917.

Sullivan, Charles. *A Companion to California Wine*. Berkeley: University of California, 1998.

Walker, Richard A. "California's Golden Road to Riches: Natural Resources and Regional Capitalism, 1848-1940." *Annals of the Association of American Geographers* 91, no. 1 (2001): 167–199.

Whiting & Berry. *A Treatise on Wines, Spirits, and Teas: With Correspondence and Certificates*. San Francisco: Towne & Bacon, 1868.

Wilkins, Mira. "The Neglected Intangible Asset: The Influence of the Trade Mark on the Rise of the Modern Corporation." *Business History* 34, no. 1 (1992): 66–99.

Zipf, George Kingsley. "Brand Names and Related Social Phenomena." *American Journal of Psychology* 63, no. 3 (1950): 342–366.

The 'disguised' foreign investor: Brands, trademarks and the British expatriate entrepreneur in Brazil

Teresa da Silva Lopes, Carlos Gabriel Guimarães, Alexandre Saes and Luiz Fernando Saraiva

ABSTRACT

This article examines the impact of the British expatriate entrepreneur, and his processes of knowledge transfer, on the industrialization and economic development of Brazil between 1875 and 1914. It focuses on the textiles industry, and combines original trademark data with conventional trade and investment statistics, and also case study analysis about firms and their entrepreneurs. It argues that British investment in Brazil was higher and had a deeper impact on economic development than considered by existing research, as expatriate entrepreneurs 'disguised' a substantial amount of foreign investments by acting as shareholders and top managers of newly established local businesses.

1. Introduction

This article provides a new approach to the study of the impact of British trade and invest-ment on the economic development of Brazil. By using trademark registration data collected for the first time, it analyses the impact of knowledge transfer by British businesses and British expatriate entrepreneurs established in Brazil on the development of brands and a domestic textiles industry.[1] It focuses on the period from 1875 to 1914, when Britain was the main trader and foreign direct investor in Brazil, and when textiles were the most impor-tant category of goods imported from Britain. During this period, the textiles industry took off in Brazil and became the most important manufacturing sector in the country.[2] This article aims to answer the following questions: How important is the expatriate entrepreneur in explaining the processes of knowledge transfer between countries, and in influencing eco-nomic development? Does trademark data provide new insights on the impact of foreign direct investment and trade by a developed country such as Britain into a developing country such as Brazil at the end of the nineteenth century and in the early twentieth century?

Knowledge transfer relates to the process through which one unit (e.g. individual, group, department, or division) is affected by the experience of another. One example of knowledge transfer is the passing of organisational best practices and skills by an expatriate working for a subsidiary of a firm in a foreign country, where that kind of knowledge does not exist (e.g. knowledge of the functioning and operation of certain machinery). Knowledge is a powerful differentiator from competitors, may lead to extraordinary firm performance, and ultimately to economic development and prosperity.[3] As an intangible asset, knowledge can provide future benefits which do not have a physical or financial embodiment.[4] This study focuses essentially on the processes of marketing knowledge transfer, which is the knowledge associated with the 'intelligence' and the skills behind the marketing methods, such as the management of brands and distribution channels.[5] However, other types of knowledge are also considered: technological knowledge, associated with technological innovations; managerial knowledge, associated with administrative processes such as book-keeping; and entrepreneurial knowledge, associated with investment opportunities and risk-taking. While marketing and technological knowledge can be protected legally through trademarks and patents, other forms of knowledge transfer such as staff training, and book-keeping accounting practices, among other administrative processes, are more difficult to protect legally.

The expatriate entrepreneur is considered here to be the sender in the process of knowl-edge transfer.[6] He has additional characteristics to those of the traditional entrepreneur, who is someone who specialised in taking judgmental decisions about the coordination of scarce resources with an economic aim, and under conditions of uncertainty.[7] An expatriate is someone who is a citizen of one country but resides in another on a long-term (but not necessarily on a permanent) basis. An expatriate may have dual nationality (i.e. they may also be citizens of the country in which they reside). They have the ability to manage effec-tively in culturally diverse settings, and to network internationally, and they have the breadth of experience and mental flexibility, which is promoted by mobility both within firms and between firms.[8] This mental flexibility is encouraged by an educational background empha-sising independent critical judgement rather than role-learning.[9] These are important ena-blers for entrepreneurs to establish relationships in foreign markets, and act as senders of facilitators in processes of knowledge transfer between countries.

The main recipients of the knowledge are the organisations and the workers operating in one of the activities within the textiles industry value chain, such as manufacturing, or in wholesaling, brokerage, distribution or retailing.[10]

There is no universal criteria for measuring and obtaining evidence about knowledge transfer. The appropriate criteria depend on various factors such as the type of knowledge being transferred, the context, and types of sender and receiver. Some researchers use objec-tive measures such as archival data on the increase in the numbers of patents to measure the speed of knowledge transfer in processes of technological innovation.[11] In a similar way, this study draws on trademark data to look at the processes of knowledge transfer associated with marketing knowledge.[12] Trademarks are considered here to be a proxy for initiatives by entrepreneurs to develop differentiation for their goods through the creation of brands and their legal protection.[13]

This study draws on trademark data collected for the first time in Brazil. Three types of sources were used: Série Indústria e Comércio – IC3 [Arquivo Nacional, Rio de Janeiro], *Diário Oficial*, and Boletim da Propriedade Industrial [Biblioteca Nacional, Rio de Janeiro). Brazil was quite advanced in enacting its first trademark law in 1875, before countries such as Argentina, Bolivia, Colombia, Costa Rica, Cuba, Mexico, Peru, Portugal, Uruguay, and Venezuela.[14] However, a system of classification of marks by industry was only introduced in 1923.[15] Until then, marks appeared filed and registered in alphabetical order by type of product (e.g. biscuits [*biscoitos*] and beverages [*bebidas*] were filed under the letter 'B'). In Britain, a classification system was in place since the trademark registration system began in 1876. Britain was relatively late among the most developed countries to introduce a registration system for its marks, and because it had a particularly strict process for examining registrations, the registrations scheme, and its published data, came to enjoy great stability. Because of its effectiveness, and also in order to facilitate international comparative analysis, the British system of classification of marks (with 50 classes) is used here in the study of Brazilian trademark registrations.[16]

The article is organised into five sections: following the introduction, section two provides an overview of the British trade and foreign direct investment in Brazil from 1875 to the start of World War I. Section three introduces new trademark data about Brazil and provides general trends and comparisons with other countries, where data has already been collected. It also discusses the origins and development of trademark law in Brazil. Section four draws on original trademark data at firm level and, combined with other research about the firms and the entrepreneurs, analyses the origins of the various textiles firms registering trademarks, and contrasts the various ways through which British expatriate entrepreneurs invested in the industry. Finally, section five provides some conclusions, and addresses the questions raised in the introduction.

2. Tangible investments in Brazil

2.1. Impact of British trade

Some researchers argue that while Britain was the main investor and trade partner of Brazil before World War I, that did not necessarily contribute significantly to positive spillovers and economic development. That contrasts with the British presence in countries such as Australia and South Africa, which were part of the former British Empire, and where there is a general agreement that they generated positive spillovers which contributed to economic development.[17] Several arguments have been put forward to explain the relatively limited amount of positive spillovers in Brazil.[18] The education of indigenous managers is considered to have led foreign firms to keep the top management in the hands of expatriates.[19] The economic, social and political structure of Brazil and its business elites are considered to have constrained modernisation.[20] The dominant business elites in Brazil are also mentioned as having focused on the production of raw materials, and therefore having been less open to the absorption of new technologies, organisations, and new modes of doing business and selling products.[21] The foreign presence is also observed to have destabilised the economy, making it more dependent in the long-term on foreign institutions.[22] Irrespective of these arguments about the impact of British investment and trade in Brazil, it is a fact that Britain was its main trading partner and investor during the period of analysis, and that, by then, the country already had its own state and institutions in place.[23]

Even though there was a decrease in the share of British imports into Brazil over time, Britain remained the principal source of Brazilian imports until the beginning of the First World War.[24] Textiles (cotton, wool, jute and linen) were the main category of goods imported from Britain, but other categories, in particular metals (iron and coal), and also machinery (steam machines), increased over time.[25] The decrease of British imports was the result of several factors. One factor related to the protectionist tariffs introduced in Brazil at various periods from the 1870s, as a way to increase the country's revenue (in view of the financial burden caused by the Paraguay War), to protect local production, and to promote local entrepreneurship (in particular from the late 1880s).[26] Other factors contributed to this evolution, such as the devaluation of the Brazilian currency (mil réis) against the British currency (£) in the 1890s and the first decade of the Brazilian Republic, and that made imports become very expensive. Another reason was the increase of imports of raw jute by Brazilian textiles merchants directly from a new source –Calcutta in India- which allowed them to avoid the British middlemen.[27] Additionally, there was an increase in competition from other nations such as the US and Germany.[28]

2.2. British direct investment in Brazil

Brazil was an attractive market for British investors because of the stability of economic and political relations that existed between the two countries, which were guaranteed through the Empire and the old alliance Britain had with Portugal, the coloniser country.[29] There were also strong links between the Brazilian state and the Rothschild Bank, a leading British financial institution at the time.[30]

   Brazil was a main market for British investors in government securities, representing more than half of the investment in Brazil up to 1880s. Thereafter, British investment predominantly targeted manufacturing and services, particularly in railways, public utilities, and banks.[31] By the end of the nineteenth century Britain represented 78% of total foreign investment in Brazil, remaining the main investor in the country until World War I, when it was responsible for 53% of the total investment.[32] The decrease of British investment over time was essentially due to the rising competition from other countries such as the US, Canada and France.

   The first attempt to develop a cotton manufacturing industry in Brazil was in 1750 while Brazil was part of Portugal. The cotton mill owners in Portugal had lost their home market as a consequence of the Methuen Treaty with Britain and were determined that they should keep the market of their Brazilian colony for themselves. They persuaded the Portuguese Government to pass legislation prohibiting the manufacture of cotton cloth in Brazil, with the exception of the most common and coarsest cloth as used by the slaves. This act was passed in 1807 and rigorously enforced. This state of affairs continued until 1846, as in 1822, when Brazil obtained its independence, no changes were made. It was only in 1846 that the Brazilian Government gave a number of concessions to factories, amongst which the free importation of machinery was the principal one.[33]

   Until the 1890s, the trade policy inherited from the Empire provided Britain with better tariffs for inputs, such as the cotton used in the textiles industry, and also with tariffs exemption in the Brazilian imports of machinery and industrial equipment. This scenario explains the increase in imports of machinery used in the textile industry during this period.[34] The increase in tariffs imposed on imports in the late nineteenth century could have worked as a strong incentive for British businesses to reduce exports and invest directly in manufacturing in Brazil, but that was not the case. Instead, there was a moderate increase in British foreign direct investment into Brazil, and exports only decreased slightly. The attractiveness of the market did not justify the different types of risk that firms might incur if they engaged in foreign direct investment instead of using arm's-length modes of entry. Nonetheless, tariff protection triggered an increase in manufacturing in the Brazilian textiles industry, and therefore, increased the risk incurred by British financiers and entrepreneurs doing business with Brazil. By the end of World War I the domestic production of textiles corresponded to 75% of the national consumption of cotton goods.[35]

3. Intangible investments in Brazil

3.1. Origins of the trademark law in Brazil

Brazil has historically been influenced by the legal rules and institutions from a far more diverse array of jurisdictions than is usually assumed for the creation of commercial and trademark law in the nineteenth century.[36] From the enactment of the French Civil Code in 1804, with the start of the Napoleonic Wars, the French juridical influence became almost universal in the world, and Brazil was no exception. But the Portuguese inheritance is also considered central to the establishment of the guidelines for Commercial Law of 1850.[37] Other countries that influenced Brazilian commercial law were Spain, the Netherlands, and also England.[38] With these multiple influences the members of the Brazilian elite aimed to create legislation that would enhance trade and investment relations in particular with those countries.[39]

The first law created that dealt with intellectual property in Brazil dates back to 1809. This was the result of the arrival of the Portuguese Royal Family to Brazil and the incentives created by the Crown for entrepreneurs to innovate.[40] But it is only in 1875 that a system of registration of trademarks emerges in Brazil.[41] This was also relatively early even when compared with more industrialised countries such as Britain and the US.[42] Great economic and social transformations occurred in Brazil around this period. A new aristocracy associated with coffee production emerged, the slave trade ended, and there was a vast increase in European immigration. These factors contributed, to a certain extent, to the development of mass production and the emergence of a consumer society, and to the need to have a more effective legal system to protect both technological and marketing innovations, through patents and trademarks.[43]

The determining motivation for the Imperial Government of Brazil to create a legislation for trademarks is associated with a case of imitation of a snuff brand in 1874. Known as the 'Moreira & Cia. vs. Meuron & Cia.' case, it was filed in Bahia by Meuron Cia., owner of a well-known snuff brand Rapé Areia Preta. The lawsuit was against Moreira & Cia., another snuff producer, for creating a very similar brand Rapé Areia Parda. The Court found that neither Criminal nor Commercial Law of 1850 provided enough grounds to protect the owner of the original brand. As a result, Moreira & Cia., the imitator, sued Meuron & Cia. for damaging the reputation of his business.[44] This debate encouraged the Imperial Justice Commission to create new legislation to protect brand innovation. In spite of receiving criticism in the Chamber of Deputies, associated with claims that the country already had property laws and did not need another one, the new trademark law was approved on 23 October 1875.[45] Meuron & Cia. became the first firm to register a trademark in Brazil: Fábrica Rapé Area Preta snuff, deposited in Junta Commercial in November 1875, approximately one month after the law was passed.[46]

Brazilian trademark law relied extensively on French law. France had also been very influential in the development of trademark law in many other countries such as Britain, the US, and Portugal.[47] This is because it had been one of the first countries to develop trademark legislation, in 1856.[48] The new law sought the protection of French-owned names in foreign countries by establishing a principle of reciprocity to be guaranteed by treaty. France led other countries to participate through the creation of bilateral agreements, and precipitated related legislation being passed.[49]

In 1883 Brazil was a signatory country of the Paris Convention.[50] The motivations to sign this convention by a country just starting to industrialise were essentially linked to the strong British presence in Brazil, and also to the conviction by the Brazilian Crown, that joining this Convention could bring stronger links with developed countries and also technological progress to Brazil.[51] Joining this Convention meant that the Imperial Government had to tailor its own legislation to agree with the international terms set out in the Paris Convention and also in areas where domestic law was silent until then.[52] This led to the promulgation of a new law for trademarks on 14 October 1887.[53] Article 6 defined that brands should be accepted in countries that were signatories of the Paris Convention. Additionally, Article 12 required that the signatory countries should create a national institution to archive the registers of industrial properties and trademarks. Thus, from 1887 the Commercial Tribunal of Rio de Janeiro centralised registrations of all trademarks in the country. The Monarchy, survived only two more years.

The Proclamation of the Republic in 1889, and the promulgation of the 1891 Constitution led once again to changes in trademark law. The new legislation followed a federalist perspective to meet the principles of the new Republican Constitution. The laws of 1890, 1894 and 1898 strengthened the Provincial jurisdiction in the trademark processes. New changes to trademark law took place in 1904. These essentially toughened the punishment for imitation, and established that these could lead to fines, and in some circumstances to jail.[54] Little was done with the institutional structure, i.e. the registration remained under the state jurisdiction, however, the Commercial Tribunal of Rio de Janeiro (later renamed Board of Trade), continued to receive all Brazilian trademark registrations.

The next important revisions in Brazilian trademark law took place in 1923. The new law provided a deeper reformulation in the legislation on trademarks. The decree created the General Directory of Industrial Property, which was in charge of patent and trademark registrations. The most important innovation that the Directory presented was the classification of trademarks in 50 classes where entrepreneurs could apply for registrations.[55]

3.2. The Data

The patterns of trademark registration in Brazil during the period of analysis were substantially different from those of more industrialised countries such as Britain, the US, and France. Table 1 provides information about the first year of registration for each of these countries, the total number of trademark registrations in absolute terms in those countries during the period 1876–1913, and also the number of registrations weighted by population.

The different registration patterns reflect the different institutional environments, and also economic, political and social phenomena such as globalisation waves, the two World Wars, technological progress, cyclical fluctuations of the economies, and the different levels of competition and industry concentration.[56] The relatively low number of registrations, when compared with the other countries in Table 1, is associated with various factors. First, Brazil's economy relied extensively on the production and exports of raw materials and foodstuffs, in particular rubber, coffee and cotton, and these products tended to be sold

Table 1. Number of trademark registrations per country for select countries, 1876–1913.

Country	First Year of registration	Total Domestic Trademark Registrations (TMs) 1876–1913	TMs/ Population (000 at mid-year)
Brazil	1875	14,956	0.02
United States	1870/1905	93,823	0.04
Britain	1876	147,322	0.10
France	1856	354,150	0.23

Source: Calculated using registration data from: Brazil – *Diário Oficial, Série Indústria e Comércio* 9X, IC3 [Arquivo Nacional do Rio de Janeiro], and *Boletim da Propriedade Industrial*; Britain - *Annual Report of the Patent Office*; United States – *Index of Patents and the Official Gazette of the US Patent Office*; France – between 1858 to 1883: III.8.3 [The Paris Archive]; from 1884 – *Bulletin Officiel de la Propriété Industrielle & Commerciale*. Population data, based on Angus Maddison, *Historical Statistics of the World Economy: 1–2008AD* (2010).

both domestically and in foreign markets unprocessed and unbranded.[57] Second, the administrative procedures for registration of trademarks were not straightforward or compulsory, creating no clear incentives for firms to register trademarks.[58] Figure 1 below shows the total annual number of total trademark registrations in Brazil from 1875 to 1913.

From the turn of the century, a series of external factors led to the fast increase in registrations. Economic conditions created by the growth in international coffee trade indirectly caused the development of the textile industry, in particular used for bagging coffee.[59] Additionally, from 1905 changes in the law which toughened the punishment by imitators encouraged many businesses to register their trademarks for the first time.[60] Apart from that, in 1906 Brazil joined the Pan American Union, formed by several Pan American States.[61] This convention encouraged firms to register trademarks in Brazil as they became automatically protected in other countries that were part of the Union. As a result, the number of Brazilian firms registering trademarks more than doubled between 1905 and 1907. In a similar way, registrations in Brazil of firms from Pan American countries also increased from 3.5% of the total number of registrations in 1905 to 27% in 1907. The first industry census in Brazil in 1907, and the National Exhibition of 1908 also contributed to a boost in registrations.[62] The National Exhibition of 1908 was set up to celebrate the centenary of the opening of Brazilian Ports to international trade and the end of the monopoly of the Portuguese. This Exhibition was organised by sections, according to the industry. Exhibitors were encouraged to provide as much information as possible about the origin of their products and their costs. This motivated entrepreneurs to register trademarks as a way to provide that information.[63]

The analysis of trademark registrations by country of origin shows that in Brazil the percentage of foreign registrations was quite significant when compared to other countries. For example, in 1895 it corresponded to 41%, while in France it was only 8.74% in the same year. While in 1905 that number had decreased to 31.4% in Brazil, in France it had also decreased to 6.15%.[64] Both in 1895 and 1905 the main foreign country registering trademarks in Brazil was Britain.[65] From 1875 to 1892 the main classes of registrations in Brazil were tobacco (26.4%), chemical substances used in medicines (18.5%), food and drink (12.6%) and textiles (10%).

Textiles is one of the industries that formed part of the industrialisation process of Brazil, which only took place in the 1880s. The abolition of slavery in 1888 and the proclamation of the Republic in Brazil in 1889 brought economic and political conditions favourable to this industrialisation.[66]

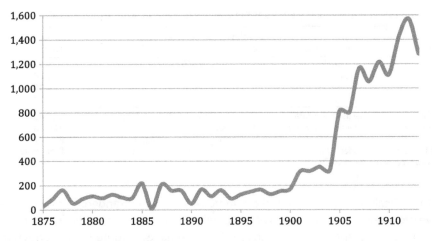

Figure 1. Number of Total Trademark Registrations in Brazil, 1875–1913.
Source: *Diário Oficial, Relatórios do Ministério da Agricultura*, various years.

Apart from participating in the various activities associated with the textiles value chain, British expatriate entrepreneurs also had a key role in the development of supporting industries.[67] They built a substantial part of the transport system on which the textiles industry was to depend for the receipt of raw materials and access to markets.[68] British banks such as the London and Brazilian Bank and The English Bank of Rio de Janeiro (later renamed British Bank of South America) provided credit and loans that enabled Brazilians to invest in textiles manufacturing. While Salvador da Bahia and surrounding areas, and Minas Gerais were the early centres for the production of textiles, from the 1880s Rio de Janeiro and São Paulo took that position. As coffee production concentrated more people in the south-central regions, the mills moved closer to the consuming centres and away from the north-eastern sources of raw materials.[69]

4. British knowledge transfer into Brazil: the case of textiles

When businesses possess competitive advantages based on specific knowledge, associated for example with a superior technology or a successful brand, issues of replicability and imitation often arise. In order to capture the value of knowledge assets associated with brand innovations which have the potential to become successful, and to minimise the risk of imitation, firms tend to register trademarks and protect them legally. As mentioned in the introduction, trademark registrations are used here as proxies for successful brand and technological innovations in the Brazilian textiles industry. Table 2 identifies the main registrants of textiles trademarks in Brazil from 1875 to 1913. The criteria for inclusion of the firms in this table relied on their number of registrations. Firms with 13 or more registrations during this period of analysis were included in the sample. They corresponded to 30% of the total registrations in textiles during the period of analysis. Some of these firms were of large size, others of small size. Table 2 provides information about their country of origin, the date they were established in Brazil, the country of origin of their shareholders and managers, the date of the first trademark registered by each one, and the total number of registrations by each one of these firms during the

Table 2. Main registrants of textiles trademarks in Brazil, 1875–1913.

Firm	Origin	Set up in Brazil	British shareholders?	British Managers?	First Trademark	Total Trademarks
1. Brazilian Branches of British Multinational Firms						
Edward Ashworth & Co	UK	1840	Yes	Yes	1879	61
J. & P. Coats Limited	UK	1879	Yes	Yes	1879	35
Clark & Co	UK	1891	Yes	Yes	1880	50
Oscar Philippi & Co	UK	1865	Yes	Yes	1902	14
2. Brazilian Firms with British Ownership and Control						
Smith & Youle/ Youle & Cia.	BRA	1880	Yes	Yes	1881	31
John Moore & Co	BRA	1959	Yes	Yes	1885	36
3. Brazilian Firms with Mixed Foreign (British, Non-British) and Brazilian Ownership and Control						
Companhia de Fiação e Tecidos Confiança Industrial	BRA	1884	Yes	Yes	1901	72
Companhia de Fiação e Tecelagem Carioca	BRA	1884	Yes	Yes	1889	51
Companhia de Fiação e Tecidos Corcovado	BRA	1889	Yes	Yes	1901	26
Companhia Petropolitana de Tecidos	BRA	1873	Yes	Yes	1888	36
Blum & Cia.	BRA	1896	Yes	Yes	1904	31
Companhia de Tecidos Paulista	BRA	1891	Yes	Yes	1907	42
4. Brazilian Firms/Representation with Foreign but Non-British Ownership and Control						
J. Pabst & Co.	BRA	1889	No	No	1910	30
M. P. Do Azevedo Junior	BRA	1891	No	No	1900	13
Secco & Co.	BRA	1900	No	No	1907	15
Les Fils de Cartier Bresson	FRA	n.a.	n.a.	n.a.	1877	25

Sources: *Almanak Administrativo, Mercantil e Industrial do Rio de Janeiro* (Laemmert, various years).
n.a – not available.

period of analysis. The largest registrants are not necessarily the most innovative firms, or firms whose brands were more likely to be imitated. But registration activity certainly reveals an awareness of the power of brands as a source of firms' competitiveness.[70]

Four groups of firms have been identified in terms of the country of origin of the shareholders and managers as illustrated in Table 2: group 1 – Brazilian Branches of British Multinational Firms, with British Management. In these cases, the Brazilian branch is a subsidiary of a British firm and both the shareholders and managers operating in Brazil are British expatriates; group 2 – Brazilian Firms with British Ownership and Management Control. Here firms are registered in Brazil and both the shareholders and the top managers are British expatriate entrepreneurs; group 3 – Brazilian Firms with Mixed Foreign, including British and Non-British, and Brazilian Ownership and Control of Management. Here the Brazilian firm is created and managed by shareholders and managers from multiple countries, one of which is Britain; and finally, group 4 relates to cases of Brazilian Firms with Foreign, but non-British Ownership and Control of Management, and to cases of Brazilian registrations by foreign firms with no branches in Brazil. In most cases these are firms established in Brazil by European entrepreneurs, in particular from Portugal, or entrepreneurs from other Latin American countries. It also includes a case of a French firm which registered trademarks in Brazil without setting up a subsidiary or hiring an agent formally. Other combinations with regard to the country of origin of the owners and the managers do not seem to appear on the top list of registrants of trademarks during the period of analysis. For example, among the top registrants there are no cases of Brazilian firms in the textile industry where both shareholders and managers are of Brazilian origin.

Some trends emerge from an analysis of Table 2. The first trend relates to the ownership and control of management of these firms, which led to their classification in four categories as explained above. All top trademark registrants in textiles had, throughout the period of analysis, foreign, and in particular, British expatriate entrepreneurs involved as shareholders, top managers, or both. British expatriate entrepreneurs either acted as shareholders, or top managers, or both. This meant that strategic decision taking by these textiles firms took advantage of the knowledge provided by British expatriate entrepreneurs. In the late-nineteenth and early-twentieth century the British education system was more advanced than that in Brazil. British entrepreneurs were more likely to have superior technological and marketing knowledge, and also marketing skills, in particular marketing knowledge associated with the management of brands and distribution channels. They also had superior managerial knowledge of administrative processes such as the management of labour force and bookkeeping.[71] British entrepreneurs and engineers understood in systematic ways phenomena such as air pressure, the force of a lever, and the problem of friction, which were crucial for the effective installation and operation of machinery used in textiles manufacturing. They tended to have training in areas such as accounting, bookkeeping, and management and control of wages.[72] They also had experience in entrepreneurial ventures carried out throughout the British Empire, which provided them with a unique ability based on experience to identify investment opportunities, often in risky environments. They were also part of international networks which permitted the businesses to be financed in the best way possible.[73]

During this period, Great Britain supplied the bulk of the specialised labour force required by the textiles industry in Brazil, including technicians to supervise or install the equipment and manage factory operations, as well as skilled textile workers, in particular master spinners and weavers, to operate the mills. British expatriate entrepreneurs had knowledge associated with the installation and operation of the machinery used in textiles factories, which they transferred through training to the locally hired workforce. British entrepreneurs also influenced the Brazilian entrepreneurial spirit in other industries through their networking with local business elites and through the creation of business associations such as The Industrial Center of Brazil (Centro Industrial do Brazil), and the Engineering Club (Clube de Engenharia), both in Rio de Janeiro.[74]

The 16 firms in Table 2 include the oldest, largest, and most capital-intensive textile firms in Brazil.[75] They registered a total of 568 trademarks which, as already mentioned, corresponded to 30% of the total trademarks registered in textiles during the period 1875–1913, where the total number of registrants was 792 firms. Of these main registrants from Table 2, groups 1 to 3, with British control or management in some form (Brazilian Branches of British Multinational Firms; Brazilian Firms with Mixed British and Brazilian Ownership and Control; and Brazilian Firms with Mixed Foreign (British and Non-British), and Brazilian Ownership and Control of Management) correspond to 90% of registrations within the sample, indicating that the British expatriate entrepreneurs were very involved in the management of firms which registered trademarks. They transferred three main types of knowledge: technological and marketing knowledge; managerial knowledge; and entrepreneurial knowledge.

Firms such J. & P. Coats, were important in the development of the Brazilian textiles industry transferring all these different types of knowledge. J. & P. Coats was then a leading multinational company worldwide, using marketing techniques and technologies which were among the most advanced in the world. This multinational firm first entered Brazil via exports and the use of external agents, Lidgerwood Manufacturing Company Ltd, and Adolf Spann and Co. In 1907 it set up a plant in Brazil – Companhia Brasileira de Linhas para Coser (Brazilian Thread Co.), in the region of São Paulo, as a way to overcome tariffs.[76] The top management were all British, and 30 Scottish workers were first sent to Brazil to train the local labour force.[77] Its sales were widespread all over the country.[78] J. & P Coats was also a very aggressive marketer and advertiser.[79] As early as 1879, soon after J. & P. products entered the Brazilian market through exports, the firm was advertising its brands in the press aggressively using sentences such as 'Unquestionably the best quality thread among those produced in Europe and the USA'. They also used direct comparative advertising mentioning competition 'Many people use the brand of thread Alexandre, thinking that these have similar quality to Coats, but in reality these are not as strong as Coats'. Other adverts include 'Coats thread is the best in the world!!! Only sold in reputed shops'; 'Coats thread the strongest and cheapest'.[80]

A firm registered as Brazilian but founded by British expatriate entrepreneurs, which was very important in transferring marketing knowledge, technological knowledge and entrepreneurial knowledge was Smith & Youle. This firm was established in Brazil in 1880 by two British expatriates who also acted as managers. These entrepreneurs had strong international networks derived from their work as agents for British trading companies.[81] The firm imported textiles into Brazil (wool, cotton and linen cloth), and also other goods and services including iron, steel and copper, and insurance. One of its shareholders, Frederick Youle, became a manager of Companhia Manufactora Fluminense in 1891.[82] Companhia Petropolitana de Tecidos, which is an example of a Brazilian firm with mixed foreign (British and non-British) and Brazilian ownership and control, and which was founded by a Cuban entrepreneur in

1873, employed 44% foreign labour, including three British top managers. These had entrepreneurial, in particular administrative knowledge, and technological knowledge.[83]

The oldest firms operating in the textiles industry tended to have a smaller number of shareholders, forming closed societies, usually centred around the founder of the firm and his relatives. An example is Companhia de Fiação e Tecidos Aliança founded in 1880 with three shareholders, two of whom were Portuguese and one British. It produced fine fabrics.[84] In contrast, Companhia de Fiação e Tecidos Corcovado established in 1889 had 80 shareholders originally from various countries, including Brazil, Britain and Portugal; and Companhia São Félix established in 1891 had 40 shareholders.[85]

These leading registrants of textiles trademarks also had interlocked shareholdings and management. Edward Ashworth & Co. was a British merchant company from Manchester which first exported to Brazil since 1840 through wholly-owned distribution channels.[86] In 1891 the firm set up its first textiles manufacturing plant in São Paulo with British expatriate entrepreneurs. In 1907 a second plant was built, also in the region of São Paulo, for the production of cotton textiles, jute and shoes.[87] By the beginning of World War I, Edward Ashworth had expanded substantially, having invested in other Brazilian textiles firms such as Companhia Taubate Industrial.[88] Another example is Companhia Fluminense's Comendador Soares, a Brazilian merchant, who also owned a hardware shop and had been a member of the Brazilian parliament in Minas Gerais and a Director of Banco de Comércio. He was the main shareholder of the firm, and was also a shareholder of Companhia de Fiação e Tecidos Pau Grande (later renamed Companhia América Fabril) until 1890.[89] Henry Whittaker was a founding shareholder of Companhia de Fiação e Tecidos Aliança in 1880, jointly with Portuguese shareholders, José Augusto Laranja and Joaquim C. de Oliveira e Silva. In 1885 he became a shareholder of Companhia Industrial Mineira, an old established textiles company in the region of Minas Gerais. Andrew Steele was also a shareholder of this company, as well as being a shareholder of Bandeira & Steels Co. Cotton Spinners.[90]

During the period between 1878 and 1893 funds and knowledge accumulated in the textile import/export trade were a major source of capital for the establishment of the early mills, in particular in Rio de Janeiro. These merchants corresponded to 47.4% of the shareholders of textiles firms.[91] An illustration is the Import/Export firm Santos, Peixoto & Cia. owned by three shareholders, one British (John Sherrington) and two Brazilian (Antônio Felício dos Santos and José Rodrigues Peixoto). These entrepreneurs were behind the establishment of Companhia de Fiação and Tecelagem Pau Grande (later renamed Companhia América Fabril).[92]

Banks, specifically foreign banks operating in Brazil to support international trade, often took an active role in the financing of textiles firms and they usually nominated some of their own managers for their executive boards.[93] For example, Banco Comercial do Rio de Janeiro owned 17% of the shares of Empresa Confiança Industrial; Banco Internacional (later renamed Banco Nacional do Brasil) provided 26% of the capital of Progresso Industrial. The presence of Banco Comercial as a major shareholder of Companhia Confiança Industrial involved the participation of two bank managers, Conde São Salvador de Matosinhos, one of the main merchants in Rio de Janeiro, and Salgado Zenha, also a shareholder of an import/export business Zenha & Silveira. During the 1880s, the director of the English Bank of Rio de Janeiro was also on the board of directors of Companhia de Fiação e Tecelagem Carioca.[94]

Table 3. Types of textiles registrants: importer/broker/distributor/retailer vs manufacturer.

Type of Trademark	1875–1889	1889–1904	Total
Importer/Broker/Distributor/Retailer			
Britain	63	43	106
Brazil	57	131	188
Other foreign	7	32	39
Sub-Total	127	206	333
Manufacturer			
Britain	14	57	71
Brazil	48	169	217
Other foreign	9	57	66
Sub-Total	71	283	354
Total	198	489	687

Source: Based on trademark registration data from IC3 Arquivo Nacional; *Diário Official* (various years).

The types of trademarks registrations in textiles show a clear pattern over time from more importer/broker/distributor/retailer trademarks to more manufacturing trademarks. Table 3 illustrates the evolution of textile registrations for these two types of registrants using two different benchmark periods 1875–1889 and 1889–1904. Importers, brokers, distributors and retailers of trademarks are intermediaries between the producer and the consumer and, in the present case, register trademarks. Manufacturing trademarks are those where the brand and the intellectual property associated with it belongs to the producing firms which also register the trademarks.

In the period 1875–1889 there were fewer registrants of trademarks and the percentage of registrations by importers, brokers, distributors and retailers was 64%. The larger Brazilian textile-importing firms had permanent buying connections in European cities, especially Paris and Manchester, and the buyers often visited those markets. Purchase orders were placed by correspondence or by resident agents and travelers visiting the markets. The advantage of offering goods personally instead of by means of letters was greater in Brazil than in other countries as the domestic manufacture did not supply the bulk of the textiles consumed. For these reasons, it was extremely important for the resident agent or traveler to have knowledge about the textiles business, instead of simply being a good sales representative or salesman. Often imported textiles had brands. However, importers in Brazil preferred to have goods put up under their own private brands, this being advantageous to them in establishing reputation and in competing with other importers. When goods were difficult to obtain, merchants bought goods with established brands. In such cases it was the manufacturer's responsibility to advertise the goods to the manufacturer who desired to have his brands purchased by the Brazilian consumer.[95]

Over time the number of registrations by importers, brokers, distributors and retailers decreased, corresponding to 42% during the period 1889–1904. This was associated with the fact that many new domestic firms were founded which produced own brands, which were able to compete with British imported goods sold in Brazil. Additionally, the main country of origin of the merchants registering trademarks relating to 1875–1889 (by importers, brokers, distributors and retailers) was Britain. In contrast, during the period 1889–1904 most registrations of trademarks were by manufacturers; these tended to be owned by Brazilian firms with British and other foreign governance, and which were totally or partially managed and owned by British expatriate entrepreneurs.

5. Conclusion

As highlighted by Mira Wilkins, in the late nineteenth century there was a significant amount of British foreign investment carried out around the world, but its quantitative significance still remains understated and not clear.[96] This study contributes to that discussion by showing that a substantial amount of foreign investment was 'disguised' as local investment and carried out by British expatriate entrepreneurs. They transferred knowledge which was facilitated through a range of institutional and governance arrangements that pre-date Chandlerian big business.[97] They were key traders and investors in developing countries, using a multitude of organisational forms which ranged from arm's-length relations, to inward foreign direct investment, and also the establishment of domestic businesses. These businesses registered as local by expatriate entrepreneurs are an illustration of foreign investment which is not accounted for by any statistics of foreign direct investment or trade. Expatriate entrepreneurs were key agents in processes of transfer of marketing knowledge, and also technological, managerial, and entrepreneurial knowledge. They had an important contribution in the establishment of new industries such as the textile industry in Brazil, and also to influencing economic development. British expatriate entrepreneurs tended to take roles as shareholders, as top managers, or as both. A substantial part of the capital used to fund those businesses came from banks some of which were British; and they relied substantially on their international social networks to procure machinery and other materials, and also to sell their finished products abroad. Expatriate entrepreneurs and managers made crucial contributions in shaping marketing strategies and practices in the industry, particularly through the use of more direct distribution methods, innovative and often aggressive marketing techniques, and the creation of brands and protection of its intellectual property. British expatriate entrepreneurs further helped increase the absorptive capability associated with knowledge transfer by investing in related industries, such as utilities, transport, and banking, by investing in education and training of the workforce, and by helping to create industrial associations for entrepreneurs to network.

This study also contributes to the literature which aims to show that trademark data can be crucial to provide new insights and explanations of different economic phenomena. The original trademark data collected for the first time on Brazil confirms when new industries such as textiles emerged, and complements existing literature on the subject by highlighting that a significant part of British investment in Brazil during the period 1875–1914 was in fact 'disguised' as domestic investment. British expatriate entrepreneurs were present in the establishment of the oldest companies and most active registrants of trademarks in Brazil, but most of the companies they established were registered as domestic. The knowledge they transferred to the country in various forms had a much more significant impact on the country's industrialisation and economic development than usually considered by conventional explanations of British investment in Brazil during the second industrial revolution.

Notes

1. While this is the first study which draws on trademark data from Brazil, there is an emerging group of scholars in Latin America using historical trademark data to explain different economic, political and social phenomena. See for instance Lluch, "Marca Registrada: Reflexiones sobre el Uso de las Marcas"; Escobar, "Female Entrepreneurship."

2. In 1907 the Brazilian textiles industry (including cotton, jute, wool, silk and linen) employed 34.2% of the total labour force in the country working in manufacturing, used 40.2% of the machinery, and 40.4% of the total capital employed in manufacturing. Throughout the twentieth century the contribution of the textiles industry to GDP was overall quite significant within manufacturing, but decreased over time. Suzigan, *Indústria*, 129; Versiani e Suzigan, *O Processo Brasileiro*: "Tabela 3 – Participação Relative dos Géneros da Indústria de Transformação no Valor da Transformação Industrial, 1919–1980," 31.

3. Knowledge can be tacit and sticky or explicit and smooth. For the purposes of this article they are analysed jointly. Teece, "The Market for Know-How," 81–86; idem "Capturing Value," 55–79; Nonaka and Takeuchi, *The Knowledge-Creating*.

4. Lev, *Intangibles*, 5–7.

5. Lopes, *Global Brands*.

6. Wilkesmann and Wilkesmann, "Cultural Characteristics."

7. Lopes and Casson, "Entrepreneurship and the Development."

8. See for example Eakin, "British Imperialism and British Enterprise in Brazil."

9. Casson, *Enterprise and Competitiveness*, 80. A social background devoid of extreme political, racial or religious intolerance is considered to encourage flexible thinking.

10. When there is no related knowledge within the organisation, absorption of new knowledge transferred can only take place if the sender (e.g. in this case the expatriate entrepreneur) stays in the organisation long enough to give time for knowledge to be transferred successfully through training and also through social interaction. Kedia and Bhagat, "Cultural Constraints"; Minbaeva, "Knowledge Transfer."

11. See for example Cantwell, *Technological Innovation and Multinationals;* idem; "The Globalization of Technology"; Almeida "Knowledge Sourcing"; Jaffe et al., "Geographic Localisation"; Almeida and Kogut, "The Exploration of Technological"; Phene, Madhok and Liu, "Knowledge Transfer"; Tsai, "Knowledge Transfer."

12. Lopes, *Global Brands*; Lopes and Guimarães, "Trademarks and British Dominance."

13. While brands can be beneficial to businesses, consumers and society in general by, for example, protecting the manufacturer from imitation through the registration of trademarks and helping consumers to simplify decision taking, they can also contribute to block innovation, creating barriers to entry, and manipulate consumers minds and be wasteful. Lopes, "Brands and the Evolution."

14. The first trademark law for these countries was passed in the following years: Argentina – 1876; Bolívia – 1893; Colombia – 1890; Costa Rica – 1896; Cuba – 1884; Mexico – 1884; Peru – 1892; Portugal – 1883; Uruguay – 1877; and Venezuela -1877. Mathur and Patel, *World Development*: Annex 3.

15. Decreto Lei, no. 16,264 (19 December 1923).

16. Textiles marks appear registered in several classes as this was a key industry in Britain's economy at the time, being a key component of British International trade. Out of the 50 classes, textiles and related products appear registered in 15 (class 23 to class 36, and class 38), and include products such as cotton, linen, jute, silk and wool. Lopes and Guimarães, "Trademarks and British Dominance": 798; Rogers, *A Guide to the Patent Office*.

17. Jones, *Multinationals and Global*, 255; Feinstein, "Britain's Overseas." About the British informal Empire see, for example, Brown, "Informal Empire in Latin America."

18. See as an illustration Haber, *How Latin America Fell Behind;* Cardoso and Faletto, *Dependencia y Desarrollo*; Evans, *Dependent Development*.

19. Stein, *The Brazilian Cotton*. Several authors disagree with this view. See for example Medina et al., *Beyond Imported Magic*; Stepan, *Picturing Tropical Nature*; Joseph, Le Grand, and Salvatore, *Close Encounters of Empire*.

20. Cardoso and Faleto, *Dependência e Desenvolvimento*; Furtado, *Formação Económica*; Fernandes, *Capitalismo Dependente*; Mello, *O Capitalismo Tardio*; O'Brien, "Path Dependency"; Haber, *How Latin American Fell*.

21. Cottrell, *British Overseas*; Stone, *The Composition and Distribution*; Platt, *Britain's Investment Overseas*; Ridings, "Business Associationalism."

22. Tavares, *Da Substituição de*; Prado Jr., *História Econômica do Brasil*. Beatty (2015) makes a similar argument about how the US were leading registrants of patents in Mexico, having transferred knowledge and technologies into the country. He argues, however, that all these investments greatly contributed to Mexico remaining technologically dependent on the US in the long-term. Beatty, *Technology and the Search for Progress*.

23. Gonçalves, *Evolução das Relações Comerciais*, 48; Needell, "The State and Development"; Love, "The Brazilian Federal State"; Manchester, *British Pre-Eminence*; De Fiore and De Fiore, *The British Presence in Brazil*. Edgerton (2006) considers that the cultural and economic gap developed by countries such as Brazil cannot be explained solely by looking at the history of technological invention and innovation. His argument is that, for countries affected by Imperialism and Colonialism, discussions should focus on the importance of 'things', and the fact that these countries followed different paths of industrialisation, in many cases resulting from their own choice to industrialise later. Edgertson, *Shock of the Old*, 39.

24. Britain's share decreased from about 46% of total imports during the period 1880-1884 to about 32% by 1910–1913. Gonçalves, *Evolução das Relações Comerciais*: 48.

25. *Trade and Navigation – Accounts Related to Trade and Navigation of the United Kingdom*.

26. The Brazilian tariff system was then considered one of the most complicated in the world. Many British and other European textile exporters had to hire own staff, with expertise on Brazilian tariffs, as it was quite impossible to operate in that market intelligently without such knowledge. The tariffs on imports reduced the national cost to produce in Brazil. Electricity, inputs and skilled labour were very expensive in Brazil in comparison with industrialised countries. Decree no. 3,396 (24 November 1888); Decree no. 25 (30 December 1891); Stein, *The Brazilian*: 85; Suzigan, *Indústria Brasileira*: 155; Versiani, "Industrial Investment"; Needell, "The State and the Development under the Brazilian Monarchy," 79–99; Love, "Brazilian Federal State in the Old Republic": 100–115; Garry, "Textile Markets," 18.

27. Reis, *O Imposto de Importação*. Firms such as Companhia de Fiação e Tecidos Aliança, Companhia América Fabril, and Companhia Progresso Industrial do Brasil, are among the leading firms producing jute. Clark, "Cotton Goods in Latin America," 6, 60.

28. The US did not have an Empire, and Brazil was one of the few foreign markets of large size where they could be assured a reasonably high level of sales. Bulmer-Thomas, "British Trade," 6.

29. Rippy, *British Investments*, 25; Kenwood and Lougheed, *The Growth of the International*, 27–28; Stone, "British Direct and Portfolio," 695.

30. Guimarães, *A Presença Inglesa*.

31. Stone, "British Direct and Portfolio Investment," 694–695; Levy and Saes, "Dívida Externa Brasileira," 50; Levy, "The Banking System"; Born, *International Banking*.

32. Rippy, *British Investments*, 151, chapter 14; Bethell, *História da América Latina*; Castro, *As Empresas Estrangeiras*, 98–99. British Investment becomes more diversified in Latin America in the early twentieth century, and Argentina becomes the main host country, receiving large investments in the production of wheat and cattle. Railways, which connected the producing areas to Buenos Aires, and also public utilities, were important industries receivers of British foreign investment until World War I. Lanciotti and Lluch, "Gran Bretaña y Argentina"; Miller, "Britain and Latin America"; Castro. *As Empresas Estrangeiras no Brasil*, 37–88, 64–66, 78–79, 98–99, 116–122.

33. In 1865 a report about textile factories in Brazil mentioned that there were nine factories employing 768 people. In 1884 there were 46 plants. In 1875 there were 30, in 1881 there were 51, 109 in 1905, and 137 in 1910. Pearse, 'Brazilian Cotton': 26; *Diário Oficial*, Rio de Janeiro (13 March 1883); Branner, *Cotton in the Empire*; Graham, *Britain at the Onset*, 38–39.

34. In 1893, for example, textile machinery imported from Britain represented 42.5% of all textiles machinery imported by Brazil. Suzigan, *Indústria Brasileira*: 152.

35. Stein, *The Brazilian*, 117; Cain and Hopkins, *British Imperialism*, 305.

36. Pargendler, "Politics in the Origins," 842.

37. Lisboa, *Princípios de Direito Mercantil*.

38. Vampré, *Tratado Elementar de Direito Comercial*, 34.

39. 'Speech of Senator D. Manoel', *Senate Records* (1 June 1860): 13, as cited in Pargendler, "Politics in the Origins," 846.

40. With the independence of Brazil in 1824, the Constitution, article 179, also includes intellectual property rights. After the proclamation of the Republic in 1889, the new Constitution renewed the protection of intellectual property. Vieira, *Propriedade Industrial,* chapters 2 and 3.

41. Decree nº 2,682 (23 October 1875). Some of its characteristics include: that marks must be distinctive; the registrant is able to claim ownership in case of litigation; first to file has ownership but there is the possibility of proof of prior ownership; trademark registrations have a term of 15 years. The law is applicable to foreigners who have factories in Brazil; and also applicable to foreigners without establishments in Brazil but whose countries have diplomatic conventions which grant reciprocity to the national marks.

42. In Britain a new trademark law was also enacted in 1875 with registrations starting in 1876. In the US there was a system of registration in place by states between 1870 and 1880 (being declared unconstitutional from 1880 until 1904), but national law only came into place in 1905. Lopes and Duguid, *Brands, Trademarks,* chapter 1; McClure, "Trademarks and Unfair Competition"; idem, "Trademarks and Competition"; Khan and Sokoloff, "History Lessons: The Early Development."

43. Wilkins, "The Neglected"; Chandler in *Scale and Scope* (1990) identifies a sequence of changes in business practices during this period – in large scale production, in the integration of professional management, and in mass marketing and distribution, which enabled new ways of packaging, branding and advertising. Chandler, *Scale.*

44. '*Moreira & Cia. vs. Meuron & Cia*' Tribunal de Comércio da Bahia, (16 April 1874), 28–29.

45. Nogueira and Fischer Jr., *Tratado Theórico e Prático,* 26.

46. Trademark nº 1, *Junta Comercial da Capital do Império – Registro das Marcas* (19 November 1875), *Série Indústria e Comércio* 9X, IC3 [Arquivo Nacional do Rio de Janeiro].

47. Lopes and Duguid, *Brands, Trademarks*: chapter 1.

48. Another country which developed new trademark law around this period is Spain. Sáiz and Fernández Pérez, "Catalonian Trademarks."

49. France remained the country with the largest number of registrations per year until the mid-twentieth century, both in total and per capita terms. Greeley, *Foreign Patent and Trademark,* 223; "Convention Between UK and Brazil"; Lopes and Duguid, *Brands, Trademarks*: 15.

50. Before then, the government had already signed some bilateral declarations to share the protection of trademarks from 1876 to 1881: the first agreement occurred with France (consolidated in the Decree nº 6,237 (21 June 1876), followed by declarations with Belgium (consolidated in the Decree nº 6,567 (8 November 1876), Germany (12 January 1877), Italy (21 July 1877), the Netherlands (27 July 1878) and Denmark (25 April 1881). Agapito de Veiga Jr. *Marcas de Fabrica.* Decree nº 1,628 (23 Outubro, 1875): Acordos Diplomáticos.

51. Bodenhausen, *Guide to the Application*; Barbosa, "Developing New Technologies."

52. Decree nº 9,233 (28 July 1884); Nogueira and Fischer Jr. *Tratado Theórico,* 56.

53. Decree nº 3,346 (14 October 1887).

54. Decree nº 1,236 (24 September 1904); Nogueira and Fischer Jr., *Tratado Theórico,* 27, 29, 265–275.

55. The Directory launched the journal *Propriedade Industrial* (Industrial Property) to publicise the trademarks and patents registered, and to publish news and relevant research on the topic. Decree nº 16,264 (19 December 1923).

56. For example, for the period 1894 until 1896, while in France all the trademark applications resulted in registrations in Britain only an average of 34% of applications resulted in registrations. The relatively low number of registrations in the US is very much connected to the fact that the US Patent and Trademark Office (USPTO) took years to introduce a reliable system of categorisation for marks. In 1870 federal trademark law passed, bringing with it federal registration. Nine years after it was passed, however, the Supreme Court declared the federal law unconstitutional. A new US federal law was enacted in 1905. In the interim, however, the Patent Office continued to register marks from US firms. The 1905 law proved more robust than its predecessor, and led to a spike in trade mark registrations after which registrations continued at a significantly higher rate than during the legal 'interregnum' of 1880–1904. Lopes and Duguid, *Brands, Trademarks,* chapter 1; Preeley, "Statistics Regarding the Grant," 242–245; Lopes, and Guimarães, "Trademarks and British Dominance."

57. Gonçalves, *Evolução das Relações Comerciais.*
58. Decree nº. 1,628 (23 October 1875): articles 2, 16 and 17.
59. Dean, *The Industrialization;* Suzigan, *Indústria Brasileira.*
60. Decree nº. 5,424 (10 January 1905): article 2.
61. This convention which took place in Rio de Janeiro, focused on several topics, including the registration or deposit of drawings, and models made in the country of origin, and its applicability to the other countries of the Union. The countries participating in this Convention were: Brazil, Ecuador, Paraguay, Bolivia, Colombia, Honduras, Panama, Cuba, Peru, El Salvador, Costa Rica, Mexico, Guatemala, Uruguay, Argentina, Nicaragua, the US, and Chile. There were some exceptions as established by the Mexico Pan American Convention in 1902. A proposal was put forward for the creation of classes of trademark registrations, as a means of standardising registration procedures throughout the American continent. "Report of the Delegates of the United States."
62. The Brazilian Industry census took place between 1905–1907. Several adverts were published in 1906 highlighting how important it is for firms to register their businesses in the census. "O Brasil em 1906," *O Fluminense* (2 December 1905): 1; "Inquérito Industrial," *O Commentário* 4, no.3 (Rio de Janeiro, 1906): 60; "Brazil National Exhibition," *The South American Journal and the Brazil and River Plate Mail*, 64 (January–June 1908): 53 [Baker Library Historical Collections. Harvard Business School]; Wright, *The Brazilian National Exposition of 1908.*
63. "Relatório do Ano de 1895," *Brasil – Ministério da Agricultura* (Rio de Janeiro, 1896); "Relatório do Ano de 1907", *Ministério da Agricultura* (Imprensa Nacional, 1908), 24–28.
64. IC3 (Arquivo Nacional); "Relatório do Ano 1907," *Ministério da Agricultura* (Imprensa Nacional, 1908), 24–28; *Bulletin Officiel de la Propriété Industrielle & Commerciale.*
65. In 1895, 13 trademarks out of a total of 130 were registered by British firms. Similarly, in 1905, 35 trademarks out of 517 were registered by British firms.
66. Before then, various factors inhibited industrialisation. These included, the presence of a society historically dominated by slavery, an economy highly reliant on coffee production, legislation which redirected labour to industries considered key to the economy such as mining, a lack of local entrepreneurial skills to enable Brazilian businesses to compete with British business, the scarceness of skilled labour force, and the inadequacy of the existing transport system. Saes, "A Controvérsia sobre a Industrialização"; Furtado, *Formação Económica;* Baer, *Industrialization and Economic Development;* Leff, *Underdevelopment and Development;* idem, *Reassessing the Obstacles to Economic Development*, 57–58, 131, 133; Becket, *Empires of Cotton*, 169–170.
67. This investment was more prominent in other industries such as the manufacture of wheat flour. Paiva Abreu, "British Business in Brazil," 396.
68. Summerhill, *Order Against Progress;* Lewis, "Railways and Industrialisation."
69. Stein, *The Brazilian*, 20–21; Carone, "Selecção, Notas e Bibliografia," 17.
70. For studies that link trademark registration activity with patents registration activity and technological innovation see for example Lopes and Guimarães, "Trademarks and British Dominance"; Helmers and Rogers, "Trademarks and Performance in UK Firms."
71. Lopes, *Global Brands.*
72. See for example Jacob, *The First Knowledge Economy.*
73. Pearse, "Brazilian Cotton," 30.
74. Graham, *Britain at the Onset,* 138; Abreu, "British Business in Brazil," 389; Hamblock, "Report on Economic," 310, 311.
75. Haber, "Business Enterprise."
76. *Almanak Administrativo Mercantil e Industrial do Rio de Janeiro* (Laemmert, 1879), 47; idem (Laemmert, 1891), 856; Rose, *Firms,* 173–174. By then it was already a fully-fledged multinational with mills over 16 countries, 60 branches and 150 depots. Kim, "Coats as a Multinational"; Graham, *Britain at the Onset of Modernization in Brazil*, 144.
77. "Linhas Para Coser: Empire of Thread," *Brazilian Business 39*, no. 7 (July 1959), 34–35.
78. Between 1898 and 1914. J. & P. Coats was selling to the following places in Brazil: Bahia, Pernambuco, Porto Alegre, Rio de Janeiro, Rio Grande, São Paulo, Desterro, Curityba, and Para. "Ledgers for J. & P. Coats Ltd, Central Agency" (GB28/UGD/199/2), [J. & P. Coats Archives].

79. Westall, "The Competitive Environment," 215.
80. "Linha Coats," *Diário de Pernambuco* (6 October 1879), 2; "Linha Coats Não Tem Igual," *Gazeta de Notícias* (20 January 1880), 6; "Linhas Brancas de Côres da J. P. Coats," *O Libertador* (11 July 1883), 4.
81. Smith & Youle appears in the Almanak Laemmert as 'Dealer Farm Wholesale'; 'Alfred F Youle, Admnistrador of the British Subscription Library'; 'Agent in Rio de Janeiro's city of the Guardian Fire and Life Assurance Co (Capital £ 2,000,000)'; 'Agent in Rio de Janeiro's city of the The British and Foreign Marine Co. Limited (Capital £ 1,000,000)'. *Almanak Administrativo, Mercantil e Industrial do Rio de Janeiro* (Laemmert, 1882), 250, 350, 657, 662.
82. "Indicador," *Almanak Administrativo, Mercantil e Industrial do Rio de Janeiro* (Laemmert, 1880), 156, 224, 818; idem (Laemmert, 1884), 783, 1,252, 1,326, 1,648; idem (Laemmert, 1885), 722, 1,468.
83. Mesquita, "A Formação Industrial," 50–51.
84. Birchal, "O Empresário Brasileiro," 2.
85. Monteiro, *Empreendedores*.
86. Apart from textiles they also traded Brazilian goods such as coffee, which they distributed through their branches in Brazil, and in various parts of Europe. "Listagem dos Negociantes Estrangeiros," *Almanak Administrativo Mercantil e Industrial do Rio de Janeiro* (Laemmert, 1868), 500; "Coluna Tribunais," *O Globo* (18 July 1876), 3.
87. "Listagem dos Negociantes Estrangeiros," *Almanak Administrativo, Mercantil e Industrial do Rio de Janeiro* (Laemmert, 1868), 500; idem, (Laemmert, 1880), 500; idem (Laemmert, 1885), 94; "Exportações – Embarcações Despanhadas no Porto do Rio de Janeiro," *Diário do Rio de Janeiro* (20 Outubro 1869), 3; *The Rio News* (24 July 1882), 7; Ellison, *The Cotton Trade,* 250.
88. Ricci, Carniello and Dias, "British Investment in Brazil."
89. Weid, "Estratégias Empresarais."
90. Birchal, "O Empresário Brasileiro," 9; *O Industrial* (16 November 1881), 4; *The Anglo Brazilian Times* (24 December 1881), 2; *Gazeta de Notícias* (9 January 1885), 1.
91. Monteiro, *Empreendedores*, 287.
92. Ibid., 36; Elizabeth von der Weid, *O Fio da Meada*.
93. The stock market was still under-developed. Stein, *The Brazilian*, chapters 3, 6.
94. Levy, *A Indústria*, 150, 153; Monteiro, *Empreendedores*, 296.
95. Garry, "Textile Markets of Brazil," 46–47.
96. Wilkins, "The Free-standing Company."
97. Chandler, *Strategy and Structure*.

Acknowledgments

This project benefitted from the financial support of the British Academy (Research Grant BM130264). The trademark information about Britain, France and the US was collected as part of an Economic and Social Research Council project grant held by Teresa da Silva Lopes (Research Grant RES-062-23-0,193). Bruna Dourado provided invaluable research assistance in the fieldwork undertaken for this research. Elizabeth Santos Souza and also Beatriz Lanna and Amanda Marinho contributed to the development of the trademark database. We would like to thank Mark Casson and three anonymous referees for very helpful comments to earlier versions of this article.

Disclosure statement

No potential conflict of interest was reported by the authors.

Funding

This work was supported by British Academy [grant number BM130264], Economic and Social Research Council [grant number RES-062-23-0193].

References

Abreu, Marcelo Paiva. "British Business in Brazil: Maturity and Demise, 1850-1950." *Revista Brasileira de Economia* 54, no. 4 (2000): 383–413.

Almanak Administrativo Mercantil e Industrial do Rio de Janeiro. Rio de Janeiro: Laemmert, 1844, 1866, 1868, 1879, 1880, 1882, 1884, 1885, 1891.

Almeida, Paul "Knowledge Sourcing by Foreign Multinationals: Patent Citation Analysis in the US Semiconductor Industry." *Strategic Management Journal* 17 (1996): 155-165.

Almeida, Paul, and Bruce Kogut. "The Exploration of Technological Diversity and the Geographic Localization of Innovation." *Small Business Economics* 9, no. 1 (1997): 21–31.

Baer, Werner. *Industrialization and Economic Development in Brazil III*. Homewood, Illinois: Richard D. Irwin, 1965.

Barbosa, Denis Borges. "Developing New Technologies: A Changing Intellectual Property System. Policy Options for Latin America." *Sistema Económico de la America Latina*. Nações Unidas: SELA, 1987.

Bastos, Wilson Lima. *Mariano Procópio Ferreira Lage: Sua Vida, Sua Obra, Sua Descendência, Genealogia* [His Life, His Work, His Offspring, Genealogy]. Juiz de Fora: Edições Paraibuna, 1991.

Beatty, Edward. *Technology and the Search for Progress in Modern Mexico*. Oakland: University of California Press, 2015.

Becket, Sven. *Empires of Cotton – A Global History*. New York: Alfred A. Knoff, 2014.

Bethell, Leslie. *História da América Latina*, 1870-1930 [History of Latin America – 1870–1930] 4, São Paulo: Edusp, 2001.

Birchal, Sérgio de O. "O Empresário Brasileiro - Um Estudo Comparativo." [The Brazilian Entrepreneur- A Comparative Study] IBMEC – Working Paper. Minas Gerais, 2004.

Bodenhausen, G. H. C. *Guide to the Application of the Paris Convention for the Protection of Intellectual Property*. Geneva: BIRPI, 1967.

Born, Karl Erish. *International Banking in the 19th and 20th Century*. Verlag: Berg, 1984.

Branner, John C. *Cotton in the Empire of Brazil*. Washington D.C.: Government Printing Office, 1885.

"Brazil National Exhibition." *The South American Journal and the Brazil and River Plate Mail*, 64 (January-June, 1908): 53 [Baker Library Historical Collections. Harvard Business School].

Brown, Matthew, ed. *Informal Empire in Latin America: Culture, Commerce, and Capital*. Oxford: Blackwell, 2008.

Bulletin Officiel de la Propriété Industrielle & Commerciale. Paris: Ministère du Commerce, 1876–1913.

Bulmer-Thomas, Victor. "British Trade with Latin America in the Nineteenth and Twentieth Centuries." University of London, Institute of Latin American Studies – Occasional Papers 19, 1998.

Cain, Peter J., and A. G. Hopkins. *British Imperialism: Innovation and Expansion, 1688–1914*. London: Longman, 1993.

Cantwell, John A. *Technological Innovation and Multinational Corporations*. Oxford: Basil Blackwell, 1989.

Cantwell, John A.. "The Globalisation of Technology: What Remains of the Product Cycle Model?" *Cambridge Journal of Economics* 19, no. 1 (1995): 155–174.

Cardoso, Fernando Henrique, and Enzo Faletto. *Dependência e Desenvolvimento na América Latina. Ensaio de Interpretação Sociológica* [Dependency and Development in Latin America. A Sociological Interpretation]. Rio de Janeiro: LTC, 1970.

Carone, Edgard. "Selecção, Notas e Bibliografia [Selection, Notes and Bibliograpgy]." In *Evolução Industrial do Brasil e Outros Estudos* [The Industrial Evolution of Brazil and Other Studies], edited by Roberto Simonsen, 9–11. São Paulo: Editora Nacional e Universidade de São Paulo, 1973.

Casson, Mark. (1990), *Enterprise and Competitiveness*. Oxford: Clarendon Press, 1990.

Castro, Ana Célia. *As empresas Estrangeiras no Brasil, 1860–1913* [Foreign Firms in Brazil 1860–1913]. Rio de Janeiro: Zahar, 1979.

Celso, Affonso. *Marcas Industriaes e Nome Commercial* [International Marks and Commercial Names]. Rio de Janeiro: Imprensa Nacional, 1888.

Chandler, Alfred D. *Strategy and Structure: Chapters in the History of the Industrial Enterprise*. Cambridge, Mass: MIT Press, 1962.

Chandler, Alfred D. *Scale and Scope: The Dynamics of Industrial Capitalism*. Cambridge, Mass: Harvard University Press, 1990.

Clark, W.A. Graham. "Cotton Goods in Latin America – Brazil, Colombia and Venezuela." *Department of Commerce and Labor - Bureau of Manufactures*, 36, 1910: 60.

"Coluna Tribunais [Column Courts]." *O Globo*. (18 July 1876): 3.

"Convention Between UK and Brazil." *Manchester and Lancashire General Adviser* (4 April, 1874).

Cottrell, P. L. *British Overseas Investment in the Nineteenth Century*. London: Macmillan, 1975.

De Fiore, Elizabeth, and Ottaviano De Fiore, eds. *The British Presence in Brazil, 1808-1914*. São Paulo: Editora Pau Brasil, 1987.

Decree nº 2,682 (23 October 1875).

Decree nº 25 (30 December 1891).

Decree nº 3,346 (14 October 1887).

Decree nº 3,396 (24 November 1888).

Decree nº 9,233 (28 July 1884).

Decree nº 1,236 (24 September 1904).

Decree nº 5,424 (10 January 1905).

Decree nº 16,264 (19 December 1923).

Decree nº 1,628 (23 October 1875).

Dean, Warren. *The Industrialization of São Paulo, 1880–1945*. Austin: University of Texas Press, 1969.

Diário Oficial, (13 March 1883). Rio de Janeiro: Imprensa Nacional, Ministerio da Fazenda.

"Empire of Thread." *Brazilian Business* 39, no. 7 (July 1959): 34-35.

"Exportações – Embarcações Despanhadas no Porto do Rio de Janeiro [Exports – Vessels from Rio de Janeiro Harbour]." *Diário do Rio de Janeiro* (20 Outubro 1869): 3.

Eakin, Marshall C. "Business Imperialism and British Enterprise in Brazil: The St. John d'el Rey Mining Company, Limited, 1830-1960." *The Hispanic American Historical Review* 66 (1986): 697-742.

Ellison, Thomas. *The Cotton Trade of Great Britain*. London: Effingham Wilson, 1886.

Escobar Andrae, Bernardita. "Female Entrepreneurship and Participation Rates in Nineteenth Century Chile." *Estudios de Economía* 42, no.2 (December, 2015): 67-68.

Evans, Peter. *Dependent Development: The Alliance of Multinational, State, and Local Capital in Brazil*. Princeton: Princeton University Press, 1979.

"Faleceu o Negociante António Xavier Carneiro, Português [The Merchant António Xavier Carneiro, Portuguese, has Passed Away]." *Gazeta de Notícias – Rio de Janeiro*. (21 May 1902): 4.

Feinstein, C. "Britain's Overseas Investments in 1913." *The Economic History Review* 43, no. 2 (1990): 288–295.

Fernandes, Florestan. *Capitalismo Dependente e Classes Sociais na América Latina* [Dependent Capitalism and Social Classes in Latin America]. Rio de Janeiro: Zahar, 1973.

Furtado, Celso. *Formação Económica do Brasil* [Economic Formation of Brazil]. São Paulo: Companhia Editora Nacional, 1968.

Garry, L. S., "Textile Markets of Brazil." *Department of Commerce – Bureau of Foreign and Domestic Commerce* 203, 1920.

Gazeta de Notícias (9 January 1885): 1.

Gonçalves, Reinaldo. *Evolução das Relações Comerciais do Brasil com a Inglaterra, 1850–1913* [Evolution of Trade Relations between Brazil and Great Britain, 1850–1913]. Rio de Janeiro: UFRJ, 1982.

Graham, Richard. *Britain and the Onset of Modernization in Brazil 1850–1914*. Cambridge: Cambridge University Press, 1968.

Greeley, Arthur Philip. *Foreign Patent and Trademark Laws*. London: Abel and Imray, 1883.

Guimarães, Carlos Gabriel. *A Presença Inglesa nas Finanças e no Comércio no Brasil Imperial* [The British Presence in the Finances and Trade of Imperial Brazil]. São Paulo: Alameda, 2012.

Haber, Stephen H. "Business Enterprise and the Great Depression in Brazil: A Study of Profits and Losses in Textile Manufacturing." *Business History Review* 66, no. 2 (Summer, 1992): 335-363.

Haber, Stephen H. *How Latin America Fell Behind: Essays on the Economic Histories of Brazil and Mexico, 1800–1914*. Palo Alto: Stanford University Press, 1997.

Hamblock, E. "Report on Economic and Financial Conditions in Brasil." *Diplomatic and Commercial Reports*, 1922.

Helmers, Christian, and Mark Rogers. "Trademarks and Performance in UK Firms." In *Trademarks, Brands, and Competitiveness*, edited by Teresa da Silva Lopes, and Paul Duguid, 55–76. London: Routledge, 2010.

"Inquérito Industrial [Industrial Survey]." *O Commentário* 4, no.3 (Rio de Janeiro, 1906): 60.

Jacob, Margaret C. *The First Knowledge Economy – Human Capital and the European Economy, 1750–1850*. Cambridge: Cambridge University Press, 2014.

Jaffe, Adam, Manuel Trajtenberg, and Rebecca Henderson. "Geographic Localization of Knowledge Spillovers as Evidenced by Patent Citations." *The Quarterly Journal of Economics* 108, no. 3 (1993): 577–598.

Jones, Geoffrey. *Multinationals and Global Capitalism*. Oxford: Oxford University Press, 2005.

Joseph, Gilbert M., Catherine C. LeGrand, and Ricardo D. Salvatore, eds. *Close Encounters of Empire – Writing the Cultural History of U.S.-Latin American Relations*. Durham: Duke University Press, 1998.

Junta Comercial da Capital do Império – Registro das Marcas [Trade Register Office of the Capital of the Empire – Trademark Registrations]. 19 November, 1875. IC3, Album 4 [Rio de Janeiro: Arquivo Nacional].

Kedia, B. L., and R. S. Bhagat. "Cultural Constraints on Transfer of Technology Across Nations: Implications for Research in International and Comparative Management." *Academy of Management Review* 13, no. 4 (1988): 559–571.

Kenwood, A. G., and A. L. Lougheed. *The Growth of the International Economy, 1820–1990*. London: Routledge, 1992.

Khan, B. Zorina, and Kenneth L. Sokoloff. "History Lessons: The Early Development of Intellectual Property Institutions in the United States." *Journal of Economic Perspectives* 15, no. 3 (2001): 233–246.

Kim, Dong-Woon. "Coats as a Multinational before 1914." *Business and Economic History* 26, no. 2 (1997): 526–539.

Lanciotti, Norma S., and Andrea Lluch. "Gran Bretaña y Argentina: Inversiones, Empresas y Relaciones Económicas, 1870-1975c. Balance Historiográfico y Agenda de Investigatión [Great Britain and Argentina: Investments, Firms and Economic Relations, 1970–1975c. Historical Overview and Research Agenda]." Universidad de San Andrés - Working Paper 48, 2009.

"Ledgers for J. & P. Coats Ltd, Central Agency" (GB28/UGD/199/2) [Glasgow: J. & P. Coats Archives], 1889-1959.

Leff, N. H. *Underdevelopment and Development in Brazil - Economic Structure and Change 1822-1947*. vol. 1. London: Allen & Unwin, 1982.

Lev, Baruch. *Intangibles: Management, Measurement and Reporting*. Washington DC: Brookings, 2001.

Levy, Maria Barbara. *A Indústria do Rio de Janeiro Através das Suas Sociedades Anónimas* [The Industry of Rio the Janeiro through its Limited Companies]. Rio de Janeiro: UFRJ, 1994.

Levy, Maria Barbara, and Flávio Saes. "Dívida Externa Brasileira 1850-1913: Empréstimos Públicos e Privados [Brazilian Foreign Debt 1850–1913: Public and Private Loans]." *História Econômica e História de Empresas* 4, no. 1 (2001): 48–91.

Levy, Maria Barbara. "The Banking System and Foreign Capital in Brazil." In *International Banking 1870-1914*, edited by Rondo Cameron, and V. I. Bovykin, 351–370. Oxford: Oxford University Press, 1991.

Lewis, C. M. "Railways and Industrialisation: Argentina and Brazil, 1870-1929." In *Latin America: Economic Imperialism and the State*, edited by C Abel, and CM Lewis, 199–230. London: Athlone, 1985.

"Linha Coats." [Coats Thread] *Diário de Pernambuco* (6 October 1879): 2.

"Linha Coats Não Tem Igual [Coats Thread has No Equal]." *Gazeta de Notícias*. (20 January 1880): 6.

"Linhas Brancas e de Côres da J. P. Coats [White and Coloured Thread of J. P. Coats]." *O Libertador*. (11 July 1883): 4.

Lisboa, José da Silva. *Princípios de Direito Mercantil* [Principles of Commercial Law]. Rio de Janeiro: Imprensa Nacional, 1874.

Lluch, Andrea. "Marca Registrada: Reflexiones Sobre el Uso de Las Marcas Comerciales, El Consumo y La Comercialización de Bienes en El Mundo Rural Argentino, 1900-1930 [Registered Trademark: Reflections on the the the Use of Commercial Trademarks, The Consumption and Trade of Argentian Rural Goods, 1900–1930]." *Mundo Agrario* 13, no. 26 (2013): 1–18.

Lopes, Teresa da Silva. "Brands and the Evolution of Multinationals in Alcoholic Beverages." *Business History* 44, no.3 (2002): 1-30.

Lopes, Teresa da Silva, and Mark Casson. "Entrepreneurship and the Development of Global Brands." *Business History Review* 81 no. 4 (2007): 651–680.

Lopes, Teresa da Silva. *Global Brands*. New York: Cambridge University Press, 2007.

Lopes, Teresa da Silva, and Paul Duguid, eds. *Brands, Trademarks and Competitiveness*. London: Routledge, 2010.

Lopes, Teresa da Silva, and Paulo Guimarães. "Trademarks and British Dominance in Consumer Goods, 1876-1914." *Economic History Review* 67, no.3 (2014): 793-817.

Love, Joseph L. "The Brazilian Federal State in the Old Republic, 1889-1930: Did Regime Change Make a Difference?" In *State and Nation Making in Latin America and Spain – Republics of the Possible*, edited by Miguel A. Centeno and Agustin E. Ferraro, 100–115. Cambridge: Cambridge University Press, 2013.

Manchester, Alan K. *British Pre-Eminence in Brazil: Its Rise and Decline*. Chapel Hill: University of North Carolina Press, 1933.

Mathur, Gautam, and Surendra J. Patel. *World Development 7*. Oxford: Pergamon Press, 1979.

McClure, Daniel M. "Trademarks and Unfair Competition: A Critical History of Legal Thought." *The Trademark Reporter* 69 (1979): 305 – 356.

McClure, Daniel M. "Trademarks and Competition: The Recent History." *Law and Contemporary Problems* 59 (1996): 13-43.

Medina, Eden, Ivan Costa Marques, and Christina Holmes, eds. *Beyond Imported Magic*. Cambridge MA: The MIT Press, 2014.

Mello, João Manuel Cardoso de. *O Capitalismo Tardio* [Late Capitalism]. São Paulo: Brasiliense, 1982.

Mesquita, Pedro P. A. "A Formação Industrial de Petrópolis: Trabalho, Sociedade e Cultura Operária, 1870-1937 [The Industrial Formation of Petropolis: Work, Society and Working Class Culture, 1870–1937]." Dissertation, Universidade Federal de Juíz de Fora, 2012.

Miller, Rory. *Britain and Latin America in the Nineteenth and Twentieth Centuries*. London: Routledge, 1993.

Minbaeva, D. B. "Knowledge Transfer in Multinational Corporations." *Management International Review* 47, no. 4 (2007): 125–144.

Monteiro, Ana Maria. "Empreendedores e Investidores em Indústria Têxtil no Rio de Janeiro, 1878-1895 [Entrepreneurs and Investors in the Textiles Industry of Rio de Janeiro, 1878–1895]." PhD diss., Universidade Federal Fluminense, 1985.

"Moreira & Cia. *vs.* Meuron & Cia." *Tribunal de Comércio da Bahia* (16 April 1874): 28-29.

Needell, Jeffrey D. "The State and Development Under the Brazilian Monarchy, 1822–1889." In *State and Nation Making in Latin America and Spain – Republics of the Possible*, edited by Miguel A. Centeno, and Agustin E. Ferraro, 79–99. Cambridge: Cambridge University Press, 2013.

Nogueira, J. L. de Almeida, and Guilherme Fischer Jr. *Tratado Theórico e Prático de Marcas Industriais e Nomes Commerciais* [Theoretical and Practical Treaty of Industrial Trademarks and Commercial Names]. São Paulo: Hennie Irmãos, 1910.

"O Brasil em 1906 [Brazil in 1906]." *O Fluminense*, (2 December 1905).

O'Brien, Patrick. "Path Dependency, or Why Britain Became an Industrialized and Urbanized Economy Long before France." *The Economic History Review* 49, no. 2 (1996): 213–249.

O Industrial (16 November 1881): 4.

Pargendler, Mariana. "Politics in the Origins: The Making of Corporate Law in Nineteenth-Century Brazil." *American Journal of Comparative Law* 60, no.3 (Summer, 2012): 805-850.

Pearse, Arno S. "Brazilian Cotton – Being the Report of the Journey of the International Cotton Mission through the Cotton States of São Paulo, Minas Geraes, Bahia, Alagoas, Sergipe, Pernambuco, Parahyba, Rio Grande do Norte." In *International Federation of Master Cotton Spinners and Manufacturers' Association* (March – September). Manchester, NH: Taylor Garnett Evans & Co., 1921: 38–39.

Phene, A., A. Madhok, and K. Liu. "Knowledge Transfer within the Multinational Firm: What Drives the Speed of Transfer?" *Management International Review* 45 (2005): 53–74.

Platt, D. C. M. *Britain's Investment Overseas on the Eve of the First World War*. New York: St. Martins Press, 1986.

Prado, Caio, Jr. *História Econômica do Brasil* [Economic History of Brazil] 43. São Paulo: Brasiliense, 2012.

Preeley, Arthur P. "Statistics Regarding the Grant of Patents and Registrations of Trademarks." *Foreign Patent and Trademark Laws – A Comparative Study*. Washington D.C.: John Byrne & Co., 1899.

Reis, Marcelo. *O Imposto de Importação e suas Alíquotas: Da Tarifa do Império à Tarifa Externa Comum* [Import Tariffs: From Empire Tariffs to Common Tariffs to Foreign Entities]. Ebook: Revolução, 2015.

"Relatório do Ano de 1907 [Report for the Year of 1907]." *Brasil - Ministério da Agricultura, vol. 1*. Rio de Janeiro: (Imprensa Nacional, 1908): 24-28. IC3 [Rio de Janeiro, Arquivo Nacional].

"Relatório do Ano de 1895 [Report for the Year of 1895]." *Brasil - Ministério da Agricultura* [Ministry of Agriculture]. Rio de Janeiro: Imprensa Nacional, 1896. IC3 [Rio de Janeiro, Arquivo Nacional].

"Report of the Delegates of the United States to the Third International Conference of the American States held in Rio de Janeiro, 21 July to 26 August 1906." Washington: Government Printing Office, 1907.

"Retrospecto Comercial [Trade Overview]." *Jornal do Comércio* (1885): 37.

Ricci, Flávio, Monica Franchi Carniello, and Nelson Wellhausen Dias. "British Investment in Brazil: Edward Ashworth, a Case Study." *Revista Brasileira de Gestão e Desenvolvimento Regional* 8, no.3 (Sept. – Dec. 2012): 283-306.

Ridings, Eugene W. "Business Associationalism, the Legitimation of Enterprise, and the Emergence of a Business Elite in Nineteenth-Century Brazil." *Business History Review* 63, no. 4 (1989): 757–796.

Rippy, Fred. *British Investments in Latin America, 1822–1949*. New York: Arno Press, 1966.

Rose, Mary. *Firms, Networks and Business Values*. Cambridge: Cambridge University Press, 2000.

Saes, Flávio A. M. "A controvérsia sobre a industrialização na Primeira República [The Controversy about the Industrialization during the First Republic]." *Estudos Avançados* 3, no.7 (1989): 20-39.

Sáiz, Patricio, and Paloma Fernández Pérez. "Catalonian Trademarks and the Development of Marketing Knowledge in Spain, 1850-1946." *Business History Review* 86 (2): 239-260.

Stein, Stanley J., and The Brazilian Cotton Manufacture. *Textile Enterprise in an Underdeveloped Area, 1850–1950*. Ithaca: Cornell University Press, 1957.

Stepan, Nancy Leys. *Picturing Tropical Nature*. Ithaca: Cornell University Press, 2001.

Stone, Irving. "British Direct and Portfolio Investment in Latin America Before 1914." *The Journal of Economic History* 37, no. 3 (1977): 690–722.

Stone, Irving. *The Composition and Distribution of British Investment in Latin America, 1865 to 1913*. New York: Garland Publishing, 1987.

Summerhill, W. R. *Order Against Progress: Government, Foreign Investment and Railroads in Brazil, 1854–1913*. Palo Alto: Stanford University Press, 2003.

Suzigan, Wilson. *Indústria Brasileira – Origem e Desenvolvimento* [Brazilian Industry – Origin and Development]. São Paulo: Hucitec, 2000.

Tavares, Maria da Conceição. *Da Substituição de Importações ao Capitalismo Financeiro* [From Import Substitution to Financial Capitalism]. Petrópolis: Vozes, 1972.

The Anglo Brazilian Time (24 December 1881): 2.

The Rio News (24 July 1882): 7.

Trade and Navigation - Accounts Related to Trade and Navigation of the United Kingdom for Each Month the Year House of Commons, Ordered, by The House of Commons, to be Printed 1875–1914.

Tsai, W. "Knowledge Transfer in Intra-Organizational Networks: Effects of Network Position and Absorptive Capacity on Business Unit Innovation and Performance." *Academy of Management Journal* 44 (2001): 996–1004.

Vampré, Spencer. *Tratado Elementar de Direito Comercial* [Elementary Treaty to Commercial Law], 34. Rio de Janeiro: F. Briguiet & Cia, 1922.

Veiga Jr., Didimo Agapito de. *Marcas de Fabrica* [Manufacturing Trademarks]. Decree n° 1628 - Acordos Diplomáticos (23 Outubro), 1875.

Versiani, Flávio Rabelo. "Industrial Investment in an 'Export' Economy: The Brazilian Experience Before 1914." *Journal of Development Economics* 7, no.3 (September, 1980): 307-329.

Versiani, Flávio, and Wilson Suzigan. *O Processo Brasileiro de Industrialização: Uma Visão Geral* [The Brazilian Process of Industrialization: An Overview]. Brasília: Universidade de Brasília, 1990.

Vieira, Marcos Antonio. *Propriedade Industrial: Marcas – História, Legislação, Comentários, Jurisprudência* [Industrial Property: Trademarks – History, Legislation, Observation, Legislation]. Rio de Janeiro: Lumen Juris, 2006.

Weid, Elizabeth von Der. "Estratégias Empresarais e Processo de Industrialização: A Companhia América Fabril, 1878-1930 [Business Strategies and Industrialisation Processes: Companhia América Fabril, 1878-1930]." *H-Indústria – Revista de História de La Indústria Argentina y Latino Americana* 3, no.5 (2009): 1-33.

Weid, Elisabeth von der, and Ana Marta Rodrigues Bastos. *O Fio da Meada: Estratégia de Expansão de uma Indústria Têxtil, Companhia América Fabril, 1878–1930* [The Thread of a Ball: Expansion Strategy of a Textile Firm, Companhia América Fabril, 1878–1930]. Rio de Janeiro: Editora Casa de Rui Barbosa, 1986.

Westall, Oliver M. "The Competitive Environment of British Business, 1850-1914." In *Business Enterprise in Modern Britain. From the Eighteenth to the Twentieth Century*, edited by Maurice W. Kirby, and Mary B. Rose, 207–235. London: Routledge 1994.

Wilkesmann, U., H. Fischer, and M. Wilkesmann. "Cultural Characteristics of Knowledge Transfer." *Journal of Knowledge Management* 13, no. 6 (2009): 464–477.

Wilkins, Mira. "The Free-Standing Company, 1870-1914: An Important Type of British Foreign Direct Investment." *The Economic History Review* 41, no. 2 (1988): 259–282.

Wilkins, Mira. "The Neglected Intangible Asset: The Influence of the Trade Mark on the Rise of Modern Capitalism." *Business History* 34, no. 1 (1992): 66–95.

Wright, Marie Robison. *The Brazilian National Exposition of 1908*. Philadelphia: G. Barrie & Sons, 1908.

Brands in the Basque gun making industry: The case of ASTRA-Unceta y Cía

Igor Goñi-Mendizabal (iD)

ABSTRACT
Basque gun making was an exception in early twentieth-century Spanish industry due to its high proportion of exports. The intense growth of handgun production during those years resulted from several factors such as Spanish patent law, the revolution in transport and communications, the electrification of manufacturing and the organisation of the sector as an industrial district. This article aims to analyse the role that brands played in this success, employing not only quantitative information but also the correspondence of one of the most important manufacturers of that time. Beyond counterfeiting, Basque gun making showed extraordinary marketing performance in which branding strategies were decisive for its success.

1. Introduction

The production of guns in Spain at the beginning of the twentieth century was divided into two fields clearly delimited by the type of demand they supplied and the ownership of the firms. State-owned factories devoted to the supply of the Spanish army were located in different parts of the country, such as Oviedo (rifles and machine guns), Toledo (ammunition) and Seville (artillery). In contrast, the firms belonging to private industry that, with few exceptions, produced light firearms exclusively for the civilian market were geographically concentrated in the valley of the Deba River in the Basque province of Gipuzkoa, particularly in the town of Eibar.

One of the most outstanding points of this industry during the first decades of the twentieth century was its marked export orientation. Thus, gun making was an exception in a Spanish industry distinguished by its lack of competitiveness abroad. The Basque production of arms increased at a high rate in the context of the first wave of globalisation, matching some of the main European production centres. This rapid growth of export sales has been explained as resulting from the successful counterfeiting strategy followed by Basque manufacturers, which offered cheap versions of foreign known handgun models.[1] Unfortunately, due to the poor quality of most of these products, guns of Spanish origin gained a bad reputation in the international markets that remained.[2]

However, beyond counterfeiting, this production growth was the outcome of a combination of factors that favoured the increase in international demand and the capacity of the Basque gun making industry in response to the new challenges. Spanish patent law, the revolution in transport and communications and the electrification of manufacturing were some of these key factors.

Another feature that characterised the Basque gun making industry at that time was its configuration as an industrial district in which, through intense subcontracting activity, several small- and medium-sized firms manufactured a wide range of pistols, revolvers and shotguns. This structure provided to the whole district a high grade of flexibility to adapt to variations in demand and to customer preferences, increasing its competitiveness.

The presence of a relatively large number of companies operating in the same market and offering products of similar characteristics brought about the proliferation of trademarks as a means of differentiating their products from their neighbouring competitors. As a result, a high percentage of the trademarks historically used for handguns all over the world were of Basque origin. For instance, 292 of the 1035 different names given to pistols and revolvers identified by Hogg and Weeks were attributed to Basque manufacturers (324 were from the US, 106 from Germany, 68 from France and 66 from Belgium), an impressive figure for such a small region.[3]

Trademarks are names or logos that are legally protected, giving the owners the exclusive right to use them for the commercialisation of their products. Their main function is to inform the customers about the origin of the product, helping them to be better informed about their purchases and avoiding unfair competition by other producers. Registry of the trademark is the factor that provides legal protection to the user of that name or logo. The term brand, in contrast, has a broader and more complex meaning. A brand is a trademark that has incorporated social and cultural values. Thus, a brand would represent not only a legal instrument for product differentiation but also an identity or social status to which consumers can feel attracted. A brand has the distinct feature of being able to transfer the fidelity of the customer from one product to another. A trademark can be transformed into a brand through improved reputation, which can be achieved by offering a higher quality product or by promoting the brand by other means such as advertising or independent certifications.[4]

In the case of Basque gun making, guns were commonly commercialised with trademarks that were not registered by manufacturers. Occasionally, the trademarks used were owned by intermediaries, and these traders might have their trademarks registered in other countries. However, several trademarks also were never registered, or their registration was postponed, although they had already been used by manufacturers. Therefore, for clarity, we will use the term 'non-registered trademarks' (NRTMs) for these cases, and the term trademark (TM) to refer to cases in which registration has been certified.

The main aim of this article is to assess the role played by trademarks and brands in the growth experienced by this industry during the early decades of the twentieth century. Our main hypothesis is that Basque gun manufacturers supplemented their lack of capital and technology with an extraordinary performance in marketing and branding.

For that purpose, after devoting the first part of this article to the historical background of gun making in the Basque country, we analyse a sample of NRTMs and TMs used by Basque producers and dealers. Our main goal is to identify patterns to support conclusions concerning not only the branding but also the marketing strategies followed by Basque gunsmiths.

We want to verify thereby whether trademarks were an effective instrument to address the bad reputation acquired by Basque guns in foreign markets during that period.

In the third section of this article, we focus on the case of *ASTRA-Unceta y Cía*, one of the most important and significant firms in this sector in Spain. Through the correspondence of this company, we approach the motivations of the branding strategies followed by the Basque gun making industry. This family firm operated not only in the civilian but also in the military market, always trying to compete by producing higher quality handguns.

2. Historical background of Basque gun making industry

Due to its iron ore deposits and other favourable features, the Basque Country has had a very long tradition of ironworking and manufacturing. One industry that stood out was the weapons-making industry. Basque smiths started producing firearms at the beginning of the sixteenth century, and the Spanish Crown's huge demand helped to foster this industry during the early modern age. After 1573, the King of Spain gave the name of 'Royal Factories' to all of the workshops devoted to producing firearms which had their headquarters in Placencia de las Armas, also known as Soraluze in Basque. This was not a real factory but rather an administrative centre from which the King's officials controlled the production process and where the finished guns made by nearby gunsmiths were sent to for storage. Thus, production tended to concentrate in a limited number of villages located around Placencia de las Armas. Together they constituted the Basque gun making region. These villages and towns were Eibar, Elgoibar, Ermua, Elgeta, Zaldibar, and Placencia de las Armas itself.

However, by the end of the eighteenth century, the Crown distrusted the weak strategic location of the factories, so close to the French border, and decided to create a new factory in Asturias in 1794, the so-called *Royal Factory of Oviedo*. From that moment on, this new facility gradually became the main firearm supplier for the Spanish army and the most important competitor in the Basque gun-manufacturing sector in the struggle for governmental military orders.

In the nineteenth century, as the importance of military contracts decreased, the magnitude of private business began to grow due to the increasing demand for handguns and shotguns. Basque gunsmiths had to improve their skills to introduce the latest technical innovations requested by their clients, such as percussion locks. In this process, the town of Eibar became the most important production centre of the region because its gunsmiths were able to adapt to these changes.

Despite the official persistence of the traditional system, the government actually started to purchase certain war materials through some Basque manufacturers who acted as intermediaries for local workshops. The Royal Factories in the Basque Country and the Royal Factory of Oviedo had to respect the traditional distribution of work and the wages stated by the guilds. In contrast, private intermediaries could negotiate the conditions of the contract with the workshops that they wanted without considering any equal distribution of production, as the Royal Factories did. As a result, the prices offered were more competitive.

Unfortunately, the production of military guns was limited to the scarce state purchases, preventing the modernisation of Basque firms that did not dare to make huge investments. Once the military manufacturing was liberalised in 1860, and due to new contracts, modern and larger companies appeared in the region. Some of these new contracts stemmed from the Spanish ordnance's progressive adoption of technological innovations such as percussion locks, rifled barrels and, finally, breech-loading systems. As a result, the old Royal Factories lost their original function and the headquarters building was used as a Proof Bank, namely a quality control institution for some years, until it was definitively closed down in 1865. Additionally, some factories and workshops of the region manufactured shotguns and small pistols of one or two shots to attend the relatively low demand of the civilian market. Most of these pistols did not have any mark or identification of the manufacturer because they were legally forbidden.[5]

However, during the Third Carlist War (1872–1876), a civil conflict whose actions occurred mostly in the Basque Country, those modern factories fell under the control of the rebel Carlist forces. After the war, most of the Basque gun making firms hoped to resume their military business, but new contracts did not appear. The government was reluctant to promote an industry in a region that had led a revolt against its authority.

In this situation, Basque gun making firms decided to specialise in producing hunting shotguns and self-defence pistols for the civilian market at a time when the demand for this type of product was beginning to increase. As seen in Table 1, over 30 years, the gun production in Eibar increased fourfold due to the rising sales of revolvers. Although revolvers were also used for military purposes, only limited quantities were purchased because only officers and some auxiliary troops were permitted to carry them. *Orbea Hermanos*, for example, sold quantities of revolvers to the Spanish army but, despite being beneficial for one company, this demand was not sufficient to support the whole industry. Therefore, most revolvers manufactured in Eibar were small and designed to be kept in a pocket rather than carried in a holster.

Although the production of shotguns does not seem to have been as important, their monetary value was comparatively higher. Conversely, the majority of pistols referred to in Table 1 are one- or two-shot types and not semi-automatic ones, which were not manufactured before the beginning of the twentieth century. The fast growth of semi-automatic pistol manufacture pushed Eibar to the second position among the main gun making districts in Europe. In 1905, Liège (Belgium) was the leader, with an output of 2,682,111 guns, followed by Eibar with 450,867. Birmingham (UK) was in third place with 337,457, and the last was Saint Etienne (France), with 63,929.[6] The preponderance of handguns became the distinctive feature of Basque gun manufacturing, reaching 90.8% of total production by 1909. In the Belgian industry of Liege, for instance, handguns accounted for less than 40%.[7]

Table 1. The total production of guns in Eibar by gun type in 1881, 1891, 1901 and 1909.

Gun type	1881 Units	1881 %	1891 Units	1891 %	1901 Units	1901 %	1909 Units	1909 %
Shotguns of all types	34,457	25.9	39,004	24.8	62,649	23.2	44,492	8.9
Pistols*	77,066	57.8	51,257	32.6	32,072	11.9	25,747	5.1
Revolvers	21,097	15.8	65,434	41.7	173,587	64.2	429,308	85.7
Rifles, cartridges and Remington carbines	598	0.4	1,345	0.9	1,954	0.7	1,420	0.3
Production total	133,218	100	157,040	100	270,262	100	500,967	100
Index	100		118		203		376	

*It mainly refers to pistols of one or two shots. Semi-automatic pistol manufacturing started at the beginning of the twentieth century.; Source: Mujica, Monografía histórica de la Villa de Eibar.

The integration of the world market is also one of the factors that explain the expansion of Basque gun production. The first telegraph station was built in Eibar in 1883, and the railway arrived in the town in 1887, providing Basque gunsmiths with the opportunity to access distant markets that they had never reached before. Electrification has been noted as another element to be considered. Dependence upon the waterpower supply in such a narrow valley constrained the factories to a very limited space, but electricity allowed the industry to respond to the increasing demand by opening new workshops and factories.[8]

The gun making industry of Eibar was configured as an industrial district in which cooperation and competition coexisted among the industry agents. No very large companies existed; rather, a wide network of small workshops produced pieces for medium-sized assembling factories.[9] Table 2 shows the configuration of the district. Gun making was the main activity of the town, considering that the actual population at the time was 11,000. The average size of companies manufacturing handguns was greater than that of those producing shotguns. Because high-quality workers were not so necessary, pistol and revolver makers integrated most of the production process within the same building and took steps towards mass production and standardisation. In contrast, shotguns were still higher-quality craftsmanship products and were primarily manufactured by gunsmiths in small workshops. For instance, in 1914, before the war, the largest companies were *Orbea y Cía*,[10] with a staff of 400 workers, and *Garate, Anitua y Cía*, with 200; both were handgun manufacturers. Victor Sarasqueta owned the largest shotgun factory in the town, employing 63 people.

Another characteristic of this industry was the persistence of piece work in these subcontracting relationships, a practice considered by workers to be a right that they deserved as gunsmiths. Visitors to Eibar at that time described how workers, most of them socialists, used to work in advance on Sunday morning to wake up later on Mondays.

Although we have defined Eibar as a Marshallian industrial district in previous works, the presence of relatively large companies such as the abovementioned *Orbea y Cía* or *Garate, Anitua y Cía* could make this asseveration arguable.[11] Markusen defined four types of industrial districts, i.e. the Marshallian district and its Italianate variant, the hub-and-spoke districts, the satellite industrial platforms and the State-anchored industrial districts.[12] The case of Eibar fulfils almost all of the features attributed not only to Marshallian districts but also to some of the additions described by Becattini for Italian districts. The main point of discussion could be the size of the firms. In the hub-and-spoke districts, the structure is dominated by some large and vertically integrated companies surrounded by suppliers; in contrast, in the Marshallian and Italianate districts, the structure is dominated by small sized and locally owned firms. Our thesis is that in 1914, Eibar was a hub-and-spoke district immersed in a

Table 2. The gun making industrial district of Eibar in April 1914.

	Firms	Workers
Shotguns	12	150
Pistols	16	475
Revolvers	24	1.020
Pistols and revolvers	6	459
Total (gun making)	58	2.104
Big foundries	3	114
Small foundries	6	48
Total (iron forging)	9	162

Note: Eibar at that time had a population of 11,000.
Source: Eibar municipality archive.

process of transformation into a Marshallian one. The largest firms of the district had started their businesses in the mid-nineteenth century (*Orbea y Cía c.* 1860, *Gárate, Anitua y Cía. c.* 1850), but most of the rest of the companies were spin-off workshops that had initiated their activity and increased their size during the first years of the twentieth century. Consequently, other Marshallian features were added during those years such as the reinforcement of unions, the commitment of the local government to the development of the industry and the creation of common institutions such as the Gunsmithing School (1913) or the Official Proof Bank (1916).

The most relevant feature of gun making, which was truly uncommon in Spanish industry, was the significance of exports that reached almost 80% of the production This success must be ascribed mostly to handguns and not to shotguns because the market for the latter was primarily national. This high degree of competitiveness abroad has been explained as a product of the combination of three factors that determined the strategy followed by Basque firms.[13] The first one was the low level of protection given by Spanish patent law to foreign designers. If the patent was not put into practice in a three-year term, techno-logical information became public and anyone could use it.[14] This approach was used by less developed countries to catch up with the leaders, thus promoting the imitation of foreign technology.[15]

The second factor was the absence of any compulsory proof in Spain. In other countries, all guns had to undergo statutory testing – 'proof' - before being introduced to the market. Once the proofs were passed, the Official Proof Bank stamped a mark on the gun, and these marks were often recognised abroad by international agreements.[16] However, not all coun-tries possessed this type of institution or signed these agreements. When a gun was exported from a country without compulsory proof to one with it, the gun had to pass only a slight functioning exam. Eventually, these two factors provided Basque gun makers the chance to produce low-cost imitations of European and American handguns.

Finally, the configuration of the sector as an industrial district, with its network of small- and medium-sized companies, permitted a wide variety of guns to be offered and great flexibility to adapt the production to any change in demand or customer tastes. There were no economies of scale in Eibar gun production, but there were economies of scope. Regretfully, the specialisation in this type of low-quality gun resulted in the discrediting of Spanish guns, in other words, Basque guns, in international markets. For those companies that were trying to compete, increasing the quality of their products to overcome that poor reputation became a difficult task.

During the First World War, after months of crisis due to uncertainty generated by the outbreak of the conflict, exports of Basque pistols and revolvers brought production to historically maximum levels (see Figure 1). During the four years of war, almost two million pistols and revolvers were purchased, largely by the British and French armies but also by Italy and Romania. This huge and unusual military demand for handguns was a consequence of the special features of trench warfare during the conflict. When soldiers faced the enemy in close combat in a muddy, narrow trench, they preferred the handling of a small firearm to that of a long, heavy rifle. The most successful product in this period was the Eibar-type pistol, also known as the Ruby pistol due to the TM used by one of the manufacturers. This handgun was a cheap copy of the Browning system pistols manufactured in Belgium by the *Fabrique Nationale d'armes de Guerre* and in the US by the *Colt Firearms Co.*[17] The most imi-tated model was the Browning 1903 and almost all of the copies ever made of this pistol

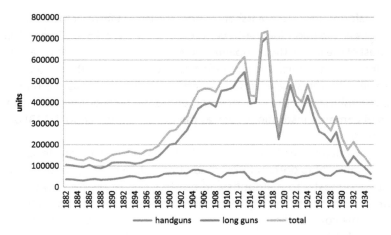

Figure 1. Sales of the gun making industry of Eibar 1880–1935. Source: Arzac, *Evolución de la industria* and Mujica, *Monografía histórica*.

were produced by Basque manufacturers.[18] Despite the efforts made by the Belgian company to prevent this unfair competition, rather conveniently the Spanish patent law protected Basque manufacturers, allowing the production of the Eibar-type pistol to continue.[19]

The poor quality of many of these pistols increased the bad reputation of Basque guns after the war, and the international markets were full of them. At the same time, in the post-war era, the governments of almost every country began to apply protective commercial policies to resuscitate their own industries. Thus, the export markets that had been the main destination of Basque guns became less profitable, and firms tried to survive the crisis by turning their attention to the home market.

Unfortunately, in the early 1920s, Spain was immersed in the so-called *Pistolerismo* phenomenon, during which strikes, demonstrations, quarrels between different trade unions and labour conflicts were solved using pistols and revolvers. In addition to repressive police measures, the government implemented restrictive legislation on gun production and trade. Despite the complaints of the Basque manufacturers and the municipalities of the gun making region, the government did not reverse its decision; thus, the gun making industry also had to face an intensive reduction of sales in the domestic market.

At that time, the Spanish compulsory Official Proof Bank also started its activity. This collective institution had been a dream pursued by some manufacturers and workers of the district, whose goal was to increase the average quality of the guns made in Eibar. Consequently, and after some delays, the former low-quality production pattern was abandoned; it was clear that new strategies were needed.

Some of the companies, taking advantage of the government policy to promote industries that did not exist in Spain, decided to undertake diversification processes. They chose products that could be adapted to their machinery and workers, such as bicycles, sewing machines, shaving razors or machine tools. That decision was not random, because some American, French and Belgian firms had already taken the same path years before.[20]

Others, drawing on experience and financial capability achieved during the war, started to design high-quality ordnance weapons to be offered to army and police trials. There were also firms that, having achieved some recognition during the war, opted to act as intermediaries selling smaller manufacturers' products, not only guns, under their better known own brand. Finally, other firms looked for new markets, such as the Balkans or China. Because Spanish law did not lessen its restrictive measures in the 1930s, these trends were reinforced until the Spanish civil war broke out in 1936.

The beginning of the Francoist dictatorship intensified the diversification process. Only three firms remained as handgun manufacturers and, although shotgun production flourished in the 1960s, other products, such as bicycles, scooters, domestic electric appliances and machine tools, became more important for the local industry. The crisis of the 1970s and 1980s almost led to the complete disappearance of gun making activity. There is no Basque handgun company today, and shotgun production remains but primarily survives by attending to demand for custom-made, high-quality products.[21]

3. Marks, trademarks and brands

Like other craftsmen of the Middle and modern ages, firearms gunsmiths used to mark their products with their own names to promote the quality of their craftsmanship. This practice was very common in the case of those gunsmiths who worked individually for the private market, and there are many examples of these marks dating back as far as the sixteenth century.[22] In the case of Basque gun makers, because this private production did not appear again until the eighteenth century, the marks of the modern age that we know today correspond to the gunsmiths of those years.[23]

During the seventeenth century, Basque firearm production remained under the tight control of the Crown, with no private merchant involved. At that time, not only the guns but also every piece received at the Royal Factory had to be tested. At least since the beginning of the eighteenth century, these guns were stamped with a mark or marks that certified that the gun had been accepted by Royal officials. Flintlocks made since 1780 also showed the mark of the craftsman responsible for that part of the gun.[24]

Nevertheless, after the liberalisation of the gun making industry and the foundation of new modern factories, change began to occur. At that time, international gun designers assigned their own names to their new mechanical systems and created companies to exploit their patents; the firms' commercial names also included the patentees' names. That approach was how some brands were created. For example, the 'Colt system revolver', patented by Samuel Colt in 1835 and manufactured by *Colt's Patent Firearms Manufacturing Company*, soon became the 'Colt revolver' or only 'Colt'.[25]

Basque manufacturers in the 1880s, when patenting their guns, started to include not only their commercial names but also specific designations concerning the technical system of the gun. For example, in 1883, *Orbea Hermanos*, one of the most important factories in Eibar, patented a revolver based on Smith & Wesson models and named it ONA, the Basque word for 'good'. This revolver was accepted by the government as the ordnance revolver for the military in 1884 and for the navy in 1885.[26] Similar examples were EUREKA (1888, Narciso Zulaica), ERREXA (1888, *Orbea Hermanos*), BOTA CILINDRO (1890, José Crucelegui) and EGOKIA (1890, Víctor Sarasqueta).[27] However, because there was no trademark registration, we cannot consider them trademarked.

The huge growth of Basque revolver production in the late nineteenth century promoted the need for differentiation because, although the diversity of the models made was not particularly broad, the number of manufacturers was increasing very quickly.[28] Because most of the new workshops were run by former workers of larger firms, it is not surprising that the models that they manufactured were similar to those made by their past masters.

The first TM concerning gun manufacturing at the Spanish Registry Office was inscribed not by a Basque manufacturer but by a Catalonian one. Although most of the industry was located in the Basque Country, there were manufacturers in Barcelona who mostly acted as traders. That is true of Eduardo Schilling, who registered the drawing of a boar for shotguns in 1895. The first Basque gun making TM, which was registered in the same year, was surprisingly not owned by a proper manufacturer but by the Proof Bank of Eibar. This institution was created to certify the minimum quality of the products, but taking the test was voluntary. As mentioned, compulsory proof was not established until 1923. These TMs were related to the proofs that should be made: '2ª P' (second proof), 'Pº' (tested?) and 'EX' (examined?).[29]

To perform a deeper analysis, we established a sample of 690 gun making NRTMs and TMs used by Spanish firms. Our main source is the thorough study made by Juan L. Calvó of Spanish gun making patents and TMs registered in Spain, which we compared with other sources.[30] The total number of TMs in the sample is 359; although some of the others might also have been registered abroad. Some of these NRTMs could also have been owned by dealers in foreign countries; however, they were exclusively used for marketing Spanish guns. The results are shown in Tables 3–7.

The information contained in Table 3 is consistent with the previous explanation of the gun making industry. Despite exceptions such as Barcelona or Madrid, the majority of the NRTMs and TMs concerning guns were registered or used by Basque companies, most of them located in Eibar. Table 4 refers to the characteristics of the NRTM and TM used.

Table 3. Spanish gun making NRTMs and TMs by the location of the firm (1883–1936).

LOCATION	NUMBER	%
Eibar	561	81.3
Barcelona	34	4.9
Ermua	29	4.2
Gernika-Lumo	20	2.9
Elgoibar	19	2.8
Placencia del as armas-Soraluze	11	1.6
Madrid	4	0.6
Not identified	3	0.4
Zumarraga	3	0.4
Liege-Eibar	3	0.4
Bergara-Eibar	2	0.3
Markina	1	0.1
	690	100

Table 4. Gun making NRTMs and TMs by language (1883–1936).

LANGUAGE	NUMBER	%
Spanish	180	26
Acronyms	157	22.7
English	121	17.5
Basque	39	5.6
French	35	5.1
Others	30	4.3
Combination of languages	29	4.2
Latin	24	3.5
Not identified	75	11
	690	100

Table 5. Gun making NRTMs and TMs by product.

PRODUCT	NUMBER	%
Ammunition	7	1.0
Powder	3	0.4
Barrels	6	0.9
Frame/action bar	1	0.1
Locks	1	0.1
Choke makers	1	0.1
Engravers	1	0.1
Polishers	1	0.1
Stocks	1	0.1
Special steel	1	0.1
Pieces	**23**	**3.3**
Target pistol	2	0.3
Alarm guns	1	0.1
Carabines	13	1.9
Gun cane	1	0.1
Guns of any type	237	34.3
Guns except shotguns	1	0.1
Guns/ammunition	17	2.5
Guns/iron furniture	3	0.4
Guns/tools/machines	2	0.3
Pistols	178	25.8
Pistols/revolvers	12	1.7
Revolvers	101	14.6
Revolvers/shotguns	2	0.3
Shotguns/pistols	1	0.1
Shotguns	61	8.8
Guns	**632**	**91.6**
Not identified	**35**	**5.1**
	690	100.0

Table 6. Trademarks registered by gunsmiths' craft unions.

TM	UNION (Spanish)	UNION (English)
S.A.	Sociedad de Acicaladores-choqueadores	Society of choke makers and primpers
S.G.	Sociedad de Grabadores	Society of engravers
S.B.	Sociedad de Basculeros	Society of action/frame makers
S.Cs.	Sociedad de Cañonistas	Society of barrelmakers
S.C.	Sociedad de Cajeros	Society of stoke makers
S.P.	Sociedad de Pulidores	Society of polishers
S.LL.E.X.	Sociedad de Obreros Llaveros de Ermua	Society of lockmakers of Ermua

Table 7. Gun making NRTMs and TMs by year.

PERIOD	NUMBER	%
1883–1899	19	2.8
1900–1910	97	14.1
1911–1920	181	26.2
1921–1930	197	28.6
1931–1936	25	3.6
1940–1960	8	1.2
Not identified	163	23.6
	690	100

Although the number of them written in Spanish is significant, the more relevant fact is that the rest are acronyms or are expressed in non-Spanish languages, such that the origin of the gun could not easily be guessed by a foreigner. We wonder whether the Basque language could be identified by the customers of the time and consequently linked with Spanish guns. However, it is evident that the main aim of this branding strategy was to enter foreign markets. As we will see, Basque manufacturers tried not only to copy the counterfeited foreign original models' TMs but also to hide the Spanish origin of the guns.

Table 5 shows the NRTMs and TMs included in the sample classified according to the product for which they were registered or the type of gun for which we know they were used. Although some of the TMs were registered with the purpose of being used for pieces or material related to gun making, most were registered for use in guns in general or specifically for pistols and revolvers. TMs for shotguns were not so common. Perhaps the name of the gunsmith, which was usually included in the company's commercial name, was sufficient for customers to identify the origin of the gun and to certify its quality.

It is interesting to consider some of the TMs included in the first group concerning parts of the guns. Some of them were used by local gun makers' trade unions to fight against the pressure of larger manufacturers. As previously mentioned, at the beginning of the twentieth century, the inner organisation of the district still resembled that of the Royal Factories due to the subcontracting of smaller workshops by the larger firms for the manufacturing of parts. To avoid a negative lowering of prices, the craft unions tried to regulate the market within the district, which is why they registered a TM for each of the main actions or processes needed to build a gun. The purpose of this measure was to oblige larger factories not to use in their guns any part that did not hold the established mark, an action that somehow returned them to the times of the guilds. Interestingly, the role played by Unions in the development of collective and certification marks has been noted by Duguid for the US.[31] These TMs were registered by unions in 1903.

In some cases, we know the registry date of the TM; in others, we know when that NRTM was used and who the manufacturer of the handgun was. Thereby, table shows that most of them were registered or at least used in the first two decades of the twentieth century. Despite the high number of NRTMs for which we cannot confidently determine a date, we assume that most of them can be included in the period 1910–1930.

What types of TMs were used by Basque gun manufacturers? In the case of shotguns, the use of the Spanish language for TMs was more common, considering that Spain and some Latin American countries were the main target market for this sort of gun. The TMs usually referred to animals or hunting and were usually accompanied by a drawing: for example, FAISAN (pheasant), LA PALOMA (the pigeon), LA IMPERIAL (the imperial), LA ESPECIAL (the special), SAN EUSTAQUIO (Saint Eustatius), SIN RIVAL (without rival), EL PATO (the duck), LA SORDA (the woodcock), PARA TODOS (for everybody), LONGINES, EL CONEJO (the rabbit), EL LEON (the lion), and EL CASTOR (the beaver). The Basque language was also used: GOGOR (hard), BETI-GOGOR (always hard), EDER (beautiful) and INDARDUN (powerful).

In contrast, pistols and revolvers were sold all over the world. In this case, foreign languages, particularly English, were widely used. One of the reasons was to ease the purchase by a foreign customer by showing culturally closer brand names. Counterfeiting was also a motivation because some of the TMs tried to resemble foreign manufacturers' brands. For instance, *Bonifacio Echeverría* of Eibar started to manufacture a pistol called STAR that, beyond the close spelling, externally resembled the Austrian STEYR pistol.

Finally, one of the main causes of this branding strategy was to avoid the effects of the worldwide reputation for bad quality acquired by Spanish manufacturers in previous years. Customers used to link Spanish guns to cheap, poor-quality products and thus, although the quality had already improved in many cases, the Basque firms felt the need to hide the real origin of the guns. This type of attitude is common when agents are dissatisfied with the ascribed collective reputation they possess.[32] Occasionally, the words used were not real English but resembled that language to non-English speakers, and mistakes or misspellings were common.[33] The use of acronyms of gunsmiths' names was also common.

Once the language had been chosen, almost any topic could be used for a brand: mythology, geography, gun type, historical events or locations. Here are examples: BRISTOL, WALMAN, PHOENIX, DIANE, HOPE, ALLIES, RUBY SIX, ANGLO OTTOMAN, INDIAN, DOUGLAS, LOOKING GLASS, SHARP SOOTER,[34] LIBERTY, PARAMOUNT, DREADNOUGHT, SCOTLAND, TRUST, ROYAL NOVELTY, POKER POSSESIVE, THE BEST SHOOTING PISTOL, PATHFINDER and PROTECTOR. Because, at that time, some of the most renowned brands were also related to specific mechanical systems and ammunition calibres, some firms saw the opportunity to take advantage of this link when using the same cartridge or a similar gun shape. For example, related to the Smith & Wesson revolver system, there were SMITH AMERICANO and ESMIT (misspelling of Smith), and for Browning, BRON-AUTO, BRON-SMALL, BRON-PETIT, BRON-SPORT, BROM, BROM-PETIT and BROMPETIER. One of the smaller revolvers made in Eibar was the so-called Velodog,[35] which was made in a wide variety of systems producing the following combinations: VELO-BRING, VELOBROG, VELO-BROM, VELO-BROW and VELO-MITH.

The brand and occasionally the commercial name could be seen primarily in two places on the handguns. On pistols, the TM was stamped on the slide, and occasionally more information was added: a real or conveniently modified commercial name, an indication of a supposed patent right or the city of origin. Revolvers do not have a very wide surface for inscriptions, so TMs used to appear on the frame or the barrel of the gun. The other place where the brand could be seen was the grip. Because the grip plates were usually made with softer materials such as wood, rubber or gutta-percha, the firms had the opportunity to show more elaborated designs of their brands, such as logos, drawings and artistically written acronyms at a relatively low cost. Some companies also used buffalo horn or mother-of-pearl for special purchases or custom-made pistols. In the 1920s, plastic materials such as celluloid were also introduced.[36]

The handguns were not always introduced to the market by the producers themselves, and they were occasionally sold to intermediaries. Depending upon the market to which the guns were to be sent, the trader could ask the producer to mark the guns with a particular TM of his own or one chosen for the moment. Occasionally, the dealer bought the pistols in advance and did not yet know to which market they were supposed to be sent. In those cases, the trader could ask for 'neutral' pistols, that is to say, pistols without any type of mark. Later, the intermediary company marked the guns according to its interests.

Beginning in 1923, when testing guns at the Proof Bank became compulsory, marks denoting that the gun had passed the test were stamped on the frame and fundamental parts of the gun, such as the barrel or the cylinder. These symbols report the type of proof made and the institution that certified it. These proof marks denote not only the quality specified by authorities to ensure the security of customers when using the gun but also the origin of the gun, because any buyer can identify the proof marks from Eibar or any other proof bank in the world. Therefore, the Proof Bank was not only an instrument that improved collective reputation but also an institution that gave a collective brand to the products of the district.[37]

4. Marketing and advertising

One of the features of early twentieth-century Eibar that astonished contemporary visitors to the town was the humble appearance of the businessmen and their successful performance in foreign markets. Some of these manufacturers were owners of factories that only a few years before were small workshops devoted to the manufacturing of parts for larger factories. They might have had good gunsmithing skills, but they lacked significant experience in marketing. Some of them hardly spoke Spanish, let alone English or French, but this limitation was not considered an obstacle to travelling abroad.

The arrival of new and better-trained generations of managers to the companies at the beginning of the twentieth century started to change this situation, but some companies found a solution by hiring foreign polyglot export managers. Another means of overcoming these difficulties was to develop business through the intermediation of dealers. This type of trading company is common to industrial districts, and their main role is to link the production of the district to the needs of the market. These intermediaries occasionally were not from Eibar. However, several cases exist of local manufacturers that also acted as intermediaries, largely those who had a renowned brand in the market and could ensure better purchases.

Interestingly, in the case of these guns destined for the civilian market, the manufacturers considered that the best way to sell their products was through commercial representatives. These salesmen were required to visit the potential customers with a batch of products to show the actual functioning of the firearm.

Advertising is considered an important means to improve the outcome of a company and is closely linked to the development of a brand[38] Since the eighteenth century, advertising has also been a means of relating brands to the way of life of successful social groups, thus trying to promote emulation among consumers.[39] In the case of the Basque gun making industry further research is needed but herein we present first provisional conclusions on this topic. One of the earliest and more interesting advertisements we have found is shown in Figure 2. It was published by *Orbea Hermanos* of Eibar in 1886, in the *Anuario del comercio, de la industria, de la magistratura y de la administración*, a guide that included addresses and information of administrations and companies of Spain. The text of the advert remarks on the following features: the awards received in some fairs for 'the superiority of its products'; the factory was the oldest of Eibar and their products had the same quality but a lower price than those of foreign competitors; the high quality of the machinery used at their facilities; the ownership of the patent of a redesigned Smith & Wesson revolver; and the fulfilment of the government requirements for the revolvers used by army officers. Finally, the advert also included a transcription of the royal order that recommended that revolver as the best for the Army.

However, this one-page advertisement is an exception because most of them were small-sized ones, and they did not include so many details. The same company published some of these smaller ads in the general press (Figure 3). Interestingly, the word 'Smith' had a more remarkable presence on this advertisement than the commercial name itself, 'Orbea hermanos y Comp.ª' The text refers to the high quality and cheapness of their revolvers, quoting again that they could compete with the best of the American factories.

This company was trying to overcome the low-quality reputation of Spanish guns in the home market by claiming to have improved an American model and offering it at a better

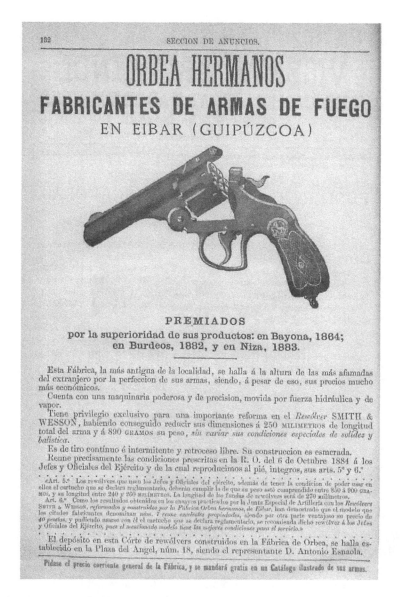

Figure 2. Orbea Hermanos advertisement. Source: *Anuario del comercio, de la industria, de la magistratura y de la administración, 1886*. National Library. Spain.

price. The reference to the certification given by a reputable institution such as the Spanish army tries not only to enhance the reputation of the brand but also to favour an emulation spirit among the non-military customers.

One means of promoting own brands in pursuit of this emulation goal was to obtain some type of patronage from the elite of society. At that time, hunting and shooting contests were frequently practiced by the aristocracy. King Alfonso XIII himself used to organise and attend this type of event. Víctor Sarasqueta, the most important shotgun maker at the beginning of the century, was a good shot, and press reports tell of the 'duels' he had with the king

Figure 3. Orbea Hermanos advertisement. Source: *El Imparcial*, 26th March 1892. National Library. Spain.

Figure 4. Victor Sarasqueta advertisement. Source: *El Imparcial*, 24th July 1914. National Library. Spain.

at pigeon shooting ranges. They became good friends, and Víctor Sarasqueta was appointed official supplier for the king and his aunt the *Infanta* Isabel, a fact that was consequently added to their adverts (see Figure 4).

Shooting contests themselves had an important promotional role if a gun of your man-ufacturing had been used by the champion. That potential result is why some companies used to sponsor the competitors, providing specially designed pistols or shotguns free or, as seen in the case of Víctor Sarasqueta, becoming competitors themselves.

5. The case of ASTRA-Unceta y Cía (1908–1952)

This company was founded in Eibar in 1908 by Juan Esperanza, a mechanic from Zaragoza, and Juan Pedro Uncetabarrenechea,[40] born in Eibar and owner of an ironmonger's shop. The official name given to this general partnership firm was *Juan Esperanza and Pedro Unceta*, and the main aim established in the foundation document was the mechanical production of diverse articles and the manufacturing of iron and steel. The workshop began operating in 1910, manufacturing parts for other handgun manufacturers of the town and, after a year, the staff of the company reached sixteen workers and eight apprentices.

5.1. Looking for a brand: The Victoria pistols (1911–1914)

The manufacturing of complete pistols started in June 1911. The model produced was based on the designs patented by Pedro Careaga following the Browning pattern. This handgun, considering its characteristics, seems to be the first Eibar-type pistol ever made.[41] It also had a special feature patented by Juan Esperanza, a loaded chamber indicator named *Hope*.[42] Using this indicator, the shooter could easily know whether the chamber of the gun had a cartridge inside. This name was registered as a TM and was stamped on the barrel of the pistol in a visible place.

To ensure good business, *J. Esperanza y P. Unceta* marketed this new pistol through the firm *Eduardo Schilling S. en C.* of Barcelona, one of the most important gun-trading companies in Spain. The agreement established that *E. Schilling* would become the exclusive seller of the pistols in the Spanish and Portuguese markets in exchange for a monthly purchase of 1500 units. The pistols were sold under the TM *Victoria*, and they had a very good level of acceptance in the market. Due to the increasing demand, the initially established production and sales levels were soon exceeded, and new agreements had to be made between the two firms. This growth was not only a result of the greater Spanish demand but also a consequence of the exports to other European markets. *J. Esperanza y P. Unceta* still followed the same strategy, conceding sales exclusiveness to other firms and staying away from marketing processes. Eduardo Schilling thereby won the concession for the French and German markets, and another firm, *Thieme & Edeler*, obtained exclusivity for Belgium and Austria.[43]

Table 8 shows the distribution of the sales made by *J. Esperanza y P. Unceta* to its customers. As seen, except for the sales made at the factory itself and the scarce purchases made by countries that were not under an agreement, nearly the entire production was marketed by the two dealer companies. In the case of sales made in the factory, Spain being an exclusive market for *E. Schilling*, *J. Esperanza and P. Unceta* had to pay the distributor's margin of profit to that company.

To sell *J. Esperanza y P. Unceta*'s pistols, *Thieme & Edeler* registered the *Victoria* and *Victoria Arms C°* TMs in Belgium[44] Occasionally, as previously noted, these trading companies asked the producers to stamp their own marks on the pistols, and *Thieme & Edeler* was no exception. Some of the pistols sent to this dealer were marked as *Dewaf* or *Belgium*, thus hiding their Spanish origin. As previously explained, when a gun was imported from a country without a compulsory proof bank to one that did, the guns had to pass tests. Thereafter, they received the official stamp to be sold in that country. To avoid extra costs, locally manufactured guns were thoroughly tested before and after being completely finished, but for those coming from abroad, the proof tests were easier to pass. In these cases, the officials of the bank only shot all of the cartridges once, and although they were guns of lower quality, they did not

Table 8. *J. Esperanza and P. Unceta*'s sales distribution by customers.

	September–December 1912		January–May 1913	
	Pistol quantity	%	Pistol quantity	%
Eduardo Schilling s. en C.	3705	56.40	5599	53.25
Thieme y Edeler	2787	42.43	4793	45.59
Others	69	1.05	99	0.94
J. Esperanza y P. Unceta (direct sales at the factory)	8	0.12	23	0.22
Total	6569	100	10,514	100

Source: Compiled by the author. Correspondence of J. Esperanza y P. Unceta 1912–1913. Esperanza y Unceta Fund AG.

show any damage because some of the chemical operations executed at the end of the manufacturing process reinforced the steel. In the long term, most of these guns were not very reliable.

Although *Victoria* pistols are considered to be of the best quality among the Eibar-type pistols, this strategy of deceiving the customers was also used.[45] The most remarkable example of this strategy was the following inscription that appeared on some pistols sent to *Thieme & Edeler*:

Manufacture Liégeoise d'armes á feu-soc-du

Liége (Bélgique) Patent Nº51.350

E. Schilling also sold pistols with other TMs, i.e. *Muxi*, *Scott* or *Brunswig*, which were not registered in Spain, but we cannot certify whether those purchases were made following the same strategy. Perhaps *E. Schilling* only wanted to make the pistols more attractive to a certain specific market; regardless, the company was clearly not particularly predisposed to show the real origin of the guns.

The coexistence of these two trading companies was not as harmonious as the Basque company would have desired. *E. Schilling* frequently complained about sales made by the Belgian firm in territories assigned to *E. Schilling*, particularly in France. Once these infringements were proven, the relationship with *Thieme & Edeler* cooled, and finally, in 1914, *J. Esperanza y P. Unceta* agreed to cancel the contract.

The success of the sales consequently led to a fast increment of the labour staff, which grew to 120 workers in 1913. The prospects of the business improved when the retired military officer Venancio López de Ceballos, Count of Campo-Giro, reached an agreement with the company giving it the manufacturing rights to his newly designed semi-automatic pistol. This arrangement was a good deal for the company because this pistol had just been declared the service handgun by the Spanish army.

To face this new challenge, and short of room in its facilities in Eibar, the company decided to move to Gernika-Lumo (Bizkaia), better known as Guernica in its Spanish spelling. The local authorities of this town had offered the company a new building free as an allowance to promote the industrialisation of what at that time was a rural medium-sized town of 4000 people. The move to Gernika-Lumo was not as peaceful as the owners most likely intended when they planned it. Only three months after arriving in the new location, the workers started a strike that lasted for a month. As a result, almost all of the staff returned to Eibar, leaving the company in a very complicated situation. Nevertheless, the firm managed to recover by hiring and training local workers and resumed its regular production throughout the following year.[46] Another consequence of the move of the company to Gernika-Lumo was that Rufino, one of the sons of Juan Pedro Unceta, replaced his father in the business. Due to this change, which was not registered until 1919, the firm's name was altered to *Esperanza y Unceta*.

The success of the *Victoria* pistols soon encountered the menace of counterfeiting. The strategy of imitation was applied not only to foreign designs but also to other products of the Basque gun making district of Eibar. Technical innovations, successful brands or emerging markets could hardly be kept secret in such a small town. Workers of different factories were usually friends or relatives, and strong competition provided incentives for betrayal. This environment, which was not well regarded by company owners as individuals, was the crucial factor that gave strength and competitiveness to the whole district. Thus, on 10 March 1914, Pedro Careaga wrote a letter to his patent agent asking him to explore the possibility of suing two manufacturers under the accusation of patent infringement.[47] This type of problem also emerged in the case of TMs and was an issue that concerned the manufacturers when they found out the registry of TMs such as *Walki-Vincitor*, *Vincitor* or *Victoriosa* by other gunsmiths of the town.[48]

However, the *Victoria* TM itself was the source of some discussions between the manufacturers and the traders from Barcelona. At the beginning of the business, Juan Esperanza and Pedro Unceta, when negotiating their agreement with *E. Schilling*, wondered what the TM of their new pistols should be, and *E. Schilling*, among other names, suggested *Victoria*. The manufacturers liked it and agreed to use it for their pistols. Later, when they applied to register the TM, it was denied because the similar *La Victoria* TM had been the property of *E. Schilling* since 1906.

Although they tried to retrieve the TM that they claimed to own, *E. Schilling* refused to provide it and asked for exclusive use of the brand in Europe. As a result, *J. Esperanza y P. Unceta* determined to use another TM for its products because the company did not want to promote one that it did not own. The new TM chosen was *Astra*, which would be the brand of almost all of the products manufactured by the company for the rest of its life. This decision also allowed the company to regain control over the marketing of its products.

5.2. *ASTRA: Building the brand (1921–1936)*

Although at the beginning of the First World War, the company still sold quantities of *Victoria* pistols to *E. Schilling*, it tried to conduct the rest of the purchases with the *Astra* TM, and most of the sales made during the war to France and Italy were so executed. Nevertheless, when trying to negotiate its first firm contract with the French army in 1914, the company was forced to offer its pistols under different NRTMs. All of the approaches to the French government were made by several intermediaries, each of them with a different representation contract. As a result, the French government could have been offered different prices for the same pistol.[49] To avoid this type of interference, *J. Esperanza y P. Unceta* suggested other NRTMs to its representatives, such as *Stosel*, *Scoot* and *Marne*.[50] It also sold unmarked pistols to the French firm *Manufacture Française d'Armes et Cycles* of Saint Etienne but not for the military market. Sales made to the French and Italian governments during the war totalled over 100,000 units. In order to assess properly the performance of the firm during this period, we should add to that total the Campo-Giro pistols purchased by the Spanish government, which amounted to 13,617 guns.

As a summary, Table 9 shows the NRTMs and TMs stamped on the products of this company during this period.

Table 9. NRTMs and TMs used for J. Esperanza y P. Unceta pistols.

TMs registered (registry year in Spain)	NRTMs and TMs used by intermediaries	
Victoria (1911; rejected)		
Fortuna (1911)	T.E.	Muxi
Hope, special dispositive (1912)	Manufacture liegeoise d'armes à feu	Salso
Indian (1914)	The automatic Lexton	Scoot
Infalible (1914)	Brunswig	Caminal
Astra (1914)	Marne	Indian
La Pajarita (1915)Coq (1920)		Infalible

The analysed correspondence of the company certifies that it attempted to register internationally some TMs such as *Indian*, *Infalible* and *Astra*. However, we currently lack reliable information concerning the answer given to those applications or the procedure followed with the rest of the TMs registered in Spain. Similarly, the letters do not offer any information about the status of the TMs used by intermediaries, and we do not know whether they were registered in other countries. The manufacturers just stamped the brand their customers requested.

In 1921, one of the owners, Juan Esperanza, decided to leave the firm and thereafter a new partner entered the company. He was Canuto Unceta, Rufino's cousin. Consequently, the company had to change its name again, becoming *Unceta y Compañía*.

During the interwar period, when the gun making industry was immersed in an intense crisis, *Unceta y Cía*'s main business strategy was to design high-quality handguns for the Spanish government, but the death of the Count of Campo-Giro in a horse-riding accident in 1916 forced the company to develop its own handgun model. The pistol submitted, the *Astra* model 400, won the official trial of 1921 and was declared the ordnance pistol for the army. The new handgun resembled the Campo-Giro in some features, particularly in the tubular shape of the slide, which became a distinctive characteristic of this company's pistols.[51]

Following the army, other military and police institutions, which had only used revolvers until that time, decided to adopt semi-automatic pistols as side arms for their members. In almost all of the trials, *Unceta y Cía* was the winner, except in that of the *Guardia Civil*, the Spanish gendarmerie force, which was won by *Bonifacio Echeverría*'s *Star model A* pistol.[52] This specialisation in the design and production of high-quality military handguns encouraged the company to offer its products to a wider range of governments, primarily in Latin America, winning trials in Ecuador, El Salvador and Colombia. These achievements provided the company with the opportunity to reinforce the brand. Every time it won a trial, it asked the government for official certification of the results and proofs so that it could use them as an asset for promotion.

Another indication of the fact that the firm was trying to build a distinctive brand was the change in the naming of its pistols by adding a number to the *Astra* brand.[53] Thus, it offered the *Astra* 200, a good-quality Eibar-type pistol; the *Astra* 300, a small version of the above-mentioned *Astra* 400; the *Astra* 500, the service signal-pistol in the army; the *Astra* 700, a low-quality pistol for militiamen; and the *Astra* 900 series, copies of the *Mauser* pistols. The *Astra* 600 and *Astra* 800 models were produced during the Second World War.[54]

Advertising was also a strategy followed by the company to enhance the *Astra* brand. The correspondence of the company includes several references to the hiring of advertising space in national and foreign publications. Figure 5 shows one of a series of advertisements published in the official publication of the so-called Somaten, but similar ads were also published in the general press of that time. The Somaten was a traditional militia of Catalonia that was reinforced during the *pistolerismo era* and used by authorities as a tool of repression against unions. Unlike most civilians, its members had the right to own a firearm. After the *coup d'état* of General Primo de Rivera in 1923, the government established the extension of this militia to all of the Spanish provinces, creating a new market niche for gun making companies. The text can be translated as follows:

> Somatenes. If you must buy a handgun, you must see the National Pistol ASTRA. Winner of the trial held by the Minister of War, the 'ASTRA' pistol challenges any pistol that claims superiority.

Figure 5. Esperanza y Unceta advertisment. Source: *El Somaten,* September 1923. National Library, Spain.

> Distrust any gun that does not offer our guarantee. … Advertising is not sufficient; other brands must prove their quality, and nobody can prove that there is a pistol better than our 'ASTRA' pistol.

Thereafter, the text quotes all of the institutions that designated the pistol for official use and the royal orders by which it was approved.

In this case, it is evident that the company was trying to take advantage of its newly conquered position as a supplier of the official service pistol, 'reglamentaria', a word that is noted particularly in the advert. It appears clear that the advertisers wanted their customers to feel like real policemen and that there would be nothing better for them than to hold the same pistols that the military did. The brand also has a prominent presence and it is specifically highlighted. Conversely, other manufacturers' advertisements in the same magazine just noted the quality of the gun to attract these potential buyers.

Figure 6. Sample of Unceta y Cía. advertisements. Source: *Crónica*, 1932–1933. National Library. Spain.

However, the company was not very happy with the outcome of this campaign and rescinded the publishing contracts months later. They explained their disappointment to their representative in Madrid:

> It is okay to advertise, but as you see, the sales are not related to the expense made. The promotion made by advertising must be continued with the personal work of travelling salesmen and representatives, but regretfully, nothing has been done by the date. We do not know for sure, but we suspect that there is more than one province capital that has no ASTRA pistols in its armouries; naturally, this is a consequence of the lack of salesmen, and maybe also a consequence of the lack of mailing. All that must be studied to give a big push to the businesses.[55]

During the early 1930s there also were interesting advertisements promoting the smaller size *Astra* 300 pistol in the home market (Figure 6). The messages transmitted in these ads are related to self-defence: 'Defend yourself. The best defence for your money is an ASTRA pistol', 'At home you should not miss the famous ASTRA pistol', and 'Do not let time go by without the defence of an ASTRA pistol'.

The prestige obtained by winning those trials also gave the company an opportunity to implement other types of business strategies. Taking advantage of the financial strength given by the profits earned during the war, it started to act as an intermediary for other Basque manufacturers, offering a wide catalogue of guns such as pistols, revolvers and shotguns and gradually adding other products that were not directly related to gun making.[56] Most of these products were sold under the *Astra* TM, the only exception being some pistols and revolvers that bore the *Union* TM. The low-price Eibar-type pistols were named the *Astra* 100, *Astra* 1000 or *Union*; the revolvers were called *Astra* or *Union* of first, second or third quality; and the shotguns were given the *Astra* TM and numbers of the series 700 and 800.[57]

Although these subcontracted products gave the company the occasion to enter new markets and to grasp opportunities for its own high-quality handguns, the firm had to face the risk of the discrediting that the low quality of some of them could cause. It frequently received complaints about guns that did not function properly. In the correspondence, we do not find any explanation addressing the apparent contradiction of this strategy. However, considering that these lower quality pistols were not very bad and that they were not sold in Spain, our conclusion is that the company felt that the risk of discredit was not high compared with the benefits of the business.

The Proof Bank of Eibar was the origin of another type of problem. In 1923, the proofs became compulsory, and these subcontractors had to prove their guns in that establishment before sending them to Gernika-Lumo. The Proof Bank was reluctant to stamp the official marks on any pistol tested there under a TM not owned by the manufacturer itself. *Unceta y Cía* suggested overcoming any trouble by using unmarked cover plates for the pistols' hand grips and having the subcontractor lightly stamp its initials on the frame, a mark that thereafter could easily be erased in Gernika-Lumo.[58] These precautions were also extended to 'Eibar' as the place where the guns were manufactured so that the customers would not mistake those handguns as actually having been manufactured in Gernika-Lumo.[59] By that time, the company was not ashamed of the Spanish origin of its guns and always stamped the legend *Unceta y Compañía-GUERNICA (Spain)* on its pistols, but it seems that Eibar still had a poor reputation in the market.

To be consistent with the wide variety of products offered in its catalogues, *Unceta y Cía* used to introduce itself as a large manufacturer. When foreign dealers visited the factories, the owners used to show them the nearby *Talleres de Guernica* and *Joyería y Platería de Guernica*, which were also their investees, as though they were all part of the same factory.[60]

5.3. *Royal pistols for Japan*

One means that the company found to overcome the crisis that the gun making industry was suffering in the 1920s was to extend its operations to new markets that had been vaguely explored in previous years. Following this strategy, the firm began to sell pistols, most of them subcontracted Eibar-type models, to Japanese trading companies.[61] *Unceta y Cía* was not the only Basque manufacturer operating in that market, *Bonifacio Echeverría* and *Beistegui Hermanos* being the main competitors there.

For these sales to the Asiatic market, *Unceta y Cía* initially used the *Royal* TM. Apparently, the owners thought that this TM had not yet been registered or, at least, that the former owner had not paid the fees for the renewal. However, in fact, it belonged to *Beistegui Hermanos*, its main competitor in that market.

The industrial district of Eibar was not a good place to keep a secret, and eventually, it was revealed. *Alday y Cía* was the main supplier of hand grip covers for the Basque handgun manufacturers, and both *Unceta y Cía* and *Beistegui Hermanos* bought *Royal*-branded grip covers there. One day, unadvisedly, the owners of *Alday y Cía* commented to *Beistegui Hermanos* that *Unceta y Cía* was purchasing these covers and consequently they asked for compensation.[62] Initially, *Unceta y Cía* tried to overcome the obstacles imposed by *Beistegui Hermanos* by sending the grip covers to Japan from other country, but it finally had to accept an agreement. In that deal, it renounced not only the right to sell any pistol under the *Royal* TM but also the right to claim any compensation for the damages that any previous patent usurpation made by *Beistegui Hermanos* might have generated for *Unceta y Cía*. In exchange, *Beistegui Hermanos* would not pursue any legal action against it.

This situation was difficult for *Unceta y Cía* to manage. The firm had already established a steady relationship with some Japanese traders and was not keen to change the brand in which it had invested so much money.[63] However, the demand continued to increase and this business turned into one of the most outstanding stories in the history of the Basque gun making industry.

In 1927, *Unceta y Cía* sent Ernest Borchers, its newly hired German export manager, to Japan to strengthen commercial ties with its Japanese customers and to obtain better knowledge of that market. After a long journey through Europe and Asia, he arrived in Japan and met those Japanese clients to realise that they were only acting as re-exporters. The final destination of the guns was not Japan but China, which was immersed in a civil war.[64] He also realised that the most demanded guns in that country were the Mauser-type pistols and that two of the company's competitors, *Beistegui Hermanos* and *Bonifacio Echeverría*, were already aware of that fact. This gun used a powerful cartridge and had a detachable shoulder stock. Due to these features, being a pistol, it could be sold as a commercial gun in China, overcoming the embargo imposed by international powers. However, once the stock was attached to it, the pistol was transformed into a carbine and could be used as a war weapon.

As a result, the three Basque companies developed their own copies of the Mauser pistol with a detachable shoulder stock. Although the calibre and external shape of the pistol were the same, internally the mechanics were different.[65] Furthermore, they developed a device that provided a fully automatic fire option that transformed the pistol into a sub-machine gun. Later, innovations were added such as a detachable 20-shot magazine or a rate-of-fire retarder.[66] Thus, they technically improved the original model at a lower cost than the German manufacturer, whose production was limited by the Versailles Treaty.

This example epitomises what has become a statement in Eibar descriptive of its industry: copy and improve.

Unceta y Cía's best customer was Chan Kai Shek's Government of Nanking. To facilitate business, the firm decided to create a subsidiary firm in Shanghai, the *Astra China Company*. The sales made through this firm reached more than $50,000 between July 1932 and July 1933.[67] The correspondence related to this company ended in 1934; thus, it appears to have survived for only three years. The reasons for this company definitively shutting down are unclear.

After the outbreak of the Spanish Civil War (1936–1939), the activity of the factory was controlled by republican authorities, and all of the production was dispatched to the armed forces of the autonomous Basque government. The infamous bombardment of Gernika-Lumo by the German Condor Legion in April 1937 did not affect the facilities of the factory; thus, the factory was militarised shortly after the occupation of the town by Franco's troops, and production resumed two months later. During the rest of the war, the firm manufactured 28,000 pistols, 130,000 parts for machine guns and 347,000 pieces of diverse material.

5.4. *ASTRA-Unceta y Cía (1952)*

Once the war was over *Unceta y Cía* faced difficulties. As the only pistol supplier of the army, the company remained mobilised, in other words under military control, and commercial trade was forbidden. Soon, after hard negotiations, the prohibition was relaxed and the company could sell guns to the Axis countries. The firm could operate this business so successfully because it had almost no competitors in Spain. The Spanish government only gave permission to resume handgun manufacturing to those factories that could perform the whole production process in the same factory. Thus, the traditional subcontracting system was cut off by the new legislation. Only three companies fulfilled the new requirements, *Bonifacio Echeverría*, *Gabilondo y Cía* and *Unceta y Cía*, and only the latter was in a condition to respond to the handgun demand coming from Germany. The first purchase was made in 1940, and the last one in 1944. The total reached 106,454 pistols.[68] *Bonifacio Echeverría* was finally able to enter the business and sold 45,965 pistols, most of them to Germany but also quantities to Bulgaria.[69]

The confluence of several factors at the end of the Second World War brought great complications to the firm. Therefore, the company had to make relevant decisions concerning business strategy and the structure of the company.

One of the most important factors was the abrupt reduction of exports due to the defeat of Nazi Germany in the war and the economic blockade established by the allied countries to Francoist Spain during those years. The situation in the national market was no better. The Spanish army called for a new service pistol trial and this time, after 30 years of victories, the pistol submitted by *Unceta y Cía* was defeated by *Bonifacio Echeverría*'s STAR pistol. This company, which also manufactured sub-machines guns, thereby became the main light weaponry supplier for the Spanish military and police forces until the 1980s.

With almost no trade either abroad or in the home market, the business was limited to scarce individual sales, and *Unceta y Cía* faced an untenable situation. During these two years, production did not stop, and the stores of the factory were full of unsellable pistols. Eventually, new investors came to rescue the company. The most important of them was the *Banco de Vizcaya*, one of the main banks of the region, which had long experience with industrial business. The new capital was used to implement a productive diversification project to reduce the proportion of the guns in the business of the company. The products chosen were pneumatic tools, such as jackhammers for mining and public works, and accessories for textile machinery. The products were to be sold as *Astra* brand goods.

The effects of the addition of these new products on the company sales were immediate. By 1948, the guns had reduced their presence in the firm's sales to 28.5%, whereas the new fabrications together reached 48.1%.[70] All of those new products were also sold under the *Astra* brand. This diversification process required more investment, and the social capital of the company was increased from 5 million pesetas to 7.5 million pesetas in 1950 and thereafter augmented again to 22.5 million. This growth did not change the shareholding structure of the company because the new shares were acquired by the former partners. As an ultimate upgrade of the *Astra* brand, the Board of Directors of the company decided to change its name to *ASTRA-Unceta y Cía, S.A.* in 1952.[71] Since that time, everyone in Gernika-Lumo and in the whole Basque Country has used the name *Astra* to refer to the company and the factory itself.

The following years are a story of decline. Although handguns recovered their weight in the company's manufacturing in the 1960s, and they produced several successful models but they were the exception rather than the rule. The international competition became more exigent, and the company did not respond to it appropriately, either technically or commercially. Nevertheless, *Astra* continued to be the brand of the company until it was

definitively shut in 1997. This problem was shared by the other two Basque handgun manufacturers, and by the beginning of the twenty-first century, this business had
disappeared.

6. Conclusion

At the beginning of the twentieth century, the Basque gun making sector was structured
as a Marshallian industrial district formed by several small- and medium-sized companies.
Lacking direct government support, these workshops and factories had neither the financial
capability nor the technical skills and machinery to compete with the mass production of
American and European factories. Thus, taking advantage of the opportunities provided by
Spanish legislation, their main strategy was to sell cheap copies of successful foreign handgun models. As a result, two types of needs appeared concerning brands. On the one hand,
they had to differentiate their products from those of their neighbouring competitors, which
carried a proliferation of TMs, regardless of whether they were registered. On the other hand,
as Basque guns gradually started to attract a bad reputation in the markets for their low
quality and poor reliability, companies tried to hide the products' origin using TMs expressed
in foreign or not easily recognisable languages. This branding strategy is fundamental to
understanding the success of the Basque pistols in the foreign markets and the outstanding
growth of its production in such a short period. As mentioned previously, the great importance that the exports had in the gun making industry was considered extraordinary by
contemporary witnesses and an exception in the uncompetitive Spanish industry. Moreover,
this unusual outcome was the result of not only the low prices of the Basque firearms but
also the unexpectedly good marketing performance of the gun makers themselves.

The counterfeiting strategies followed coincide with those described by Da Silva and
Casson but with a distinctive feature that the people of Eibar use, noted by the motto 'copy
and improve'.[72] When imitating foreign designs, modifications were made to avoid producing
exact copies not only to respond to the aim of not being sued by patent owners but also to
improve shortcomings of the original designs. Despite the financial and technical disadvan-
tages, they had sufficient skills to observe those limitations and to solve them to gain advantage in the markets. That was true of the Eibar- and Mauser-type pistols, which embodied
innovations that improved the imitated product.

The case of *J. Esperanza y P. Unceta*'s early years demonstrated that this counterfeiting
strategy was occasionally followed not only due to the manufacturer's decision but also
because of the demands made by intermediaries and traders. In the case of the *Victoria*
pistols, we saw that the firm had a solid intention to build its own brand but that it failed
due to the less fair practices of the dealers.

Specialising in the supplying of military firearms gave *Unceta y Cía* the opportunity to
obtain an external independent judgement of its products. Setting aside the significance
that the government purchases could have had for the revenues of the company, it is evident
that the firm thus obtained a reputation for its brand that gave it the chance to act as a
successful gun dealer. Because of the credit acquired, it could extend its operations to products other than guns.

Another behaviour that we have ascertained is that the gun making companies tended
to use TMs on their products before registering them, as occurred in the case of the *Victoria*
and *Royal* pistols. We do not know whether the registry came only once the brand had

displayed a certain level of efficiency in the market and not earlier or that the delay resulted only from negligence or naivety.

The advertising examples showed in this article demonstrate that branding was clearly present in the marketing policy of the company during those years. We can also confirm that several brands built in the Basque gun making industry remain in the market although not related to this activity. For instance, *Orbea* and *BH* (Beistegui Hermanos) retain good reputations as bicycle brands, and *Olave, Solozabal y Cía* produces staplers and other office goods with the same brand it used for its revolvers 80 years ago, namely *EL CASCO* (the helmet).

Astra also remains in two different ways. After its final closure in 1997, the company's factory in Gernika-Lumo stood abandoned for years, and the regional government's plans were to pull it down to build houses. On 25 December 2005, a group of youngsters entered the factory and occupied the building; therefore, the decision was changed to make it a cultural centre called *Astra Kulturarako Fabrika Soziala* ('Astra social factory for culture').[73] Furthermore, the *Astra* TM returned years ago as a gun brand in Switzerland. The *Astra Defense* Company thereby introduced itself as the genuine descendant of a long tradition started in the Basque Country.[74]

Notes

1. Castells, *Los trabajadores.*
2. 'Around 1990, I walked into a gun shop and began chatting with the man behind the counter. He was a knowledgeable gun owner and a big-game hunter and had been in the business for years. ... As we examined a shotgun together, I suggested to him that for half the money, you could buy a gun in Spain that was made to measure, with better wood, better engraving, and better overall workmanship. "Well, maybe," he replied, "but Spanish steel is always suspect." That statement sums up the greatest problem to plague Spanish gun makers in this century. For a variety of reasons, Spanish steel has acquired a stigma. It is a demon that steadfastly refuses to be exorcised.' Wieland, *Spanish Best*, 121–122.
3. Hogg and Weeks, *Pistols of the World*, 286–306.
4. Casson and Wadeson, *Export Performance*, 36; Davis and Maniatis, "Trademarks, Brands and Competition," 119–121; Helmers and Rogers, "Trademarks and Performance," 56; Higgins, "Trademarks and Infringement," 103–104; Schwarzkopf, "Turning Trademarks," 165–166.
5. Calvó and Jiménez, *1840–1940, Cien Años*, 15.
6. L'Armurerie liegeoise, 1 January 1906, 882. There was another gun making district in Brescia (Italy) but no information is available on its production figures for those years.
7. In 1906 the figure was 37% and in 1907 it decreased to 32%. L'Armurerie liegeoise, 1 March 1908, 1048.
8. Catalán, "Capitales modestos."
9. Echevarría, *Viaje por el País*, 18–19.
10. This was the name of the former *Orbea Hermanos.*
11. Goñi-Mendizabal *Eibar y la industria.*
12. Markusen, "Sticky Places." For Spanish industrial districts see also Catalan, Ramón-Muñoz and Miranda, *Distritos y clusters.*
13. Goñi-Mendizabal, "Evolución de la industria."
14. Gun designers, for example John M. Browning, Georg Luger and so on, patented their gun systems in Spain, looking for protection that they did not receive. For the Spanish patent system, see Sáiz González, "Invención, patentes e innovación."
15. Da Silva and Casson, "Brand Protection," 308.
16. Some American firms, due to their reputation for high quality, received the same international recognition as the European proof banks.

17. 'The shape of the safety catch also changed, and it became a large, bulbous, ribbed item, which always looks as if it were made by the blacksmith's apprentice while the blacksmith was out. … The material was often of poor quality, and the workmanship was equally poor; … In fairness it must be said that not every "Eibar" pistol was cheap and nasty; many reputable firms owe their start or at least their subsequent well-being to the "Eibar" pattern of pistol, and produced quality weapons right from the start. But, regrettably, it is true that in this particular product, the shoddy outnumbers the good by a wide margin.' (Hogg and Weeks, *Pistols of the World*, 13)
18. Ezell, *Handguns of the World*, 229–231.
19. Calvó, *La Industria Armera*, 144.
20. Henning and Witkowski, "The Advertising."
21. Wieland, *Spanish Best*.
22. Lavin, *A History of Spanish Firearms*, 266.
23. Most of the marks published by Lavin (*A History of Spanish Firearms*) in the appendix of his book were from the late eighteenth and early nineteenth centuries. All the marks are of two types: the name of the gunsmith under a crown and the drawing of an animal.
24. Calvó, *La Industria Armera*, 58.
25. For the use of patents as trademarks see Higgins, "Forgotten Heroes," 274–277.
26. This was one of the few contracts signed by the government with Basque manufacturers in the last decades of the nineteenth century (Calvó, *La Industria Armera*).
27. ERREXA is the Basque word for 'easy'; BOTA CILINDRO is a strange combination of two Spanish words meaning 'boot cylinder'; and EGOKIA means 'appropriate' in the Basque language. The last brand was used to designate the system used in cane shotguns manufactured by Víctor Sarasqueta.
28. This growth in the number of trademarks was not exclusive to the gun making industry. González Sáiz and Fernández Perez, "Catalonian Trademarks," 255.
29. Calvó, *La Industria Armera*.
30. Calvó, *La Industria Armera*; Hogg and Weeks, *Pistols of the World*; Larrañaga, *Armeros Vascos*.
31. Duguid, "A Case of Prejudice?," 317–318.
32. Casson and Wadeson, *Export Performance*, 39–40.
33. Hogg and Weeks, *Pistols of the World*, 28.
34. The spelling was incorrect in the registered trademark.
35. These small revolvers were conceived as a defence for cyclists against wild dog attacks. The name comes from the combination of the French word *veló* (bicycle) and the English word dog.
36. Antaris, *Astra Firearms*, 82–83.
37. The role of these certifying institutions on reputation has been highlighted by Casson and Wadeson, *Export Performance*, 37–38.
38. Wilkins, "The Neglected Intangible," 69; Schwarzkopf, *Turning Trademarks*.
39. Casson and Wadeson, *Export Performance*, 41–42 .
40. Uncetabarrenechea is a Basque compound surname that means approximately 'the house inside the area full of ivy'. It is common to abbreviate long Basque names, so in this case they used the shorter Unceta.
41. This patent, in which the pistol was called PISTO ESTOC, was the first to show the characteristic features ascribed to Eibar-type pistols (Calvó, *La Industria Armera*, 151–152).
42. Calvó, *La Industria Armera*, 188.
43. For further information on E. Schilling and Thieme&Edeler see Calvó, *La Industria Armera*, 317–319.
44. Gadisseur and Druart, *Le qui est qui*, 263.
45. Hogg and Weeks, *Pistols of the World*, 244.
46. Etxaniz, "Gernika-Lumo."
47. The pistols that he complained about were the *Titanic*, made by *Faustino Arteagoitia*, and the *Stossel*, produced by *Beistegui Hermanos*. Letter by Pedro Careaga to Gerónimo Bolibar, Barcelona, 10/03/1914, Letter Copying Book (LCB) n. 7, Esperanza y Unceta Fund, Gernikazarra Archive (GA).

48. Letter by J. Esperanza y P. Unceta to Eduardo Schilling, Barcelona, 07/04/1914, LCB n. 7, Esperanza y Unceta Fund, GA.
49. Letter by J. Esperanza y P. Unceta to Ponciano Azanza from Brussels, then in Bayonne, 09/10/1915, LCB n. 13, Esperanza y Unceta Fund, GA.
50. The latter was a clear opportunistic reference to the battle in which the French troops stopped the German advance in 1914.
51. That is why these pistols were colloquially called 'puro', that is to say cigar; Ezell, *Handguns of the World*, 539; Hogg and Weeks, *Pistols of the World*, 245.
52. Astra pistols became the service handguns of the *Carabineros* (frontier guards) and prison guard corps in 1921 and of the navy in 1923. The air force, once created as an independent entity in 1931, adopted the Astra 400 pistol too (Antaris, *Astra Automatic Pistols* and *Astra Firearms*).
53. They registered two new trademarks in 1923, *Nacional* and *España*, but they were never actually used.
54. An Astra 600 pistol was offered in *Unceta y Cía* catalogues in the late 1920s, but in all the books related to handguns, this model is only mentioned for Second World War production.
55. Letter by Unceta y Cía to Vicente Valero de Bernabé, Madrid, 09/02/1925, LCB n. 51, Esperanza y Unceta, GA.
56. Some of these products (e.g. pliers and counter scales) were the result of diversification projects implemented by the firm.
57. The model numbers were 720, 730, 740, 750, 760, 780, 790, 800, 801, 804, 805, 810, 811, 820, 821, 830 and 831. We have references to the use of the numbers 1000, 2000 and 3000 for shotguns as well.
58. Letter by Unceta y Cía to Norberto Arizmendi, Eibar, 15/12/1930, LCB n. 81, Unceta y Cía Fund, GA.
59. Letter by Unceta y Cía to Tomás Urizar, Eibar, 9/12/1936, LCB n. 81, Unceta y Cía Fund, GA.
60. Letter by Unceta y Cía to The Ohashi Trading Company, Kobe, 17/11/1926, LCB n. 62, Unceta y Cía Fund, GA.
61. These firms were not always ruled by the Japanese and most of them were located in Kobe. See Goñi-Mendizabal, "Imitación, innovación y apoyo institucional" and "De Esperanza y Unceta."
62. Letter by Unceta y Cía to Alday y Cía from Eibar, 5/07/1926, LCB n. 60, Unceta y Cía Fund, Gernikazarra Archive.
63. Letter by Unceta y Cía to Ohashi Trading Company from Kobe, 30/08/1926, LCB n. 60, Unceta y Cía Fund, Gernikazarra Archive.
64. Chan, *Arming the Chinese*; Lary, *Warlord Soldiers*.
65. Since the Mauser c96 pistol was an old gun, the copy of the external shape of the gun did not pose any patent infringement. Bonifacio Echeverría did not follow the two others and only adapted one of his models to the Mauser caliber, also by adding a detachable wooden stock.
66. Mortera, *Las pistolas españolas*; Nelson and Musgrave, *The World's Machine Pistols*.
67. Goñi-Mendizabal, "De Esperanza y Unceta."
68. Antaris, *Astra Automatic Pistols*.
69. Antaris, *Star Firearms*.
70. The remaining sales were products sold as intermediaries (22%) and store surpluses (1.4%).
71. The other two competitors made the same decision, becoming *LLAMA-Gabilondo y Cía* and *STAR-Bonifacio Echeverría*.
72. Da Silva and Casson, "Brand Protection," 292–293.
73. http://www.astragernika.net/
74. http://www.astra-arms.ch/

Disclosure statement

No potential conflict of interest was reported by the author.

Funding

This work was supported by the Eusko Jaurlaritza under [grant number IT-807-13], [grant number IT-897-16].

ORCID

Igor Goñi-Mendizabal 🅘 http://orcid.org/0000-0003-1826-439X

References

Antaris, Leonardo M. *Astra Automatic Pistols*. Sterling, CO (USA): Firac, 1988.

Antaris, Leonardo M. *Star Firearms*. Davenport: Firac, 2001.

Antaris, Leonardo M. *Astra Firearms*. Davenport: Firac, 2009.

Arzac, Paul, and Juan Ignacio. *Evolución de la industria armera de Eibar* [Evolution of Eibar gunmaking industry]. San Sebastián: Cámara de Comercio, Industria y Navegación de Guipúzcoa, 1976.

Calvó, Juan L. *La Industria Armera Nacional 1830–1940. Fábricas, Privilegios, Patentes y Marcas* [National gunmaking industry 1830–1840. Factories, privileges, patents and trademarks]. Eibar: Comisión Ego Ibarra, 1997.

Calvó, Juan Luis, and Eduardo Jiménez Sánchez-Malo. *1840–1940, Cien Años de Pistolas y Revólveres Españoles* [1840–1940, One hundred years of Spanish pistols and revolvers]. Pontevedra: CID-Asociación Española de Coleccionistas de Armas Antiguas y Recuerdos Históricos, 1993.

Casson, Mark, and Nigel Wadeson, "Export Performance and Reputation", In *Trademarks, Brands and Competitiveness*, edited by Teresa da Silva Lopes and Paul Duguid, 31–55. Oxford (UK): Routledge International Studies in Business History, 2010.

Castells, Luis. *Los trabajadores en el País Vasco (1876–1923)* [Workers in the Basque Country (1876–1923)]. Madrid: Siglo XXI Editores, 1993.

Catalán, Jordi. "Capitales modestos y dinamismo industrial: Orígenes del sistema de fábrica en los valles guipuzcoanos, 1841–1918." [Modest capitals and industrial dinamism: origins of the factory system in the valleys of Gipuzkoa, 1841–1918]. In *Pautas regionales de la industrialización española (siglos XIX y XX)*. Barcelona: Ariel, 1990.

Catalan, Jordi, Ramon Ramón-Muñoz, and José Antonio Miranda (eds.). *Distritos y clusters en la Europa del Sur* [Districts and clusters in southern Europe]. Madrid: Lid, 2012.

Chan, Anthony B. *Arming the Chinese. The Western Armaments Trade in Warlord China, 1920–1928*. Vancouver (Canada): University of British Columbia Press, 1982.

Davis, Jennifer, and Spyros Maniatis. "Trademarks, Brands and Competition." In *Trademarks, Brands and Competitiveness*, edited by Teresa da Silva Lopes and Paul Duguid, 119–137. Oxford (UK): Routledge International Studies in Business History, 2010.

Duguid, Paul. "A case of Prejudice? The Uncertain Development of Collective and Certification Marks." In *Business History Review*. 86 vols, edited by Teresa da Silva Lopes and Paul Duguid, 311–333. Cambridge, Massachusetts (SA): Cambridge University Press, 2012.

Echevarría, Toribio. *Viaje por el País de los Recuerdos* [A Journey through the Country of Rememberings]. San Sebastián: Sociedad Guipuzcoana de Ediciones y Publicaciones, 1990.

Etxaniz, José Ángel. "Gernika-Lumo, 1913, Industrialización, movimiento obrero y conflicto social: la huelga de Esperanza y Unceta." [Gernika-Lumo, 1913, Industrialization, labour movement and social conflict: the strike at Esperanza and Unceta]. In *Vasconia, no. 30. Cuadernos de historia-geografía*. Donostia: Eusko Ikaskuntza, 2000.

Ezell, Edward C. *Handguns of the World*. Harrisburg, PA (USA): Stackpole Books, 1983.

Gadisseur, Guy, and Michel Druart. *Le qui est qui de l'Armurerie liégeoise, 1800–1950* [The Who's who in the Liege gunmaking industry, 1800–1950]. Biarritz: Éditions du Pécari, 2005.

Goñi-Mendizabal, Igor. "Imitación, innovación y apoyo institucional. Estrategias de penetración en los mercados internacionales de las empresas armeras vascas durante el Siglo XX." [Imitation, innovation and institutional support. Basque gunmaking companies' strategies to penetrate international markets.] In *Revista de la Historia de la Economía y de la Empresa*, no. 2, edited by Eugenio Torres, 207–233. Bilbao: Archivo Histórico del BBVA, 2008.

Goñi-Mendizabal, Igor. "De Esperanza y Unceta a ASTRA-Unceta y Cía., S.A., una empresa armera ante el mercado internacional (1908–1970)." [From Esperanza and Unceta to ASTRA-Unceta y Cía., S.A.; a gunmaking company in the international market (1908–1970)]. *Revista de historia industrial* 18, no. 40 (2009a): 51–93.

Goñi-Mendizábal, Igor. "Eibar y la industria armera: evidencias de un distrito industrial." [Eibar and the gunmaking industry: evidences of an industrial district]. *Investigaciones de Historia Económica* 6, no. 16 (2010): 101–133.

Goñi-Mendizabal, Igor. "Evolución de la industria armera vasca (1876–1969): un enfoque a largo plazo." [Evolution of the Basque gunmaking industry (1876–1969): a long term view.] In *Del metal al motor. Innovación y atraso en la historia de la industria metal-mecánica española* [From metal to motor. Innovation and backwardness in the Spanish metal and mechanical industries], edited by P. Pascual and P. Fernández Pérez, 385–432. Barcelona: Fundación BBVA, 2007.

Helmers, Christian, and Mark Rogers. "Trademarks and Performance in UK Firms." In *Trademarks, Brands and Competitiveness*, edited by Teresa da Silva Lopes and Paul Duguid, 55–75. Oxford (UK): Routledge International Studies in Business History, 2010.

Henning, Robert A., and Terrence H. Witkowski. "The Advertising of E. Remington & Sons: The Creation of an Iconic Brand, 1854–1888." *Journal of Historical Research in Marketing* 5, no. 4 (2013): 418–448.

Higgins, David M. "Forgotten Heroes and Forgotten Issues: Business and Trademark History during the Nineteenth Century." In *Business History Review*. 86 vols, edited by Teresa da Silva Lopes and Paul Duguid, 261-285. Cambridge, Massachusetts (SA): Cambridge University Press, 2012.

Higgins, David M. "Trademarks and Infringement in Britain, c. 1875-c31900." In *Trademarks, Brands and Competitiveness*, edited by Teresa da Silva Lopes and Paul Duguid, 102-118. Oxford (UK): Routledge International Studies in Business History, 2010.

Hogg, Ian V., and John Weeks. *Pistols of the World*. London: Arms and Armour Press, 1978.

Larrañaga, Ramiro. *Armeros Vascos, Repaso Histórico- Raíces y Desarrollo* [Basque gunsmiths, Historical Review-Roots and Development]. Eibar: Ego Ibarra Batzordea, Ayuntamiento de Eibar, 2001.

Lary, Diana. *Warlord Soldiers. Chinese Common Soldiers, 1911–1937*. Cambridge, MA: Cambridge University Press, 1985.

Lavin, James D. *A History of Spanish Firearms*. London: Herbert Jenkins, 1965.

Markusen, Ann. "Sticky Places in Slippery Space: A Typology of Industrial Districts." *Economic Geography* 72 (1996): 293–313.

Mortera Pérez, Artemio. *Las pistolas españolas tipo 'Mauser'* [Spanish 'Mauser type' pistols]. Valladolid: Quirón Ediciones, 1997.

Mujica, Gregorio de. *Monografía histórica de la Villa de Eibar* [Historical monograph of the city of Eibar]. 1908. 3rd ed. Eibar: Ayuntamiento de Eibar, 1984.

Nelson, Thomas B., and D. Musgrave. *The World's Machine Pistols and Submachine Guns (1964–1982)*. Hong Kong: Chesa, 1981.

Sáiz González J. Patricio. *Invención, patentes e innovación en la España contemporánea* [Invention, patents and innovation in contemporary Spain]. Madrid: Oficina Española de Patentes y Marcas, Ministerio de Industria y Energía, 1999.

Sáiz González, Patricio, and Paloma Fernández Perez. "Catalonian Trademarks and the Development of Marketing Knowledge in Spain, 1850-1946." In *Business History Review*, edited by Teresa da Silva Lopes and Paul Duguid. Vol. 86, 239–260. Cambridge, Massachusetts (SA): Cambridge University Press, 2012.

Schwarzkopf, Stefan. "Turning Trademarks into Brands. How Advertising Agencies Practiced and Conceptualized Branding, 1890-930." In *Trademarks, Brands and Competitiveness*, edited by Teresa da Silva Lopes and Paul Duguid, 165-193. Oxford (UK): Routledge International Studies in Business History, 2010.

Da Silva, Teresa, and Mark Casson. "Brand Protection and the Globalization of British Business." In *Business History Review*. 86 vols, edited by Teresa da Silva Lopes and Paul Duguid, 287–310. Cambridge, Massachusetts (SA): Cambridge University Press, 2012.

Wieland, Terry. *Spanish Best: The Fine Shotguns of Spain*. Camden, Maine (USA): Countrysport Press, 2001.

Wilkins, Mira. "The Neglected Intangible Asset: The Influence of the Trade Mark on the Rise of the Modern Corporation." *Business History* 34, no. 1 (1992): 66–95.

L'Armurerie Liégeoise, Organe mensuel de l'«Union des Fabricants d'armes» et du Musée d'Armes de Liége [L'Armurerie Liégeoise, Monthly organ of the "Union of Manufacturers of arms" and of the Arms Museum of Liège]. Liége (Belgium): Union des Fabricants d'armes, 1906–1908.

Cheese trademarks: Italian dairy firms' practices during the 20th century

Ilaria Suffia (ID), Andrea Maria Locatelli (ID) and Claudio Besana (ID)

ABSTRACT

Trademarks have recently become a very useful source for business historians. This longitudinal analysis of the twentieth-century trademarking activities of the most important Italian dairy firms of the era, namely Galbani, Invernizzi and Locatelli, demonstrates that trademarks were used both as a protective weapon against competitors and as an innovation carrier to open up new markets. This article also argues that trademark registrations had another dual purpose – not only were they used as buffers against negative shocks but they were also used to support periods of economic growth. A fundamental finding of this work is that trademarks, across various types of registrations, were closely connected to the features on which the companies based their sales strategies.

1. Introduction

Researchers have recently reemphasized the importance of brands and trademarks for businesses,[1] especially in a world of growing competition,[2] proliferating imitators and counterfeiters.[3] A brand is a vital intangible asset for firms pursuing long-term strategies, supporting their growth, sustaining their processes of globalization, and strengthening their efficiency.[4] It is defined as 'a legally defensible proprietary name, recognized by some categories of consumer as signifying a product with dimensions that differentiate it in some way from other products designed to satisfy the same need'.[5] A trademark is the 'aspect of the brand that gains legal protection through registration'.[6] Scholarship in the field highlights the economic advantages bestowed by this protection instrument and, from the 1980s, companies started to include trademarks in their balance sheets, so they increasingly became a 'tangible' asset for enterprises. In the wake of this development, trademark studies garnered new appeal and attracted a new wave of researchers. There remains significant space to explore, however, particularly because collecting complete data on trademarks is an 'immense' and 'daunting' challenge.[7] Hence, brand and trademark discussions, over the last twenty years, were often focused on firm-specific studies and they did not offer a longitudinal analysis of registrations at either the sectoral or national level.

This study represents a first step towards a more complete understanding of this phenomenon in Italy. While concentrating on a traditional area of the field, it nonetheless moves the approach forward. Firstly, it provides a database of the trademarks recorded by the most important Italian companies operating in the dairy sector, with data ranging from the late nineteenth century to the early twenty-first century (1890–2015 to be precise). It also takes into account the fact that the literature pointed out that trademarks were vital to the growth of convenience goods, among others, dairy products.[8] The cases under consideration relate exclusively to the dairy industry.

The goal of this research is to supply a longitudinal analysis of trademark registrations, identifying any emerging patterns followed by firms. In terms of business strategies, it establishes that trademarks were utilized as 'weapons' against competitors, so they were a protection policy. Otherwise, their role was to create new market segments, exploiting product and process innovations. The long-term analysis, then, suggests that companies' behavior in their trademarking activity was also influenced by the national and international economic contexts. Indeed, the data shows that companies were most inclined to register a trademark in the period after adverse economic shocks but that they were also employed as supportive and stimulating mechanisms during periods of consumer growth. Furthermore, from the beginning of the twenty-first century, there was a rise in registrations linked to the entry of foreign capital into the Italian dairy industry as well as to increasing competition in the market.

Additionally, the study offers an overview of what companies recorded. In general, a trademark can be a name, a term, a symbol, an image, a design, a sentence or a combination of these and, in this sense, the type of trademark reflects the meaning of the protection strategy of the company. The most protected element was product name, but images and designs were also a feature of many registrations. In particular, both trademark types carried very specific 'messages'. They focused on certain aspects, such as naturalness and the high quality of goods, while simultaneously emphasizing specific values relating to rural tradition and Italian cultural history.

Finally, the analysis raises one last issue: that of the longevity of trademarks. It is immediately apparent that the registrations split in two categories: first, or new, trademarks and renewals of existing trademarks. In particular, the data show that renewals are more prevalent in this new millennium. This reflects the effects of increased competition and the need of companies to protect their products and position in the market. Future research on 'enduring' trademarks may well build on these early findings and provide further insight into how trademarks could accumulate value over time.

The study concentrates on three of the most important Italian dairy firms of the twentieth century: Galbani, Invernizzi and Locatelli. In 1921, Galbani was the ninth largest Italian dairy enterprise in respect of capital and total assets. Six years later, in 1927, it was the third largest. The company continued to grow and it was the Italian sectoral leader in 1960, 1972 and 1983.[9] Locatelli and Invernizzi were among the ten most important cheese industry firms from the 1950s.[10] Each of these three companies was eventually sold to foreign industrial groups. Even though they were acquired by several groups, namely Nestlé, Kraft, Besnier and Lactalis, data from Mediobanca indicate that their trademarks continued to be market leaders.

The article is based on a database of dairy trademarks registered by Galbani, Locatelli and Invernizzi, this database has been created by the authors and it is based on the records held by the Italian State Archive and the Italian Patents and Trademarks Office. In total, about 1,200 brands were filed from 1890 to 2015.

The article is organized according to a number of distinct but closely related sections. Initially, it sketches the development of the Italian dairy sector during the period under consideration. It then focuses on the creation of the diary trademarks database before presenting an analysis of the trademark activities of the firms, divided by phases. There is a brief illustration of the registration path followed by each company, highlighting the differences between them. The next section outlines the types of trademarks used, and offers some insights into the strategies pursued by each firm. There is also space dedicated to the question of the durability of trademarks. In conclusion, the article seeks to present an enlightening overview of the trademarking activity of the Italian dairy industry from the late nineteenth to early twenty-first century.

2. A long-term perspective on the Italian dairy industry and the place of Galbani, Invernizzi and Locatelli

The structure and shape of the Italian cheese industry in the late twentieth century was the result of a century of change and development.[11] Since the unification of the country in 1861, Italian dairy producers have created highly differentiated products which they supplied to diverse markets. Lombardy was the most important region for both traditional production techniques and those relying on empirical experiments. Parmesan cheese was produced in southern Lombardy. In the mountainous territory of the province, dairy farmers made soft cheeses and sold them in local markets. Some transhumant herdsmen integrated dairy production with cattle breeding activities thus linking the mountains and plains. In the latter decades of the 1800s, these families of farmers moved permanently to the irrigated plains. At the same time, the development of communication systems, especially railways, fostered growth in the international trade of *stracchini*, especially wheels of *gorgonzola*.[12] With production of these cheeses growing in the entire Lombardy-Piedmont plateau between the Adda and the Sesia, the problem of aging the cheese arose, as they had to be matured for several months. So, farmers and traders in the area of Lecco (Lake Como) started to specialise in the seasoning and marketing of a typical local cheese, *stracchino*, taking advantage of the location of natural caves that guaranteed excellent ripening.[13]

The beginning of Locatelli and Invernizzi experience in the second half of the 1800s was within this relationship between the mountains and the plains. Locatelli was founded as a modest business aging soft cheeses in caves. Thanks to the efforts of Giovanni Locatelli and his five children, it grew quickly. By 1885 there was already a branch in London and, in 1897, a second branch opened in Buenos Aires. For over 30 years, the company developed as a family business creating a large commercial network in the exportation of other Italian cheeses, such as *grana* and *pecorino romano*, which were increasingly requested by Italian immigrants in the Americas. Carlo Invernizzi produced cheeses with milk from his own herd. In 1908, one of Carlo's eight children, Giovanni, separated from the family business. Six years later, Giovanni was able to move his business to the town of Melzo, near Milan, where he set up a production unit of a significant size. Experienced in packaging *stracchini* and other soft cheeses particularly enjoyed by consumers, Giovanni sold a significant share of his products on the Milan market through middlemen wholesalers. Large quantities of goods were picked up by his dealer in Genoa, while some of the cheeses produced by his dairy factory were sold in the French Riviera.

The construction of a commercial network and the horizontal integration of production systems permitted the development of several firms, including Galbani.[14] The firm's business began with modest sales of dairy products in 1882. Its headquarters were in Ballabio, near Lecco. The key force in the company was not the family as a unit, but an individual entrepreneur, Egidio Galbani. He replaced his father Davide in the 1880s and headed the company for the next 30 years. He did not limit himself to being a salesman. Egidio soon started producing his own cheeses, which were related to the typical cheeses of the area. He also aimed to imitate the soft 'luxury' French cheeses which, at that time, were imported from the country on the other side of the Alps in large quantities. After choosing to dedicate the company to packaging cheese that it created and produced, Galbani needed to open a new plant in an area that could guarantee greater availability of milk to process throughout the year.[15] Since the 1880s, cheese imitating the French and Swiss specimens was produced in order to appeal to more distant markets. The further expansion of production was determined by the ability to successfully select and mature dairy products of a consistently high quality and to ensure connectivity and continuity in the production chain, from milk production to cheese production to the distribution of goods. The drive to increase sales volumes and ensure a reliable flow of production throughout the whole year required new production sites within easy access of both raw materials and the commercial market in Milan. The move towards an integrated industrial cycle required investment in product advertising, while entrepreneurs formed a nationwide sales network through deposits and commercial representatives. During this first stage of modernization, advertising consisted of the distribution of company catalogues and the packing.

Major industrial development in the 1920s, in concert with the creation of a network of subsidiaries and sales companies at emigration departure points, resulted in a net increase in exports (which accounted for 30–50% of total production). In the 1930s, the production of cheese was concentrated in Northern Italy, which accounted for around 75% of the national total. The global production of cheese was estimated to amount to 2,230,000 quintals. *Grana* was the most prolific variety with production of 585,000 q., followed by kneaded-curd products such as *caciocavallo* and *provolone* (161,000 q.), *gorgonzola* (184,000 q.), *asiago* (131,000 q.), *montasio* (133,000 q.) and 'Swiss' cheeses such as *emmenthal* and *sbrinz* (129,400 q.). The production of fresh and short-ripening soft cheeses was affected by the shortcomings of refrigerators in the chain of distribution and by the lack of fridges in Italian households. There were 18,678 industrial plants processing milk products, 4,800 of which were concentrated in Lombardy.

Until the 1950s, the entire food industry, including the dairy sector, followed a path of slow change based on a combination of low level of domestic consumption and protectionism. Exports were always based on the demand of emigrants. Italian dealers controlled this market but they faced competition from Italian products made abroad. During the 'Golden Age' the consumption basket changed in line with the models of other Western countries, but the most important changes in the food industry occurred in the 1960s. This was especially so in the North where firms improved industrial processing and, at the same time, retained the agriculture–industry connection.

In the milk-dairy sector, Lombardy continued to be the region contributing the most to domestic production, with a share close to 30%. The volume of milk processed increased from 37 million hectolitres in 1951 to 50 million hectolitres in 1962. In 1963, this figure fell to 42 million hectolitres, but had risen again to 52.2 million hectolitres by 1967. According to data collected by Assolatte, at the end of the 1960s around 47,280,000 quintals of milk were used in industrial processing, almost exclusively for consumption in family homes.

The 1961 production census identified a record-high number of industrial businesses: 3,417 with 23,750 workers. Ten years later, a similar census recorded 2,834 plants with 23,057 workers. The fall in the number of businesses amounted to 30% in a decade, whereas the equivalent decrease for the food sector as a whole was only 13.7%.

The sector was consolidated in the 1960s before suffering the negative effects of the 1973 oil crisis, although it was less badly affected than other sectors. A reliable statistical framework is available from the 1970s. A comparative analysis of the food sector is possible for turnover, i.e. a variable with a homogeneous identity. Lucio Sicca, in 1977,[16] estimated the concentration of production on the basis of the value of revenue consumption of all food industry sectors for the year 1974. The cheese and butter industry emerged at the top of the chain of food products. Overall the top six products (cheese and butter, bread, wine, olive oil, milk, grain meal) accounted for over 52% of the value of the market's consumption of processed products. It should be noted that these were all products estimating from a national agriculture sector characterized by a trade deficit and a low level of technological application. The data show that the food industry was concentrated in northern Italy. According to Sicca's survey, Galbani was the leading food company in terms of internal turnover, with 177.5 billion lire in 1974. Invernizzi (74.4 billion lire) was at 11th and Locatelli (72.5 billion lire) ranked 12th, while the other companies in the sector occupied lower positions: Polenghi Lombardo (49.0) – 21st; Parmalat (45.0) – 26th; Nestle (38.9) – 29th; Kraft (30.0) – 35th; Latterie Coop Riunite (25.0) – 40th; Latterie Sorinesi (20.5) – 47th and finally the Prealpi (16.0) – 65th. Instead, regarding the revenue generated, Galbani was second; while the public enterprise Società Meridionale Elettrica (SME) was 1st and the Nestlé Italia group was fifth.

In 1979 the food industry had a gross turnover of 40.47 trillion lire. The added value at factor cost was equal to 7,163 billion lire with an added value/turnover of 17.7%. The number of workers in the sector was estimated at 432,800, of whom at least half worked in businesses with 20 employees. There was an increase in the relative weight of the food industry, and specifically the dairy industry, in the overall industrial system in the 1950s and 1960s before its importance declined in the 1970s. This trend was even more pronounced when measured in the context of the Italian relationship with other European Economic Community (EEC) countries. This was because of the lower growth in the Italian consumption of processed products and the national trade deficit position. Umberto Bertelè and Francesco Brioschi, using figures for 1979, compiled sales rankings for each product classes although they excluded certain artisanal activities.[17] The dairy industry had a turnover of 3,733 billion lire, placing it behind the canned food and pasta sectors.

Turnover and gains decelerated during the 1970s, and during the second half of the decade several corporate restructurings were unsuccessful. This was at least partly due to the persistent crisis in the supply of raw materials and the high rate of balance of trade deficit. Labour and transport costs increased while new competition simultaneously emerged from EEC producers who had access to the Italian domestic market since the end of the transitional period following agreements to open borders. Firms with a high level of debts started restructuring processes with two alternative strands: either the creation of large multi-divisional companies or the sectoral specialization. In addition, some companies which enjoyed a high rate of exports were absorbed by public groups, such as Ente Finanziario Industria Meccanica (Efim) and SME. Furthermore, modernization of the distribution system of supermarkets and hypermarkets as they spread nationally meant that the internal distribution network of companies represented a cost factor rather than a competitive advantage.

In the mid-1980s, the Italian agro-industrial sector underwent profound transformations associated with the development of large 'horizontal technologies': microelectronics and biotechnology. The roles of industrial research, engineering and consulting services grew in importance as food companies had to contend with an intensification of competition in the food industry. On the other hand, the inflow of foreign capital was significant. During this decade, foreign groups conducted several acquisitions. The takeover of Invernizzi (founded in 1908) by the American company Kraft (1985) and that of Galbani (founded in 1920) by the partnership Ifil-Danone (1989) were the most important events.[18] The final effect of modification was the development of business groups that featured a set of companies under the control of a single economic center. The structures of the industrial groups were complex and they employed varied strategies. In addition, there were financial links between different groups.

The effect of the dynamics of concentration in the dairy sector was that national groups traditionally linked to the food sector came under pressure from conglomerate groups of both financial and industrial corporations which sought not only to compete in the existing food market but to extend into new market spaces.

3. An overview of registrations: creating the data-set

The Italian State Archive [Archivio di Stato] (hereafter ISA) holds a trademark database that runs from 1869 to 1980; trademarks filed after 1980 are recorded in the Italian Patents and Trademarks Office [Ufficio Italiano Marchi e Brevetti] database (hereafter IPTO). The ISA database includes several items of information, including trade number, trademark owner, description of the trademark, type of brand, brand location and date of registration. It also provides a link to an image of the original registration document.[19] The structure of the IPTO database is quite different. It provides a search page and it is possible to navigate the data by code, by date, by province, by text, by owner and, finally, by type. In contrast to the ISA's records, it uses classes to identify types of trademarks. The records in the IPTO database contain even more information than those of the ISA. In fact, they include the whole history of each trademark, with previous and next registrations.[20] In that regard, it is important to note that every record had a unique registration number and so each renewal had its own number.[21] In total, from 1869 to 1980, almost 2,200 diary industry trademarks were recorded,[22] but unfortunately, and unlike the data from ISA database, it is not possible to estimate the total number of cheese trademarks included in the IPTO database from 1980.[23]

The cheese trademarks owned by Galbani, Locatelli and Invernizzi, filed from 1890 to 2015, total about 1,200.[24] In particular, the ISA database holds 471 trademarks and it is interesting to note that about 35% of these registrations were taken in a relatively short period from 1945 to 1950. The IPTO database details almost 800 brands.[25] According to the range of data displayed in this database, nearly 10% of its records – in particular, 68 trademarks taken out between 1938 and 1979 – form part of the registration history of others' records. These 68 trademarks had all been used at least once before 1980 and were now being renewed.[26] Furthermore, among the IPTO data there are 14 applications that are currently waiting to be approved.[27] It is interesting to note that applications are not always successful, as in the case of two Galbani requests, one of which was rejected in 1995 and the other in 1999. The first case concerned the classification of a new *mozzarella* type product and the introduction of a logo and the complicating factor was the claim made for the new cheese. The proposed title of the trademark was: 'la prima mozzarella ai gusti – la premiere mozzarella aromatisee – die erste gewurzte mozzarella – la primera mozzarella con especias' [the first flavoured mozzarella]. The second case, four years later, also concerned a slogan for a Galbani mozzarella: 'la mozzarella più mozzarella che ci sia' [the best mozzarella that exists]. The brand was a strong one, but it was unfair to the competition and had significant implications for consumers; it is possible that it was rejected for both these reasons.

Figure 1 represents in one entity the data from the two main databases and it provides a complete picture of the firms' registrations over time. As part of a closer look at the whole set of registrations, it will be useful to establish some preliminary contextual parameters. Firstly, Figure 1 illustrates that while about 40% of the total records concerned here were filed between 1890 and 1964, the majority of brands were filed after 1980: 683 brands, or about 55% of total trademarks, were approved between 1980 and 2015.[28] To some extent, this figure exemplifies the difference between the two databases. The IPTO database uses, as highlighted, a different system of classification to subdivide the categories of brands more widely than does the ISA database. Furthermore, 1965 is the last year for which the ISA database holds records for the three firms studied and they refer to eight registrations in 1965, seven of them filed by Locatelli and one by Galbani. Unfortunately, this void cannot presently be filled by any other sources.[29] The IPTO database recognizes only 51 new trademarks from 1966 to 1979, but this does not represent complete coverage of activity during the period.[30] So, the interruption in the ISA series certainly contributes to the drop in recorded registrations between 1965 and 1979 and this had to be taken into account in the analysis below. Indeed, the extant figures suggest that the frequency of records was rather low in this period, accounting for only 5% of the total, but they cannot be taken at face value.

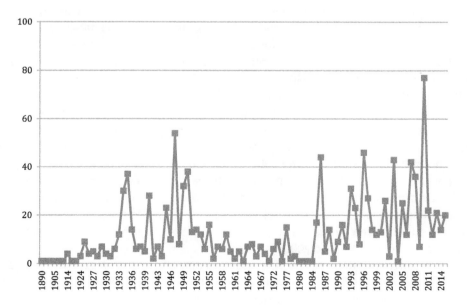

Figure 1. Registrations by Galbani, Invernizzi and Locatelli (1890–2015).
The graph does not include brands that have not yet been approved and registered. Table 2 also provides the series of trademarks per period. Sources: elaborations from ISA, https://dati.acs.beniculturali.it; and IPTO, www.uibm.gov.

Another general note about the series is that the data also point towards generally limited trademarking activity between the 1950s and the 1980s. In large part, this was due to the truncated ISA records, but the point here is to emphasize that the decrease in registrations was already evident at the beginning of the 1950s, that is, before ISA records ceased.

Finally, despite these last remarks, the data clearly demonstrate that trademarking activity increased in the late twentieth century. This growth was then maintained into the twenty-first century and intensified from around 2010.

4. Registrations over the long term (1890–2015)

This section provides a long-term overview on the trademark activity of Galbani, Locatelli and Invernizzi, along with the development of the enterprises. Figure 1 displays that the registrations do not follow a specific long-term path, but it is possible to note that there were two main periods of activity: the first was between 1931 and 1950 and the second started in 1986 and continues still. In general, the data show a high level of volatility that was probably linked to particular business product strategies. These followed a common policy in terms of support and market expansion but they differed in timing and development.

Before the 1950s, growth spurts seem to be linked to two opposing business cycles. On one hand, increasing registrations occurred during periods of economic recovery after adverse economic shocks, such as after WWI, the Wall Street crisis of 1929 – the effects of which were not felt in Italy until 1931 – and WWII. On the other hand, depositing trademarks could be considered a business strategy based on anticipation of future boom periods. To a certain extent, such a policy would explain and justify the dynamic trademark growth before the two wars and at the beginning of the 1950s, i.e. at the start of the Golden Age.[31] The high rates in 1945 and in 1947 have a further explanation. In general, the first step in securing a trademark is to submit a request. There is always a delay between the request and the registration. Galbani's 1943 applications had to wait approximately two years and seven months to be processed, while for applications made in 1945, the delay time was 883 days.[32] So, these delays were also a contributory factor in the sudden growth of registrations during the second half of the 1940s.

From the 1980s, the increasing trademarking activity reflects concomitant difficulties, in the business cycle in general and, in particular, in the dairy sector. The oil crisis, and accompanying increases in production costs – above all in transportation – and intensifying competition from European dairy industries raised the protection level of the firms. Somehow, the trend of trademarking after the 1980s displayed the same traits as that of the period between the 1930s and 1940s: both phases started with a recovery after a significant period of crisis before suffering several shocks. Individual peaks also followed a similar pattern in the two phases. In fact, the average delay between request and registration of each trademark was about 900 days in both eras. The delay extended to about 2,000 days for requests filed in, for example, 1999 and 2000.[33]

In accordance with these trends, the long-term path of registrations can be divided into three main phases. The first phase started in 1890 with the first record and it ended after WWII, when the level of registrations declined. Thereafter came a fairly fallow phase from the 1950s to 1970s, linking the two main periods. It was characterized by a steady but low level of registration, at under 20 filings annually. Finally, the last phase took place post-1980s and it carried the highest share of registrations in the series, with 2010 the pinnacle overall. The following analysis attempts to explain the relationship between the long-term evolution of registrations, the history of the companies and their respective strategies.

4.1. The first phase (1890s–1940s)

Galbani was, as already noted, the first of the three companies reviewed in this article to register a trademark, in 1890. In contrast to Galbani, it took Locatelli some time to fill its first record. The first Locatelli trademark was registered in 1910. The slower adoption of a trademark was due to the fact that the company started as a commercial business, not as a producer. Only around WWI, when the company became a producer, did its trademarking activity start. Slow start notwithstanding, Locatelli marks are still regularly filed, with a new request pending as of February 2016.

Invernizzi was the last of our three subjects to register its goods – its first trademark was filed in 1924. A factor in this lag was Giovanni's later entry to cheese production in about 1914. Like the other firms, Invernizzi trademarks still survive. Its most recent registration was recorded in May 2014, but at the time of writing it was waiting on two registrations requested in November 2015 and March 2016.

Before 1931, only 47 registrations had been deposited, most of them during the 1920s. There were only six registrations before WWI; this means that there was less than one trademark per year for at least 20 years. The four new trademarks in 1914 were interesting, because these can be taken as an early indication of increasing company needs in terms of product protection or development. This strategy seems to have been consolidated during the 1920s. In this period, the number of trademarks registered in a single year was never more than ten, but there was a definite move away from solitary registrations, at least for Galbani. In 1925, nine trademarks were introduced, eight by Galbani and one by Locatelli.

During the first years of the twentieth century, the industrial development of Galbani and Locatelli was focused on horizontal integration combined with the expansion of business strategies. Galbani's business grew during the early years of the 1900s thanks to the production of cheeses typical in the tradition of the Bergamo Pre-Alps area (*taleggio, quartirolo, robiola*), but especially thanks to the creation of new products over a range of qualities and prices. The most famous and the most widely sold was certainly 'formaggio Bel Paese' [Bel Paese cheese], created in 1906, a soft cheese that aged quickly, made to compete with French cheeses and therefore, at least initially, intended for a consumer with a certain spending power. When producing these and other cheeses, Galbani followed practices from the other side of the Alps, aiming to package cheeses with consistent characteristics. They were also promoted with advertising campaigns (choice of name, particular packaging with a careful selection of images), and they needed to be available in almost all Italian commercial markets, being distributed through a network founded on warehouses and representatives placing the product in shops in various cities.

Galbani reached the pinnacle of its expansion at the end of the 1920s. For reasons that are not clear, Egidio Galbani transferred control of his company in 1926, selling his share of 65% to the Invernizzi brothers.[34] The firm became the incorporated company Egidio Galbani. The constant growth of the company in the early twentieth century needed new and significant funding which was provided from outside of the circle of family members.[35]

In 1922, the incorporated company had reached a remarkable size: it produced 11,500 quintals (hereafter q) of cheese annually, exporting 800 q each year. The business was further increased with the opening of a factory in Certosa di Pavia in the same year. Experimentation with new products continued, beginning with the production of processed cheeses. Exports also grew, and in 1925 they exceeded sales in the Italian market. International sales, whose main destinations were France, Germany and the United States, were supported by the Locatelli sales network abroad. Production capacities of the plants (in Melzo and Certosa di Pavia) allowed Galbani to be the second-largest operator in Italy in the dairy/cheese industry.[36] In 1930 the firm manufactured about 1,500 hectoliters (hereafter hl) of milk per day, and 450,000 hl per year.

Locatelli's growth in the first years of the 1900s led the company to manage no less than 12 dairy factories after WWI. The factories specialized in the production of butter, 'Swiss use' cheeses, such as *sbrinz* and *emmenthal*, and *provolone*.[37] They also worked aging *grana*, managing a cheese factory in Reggiano. Particularly active in exporting *pecorino* to the Americas, the Locatellis began working in the production of this cheese thanks to their plants in Sardinia and invested further to purchase of a farm over 1,100 hectares near Rome.

This development resulted in significant change for Invernizzi in 1928. In that year, the company took the name Caseificio Giovanni Invernizzi, after buying a plant specialized in the production of *emmenthal*.[38] Also in 1928, the company chose to customize its production with the creation of a successful logo of a child licking his fingers. Because it was during the Fascist era, this child took on the name of 'Moretto'.

This period of development was characterized by a lower level of protection but that in turn led directly to the first main phase in branding in the 1930s. This phase began in 1931 with three registrations before a rapid increase in activity resulted in 37 trademarks in 1935. However, this was only a single wave because after that, and within two years, the number of registrations fell back to six. Another high point was reached in 1940, and the graph illustrates that there were a series of short cycles before, during and after WWII. It took only one year, from 1946 to 1947, to reach the second maximum point of the whole sequence.

On the eve of WWII, Galbani was solidly controlled by the Invernizzi brothers and had eight production factories and a range of over 100 products including cheeses and cured meats. It was a large company that operated in an extremely divided sector. The distribution network of the enterprise covered the entire national territory: there was even advertising promotion on a national scale. In the 1930s, the state radio organization agreed a contract to insert advertising messages into the normal programming of various broadcasts.

In the same decade, Locatelli concentrated its activity on the domestic market,[39] and on the production of fresh cheeses, through the purchase of a plant in Robbio Lomellina (Pavia) in 1935.[40] The enterprise also concentrated on products for children: 'il formaggino Mio'. Several successes confirmed a new production horizon after World War II, including that of 'formaggino Mio'.

In the 1930s, i.e. at the beginning of the period under consideration, Invernizzi extended its range of products to processed cheeses, imitating Swiss products.[41] This helped in increasing the trademarking activity of the company. The war years were particularly trying for the firm, in part because its founder died, and he had long centralized all the main entrepreneurial function in himself. Military supply contracts and the abilities of Romeo Invernizzi, who replaced his father in managing the company, allowed the business to survive this challenging period without overly negative consequences. Above all, Romeo, who was named general director in 1947 and managing director in 1953, led a new expansion of the company just after WWII. An important step in this direction was the entry in the *gorgonzola* production, in 1947, with a product that aged faster and was therefore creamier. In 1948, a contest was created to give a name to the 'gorgonzola Invernizzi', with a prize of 150,000 lire, a large sum at the time.

4.2. The second phase (1950s to 1970s)

The general elevated trademark activity during the 1930s and 1940s started to decline fast in the 1950s. The previous high registrations level was a first reason of that fall, but the companies' internal struggles further help to explain it. Competition, both foreign and domestic increased in these years and Locatelli was under such pressure that it surrendered itself to the Swiss multinational Nestlé in 1962.[42]

The lack of data on registrations in the period between the mid-1960s and 1970s prevents further investigation of the firms' trademarking activity. But, analyzing the data on the top 10 Italian dairy companies by share capital and assets in three benchmark years (1952, 1960 and 1972) demonstrates that the companies studied grew considerably. Table 1 recaps the figures for Galbani, Locatelli and Invernizzi.[43]

Indeed in 1952, Galbani and Locatelli were already in the top 10 list.[44] Galbani was second and Locatelli, at that time operating under the name of Lir-Latterie Industriali Riunite, was seventh. Within 10 years, Galbani reached the top spot, Locatelli went as far as third and Invernizzi joined the top 10. Galbani maintained its leadership position into the 1970s, while Locatelli and Invernizzi both made progress. In 1972, Locatelli occupied the second rung on the ladder and Invernizzi was not far behind in sixth place. The data also display that between 1960 and 1972 there was a strong growth in assets, taking into account the level of inflation and devaluation in this period.

In particular, the Galbani's widespread commercial organization created a competitive advantage for the firm after WWII. The company's warehouses and vehicles were able to efficiently supply a distribution system that, in 1961, was still based on small trade: there were almost 130,000 retail vendors of food products, potential clients of the dairy industry, while there were only 100 supermarkets operating in Italy.

Locatelli, during the 1960s, supported the sales of its goods using innovative and promotional campaigns and after the incorporation in Nestlé was the first outfit to introduce *mascarpone* to the Italian market. *Mascarpone* is a soft cheese, and it was packaged in trays.

Table 1. Rank position of Galbani, Invernizzi and Locatelli (1952, 1960, 1972).

Year	Rank Position	Company	Share capital	Assets
1952	2	Egidio Galbani	468,000	4,097,610
1952	7	Lir – Latterie industirali riunite (after Locatelli)	4,000	1,003,745
1960	1	Egidio Galbani	1,500,000	17,338,756
1960	3	Locatelli	1,000,000	8,293,885
1960	7	Invernizzi	300,000	2,169,162
1972	1	Egidio Galbani	4,500,000	51.862,063 (1971)
1972	2	Locatelli	4,000,000	22.095,407 (1971)
1972	6	Invenizzi	1,500,000	9,239,693 (1971)

Source: Fumi Gianpiero, The Rise and Decline of a Large Company, pp. 357–359.

This important product innovation was designed to improve – or at least maintain – the market share of this kind products.

Invernizzi became a joint stock company in 1953. At the same time, a new development strategy was initiated, the core of which was to create a direct sales network. The method used was off-truck sales, implemented by company representatives who visited retailers several times per week to deliver the goods and promote the company's various products. In 1977, this product distribution system reached its peak with 147 warehouses located in large and small centres on the Italian peninsula and almost 1,800 sales agents working in all areas of the country. Growth in sales was facilitated by the success of processed cheeses, especially in the south. The sales of fresh products increased in the 1960s, when refrigerators began to be a common appliance in the houses of Italian families. Indeed, this development was positive for the whole dairy industry, including Locatelli and Galbani.

Advertising campaigns were also important, and were initially entrusted – as, for example, in Galbani – to radio and then television. During the campaigns, up to 70 messages per day were aired, accompanied by catchy jingles with simple refrains. There were ads at the brand level, identifying easy-to-memorize names, but which allowed company products to be distinguished. For that, names were given to cheese types. For example *robiola* became 'Invenizzina', and the same was done to a processed cheese that became 'Milione', a name that referred to the adventures of a character from the most popular comic book for children, 'Corriere dei piccoli'. The company's range of products also expanded during the 1950s. In 1957, the firm entered the cow's milk mozzarella sector, introducing the brand 'Mozzarella Carolina'. Moreover, by selling products carrying its brand name but produced by others, the company met two objectives: expanding the range of products on offer to customers (e.g. *pecorino* cheese), and meeting peaks in demand without having to enlarge its own plants. Invernizzina's fortunes were generally positive in the 1950s and 1960s. During this period, the company could exercise considerable contractual power in its dealings with milk producers and purchasers, who were almost always small commercial businesses. Domestic competition was very strong, but its sales network and goods, strengthened and reinforced by strong advertising campaigns, created a large competitive advantage. Promoting the company names as a guarantee for its mass-market products was the strategy pursued in the next decade (1970s), introducing, for example, the jingle 'Invenizzi invernizzina che bontà' [Invernizzi little invernizzi that goodness]. In the same period, the company promoted several plans to differentiate its product range. The strategy was to transform traditional rural products into mass-market goods, i.e. standardized commodities. So, 'Mozarì', a *mozzarella* in UHT packaging, was created. For the first time, an Invenizzi good was addressed only to large retailers.

The context emerging in the 1950s–1970s period well introduces the increasing importance in the trademark activities displayed in the last part of the twentieth century and, above all, in the first 15 years of the 21st century. In general, the registrations trend starting in the 1980s shows similar characteristics to the first main phase. There are several peaks with the higher reaches – above 40 registrations – in 1986 (44 trademarks), 1996 (46 trademarks), 2003 (43 trademarks), 2007 (42 trademarks) and 2010 (77 trademarks).

4.3. The third phase (1980s–2015)

From the mid-1980s, there were increasing levels of foreign capital invested in the Italian dairy industry while large retailers, including a significant French element, became more prominent. National and foreign groups devised different acquisition plans, but in the end the Italian enterprises were incorporated in the French group Lactalis.

In 1986, the best-performing Italian industry was Galbani with approximately 1,288 billion lire in revenue and, in 1989, the company joined the Danone group. This was part of a plan to strengthen its presence in the European market and involved the creation of a new line of cheese under the 'Vallelata' brand. In 2002, Galbani returned to autonomous management; the BC Partners fund acquired all the production machinery of Galbani and provided the company with continuity in management. A few years later, there was another switch in the management of the business. Initially, two new companies, bigG Srl and bigG logistica Spa, were created to manage distribution. Another holding, Gruppo Galbani Spa, was then established and became part of the French group Lactalis in 2006.[45]

The acquisition of Galbani opened the way for Lactalis to dominate the Italian dairy sector.[46]

In 1985, Luigi Invernizzi, son of the then octogenarian founder Giovanni, sold the company to Kraft Food Spa. In the latter half of the 1980s, the Nestlé group invested heavily in the production of fresh cheeses, creating a new industrial plant,[47] but a decade later, in 1998, the family group Besnier purchased the Locatelli brand and the Nestlé dairy branch. The Locatelli trademark is now part of the Lactalis group.[48] In December 2003, the French group Lactalis bought this brand from Kraft.

These governance changes in Galbani and Invernizzi (similar to those experienced by Locatelli in the 1960s) may have several explanations. The ownership change can be explained by a classic problem of the family business, namely the transition to a 'third property' in the absence of members of the founding family with entrepreneurial initiative. However, other factors may also have been at play. Multinational plans guarantee employment levels and, at the same time, incorporation in a multinational ensured integration of productive lines and market targets by exploiting each company's patents and brands. In addition, both Galbani and Locatelli were facing a new challenge: the transformation of the Italian retail system.[49] Until the end of the 1970s the sale of food products was based on an extensive distribution network, one that Invernizzi and Galbani mastered effectively. By the 1980s the situation had changed as the advent of supermarkets and large retail chains generally, forced these dairy industries to engage with processes designed to influence the trends of consumption. In short, Invernizzi and Galbani were no longer the main actors in their own market.

Other important factors in this period were cyclical Italian agricultural crises along with the development induced by growing economic European integration and by the internationalization of markets. These forces were negative factors pushing the reorganization of the sector. Moreover, the Italian food system remained linked to the 'modernization of mass consumption', while other Western countries began to change the paradigm of production and consumption patterns began to point to what has been described as 'typicality'.[50] Nonetheless, the increased trademarking activity of Galbani, Invernizzi and Locatelli after the French acquisitions demonstrates that these companies also started to move towards commercial strategies that were more closely focused on protection, in particular the protection of certain values, among these, typicality.

4.4. Trademarks by companies

Galbani owned the highest number of trademarks and had been the first to file one: 'Robiola Galbani', which was registered on 5 April 1890. In total, about 855 trademarks of the 1,200 analyzed belonged to Galbani. So, the registration activity of this company clearly reflects that of the general trend depicted in Figure 1.[51]

Locatelli filed 148 trademarks between 1910 and 2015 (Figure 2).[52] The company trend seems to follow the broad path of registrations, with a concentration in the mid-1930s, after WWII and post-1980s, with its annual peaks also coinciding with the general pattern. Its high-water trademark was 2010, as was the case with its competitors. Finally, there was an interesting relative maximum in 1965, consisting of seven records, which might have been the result of a reorganization implemented after the surrender of the enterprise to Nestlé. In fact, about 65% of all Locatelli trademarks were registered after 1963. So, in terms of product protection it seems that the Swiss multinational was more active than the previous Italian owner.

Invernizzi trademarks accounted for about 17% of the total of registered trademarks,[53] but its trademarking history is somewhat different from those of Galbani and Locatelli (Figure 3). Invernizzi was the last of the three to brand its goods. Its first registration, in 1924, was that of 'Formaggio Martesana' [Martesana Cheese], which is the name of one of the canals of Milan. Invernizzi, in contrast to its two rivals, conducted the majority of its registrations before 1964, by which point 68% of its activity had taken place. Invernizzi, like the others, intensified its trademarking campaign in the 1930s, but unlike the others, its second and most important peak was in 1950 rather than in 2010. The company's level of trademarking has remained stable since the turn of the twenty-first century, whereas for Galbani and Locatelli there have been at least two points of significant upsurge, in 2003 and in 2010. Again, the limitations of the databases are a factor in these differences. Nevertheless, they suggest the adoption of a low-level protection approach in recent years. In addition, the

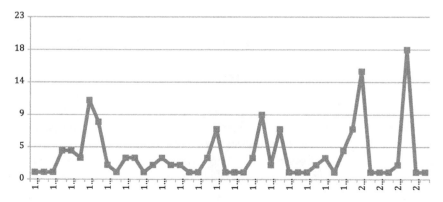

Figure 2. Locatelli trademarks (1910–2015).
Source: elaborations from ISA, https://dati.acs.beniculturali.it and IPTO, www.uibm.gov.

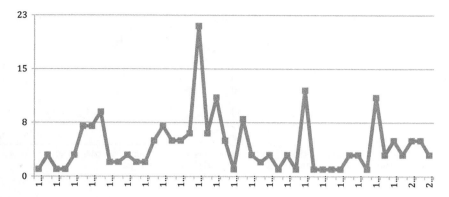

Figure 3. Invernizzi trademarks (1924–2014).
Source: elaborations from ISA, https://dati.acs.beniculturali.it and IPTO, www.uibm.gov.

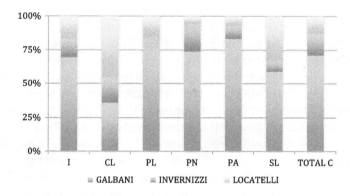

Figure 4. Trademarks by type of registration and by Company. Source: elaborations from ISA, https://dati.acs.beniculturali.it and IPTO, www.uibm.gov.
Notes: Legend: I = image; CL = company logo; PL = product logo; PN = product name; PA = packaging; SL = slogan; TOTAL C = total by company.

lack of any noticeable increase in registrations after 1996 also indicates Invernizzi's diminishing interest in this activity.

5. Trademarks Types[54]

Companies registered different kind of trademarks, according to their product and sales policies. The registration could relate to an image;[55] a logo, both of the company and the product; the name of the product; the product packaging; and, finally, an advertising slogan (Figure 4). Table 2 shows the trademarks registered by type per period.

In approximately 47% of cases the trademarks concerned the product name. For example, the name of 'Campione' [Champion] cheese was deposited by Locatelli in 1963. In particular, product name was the most protected product feature between 1965 and 1969, when almost 60% of the registrations filled were of this type. Moreover, product name was also the most frequently registered feature in other periods: it accounted for 53% of records filed in the period 1945–1964 and 52% in 1980–1999. Its importance was remarkable also in the period

Table 2. Type of trademarks per period by Galbani, Invernizzi and Locatelli (1890–2015).

PERIOD	I	CL	PL	PN	PA	SL	Total
1890–1914	8			1	1		10
1915–1929	14		3	15	1		33
1930–1944	66	5	7	76	10		164
1945–1964	89	9	10	144	18	3	273
1965–1979	18	3		35		3	59
1980–1999	85	15	24	144		11	279
2000–2015	191	9	23	140		11	374
TOTAL	471	41	67	555	30	28	1192

Notes: Legend: I = image; CL = company logo; PL = product logo; PN = product name; PA = packaging; SL = slogan.
Source: elaborations from ISA, https://dati.acs.beniculturali.it and IPTO, www.uibm.gov.

between WWI and the end of WWII: between 1915 and 1944 names made up more than 45% of product registrations.

A number of themes emerged from an analysis of the product names. A name was chosen to highlight specific features, namely naturalness and high quality, but also ties with territory, rural tradition and Italian cultural history. In 1950, for example, Galbani filled a cheese named 'Buongustaio' [Gourmet]. Furthermore, one of Galbani's first trademark was 'Robiola di Melzo',[56] deposited in 1901. In the same way, Invernizzi registered 'Formaggio Melzo' [Melzo Cheese] (1946), 'Gorgonzola di Melzo' [Gorgonzola of Melzo] (1946), 'Duomo' (1951) [Dome] and 'Ambrosiano' (1951).[57] Locatelli protected its 'Mozzarella della salute' [Mozzarella Health] in 1959. Several names invoke the Alps or a rural context: 'Bucaneve' [Snowdrop] (Galbani, 1949), 'Crème du Mont Blanc' [Mont Blanc Cream] (Galbani, 1926), 'Agreste' (Galbani, 1940), and 'Crema di pastorella' [Pastorella Cream] (Locatelli, 1959). 'I promessi sposi' [The Betrothed], a traditional Italian novel written by Alessandro Manzoni, and its settings, inspired a series of cheese names, among them 'Lucia' (Galbani, 1934), the name of the female protagonist. Finally, each enterprise prioritized its best-known cheese, so that the product name could itself be leveraged against competitors. A case in point is *robiola* cheese and its varieties, including 'Robiola Galbani', 'Robiola Invernizzi' and 'Robiolina Locatelli' [Little robiola Locatelli].[58] Part of the strategy of protecting product name related to the protection of new goods, and its value became apparent after WWII when the market expanded dramatically and competition increased significantly.

The second type of registration concerns images by which customers could identify the products. In 1933, for example, Galbani chose to use a shamrock to label a cheese named 'Trifoglio' [i.e. shamrock]. As for the product name, the images were strongly redolent of the characteristics listed above. There were pictures referring to mountains and pastures, farmers and livestock, e.g. a mountain featured in 'Taleggio Valsassina' (Galbani, 1935). A pasture was the theme of 'Formaggio Segreto delle Alpi' [Secret Cheese of the Alps] (Invernizzi, 1926). The images supported the role of the name in the companies' strategies to create an identity for each product, so that it was not only a cheese but also a healthy way of life, in the best traditions and culture of the country. The use of images became especially prominent in the twenty-first century: 40% of images were filed since 2000 and they accounted for more than the half of the total trademarks registered in this period (51% of total brands filed after 2000). This kind of trademark was also the most important before WWI, and remained crucial during the inter-war period. In general, the increasing importance of images illustrates how the companies attempted to capture consumer attention: by encouraging a quick glance to invite instinctive purchase.

The product logo and the company logo were also a subject of protection, but at 10% their importance in the context of the total brands registered is not hugely significant. In this case, the companies had other instruments to provide the required protection, particularly images and product name. Moreover, the company name was often linked directly to products, so it became part of the trademark.

Product packaging registrations were much less frequent at just 2.5% of the total cases and this kind of trademark was used only prior to WWII. Indeed, post-war mechanization of production processes and standardization of packaging techniques led the companies to abandon this kind of protection. The emergence of slogans points to a movement in an alternative direction. They became regular features just after WWII and gained increasing importance in the later part of the twentieth century. The slogans promoted the cheeses as universally appealing and stressed their healthy characteristics: 'Bel Mondo il formaggio per tutto il mondo' [Bel Mondo the cheese for the whole world] (Invernizzi, 1950) and 'Il Gorgonzola di facile digestione' [Gorgonzola easy to digest] (Invernizzi, 1950). Slogans, along with images, account for all the brands currently waiting to be approved.

According to the firms' history, trademarks were mainly aimed at the Italian market. In some cases, the companies required an extension of protection to foreign countries. For example, in February 1965, Locatelli deposited a request for the registration of 'Genziana', a 'pasteurized cheese', with a 'special note' indicating: 'protection extended to France under the Italian–French Agreement of 8 January 1955'.[59] In general, the company name was prioritized in foreign markets.[60] In these circumstances, the firm logo became the 'export' trademark and the product brand – essentially an Italian name – was used as an intangible asset to confirm, on the one hand, the Italian taste of the product and, on the other hand, the set of values related to the product itself.

Nevertheless, the export activity of the companies was also supported by the use of some international names. For example, as early as the 1920s, Galbani deposited 'Butterkäse', 'Block Chester', 'Crème du Mont Blanc', 'Galbani Kaese', 'Kraft Cheese' and 'Mexican Cheese'. In the 1930s, the company added further to its collection of foreign 'names': 'Erbo Cheese', 'Fromage des Laumes', 'Garda Cheese' and 'Melzo Cheese' and Invernizzi registered its cheese 'Cartableu'. Between the mid-1950s and mid-1960s, Locatelli introduced trademarks named 'Cottage', 'Napoleon' and 'Kremli' and, in the same period, Galbani and Invernizzi registered, respectively, 'Alpen-toast' and 'Bick'.[61] In the broader context, however, these foreign names were only a small minority of the companies' trademarks.

Galbani were trendsetters in many respects. The most interesting issue in this case is the use of slogans, which the company started adopting in the 1950s. The trademark 'cremino galbani formaggio di lunga vita' [Galbani 'small cream' cheese for long life] was realized for the first time in July 1951 and it was renewed until 2010. It is interesting to note that it includes different aspects of the company's protection strategy: the company name and the healthy idea of the product. Another issue is a long-lasting life, because this trademark is over 60 years old and it appears that the company will maintain it for a long time to come. Other slogans were developed during the 1970s (one), 1980s (two) and 1990s (two) and all had several renewals bringing them up to the current day. In fact, the last renewal dated to 2015 and covered a company slogan that promotes the long-life activity of the firm at the top level: '[Galbani] dal 1882 n° 1 in Italia' [Galbani from 1882 number 1 in Italy]. An alternative, 'Galbani ispirazione Italiana dal 1882' [Galbani Italian inspiration from 1882] is awaiting approval. Galbani was also the firm most interested in packaging branding. Twenty five of

30 packaging trademarks were Galbani initiatives but, as we have seen, the protection of packaging did not retain the same significance after the war and attention switched elsewhere.

Invernizzi focused on product name trademarks more than the other two enterprises and almost 59% of its records were in this category. The company's branding efforts were most concerted in the mid-twentieth century, before which point product name trademarks were more popular.

Locatelli invested more in its company logo than Galbani and Invernizzi. This strategy offsets the smaller number of trademarks directly related to company products. Significant efforts were also put into the use of slogans. For example, Locatelli adopted the slogan 'Il Re dei formaggini per grandi e piccini' [The King of cheese for young and old] (1965) to support its cheese. In particular, this brand referred to a special kind of cheese created for children. It was named 'Formaggino Mio' [Mio Cheese]. The enterprise's slogans also referred to the quality of its production processes. Two such slogans were: 'locatelli fa le cose per bene' [locatelli does things right] and 'esperienza locatelli dal 1860' [locatelli experience since 1860]. The latter reflects the practices of one of Locatelli's competitors, Galbani, which promoted a similar trademark. Locatelli trailed after Galbani, however, only registering its trademark in 1983.

6. 'Enduring' trademarks[62]

The general trend is obtained by counting each registration, but as outlined above a trademark can have a 'history'. In other words, a trademark can have undergone more than one assignment. So, a registration can take the form of either a first trademark or a renewal of an existing trademark. The literature refers to these registrations as 'enduring' trademarks.[63]

'New' or original trademarks account for 50% of total registrations; the other half of registrations were renewals. This could potentially mean that each trademark had one renewal. In reality, as we shall see, some trademarks have been registered multiple times while others were never renewed.

Figure 5 shows that all trademarks registered before WWI were new and belonged to Galbani, while in this period both Locatelli and Invernizzi were only commercial businesses. More than 60% of the total of new registrations were filed before 1964. In particular, the period after WWII saw the highest quota of first registrations, with about 29% of the total of new trademarks filed at this point. According to the history of the development of the dairy sector and its constituent firms, the post-war period was one of great change, characterized by increasing competition and innovation, both in types of goods and in production processes. So, companies were encouraged to use trademark security to defend their new products.

Despite the gaps in the data for the period between 1965 and 1979, the graph shows that about 76% of registrations filed in these years were new trademarks. However, it also underlines that several trademarks registered after 1980 had a prior history.[64]

In the 1980s, there was a turnaround: renewals outnumbered first trademarks. This reversal was particularly pronounced afterwards, since when 295 of 374 registrations were renewals. At present, this analysis cannot delve deeper into the issue of enduring trademarks. However, these preliminary insights clearly show the shift in the companies' policies and, at least for

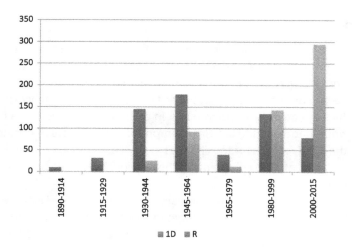

Figure 5. Number of first trademarks and renewed trademarks by period (1890–2015). Source: elaborations from ISA, https://dati.acs.beniculturali.it and IPTO, www.uibm.gov.
Notes: Legend: 1D = first registration; R = renewal.

now, it seems reasonable to suggest that the increasing level of renewals reflects the idea that new protective strategies needed to focus on a typicality based in the past. What we can state with certainty is that companies used renewals to keep 'old' trademarks alive so as to emphasize the role of tradition and capitalize on consumers' recognition of already well-known goods. Finally, the evidence to be gleaned from the data for each enterprise allows us to make some further remarks.

Galbani's history reflects the general trend, but it had more renewals (448) than first trademarks (407). The company has certainly concentrated more on renewals than original registrations in the twenty-first century. The most frequently renewed products were 'Bel Paese' and 'Taleggio Galbani". 'Bel Paese' was highly prized as the enterprise's most popular cheese. The frequent renewal of 'Taleggio Galbani' underlines the need to protect *taleggio* goods which were also offered by competitors, among them Invernizzi.[65] So, in this case the uniqueness of the product was guaranteed by the use of the firm's name. The same strategy, albeit with fewer renewals, was also followed for another cheese: 'Robiola Galbani'.

The 'first brand' proportion of Invernizzi's trademarks was higher than renewals: about 70% of Invernizzi's brands were 'new'. Nevertheless, only three new trademarks have been registered since 1980: one in 1980 itself, one in 1987 and one in 1988. This confirms the pattern of branding development engaged in by Invernizzi and its decline in more recent years. Among the Invernizzi cheeses, 'Robiolina Invernizzi' is an interesting case. From 1926 to 2008 there were no fewer than 14 renewals of this product. This displays the high value that the company attached to it.

Locatelli also had more 'first' brand registrations (82) than renewals (66). Locatelli, however, lagged behind in the registration of new trademarks. In its case, the suspension of new brands started in 2008. The last new trademarks concerned an image, referring to *burrata*, a fresh cheese, made with cow's milk, with spun dough, similar to mozzarella but with a much softer texture. This brand was also associated with the idea of a 'cuore morbido di crema' [soft heart of cream].

7. Conclusions

This article presents the first longitudinal analysis of the cheese trademarks established by three of the most important Italian dairy enterprises. It covers the entire chronological period of the dairy trademarking activity of these companies, from 1890 almost to the present day. The data are based on two official sources: the first is the Italian State Archive and the second is the Italian Office of Patents and Trademarks. In offering an overview of a century and a quarter of the firms' trademarking activity, it emphasizes the theme of business evolution and examines the main reasons for the changes in trademarking encountered over time. It also provides further context by pinpointing the relationship between these changes and wider economic events.

The dairy sector, and the food sector generally, is a 'traditional' field in trademark studies, especially because trademarks offer advantages for both consumers, by promoting tangible and intangible characteristics of products and reducing search costs, and for producers, by providing protection for goods and contributing to the opening new markets. The analysis of these cases confirms that firms used trademarks in both these two different ways, but always with the overall goal of maintaining or improving their competitiveness as well as gaining the long-term loyalty of consumers.

The companies analyzed commenced their trademarking activity at an early point in their development, just as they started production. Trademarks were employed as a weapon against competitors in the 1930s, post-WWII and again after the oil crisis, all times of increasing domestic and foreign competition. Indeed, it is no coincidence that the trademarking paths of each enterprise follow the same general trend. Meanwhile, trademarks became a complementary instrument, along with patents, in safeguarding new technologies in products and in production processes, in other words, in protecting innovations. This strategy was particularly prevalent after WWII, and revolved around new technologies in refrigeration and innovations in packaging. In the context of wider economic phenomena, trademarking registrations represented a response to negative shocks, but they were also utilized in efforts to expand markets or initiate new commercial opportunities, such as in the period after WWII.

Companies employed different typologies of trademarks – from product names and logos to images and packing designs – through which they communicated information, and moreover values, to consumers. Product names and images were the most frequent kinds of trademarks. In particular, product names dominated trademark registration for most of the twentieth century, especially during its second half, while images and designs were dominant in the early start of companies' trademarking activity as well as in the new millennium. At any rate, by using trademarks as a communication tool, customers were supported in their purchasing decisions and firms established a direct link with them, based on long-lasting trust. Building on the firms' rural origins, the characteristics incorporated in dairy trademarks related to the naturalness of products and the high quality of both raw materials and final goods. Furthermore, territorial ties, Italian cultural history and rural tradition were also standout features, embodied in product names and carried through images or designs.

Finally, the data suggest that dairy firms coped with increasing level of competition by regularly introducing 'new trademarks' until the 1980s, especially after WWII. However, during the last two decades of the twentieth century and, above all, in the twenty-first century, a new strategy based on the renewal of existing trademarks emerged. This change underlined the beginning of a different direction in protection policies. Indeed, from the mid-1980s onwards firms focused their attention on the role of tradition and on long-lasting relations with well-known goods, all that throughout 'enduring' trademarks.

In an overall sense, this research has added to the body of knowledge of trademarks in business history and their role in business development. Granted, the findings are based on three case studies, but the data refer to leading actors in the Italian dairy industry since the late nineteenth century. Thus, the article provides a valuable vantage point on the entire sector. As a first study, it only goes far in addressing certain problems, such as the question of the effects of trademarks on the level of globalization of firms, the degree of success or failure of trademarks and the commercial value of trademarks. However, the abundance of information contained in the source material means that a step-by-step analysis of these issues can be undertaken in future studies.

Notes

1. See Lopes and Duguid, 'Introduction: Behind the Brand', 235; Higgins, 'Forgotten Heroes and Forgotten Issues', 261.

    Furthermore, for an exam of the business history of brands in Europe see Bonin et al., *European Business and Brand Building*, and for a historical review of the concept of branding see, for example, Bastos and Levy, 'A History of the Concept of Branding', 347–368.

2. This is the main point underlined by Teresa da Silva Lopes and Paul Duguid in their book entitled *Trademarks, Brands, and Competitiveness*.

3. The relationship between trademarks and the issue of imitations and counterfeits is analysed in Lopes and Casson, *Brand Protection*.

4. Several studies highlight the role of brands and trademarks for firms. For example, see: Higgins, 'Forgotten Heroes and Forgotten Issues', 263; Sáiz and Fernández Pérez, 'Catalonian Trademarks', 239; Lopes, *Global Brands,* 5, Lopes, 'The Growth and Survival', 595, Duguid, 'A Case of Prejudice?', 312.

    See also: Wilkins, 'The Neglected Intangible Asset', 66–95; Petty, 'From Label to Trademark', 129–153.

    Moreover, for a long-term study on the concept of brand see: Moore and Reid, 'The Birth of Brand: 4000 Years of Branding', 419–432 and Jones and Morgan, *Adding Value*.

    Finally, for some insights on the cultural approach of brands see: Cayla and Arnould, 'A Cultural Approach to Branding' and Askegaard, 'Brands as a Global Ideoscape'.

5. Lopes, *Global Brands*, 5. So, it is important to note that 'brand and trade marks are closely connected'. They are similar because they 'help producers differentiate their products from rivals', but they differ in some aspects. In particular, brands do not give property rights and they convey specified messages; Barnes and Higgins, 'Brand Image, Cultural Association and Marketing', 4. So, companies converted their products into brands with 'personalities' that expressed what the 'consumer wished to be', Fitzgerald, 'Marketing and distribution', 397. For more details in the distinction between brands and trademarks see Mercer, 'A Mark of Distinction'.

6. Lopes and Duguid, *Trademarks, Brands, and Competitiveness*, 1.

7. Sáiz and Fernández Pérez, 'Catalonian Trademarks', 239; Duguid, Lopes and Mercer, 'Reading Registrations', 10.

8. Higgins, 'Forgotten Heroes and Forgotten Issues', 263. More details in Wilkins, 'When and Why', 25–26.

    Examples of other studies on food history include Lopes, *Global Brands*; Duguid, 'Developing the Brand', 405–441; Battilani and Bertagnoni, 'The Use of Networks in Marketing', 31–57.

9. Source: IMITA.db – Archivio Storico delle Società per Azioni Italiane; cfr. https://imitadb.unisi.it/.

10. *Ibid.*

11. In general, for an overview on the Italian economic development see Zamagni, *The Economic History of Italy, 1860–1990*; Cohen and Federico, *The Growth of the Italian Economy, 1820–1960*. Other information about the Italian economy can be found in Toniolo, *The Oxford Handbook of the Italian Economy since Unification*.

    Furthermore, on the evolution of the Italian enterprises see: Colli and Vasta, *Forms of Enterprise in Twentieth Century Italy*; Giannetti and Vasta, *Evolution of Italian Enterprises in the Twentieth Century*; Amatori and Colli, 'European Corporations'; Aganin and Volpin, 'The History of Corporate Governance in Italy'; Colli et al., 'Mapping Strategy, Structure, Ownership and Performance in European Corporations'; Colli and Vasta, 'Large and Entangled: Italian Business Group in the Long Run'; Colli et al., 'Long-term Perspectives on Family Business'; Toninelli and Vasta, "Opening the Black Box of Entrepreneurship".

12. Besana, *Tra agricoltura e industria*. See also Fumi, *Una grande impresa cooperativa*.

13. On Italian dairy development see Ferrari, *L'industria del latte in Italia*; Besana et al., *Cheese Manufacturing in the Twentieth Century*. For Lombardy see Mandressi, 'La nascita del caseificio industriale in Lombardia' and Besana, *Tra agricoltura e industria*.

14. It is interesting to note that the Galbanis were related to the Locatellis.

15. It therefore moved to lower altitudes, beginning to manage a modest facility in a town near the Lombardy capital, with access to the Milan–Venice railway. The new headquarters of the Galbani business was located in an area where the dry Lombardy plains, a realm of sericulture, began to benefit from the advantages of irrigation, in a city that represented a point of transfer of the *bergamini* transhumance to the mountains. For some time, Galbani continued to send packaged cheese to the small hillside town of Ballabio (Como), for aging in the Pre-Alps – Grigne caves. In 1898, its dairy factory was equipped with a steam boiler and a refrigerating plant. It was still a plant with limited production capacity that probably processed 50 hectoliters of milk per day, a rather small amount, but one that produced more than eight times what a traditional hut dedicated to the production of butter and *grana* cheese could produce; Colli, *Galbani Egidio*, 363–367; Mantegazza, *Locatelli*, 345–348.

16. Sicca L., *L'industria alimentare in Italia*. Instead, on the role of the European Common Agricultural Policy (CAP) see Stranieri and Tedeschi, 'The Influence of the European Institutions', pp. 95–111.

17. Mediobanca, Dati cumulativi.

18. Ifil was a holding company owned by the family Agnelli (Fiat) with diversified investments in many companies including some foods firms; Besana and Locatelli, 'Italian Family Business and Multinationals', 123–128.

19. Source: elaborations from https://dati.acs.beniculturali.it.

20. See: https://www.uibm.gov.it

21. For example, on 16 January 1970, a biscuit industry named Bistefani Biscottificio Santostefano S.P.A. deposited the trademark 'Chateau Doré' for the first time, with the number 255,050. On 27 November 1992 it was renewed and it was registered with the number 581,133; Source: elaborations from IPTO, http://www.uibm.gov.it.

    It seems also useful to add that the trademark number is a serial number. The first mark registered refers to a 'castor oil' produced by I.G. Schmidt fu Giorgio, in 1869. Opposite, among the first cheese trademark there is that of the 'etichetta con impressa la parola *Fromage des Alpes* ed altre iscrizioni relative a tale prodotto' [label with imprinted word *Fromage des Alpes* and other inscriptions relating to that product], deposited by 'Ditta Molli G.A. e C.I.' in 1880; Source: elaborations from ISA, https://dati.acs.beniculturali.it.

22. See: ISA, https://dati.acs.beniculturali.it. In particular, this figure refers to trademarks the description of which incorporates the words: cheese, dairy and butter. The ISA database doesn't facilitate a historical sequencing of dairy marks, but it gives useful information about the total amount of registered trademarks in this sector.

23. In the IPTO database the cheese marks are identified with the class number 29, but a large volume of other goods is also included in this class. So, it is difficult to assess the real quota of cheese in number 29 group; Source: elaborations from https://www.uibm.gov.it

24. The series of cheese registrations included each trademark, i.e. each number of trademark recorded in the ISA and in the IPTO databases. This means that, for the moment, there is no distinction between new brands and renewed trademarks.

   The data were collected from the ISA database using specific keywords, such as cheese, dairy and butter, and by name of the owner.

   The IPTO database was searched by owner or by text: by owner including the three company names and by text including specific words, such as Galbani, Locatelli and Invernizzi. Supply information has been obtained using others key words, such as Nestlé, Kraft Food, Danone. Finally, only brands identified as 29 and 30 classes are taken into consideration; Source: elaborations from https://dati.acs.beniculturali.it and www.uibm.gov.it.

25. Among these 800 trademarks, 45 were already present on the ISA database. Thus, the analysis which follows will be based on 755 IPTO registrations.

26. Sources: elaboration from ISA, https://dati.acs.beniculturali.it, and IPTO, www.uibm.gov.it.

27. There are currently a number of trademark requests which are in the process of being registered: Invernizzi is waiting on two requests, Locatelli, four and Galbani, eight. The data are updated to November 2016; Source: personal analysis of sources.

28. Source: elaborations from ISA, https://dati.acs.beniculturali.it, and IPTO, www.uibm.gov.it.

29. The lack of brands in this database could be the result of a delay in its completion. Furthermore, because of the nature of these historical sources, it is possible that part of the data was dispersed. Future research into this material might be able to remedy this.

30. In fact, this data (51 brands) refers to previous renewals of trademarks registered only after 1980 in the UIBM database.

31. More figures and data on Italian economic development are in Brandolini and Vecchi, *Standards of Living*, 227–248.

   Furthermore, for an overview on the history of consumer culture in modern Italy see Scarpellini, *Material Nation*.

32. Source: elaborations from ISA, http://dati.acs.beniculturali.it.

   The delays were similar for the others two enterprises. For example, for Invernizzi there were more than 1000 days of delay before a request made in the second half of 1943 was fulfilled. However, this phenomenon was even more severe for Locatelli in 1944, from which point they experienced a 1,134 day delay; *Ibid*.

33. Source: elaborations from IPTO, www.uibm.gov.it.

34. They should not be confused with the Invernizzi who owned the Invernizzi cheese industry. The Lecco entrepreneur remained honorary president of the company that he had founded and developed until 1928.

35. The incorporated Egidio Galbani was created with capital equal to two million lire and its headquarters were in Milan. Egidio and his brother Giuseppe owned two thirds of the shares. Egidio was named President, but the role of CEO was given to Rinaldo Invernizzi. Rinaldo entered Galbani with his own brothers Achille and Ermenegildo. The Invernizzis were part of a family of *bergamini* from the Valsassina who were permanently established on the plateau: they worked in their father's company, Antonio Invernizzi s.a., which managed a plant that had served Galbani for many years in the Pavia area. Furthermore, the company capital was increased to 10 million lire, thanks to help from a consortium of banks led by the Banca della Svizzera Italiana in Lugano.

36. Indeed, the sector was still led by Polenghi Lombardo; Fumi, 'The Rise and Decline of a Large Company', 337–362.

37. It is interesting to note that Locatelli's factories also controlled a cured pork meat factory, which manufactured meats from pigs raised on by-products from the dairy industries.

38. The plant was located in Caravaggio in the Lower Bergamo area, bordering the Cremona area.

39. That strategy was essentially due to the collapse of international trade, but it turned out to be beneficial to Locatelli's development.

40. This plant was established by one of Locatelli's competitors: Egidio Galbani.

41. Taking advantage of the strong competitive advantages cheese factories enjoyed over milk producers, the firm continued to record substantial profits, accumulating resources used for the purchase of rural land and farms.
42. That was the result of deficiencies in competitive skill compared to rivals from larger companies which, in this period, were better organised in terms of production and commerce; Rama and Pieri, *The European Dairy Industry*. Nonetheless, Nestlé assigned executives roles to various members of the family at Locatelli.
43. Furthermore, when considering these values it is important to note that Italian family-owned companies usually underestimated their capital. So, it is likely that these three companies had greater capital available to them than is listed here.
44. Galbani was already in this list in 1921, in ninth position. Six years later, it was third and from 1936 it gained second position; Fumi, 'The Rise and Decline of a Large Company', p. 357.
45. Galizzi and Linda, 'Strategie di internazionalizzazione dell'industria alimentare', 23–45.
46. Bianchi and Leroy, *International Handbook on Industrial Policy*. See also Goto, 'Business Groups in a Market Economy'.
47. At the same time, the firm abandoned the production of cured pork meat in Moretta (Cuneo).
48. Brioschi, *Strutture proprietarie e comportamento concorrenziale del sistema industriale italiano*, 67–89.
49. Alò and Bedetti, *Il business in tavola*, 48–56.
50. Bertelè and Brioschi, Il sistema agricolo-alimentare; Ceccarelli et al., *Typicality in History: Tradition, Innovation and Terroir*.
51. These remarks are based on personal processing of the evidence presented at https://dati.acs.beniculturali.it and at www.uibm.gov.it.
52. The following analyses are based on elaborations from ISA, https://dati.acs.beniculturali.it and IPTO, www.uibm.gov.it.
53. There are a total of 194 Invernizzi brands; Source: elaborations from ISA, https://dati.acs.beniculturali.it and IPTO, www.uibm.gov.it. The following analyses are based on the same sources.
54. In general, the data of this section are based on data included in ISA, https://dati.acs.beniculturali.it and IPTO, www.uibm.gov.it.
55. In this typology are included both images and designs.
56. Source: elaborations from ISA, https://dati.acs.beniculturali.it and IPTO, www.uibm.gov.it.
57. Source: *ibid*.
   'Duomo' and the word 'ambrosiano' both mean something linked to Milan. Moreover, other references to Milan and the production area of Melzo include: Duomo [Dome – as associated with Milan], 'Stracchino Duomo' [Dome stracchino] (1961), 'Fontina di Melzo', 'Il Bel Paese di Melzo' [The Beautiful Village of Melzo] (1931), 'Verde di Melzo' [Green of Melzo] (1939).
58. Source (for all the citations): elaborations from ISA, https://dati.acs.beniculturali.it.
59. Source: elaborations from ISA, https://dati.acs.beniculturali.it and IPTO, www.uibm.gov.it.
60. In several cases, the company name was added as the product name, creating a trademark in which both aspects were covered. For example, Locatelli registered both 'Moregal' and 'Moregal Locatelli', in 1947; *Ibid*.
61. *Ibid*.
62. In general, the data of this section are based on the ISA and IPTO databases; cfr https://datiacsbeniculturaliit, and www.uibm.gov.it.
63. For example, 'of the approximately 6000 trademarks applied for residents in Catalonia between 1850 and 1905, 60, or roughly one percent, were still in force in 2010'; Sáiz and Fernández Pérez, 'Catalonian Trademarks', 257.
64. Remember that neither of the two databases includes registrations for this period, but they have been derived from the history of the brands filed after 1980 in the IPTO database.
65. Invernizzi, in fact, also registered its own 'Taleggio Invernizzi'.

Disclosure statement

No potential conflict of interest was reported by the authors.

ORCID

Ilaria Suffia (iD) http://orcid.org/0000-0003-1197-0275
Andrea Maria Locatelli (iD) http://orcid.org/0000-0001-5154-1323
Claudio Besana (iD) http://orcid.org/0000-0002-8732-0992

References

Aganin, A., and P. Volpin. "The History of Corporate Governance in Italy." In *The History of Corporate Governance around the World*, edited by R. K. Morck, 325–361. Chicago: University of Chicago Press, 2005.

Alò, C., and R. Bedetti. *Il business in tavola. Come cambia l'industria alimentare* [The Business on the Table. How Does the Food Industry Change]. Milano: Edizione il Sole 24 ore, 1988.

Amatori, F., and A. Colli. "European Corporations: Ownership, Governance, Strategies and Structures. a Review of Five Countries: United Kingdom, Germany, France, Italy and Spain." In *The European Enterprise: Historical Investigation into a Future Species*, edited by Schroeter H., 23–36. Berlin: Springer Verlag, 2007.

Askegaard, S. "Brands as a Global Ideoscape." In *Brand Culture*, edited by J. Schroeder, and M. Salzer-Mörling, 91–102. London: Spon Press, 2006.

Barnes, F., and D. M. Higgins. "Brand Image, Cultural Association and Marketing: 'New Zealand' Butter and Lamb Exports to Britain, C. 1920-1938." *Business History* (2017): 2–28. doi:10.1080/00076791.2 017.1344223.

Bastos, W., and S. J. Levy. "A History of the Concept of Branding: Practice and Theory." *Journal of Historical Research in Marketing* 4, no. 3 (2012): 347–368.

Battilani, P., and G. Bertagnoni. "The Use of Networks in Marketing: The Italian Co-Operative Experience." *Journal of Historical Research in Marketing* 7, no. 1 (2015): 31–57.

Bertelè, U., and F. Brioschi. *Il sistema agricolo-alimentare in Italia* [The Agricultural-food System in Italy]. Bologna: Il Mulino, 1976.

Bertelè, U., and F. Brioschi. *L'economia agro-alimentare italiana* [The Italian Agri-food Economy]. Bologna: Il Mulino, 1981.

Besana, C. *Tra agricoltura e industria. Il settore caseario nella Lombardia dell'Ottocento* [Between Agriculture and Industry. The Lombardy Dairy Sector in Nineteenth Century]. Milano: Vita e Pensiero, 2012.

Besana, C., and Andrea Maria Locatelli. "Italian Family Business and Multinationals in the Eighties of the 20th Century. Invernizzi/Kraft and Galbani/Danone." In *The French Economic History Review* 1, no. 3 (2015): 116–129.

Besana, C., R. D'Errico, and R. Ghezzi, eds. *Cheese Manufacturing in the Twentieth Century. the Italian Experience in an International Context*, 95–112. Bruxelles: Peter Lang, 2017.

Bianchi, P., ed. *Antitrust e gruppi industriali* [Antitrust and Industrial Groups]. Bologna: Il Mulino Bologna, 1988.

Bianchi, P., and S. Leroy, eds. *International Handbook on Industrial Policy*. Cheltenham-Northampton: Edward Elgar, 2006.

Bianchi, P., and G. Gualtieri. "Concorrenza e potere di mercato: acquisizioni e fusioni in Italia." [Competition and market power: acquisition and mergers in Italy]. In *Antitrust e gruppi industriali*, edited by P. Bianchi, 162–188. Bologna: Il Mulino, 1988.

Bonin, H., L. Segreto, A. K. Lozminsky, C. Manera, and M. Pohl eds. *European Business and Brand Building*. Bruxelles-New York: Peter Lang, 2012.

Brandolini, A., and G. Vecchi. "Standards of Living." In *Oxford Handbook of the Italian Economy since Unification*, edited by G Toniolo, 227–248. Oxford: Oxford University Press, 2013.

Brioschi, F. "Struttura proprietarie e comportamento concorrenziale del sistema industriale italiano [Ownership Structures and Competitive Behavior of the Italian Industrial System]." In *Antitrust e gruppi industriali*, edited by P. Bianchi, 221–233. Bologna: Il Mulino, 1988.

Cayla, J., and E. Arnould. "A Cultural Approach to Branding in the Global Marketplace." *Journal of International Marketing* XVI, no. 4 (2008): 86–112.

Ceccarelli, G., A. Grandi, and S. Magagnoli eds. *Typicality in History: Tradition, Innovation and Terroir*. Brussels: PIE Peter Lang, 2013.

Chiapparino, F., and R. Covino. *Consumi e industria alimentare in Italia dall'Unità a oggi: lineamenti per una storia* [Consumption and Food Industry in Italy from Unity to Today: Outlines for a History]. Palermo: Giada, 2002.

Cohen, J., and F. Giovanni. *The Growth of the Italian Economy, 1820–1960*. Cambridge: Cambridge University Press, 2001.

Colli, A. "Galbani, Egidio." In *Dizionario Biografico Degli Italiani* [Italians' Biographical Dictionary]. Vol. 51 363–367, 1998. http://www.treccani.it/enciclopedia/egidio-galbani_(Dizionario-Biografico)/

Colli, A. *The History of Family Business 1850–2000*. Cambridge: Cambridge University Press, 2003.

Colli, A., and M. Vasta, eds. *Forms of Enterprise in 20th Century Italy: Boundaries, Structures and Strategies*. Cheltenham- Northampton: Edward Elgar, 2010.

Colli, A., and M. Vasta. "Large and Entangled: Italian Business Group in the Long Run." *Business History* 57, no. 1 (2015): 64–96. doi:10.1080/00076791.2014.977872.

Colli, A., M. Jes Iversen, and A. de Jong. "Mapping Strategy, Structure, Ownership and Performance in European Corporations: Introduction." *Business History* 53, no. 1 (2011): 1–13.

Colli, A., C. Howorth, and Mary Rose. "Long-Ter Perspectives on Family Business." *Business History* 55, no. 6 (2013): 841–854. doi:10.1080/00076791.2012.744589.

Duguid, P. "Developing the Brand: The Case of Alcohol, 1800-1880." *Enterprise & Society* 4, no. 3 (2003): 405–441.

Duguid, P. "A Case of Prejudice? The Uncertain Development of Collective and Certification Marks." *Business History Review* 86 (2012): 311–333.

Duguid P., T. da Silva Lopes and J. Mercer, "Reading Registrations. An Overview of 100 Years of Trademark Registrations in France, the United Kingdom, and the United States." In *Trademarks, Brands, and Competitiveness*, edited by T. da Silva and P. Duguid, 9–30. New York: Routledge, 2010.

Ferrari, P. *L'industria del latte in Italia* [The Milk Industry in Italy]. Piacenza: Camera di commercio, industria, artigianato e agricoltura, 1970.

Fitzgerald, R. "Marketing and Distribution." In *The Oxford Handbook of Business History*, by Jones G. and J. Zeitlin, 369–419. Oxford: Oxford University Press, 2007.

Fumi, G. "Una grande impresa cooperativa nell'industria alimentare: la Latteria Soresinese (1900–1940) [A Large Cooperative Enterprise in the Food Industry: The Soresinese Latteria (1900–1940)]." In *Oro bianco. Il settore lattiero-caseario in Val Padana tra Ottocento e Novecento*, by P. Battilani and G. Bigatti, 369–445. Lodi: Giona, 2002.

Fumi, G. "The Rise and Decline of a Large Company: Polenghi Lombardo." In *Cheese Manufacturing in the Twentieth Century. the Italian Experience in an International Context*, edited by Besana C., R. D'Errico, and Ghezzi Renato, 337–362. Bruxelles: Peter Lang, 2017.

Galizzi, G., and R. Linda. *Strategie di internazionalizzazione dell'industria alimentare europea* [Internationalization Strategies of the European Food Industry]. Milano: Cassa di risparmio delle province lombarde-Editori Laterza, 1989.

Giannetti, R., and M. Vasta, eds. *Evolution of Italian Enterprises in the 20th Century*. Heidelberg: Physica-Verlag, 2006.

Goto, A. "Business Groups in a Market Economy." *European Economic Review* 19, no. 1 (1982): 53–70.

Higgins, D. M. "Forgotten Heroes and Forgotten Issues: Business and Trademark during the Nineteenth Century." *Business History Review* 86 (2012): 261–285.

Jones, G., and N. J. Morgan, eds. *Adding Value: Brands and Marketing in Food and Drink*. London: Routledge, 1994.

Lopes da Silva, T. and M. Casson. "Brand Protection and the Globalization of British Business." *Business History Review* 86, (2012): 287–310.

Lopes da Silva, T. and P. Duguid, eds. *Trademarks, Brands, and Competitiveness*. New York: Routledge, 2010.

Lopes da Silva, T. and P. Duguid. "Introduction: Behind the Brand." *Business History Review* 86, (2012): 235–238.

Lopes da Silva, T. "The Growth and Survival of Multinationals in the Global Alcoholic Beverages Industry." *Enterprise & Society* 4, no. 04 (2003): 592–598.

Lopes da Silva, T. *Global Brands: The Evolution of Multinationals in Alcoholic Beverages*. New York: Cambridge University Press, 2007.

Mandressi, F. "La nascita del caseificio industriale in Lombardia [The Birth of the Dairy Industry in Lombardy]." *Annali di storia dell'impresa* 10, (1999): 565–591.

Mantegazza, A. "Locatelli." In *Dizionario biografico degli italiani*. Vol. 65, 345–348, 2005. Mandressi: http://www.treccani.it/enciclopedia/locatelli_(Dizionario-Biografico)/

Mediobanca. *Dati cumulativi di 1743 società italiane* [Cumulative Data of 1743 Italian Enterprises]. Milano: Mediobanca, 1990.

Mercer, J. "A Mark of Distinction: Branding and Trade Mark Law in the UK from the 1860s." *Business History* 52, no. 1 (2010): 17–42. doi:10.1080/00076790903281033.

Moore, K., and S. Reid. "The Birth of Brand: 4000 Years of Branding." *Business History* 50, no. 4 (2008): 419–432.

Petty, R. D. "From Label to Trademark. the Legal Origins of the Concept of Brand Identity in Nineteenth Century America." *Journal of Historical Research in Marketing* 4, no. 1 (2012): 129–153.

Rama, D., and R. Pieri. *The European Dairy Industry: Consumption Changes, Vertical Relations and Firm Strategies*. Milano: Franco Angeli, 1995.

Sáiz, P., and P. Fernández Pérez. "Catalonian Trademarks and the Development of Marketing Knowledge in Spain, 1850-1946." *Business History Review* 86, (2012): 239–260.

Scarpellini, E. *Material Nation. a Consumer's History of Modern Italy*. Oxford: Oxford University Press, 2011.

Sicca, L. *L'industria alimentare in Italia* [The Food Industry in Italy]. Bologna: il Mulino, 1977.

Stranieri, S., and P. Tedeschi. "The Influence of the European Institutions and Policies and the Italian Dairy Sector." In *Cheese Manufacturing in the Twentieth Century. the Italian Experience in an International Context*, edited by Besana C., R. D'Errico, and Ghezzi Renato, 95–112. Bruxelles: Peter Lang, 2017.

Toninelli, P. A., and M. Vasta. "Opening the Black Box of Entrepreneurship: The Italian Case in a Historical Perspective." *Business History* 56, no. 2 (2014): 161–186. doi:10.1080/00076791.2012.745068.

Toniolo, G., ed. *The Oxford Handbook of the Italian Economy since Unification*. Oxford: Oxford University Press, 2013.

Wilkins, M. "The Neglected Intangible Asset: The Influence of the Trade Mark on the Rise of the Modern Corporation." *Business History* 34, no. 1 (1992): 66–95.

Wilkins, M. "When and Why Brand Names in Food and Drink?." In *Adding Value: Brands and Marketing in Food and Drink*, by G. Jones and N. J. Morgan. London: Routledge, 1994.

Zamagni, V. *The Economic History of Italy, 1860–1990*. Oxford: Clarendon, 1993.

The effects of producers' trademark strategies on the structure of the cognac brandy supply chain during the second half of the 19th century. The reconfiguration of commercial trust by the use of brands

Thomas Mollanger

ABSTRACT

The role of intermediaries in the distribution system of the cognac brandy trade changed with the choice of brand strategies by producers, thanks to the development of favorable legislation for property rights. Prior to the enforcement of trademark laws, consumers relied heavily upon the personal reputations of retailers in order to choose the spirits they drank. The recognition of producers' trademarks in the second half of the nineteenth century reconfigured the issue of trust by allowing producers to integrate forward into distribution and marketing and by allowing consumers to trust an entity that they did not know personally: producers' brands. They took over part of retailers' work and tried to monitor intermediaries so as to enhance their own name as a sign of quality.

Introduction

This article aims to demonstrate how the development of legislation favorable to property rights has, thanks to a set of laws on trademarks, accompanied the changes in the structure of commerce during the second half of the nineteenth century. We argue that the 'development of the brand'[1] has fostered the passage from a reputation-based model where the intermediaries (wholesalers, retailers) played a crucial role in maintaining the trust of the final customers to a more impersonal marketing-based model, where producers' brands play a substantial role in maintaining trust with consumers. This has resulted into a reconfiguration of the role of intermediaries. In other words, the role of intermediaries has changed regarding the modifications in the structure of the trade within the reconfigurations of the institutional context.

In order to substantiate our arguments, we concentrate our attention on the alcoholic beverages sector during the second half of the nineteenth century. The alcoholic beverages sector is particularly adapted in order to understand the issue of trust and reputation because, as opposed to technology-based industry, beverages belong to what has been described as "marketing-based industry."[2] A market of experience goods for some authors,[3] but one of singularities for others,[4] this sector is marked with the seal of intangibility and by the work of persuasion and conviction that players are supposed to do in order to convince consumers to prefer their goods to others.[5] The importance of intangible assets is all the more important as the nineteenth century was characterized by rising incomes and by increased competition. Cognac brandy, whisky, rum and gin were increasingly put in competition to win the favours of buyers. Therefore, the marketing work was enhanced by the necessity to convince stakeholders to prefer one type of beverage to others. The cognac brandy trade is all the more relevant as this sector is totally forgotten by historians. Apart from geographical approaches,[6] and some individual business histories, the cognac brandy trade has never been studied.[7] On the contrary, whisky,[8] sherry,[9] as well as beer,[10] have been tackled by business historians enhancing the changes in the structures of the trade thanks to the growing regulation of the markets of wines and spirits. The distributive slope of cognac brandy is totally unknown.

The nineteenth century was a crucial time in the evolution of the marketing of consumer goods. Trademarks and brands played a crucial role in this perspective. Prior to the development of brands, the distribution of goods was organized around the capacity of the retailers to produce trust. The name of the producer was rarely known at the end of a commodity chain. The institutional context was not able to ensure the quality of the goods that were distributed in the shops. In most cases, it was not the brand of the producer in Cognac that was burnt on the barrels and that was marketed in the final shops. On the contrary, wines and spirits retailers of London were creators of their own brands, often from obscure mixtures that took place in cellars or in warehouses. Therefore, to gain the consumer's trust, wines and spirits retailers used special marketing tools in order to promote, not the brands of the producers, but their own. As Mary Eschelbach Hansen did for the grain market in the United States during the second half of the nineteenth century, here we test the assumption that the personal reputation of retailers was of lesser value to create trust after the development of a trademark law in the 1870s.[11] The trust of final consumers was no longer gained by the capacity of the retailers to produce trust in their personal networks. The 'object of trust' was transferred upwards in the supply chain to the hands of producers. This was possible thanks to changes in the institutional context and in the rules of the game. Henceforth, the producer was able to enforce his name by taking the power in the supply chain. The trademark laws resulted in a vertical integration by producers into distribution and marketing. The capacity of the producer to 'brand' his goods and to create goodwill that was able to generate trust would have been impossible without institutional guarantees. It is precisely during the second half of the nineteenth century that these guarantees emerged.

The aim of our article is to understand how branding and the issue of trademarks reconfigure the issues of trust and reputation. To what extent do brands and trademarks influence the distribution and marketing of alcoholic goods? How have the laws on individual trademarks been interpreted and used by the commercial actors? How have the changes in the institutional context displaced the "object of trust" from the hands of retailers into the hands of the producers? Did trademarks replace the role played by retailers' reputation in creating trust?

To answer these questions, this study has used the complete archives of the French cognac house Hennessy (law cases, commercial correspondence, accounting books) and has been complemented with the commercial press of that time *(Ridley & Co.'s Monthly Wine & Spirit Trade Circular, Wine Trade Review)*, collections of ephemera and law reports.

This article is divided into four parts. The first part aspires to consider the relationship between the notions of trust, branding, trademarks and reputation particularly from an institutionalist perspective. The second part will describe the distribution channels of the first half of the nineteenth century and the key role played by retailers in promoting the beverages. In the third part we try to analyze the changes in the institutional context during the second part of the century, particularly the development of favorable legislation for property rights which is essential for the emergence of branding and new marketing tasks. Finally, we demonstrate what effects these changes have produced regarding the issue of commercial trust.

The issue of trust through trademarks' lens: How to link trust, reputation, trademarks and brands

The supply side of markets has mainly attracted attention from economists, business historians and economic historians.[12] This has led to the underestimation of the role of the demand side in two ways: first, by forgetting the role of the consumers in shaping the works of entrepreneurs; and second, by putting aside the importance of marketing in the rise of modern corporations. However, since the 1990s, increasing attention has been focused on the importance of intangible assets. The article of Mira Wilkins has played a 'pioneer effect' by enhancing the role of trademarks in the rise of the modern enterprise.[13]

Trademarks and brands are only one element in the vast body of what can be gathered under the umbrella of 'intangible assets'. Intangible assets were at work very early in order to produce commercial trust.[14] Studies on commercial trust by modernist historians have enhanced the role that reputation plays in the coordination of economic activities.[15] Because 'real' markets do not correspond to the model of pure and perfect competition described by economists, in order to be structured, they need devices. It is all the more important for markets where institutions do not play an important role in reducing uncertainty that weigh upon traders. Avner Greif has demonstrated how reputation, defined as information circulating through personal networks about individuals, plays a key role as a social device to detect who is dishonest and to punish opportunist behavior.[16] In the reflections on the need of imperfect markets for devices so as to function, reputation plays a central role. In other words, 'the radical uncertainty' which characterizes markets observed by sociologists and historians,[17] and which reduces the ability of economic actors to trade (by lack of information about and trust in commercial partners), requires the intervention of third parties, social or institutional (for example thanks to trademarks and brands[18]), in order to resolve the problem of asymmetric information. Reputation plays an essential role in acting as a signal on such markets so as to create trust. In his study on 'The market for lemons', Akerlof has enhanced the link between signal and trust.[19] By analyzing in detail the functioning of the market for second-hand cars and by asking how a consumer can trust the seller in a context of asymmetric information, Akerlof shows that without signals of quality, the buyer is totally unable to trust the seller because of the distrust due to the gap than can exist between the speech of the seller and the true state of the car. Over the long run, this dead-end situation can provoke the disappearance of the market because uncertainty stops economic exchange. The solution to create trust is to equip the market with devices in which the buyer can trust.[20] Among these multiple devices able to signal the quality of the goods, reputation is only one form of intangible asset that is able to produce trust between commercial partners. Akerlof also underlines market regulations, licensing practices and, of course, brands and trademarks.

In the same way as reputations, brands and trademarks are able to act as signals and to make possible the economic exchange by solving the problem of uncertainty. Trademarks can be seen as the remedy to the limit of reputation which was easily faked when extended outside the limits of the personal networks of economic actors. Traditionally, the importance of trademarks is underlined in two ways. The first concerns the consumer's interest. Trademarks act as sign of quality. They facilitate the recognition of peculiar goods and producers. Moreover, the use of a trademark transfers the liability of the economic exchange to the actor that is at the origin of the brand. It pushes the trademarks' owners to do their best to respect a constant quality. Trademarks and brands also contribute to limit the search costs on the buyer's side by facilitating comparisons. The second way consists of enhancing the interest of trademark on the producer's side. As Teresa da Silva Lopes and Paul Duguid have stated, trademarks "have the capacity to shape consumer's interests and tastes and to develop loyalty."[21] Trademarks, by their institutional (legal) recognition, allow the trademarks' owners to protect their intangible assets. Trademarks appear to act efficiently in conveying reputations that were operated in personal networks in former times. This is particularly true when distribution networks tend to extend and undermine the traditional familiarity between the seller and the buyer.[22]

As Mira Wilkins has noted, the use of trademarks in the management of intangible assets during the nineteenth century responded to changes due to the extension of markets outside of their zones of influence, where the personal reputations of locals actors played the role of regulators.[23] By recognizing the legal value of the intangible assets that were formerly embodied in reputations and networks, the institutional context allows firms to control their outputs in regions where they are not present. Trademarks and brands allow impersonal exchanges by "transferring" the object of trust from the personal contacts into a legal entity.

Trademarks and brands help to reduce costs of transactions and contribute to install trust between partners. The great advantage of the trademark system is that it offers a legal protection to the merchants who have registered their brands. Branding represents a strong weapon to take power into the supply chains and to be able to dictate the rules to the other components of the chain. The role of trademarks and reputation in gaining trust from commercial partners changed with institutional contexts. If reputation, through individual networks, plays a crucial role in markets characterized by uncertainties on the quality of the products and on the credit of the potential partners, however, with the growing regulation of markets during the nineteenth century, its role as a means of coordination is supposed to decline. In other words, the progressive regulation of markets, through growing institutionalization, would have replaced the role played by personal reputations and personal networks. The emergence of legislation favourable to property rights after the 1850s tends to reconfigure the issue of trust and reputation because it reinforces the institutional guarantees in regard to the traditional model of coordination based on reputation and personal networks. The aim of this article is precisely to understand the influence of the institutional changes of the second half of the nineteenth century, particularly the emergence of a trademark law, on the reputation-based system of coordination and, finally, on commercial trust.

The *ex-ante* distribution of cognac brandy: a reputation-based model

By 1850 the spirits trade was organized around a long supply chain, going from the growers in the Charente region to the final consumers in London or overseas (see Figure 1). This chain was lengthened due to the increase in volume of the cognac brandy trade. If specialization

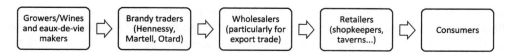

Figure 1. Diagram of Cognac brandy supply chain.

of the components of the chain in the wine and spirits' trade grew during the first half on the nineteenth century, however, each entity of the chain played a substantial role in the production and distribution of the products.

Upstream, the growers in the Charente region were in charge of choosing and planting a suitable vine variety and of cultivating it. Their task also consisted of making wine and, in most cases, they were also responsible for the distillation of the surplus harvest or by intentionally directing a portion of the harvest to distillation. Growers kept the brandies in their personal cellars and warehouses, waiting to propose samples in weekly local fairs that were held in the cantons of Charente. During these fairs, where the personal contacts played a crucial role, growers entered into contact with brandy merchants.

Brandy merchants, who were implanted in the Cognac regions, personally travelled to the fairs in order to taste the different brandy samples and to discuss the prices with the growers. These merchants collected brandies they had bought and stocked them in their own facilities. They played a crucial role in collecting the highly diverse brandies from hundreds of small family producers. The task of the merchants was, thanks to the work of cellar masters, to blend different brandies in order to create a product corresponding to the demand (the information on markets and on demand were sent to them by their agents in foreign markets who, by private correspondence, transmitted regular feedback).

The principal customers of brandy producers were wines and spirits importers (wholesalers and retailers) present in the main centres of consumption and redistribution of spirits. These importers, who also moved towards a greater specialization in the nineteenth century, placed orders with brandy merchants in the producing regions by taking into account their own stock, the state of the demand and their speculative forecasts.[24] The task of wholesalers consisted of selling wines and spirits on commission to the retail trade. In the first half of the century, they gathered different spirits in large warehouses where mixing seems to have been frequently used.[25] These warehouses played an increasing role in the world spirit trade as urbanisation grew and as London (even if declining) continued to play a significant role for the redistribution of wines and spirits for home trade and foreign markets.[26] They were subject to growing regulation during the first half of the nineteenth century, particularly in allowing the institutions to have better control over the taxation of spirits. The blending of wines and spirits held in bond in British ports was strictly controlled in the 1850s. As James Simpson remarks, it was for example illegal to blend French wines and Portuguese wines for home consumption (the legislation was less binding for wines and spirits aimed at exportation).[27] Wholesalers were an important link in connecting producers and retailers (shopkeepers, taverns, public houses) during the first half of the century.

Downstream in the commodity chain, retailers kept spirits they received in their own personal cellars in London. These cellars were the place of major manipulations in the blending and creation of spirits, in part because no legislation coerced them.[28] In order to reduce costs, or in order to create new tastes that they sold under their own names, London retailers resorted massively to the practice of mixing by emptying drums into new containers, sometimes without individualizing the origins of the spirits (on the contrary, they poured liquids into large tanks without separating the different brandies). This practice was facilitated by their key role in changing the containers of the alcoholic beverages. Until the 1870s brandy was bottled by retailers.[29] If some of them did not have recourse to mixing, this was not the case for others.[30] In his practice book dedicated to the wholesale and retail trades, Joseph Hartley enhanced the different solutions for a retailer to save transaction costs by transforming "an inferior brandy" into a brandy comparable in taste, to the top-rated brandies in the London market, those of Cognac.[31]

Such a commodity chain totally erases the name of the producers. At each stage of the chain, the product can potentially be adulterated. This situation was underlined by the type of container used by brandy merchants in Cognac to ship their goods. For the year 1849–1850, the brandy trade house Hennessy shipped to England 33,213 hectoliters in casks and only 196 hl in bottles (19,592 bottles of 0.75L). Moreover, it was not the brand name of the producer that was burnt on the casks, but the personal brand names of the importers, most of the time, only their initials. In September 1849, Richard Brothers, brandy importers of London, requested Hennessy to brand the five puncheons with the letters RB overcoming three small circles. On the same day, the invoice register of the company recorded an invoice for Walter Bovill who ordered 10 hogsheads to be branded with the initials WB. Once arrived in London, wholesalers and/or retailers changed the containers, the wholesalers by discharging liquid into large tanks and retailers by putting it into bottles. The temptation for London merchants to deliberately forget the name of the shippers was quite strong. Moreover, the demand was concentrated on young brandies, generally issued from crops which did not exceed two years. Young brandies for the year 1849–1850 represented 60% of the Hennessy's shipments in casks sent to the English market. The fact that the demand was concentrated on young brandies prevented the shippers in Cognac from respecting a constant quality, because the product of the distillation was highly sensitive to the harvest yields (which varied greatly from year to year depending on the natural conditions: frosts and vine diseases among others). In other words, the supply volatility was quite marked. As a result, there was not a strong incentive by brandy producers to sell their commodity under their own names.

In such a context, the issue of trust was based on the capacity of each element of the commodity chain to appear sufficiently trustworthy to the downstream link. Reputations in markets were achieved by the capacity of each element to meet the expectations of the commercial stakeholders. Gaining reputation within London in the premium market was achieved by quality and consistency which, in the absence of any semblance of national advertising depended on the word of mouth (personal networks). No entity was able to control the chain and to monitor the others. By simply selling their goods to foreign importers, manufacturers avoided all the difficulties and expenses of marketing to a mass of anonymous customers. Even if the public space remained fairly closed to advertising, in the few advertisements we have been able to find in the press of the first half of the nineteenth century, it was either the cognac brandy as a generic product that was highlighted, or the name of the retailers.

As James Simpson enhanced,[32] it was the reputation of individual retailers in the thousands of taverns and shops in cities such as London, Paris and New York that determined which spirits were drunk. Without institutional guarantees, consumers based their choices on the reputations of the retailers. Studies dedicated to the culture of shopping during the first half of the nineteenth century demonstrate that the task of marketing goods, of promoting them, was not invented by the manufacturers and producers but by shopkeepers and retailers. 'The manufacturer of the early nineteenth century was a man of very limited horizons.'[33] Because goods were not standardized, because no link in the commodity chain was able to control it and because no institutional device was able to guarantee the quality of the products, then, in order to supply themselves, the consumers rested upon the personal reputations of the retailers.[34] The wines and spirits market was structured around the central notion of 'clientele'. Repeated purchases were a way to ensure the reputation of stakeholders. This was all the more the case where, as we have seen, retailers were particularly open to practices of adulteration and mixing. If some retailers wanted to offer good quality products, others privileged pecuniary interests and did not hesitate to practice massive mixing and to fool customers. Wines and spirits merchants acquired an extremely bad reputation towards consumers. Scandals emerged and revealed well-crafted techniques that were able to mislead even the professionals. As a result, it is not a surprise to see the professions of wines and spirits merchants occupying the top places in the bankruptcy lists published by newspapers of the time. In order to resolve this crisis of confidence,[35] retailers used new methods of retailing and new discourses in order to enhance their integrity. Particularly by offering money-back guarantees or by enhancing scientific approvals, for example, but above all, by enhancing the origins of the products they received. To this aim, they used the names of the producers to advertise their products. Therefore, the names of producers were not total strangers to final consumers. However, no institutional regulations allowed control over the use of names. Enhancing the name of the producer was only a marketing tool in order to create trust in a market highly segmented where the question of trust was essential to solve the problem of uncertainties regarding the credit of the partners and the quality of the products. But in most cases retailers relied upon their personal reputations and skills that they developed within local communities to attract customers and to manage their clienteles.[36]

Thanks to the growing regulation of the market in the second half of the century, more particularly by the development of a trademark law that protected property rights, this 'market coordination' system, highly personalized and based on personal reputations, would undergo deep changes in what Davies has called 'the second retailing revolution.'[37] Then, as we will see, the personal character of the intermediary became less important to maintain commercial trust.

Changes in the rules of the game during the "first globalization": the evolution of legislation favorable to property rights

The growth of urbanization and the reduction of advertising taxes contributed to opening the public space more widely for business communication. The lowering of taxes on the importation of foreign spirits in England, and particularly French ones (as early as 1849 with Robert Peel, but above all with the Franco–British treaty Cobden/Chevalier in 1860), resulted in an increase in the volume of brandies in circulation. New laws on retailing (Gladstone's changes in the 1860s) multiplied the retail outlets and the consumption (for a time) of alcoholic beverages. The decreased weighting of London as a redistribution center allowed manufacturers to avoid the chicaneries in the London docks, particularly when the brandy was destined for to re-export. The improvement of living standards generated a more regular demand and new outlets for the premium market. Moreover, the context of the 'first

globalization' was characterized by an acceleration of economic exchanges, with new countries and with new economic partners. Competition increased and the need to define the
weight, the measures and the qualities on an international scale was a key preoccupation.[38]
But above all, we argue here that the major institutional change on the structure of the
cognac brandy commodity chain is the development of a favorable legislation for property
rights. Of course this change was not exclusive from the others: the passing of laws to protect
names is linked in a consubstantial way to the question of the enlargement of the frontiers
of trade. However, the appearance of a defensive property right, mainly thanks to trademark
laws, was essential for the emergence of new marketing tasks.[39]

This article focuses on the establishment of individual trademark laws. Collective trademarks are also a major component but they were not recognized until the 1890s. But even
during these years, French producers and their syndicates (as early as 1882 the Champagne
traders had their own syndicate to protect their trade) were totally unable to protect their
name abroad. That was in partly due to the difficult international coordination between
countries based on common law and countries like France based on 'codified' law. British
judges for example were totally unwilling to apply the clauses of the Madrid Agreement on
collective trademarks because the national law was not based on any precedent. We had to
wait until the first decade of the twentieth century to see the establishment of efficient
legislation of collective trademarks. As Alessandro Stanziani has pointed out, 'To sum up,
during all the nineteenth century, judicial interpretations guaranteed the protection of individual trademarks and brands but refused to take into consideration collective trademarks
and generic names.'[40] The question of collective brands received growing attention during
the last year of the nineteenth century and in the beginning of the twentieth century with
the setting of an appropriate legislation and of regional unions (the Syndicat de Défense du
Commerce des Eaux-de-vie de Cognac was created in 1901).

Trademarks, particularly in France, have a long history that is not limited to the second
half of the nineteenth century.[41] Heiresses of the corporations system, the rights to mark
were temporarily removed in 1791. However, very soon manufacturers and traders wanted
protection marks to be restored. Marks were, in their view, the only way to certify the quality
of the products that were put on the markets. Very quickly, rights were reinstated. Cutlers
and jewelers regained many of their rights in 1797–1799. The law of 22 germinal year XI
[1803] attacked the counterfeiting and usurpation of marks of artisans. This law was important because it reinforced a property right for the manufacturers. The legislation was
extended to the names of businesses and places with the law of 24 April 1824. A crucial limit
of this law was that it recognized protection only for manufactured products. Moreover, this
law concerned essentially the French case, thus offering only a very limited defence for
producers who exported their goods. This was the case with the cognac brandy trade in the
nineteenth century. The Hennessy trade house sent only 1.23% of its total output in casks
to the domestic market in 1836–1837, and 2.27% in 1851–1852.

A crucial advance in the defence of the property right for brandy merchants came with
the law of 23 June 1857. After this date brandy traders rushed to Chambers of Commerce
to register their marks. This new law sought the protection of French-owned names in foreign
countries. The nature of the countries where the marks could be registered rested upon the
diplomatic actions of the French State. Indeed, an essential preamble to the registration of
the marks in foreign countries was the agreement negotiated upstream with new states to
establish a treaty of reciprocity with regard to trade rules. The countries where brandy

merchants were able to register their trademarks rested on geopolitical bases. By the middle of the nineteenth century, a series of bilateral agreements over intellectual property was established. Russia was, in 1857, the first country with which an agreement of this kind was reached. However, the brandy trade actors were not in a hurry to register their trademarks in Russia. Hennessy waited until 1897 to register its label. More importantly for the cognac brandy trade, an agreement was passed with the United Kingdom in 1860 on the occasion of the discussions between Cobden and Chevalier for the free-trade agreement. In 1861, Hennessy thanked his London agent Twiss & Brownings for having started the process by registering its label at Stationer's Hall.[42] The treaty not only aimed to reduce the taxation that weighed upon the French wines and spirits entering the British market, but also to establish reciprocity on the subject of the property rights.[43] A bilateral agreement was also established in 1869 with the United States. Hennessy, once again, did not wait a long time to register its mark: as early as 1869 the house sent a power of attorney to its agent in the American market, Edward Blackburn, to give him the power to register the label in the Patent office of Washington. The law of 1857 was of crucial importance.

As Alain Beltran, Sophie Chauveau and Gabriel Galvez-Behar have written, 'although mod- ified in 1874, 1890 and 1920, it was a law destined to last 100 years.'[44] By adapting the laws of the property rights to the new context of the first globalization, this law was extremely useful for spirits manufacturers. However the right to register trademarks depended upon geopolitical considerations.

To find the trace of a global approach responding to the desire to standardize practices and to respond to the needs of globalization, we have to wait until the 1880s, particularly the first international conventions on property rights and trademark laws. Before these first global attempts, 'it has never been possible for businesses to draw on their home country's trademark law to protect their trademarks internationally, unless when countries where those businesses were based had formed an internationally reciprocity treaty or were part of an international convention.'[45] In 1883 the first international convention was instituted: the Paris Convention for the Protection of Intellectual Property. This convention granted reciprocal rights for registration for nationals of countries that agreed to sign the treaty. The list of signatories reveals the international dimension of the issue of property right: Belgium, Brazil, Spain, France, Guatemala, Italy, Holland, Portugal, Salvador, Serbia and Switzerland. Britain had been quite reluctant to integrate this convention because it only joined it in 1884. This convention was at the origin of the creation of the International Union for the Protection of Industrial Property. This first international meeting was followed by the Treaty of Madrid, signed in 1891, which was in line with what had been done in Paris eight years before, and the first aim of which was to facilitate the international registration of marks. 'After initial registration in their home country, a trademark proprietor could make an international reg- istration that was then passed to the required country or countries. This scheme made the international registration of marks simpler and more appealing to businesses seeking to protect their brands abroad.'[46]

The enforcement of legislation favourable to property rights through trademark law allowed the brandy merchants to enlarge their horizons by permitting them to control the distribution and the marketing of their products more efficiently. As we have shown previ- ously, the recourse to marks and brands by brandy merchants preceded the emergence of a trademark legislation. What the improvements in legislation have changed, is that they have helped to reduce the uncertainty by offering to the brandy producers a legislative device that helped them to monitor the circulation of the goods through the downstream intermediaries. This point is particularly noticeable when we try to study the court cases in which the cognac brandy trade house Hennessy was the plaintiff. Before the 1860s, the court reports in the archives of the company show that Hennessy went to the court mainly to be represented at a bankruptcy, for payment problems or for problems relating to the packaging of brandy during transport. There was no attempt on the part of Hennessy to prosecute retailers to impose its name, including in the French markets where trademark legislation was more advanced. On the contrary, after the 1860s, the name of Hennessy as plaintiff appeared more and more regarding the issue of reputation. For the first time, Hennessy systematically prosecuted the downstream links of its commodity chain who abused its name. By casting a glance at the database established by Paul Duguid on the court reports published in the commercial press that involved alcoholic beverages and by analyzing the legal archives of the Hennessy company, we have been able to identify 62 trademark cases in which Hennessy was the plaintiff between 1850 and 1910. The repartition is revealing: 11 cases between 1866 and 1873, 11 cases between 1875 and 1877, 17 cases between 1886 and 1899 and 23 cases between 1900 and 1907.

In 1869, Hennessy was the plaintiff against several Australian distributors accused of putting Hennessy cask brandy into Hennessy bottles. In 1877 the press brought out the name of Hennessy (against distributors and grocers) nine times. According to Duguid, Hennessy was the most litigious alcoholic beverage brand. As the *Wine Trade Review* reported in its edition of 15 June 1877, "Messrs. Hennessy spare no trouble or expense in prosecuting anyone who may infringe their brand." As early as the end of the 1880s Hennessy relied not only on its agents by sending them power of attorney to prosecute the forgers, but worked closely with lawyers to defend its brand. Expenditure spent on the defence of the brand was substantial: the registration and renewal of trademarks near local institutions, court fees, publication of information in the press about the risks incurred by forgers, infringement suits, contributions to transnational institution (the union of manufacturers) to send delegates on foreign markets to detect counterfeits, attorneys consultations, subscriptions to societies of trademarks' protection etc. All these elements weighed in the account books. In 1887, when for the first time a special account dedicated to the 'defence of the brand' appeared in the "Grand Livre", 17,500 francs was spent during the previous 12 months. Ten years later, the amount of expenses for the protection of the brand increased to 149,462 francs (see Table 1).

It appears that Hennessy prosecuted in order to control its packaging. Retailers resorted massively to mixing in their cellars before selling brandies under their own marks. The practice was prevalent when brandies were sent to the markets in barrels and when retailers were in charge of packaging. When Hennessy began to export in cases (mainly its best brandies[47]), the practice remained. When using both cases and casks, it reserved its best brandies ('aged' or coming from the best *'terroirs'*) for bottles, and its youngest (less than two years of aging) for casks. In 1867 Hennessy shipped 76,818 hl in casks and 21,674 hl in cases (see Figure 2). It was in 1875 that the two curves intersected for the first time. Hennessy shipped 27,901 hl in casks and 36,825 hl in cases. After 1877, shipments in cases tend to be systematically higher than the shipments in casks.

It was very tempting for retailers at first to import *Hennessy* brandy in bottles so as to stock bottles and labels, and then to import only brandies in casks (cheaper because of the lower quality) that they then used to fill the empty bottles bearing the name of Hennessy.

Table 1. Hennessy's expenditure in trademarks, 1887–1901.

Years	Expenditure in Francs
1887	17.500
1888	18.750
1889	18.750
1890	18.750
1891	18.147
1892	17.055
1893	27.740
1894	66.188
1895	69.905
1896	65.699
1897	149.462
1898	138.020
1899	97.907
1900	198.130
1901	152.998

Source: Hennessy archives, Historical Collection, Accounting Books, Grands Livres.

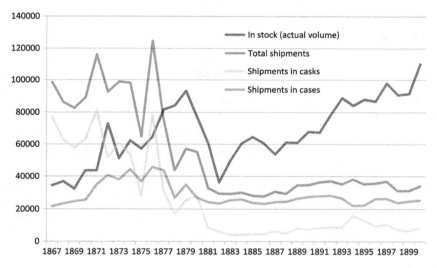

Figure 2. Shipments in casks and in cases of Jas Hennessy & Co, 1867–1900.Source: Hennessy's archives, Shipping curves.

Hennessy used the new trademark laws in order to control the packaging. Second, we note a crucial acceleration in the law reports of cases involving Hennessy as plaintiff in 1875 and in the beginning of the1890s. These trends can be explained by the turning point taken by the English courts. In the 1870s they decided to recognize and to reinforce trademark law following the Trade Marks Act of 1875,[48] and also by attempts to establish an international system of property rights at the beginning of the 1890s.

However, this institutional perspective must not convey the idea that companies are solely responsible for the construction of the markets. If the emergence of property right has enabled producers to take the power in their commodity chain, the emergence of such legislation was also decided in the name of the consumer. A lot of references enhance this idea. In 1865, the *Wine Trade Review* presented brands as a possible solution to fraud.[49] Furthermore, it is particularly telling to note that even *Ridley's* notes in the edition of January 1884 that 'the system of brands, whatever its faults may be, is supposed to act as a guarantee to the public, who are content to pay a higher figure for a branded article, rather than incur the risk of not obtaining it genuine if they dispense with the guarantee.'[50] In the same vein, the edition of 14 December 1907 of an Australian newspaper recognized the convergence of interests between proprietaries of high-class spirits and the benefit of consumers (in the name of public health): 'In other parts of the world the law for the preservation of the public health and the protection of private property in well-known brands of spirits has been vigorously upheld, with the result that the public are safeguarded in their obtaining, when required, the pure or superior spirit they ask and pay for.'[51]

Moreover, if the case of Hennessy is quite representative of the influence of the institutional changes, the use of brands and trademarks is not born with their institutional recognition. For example, the brewer Guinness was particularly active as early as the 1840s for prosecuting the imitation of its labels. As a result, the conclusion must be nuanced. If a favorable legislation had enabled the manufacturers to take control in their supply chain by being able to monitor the use of their name downstream in the supply chain, the use of the manufacturers' names had been in use since the first half of the century. What the new trademark laws had brought was a legal device that helped structurally to take control over the commodity chain.

The transfer of the 'object of trust' from retailers to the hands of producers

To what extent have these institutional changes weighed upon the classic structure of brandy distribution based on the personal reputations of the retailers?[52] Marks were in use before the establishment of trademark laws. However, by recognizing the legal value of the producers to protect their name, legislation allowed, progressively, a shift in power in the supply chain. Final customers trust not only retailers thanks to the information circulating in their personal networks, but they trust also intangibles: producers' brands. With the legal recognition of property rights, consumers can trust an entity that is not personally known to them. The progressive building of trust into the institutional context has allowed consumers to extend their judgment devices beyond their personal networks. This change of hands in the object of trust is the result of a long and slow balance of power between manufacturers and distributors.

One of the first tasks of producers after the establishment of a trademark law was to try to identify and control their outlets. Indeed, until law offered an institutional device to integrate into marketing process, a lot of brandies were stocked and circulated among different downstream stakeholders. Even if shipments of bottles grew during the second half of the century, a lot of casks continue to be sent and a significant quantity of brandies issued by Hennessy was stocked in foreign warehouses and cellars. Retailers continued to play a significant role in the packaging process of these brandies. Therefore, brandy producers had to locate this bottling abroad and to negotiate with retailers/bottlers in order to monitor their name. There were traditionally three ways for the retailers to mark the bottles they packaged: they could sell them by imposing their own marks, they could reach an agreement with the producers regarding information that can be written on the labels (allowing retailers to put their names and the names of the producers on the labels), or they can stick the labels received from the producers (mainly with only the producers' names). After the registration of its label in 1864, Hennessy tended to privilege the two last forms of labelling. Even if the trade house tended to be more integrated downstream in the marketing process, however,

Hennessy was not yet able to control all the brandies shipped by the company. In order to detect those who cheated on the labels or on the bottle contents, Hennessy had to build a very dense agency network through which information concerning markets flowed. The correspondence with the agents abroad is flooded by references to local bottling processes. As early as the 1860s, Hennessy enjoyed a partnership with the house Engs & Son, an American wholesaler, in order to package its brandies on American soil. In order to be sure that Engs & Son bottled the brandy they received in casks, Hennessy sent systematically with the casks a significant number of labels. This preoccupation to control the packaging in foreign countries was all the more important as Hennessy reserved the bottling process for its premium brandies. A retailer in a foreign market who did not respect this point could seriously damage the reputation of the producers' name.

Hennessy expressed this fear of its lack of control on its own brandies in a letter written to its London agent Twiss & Brownings in 1859:

> We are sorry to hear you have so many cases in the hands of the house at Sydney bottled in London, we have not much confidence in this mode of supplying our Brandy & we are inclined to think that it is more dangerous to our good reputation than advantageous in other respects, it would be much better to give up bottling in London with our own labels.[53]

When Twiss & Brownings reproached Hennessy for its lack of confidence in the bottling process that took place in England, the answer of Hennessy was categorical:

> it strikes us that trade mark are no longer a guarantee if they can be used by everyone ... We are aware that Messrs Bass & Co in granting to a great number of houses the privilege of using their trade mark in bottling their beer have materially increased their business, but all the 'labels' bear in a very prominent way the name of the firm which bottles, ... Mess Bass & Co had recourse to this slip when they found that it would be a perfect impossibility for them to bottle themselves the immense quantities required; it is not our case & there is perhaps not much comparison to make between the beer trade & the brandy shippers.[54]

The issue of labels was of importance because, with the increasing number of retail outlets (thanks to Gladstone's decisions), the number of sales in bottles increased significantly. Packaging brandies in bottles in the producers' region was only one way to resolve the problem. In order to control the brandies that had been shipped previously and in order to continue to meet the demand in casks, Hennessy also had to control retailers' packaging in foreign markets by ensuring that they respected the process and the labels. The decision to place the name of the producer or one of the retailers on bottles was used sparingly. Rather than erasing a name for the benefit of another, it was a combination of both that seemed to loom: 'In the writer's opinion which Mr. Thos Browning is likely to share, parties bottling ought to have their name on labels even when we allow "Hennessy's.'[55] With trademark laws, producers had to monitor the use made of their name and to enforce as much as possible their name on brandies shipped by them. What was considered as an important retailers' task in the first half of the century had become a major preoccupation of producers after the emergence of favorable legislation.

To monitor intermediaries, another element was to place the producers' names in the first line by increasing advertising.[56] The advertising of alcoholic beverages has a long history and we can find traces of it as early as the seventeenth century. The titles of the newspapers of the Ancien Regime reveal their interest in advertising: *General Advertiser, Daily Advertiser, New York Commercial Advertiser, Liverpool Commercial Advertiser*.[57] The nineteenth century is however presented as the moment when the press opened its doors more and more to the commercial press (particularly by the reduction of taxes for advertising in the early 1830s).

These new 'reputational devices' compete with traditional ways of circulating information through personal networks.[58] Even if these two ways of circulating information are not exclusive, the press offered new horizons for the communication of the manufacturers. Until the first half of the nineteenth century, when French brandy was advertised it was mainly under its generic name or under the retailers' names. When the name of Hennessy appeared in the press in the eighteenth and in the first half of the nineteenth centuries, it was only in case of new partnerships (or dissolution), in cases of prosecution (payment default) or, sometimes, in advertisements that announced the arrival of vessels transporting French brandies (it appears sometimes that the adverts mention the name of the producers). This situation endured during the first half of the nineteenth century, principally in the form of retailers' advertisements mentioning their retailing activities, sometimes underlining their integrity by enhancing the names of the producers from whom they bought.

Hennessy's expenditure during the nineteenth century is revealing. By analyzing all the account books of the company during this century, we are able to retrace the history of the company's communications. Between 1800 and 1863, no advertising cost is mentioned. It does not mean that the name of Hennessy does not appear in the commercial press of the time. But it was beyond its control. The first expenditure in advertising appears in the account books of the period 1864–1867. It is not by chance that manufacturers' interest in advertising coincides chronologically with the emergence of legislation on trademarks. In December 1864, Hennessy notes advertising expenses accrued to its Australian agent, Ross & Spowers. This case is not isolated and indicated the kickoff of a growing interest in advertising. The same expenditure appeared in 1866 and 1867. In 1871, a commission is paid to Wolfen & Co for having inserted notices and advertisements in local newspapers. The contents of these adverts are rather informative. They tended to prevent the risks of fraudulent use of bottles and brandies. These informational strategies were also persuasion strategies because they enhanced the producers' names instead of the retailers'. When the reputation of a retailer is too tainted by suspicion, its name tended to disappear in favor of the producer's name. On the other hand, when reputations of retailers are strongly established, then the name of the producer does not take the precedence over the retailers' name.

Furthermore, the process of price determination was taken away from the retailers to pass to the manufacturer.[59] Price determination was a key task of the retailers' work. Price maintenance was, for "old-style" retailers, their most important method of attracting customers and enlarging their trade.[60] The fear of Hennessy of being undersold (or oversold) was a leitmotif in the commercial correspondence. During the last decade of the nineteenth century and the first of the twentieth century, Hennessy and Martell joined forces in order to fight against the practice of underselling by retailers. They played a major role in the formation of the "Anti Cutting Association" in 1904 that aimed to discipline intermediaries. Whereas price determination was considered a key feature of the portfolio of retailers' tasks, more and more this power passed into the hands of the trademarks' owners. This would have been impossible without the legal takeover of manufacturers into commodity chains. As Susan Strasser emphasized, "with the ascendancy of branded foods, however, the manufacturers had an intense interest in what happened to their goods after they sold them."[61]

Contrary to cognac brandy producers, British brewers built special and exclusive relations with retailers. Indeed, before 1880, brewers sold almost exclusively to independent publicans. During the 1880s they sold more and more to tied houses.[62] The output was becoming increasingly concentrated in fewer firms during the second half of the nineteenth century.

This process was aided by the re-establishment of restrictive licensing laws in 1869 which encouraged brewers to secure their outlets and to acquire licensed property. Cognac producers did not use such tied houses. The comparison between the two distribution structures undoubtedly deserves more investigation. Our conclusions must be nuanced and seem relevant for the cognac brandy trade, more generally for trades where producers are situated not very far from their outlets. That was the case with brewers who were able to travel to their tied houses and to resolve disputes. An English trader could prosecute another actor on terms much broader than foreigners. Moreover, brewers were very soon able to manufacture a standard beer, particularly in the 1880s when the tied-house system grew in England. During this period cognac producers faced a huge problem of quality with the phylloxera crisis. Finally, consumption of beer was much more important than the consumption of brandy. It allowed retailers to be much more specialized than those who retailed brandies.

The increasing appearance of the producers' names in the press did not mean that the names of the retailers suddenly disappeared. The resistance expressed by retailers to the increasing weight of manufacturers in the distribution and marketing of products was tenacious. It was the case for example of Charles Tovey, an English retailer, who decided not to import cognac brandy from firms who did not wish to put his brand upon the casks.[63] In the same vein, the *Ridley's* complained in 1869 that the foreign shippers enjoyed the benefits rather than the merchants.[64]

The most reputable retailers were able to continue to sell brandies under their own brands and names. That was the case for example for the Victoria Wine and for the Gilbey companies. Both of them were able to sell brandies under the brands of the cognac shippers and under their own. A way to resist the growing power of producers' brands was also to grant a larger budget for marketing. In his study of the marketing strategies of Gilbey during the second half of the nineteenth century, Graham Reading showed to what extent the proactivity of Gilbey had not been crushed by the growing weight of producers' brands. On the contrary, Gilbey tried to adapt itself to the new commercial context and by directing its speech to consumer benefit.[65] The Victoria Wine Company, on a smaller scale, followed the same path.[66] Specialization was another answer given by retailers to the problem of mistrust they faced.[67] The question of whether or not the retail shops should sell products other than spirits, beer and wine was a current issue faced by most of the mass retailers.[68] A lot of them diverted from mass markets to concentrate on a premium market based on loyal customers.

However, not all producers intended to establish a direct link with consumers. At the sight of the growing tensions between the main cognac trade houses (Martell and Hennessy), which had a large recourse to prosecutions under new trademark laws in order to impose their names in the supply chain, and foreign wholesalers, some minor cognac trade houses tried to play on these tensions and grudges by arguing in favor of intermediaries' freedom of action. This is the case for example of two cognac companies, the Champagne Vineyards Proprietors and The Vine Growers & Co who, in their circulars, after having criticized the two giants of the trade, Hennessy and Martell, claimed: 'We again call on the Wholesale Spirit Trade not to abandon their legitimate profits as Bottlers into the hands of Cognac shippers.'[69] The content of this circular is not without strategic ambition as Hennessy and Martell gradually abandoned their shipments in barrels and increasingly resorted to prosecutions.

However, rare were retailers who sold only products under their own brands. Even the most reputable of them sold producers' brands. For example, in face of the growing powers of proprietary brands in the 1880s and in the 1890s, Gilbey's was forced to abandon its famous castle label in order to use, instead, the brands names of the producers.[70] To react to producers' integration in distribution, Gilbey tried also to integrate upstream into production by buying the long established port shippers named Croft in 1910, and by purchasing three Scotch whisky distilleries: Glen Spey in 1887, Strathmill in 1895 and Knockando in 1904. In 1895 the firm began to distil its own gin and soon the corresponding trademark, "Gilbey's Gin", became a well-known brand.

Moreover, some wine and spirit merchants succeeded in their attempts to overcome their bad collective reputation by establishing good individual reputations.[71] This depended on two major conditions. First, it was necessary to invest in intangible assets to improve their reputation. Secondly, these retailers had to focus on quality and to ensure that a brandy sold under a personal brand in Liverpool was the same as in London. They tried increasingly to standardize their products and transformed their strategies from "build to order" ones to "buyers' own brand". A lot of them were particularly fast in registering their trademarks as soon as the registrations were opened. In January 1876 Gilbey's applied for trademarks for wines, spirits and liqueurs.

The direct link that was established between producers and consumers worried trade intermediaries. In its edition of August 1869, *Ridley & Co.'s* explicitly asked "How is the middleman to exist?" In November 1889, the question of the direct link between producers and consumers still worried the wholesalers' community: 'It has long been one of the recognised, but apparently unavoidable, evils of the Wine and Spirit Trade that certain Houses ostensibly engaged in the Shipping business, should seek to go behind the back of the ordinary Merchant, and thus arrogate themselves the combined profits on the two interests. In these days when the cry is loud against the middlemen ....' In the edition of January 1870 this same review sighed over the growing interest of cognac brandy manufacturers for distribution and commercialization. However, if producers were able to communicate directly with consumers thanks to their communication and their packaging, they were not able to trade without wholesalers and retailers.[72]

How do we explain the resistance of wholesalers in a trade structure where producers were able to establish direct links with consumers without passing through the personal networks of wholesalers and retailers? Traditionally the relationship between wholesalers and retailers was extremely strong. The strength of such a relationship depended on the credit link: wholesalers gave credit to retailers.[73] This relationship based on credit was extremely difficult to overcome. Producers were not able to replace wholesalers by giving credit to retailers because they did not have sufficient resources in order to know all the traders. In this game, wholesalers were still the best. Moreover manufacturers did not necessarily want to avoid wholesalers because their personal networks helped to lessen transaction costs. As Susan Strasser has shown, when producers tried to establish direct links with retailers, wholesalers responded by buying huge quantities of generic goods on which they applied their own brands.[74]

Finally, in facing the growing power of producers' brands, retailers and wholesalers tried to gather them in order to lobby the authorities and keep some of their former functions. The question of the bottling in bond for home consumption was a crucial one. As early as 1868 the *Ridley & Co.'s* regretted that "the tendency of the trade is towards the sale of wines bottled by the shipper". Retailers and wholesalers tried to lobby and get their right to bottle from their own warehouses recognized. Merchants and brokers were worried about the fact that they were forbidden to bottle foreign wines and spirits in bond for home consumption. Finally in 1878 their claims had been received and they were again authorized, under the supervision of the customs officials, to bottle in bond for home consumption.

Conclusion

Generally, studies on trademark laws have adopted a legal perspective. What must now be put in the diaries of business historians is the question of the interpretation, the application and the uses of legal devices, particularly by focusing our attention on business archives in order to understand the efficiency of the law and its effects on business behaviour. In this respect, an institutionalist perspective can bring, we think, a real benefit. The sector of alcoholic beverages was very concerned by the issue of trademarks because these institutional devices created landmarks and acted as signals in order to create trust in an industry particularly affected by mistrust between the stakeholders. By focusing on the cognac brandy trade, a trade crucially abandoned by historians, this study tends to bring some answers.

The role of intermediaries in the brandy market changed with the establishment of new rules of the game in the second half of the nineteenth century. Until the growing regulation of the market, wholesalers and retailers played an active role in the commercialization of the products. They received brandies and were authorized to package and brand them according to their personal strategies. The manufacturer was a man of very limited horizon. He acted as a commissionaire in the service of his constituents and knew very little of the markets outside his immediate area. He relied on his personal networks of wholesalers, merchants, retailers and agents to receive information on trends and to adapt the products. His horizon was limited to the link situated directly downstream in the supply chain. The very slow communication made a possible integration into distribution and commercialization difficult. By simply selling their brandies to a principal, the manufacturers in Cognac avoided the difficulties and expenses of marketing them to a "mass market" and were not held responsible in the eyes of consumers. The key agent in such a supply chain was the wholesaler who was in charge of the physical work of distribution and took the responsibility for the product promotion.

The establishment of new 'rules of exchange' changed the traditional balance of power in the supply chain. Globalization highlighted unfair competition and problems which lead to the recognition of intangible property rights. Because trade intermediaries were accused of putting in danger the public health and because fraud became more and more common (globalization puts into competition products that were previously unaware of their mutual existence), regulation was concentrated on the question of creating trust among different stakeholders and establishing institutional benchmarks, among which were trademarks. The commercial horizon of cognac producers had been deepened[75] thanks to the growing regulation of the brandy market in a context of globalization and the omnipresence of fraud. Some of the intermediaries' functions had been taken over by manufacturers. Bottling, branding, retail price fixing and the responsibility for quality were transferred upstream to the hands of brandy manufacturers. The boundaries of the firm expanded. Agents received new powers (detection of fraud, reception of powers of attorney in order to prosecute) and new functions were created in companies (advertisers, lawyers). Producers stopped acting as agents for principals and began to play a proactive role. The study of the archives of the cognac brandy trade house Hennessy makes it possible to understand better the process of adaptation of an economic actor who was not integrated into distribution and marketing to a brand strategy. Macroeconomic data on trademarks and the analysis of the press of the time, with a concern for comparison, allow avoiding the idiosyncratic pitfalls and to enlighten the microhistory through a global lens.

By transferring upstream the liability of the quality of the products, the object of the commercial trust changed: it progressively switched from the hands of retailers to the hands of manufacturers. Consumers relied not only on personal reputations of retailers but also trusted producers' brands. From a system based on personal relations, we move towards a more 'impersonal' model where trust is not only based on personal relations but on abstract entities: producers' brands.

Notes

1. Duguid, "Developing the brand", 405–441.
2. Lopes, *Global Brands*, 326.
3. Nelson, "Information and consumer behavior", 311–329.
4. Karpik, *L'économie des singularités*.
5. Wilkins, "When and why brand?", 15–40.
6. Bernard, *Le Cognac à la conquête du monde*.
7. Butel and Huetz de Lemps, *Hennessy*.
8. Morgan and Moss, "The marketing of Scotch whisky", 116–131.
9. Simpson, "Too little regulation?", 367–382.
10. Cabras and Higgins, "Beer, brewing, and business history.".
11. Hansen, "Middlemen in the market for grain:", 59–72.
12. According to Daniel Roche, "Economic historians work especially on the side of production and manufacturing, more rarely on the side of the trade". Roche, *La Culture des apparences*, 16. See also Corley, "Marketing and business history", 93–115.
13. Wilkins, "The neglected intangible asset".
14. Fontaine, *L'économie morale*.
15. Hancock, *Oceans of Wine*; Trivelatto, *The Familiarity of Strangers*.
16. Greif, "Reputation and coalition in medieval trade", 857–882.
17. Keynes, *The Collected Writings. VIII*.
18. Arrow, "Uncertainty", 941–973.
19. Akerlof, "The market for 'lemons'", 488–500.
20. Karpik, "Dispositifs de confiance et engagements crédibles", 527–550.
21. Lopes and Duguid, "Introduction".
22. Higgins, "Trademarks and infringement in Britain", 103.
23. "When the separation between producer and buyer occurs, the name and reputation become intangible property rights that require legal support." Wilkins, "The neglected intangible asset", 68.
24. Their tendency to speculate made it all the more important that they were able to keep large stocks of brandy in huge warehouses. They were able to weigh on the exchanges and to play a significant role in the negotiations on prices.
25. *The Wholesale and Retail Wine & Spirit Merchant's Companion* written by Joseph, Hartley, first published in 1835 (republished in 1839) is particularly revealing of the taste of spirit trade intermediaries for mixing and adulterating the products they received.
26. Eaton, "Warehouses and warehouse districts", 17–26; Rose, *Firms, Networks and Business Values*, 72–73.
27. Simpson, *The Emergence of a World Industry, 1840–1914*, 92.
28. Shaw, *Wine, the Vine and the Cellar*.
29. Mui and Mui, *Shops and Shopkeeping*; Cox, *The Complete Tradesman*.
30. Mitchell, *Tradition and Innovation*.

31. Hartley, *The Wholesale*, 65–66.
32. Simpson, *The Emergence*.
33. Porter and Livesay, *Merchants and Manufacturers*, 3.
34. Wenger, *A Country Storekeeper in Pennsylvania*.; Stobart, *Sugar & Spice*; Atherton, *The Frontier*; Willan, *An Eighteenth-Century Shopkeeper*.
35. Paul Duguid noted that the profession of wines and spirits merchant, at least during the first half of the nineteenth century, was described as "the most rotten set in London".
36. Jefferys, *Retail Trading in Britain*.
37. Davis, *A History of Shopping*.
38. Stanziani, *Rules of Exchange*.
39. Chandler, *Scale and Scope*.
40. Stanziani, *Rules of Exchange*, 152.
41. Duguid, "French connections", 3–37.
42. "We are quite disposed to register our labels both here & in England but we are at a loss how to fill up the paper you have sent us." Hennessy Archives, Cognac, Historical collection, Register of letters "Twiss & Brownings", 1 March 1861.
43. Bently, "The making of modern trade marks law"; Higgins, "Forgotten heroes", 261–285; Mercer, "A mark of distinction", 17–42.
44. Beltran, Chauveau and Galvez-Behar, *Des brevets et des marques*.
45. Lopes and Casson, "Brand protection", 13.
46. Ibid., 14.
47. In 1849, Hennessy signals to its English agent Twiss & Browning: "You have sent us an order for 50 cases of New Brandy (1848) we have hitherto objected to ship such young Brandies in bottle as they can really do us no credit." (8 September 1849).
48. "By this act, registration conferred upon the proprietor 'prima facie' evidence of his right to the exclusive use of such trade mark." (Higgins, "Trademarks and infringement in Britain, c.1875–c.1900", 106).
49. *Wine Trade Review*, 18 February 1865, cited by Duguid, "Developing the brand", 411.
50. Cited by Simpson, "Selling to reluctant drinkers: the British wine market, 1860–1914", 80–108.
51. *The Newsletter: An Australian Paper for Australian People*, Sydney, 14 December 1907.
52. Akehurst and Alexander, *The Emergence*; Tamilia. "History of channels of distribution".
53. Hennessy Archives, Historical Collection, Register of letters "Twiss & Brownings", 22 June 1859.
54. Ibid., 29 October 1864.
55. Ibid., 28 March 1864.
56. Laird, *Advertising Progress*.
57. Brown, *Victorian News and Newspapers*, 15.
58. Taylor, "Privacy, publicity, and reputation", 679–701.
59. Jefferys, *Retail Trading in Britain*, 38.
60. Yamey, "The origins", 522–565.
61. Strasser, *Satisfaction Guaranteed*, 269.
62. Higgins and Verma, "The business of protection".
63. Duguid, "Developing the brand", 424.
64. Edition of August 1869. Cited by James, Simpson, *The Emergence of a World Industry*, 99.
65. Harding, "'Competition is useless'", 44–67.
66. Briggs, *Wine for Sale*.
67. Alexander, "The study"; Shaw, *The Evolution of Retail Systems, c. 1800–1914*.
68. Much, "Public houses", 1–19.
69. British Library, London, *Ridley & Co.'s Monthly Wine and Spirit Trade Circular*, January 1870.
70. Unwin, *Wine and the Vine*.
71. Duguid, "Preface: In vino veritas?".
72. Chapman, *Merchant Enterprise in Britain*.
73. Cochoy, *Une histoire du marketing*.
74. Strasser, *Satisfaction Guaranteed*, 20.
75. Koehn, *Brand New*; Tedlow, *New and Improved*.

Acknowledgement

I thank Hubert Bonin for his management, the Hennessy Company for its support and access to archives and the University of Bordeaux for accompanying me.

Disclosure statement

No potential conflict of interest was reported by the author.

References

Akehurst, Gary, and Nicholas Alexander, eds. *The Emergence of Modern Retailing 1750–1950*. London: Frank Cass, 1999.

Akerlof, George. "The Market for "Lemons": Quality Uncertainty and the Market Mechanism." *Quarterly Journal of Economics* 84, no. 3 (1970): 488–500.

Alexander, Andrew. "The Study of British Retail History: Progress and Agenda." In *The Routledge Companion to Marketing History*, edited by D. G Brian Jones and Mark Tadajewski, 155–172. London: Routledge, 2016.

Arrow, Kenneth. "Uncertainty and the Welfare Economics of Medical Care." *American Economic Review* 53, no. 5 (1963): 941–973.

Atherton, Lewis. *The Frontier Merchant in Mid-America*. Columbia, SC: University of Missouri Press, 1971.

Beltran, Alain, Sophie Chauveau, and Gabriel Galvez-Behar. *Des brevets et des marques. Une histoire de la propriété intellectuelle* [Patents and Trademarks. A history of intellectual property]. Paris: Fayard, 2001.

Bently, Lionel. "The Making of Modern Trade Marks Law: The Construction of the Legal Concept of Trade Mark (1860-80)". In *Trade Marks and Brands: An Interdisciplinary Critique*, edited by Lionel, Bently, Jennifer Davis and Jane C. Ginsburg, 3–41. Cambridge: Cambridge University Press, 2008.

Bernard, Gilles. *Le Cognac à la conquête du monde* [The Cognac, to the Conquest of the World]. Pessac: Presses Universitaires de Bordeaux, 2011.

Briggs, Asa. *Wine for Sale. Victoria Wine and the Liquor Trade, 1860-1984*. Chicago, IL: Chicago University Press, 1985.

Brown, Lucy. *Victorian News and Newspapers*. Oxford: Oxford University Press, 1985.

Butel, Paul, and Alain Huetz de Lemps. *Hennessy, histoire de la société et de la famille, 1765-1990* [Hennessy, History of the Company and of the Family, 1765-1990]. Cognac: Hennessy editions, 1999.

Cabras, Ignazio, and David Higgins. "Beer, Brewing, and Business History." *Business History* 58, no. 5 (2016): 609–624.

Chandler, Alfred. *Scale and Scope. The Dynamics of Industrial Capitalism*. Cambridge, MA: Harvard University Press, 1990.

Chapman, Stanley. *Merchant Enterprise in Britain. From the Industrial Revolution to World War I*. Cambridge: Cambridge University Press, 1993.

Cochoy, Franck. *Une histoire du marketing. Discipliner l'économie de marché* [A History of Marketing. Disciplinating the Market Economy]. Paris: La Découverte & Syros, 1999.

Corley, A. B. "Marketing and Business History, in Theory and Practice." In *The Rise and Fall of Mass Marketing*, edited by Richard Tedlow and Geoffrey Jones, 93–115. London: Routledge, 1993.

Cox, Nancy. *The Complete Tradesman: A Study of Retailing, 1550–1820*. Aldershot: Ashgate, 2000.

Davis, Dorothy. *A History of Shopping*. London: Routledge & Kegan Paul, 1966.

Duguid, Paul. "French Connections. The International Propagation of Trademarks in the Nineteenth Century." *Enterprise and Society* 10, no. 1 (March 2009): 3–37.

Duguid, Paul. "Developing the Brand: The Case of Alcohol, 1800-1880." *Enterprise and Society* 4, no. 3 (September 2003): 405–441.

Duguid, Paul. "Preface: In Vino Veritas?". In *Locating Global Advantage. Industry Dynamics in the International Economy*, edited by Martin Kenney and Richard Florida. Stanford: Stanford University Press, 2004: XIII–XXV.

Eaton, Leonard. "Warehouses and Warehouse Districts in Mid-American Cities." *Urban History Review* 11, no. 1 (1982): 17–26.

Fontaine, Laurence. *L'économie morale. Pauvreté, crédit et confiance dans l'Europe préindustrielle* [Moral Economy. Poverty, Credit and Trust in Pre-industrial Europe]. Paris: Gallimard, 2008.

Greif, Avner. "Reputation and Coalition in Medieval Trade. Evidence on the Maghribi Traders". *Journal of Economic History* XLIX, no. 4 (1989): 857–882.

Hancock, David. *Oceans of Wine. Madeira and the Emergence of American Trade and Taste*. New Haven & London: Yale University Press, 2009.

Hansen, Mary Eschelbach. "Middlemen in the Market for Grain: Changes and Comparisons". *Essays in Economic and Business History* (2000): 59–72.

Harding, Graham. "'Competition is Useless': How Gilbey's Retail and Marketing Innovation Dominated the British Wine and Spirit Market, 1857–1922." *History of Retailing and Consumption* 2, no. 1 (2016): 44–67.

Higgins, David. "Forgotten Heroes and Forgotten Issues: Business and Trademark history during the Nineteenth Century." *Business History Review* 86 (2012): 261–285.

Higgins, David, and Shraddha Verma. "The Business of Protection: Bass & Co. and Trade Mark Defence, c. 1870–1914." *Accounting, Business & Financial History* 19, no. 1 (2009): 1–19.

Higgins, David. "Trademarks and Infringement in Britain, c.1875–c.1900". In *Trademarks, Brands and Competitiveness*, edited by Teresa da Silva Lopes, and Paul Duguid, 102–118. New-York/London: Routledge, 2010.

Jefferys, James. *Retail Trading in Britain, 1850-1950. A Study of Trends in Retailing with Special Reference to the Development of Cooperative, Multiple Shop and Department Store Methods of Training*. Cambridge: Cambridge University Press, 1954.

Jones, Brian D. G., and Mark Tadajewski, ed. *The Routledge Companion to Marketing History*. London: Routledge, 2016.

Karpik, Lucien. "Dispositifs de confiance et engagements crédibles." [Trust Devices and Credible Commitments] *Sociologie du travail* 38, no. 4 (1996): 527–550.

Karpik, Lucien. *L'économie des singularités* [The Economy of Singularities]. Paris: Gallimard, 2007.

Keynes, John Maynard. *The Collected Writings. VIII, A Treatise on Probability*. London: Macmillan for the Royal Economic Society, 1973.

Koehn, Nancy. *Brand New: How Entrepreneurs Earned Consumers' Trust from Wedgwood to Dell*. Boston, MA: Harvard Business Review Press, 2001.

Laird, Pamela. *Advertising Progress. American Business and the Rise of Consumer Marketing*. Baltimore: The Johns Hopkins University Press, 1998.

Lopes, Teresa da Silva. *Global Brands. The Evolution of Multinationals in Alcoholic Beverages*. Cambridge: Cambridge University Press, 2007.

Lopes, Teresa da Silva and Mark Casson. "Brand Protection and Globalisation of British Business". *Business History Review* 82, no. 2 (June 2012): 287–310.

Lopes, Teresa da Silva and Paul Duguid, ed. *Trademarks, Brands and Competitiveness*. New-York/London: Routledge, 2010.

Lopes, Teresa da Silva, and Paul Duguid. "Introduction. Brands and Competitiveness". In *Trademarks, Brands and Competitiveness*, edited by Teresa da Silva Lopes and Paul Duguid, 1–8. New-York/London: Routledge, 2010.

Mercer, John. "A Mark of Distinction: Branding and Trade Mark Law in the UK from the 1860s." *Business History* 52, no. 1 (2010): 17–42.

Mitchell, Ian. *Tradition and Innovation in English Retailing, 1700 to 1850: Narratives of Consumption*. Aldershot: Ashgate, 2014.

Morgan, Nicholas, and Michael Moss."The Marketing of Scotch Whisky. An Historical Perspective". In *The Rise and Fall of Mass Marketing*, edited by Richard Tedlow and Geoffrey Jones, 116–131. London: Routledge, 1993.

Much, Alistair. "Public Houses as Multiple Retailing: Peter Walker & Son, 1846-1914." *Business History* 48, no. 1 (2006): 1–19.

Mui, Hoh-Cheung, and Lorna H. Mui. *Shops and Shopkeeping in Eighteenth Century England*. London: Routledge, 1989.

Nelson, Philip. "Information and Consumer Behavior." *Journal of Political Economy* 78, no. 2 (1970): 311–329.

Porter, Glenn, and Harold C. Livesay. *Merchants and Manufacturers. Studies in the Changing Structure of the Nineteenth-Century Marketing*. Chicago, IL: Ivan R. Dee, 1971.

Roche, Daniel. *La Culture des apparences. Une histoire du vêtement XVIIème-XVIIIème siècle* [Culture of Appearances. A History of Clothing, XVII-XVIIIth Century]. Paris: Le Seuil, 1991: 16.

Rose, Mary. *Firms, Networks and Business Values. The British and American Cotton Industries since 1750*. Cambridge: Cambridge University Press, 2000: 72–73.

Shaw, Thomas George. *Wine, the Vine and the Cellar*. 2nd ed. London, 1864.

Shaw, Gareth. *The Evolution of Retail Systems, c. 1800-1914*. Leicester: Leicester University Press, 1992.

Simpson, James. "Selling to Reluctant Drinkers: The British Wine Market, 1860-1914." *The Economic History Review* 57, no. 1 (2004): 80–108.

Simpson, James. "Too Little Regulation? The British Market for Sherry, 1840-90." *Business History* 47, no. 3 (2005): 367–382.

Simpson, James. *The Emergence of a World Industry, 1840–1914. Creating Wine*. Princeton: Princeton University Press, 2011.

Stanziani, Alessandro. *Rules of Exchange. French Capitalism in Comparative Perspective, Eighteenth to Early Twentieth century*. Cambridge: Cambridge University Press, 2012.

Stobart, Jon. *Sugar & Spice. Grocers and Groceries in Provincial England, 1650-1830*. Oxford: Oxford University Press, 2013.

Strasser, Susan. *Satisfaction Guaranteed. The Making of the American Mass Market*. New-York: Pantheon Books, 1989.

Tamilia, Robert. "History of Channels of Distribution." In *The Routledge Companion to Marketing History*, edited by D. G. Jones Brian and Mark Tadajewski, 173–202. London: Routledge, 2016.

Taylor, James. "Privacy, Publicity, and Reputation: How the Press Regulated the market in Nineteenth Century England." *Business History Review* 87, no. 201 (2013): 679–701.

Tedlow, Richard S. *New and Improved, The Story of Mass Marketing in America*. New-York: Basic Books Inc, 1990.

Trivelatto, Francesca. *The Familiarity of Strangers. The Sepharadic Diaspora, Livorno, and Cross-Cultural Trade in the Early Modern Period*. New Haven & London: Yale University Press, 2009.

Unwin, Tim. *Wine and the Vine. An Historical Approach*. London: Routledge, 1996.

Wenger, Diane A.. *A Country Storekeeper in Pennsylvania. Creating Economic Networks in Early America, 1790-1807*. University Park, Pennsylvania: The Pennsylvania State University Press, 2008.

Wilkins, Mira. "The Neglected Intangible Asset: The Influence of the Trade Mark on the Rise of the Modern Corporation." *Business History* 34, no. 1 (January 1992): 66–95.

Wilkins, Mira. "When and Why Brand Names in Food and Drink?". In *Adding Value. Brands and Marketing in Food and Drink*, edited by Geoffrey Jones and Nicholas J. Morgan, 15–40. London: Routledge, 1994.

Willan, T. S. *An Eighteenth-Century Shopkeeper. Abraham Dent of Kirkby Stephen*. Manchester: Manchester University Press, 1970.

Yamey, Basil. "The Origins of Resale Price Maintenance: A Study of Three Branches of Retail Trade". *Economic Journal* 52 (1952): 522–565.

Disney in Spain (1930–1935)

Jose Bellido and Kathy Bowrey

ABSTRACT

This article looks at the ways in which the global brand par excellence – Mickey Mouse – spread throughout Spain in the early 1930s. In tracing the creative and commercial interplay with the Mickey character we show how the Disney Company failed to obtain any significant intellectual property rights in its own name or obtain a sympathetic hearing by Spanish patent and trademark officials. Yet this was undoubtedly a period of significant global development of the Disney brand. With the attempt to explain such an apparent contradictory situation, this article highlights the importance of the management of particular struggles in the flux of desires, appropriation and investments that contributed to the emergence of the elusive 'merchandising right'.

'The route taken by Mickey Mouse is more like that of a file in an office than it is like that of a marathon runner.'[1]

Introduction

Today it is common for Mickey Mouse to be characterised as one of the most important, if not *the* most important, intellectual property assets of the modern era. The iconic status enjoyed by the character has led to the adoption of Mickey Mouse as the quintessential North American rodent, let loose by the Disney corporation upon the rest of the world.[2] Global familiarity with the character provides an opportunity to talk about the extension, globalisation and congestion of intellectual property rights, serving as a magnet for criticism and political claims about the nature and extent of corporate and legal power wielded over our everyday lives.[3] However, this reading has eclipsed many interesting historical angles, and in particular the ways in which a whole new set of contractual arrangements and business configurations were put in place to support the emergence of this figure as a global merchandising legend, and how these arrangements interacted with the development of intellectual property practices.

By looking at the specific case of Spain, this article explores the rise of Mickey Mouse from trademark to brand. Our study challenges the ways in which business history scholarship has focused on the importance of intangible rights to the development of the multinational and growth of global consumerism. Although we agree on the importance of trademarks to the emergence of the multinational firm,[4] we think that there is a tendency to oversimplify the processes by which trademarks become intangible assets of the multinational corporation. The presumption underpinning much of that literature is that North American firms were naturally entitled to trademark protection in overseas territories and could easily obtain registrations and enforce these overseas with relative ease. We would like to move away from any idealised role of law presented there, where brands are often depicted as the development of legal 'rights' asserted by the multinational. The distinction between the trademark and the brand has become common in marketing literature.[5] It is described by Stefan Schwarzkopf in the following way. The trademark is treated as 'a purely legal entity, operating in a commercial context'; and the brand is 'embodied in icons which are protected by trademarks, while being embedded in cultural as well as commercial contexts'.[6] The strength of the distinction is derived from its attempt to draw attention to the importance of managerial and advertising expertise and other cultural factors that underpin trademark value, awareness and longevity. Again, we are sympathetic to this objective, but we think that in relegating the trademark to the 'purely legal' sphere, the distinction often fails to capture the historically specific forms of relations emerging between culture, economy and the law that caused intangible properties to become valuable. This is especially interesting in the case of the Disney corporation in Spain, as the company did not own any of the significant trademarks or design rights, or enforce any copyright protection, in the period we study – and yet the Disney brand still succeeded. This suggests that we need to look more carefully at the dynamics of the interrelationship between property and contract and the logistics that enabled and shaped the internationalisation of intellectual property 'rights'. In particular, it is important to explore the ways in which appropriation and investment coalesced historically and how trademark and licensing arrangements facilitated the making of business configurations that contributed to the rise of the global brand.

International intellectual property in the early 1930s

At the outset it is important to note that there were two relevant treaties in this era for the protection of North American intangible property abroad. The Paris Convention for the Protection of Industrial Property (1883) afforded protection to patents, trademarks and industrial designs of nationals of convention countries, on the same terms as available to their own citizens.[7] The US joined the convention in 1887, which meant that North American firms could apply for patent, design and trademark registration in accordance with the laws that applied in the jurisdiction where they sought protection.[8] As we shall see, in the early 1930s Disney did not seem particularly interested in applying for design or trademark protection in Spain. However, a high degree of enthusiasm for the popular film character led to extensive commercial appropriation and assimilation of the character into Spanish folklore. Following from this, significant trademark registrations and design rights came to be held by Spanish traders. But when Disney complained, the rights of domestic traders were upheld by Spanish officials. It is therefore important to follow the history of these local traders who first manufactured Disney products and registered trademarks and designs to support their trade in order to consider how their profile and alignments rapidly changed at a very early stage.

The Berne Convention for the Protection of Literary and Artistic Property (1886) was the treaty that facilitated international copyright protection. Although the US had not signed this copyright treaty, the Berlin Revision of 1908 provided a 'backdoor' solution for North American authors and artists.[9] Non-signatory countries could qualify for protection by issuing identical release dates for the publication in the US and a Berne Union country.[10] American authors and artists were also entitled to protection under Article 50 of the Spanish Copyright Law 1879, following US recognition of Spain as a 'proclaimed country' from 1895.[11] However, they were only entitled to protection as known to Spanish copyright law. It was not at all clear that cartoon characters which began their life as artistic works or drawings, known to the Spanish public through reproduction on film, could be protected from unauthorised industrial application.[12] Contrary to the contemporary understanding of 'intellectual property' as one comprehensive legal category that protects a wide array of intangible creations and products, in this era there was no such umbrella construct. Furthermore, as Bently and Sherman have discussed, the two international intellectual property treaties contributed to a bifurcated perception of legal rights, and along with this, a distinction between original authors and inventors and their respective protections.[13] In turn, they were seen as piecemeal and limited avenues of protection, depending upon an intangible creation's precise origin, form of manifestation and technicalities of specific copyright, design, patent and trademark laws.

In the 1930s, outside the established book, newspaper and music publishing industries, few corporations had the strategic insight and the managerial infrastructure in place to arrange for effective foreign copyright protection, even assuming that this was available for film characters. Yet what our study reveals is how rights and relations were still able to be asserted through licence agreements entered into with local manufacturers and traders, regardless of the formal legal credentials of Disney's copyright and industrial property ownership claims. These processes of negotiation and selection of local traders that had already established a market advantage led to the initial deployment of Disney agents and the appointment of licensees who ironically became more interested in trying to control the circulation of Disney products in Spain than Disney itself. In fact, as we shall see, licensees developed a more active role in opposing further Spanish Mickey registrations immediately after their appointment. So, rather than narrating a clear development of legal protection and expansion underpinning the transition from trademarks to brands, this history shows a more complicated assemblage of contacts, arrangements and appointments. Despite (or precisely because of) the limitations of intellectual property protection in Spain, the interactions between Disney and local commercial enterprises triggered a set of particular relations in which the object or property transacted was not just the use of a sign but the timely provision of specific services, publicity and information regarding the availability of Disney characters. The establishment of distinct managerial and contractual arrangements with affiliated local traders fragmented and dispersed earlier playfulness with the character. Combined with the rise of the international advertising firms that coordinated publicity campaigns and releases, these business and legal strategies helped secure a strong connection between Mickey, Disney and Disney-affiliated enterprises. Marketing ventures centring on licensed products, magazines and catalogues captured the imagination of fans and channelled goodwill into modes of consumption that served to reinforce authorised readings of signs, precipitating a shift from trademarks to brands and making the idea of a global franchise possible.

In tracing the ways Disney adapted to the cultural, legal and business conditions of 1930s Spain, we show the importance of managerial strategies, the emergence of commercial and legal infrastructures, and the contingent use of 'borrowed' local knowledge and expertise, to the emergence of international brand consciousness in the early twentieth century. We argue that contrary to what is often claimed by Disney's many critics, the remarkable success of the enterprise was not attributable to the unfolding of any grand corporate plan lying behind Mickey's endless iterations, set loose from a Californian home base. Rather, the enterprise was, for its time, unusually adept and flexible in embracing and enrolling local interests and enterprises open to business negotiation and collaboration that allowed the firm to capitalise on relevant manufacturing and trading opportunities, developing new forms of professional marketing and licensing expertise. Sensitivity to cultural, legal and economic contingencies was central to this success. It was the variety of these connections, modulations and interactions, more than any development of international intellectual property protection, that laid the foundation for the far more extensive intellectual property claims that came to distinguish the enterprise later in the twentieth century.

Of mice and magic

In December 1930 Carlos Gea contacted a distinguished trademark agent, Alfonso Ungría,[14] with the idea of registering a peculiar sign in the Spanish Patent and Trademark Office.[15] Gea was a well-known figure of the citrus industry in Valencia,[16] one of those entrepreneurs who had contributed to making the fruit desirable all over the world.[17] Although the fruit came from orange groves near Valencia, its production was mainly destined for export.[18] So, he decided to distinguish his products with a pictorial representation of a mouse, described in his application as 'popularised on films'.[19] That mouse was none other than the famous character Mickey, with the long shoes and the oval buttons on his shorts. The following legend was inscribed above this figure, in case of any doubt: 'Mickey Oranges' (see Figure 1).[20] The application was particularly significant because trademark registrations, printed labels and artistic design packaging were among the material features that allowed oranges to shift from simple agricultural products to marketable commodities.[21] If there was one product or trade that epitomised Spain in this period, it was the orange.[22] These Valencia oranges were for international distribution and the first Mickey trademark registration in Spain was in class four of the nomenclature: oranges.[23]

Gea's interest in the packaging of his oranges for export shows the international spread of an American 'paradigm shift' in the packaging and marketing of mass market and consumer products.[24] If there was an association that could make the products more attractive to the consumers, and in particular to Americans, it was the celebrity of the moment: Mickey Mouse.[25] In developing the international market for citrus, Gea sought to combine the local and the global, to create a 'context of consumption'[26] by linking the local product to a famous image to catch the attention of distributors and consumers. Less than two weeks after the application, 'Mickey Oranges' was published in the Spanish official trademark gazette.[27] No opposition was filed and having passed all the requirements stipulated in the corresponding trademark law,[28] the application was successful.[29] In February 1931 a registered trademark was granted to Carlos Gea for 'Mickey Oranges'. This was the first Mickey Mouse mark introduced into the Spanish Patent and Trademark Office and Gea was given a certificate of registration that constituted a *juris tantum,* a rebuttable presumption that the

Figure 1. Spanish registered Trademark 83,398.
Courtesy of Archivo Histórico OEPM.

property right noted on the register was valid.[30] Soon another application followed suit. This application came from a rival citrus entrepreneur from the same province.[31] However, there were some differences in the label design. Instead of a verbal reference to the character, the new application relied on an overall visual connection, showing the delightful mouse juggling oranges.[32] In order to avoid being held confusingly similar, the application transliterated the word 'mouse' ('maus') and dropped one letter to become 'Micke' (see Figure 2).[33] However, these efforts were not enough. Although crate labels decorated with Mickey in full juggling mode captured the trade connection even better than the first sign, arriving a few weeks later at the office meant that the registration was limited to fruits *except* oranges.[34]

The chances of making a difference in a competitive marketplace resided not in having an exclusive right to a Mickey mark but in the productive use of the figure to advertise products. Mickey was so popular a film character that, as with Felix the Cat a few years

Figure 2. Spanish registered Trademark 84,619.
Courtesy of Archivo Histórico OEPM.

earlier,[35] he generated a marketing craze. Throughout the early 1930s images of celebrities were used to advertise a huge range of products, including sweets and other junk food available for purchase, much of which was individually wrapped and sold in corner stores. For instance, one American parenting manual from 1928 was so concerned by the health implications of this development that the book recommended mothers combat children's resistance to unhealthy foods by mastering the art of 'selling food to children' themselves: 'Why not name a few dishes after these heroes? Why not 'Babe Ruth's Home Plate' or 'Mary Pickford's Beauty Compound'?'[36] This strategy was suggested as the foundation for an ambitious campaign to get children to eat spinach three times a week. Spanish Mickey fruit labels reflected a similar interest in 'updating' the image of traditional foods, such as the humble orange, in the face of the increasing availability of new manufactured snack foods. Soon, Pedro Monsonis, another well-known citrus entrepreneur from the same Spanish region,[37] labelled his oranges with trade material depicting two Mickeys pulling a giant orange apart.[38] His label also included what some commentators have identified as a trademark constant: the introduction of quality indicators (see Figure 3).[39] Another key figure in the Spanish citrus industry, José Ventura, also tried to create an emotional attachment to his products by using the figure of the lovable mouse. Ironically, the proliferation of similar signs and the particular dynamic context from which these marks sprang paved the way for a creative contest in

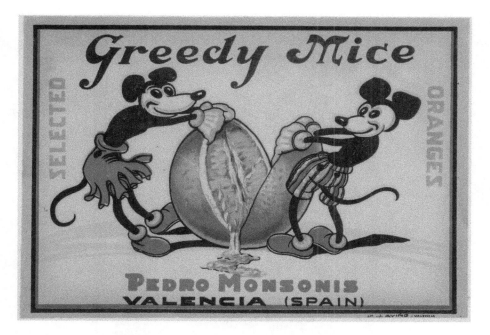

Figure 3. Pedro Monsonis (Valencia) – Unregistered Label.
Courtesy of Rafael Llop.

which the victorious protagonist was undoubtedly Mickey. In popular terms, the mouse had definitely defeated the cat (see Figure 4).[40]

While fruit labels began as marketing tools directed at retailers and distributors, with the trademark most visible on the packing crates, Mickey was also deployed as a signalling device to individualise oranges themselves.[41] In 1930, a citrus export group from Valencia and Alcoy was granted permission to install a new machine that issued silk and tissue paper to wrap and pack oranges.[42] For some citrus entrepreneurs, Mickey became an ideal mark to be used in orange wrappers because he could distinctively personalise the humble, individual orange. Moreover, his popularity was imagined to be a magnet to attract the consumer's eye to their oranges, marking their goods out from the near identical produce of the other traders.[43] The sign was specifically designed to help distinguish the oranges in fruit shops. In that sense, it marked a crucial stage in the transformation of oranges into commodity products.[44] Since crates were easily discarded by retailers or distributors, enfolding the orange in wrapping paper helped the trademark to survive shipment contingencies. As we can see from the illustrations, both crate labels and orange wrappers appealed to the foreign eye.[45] The accompanying messages were not written in Spanish but in the language of the importing country in which these oranges were going to be sold. [46]

Mickey was seen as a naughty, magical film star, a distinctive cultural artefact that came to represent an object and an anthropomorphic subject in one. He was described by American film critic, Leonard Maltin, in these terms: 'Now his eyes had irises and pupils, which meant that they looked more realistic, more human and could effect a greater range of expression, perhaps it might be imagined that Mickey Mouse was also in possession of a soul.'[47] Anthropomorphism has been well studied in anthropology, psychology and

Figure 4. José Ventura Oranges (Alcira) – Unregistered Label.
Courtesy of Museo de la Naranja de Burriana.

marketing literature.[48] As evidenced in cave drawing and folklore, attributing human qualities to inanimate objects was considered a universal phenomenon. It helped children interact with and relate to the non-material world and to understand the social order.[49] Anthropomorphism was, however, also particularly useful to advertisers who, by their selection, sought to invest otherwise mundane goods with a range of emotional qualities to make them appear more interesting and attractive. In trademark terms figurative marks were readily recognisable, often bearing known qualities that can be appropriated to the product that adopts the sign.[50] However, whilst traditionally the tiger, for example, might signal strength, the arrival of cinema brought with it the capacity to communicate emotional qualities on a mass, cross-cultural scale.

A glance at these fruit labels and orange trademarks evidences what Henry Jenkins once described as the logic of emotional intensification that shapes most popular culture.[51] Mickey was interviewed, had birthdays and cool fan clubs.[52] The character was simultaneously traded, read and transacted. In that specific sense, Mickey was a feisty companion to play with, to learn and to have 'fun' with. The broader media interest in Mickey, making the mouse 'one of us',[53] was a trend highly visible in Spanish newspapers and magazines.[54] This cultural activity only further invested registered and unregistered Mickey-inspired trademarks with commercial value wherever the reportage extended, and this in turn encouraged further appropriations.

The uses of enchantment

Mickey's media ubiquity generated distinctive local effects. Imaginings of the mouse were quickly merged with local folktales, stories, and myths already in place in Spain. For instance, newspapers reported Mickey's engagement in traditional festivals.[55] To some extent it could be argued, as Rosemary Coombe suggests, that 'texts protected by intellectual property laws […] are cultural forms that assume local meanings in the lifeworlds of those who incorporate them into their daily lives.'[56] Yet there is an important issue to be noted here: as discussed above, there were no Spanish intellectual property rights held by Walt Disney in the early 1930s.[57] Disney lodged no trademark or design registrations. Copyright in an artistic work did not prevent industrial uses of a derivative design. Neither was a corporate strategy clearly established to directly profit from the mouse beyond the money the animated cartoons could generate outside of the US. There were some ad hoc merchandising arrangements in place across Europe, such as the licensing of a Mickey Mouse doll made by the British company Deans and Sons in 1929,[58] where Deans had registered the design rights in their own name.[59] More permanent arrangements were beginning to be considered with Disney's engagement of an agent, William Banks Levy, in London in 1930.[60] Levy had previously worked as general manager for Powers Cinephone, a company that manufactured sound equipment for the cinema that was used by Disney from 1929.[61] He was tasked with licensing Mickey in the UK.[62] There was a similar arrangement with US toymaker Georg Borgfeldt & Co, who had also registered German Mickey trademarks in association with Disney in 1930.[63] Yet for the most part Disney was playing catch-up in Europe – reacting to, rather than initiating, international merchandising activity. In this regard, although North American corporations were effectively exploring patent pools and seeking trademarks which impacted upon the development of various industries,[64] in this era the activity appears to have been limited to attempts at developing managerial control over the technologies of mass manufacturing abroad. It needs to be noted that one of the techniques adopted in the 1930s that aided syndication by allowed for a speedy Trans-Atlantic transmission of imagery was the dry mat or matrix.[65]

Contemporary cultural studies and intellectual property scholars often criticise Disney as housing corporate plans to appropriate and homogenise national folklore, particularly after the success of the film *Snow White and the Seven Dwarfs* (1937).[66] But the dynamic in Spain was precisely the opposite. There was no plan to appropriate traditional narratives and folk tales. However, Mickey's popularity unintentionally brought the mouse into interaction with local myths and legends. Suitably nicknamed 'Ratón Miguelito',[67] the first encounter the Spanish Mickey had with a local narrative was with another anthropomorphic mouse: a character from an anonymous fairy tale legend known as '*Ratón Pérez*'.[68] Unlike Mickey, Pérez was a tooth fairy in a tale that had its origins in oral tradition and had made an appearance in the printed world via a book written by Luis Coloma in 1902.[69] The meeting between mice was so productive for the Spanish and Latin American media that some commentators rebranded Mickey (or Miguelito) as Ratón Pérez, while others preferred to think of a battle between them.[70] These games of free association also influenced some corporate attempts to register a new Mickey trademark. In the summer of 1931 the Spanish Patent and Trademark Office received a trademark application depicting a grotesque version of Mickey Mouse playing the fiddle (see Figure 5).[71] While it is possible to recognise the Mickey image from the film released by Disney in 1930,[72] the striking point to note here is that the application

Figure 5. Spanish registered Trademark 86,388.
Courtesy of Archivo Histórico OEPM.

was not made by the US company itself but by a company located in Barcelona, the record and publishing company Odeon S.A. Represented by the doyen of Spanish trademark agents, Alberto de Elzaburu,[73] the application was for a label to be applied on discs in order to distinguish a song written by Harry Carlton.[74]

Curiously, and somewhat ironically, the trademark combined the names Mickey Mouse and Ratón Pérez to fix the connection in the mind of Spanish consumers.[75] However, the impression did not last. No Spaniard today would identify Mickey with Pérez. Each mouse came to lead a distinctive commercial life. A plausible explanation as to why the two characters came to be distinguished over the years is not to be found by reading the records of the law courts. No case was ever brought to delineate what was public and what was private around any intangible property rights that could be claimed. However, it might be possible to hypothesise an answer outside of positive law.

In the 1920s and 30s cinemas would rent films from distribution companies, and film trade magazines and 'film exploitation services' provided creative marketing advice and advertised strategies to independent cinema owners to accompany new and popular releases.[76] With the arrival of children's films and Saturday children's matinees, children-centred social activities were also encouraged. These could involve talent contests, competitions, fancy-dress and tie-ins with local businesses. The Mickey Mouse fan club owes its heritage to this practice.[77] Though presented as innocent, family-oriented community activity, it is a good example of the commodification of play, where spontaneous, 'natural' social behaviour of children that has little direct economic value comes to be organised into social activity that is much more economically productive. The fan club and the overall interest in Mickey played a critical role in constructing a distinctive cultural popular icon, a media personality, consequently helping to differentiate the authorised character from that of other local legends.[78] Fan clubs provided an opportunity for the social regulation of fans. Guided by the Disney campaign booklet, the clubs helped promote desired readings of the character and to 'correct' unwelcome local associations, such as the connection with Ratón Pérez. Fan clubs played a normative role in delineating property boundaries and investing trademarks with preferred meaning. By 1932 Mickey Mouse clubs boasted more than a million members.[79] Spain was not an exception.[80] The Mickey fan club not only contributed to making sales,[81] it facilitated Mickey's universal appeal at the grassroots, removing the cultural resonance of local attempts to ascribe different characteristics to the popular figure so he could 'correctly' function as an international brand. Clubs were, however, only one of the important means by which consumers were directly linked to the production, marketing and distribution of Mickey Mouse as a distinctive form of intangible property.[82]

Toys, sweets and biscuits

Toys, cigarette cards and sweets associated with popular children's film characters were an obvious tie-in.[83] As Kenneth Brown has recently noted in relation to toys, all these objects constitute the epitome of a modern consumer good: 'a non-essential item subject to a demand that fluctuates not only with the availability of disposable income but also according to the whims of popular taste and fashion'.[84] The commercial value of tie-ins was noted by Roy Disney: 'The sale of a doll to any member of a household is a daily advertisement in that household for our cartoons and keeps them all Mickey Mouse Minded.'[85] The orange trader's distinctive marketing plan was significantly undermined when Spanish candy bars bearing Mickey Mouse also emerged to compete for consumer attention. Mickey also started to take the form of distinctive toys, locally made. One citrus entrepreneur astute enough to see profit in these media flows was Rogelio Sanchís Bernia (1888–1936), who supplemented his citrus trade by making toys in a small town in the region of Valencia.[86] In the late 1920s his toy company, La Isla, was getting a name for making distinctive toys representing Hollywood film and cartoon stars such as Felix the Cat, Laurel & Hardy and Buster Keaton.[87] Immediately after Mickey was released, he incorporated the mouse into his portfolio of tinplate sparklers and wind-up toys (see Figure 6).[88] What made these toys remarkable was not that they were – as one collector says – 'the finest Disney wind-ups ever made'.[89] Rather, their most interesting feature was how they became to be considered as 'Disney toys'. The combination of distinctiveness and local imagination was not only attractive to children – Disney representatives in Europe appear to have been so enchanted with Rogelio's toys that, instead of suing him, they decided to enrol him as a licensee.[90]

It should be remembered that it would have been difficult for Disney to sue. The La Isla toy could not be described as an unauthorised appropriation of Mickey or a 'piracy', given that Disney had still failed to register any trademarks or design rights in Spain, and the scope of copyright protection for industrial objects was at best, undetermined. Indeed, if Disney

Figure 6. Minnie Mouse carrying Felix in a cage (R.S. La Isla Toys).
Courtesy of Hake's Americana & Collectibles.

had lodged applications for industrial rights, as will be discussed shortly, it is not clear how any registrations would have been determined. Yet, such was the confidence of the Disney company's entitlement to authorise all Mickey-related enterprise that in September 1934 the new Disney representative for Spain, Portugal and Italy, Pierre de Beneducci, granted La Isla one of the first Disney licences for Spain.[91] While close analyses of early Disney contractual arrangements are scarce, probably due to the restrictions of access imposed by corporate archivists and lawyers,[92] these documents are an invaluable source for considering the ways in which intellectual property 'rights' were conceived, negotiated and constituted in this period. The Spanish 1934 contract appears to have been Disney's main attempt to assert intangible 'rights' over what were aspirationally described as 'Disney creations'. This generic term elides the legal definitional problem of the rights constituted by the agreement. The content of the rights came to be defined by the business practices engaged to commodify the 'creations'. Interestingly, Disney placed itself under the specific obligation to provide samples and models that might be suitable for character merchandising to the licensee. In return, La Isla conceded by giving Disney the right to approve the Disney products they created. The constant exchange of information and materials authorised by the contract created a dynamic logistical network that generated the possibilities for exploitation and creation of 'intellectual property' value. Although the contract included a security clause, the commission fee paid by the Spanish licensee was significantly low (5%), a term that surely made the engagement attractive to the local manufacturer. Another element that made the contract particularly interesting was the careful way in which it limited the scope of the right to manufacture 'Disney creations'. Disney framed the right as only covering tin plate and mechanical toys. This confinement followed a similar logic to that of the trademark registry, carving out the specific goods and services for the constitution of a trademark, while leaving open the potential for other exclusive licensing arrangements that could arise utilising other equipment and plant.

In sum, the La Isla contract illustrated an early Disney synergistic business practice,[93] an attempt to strengthen the marketing chain by enlisting entrepreneurs who were already manufacturing Disney products locally. Rather than being a threat, unlicensed Spanish 'pirate' activity initially helped develop the value of the Disney brand in Spain. It made more commercial sense to work with existing channels and bring them into the fold. Outsourcing manufacturing also avoided the administration and costs associated with tariffs on imported goods and with establishing new distribution and retail chains.[94] This low-key strategy allowed the company to quickly and efficiently establish a presence in new areas, connecting the US company with a much broader class of goods and services. An association with Disney was facilitated, regardless of the actual origins of the product design and manufacturing. Instead of using the law defensively, an informal use of intellectual property claims served as a framework to set up the conditions for international production and distribution going forward. These local engagements are also credited with providing a feedback effect for Disney's future creativity. As Forgacs has observed:

> [I]t is likely that the success of character licensing and merchandising, which took off almost immediately after the film debut of Mickey Mouse in 1928, played a part in shifting Disney animation towards both cuteness and a more 'family'-oriented product because it demonstrated the potential of the toys and gadgets market as a source of additional revenue. The syndication to newspapers and magazines of cartoon strips (handled by King Features Syndicate) and the licensing arrangements with foreign publishers probably reinforced this feedback effect on the Studio, because they confirmed the worldwide success of the core Disney characters (Mickey,

Goofy, Donald, the Three Little Pigs) and encouraged the Studio to produce more characters like them who could undergo development in the comics and consumer goods markets. [95]

After the citrus entrepreneurs, the second wave of businessmen to come to the Spanish Patent and Trademark Office, hoping that a registered Mickey would distinguish their products, were the makers of biscuits and sweets. A confectionary manufacturer successfully registered the trademark 'Miki' for biscuits in 1933.[96] One year later, biscuit entrepreneur María Bea Biosca visited the patent and trademark office with similar ambitions.[97] The subject of her trademark application, a humorous drawing of Mickey Mouse with large hands and open mouth,[98] successfully passed the bureaucratic hurdles and the trademark was granted on 14 January 1935.[99] Presumably both traders applied for a trademark thinking that they had found a novel means to attract customers – real sales appeal of particular interest to children and families. However, the surprising thing is that after making the effort to navigate the bureaucratic process of registering the trademarks, both renounced their rights to their marks in 1935.[100] This action is most astonishing in the case of the second applicant, since she abandoned the trademark only two weeks after obtaining it.[101] Neither party gave an explanation as to why they had so suddenly and completely renounced their rights; it is plausible to surmise that they did so after feeling the pressure of a licensed network that was spreading across Spain, a spider's web of licensing and associated income streams underlying intangible properties. The culturally imperialistic implications of this acquiescence to Disney's ambitions were publically acknowledged when a satirical magazine in 1934 commented: 'the Arab domination in the peninsula in comparison with Mickey's expansion is a historical joke.'[102]

Globally licensed networks

Less than a decade after Mickey was born, lawyers came to recognise him as 'one of the most powerful merchandising forces in the world'.[103] And as Jane Gaines declared much later, it is a paradigmatic, textbook example of the productive use of intellectual property.[104] Disney had built a network of licensees by forging alliances locally,[105] and had developed the ambition to succeed as an international business. However, rather than reading this as the origins of a distinctive West Coast or American hegemony, we would draw attention to the role of local collaborations, networks and expertise that was central to the development of Disney's licensing activity. Global cultural awareness of this modern corporation originated from turning ad hoc relations between the US filmmaker and local businesses into a more orderly and controlled web of association. As we have seen, business ventures originated with free play that sought to capitalise on the popularity of the Mickey character in Spain, at a time when centralised control by the company was impossible. Foreign corporate enterprises were much better suited at that time to reading local demand and servicing production, wholesaling and retailing. For Mickey marks to become truly productive for Disney as a distinctive global brand that they controlled, there were other important developments and trade connections that needed to occur. The maturation of commercial dynamics that assisted Disney in securing control is best explained with reference to a particularly innovative commercial venture that took place in the early 1930s. An alliance was formed between Lambert Pharmaceutical, toy and card publisher Waddington, and Disney (See figure 7). Spanish children were given a free paper mask when their parents bought them a tube of a particular branded toothpaste (a product of increasing importance, perhaps, given the dental cavities that must have formed following the consumption of too many Mickey sweets

Figure 7. Mickey's Spanish mask (Lambert Pharmaceutical, Waddington and Disney). Courtesy of UCL Photography Department.

and biscuits!).[106] Combining the commercial forces of a toothpaste manufacturer, a paper maker and an entertainment company is an excellent example of market penetration through creative, specialist novelty marketing to children.[107] The trick of making toothpaste 'kid-friendly' was a smart advertising idea that worked well for all three parties involved.[108] Exactly the same campaign was simultaneously launched in distant places such as the United Kingdom,[109] Australia,[110] and New Zealand.[111] While it was a significant premium-based strategy in which incentive-gifts were given to consumers promoting brand loyalty, the idea of having a globally synchronised campaign was highly innovative.[112]

There are (at least) two features underlying this marketing scheme that need to be highlighted. First, the campaign could only take place thanks to the global expansion of multinational advertising agencies that had occurred in the late 1920s.[113] The infrastructure and connectivity of multinationals such as J. Walter Thompson (JWT) and their local correspondents appear to have been crucial to forging these innovative trade alliances.[114] Secondly, the masks given away (and the ads that announced them) were among the first products in Spain to incorporate the legend, 'Authorised by Walt Disney Enterprises'. Simply by giving licensed Mickey and Minnie masks for free, Disney cemented ties with consumers and educated them into the protocols of consumption. In that sense, the advertising scheme helped to shift the balance of forces in the company's favour, enabling trademark licences to become advertising tools in themselves, and in turn allowing for the further professionalisation and growth of the advertising industry in marketing 'premium brands'.[115] This facilitated the development and internationalisation of trademark practice in the following decade.[116]

That Spanish licensees perceived a change in commercial culture as being underway can be seen in trademark disputes that arose after the mysterious trademark withdrawal of the first biscuit purveyor, mentioned above. Three days after Biosca renounced her trademark on 4 February 1935, another biscuit manufacturer applied for a Mickey trademark.[117] The applicant was a company named Loste, headquartered in Tarragona and one of the best-known Spanish biscuit manufacturers of the twentieth century.[118] Curiously enough, a covering letter from the Disney representative in Europe, Pierre de Beneducci, was part of their application.[119] The letter was directly addressed to the comptroller, letting him know that they had granted the company an authorisation to use and register Mickey Mouse as a trademark in Spain for confectionary, chocolates, candies and jams.[120] Unsurprisingly, the application was opposed by the holder of the trademark 'Miki', who had been producing biscuits so labelled since 1933. He argued that there were phonetic, conceptual and visual similarities between the marks that precluded the granting of the new application under section 124.1 of the Spanish Industrial Property Code (1929).[121] Despite the force of his argument, it is unclear whose rights would have prevailed as a matter of law because, again, there was an intriguing and sudden trademark withdrawal before the decision of the comptroller was made.[122] Combined with the earlier examples, this was clear evidence of a reluctance to let the comptroller publically decide who owned what rights, in favour of the parties coming to terms under a veil of confidentially. This raises the notion of licensing arrangements operating as a form of private registration of rights, with, in the event of litigation, a practice of coming to terms with the other side to ensure the minimum amount of public oversight.

In 1934 Disney launched an annual merchandising catalogue.[123] It listed licensed products and manufacturers. It also included notation of the European branches established to manage the rights available to facilitate further licensing and revenue streams.[124] The production of an annual catalogue reinforced the idea that discrete products were connected through a chain of authorisation of 'rights' managed by Disney's agents, and that opportunities were to be constantly renewed. Over time, this coordination also made possible the idea of 'standardisation' of the Disney range. According to cultural historians and collectors, 1935 was 'the most successful year ever known to the manufacturers of the Walt Disney Character Merchandise'.[125] The curating of Disney product into a catalogue not only increased the number of products bearing Disney characters and made it easier for retailers to source desirable merchandise;[126] it also led to a new integration between products and signs that mushroomed in the Spanish marketplace and abroad.[127] It affected the meaning of signs, heralding a shift from production to merchandising, from trademark to international brand. Rather than the mark operating as a sign attached to particular goods and services, it was increasingly associated with the much more abstract, affective properties of the Mickey character which was coming to be represented in essentially the same way across the globe.[128] Mickey products such as paper masks were not just given away with toothpastes to influence purchasing choices about a particular branded toiletry product.[129] Branding came to dictate consumer choice in a different way to the past. Originally a label and recognisable trademark merely helped to communicate fitness for purpose and the source of the product, and to allow for consumer past experience to be brought to bear on consumption choice. But through the management of brand associations a chain of signs became a much more complex conduit of cultural meaning and 'symbolic capital' through its association with the Disney brand. As Pierre Bourdieu has noted:

> This economy demands a social world which judges people by their capacity for consumption, their 'standard of living', their lifestyle, as much as by their capacity for production. It finds ardent spokesmen in the new bourgeoisie of the vendors of symbolic goods and services, the directors and executives of firms in tourism and journalism, publishing and the cinema, fashion and advertising, decoration and property development.[130]

Character merchandising assisted in the development of symbolic capital, to the mutual advantage of all the authorised producers and manufacturers that appeared in the catalogue. The specific toothpaste, for instance, could then be distinguished by a characterisation and meaning that was beyond the reach of competitors. In exchange, the Disney brand was further universalised and entrenched in the global consciousness. This activity led to a complex overlaying of meanings associated with signs, and this complexity 'empowered' consumers in their consumption choices, allowing them to playfully engage with brands within the confines of corporate-sanctioned associations. Disney continued licensing without necessarily resolving all potential conflicts or obstacles posed by rights to other marks on the register and in the marketplace, and without registering its own marks across a range of classes of goods and services. Their ambiguous legal status in Spain produced more than one headache for newly established Disney licensees. In the last months of 1934 and the beginning of 1935 there were contenders, who were encouraged because there remained nothing on the register in Disney's name.[131]

Walt Disney, from Barcelona

Not everybody who applied for a Mickey trademark withdrew or abandoned their application. In March 1934, José Geis Bosch went to the patent and trademark office to register a beautiful trademark in class 44 (textiles) depicting not only Mickey but also his girlfriend Minnie (see Figure 8).[132] His application too, was opposed. What made this opposition different from the cases mentioned above was the profile of the opponent. The opposition was not raised by a Disney licensee but by Disney himself. Walter E. Disney, astonishingly described as a subject domiciled in Barcelona, formally opposed Geis Bosch's application.[133] He claimed to be the creator of the two beloved characters as evidenced by the posters and adverts he forwarded to the office. The applicant, Geis Bosch, did not desist in his attempt to register, and submitted a forceful response that attacked the form and the substance of Disney's opposition. In fact, the awkward way in which Disney had opposed the application indicated a weakness which was of strategic advantage to Geis Bosch.[134] Disney's self-description as the creator and proprietor of the characters enabled the applicant to argue a significant point of law. A trademark was an industrial property right, where ownership came from local use and registration of the sign. This was not about copyright, which arises with authorship.[135] The submission of adverts and posters for films only underlined a lack of documentary proof to support a trademark opposition. Since there was no trademark certificate that could challenge the application, Geis Bosch was granted the trademark a few months later.[136]

Another trader who frustrated Disney in registering a Mickey trademark in the Spanish Patent and Trademark Office was Manuel Osa. In November 1934, he applied for a Mickey trademark consisting of an original drawing of the mouse pouring a sparkling beverage into a narrow glass with the legend 'always order the delicious aperitif' (see Figure 9).[137] Despite (or because of) the application being limited to aperitifs and carbonated drinks, his attempt to register a trademark was opposed by Walt Disney.[138] Interestingly, Disney now included in his opposition an appendix with a copy of the US copyright certificate he received in 1931.[139] Instead of withdrawing the application, Osa defiantly contested the opposition to his application. He homed in on three major issues. Firstly, echoing Geis Bosch's argument, he used the lack of Spanish trademark registrations held by Disney as a touchstone to

Figure 8. Spanish registered Trademark 86,388.
Courtesy of Archivo Histórico OEPM.

interrogate the basis of this opposition. Secondly, he criticised the ongoing Disney licensing practices in Spain as an attempt to create a de facto monopoly which, if sanctioned by the comptroller, would undermine the very logic of trademark registration which limited rights to particular classes of goods and services. Thirdly, he suggested that a pending trademark application, recently submitted by Disney for a magazine for children, was the appropriate scope of any intangible property right Disney should be given, if any.[140] Additionally, Osa drew attention to the existence of a variety of Mickey orange trademarks already on the

Figure 9. Spanish registered Trademark 101,116.
Courtesy of Archivo Histórico OEPM.

register.[141] Osa's (or his trademark agent's)[142] argumentative strategy proved successful.[143] The comptroller determined that the lack of previous registered Spanish trademarks by Disney precluded him from opposing Osa's application.

These major defeats put Disney international licensing practices at risk. From this time onward Disney representatives paid much more attention to their trademark strategies and the contractual arrangements underpinning them in Spain.[144] In February 1935, Disney opposed a trademark application lodged by the famous Italian publisher Lotario Vecchi.[145] Although Vecchi had agreed with the Disney agent to withdraw his application,[146] Disney still filed an opposition, presumably as a shot across the bow of other traders. The defence was unnecessary since Vecchi had already withdrawn his application.[147]

Whilst legal struggles concerning trademark were a most frustrating experience for the Disney company, there were also problems with design rights. In February 1935, Disney had tried to register the mouse as a design (see Figure 10),[148] a move the company had made in several countries.[149] In Spain, the application did not go as smoothly as expected. It faced two powerful oppositions.[150] The opponents used a repertoire of arguments to persuade the comptroller of the need to reject the application as non-compliant with the technicalities

Figure 10. Spanish Design Application 482.
Courtesy of Archivo Histórico OEPM.

of Spanish law. This included highlighting that Walt Disney was obviously not resident in Barcelona, and thus in accordance with Spanish design law was not entitled to apply for industrial property protection.

A challenge was also mounted to the novelty of the design, a legal requirement akin to originality in copyright that prevented monopoly rights being granted to familiar shapes and appearances of commodities that could stifle competition. It was argued that the huge exposure of the Mickey Mouse films, advertising and other merchandise meant that any claim to novelty in the appearance of the character had long since expired. In one sense, this turned Disney's evidence of his claim to ownership against him. The development of a large and successful licensed network (and unlicensed uses) of 'intellectual property' ironically prevented him from claiming the requisite level of novelty required to register his own design right. Still, Disney insisted on submitting a copy of the US copyright certificate, which predictably led to the distinction between copyright and industrial property again being raised as an obstacle to the registration.[151] Finally, the lack of specification of the class of goods and services in which his design was going to be applied was also highlighted as an impediment to registration. Disney's application for an industrial design failed; however, an application for an artistic design was granted in December 1935, recognising the existence of a Disney representative in Barcelona. From these examples it is clear that the Spanish people truly loved this mouse, across many iterations. However, from a legal point of view, the most interesting aspect to note is that the first steps of Disney in Spain were marked by a significant struggle to ascertain *any* rights against local entrepreneurs. There was an initial successful resistance to the expansion of the Disney empire. Rather than assist Disney's ambitions, Spanish copyright and industrial property law was initially helpful in maintaining local rights and activities against the claims of the larger US corporation. But Disney was able to mobilise those local rights and capitalise on them to create an infrastructure for his international enterprise. This raises an important but familiar question about the relationship between law, culture and economy.

Conclusion

In legal literature there is a presumption that law is not only master of its own domain, but also rules over social and economic life, dictating what is possible and policing infringements and violations. Many business historians have also followed this approach. However, whilst culture and economy do not operate in ignorance of this legal will to power and influence, as the first years of Disney in Spain show, there has always been a wide scope for selection, negotiation, mediation, indifference and resistance. This essay shows how productive those processes were, without necessarily disrupting the orderly appearance of the established categories of copyright, design and trademark. While Spanish law did not appear to advance in this period to facilitate the growth of international trade, processes of appropriation, collaboration and investment advanced nonetheless, repositioning simple agricultural produce like oranges to link them to and develop a cultural economy. Thus we argue that in this period the most significant legal changes to appreciate are not those that occurred on the surface of the positive law, but the legal and commercial practices that emerged alongside it.

Our brief historical account appears to evidence a business shift in the early twentieth century – significant changes in activities and orientations whereby manufactures came to support merchandising, advertising and distribution. Along with this shift there was a corresponding change underway in the genealogy of signs, from trademarks to brands. The two are often perceived as encompassing different traditions and patterns of circulation; to signify different relationships and values. While trademark affords legal rights, associated with particular signs and attached to nominated goods, and later services, brands have been frequently defined as far more amorphous entities. Counter-intuitively, trademark ownership was not essential for effective licensing of the marks, probably to avoid being bogged down in legislative differences manifested in comparative trademark law throughout the twentieth century. Brands generated meaning and authority from their deployment and interactions with traders and the public. Accordingly, we argue that the significance of the Disney corporation as a metaphor for the evolution of intellectual property laws should not be read in terms of the idea of Disney as an aggressive rights holder from the start, stifling creativity and competition across time and space, with the advantage of a privileged position before the law. Rather, the company exemplifies a much more complex and remarkable achievement – turning a small mouse character into a famous brand and able to capitalise in the way the sign came to imbue ordinary, everyday objects and experiences with symbolic meaning. In doing so, the most important strategy was surely collaborative in nature, enrolling and learning from local entrepreneurs, consumers and manufacturers already in place before Disney's definitive corporate arrival in Europe by the mid-1930s.

Notes

1. Benjamin, *Selected Writings*, 545.
2. Kozinsky, "Mickey and Me"; Litman, "Mickey Mouse Emeritus"; Heald, "Testing the Over-."
3. Grzelak, "Mickey Mouse & Sonny Bono Go to Court"; Posner, "Response"; Depoorter, "The Several Lives."
4. Wilkins, *The Maturing* and "The Neglected Intangible"; see also Chandler, "The Emergence" and *Scale & Scope*.
5. Aaker, "Dimensions of Brand Personality"; de Chernatony and MacDonald, *Creating Powerful Brands*.
6. Schwarzkopf, "Turning Trademarks into Brands," 165.
7. Article 2 of the Paris Convention (1883); for a discussion, see generally Ricketson, *The Paris Convention* .
8. Seely, *History of the International Union*, 7 .
9. Jacobson, "The Question," 422.
10. Colino, "Copyright Protection."
11. Solberg, "Copyright Enactments," 92; see also the Spanish Royal Orders of March 1906 and 26 June 1914 regarding the copyright registration of North American citizens in Spain; Fernández Mourillo, *Legislación y Propiedad Intelectual*, 131–132.
12. Design protection of Mickey Mouse was not sufficient in the UK; see Anon., "Mickey Mouse in Court." For a similar comment on the possible existence of a legal gap, see Cabello Lapiedra and Martínez Garcimartín, *La Propiedad Industrial en España*, 123.
13. Sherman and Bently, *The Making*, 162.
14. Ungría, who had been a diplomat, became a member of the Spanish Institute of Trademark and Patent Agents in 1929, see letter Ungría to the President of COAPI, 11 September 1929 in COAPI Archives. His patent and trademark agency was founded in 1891; see 'Advert' *Diario La Vanguardia*, 1 November 1929, 4; see also Ungría, "Ley y Práctica en materia," 13–31.
15. Power of Attorney from Gea Uberos to Ungría, Valencia, November 1930; File 83, 398; AHOEPM.
16. 'Obituary' *Diario ABC*, 4 August 1972, 74.
17. Vicente Abad notes that the zenith of the Spanish orange exports was 1930; see Abad, *Historia de la Naranja*, 249.
18. References to agricultural trademarks with a suggestion that they could have been regulated differently can be found in Peraire, *La marca de fábrica. Comentarios a la legislación vigente. Jurisprudencia civil y penal* 23.
19. Trademark application from Carlos Gea Uberos, 3 December 1930, File 83, 398; AHOEPM.
20. Description of the application; File 83, 398; AHOEPM.
21. See Hudson-Richards, *The Orange Proletariat*; see also Arroyo, *Las etiquetas naranjeras*; Mir, "Etiquetas de alimentos. Frutas. Miscelánea" ; EPH/554(1)-EPH/554(18) in BN.
22. On the debate concerning the citrus industry as the main source of Spanish national wealth in the 1930s, see "La calidad de la naranja exportada," 6; Malboysson, "El maravilloso espectáculo," 25–27. That oranges conquered the Spanish imaginary is also reflected in novels (Ibañez' *Entre Naranjos*) and mascots (the 1982 World Cup mascot organised in Spain, was unsurprisingly, an orange).
23. Sánchez Pérez, *La Propiedad Industrial*, 233.
24. Twede, "History of Packaging," 117–119.
25. See *revista Gutiérrez*, 6 December 1930, 18–19; "Cosas del Cine," *La Vanguardia*, 3 January 1931, 14 ["The Star That Interests Us Now is Mickey Mouse"]; "Ecos y Noticias," *La Vanguardia*, 1 May 1931, *16*; Abad, "The Orange Trademarks," 126 (these marks had the 'clear intention of promoting the consumption of these marks among the infant population, offering at the same time the possibility of collecting different scenes of their favourite characters printed on the paper where the oranges were packed up').
26. Arvidsson, "Brands: A Critical Perspective."
27. *Boletín Oficial de la Propiedad Industrial*, X; for some references to the institutional history of trademark law in Spain, see Sáiz and Fernández Pérez, "Catalonian Trademarks."

28. *Estatuto sobre Propiedad Industrial*, aprobado por Real Decreto-Ley de 26 de julio de 1929 (Industrial Property Code, approved by Royal-Decree Law, July 1929).
29. Certificate of Registration, 21 February 1931, File 83, 398; AHOEPM.
30. See Ladas, *Patents, Trademarks, and Related Rights*, 1067.
31. Trademark application from Enrique Dealbert Nebot, File 84,619, AHOEPM, filed 11 March, 1931.
32. Description of the trademark, Enrique Dealbert Nebot, File 84,619 AHOEPM, filed 11 March, 1931.
33. Trademark Application, File 84,619; AHOEPM, filed 11 March, 1931.
34. Certificate of Registration, File 84,619, AHOEPM filed 23 July, 1931. Trademark law requires traders to stipulate a class of goods to which a particular mark will be applied and further tries to prevent a monopoly emerging that could restrict the rights of other traders in that class by allowing for more fine-grained delineations of rights for competing marks.
35. Felix the Cat and Mickey Mouse both began their corporate lives with the same New York agent, Jack Warner's former secretary, Margaret [Mintz] Winkler. See Canemaker, *Felix*, 89–95.
36. *Mother's Own Book*, 61.
37. Caballer, "Enrique Monsonís, un liberal convencido"; *Diario El País*, 8 October 2011; see also Monsonís, *Memorias incompletas* and Monsonís "Extrema preocupación."
38. Lit. J. Aviñó. Valencia, 1930. See also Mir, "Etiquetas de alimentos. Frutas. Miscelánea," 184 .
39. Abad, "The Orange Trademarks," 125.
40. De Mantilla, "Las películas de dibujos animados," 7; Centeno, "Dibujos Sonoros," 17; Gómez Mesa, *Los films de dibujos animados*.
41. For a history of these packaging devices, see Karp, "Orange Wrappers," 119–124. See also some brief comments in Hyman, *Oranges. A Global History*, 52–53.
42. Comité Regulador de la Industria del Papel, *Gaceta de Madrid*, 192, 11 July 1930, 272.
43. 'A new advertising advance was the printing of marks on the silk papers where oranges were packed up; so the advertising of a particular trademark could come sooner to consumers, who could ask for them at their particular fruit shop, if the orange had their quality requirements' in Abad "The Orange Trademarks," 125. See also Abad "La publicidad naranjera," 382.
44. Franck Cochoy has traced the material agency of 'packaging'; see Cochoy, "A Brief Theory." See also Pottage, "No (More) Logo."
45. As Vicente Abad notes, some traders 'worried about designing their marks according to the tastes of the markets to which they were addressed' in Abad, "The Orange Trademarks," 125.
46. Trademarks and labels written in a foreign language were accompanied by the name of the manufacturer and his or her locality as stated in Peraire, *La marca de fábrica*, 39.
47. Maltin, *Of Mice and Magic*, 40; as cited in Leslie, *Hollywood Flatlands*, 32.
48. See for example, Brown, *Human Universals*; Baker, *Picturing the Beast;* Levy, "Dreams, Fairy Tales, Animals, and Cars."
49. Fournier "Consumers and Their Brands," 344.
50. Mollerup, *Marks of Excellence*, 128.
51. Jenkins, *The Wow Climax*, 3.
52. Escobar, "Mickey y Minnie: dos actores internacionales" *Diario El Sol*, 4 June 1933, 8; "Aniversarios-El del nacimiento de Mickey Mouse" *La Vanguardia*, 21 October 1933, 10; "El aniversario de Mickey Mouse", *La Vanguardia*, 1 December 1934, 15; "Mickey Mouse ha cumplido ya siete años" *La Vanguardia*, 14 September 1935, 15; "Como se celebrará en el extranjero el aniversario de Mickey Mouse" *La Vanguardia*, 17 September 1935, 17.
53. "Introduction" in Craig and Morra-Yoe, *The Art of Mickey Mouse*, 8.
54. "El Teatro y el Cinema" *Ellas*, 4 September 1932, 13; "Mickey visita la exposición de Chicago" *La Vanguardia*, 30 November 1933, 12; "Quizá la sorpresa más grande que tuve durante el viaje fue al tropezar con Mickey y Minnie en Manchuli. Allí estaban, de tamaño natural y casi como quien dice coleando […]' *La Vanguardia*, 11 December 1934, 19; "Mickey demuestra entender en mecánica," *La Voz*, 18 December 1934, 7.
55. "Mickey Mouse admira las fallas valencianas" *Mundo gráfico*, 26 April 1933, 16.
56. Coombe, *The Cultural Life*, 7.

57. This is rather surprising since it is now commonly accepted that 'Mickey was created after the Disney Brothers Studio lost the rights to Oswald the Lucky Rabbit,' in Peterson, "Disney, Walt (1901–1966)," 272; see also Bain and Harris, *Mickey Mouse*, 12; Maltin, *Of Mice and Magic*, 34.

58. Tumbusch, *Disneyana*, 35; Miller, *The Dean's Rag Book Company*, 48–53. See also generally Cope and Cope, *Dean's Rag Books*.

59. Design Registration Number 750,611, Class 12; BT52/1,435; NA, filed 6 December 1929.

60. Johnson, Ehrbar, and Ghez, *Inside the Whimsy Works*, 47–48.

61. Kellogg, "History of Sound Motion Pictures," 356.

62. 'George Kamen appointed….' *Playthings*, July 1933: 60.

63. See Gerstein, "Mickey Mouse Annual"; Ghez, *Disney's Grand Tour*, 22; Barrier, *The Animated Man*, 83.

64. Serafino, "Survey of Patent Pools."

65. Bellido "King Features Syndicate, Inc. and Betts v O. & M. Kleemann Ltd. (1940)," in Bellido, *Landmark Cases*.

66. Zipes, "Breaking the Disney Spell."

67. *La Vanguardia*, 9 September 1934, 12; Chapman, "Mickey Mouse and Other Things," 271–272.

68. "El Ratoncito Pérez (Mickey Mouse) se une a los Artistas Asociados" *La Vanguardia*, 1 May 1931, 16; "Todo el mundo conoce al saladísimo Mickey Mouse, o sea el Ratoncito Pérez" in "Ecos y Noticias" *La Vanguardia*, 16 June 1931, 19.

69. See, generally Pedrosa, *La historia secreta del Ratón Pérez* .

70. Fernando G. de Mantilla 'Las películas de dibujos animados' *El Imparcial*, 7 September 1930, 7; Carlos Fernández Cuenca, 'Las películas de dibujos' *La Época*, 15 January 1931, 3; 'Mickey Mouse admira las fallas valencianas' *Mundo gráfico*, 26 April 1933, 16; Bayardi, *Ratón Pérez*.

71. Description of the trademark, Odeón, SA, File 0,086,388; AHOEPM, Filed 28 July 1931.

72. The film was *Fiddlin' Around*. See Maltin, *Of Mice and Magic*, 345.

73. Power of Attorney from Odeón, SA to Elzaburu, 21 July 1931, File 0086388; AHOEPM; the firm (Elzaburu) was founded in 1865 and was one of the most active members of the International Association for the Protection of Industrial Property since the late nineteenth century; see "Asociación Internacional para la Protección de la Propiedad Industrial" *Industria é invenciones*. 28 May 1898, n. 22, 11; see also de Elzaburu "Comentarios sobre Propiedad Industrial" *El Sol*, 5 July 1924, 6; Annuaire de l'Association internationale pour la protection de la propriété industrielle 4 (2) 1932: 77.

74. Holliss and Sibley, *Mickey Mouse*, 23.

75. "El famosísimo disco Odeón Ratoncito Pérez (Mickey Mouse) lo vende Zato, Peligros, 14" in "Noticias e Informaciones Diversas," *diario ABC*, 28 December 1930, 71.

76. 'Publicity in Practice' *The Bioscope Service Supplement*, 7 November 1928, iii; 'Selling Angles' *The Bioscope*, 12 November 1930, 31–33; 'An ideal set of publicity aids' *The Bioscope*, 18 February 1931, xiii; 'Selling the Picture to the Public. Goodwill and How to Get it' *The Bioscope*, 9 August 1929.

77. 'The principle elements of the Mickey Mouse Club scheme were outlined in a general campaign booklet published in 1930 by the Disney Company. According to the plan, exhibitors would arrange a series of Saturday matinees for children, organizing the audience for these matinees into a club built around the character of Mickey Mouse. … The club programs were not designed simply to appeal to children, but to incorporate as fully as possible the cultural activities within a community' in deCordova; "The Mickey in Macy's Window," 207.

78. See Martínez, "Apuntes para una historia de los tebeos."

79. Alcacer & Collis, "Walt Disney Company"; Thomas, *The Walt Disney Biography*, 80; Watts, *The Magic Kingdom*, 147.

80. *La Vanguardia*, 3 February 1933, 13.

81. Pellisier, "Making Sales Through Clubs," 40.

82. For an insightful reference to the first years of merchandising and the changing managerial attitudes developed by Disney, see Gadducci and Tavosanis, *Casa Disney*, 9–11.

83. As a trade journal noted in the summer of 1930, 'Mickey Mouse means business' *The Fancy Goods Trader*, July 1930, 9; see also "La enorme popularidad del ratón Mickey," *La Vanguardia*, 12 May 1933, 16.
84. Brown, *Factory of Dreams*, 110.
85. Roy Disney as quoted in deCordova, "The Mickey in Macy's Window," 205. DeCordova notes 'the Disney Company was interested in the publicity value of these items as much as the substantial royalties they would generate'.
86. 'In 1926, Sanchís started up a tin toy company at the castle, naming the firm 'La Isla.''I don't think he had any previous experience in toy manufacture,' said Wengel. 'He started in fruit packing and somehow got interested in toys. That's amazing, because the toys are of such great quality and are so complex,' in Saunders-Watson, "La Isla Toys," 20. See also generally 'Rogelio Sanchís' Oranges Fruit Crane Label' in RS.
87. Lobel, "Spanish Dancing Sparklers," ; Sellés, *Juguetes valencianos*; Avilés, *Informe*, 6.
88. Saunders-Watson, "La Isla Toys"; see also Wengel and Wengel, "Origins and Examples," 36–40.
89. Saunders-Watson, above., 22; Hillier and Shine, *Walt Disney's Mickey*, 45 ['As far as character toy making in Spain is concerned, Rogelio Sanchís is the beginning and the end. He was a genius at designing and producing toys']. See also Hendeles et al., *Partners*, 21; Bock, *Exhibiting Trauma, 29–31*.
90. Contract between Walt Disney Enterprises and Rogelio Sanchís; 6 September 1934 in RS. It is also worth noting that the cheeky incorporation of a caged Felix the Cat, carried by a mouse, in the toy clearly speaks to the supremacy of the newer character on the scene.
91. For an interesting reference to Beneducci's role in Italy, see Gadducci, Gori, and Lama, *Eccetto topolino*, 86. Disney distributed Europe into two territories and appointed two representatives. While Beneducci was in charge of Portugal, Spain and Italy, William Banks Levy and then George Kamen, were appointed to manage Disney merchandising in London; see Munsey, *Disneyana*, 81–85; see also the contract appointing Beneducci as the Disney representative in Southern Europe in 'Mondadori – 1934–1974, bb. 3' in AME.
92. On the history of these archives, see Smith, "The Walt Disney Archives."
93. Wasko goes further to claim that with Disney, 'synergy' involves establishing an 'architecture of merchandising' in Wasko, *Understanding Disney*, 159. However, we would argue that in this era the arrangements lacked the degree of solidity or permanence suggested by her structural metaphor.
94. The US Depression era 'Smoot-Hawley' Tariff Act 1930 increased tariffs on over 20,000 items, leading to retaliation by America's trading partners including Spain, who removed most favored nation treatment. See Jones, *Tariff Retaliation*, 34–67.
95. Forgacs, "Disney Animation," 366.
96. Trademark Application, File 0,093,620; AHOEPM, filed 17 March, 1933.
97. Trademark Application, File 100,578; AHOEPM, filed 27 September, 1934.
98. Description of Trademark, File 100,578; AHOEPM, filed 27 September, 1934.
99. Trademark Certificate, File 100,578; AHOEPM, filed 14 January, 1935.
100. Instancia de Renuncia, File 0,093,620; AHOEPM, filed 9 July, 1935.
101. Instancia de renuncia, File 100,578; AHOEPM, filed 1 February, 1935.
102. Huertas "Mickey y sus 55.000 amigos" *El Periódico de Catalunya*, 15 November 1998, 41.
103. Berle and Sprague de Camp, *Inventions and their Management*, 563–564.
104. Gaines described Mickey as a 'merchandising legend' in Gaines, *Contested Culture*, 158.
105. For a wonderful history of early Disney marketing in the US, see deCordova, "The Mickey in Macy's Window," 203–213.
106. "Una careta de Mickey Mouse o Minnie Mouse la obtendrá gratis con cada tubo que adquiera de crema dentífrica Listerine (con la autorización de Walt Disney-Mickey Mouse Ltd)" *La Vanguardia*, 28 December 1933, 6; 'Ya hay de nuevo caretas' *La Vanguardia*, 24 April 1934, 2; 'Ya hay de nuevo caretas' *La Vanguardia*, 22 May 1934, 7.
107. For a history of the company, see Watson, *The Waddingtons Story*.
108. As Evalyn Grumbine noted 'millions of paper masks of comic and screen stars were used as juvenile premiums. … In Great Britain Listerine tooth paste used masks of Mickey and Minnie

Mouse. Sales were doubled almost overnight. It is reported that more than 10 million masks were distributed in England alone during a period of two months' in Grumbine, *Reaching Juvenile Markets*, 87.

109. 'Masks of Mickey Mouse and Minnie Mouse can be obtained from any chemist by purchasing a tube of Listerine Tooth Paste' *The Teesdale Mercury*, 8 November 1933, 14.

110. 'For the Kiddies, while they last! Free! Mickey Mouse or Minnie Mouse- Party mask with every 1/3 tube of Listerine Tooth Paste' *The Argus*, 12 February 1934, 14.

111. 'Kiddies delighted with Mickey or Minnie Mouse Paper Masks – free with every 1/3d tube of Listerine Tooth Paste' *Akaroa Mail and Banks Peninsula Advertiser*, 22 May 1934, 2.

112. For an interesting study of similar strategies, see Robinson, "Marketing Gum," 4–44.

113. 'The advertising multinationals began arriving in Spain in the 1920s, among them Publicitas, Germany's Rudolf Mosse, Britain's Crawford, France's Havas, and from the United States, the J. Walter Thompson Company (JWT) …' in Pérez-Latre, "Spain," 1464.

114. Bravo, *Walter Thompson España*.

115. *Trademark Selection: The Management Team Method*.

116. Bellido, "Toward a History."

117. Trademark Application, File 0,102,173; AHOEPM, filed 14 February, 1935.

118. Moreno Lázaro, "La dulce transformación," 205–248 and Moreno Lázaro, "Tecnología, empresa y mercado," 15–35; Monroig, "La industria," 3.

119. Letter from Pierre de Beneducci, Representante Exclusivo en España, Italia y Portugal, 24 January 1935; File 0,102,173; AHOEPM.

120. Ibid.

121. *Estatuto sobre Propiedad Industrial*, aprobado por Real Decreto-Ley de 26 de julio de 1929 (Industrial Property Code, approved by Royal-Decree Law, July 1929).

122. Instancia de Renuncia. 9 July 1935; File 0,093,620; AHOEPM.

123. Munsey, *Disneyana*, 113.

124. The first issue of the merchandising catalogue was arranged by Disney's merchandising director Kay Kamen; see Mosley, *The Real Walt Disney*, 148–150; Bain and Harris, *Mickey Mouse*, 150; Beezy, "Good Marksmanship," 22; Thomas, *The Walt Disney Biography*, 81–82; Munsey, *Disneyana*, 107–126; Hollis, *Toons in Toyland*, 11.

125. "Mickey Mouse Looks Forward to 1936" *Playthings*, February 1936, 56.

126. "Jabón y Pasta dentífrica Mickey Mouse- Con la Autorización de Walt Disney," *La Vanguardia*, 5 November 1935, 5; 'Soon kids all over the world were clamouring for Mickey Mouse toothbrushes, drinking glasses, combs, trains, watches, and an incredible assortment of toys and figurines that would number in the hundreds by 1935 and the thousands by 1960' in Bain and Harris, *Mickey Mouse*, 15.

127. Papeles Wipa (Barcelona) was one of the licensees that began producing Mickey fountain pens and other stationary material with the film star.

128. Though discussed in relation to a later period, Henry Jenkins describes affective economics as a discourse that 'emphasizes the emotional commitments consumers make in brands as a central motivation for their purchasing decisions', Jenkins, *Convergence Culture*, 319.

129. Grumbine, *Reaching Juvenile Markets*, 87–88.

130. Bourdieu, *Distinction*, 328–329.

131. Similar trademark struggles were soon after experienced by Disney in Australia where Disney was more successful, the significance of which was noted in the USA; see *Radio Corporation Pty Ltd v Disney ('Mickey Mouse case')* (1937) 57 CLR 448; see also George G. Turri, 'Mickey Mouse in Australian High Court'; "Mickey Mouse's Rights are argued in Australia," *New York Times*, 30 April 1936, 16.

132. Trademark Application, File 98,076; AHOEPM, filed 10 March, 1934.

133. Trademark Opposition, File 98,076; AHOEPM filed 15 June, 1934. Walt and Roy Disney and their wives did tour the Continent for two months in 1935. See Ghez, *Disney's Grand Tour*.

134. Response by Geis Bosch, 4 September 1934; File 98,076; AHOEPM.

135. For a discussion of US–Spanish copyright relations, see Bellido, Xalabarder, and Casas Vallès, 'Commentary on US–Spanish Peace Treaty."

136. Trademark Opposition Decision, File 98,076; AHOEPM filed 16 March, 1935.
137. Trademark Application, File 101,116; AHOEPM, filed 22 November, 1934.
138. Opposition to the Trademark application, File 101,116; AHOEPM, filed 14 February, 1935.
139. Appendix: US Copyright Certificate Entry Class G. No. 6,499 (Walt Disney's Mickey Mouse) File 101,116; AHOEPM, filed 1 June, 1931.
140. Trademark Application, File 101,717; AHOEPM, filed 22 December, 1934.
141. Response to the Opposition, File 101,116; AHOEPM, filed 28 February, 1935.
142. Power of attorney from Manuel de la Osa to Luis María de Zunzunegui, File 101,116; AHOEPM, filed 22 February, 1935.
143. Trademark Opposition Decision, File 101,116; AHOEPM, filed 13 March, 1935.
144. Surely one of the aspects that made licensing arrangements attractive and successful was the infrastructural support given by Disney to its licensees. For instance, as Heide and Gilman observe, 'design and artwork was supplied free of charge to licensees …,' in Heide and Gilman, *Disneyana.*, 43.
145. Trademark Application, 4 December 1934, File 101.449; AHOEPM, filed 4 December, 1934.
146. Letter from Vecchi to Pierre Beneducci (Disney agent), 12 February 1935, File 101.449; AHOEPM. Some references to Vecchi in Spain can be read in Sanchis, *Franco contra Flash Gordon*, 60–61. See also Martín, *Historia del comic español: 1875–1939*, 118–133.
147. Opposition to Trademark Application, File 101.449, filed 26 Februrary, 1935; AHOEPM; Renuncia al Registro, File 101.449; AHOEPM, filed 14 March, 1935.
148. Design Application, File 482, AHOEPM, filed 15 February, 1935.
149. When tested in court, the UK design registration held by the British toy maker, Deans Rag Book Co, ultimately provided little protection for Mickey for similar reasons to those raised in the Spanish opposition; see *Deans Rag Book Company Limited v Pomerantz and Sons* (1930) 47 RPC 485; *The Times*, 18 July 1930, 5; *The Times*, 19 July 1930, 4; *The Times*, 23 July 1930, 5.
150. Opposition to Design Application, (Don Emilio Urquizo y Falcó), filed 15 May, 1935; and opposition to Design application, (Francisco Tribó Capdevila), File 482, AHOEPM, filed 1 June, 1935.
151. Following difficulties with industrial property rights, a global strategy of linking licensing with copyright is confirmed in the 1940s by a letter written by Gunther Lessing, Disney's legal counsel, to Art Arthur, Motion Picture Industry Council. He wrote: 'the patent lawyers told us that it "couldn't be done" as such licenses as we contemplated would put our trademarks in the public domain. Roy Disney and I decided that there was money to be derived from this endeavour so we based it on the copyright laws and the laws of unfair competition'; Lessing to Arthur, November 18, 1949; AMPAS.

Disclosure statement

No potential conflict of interest was reported by the authors.

* Archival sources are from collections abbreviated as follows: AHOEPM = Archivo Histórico de la Oficina Española de Patentes y Marcas, (Madrid, Spain); AME: L'archivio storico Arnoldo Mondadori Editore (Milan, Italy); AMPAS = Academy of Motion Pictures Arts and Sciences (Los Angeles, California); BN = Biblioteca Nacional de España (Madrid, Spain); COAPI = Archivo del Colegio de Agentes de la Propiedad Industrial (Madrid, Spain); NA = National Archives (Kew, UK); RS = Archivo Rogelio Sanchís (Valencia, Spain). Thanks to Patricio Sáiz, Tiziano Chiesa, Ángel Fernández González, Julia Hudson-Richards, Rogelio Sanchís, Fabio Gadducci, Emilia de la Peña, Carlos González, Didier Ghez and David Lobenstine.

References

Aaker, Jennifer L. "Dimensions of Brand Personality." *Journal of Marketing Research* 34, no. 3 (1997): 347–356.

Abad, V. *Historia de la Naranja (1781–1939)* [History of the Orange]. Valencia: Comité de Gestión de la Exportación de Frutos Cítricos, 1984.

Abad, V. "The Orange Trademarks." In *The Golden Fruit: The Spanish Citrus Industry 1781–2000*, edited by V Abad, JP Rojas, FZ Rodrigo, E Domènech, JP Andrés and M de la Taronja. Valencia: Generalitat Valenciana, 2000.

Alcacer, J & Collis D. "The Walt Disney Company (A): Corporate Strategy TN." *Harvard Business School Teaching Note*, no 795–152, (1995).

Anon, "Aniversarios- El del nacimiento de Mickey Mouse." *La Vanguardia*, 21 October 1933, 10.

Anon, "Como se celebrará en el extranjero el aniversario de Mickey Mouse." *La Vanguardia*, 17 September 1935, 17.

Anon. "Mickey Mouse in Court: Deans Rag Book Co Ltd v Pomerantz and Sons." *The Times*, 18 July 1930: 5; 19 July 1930: 4; 23 July 1930: 5.

Anon, "El aniversario de Mickey Mouse." *La Vanguardia*, 1 December 1934, 5.

Anon, "Mickey Mouse ha cumplido ya siete años." *La Vanguardia*, 14 September 1935, 15.

Anon, *Mother's Own Book*, New York, NY: The Parent's Publishing Association Inc, 1928.

Anon, *revista Gutiérrez*, 6 December 1930, 18–19.

Anon, "Cosas del Cine" *La Vanguardia*, 3 January 1931, 14.

Anon, "Ecos y Noticias" *La Vanguardia*, 1 May 1931, 16.

Arroyo, T. V. *Las etiquetas naranjeras en la Comunidad Valenciana*. [Orange Labels in Valencia] València: Conselleria d'Agricultura, Peixca i Alimentacio, 1998.

Arvidsson, A. "Brands: A Critical Perspective." *Journal of Consumer Culture* 5, no. 2 (2015): 235–258.

Avilés, P. *Informe: El museo valenciano del juguete [Report: The Toy Museum in Valencia]*. Valencia, 2012.

Bain, D., and B. Harris. *Mickey Mouse. Fifty Happy Years*. London: New English Library, 1977.

Baker, S. *Picturing the Beast: Animals, Identity, and Representation*. Manchester, NH: Manchester University Press, 1993.

Barrier, M. *The Animated Man. A Life of Walt Disney*. Berkeley: University of California Press, 2007.

Bayardi, M. A. *Ratón Pérez contra Miguelito* [Ratón Pérez vs Miguelito]. México: Secretaria de Educación Pública, 1945.

Beezy, M. C. "Good Marksmanship." *Los Angeles Lawyer* 29, no. 10 (2006): 20–26.

Bellido, J. "Toward a History of Trade Mark Watching." *Intellectual Property Quarterly* 2 (2015): 130–152.

Bellido, J., ed. *Landmark Cases in Intellectual Property*. Hart: Bloomsbury, 2017.

Bellido, J., R. Xalabarder, and R.Casas Vallès. "Commentary on US-Spanish Peace Treaty (1898)." In *Primary Sources on Copyright (1450-1900)*, edited by L. Bently and M. Kretschmer, 2011. www.copyrighthistory.org

Benjamin, W. *Selected Writings: Volume 2 Part 2. 1931-1934*. Massachusetts: Harvard University Press, 1999.

Berle, A. K., and L Sprague de Camp *Inventions and their Management*. Pennsylvania: International Textbook Company, 1937.

Bock, A. *Exhibiting Trauma: Ydessa Hendeles at the Haus der Kunst in Munich*. Quebec: Thesis Concordia University, 2004.

Bourdieu, P. *Distinction. A Social Critique of the Production of Taste*. London: Routledge & Kegan Paul, 1984.

Bravo, J. J. *Walter Thompson España. De 1927 a 1936 [Walter Thompson Spain. From 1927 to 1936]*. Madrid: J. Walter Thompson, 1978.

Brown, D. E. *Human Universals*. New York: McGraw-Hill, 1991.

Brown, K. *Factory of Dreams. A History of Meccano Ltd*. Lancaster: Crucible Books, 2010.

Cabello Lapiedra, F., and P. Martínez Garcimartín. *La Propiedad Industrial en España [Industrial Property in Spain]*. Madrid: Reus, 1945.

Canemaker, J. *Felix: The Twisted Tale of the World's Most Famous Cat*. New York: Pantheon Books, 1991.

Centeno, F. "Dibujos Sonoros." *La Vanguardia*, 23 November 1930, 17.

Chandler, A. "The Emergence of Managerial Capitalism." *Business History Review*, 58, no. 4 (Winter, 1984): 473–503.

Chandler, A. *Scale & Scope: The Dynamics of Industrial Capitalism*. Cambridge: Harvard University Press, 1990.

Chapman, C. "Mickey Mouse and other things." *Bulletin of the United States Trademark Association* 29 (1934): 271–272.

de Chernatony, L., and M. MacDonald. *Creating powerful brands in consumer, service and industrial markets*. Oxford: Elsevier, 2003.

Cochoy, F. "A Brief Theory of the Captation of Publics." *Theory, Culture & Society* 24, no. 7–8 (2007): 213–233.

Colino, R. "Copyright Protection Abroad for US Cultural Export", *Duke Law Journal*, (1962): 219–247.

Coombe, R. *The Cultural Life of Intellectual Properties*. Durham N.C.: Duke University Press, 1998.

Cope, P., and D. Cope. *Dean's Rag Books and Rag Dolls: The Products of a Famous British Publisher and Toymaker*. London: River Books, 2009.

deCordova, R. "The Mickey in Macy's Window: Childhood, Consumerism, and Disney Animation." In *Disney Discourse: Producing the Magic Kingdom*, edited by E. Smoodin, 203–213. New York: Routledge, 1994.

Craig, J., and J. Morra-Yoe, eds. *The Art of Mickey Mouse*. New York: Hyperion, 1991.

Depoorter, B. "The Several Lives of Mickey Mouse: Expanding the Boundaries of Intellectual Property Law." *Virginia Journal of Law and Technology* 9, no. 4 (2004): 8–10.

Escobar, S. "Mickey y Minnie: dos actores internacionales." *Diario El Sol*, 4 June 1933, 8.

Fernández Mourillo, M. *Legislación y Propiedad Intelectual [Legislation and Intellectual Property]*. Madrid: Reus, 1930.

Forgacs, D. "Disney animation and the business of childhood." *Screen* 33, no. 4 (1992): 361–374.

Fournier, S. "Consumers and Their Brands: Developing Relationship Theory in Consumer Research." *Journal of Consumer Research* 24, no. 4 (1998): 343–353.

Gadducci, F., F. Gori, and S. Lama. *Eccetto Topolino*. Battipaglia: Nicola Pesce Editore, 2011.

Gadducci, F., and M. Tavosanis. *Casa Disney, Autore e diritto d'autore*. Bologna: PuntoZero, 2000.

Gaines, J. *Contested Culture. The Image, the Voice, the Law*. Chapel Hill: The University of North Carolina Press, 1991.

Gerstein, D. "Mickey Mouse Annual." *Disneyana Update* 72 (2009): 48–53.

Ghez, D. *Disney's Grand Tour: Walt and Roy's European Vacation, Summer 1935*. New York: Theme Park Press, 2014.

Gómez Mesa, L. *Los films de dibujos animados [Animated Cartoons]*. Madrid: C.I.A.P, 1930.

Grumbine, E. *Reaching Juvenile Markets*. New York: McGraw-Hill, 1938.

Grzelak, V. A. "Mickey Mouse & Sonny Bono Go to Court: The Copyright Term Extension Act and Its Effect on Current and Future Rights." *John Marshall Review of Intellectual Property Law* 2 (2002): 99–115.

Heald, P. "Testing the Over- and Under-Exploitation Hypothesis: Best-selling Musical Compositions (1913-32) and Their Use in Cinema (1968-2007)." Working Paper No. 429, John M. Olin Program in Law and Economics, 2008.

Heide, R. and J. Gilman. *Disneyana. Classic Collectibles 1928-1958*. New York: Disney Editions, 1994.

Hendeles, Y., C. Dercon, C. Squiers, E. van Alphen, and T. Weski, eds. *Partners: Ydessa Hendeles*. Köln: Walter Koenig, 2003.

Hillier, B., and B. C. Shine. *Walt Disney's Mickey Mouse Memorabilia – The Vintage Years 1928–1938*. London: Octopus Books Ltd, 1986.

Hollis, T. *Toons in Toyland: The Story of Cartoon Character Merchandise*. Jackson, MS: University Press of Mississippi, 2015.

Holliss, R., and B. Sibley. *Mickey Mouse. His Life and Times*. New York: Harper & Row, 1986.

Hudson-Richards, J. "The Orange Proletariat Social Relations in the País Valenciano, 1860–1939." PhD diss., The University of Arizona, 2008.

Hyman, C. *Oranges: A Global History*. London: Reaktion Books, 2013.

Huertas, J. M. "Mickey y sus 55.000 amigos." *El Periódico de Catalunya*, 15 November 1998, 41.

Jacobson, R. "The Question of Berne Entry for the United States." 11 *Case W. Res. J. Int'l L.* (1979): 421–444.

Jenkins, H. *Convergence Culture: Where Old and New Media Collide*. New York: New York University Press, 2006.

Jenkins, H. *The Wow Climax. Tracing the Emotional Impact of Popular Culture*. New York, NY: New York University Press, 2007.

Johnson, J., G. Ehrbar, and D. Ghez. *Inside the Whimsy Works: My Life with Walt Disney Productions*. Jackson, MS: University Press of Mississippi, 2014.

Jones, Jr., J. M. *Tariff Retaliation*. Philadelphia, PA: University of Pennsylvania Press, 1934.

Karp, D. "Orange Wrappers." In *Food in the Arts: Proceedings of the Oxford Symposium on Food and Cookery*, edited by H Walker, 119–124. Devon: Prospect Books, 1998.

Kellogg, E. 'History of Sound Motion Pictures (1955)' In *A Technological History of Motion Pictures and Television* edited by R Fielding, 174–220. Berkeley: University of California Press, 1974.

Kozinsky, A. "Mickey and Me." *University of Miami Entertainment and Sports Law Review* 11 (1994): 465–470.

Ladas, S. P. *Patents, Trademarks, and Related Rights: National and International Protection* vol. 1. Boston, MA: Harvard University Press, 1975.

Leslie, E. *Hollywood Flatlands. Animation, Critical Theory and the Avant-garde*. London: Verso, 2002.

Levy, S. J. "Dreams, fairy tales, animals, and cars." In *Brands, Consumers, Symbols, and Research: Sidney J. Levy on Marketing*, edited by D. W. Rook, 67–81. London: Sage Publishing, 1999.

Litman, J. "Mickey Mouse Emeritus: Character Protection and the Public Domain." *University of Miami Entertainment and Sports Law Review* 11 (1994): 429–435.

Lobel, C. "Spanish Dancing Sparklers" *Antique Toy World*, November 2009, vol. 39, No. 11: 64.

Malboysson, E. "El maravilloso espectáculo que ofrece el puerto de Valencia." *Revista Estampa* (1930): 25–27.

Maltin, L. *Of Mice and Magic: A History of American Animated Cartoons*. St Louis: Von Hoffmann Press Inc, 1980.

de Mantilla, FG. "Las películas de dibujos animados" *El Imparcial*, 7 September 1930, 7.

Martín, A. *Historia del comic español: 1875–1939 [History of Spanish Cartoons]*. Barcelona: Gustavo Gili, 1978.

Martínez, A. M. "Apuntes para una historia de los tebeos: La civilización de la imagen (1917-1936)." *Revista de Educación-Estudios* (1968): 139–153.

Miller, N. *The Dean's Rag Book Company- The First 100 Years*. Gwent: The Dean's Rag Book, 2002.

Mollerup, P. *Marks of Excellence. The History and Taxonomy of Trademarks*. London: Phaidon, 1997.

Monroig, M. "La industria de productos Loste: Honra y orgullo de España" *Imperio: Diario de Zamora*, 18 July 1956, 3.

Monsonís, E. *Memorias incompletas [Incomplete Memories]*. Burriana: Fundación Individuo y Sociedad, 2007.

Monsonís, P. "Extrema preocupación ante la próxima campaña naranjera." In *Seis estudios sobre la coyuntura actual de la riqueza naranjera*, edited by P. Monsonís, B. Bono and M. Torres Martínez. Castellón de la Plana: Hijos de F. Armengot, 1959.

Moreno Lázaro, J. "La dulce transformación. La industria gallega española en la segunda mitad del siglo XX." *Revista de historia industrial* 19 (2001): 205–248.

Moreno Lázaro, J. "Tecnología, empresa y mercado en la fabricación española de galletas, 1790-1936." *Revista de historia industrial* 37 (2008): 15–35.

Mosley, L. *The Real Walt Disney. A Biography*. London: Grafton, 1985.

Munsey, C. *Disneyana: Walt Disney Collectibles*. New York: Hawthorn Books, 1974.

Pedrosa, J. M. *La historia secreta del Ratón Pérez [The Secret History of Pérez the Mouse]*. Madrid: Páginas de Espuma, 2005.

Pellisier, C. E. "Making sales through clubs: RH White Co. Mickey Mouse Club." *Playthings* (1932): 40.

Peraire, F. *La marca de fábrica. Comentarios a la legislación vigente. Jurisprudencia civil y penal* [Trademarks: Comments on legislation. Civil and criminal jurisprudence]. Barcelona: Impr. A. Ortega, 1927.

Pérez-Latre, F. J. "Spain." In *The Encyclopaedia of Advertising*, edited by J McDonough and K Egolf, 1464–1468. London: Taylor and Francis, 2003.

Peterson, D. K. "Disney, Walt (1901-1966)." In *The Greenwood Encyclopaedia of Folktales and Fairy Tales. Vol. 1: A-F*, edited by D. Haase, 271–275. Westport: Greenwood Press, 2008.

Posner, R. "Response to Why Mickey Mouse is Not Subject to Congestion by Michele Boldrin and David Levine." *The Economists' Voice* 1, no. 2 (2004): 1–2.

Pottage, A. "No (more) Logo: Plain Packaging and Communicative Agency." *UC Davis Law Review* 47, no. 2 (2013): 515–546.

Ricketson, S. *The Paris Convention for the Protection of Industrial Property: a commentary*. Oxford: Oxford University Press, 2015.

Robinson, D. J. "Marketing Gum, Making Meanings: Wringley in North America 1890-1930." *Enterprise & Society, no 1* (2004): 4–44.

Sáiz, P., and P. Fernández Pérez. "Catalonian Trademarks and the Development of Marketing Knowledge in Spain, 1850–1946." *Business History Review* 86, no. 02 (2012): 239–260.

Sammond, N. *Babes in Tomorrowland*. Durham N.C: Duke University Press, 2005.

Sánchez Pérez, J. B. *La Propiedad Industrial en España: Bosquejo Histórico – Legislación [Industrial Property in Spain: An overview of its history and legislation]*. Madrid: Reus, 1945.

Sanchis, V. *Franco contra Flash Gordon [Franco vs Flash Gordon]*. Barcelona: Tres I Quatre, 2009.

Saunders-Watson, C. "La Isla Toys: Radical characters of the pre-war era." *Antique Toys* (2007): 18–24.

Schwarzkopf, S. "Turning Trade Marks into Brands". In *Trademarks, Brands, and Competitiveness*, edited by T. da Silva Lopes and P. Duguid, 165–193. Oxon; New York: Routledge, 2010.

Seely, F. A. *History of the International Union for the Protection of Industrial Property*. Washington: Washington Government Printing Office, 1887.

Sellés, J. P. *Juguetes valencianos: un siglo en la historia de una industria peculiar [Toys from Valencia: A Century in the history of a peculiar industry]*. Valencia: Generalitat Valenciana, Conselleria de Cultura, Educación y Ciencia, 1997.

Serafino, D. "Survey of Patent Pools Demonstrates Variety of Purposes and Management Structures." *Knowledge Ecology Information Research Note No 6*. Washington: Knowledge Ecology International, 2007.

Sherman, B., and L. Bently. *The Making of Modern Intellectual Property Law*. Cambridge: Cambridge University Press, 1999.

Smith, D. "The Walt Disney Archives: It all Started with a Mouse." *Historical Journal of Film, Radio and Television* 16, no. I (1996): 13–17.

Solberg, T. *Copyright Enactments of the United States 1783–1906*. Washington: Government Printing Office, 1906.

Thomas, B. *The Walt Disney Biography*. London: New English Library, 1977.

Trademark selection: The management team method. New York: USTA, 1960.

Tumbusch, T. *Disneyana. Disney Merchandise of the 1930s*. Ohio: Tomart Publications, 2014.

Turri, G. G. "Mickey Mouse in Australian High Court." *Bulletin of the United States Trademark Association* 32, no. 10 (1937): 297–306.

Twede, D. "History of Packaging". In *The Routledge Companion to Marketing History*, edited by D. G. Brian Jones and Mark Tadajewski 115–129, Oxon; New York: Routledge, 2016.

Ungría, A. "Ley y Práctica en materia de Propiedad Industrial". In *Cuatro Conferencias sobre Propiedad Industrial*, 13–31 [Four Conferences on Industrial Property], edited by COAPI. Madrid: Colegio Oficial de Agentes de la Propiedad Industrial, 1950.

Viana Arroyo, T. *Las etiquetas naranjeras en la Comunidad Valenciana [Orange Labels in Valencia]*. València: Conselleria d'Agricultura, Peixca i Alimentacio, 1998.

Wasko, J. *Understanding Disney*. Cambridge: Polity Press, 2001.

Watson, V. *The Waddingtons Story: From the Early Days to Monopoly, The Maxwell Bids and into the Next Millennium*. Huddersfield: Jeremy Mills Publishing, 2008.

Watts, S. *The Magic Kingdom. Walt Disney and the American Way of Life*. Columbia, SC: University of Missouri Press, 1997.

Wengel, D., and P. Wengel. "Origins and examples of those great R.S. La Isla Toys made in Spain" *Antique Toy*." *World* 25, no. 4 (1995): 36–40.

Wilkins, M. *The Maturing of Multinational Enterprise. American Business abroad from 1914 to 1970*. Cambridge: Harvard University Press, 1974.

Zelizer, V. A. *Pricing the Priceless Child, The Changing Social Value of Children*. New York: Basic Books, 1985.

Zipes, J. "Breaking the Disney Spell." In *The Classic Fairy Tales*, edited by M Tatar, 332–335. New York: W. W. Norton & Company, 1999.

Branding, Culture, and National Identity

Part II

Branding, Culture, and National
Identity

INTRODUCTION

Cross-cultural factors in international branding

Rafael Castro and Patricio Sáiz

ABSTRACT
This is the second special issue resulting from the symposium titled 'The Brand and Its History'. This issue aims at deepening the knowledge of the historical and cultural roots of the origin, uses, and meanings of modern branding. This editorial summarises previous contributions from economic, marketing, and historical literature; presents the main findings of the seven articles included in this issue; and reflects on possible further research.

If you are not a brand, you are a commodity. Then price is everything and the low-cost producer is the only winner.[1]

Introduction

This is the second special issue coming out of the multidisciplinary research seminar and international conference session 'The Brand and Its History: Economic, Business, and Social Value', held in Madrid in 2014, and from the call for papers published in September 2015 in *Business History*. The variety of topics and number of articles received led to a double special issue with two distinct but related research lines: the first one on trademarks[2] and this one on historical and cultural factors in modern – and international – branding.

To define what is a brand is not an easy task. Even the first definition given by the American Marketing Association seems too simple and related to trademarks: 'name, term, design, symbol, or any other feature that identifies one seller's good or service as distinct from those of other sellers.'[3] Over the last 70 years, research on branding has enriched this definition through thousands of articles published by academic journals. For example, in 1998 Leslie de Chernatony and Francesca Dall'Olmo identified at least 12 main themes needed for an accurate categorisation of the broad range of definitions of 'brand' in the literature. Brand was seen as: (1) a legal instrument, (2) a logo, (3) a company, (4) a shorthand, (5) a risk reducer, (6) an identity system, (7) an image in consumers' minds, (8) a value system, (9) a personality, (10) a relationship, (11) an added value, and (12) an evolving entity.[4] This range offers only an idea of the complexity of the matter. In this 'maze' dominated by marketing scholars and brand practitioners, business history has been, and still is, under-represented.

This special issue aims at starting to fill this void. It is devoted to the historical and cross-cultural factors that influence the building, management, and meaning of modern brands over time. It comprises seven articles that discuss branding topics from an array of products, such as luxury goods and counterfeits, and from a range of countries, such as Canada and New Zealand, among others. The following sections summarise branding research topics in different fields, highlight contributors' findings, and suggest additional research paths.

Academic research on brands: an introductory survey

Brands and branding are by no means new phenomena for either academia or the business world. Branding practices have existed for millennia,[5] yet research really occurred only after World War II, with the advent of the 'consumer revolution' of post-war economic expansion.[6] However, not all fields have treated brands in the same way and with the same intensity. In the next two sections, we highlight the specific research on brands in three interrelated fields: economics, marketing, and business history.

Economics and marketing

As stated in the introduction to the first special issue,[7] mainstream economists have generally treated brands simply as trademarks; that is, as part of the consumer-choice process. How do consumers make their choices? Neoclassical consumption theory assumes that consumers are able to evaluate the quality of any good or service on the basis of their tastes and so determine what choices will maximise their utility function.[8] In other words, the consumers act in accordance with an explicit 'rational action' model of human behaviour.[9] Nevertheless, consumers are frequently uncertain about the quality of an unknown product (e.g. its strong and weak points), and to make an educated decision requires credible information that is difficult and costly to gather. Brands are signs that convey such credible information to consumers. Thus, brands – meaning trademarks – have been considered an important mechanism for overcoming market failures caused by information asymmetries.[10] To preserve brand reputation, producers are incentivised to at least maintain, if not increase, the quality of their goods or services for the benefit of consumers and markets.[11]

The evolution of the world economy in the second half of the twentieth century brought a new way of approaching the consumer-choice process that did not exactly fit the neoclassical theory.[12] Industrial advances in the first half of the twentieth century connected consumers' choices with mass production while the second half of the century brought the advent of the 'information society', in which knowledge and communication became crucial.[13] In this new framework, the assumption that the most significant product qualities such as the freshness of food are objective was challenged. Subjectivity became ever more important. Consumers no longer only bought a trademarked product to consume the good but also for the experience that the brand provided.[14] This new perspective, which certain scholars called the 'experience economy',[15] was a reminder of the 'vicarious consumption' that Thorstein Veblen described over a century ago, and which had never been sufficiently investigated by economic theory.[16] In this new economy, brands became more complex and multidimensional.[17]

New analytical proposals emerged, such as those from behavioural economics, to explore beyond the limits of neoclassical theory. As a reaction against the restrictive assumptions of marginalism, behavioural economists sought to introduce more 'realistic' perspectives regarding the behaviour of economic agents.[18] The field aimed to study how individuals make consumption, investment, and managerial decisions; and the way they interact or influence other individuals, organisations, markets, and societies. In doing so, behavioural economics depict a unification between psychology and economics.[19] It was not until the 1980s, however, that the field began to have a significant impact on scholarship, when journals on the topic appeared, such as the *Journal of Economic Psychology* and the *Journal of Economic Behavior and Organization*, and when the Society for the Advancement of Behavioral Economics was founded. Since that time, four main research topics have emerged: the consumer, the worker, the manager, and the role of ethics in business.[20]

With respect to the first topic, the one of interest for this introduction, behavioural economists have focused on the analysis of demand and consumer-choice processes. A distinctive feature of behavioural economics is its interest in collecting as much data as possible on individual decision-making as a way of testing hypotheses and obtaining results.[21] The seminal works of Herbert Simon, based on such observations, suggested that consumers do not maximise but instead 'satisfice' their decision-making processes simply because they do not have enough information or cognitive skills.[22] In the same vein, Daniel Kahneman and Amos Tversky demonstrated that consumers' behaviour could often deviate substantially from the norms of classical economic theory.[23] The development and enhancement of behavioural economics unfurled new branches of study aimed at integrating psychological aspects into decision-making processes. Behavioural economists incorporated general principles of choice from psychology, such as Herrnstein's matching law.[24] This has led to characterising consumers, when choosing among brands, as Bayesian learners who use and update their current preferences based on personal consumption experiences.[25]

Hence, branding studies have been a significant topic in academic behavioural economics over the last several decades. Most of the research focuses on brand choice and elasticity of demand.[26] In fact, the bulk of these works have examined reference prices and the effects on buyers' behaviour and brand choices, demonstrating that both consumers' choice and brand selection are particularly related to the sensitivity towards price changes, a more important factor than other emotional concepts, such as brand loyalty, that has generally been laid on the table by marketing literature.[27]

Behavioural economics rapidly connected to business disciplines, including marketing. However, marketing scholars and practitioners created a pluralistic and interdisciplinary approach towards consumer behaviour research by putting brands at the centre of their analyses. In the mid-1950s, the *Harvard Business Review* provided the first landmark on the topic: Burleigh Gardner and Sidney Levy pointed out that consumers were confronted with making choices among brands, even if they were not able clearly to discern differences among the products. They crystallised the insight that consumers are guided by brand image because 'people buy things not only for what they can do, but also for what they mean'.[28] Obvious as it may have been, the statement served to spur new directions in research.

Since then, firms have tried to build bridges to connect with consumers through brand properties. Several marketing theories have formalised this connection. In 1956, Wendell

Smith coined the concept *segmentation*. Smith explained that the market, as heterogeneous as it was, was comprised of smaller homogeneous *segments*.[29] Firms must first identify these segments to manage brands properly and reach consumers. The segmentation was limited, at the beginning, to socio-economic variables such as income, education, or civil status. As brands were increasingly developed as conveyors of emotions, practitioners and scholars considered and included new segmentation variables, such as buying behaviour, motives, values, consumer patterns, and aesthetic preferences.[30] Hand-in-hand with segmentation, Ross Cunningham defined *brand loyalty* as a unique value that no other alternative could provide. Brand loyalty is the main reason why brand-loyal consumers are willing to pay more for a certain product.[31] On the other hand, Pierre Martineau established the theoretical foundation of *brand personality*.[32] Using the example of two stores with similar products, prices, and services, Martineau demonstrated that consumers often showed partiality towards one of the stores and not the other because of its *personality*. That is, consumers will choose the store – or, in general terms, the brand – that represents their own personality and that fits with how they want to be perceived. This uniqueness led to William Lazer's *lifestyle marketing*, which is a process of establishing relationships between products offered on the market and targeted to lifestyle groups.[33]

Since the 1970s, branding conceptualisation expanded in terms of both theory and practice. There was a dramatic shift in the importance of branding to consumers' choice, and firm managers' and marketing researchers' awareness of this shift. As soon as marketers noticed that mass communication associated with mass production was failing, companies started to communicate immaterial values conveyed by the brand. It was the way to stand out from competitors, so brands had to create a meaning for their consumers.[34] In other words, companies had to *position* themselves in the minds of customers and weave a relationship with them.[35] According to Martin Kornberger, many of the global brands that are powerful today are so because, during the second half of the twentieth century, companies turned consumption into a lifestyle choice that empowered consumers. In this process, consumers went from passive recipients of messaging to active actors in branding.[36]

This clearly indicated that brands were increasingly valuable to firms. In fact, firms were eager to know this exact value. Much of this interest was initially driven by the mergers and acquisitions boom of the 1980s, when it became apparent that the purchase price paid for many firms reflected the value of their brands.[37] David Aaker gathered and unified all the concepts that had been developed over the previous decades and focused on *brand equity*.[38] He defined brand equity as a set of five categories of brand assets and liabilities linked to a brand: (1) brand loyalty, (2) brand awareness, (3) perceived quality, (4) brand associations, and (5) other proprietary assets (e.g. patents, trademarks, and channel relationships). The success of brand equity as a field of research is undeniable; since the 1990s, it has been one of the most researched areas within marketing, with thousands of articles on the topic published in academic journals.

Brand equity has been considered in many contexts, but two main ones emerged from the large volume of publications in the field: the firm-oriented side (the *financial-based perspective*) and the consumer-oriented side (the *consumer-based perspective*). The former focuses on the total value of the firm,[39] the latter on measuring how consumers react to a brand.[40] According to Christodoulides and Chernatony, *consumer-based brand equity* is 'a set of perceptions, attitudes, knowledge, and behaviours on the part of consumers that results in increased utility and allows a brand to earn greater volume or greater margins than it could without the brand name'.[41] It was the step prior to so-called *relational branding*. This field of research appeared at the end of the 1990s and developed in the early 2000s. It describes how customers create their personal relationship to a brand through their experiences, values, and communications with that brand.[42] Susan Fournier argues that a brand could be seen as a relationship partner, and that consumers could have several relationships with different brands.[43] These relationships, according to Jean-Noël Kapferer, involve deep emotional contacts and loyalty, which are awarded to a brand whose identity fits the individual perspectives of the consumer.[44]

To sum up, in less than 60 years the concept of branding evolved from ownership and reputation to brand image, symbolic values, and relationship partnering. In the second half of the twentieth century and the beginning of the twenty-first century, brands assimilated characteristics from a large array of actors. Currently, brands even 'seem human'[45] and may have a great range of personalities.[46] Overall, after marketing scholars and practitioners shifted their research focus from firms to consumers, they told us that brands define and convey aspects of ourselves,[47] our national identity,[48] and the groups that we, as consumers, desire to belong to and be associated with.[49] Thus, brands have become cultural devices that are economically relevant because consumers are willing to pay for them.[50] In an increasingly global economy in which branding is conducted on a worldwide landscape, understanding culture – and its symbols – is viewed as increasingly critical.[51] In other words, to succeed, firms must find out how 'consumers consume' in different environments.[52]

Moreover, these environments have been shifted by globalisation. Thus, it is not by chance that a main field of marketing research over the last 30 years has been how to build global brands. Among the myriad of definitions, Jan-Benedict Steenkamp, Rajeev Batra, and Dana Alden describe a global brand as one that consumers can find under the same name in multiple countries with similar and coordinated marketing strategies.[53] Most of the research, however, has concentrated on whether or not firms should standardise or customise their global marketing and branding programmes to adapt them to the different markets and cultures.[54] Some works affirm that 'globalness' creates consumer perceptions of brand superiority over local brands, and that such globalness is a stronger signal of quality over nation of origin.[55] However, several researchers have demonstrated that some consumers prefer brands with strong local connections[56]; or items that hail from countries considered to have particular expertise – for example, chocolate from Switzerland, clothing from Italy, cosmetics from France, cars from Germany, or electronics from Japan.[57] Although the debate is still open and there are no definitive results, it clearly shows the importance of the origination of the product or brand in the global economy. This is an aspect of product information with a complex effect on consumer behaviour, which is usually linked to cross-cultural and historical factors.[58]

Marketing scholars over the last few decades have developed two concepts closely related to the country image in this global environment: country of origin (CoO) and nation branding.[59] The former became increasingly important as movement towards globalisation of production intensified.[60] The seminal works on this are from the 1960s. Ernest Dichter was the first to argue that a product's CoO may have a 'tremendous influence on the acceptance and success of products'.[61] Three years later, Robert Schooler conducted the first empirical test of the concept in Central America. He found significant differences in the evaluation of products that were identical, except for the name of the country specified on a 'made in' label.[62] Since Schooler's seminal paper, the CoO effect has been the subject of a large number of studies.[63] Most of these studies have focused on measuring the significance of CoO effects for different products, but there has been no definitive consensus.[64] This lack of consensus is probably due to differences in the characteristics of the studies,[65] the product itself,[66] the image of the CoO,[67] or the recognition of brand origination.[68] In any case, research reveals that, in a global market, the sensitivity to CoO in the minds of customers has become crucial to companies. This sensitivity connects with both consumers' beliefs about a product on the one hand – based on their beliefs about the country from which the product originates[69] – and, on the other, with the symbolic and emotional meaning with respect to their feelings of national identity.[70]

One of the purposes of nation branding is to improve such feelings and emotions. The concept arose in the 1990s when Simon Anholt coined the term as the sum of perceptions of a country across six fields of national competence: exports, governance, tourism, investment and immigration, culture and heritage, and people.[71] In this vein, several scholars argue that nations, as brands, have individual identities that are unique unto themselves and that were developed historically.[72] Under the pressures of globalisation, numerous countries – developing and developed – have increasingly invested in branding in the hopes of producing images and emotions that could attract tourists, skilled students and workforce, or investments; and increase exports, international credibility, and political influence.[73] How do nations brand themselves? If nations are brands, the techniques of corporate branding could also be applied to them. According to Rebecca Hansen, nation branding could be about telling stories – constructed around the past, for example – or about developing powerful narratives of a country in order to generate cultural meanings on its products.[74] Overall, nation branding is presented as a crucial element in the economic, political, and cultural flourishing of any state, even when its actual effects have not been completely verified.[75]

Business history

As mentioned, since the 1970s branding research shifted attention from producers and products towards consumers. In this transition, brands definitely acquired economic meaning – as intangible assets – and were managed as cultural, ideological, or political objects. This new approach had necessarily to focus on cross-cultural processes that affect contemporary brands, including historical contexts and ethical concerns, among others.[76] Behavioural economists, but mainly marketing and management theorists, have produced a range of concepts and hypotheses that offer historians an opportunity to explore the processes involved in brand development over time in a more systematic way. However, that is not an easy task because, whereas analysis is possible for marketing practitioners and scholars through the use of surveys and interviews, business historians are compelled to use other sources which are often unavailable.[77]

The scarcity of sources in researching branding as emotional and cultural issues could explain, in part, why business historians extended their historical research on trademark topics. Historians generally agree with Mira Wilkins's seminal association of modern brands with the 'large-scale modern enterprise' that arose at the end of the nineteenth century and the beginning of the twentieth century.[78] Although she added a cultural dimension to the debate when discussing the role of the trademarked brand as a proxy 'face' to the consumer on behalf of modern corporation, she refrained from disentangling trademark, brand name, trade name, and company name.

In fact, historical research on branding started in the late 1980s and early 1990s. Hand-in-hand with marketing historians, business historians published in a steady stream as they became aware of the nature of brand, whose identity is built over time. This makes an historical approach particularly appropriate.[79] Often, US and UK business historians were more interested in consumer goods – such as food and drinks – than in other products, which is probably due to the key role of trademarks and branding in those sectors. *Adding Value*, edited by Geoffrey Jones and Nicolas Morgan, is a good example. Mainly devoted to corporations' branding and marketing strategies in food and beverages, the 1994 book included some chapters that addressed theoretical issues on the nature and function of brands.[80] Mark Casson called attention in this edited book to cultural and ideological dimensions of brands. According to the author, brands do more than provide information: they also transmit cultural characteristics that can manipulate consumer demand through, for example, advertising.[81] Conversely, in the same book, Vudayagiri Balasubramanyam and Mohammed Salisu suggested that advertising plays a key role in educating consumers.[82] Regardless, the compilation was a good starting point for other empirical, historical, cultural, and even ideological studies on branding to assess correctly its role in economic growth and problems with its management over time.

Similar works followed. Many focused on the reasons for the emergence of branding and its evolution within the firm,[83] particularly in six main topics: (1) the entrepreneurship's role in the creation and survival of successful brands, (2) the building and management of the corporate brand, (3) the importance of reputation, (4) the rise of nation branding, (5) the role of advertising and marketing agencies within branding, and (6) the fashion business and branding.

With respect to the first topic, several works showed the importance of entrepreneurs in discerning how economic and social changes over the last two centuries changed consumer needs and wants. Nancy Koehn assessed the brand-building strategies of Henry Heinz to answer the change in consumers' daily behaviours at the end of the nineteenth century. Heinz understood the importance of considering and exploring the demand side to compete effectively: consumers had to be able to identify the goodness – and other intangible aspects – of the product and perceived quality relative to rival goods.[84] In a following book, Koehn illustrates even earlier modern marketing and branding strategies. For example, entrepreneurs such as Josiah Wedgwood employed the power of branding in the 1760s for the production of pottery in England.[85] Teresa da Silva Lopes and Casson analysed branding processes in several countries and industries to show how key global brands usually had their origin in the eighteenth and nineteenth centuries; that is, brands were old and originated in developed countries with solid institutional frameworks. In such a brand-development process, entrepreneurship emerged not only from the traditional self-made man founding a firm but also from the hired organisation manager.[86] Finally, Terri Lonier, in her work on Quaker Oats, Coca-Cola, and Crisco, acknowledged the ability of the entrepreneurs behind these three firms in recognising the inherent value of low-cost agricultural goods and in converting them to high-revenue branded food products. However, she argued that nineteenth century brands were co-created by companies and customers, together with influencers such as wholesalers, grocers, and salesmen.[87]

Regarding the second topic, several case studies revealed how some organisations were branded as a whole and then used their names to support their product brands and boost sales. This was the case for the Scotch whisky industry. According to Stephen Jones, this industry has undergone fundamental changes in both organisation and structure since the late 1970s. Jones places corporate brand management at the core of the topic: companies used strategic corporate brand building to restructure their activities successfully.[88] In the United States, Roland Marchand and William Bird examined the strategies – internal marketing, indirect product branding, film and radio promotions – developed by corporate leaders such as General Motors, General Electric, Metropolitan Life Insurance, and Du Pont Chemicals, among others, to win public approval and build their own internal corporate culture.[89] In Britain, Michael Heller explored how Shell developed its corporate identity. Other oil companies sought to brand their products, but Shell worked to brand the company first and let its image be the guarantor of its products.[90] Dominique Barjot and Francesca Tesi analysed the creation of the Michelin brand. It is an interesting case of cultural transfer because of the deep influence of the American market in the shaping and change over time of the Michelin corporate brand – including Bibendum, the firm's icon.[91] Leigh George demonstrated how General Electric (GE) wanted to reassert its market dominance – built on innovative research and development – through an intense advertising campaign to promote its trademarks for light bulbs. Rather than identify an individual product, GE attempted to symbolise the imperceptible research and technological improvements for the public in a market in which all bulbs essentially looked the same. The particularity of the campaign – 'The Sun's Only Rival' – was that GE brands represented neither service nor electrical technology. In fact, they were related to the god of light in Persian mythology. In doing so, GE redefined what a corporate brand could be: something related to cultural connotations and an element through which the imaginary could be built.[92]

The third topic is, in part, connected to the second. According to Heller, 'the corporate brand can endorse product brands, providing indications of trust, reputation, and recognition'.[93] Reputation – as trust and recognition – is fundamental to market operations, but it is difficult to measure. It has a dual effect involving both adverse selection and moral hazard.[94] On the one hand, if purchasers cannot distinguish between the qualities of products, then they cannot compare them properly. Thus, the disparities that differentiate high-quality goods from low-quality goods remain unknown.[95] On the other hand, a supplier with a good reputation needs to preserve high quality to maintain profits over the long run.[96] In other words, reputation is difficult to earn and is related to more than the general level of quality. Reputation might rely on tangible or intangible advantages that purchasers have to trust. For instance, in a technology-intensive sector research and development could make the difference. The famous 'Intel inside' branding provides a good example of shared reputation and raises the issue of competition in supply chains when firms increase their own reputation by using certain highly reputed suppliers.[97] Peter Miskell examined the growth of healthcare products, another R&D-intensive sector, in relation to developments in the scientific understanding of diseases and treatments.[98] Reputation could also be something 'spiritual', as Lopes demonstrated for the British chocolate industry in the early forms of fair trade from the 1860s to the 1960s. In smaller and unregulated markets, organisations such as the religious Quaker Society of Friends were recognised as forms of indirect endorsement of chocolate firms and their brands and served as a good marketing strategy.[99] Lopes also showed the importance of reputation in the alcoholic beverages sector, where the association of a brand with a history and an entrepreneur who provides the customer assurances about the authenticity and reliability of the product is significant.[100] Conversely, a lack of reputation can do damage; one example is Spain's sherry producers, who failed in their response to the problems of selling their products on the British market. According to Eva Fernández, branding had no positive effects because quality producers could not stop cheap sherry imitators and their 'sherry' labels from pouring into the UK market starting in the 1920s.[101]

Reputation goes beyond the firm itself. In fact, a brand shares, to a certain extent, the reputation of its home country or region.[102] As previously stated, the interest in the idea of nation branding and related topics such as CoO took off at the beginning of the twenty-first century with the swelling of globalisation. However, Wally Olins has argued that the process is not new and that nations have branded themselves for more than two centuries.[103] Some case studies and books support Olins's argument. In the 1990s, David Head explored the mystique of the 'made in Germany' branding, an interesting example of how the manufacturing reputation of a nation is a public-good externality affecting business success.[104] Casson and Nigel Wadeson, combining economic theory with some elements of historical, sociological, and management analysis, also linked reputation and export performance and the extent to which they can be improved through institutions.[105] Denmark is one of the most documented cases. In the food and agriculture sector, David Higgins and Mads Mordhorst examined the interplay between quality, reputation, branding, and price premiums in the case of Danish butter and bacon exports to Britain between 1880 and 1938. Danish supremacy in both sectors over the British market was based on a deeply embedded institutional and industrial structure that generated a number of competitive advantages that overcame the liability of foreignness.[106] In turn, Per Hansen studied another Danish sector – furniture – in another market (the United States) between 1940 and 1970. Hansen developed a conceptual framework for analysing the relationship among nation brands, country image – promoted by public or private institutions – and product brands. He demonstrated how country image and product brand interact as a co-brand to provide a central link to consumers. In a recent book on brands, geographical origin, and globalisation, Higgins insisted on the significant role of CoO effects in international commerce, and explored how indications of origin historically emerged and evolved.[107] From the firm side, depending on the country and the product, companies can take advantage of the nation or region brand and the image of their home to strengthen their corporate and product brand.[108] The case of Barcelona and SEAT in the automotive sector shows the opposite; according to Joaquim Rius-Ulldemolins, SEAT, as a member of the Volkswagen group, systematically concealed its Catalan origins, because the idea of a Catalan (non-Spanish) industrial area did not fit with the widespread image of Spain's 'passion and leisure'.[109] Similarly, in the first volume of this special issue, Igor Goñi showed that the gun-making firms in Eibar (Basque Country) also tried to hide the geographic origins of their low-quality products by using trademarks in English and other languages.[110] In the same vein, José Antonio Miranda explained how Spanish fashion companies achieved a prominent position in the international market in the last third of the twentieth century, even though this success was not supported by a positive CoO and did not reinforce the image of Spain in the fashion market.[111]

The fifth topic explores the increasingly key role of advertising and marketing agencies in branding. According to John Mercer and Stefan Schwarzkopf, advertising agencies began to transform from trademark inertia to branding strategies during the interwar period.[112] Agencies such as J. Walter Thompson understood early the importance of knowing what consumers think, feel, and say about their consumption, and they assumed an increasingly powerful mediating role between branded goods and their consumers. Advertising agencies progressively realised that brands were connected with the hedonic, aesthetic, or ritualistic dimensions of consumption and were the result of the cultivation of distinct identities, associations, and benefits. By the late 1920s and early 1930s, several agencies developed the practical skills of how advertising could build brands. They included market and consumer research, campaign planning, positioning, segmentation, benefit marketing, and modern techniques of brand communication. This was before the rise of modern marketing in the 1960s. In other words, branding was a tool to 'create desire' and to weave relationships with consumers, as Casson pointed out in his chapter in *Adding Value*.[113] Such relationships show deep socio-cultural values that could be found even during the late nineteenth century through the use of ephemera, adverts, merchandising, or packaging concerning low-involvement brands, as Heller and Aidan Kelly demonstrated.[114]

The last topic has to do with the fashion business. Most of this particular research area barely touched on branding, but in examining the various components of fashion as a simultaneous cultural phenomenon and significant business, we realise how fashion brands were created and developed over time. Business historians have recently given attention to fashion. For example, Andrea Colli and Elisabetta Merlo focused on marketing and management practices of family and luxury businesses in Italy in the second half of the twentieth century, especially in Zegna and Armani. In line with the article by Merlo and Mario Perugini in this special issue, Colli and Merlo analysed how designers, lacking marketing and entrepreneurial capabilities, established reliable partnerships in the industry in order to expand their companies.[115] Véronique Pouillard focuses on French business with different approaches. From a legal perspective, Pouillard studies the levels of design protection in Paris and New York in the interwar years. Surprisingly, the lack of protection did not prevent New York from becoming a contender in the fashion industry.[116] Despite the American competition, French couturiers and Parisian fashion houses prevailed as main originators of women's fashions until World War II. Pouillard stresses the role of the media in disseminating the idea of *haute couture* as fulfilling consumers' desires, imaginations, and aspirations.[117] From a management perspective, she describes how Parisian fashion houses reinvented themselves as brands, capitalising on the symbolic value of haute couture and its cultural heritage in the American market of the 1950s.[118] Finally, from an institutional point of view, she analysed the activity of the *Chambre Syndicale de la Couture*, a key institution in the French fashion industry during the interwar period.[119] In recent years, several compilations have provided interesting case studies that complete our knowledge on French luxury brands,[120] explore recent highly successful Spanish brands,[121] as well as the Italian fashion system.[122] In analysing patents and trademarks, Carlo Belfanti and Merlo examined the innovative capacity of Salvatore Ferragamo, one of the leading 'made in Italy' firms in the footwear sector.[123] Stephanie Amerian focused on the pioneering efforts of Dorothy Shaver, of the Lord & Taylor department store in New York City, to promote American design, brands, and designers from the 1920s to the 1950s.[124] Finally, a recent book edited by Regina Lee Blaszczyk and Pouillard provides new interdisciplinary insights into the history of the fashion business and cultural studies through different case studies in which brands are partially addressed.[125]

Contributions in this special issue

The articles included in this special issue address the distinct concerns discussed above, especially related to the emotional, national, and cross-cultural links between brands and consumers. The two first articles refer to specific kinds of products: those that fall under luxury brands. Pierre-Yves Donzé presents a case study of the Swiss watch company Longines between the 1880s and the early twenty-first century. It is a clear example of how luxury brands were built, evolved, and globalised. Longines represents the mutation of brands from their material links – high-precision goods – to the intangible values that they want to convey: design, tradition, years of know-how, crafts, heritage, and status. As Donzé asserts: 'The first generation of global brands relied on technique, not image', but the rise of Japanese competitors, with their electronic movements far more precise than mechanical ones, compelled Swiss watchmakers to reposition their brands to luxury and to turn their watches into fashion objects and goods of social distinction. Donzé presents a case of success that leads well to the next article: a comparative study of the process of building global brands in fashion, another luxury industry.

Elisabetta Merlo and Mario Perugini present a case study of Gruppo Finanziario Tessile (GFT), the main Italian clothing manufacturer. The GFT case delves deeper into a topic addressed above: the search for reputation, which is one of the many branding issues that fashion faces.[126] GFT was a mass-production company in Italy in the 1950s. Seeking to expand abroad and to enhance its markets shares, in the 1960s and the 1970s it approached successful contemporary Italian fashion designers. The partnerships changed GFT in terms of scope and diversification and clearly benefited the designers who developed significant textile brands – based on their own names – and, after several years, became independent from their industrial partner. Merlo and Perugini tell the story of failure when GFT suffered a profound crisis in the 1990s. However, the article sheds light on how famous Italian fashion luxury and *prêt-à-porter* brands were built over time and helps to explain whether GFT or its fashion designers improved brand management.

The next three articles appeal to the sense of national belonging and to the cross-cultural connections among countries. Through a case study of two brands, Felicity Barnes and David Higgins demonstrate how it is possible to build a major brand based on CoO without trademark protection. New Zealand lamb and Anchor butter emerged during the highly volatile interwar period and prevailed in the increasingly competitive market of the United Kingdom. Their success was based on: (1) the strong cultural foundations of New Zealand and Anchor brands, built on the so-called empire connection that made them particularly appealing to British consumers; (2) accurate marketing policies from the boards – the New Zealand Meat Produce Board (NZMPB) and the New Zealand Dairy Produce Control Board (NZDPCB) – that promoted both brands together and boosted the construction of a shared British identity, enhancing similarities and carefully concealing the differences; and (3) the action of the New Zealand state, which was heavily involved in regulating, coordinating, and promoting the activities of NZMPB and NZDPCB.

Ramón Ramón examines the increasing flows of canned and branded olive oil from Europe to North America from 1870 to 1938. This expansion was the result of three factors that interconnected different sides of brands, as discussed in this introduction. The first is related to the mass migration from southern Europe at the end of the nineteenth century that boosted the consumption of olive oil in the Americas. New mass migration allowed exporting firms to appeal to cultural identification between olive oil and the home country to earn immigrants' loyalty. Not surprisingly, brands started to promote names, symbols, and label designs that evoked the 'mother country'. Migrants also became active actors in the changes in the commodity chain in the US market as a response to the demand for variety and the fluctuating costs of packaging, storing, and blending. These transformations led to the use of modern marketing and branding techniques as competitive strategies. Finally, brands helped towards solving the problem of fraud that went hand-in-hand with market growth. As a 'haven of stability – and trust – in a world with a high degree of uncertainty',[127] olive oil brands offered consumers a certain guarantee of quality in a product that could be easily adulterated.

Matthew Bellamy explores the birth of Labatt Blue, the first national lager brand in Canada. The author analyses how Labatt's marketing managers set up the 'identity' of the brand over a course of years, from the 'European' Labatt Pilsner to the 'Canadian' Labatt Blue. Pilsners had an image problem in Canada – a country where the idea of nation collided with regional, religious, linguistic, and ethnic diversity – as it did not match with the imagination of distinct segments of Canadian beer drinkers. Only after 'Pilsner' was rebranded as the flagship 'Blue' did Labatt reach the top spot in the Canadian brewing industry. This case study offers two important lessons to understand better the creation of a brand, notwithstanding that it needs to connect emotionally and culturally with consumers. First, it demonstrates how complex and difficult is the process of building a brand: it can take decades, making marketing knowledge essential. Second, it shows that such knowledge comes from a large array of actors. In the alcoholic beverages sector, the founders of firms and/or their family members were usually key in giving the brand its 'authenticity' and its 'personality'; in this case, though, Labatt had strong marketing executives who had the knowledge and skills needed to refashion the firm, confirming Lopes and Casson's findings on the role of professional managers.[128]

Valeria Pinchera and Diego Rinallo return readers to the Italian fashion industry, but they focus on the collective fashion shows that Giovanni Battista Giorgini organised in Florence from 1951 to 1965. The article critically examines Giorgini's nation-branding strategy as a promotional platform aimed at the North American market. The authors highlight the importance of collective marketing actions to earn consumers' loyalty. In this case study, Giorgini built the (inaccurate) narrative that Italian fashion was the direct heir of the Renaissance craftsmanship tradition. With the help of the foreign press, and in line with Pouillard's findings, Giorgini's nation branding succeeded in giving a more favourable country image that defined and legitimised Italian fashion in foreign markets. The research highlights two main findings not given enough attention by branding and marketing scholars. First, an accurate, ongoing, and coordinated nation-branding strategy can lead to the creation of a stable and durable CoO effect. In this case, despite the demise of Florence as a centre of craftsmanship, Italy did not lose its aura of fashion power. Second, as pointed out by Per Hansen, it is the joint effort of both firms and national institutions which co-creates and co-brands a country image in international markets.[129]

The final article in this special issue is devoted to the deep socio-cultural role of brands, in this case as a means of freedom, through counterfeiting of Western brands in Soviet Lithuania. Brigita Tranavičiūtė sheds light on how the demand for foreign counterfeit brands spread along with the Western cultural ideas that had reached the Soviet Union in the 1970s and the 1980s. She also analyses the realm of the Soviet shadow economy that covered the production and sales of the garments by using fake foreign brand logos and letterings. The story of Lithuania is a reminder of what happened in Poland after World War II when Western brands became known to local consumers: clothing such as jeans was brought into the country by tourists and then sold in flea markets.[130] However, this Lithuanian case study offers more. It is a prime example of the complexity of messages that a brand conveys. If brands define the groups that consumers desire to belong to, wearing counterfeit foreign brands or letterings in English is a clear indication of cultural freedom and personal image in a monolithic-culture country such as the Soviet Union. Neither moralising Soviet propaganda nor sanctions against people engaged in the commerce of fake Western brands could stop these practices. Her article offers a powerful allegory of the collapse of the Soviet system at the beginning of the 1990s.

Branding history: challenges and opportunities

At the end of 2015, *The Economist* presented the results of several surveys that warned about the waning faith in brands.[131] In North America, consumers said they trusted only about one-fifth of brands. In Europe, the proportion barely reached one-third. In a world in which brands ruled for more than a century, what could explain this trend? Why is old marketing fading? The answer lies with the new marketplace, which is related to the information and network society. The ease of accessing information should theoretically make consumer-choice processes easier. In the twenty-first century, some economists have turned to the Internet as the mechanism to provide a utopian marketplace where buyers and sellers would have full information.[132] Of course, even in the virtual world, full information is not possible. Even so, it is clear that changes for brands are coming because their strength as a sign of quality and their power to open people's wallets are fading.[133] What is the role of brands in this new 'perfect' marketplace? How can brands prevail? Far more important, how can business historians provide valuable analyses about changes in branding? In other words, how can the past be used to study the future of branding?

The first way has to do with the prime work of business historians. We are facing times of deep and rapid changes that are altering the relationships among firms, their brands, and their consumers. Business historians could provide significant insights into how firms managed similar problems and situations when creating and building their brands in past critical moments, including the challenges and consequences of their distinct responses. In doing so, we may be able to decode the keys that explain brand successes and failures over time. There are many cases of long-term success – Coca-Cola is probably the most prominent – and some legendary brands have recently outlasted their own firms, such as Saab or Converse, among others. These companies deserve to be researched in depth. This could open a new line of research: the study of brand failures, which is a challenging task. When researching failure, there will probably be a lack of resources at the firm level, but it would be worthwhile to explore and analyse other resources, such as media.

Another path for future research on branding history is consumption. Brands, through the emotions they convey, are the bridges between firms and consumers, but very little is known about the historical evolution of the consumer side in this story. In other words, we barely know whether consumers were active or passive actors in the building and development of brands over time. If proactive, it would be necessary to explore how individual and collective perceptions emerged, and whether public and private institutions played any roles. Business historians could lean towards historical episodes of collective construction of the ideology of brands and relational branding. The case of Soviet Lithuania in this special issue is a good example to understand how cultural, political, social, and even religious phenomena have strong consequences in the collective development of brands. The lack of resources becomes, once again, apparent, especially for the nineteenth century and earlier.

To overcome this liability, it will be necessary to adopt a multidisciplinary approach. For example, the study of marketing constructs such as *brand communities* or *subcultures of consumption* could be a strong starting point. Both concepts describe small but united groups within society that were emotionally connected with a brand. The idea of communal consumption is not new. Many enduring brands – Singer, Harley Davidson, Coca-Cola – swept along different kinds of communities, but a systematic historical research that considers other approaches, such as ethnographic or iconographic approaches, has been overlooked. Other sources could be found in market surveys provided by consultancy firms, advertising agencies, or public institutions. In doing so, business historians would contribute to the building of a comprehensive cultural history of branding.

Historical research can also explore opposite branding tendencies. One of the main topics of this special issue is the historical study of CoO and nation branding, both being responses to globalisation, and both being phenomena that seem to 'sweep away everything' in their paths. However, the growing presence of global brands in the marketplace has not terminated successful regional or local brands. On the contrary, local brands, particularly consumer-good brands, are often related to healthy small and mid-sized companies (SMEs) in all countries. The success of these local brands may rely on strong emotional connections with their surroundings – as well as premium quality and other values related to tradition and the nostalgia of 'the good old days' – that could be historically tracked. Thus, business historians would be able to identify the keys to understand how enduring local SME brands are built over time. A systematic comparison with the evolution of enduring global brands should help in elaborating a taxonomy of the factors that allow a brand to survive over time or even to pass from local to global.

Another issue for future research is the study of private label brands (PLBs) and the long-term competition with national brands; that is, the classic fight between manufacturers and wholesalers/retailers. Although it was one of our requests in the call for papers in September 2015, we did not receive any proposals on the topic.[134] Historically, PLBs represented lower-price and usually lower-quality options than competing national brands.[135] However, consumer perceptions of private labels have changed over the years, both in Europe and North America, because of the increasing reputation earned by PLBs in terms of quality and promotion.[136] Despite it being a current issue in branding studies and that PLBs appeared at the beginning of the twentieth century and gained in popularity in parallel with national brands (especially in the United States), business historians have given little attention to the topic, excepting some studies on British and American private brands.[137] Consumption behaviours are changing because of new distribution channels, such as the Internet. Additionally, some large retail companies – such as Sears, one of the first firms to adopt PLBs – are facing serious difficulties.[138] This provides many opportunities for business historians to shed light on the topic with provocative, comparative, and long-term analyses.

The final idea for this research agenda is a key issue in branding: the defence of the brand from counterfeiting. According to the Organisation for Economic Cooperation and Development (OECD), trade in counterfeit and pirated goods amounted to 2.5% of world trade – about USD 461 billion – in 2013, the equivalent of the combined gross domestic product of Ireland and the Czech Republic.[139] Counterfeiting makes up a vast global business/ problem nowadays and covers an immense gamut, from synthetic cinnamon to copies of the world's most famous electronic devices, including software piracy. However, this business is not new. Historically, innovation and imitation are two sides of the same coin, and the extension and enforcement of patent and trademark laws were not always a way to prevent counterfeiting. In that sense, there are two possible paths of research for business historians: first, to dig into the origins of counterfeiting in distinct goods and sectors and explore how the "business of fakes" has been historically set up and organised; and second, to analyse the responses of imitated firms and brands beyond the trademark legislation.

All these – and related paths – make it clear that there is plenty of room for business historians to play an active role in branding research not only by providing useful analytical and historical knowledge, which is our main goal, but also by contributing directly to current discussions in business studies regarding one of the most powerful engines of our society: brands.

Acknowledgements

The authors want to sincerely acknowledge: (1) the *Business History* editorial board, and especially Ray Stokes and Andrea Colli, for their constant support in the preparation of this two-issue symposium; (2) attendees of 'The Brand and Its History: Economic, Business, and Social Value', at the UAM Multidisciplinary Research Seminar (Madrid, 22–23 May 2014), and of our session at the International Congress of the Spanish Economic History Association (Madrid, 4–5 September 2014); and (3) the selfless professional collaboration of dozens of scholars who acted as reviewers for this two-issue symposium: Glyn Atwal, John Balmer, María Inés Barbero, Patrizia Battilani, Lionel Bently, Stephen Brown, Andrea Caracausi, Catherine Carstairs, Montserrat Casanovas, Jordi Catalan, Samir Chargui, Howard Cox, Jennifer Davis, Bert De Munck, Stephanie Decker, Timothy Dewhirst, María Fernández Moya, Gabriel Galvez-Behar, Xavier García, Francesca Golfetto, Andrew Griffiths, Tristan Jacques, Kai Lamertz, Manuel Llorca-Jaña, Laura Macchion, María Eugénia Mata, Peter Miskell, Philippe Moati, Mads Mordhorst, Jonathan Morris, Simon Mowatt, Margrit Müller, Juan Luis Pan-Montojo, Eugenia Paulicelli, Yovanna Pineda, Jordi Planas, John Potvin, Véronique Pouillard, David Rolph, Jeremy David Rowan, Peter Scott, Marina Sheresheva, Fredrik Tell, Nebahat Tokatli, Jesús-María Valdaliso, Michelangelo Vasta, Terence Witkowski, and Sergei Zhuk.

Notes

1. http://www.philkotler.com/quotes/.
2. Sáiz and Castro, 'Trademarks in Branding.'
3. The American Marketing Association completes the definition with the entry 'brand and branding:' 'a brand often includes an explicit logo, fonts, colour schemes, symbols, sound which may be developed to represent implicit values, ideas, and even personality.' American Marketing Association, 'Dictionary.'
4. Chernatony and Riley, 'Defining a 'Brand', 418–424.
5. Some examples of pre-modern brands are in Moore and Reid, 'The Birth of Brand;' Zangger, 'Chops and Trademarks;' Belfanti, 'Branding before the Brand.'
6. Bastos and Levy, 'History of the Concept of Branding,' 355.
7. See Sáiz and Castro, 'Trademarks in Branding.'
8. Babutsidze, 'How Do Consumers Make Choices?,' 752; Ramello and Silva, 'Appropriating Signs and Meaning,' 952.
9. Casson and Wadeson, 'Export Performance and Reputation,' 31.
10. Akerlof, 'The Market for 'Lemons'.'
11. Landes and Posner, 'Trademark Law.'
12. See Carter, Casson, and Suneja, 'Introduction,' xiii–xiv.
13. Ramello and Silva, 'Appropriating Signs and Meaning,' 938.
14. In fact, it is not only the experience for themselves; many people buy branded goods for the purpose of impressing others. Landes and Posner, 'Trademark Law,' 308.

15. Pine and Gilmore, *The Experience Economy*.
16. Veblen, *The Theory of the Leisure Class*. One attempt was undertaken by Yuran, 'Meaningful Objects or Costly Symbols?'
17. Moore and Reid, 'The Birth of Brand,' 420.
18. Hattwick, 'Behavioral Economics,' 141.
19. Costa, Carvalho, and Moreira, 'Behavioral Economics and Behavioral Finance,' 1–3.
20. Hattwick, 'Behavioral Economics,' 142.
21. Oliveira-Castro, Foxall, and Schrezenmaier, 'Consumer Brand Choice,' 147–148.
22. Simon, 'Rational Decision Making.'
23. Kahneman and Tversky, 'Choices, Values, and Frames.'
24. Mohaidin, 'Behavioural Economics Approach,' 411–413. The matching law states that individuals will distribute their behaviour between alternatives in the same ratio that reinforcement has been obtained for those alternatives; that is, choosing what they think will provide them the maximum possible reward.
25. Shin, Misra, and Horsky, 'Disentangling Preferences.'
26. Wells, 'Behavioural Psychology,' 1138–1144.
27. Hardie, Johnson, and Fader, 'Modeling Loss Aversion,' 379; Foxall and Schrezenmaier, 'The Behavioral Economics;' Foxall, Oliveira-Castro, and Schrezenmaier, 'The Behavioral Economics;' Foxall et al., *Behavioral Economics of Brand Choice*.
28. Gardner and Levy, 'The Product and the Brand,' 118.
29. Smith, 'Product Differentiation.'
30. See Goyat, 'The Basis of Market Segmentation.'
31. Cunningham, 'Brand Loyalty;' Chaudhuri and Holbrook, 'The Chain of Effects.'
32. Martineau, 'The Personality.'
33. Lazer, 'Symbolism and Life Style;' Berkman and Gilson, *Consumer Behavior*.
34. Roper and Parker, 'Evolution of Branding Theory,' 58.
35. Ries and Trout, *Positioning*.
36. Kornberger, *Brand Society*.
37. Leone et al., 'Linking Brand Equity,' 126.
38. Aaker, *Managing Brand Equity*; Aaker, *Building Strong Brands*.
39. Simon and Sullivan, 'The Measurement and Determinants.'
40. Keller, 'Conceptualizing, Measuring and Managing.'
41. Christodoulides and de Chernatony, 'Consumer-Based Brand Equity,' 48.
42. Brodie, Glynn, and van Durme, 'Towards a Theory;' Hampf and Lindberg-Repo, 'Branding,' 233.
43. Fournier, 'Consumers and Their Brands.'
44. Kapferer, *The New Strategic Brand Management*.
45. Aggarwal and Mcgill, 'When Brands Seem Human.'
46. Aaker, Fournier, and Brasel, 'When Good Brands Do Bad;' Swaminathan et al., 'When Brand Personality Matters.'
47. Belk, 'Possessions and the Extended Self.'
48. Dong and Tian, 'The Use of Western Brands.'
49. Han, Nunes, and Drèze, 'Signaling Status;' Casson, 'Brands: Economic Ideology,' 51; see also the contribution of Brigita Tranavičiūtė in this same Special Issue.
50. Casson, 'Brands: Economic Ideology,' 50–53. The author identifies several types of cultural characteristic: emotion, morality, allegiance, and status, among others.
51. Aaker, Benet-Martínez, and Garolera, 'Consumption Symbols,' 507.
52. Holt, 'How Consumers Consume;' Roth, 'The Effects of Culture.' The Consumer Culture Theory (CCT) is essentially concerned with the cultural meanings and social dynamics that shape consumers' experiences in their everyday lives; it has contributed to a better understanding on the matter over the last 20 years. For an overview, see Arnould and Thompson, 'Consumer Culture Theory.'
53. Steenkamp, Batra, and Alden, 'How Perceived Brand Globalness,' 53.
54. Keller and Lehmann, 'Brands and Branding,' 750; Roth, 'Effects of Global Market Conditions;' Levitt, 'The Globalization of Markets;' Holt, Quelch, and Taylor, 'How Global Brands Compete;'

Mooij and Hofstede, 'The Hofstede Model,' 85. A model that scholars have used often is Geert Hofstede's dimensional model of national culture. Hofstede, 'The Cultural Relativity.'

55.   Kapferer, *Strategic Brand Management*; Keller, *Strategic Brand Management*; Holt, Quelch, and Taylor, 'How Global Brands Compete.'

56.   Shimp and Sharma, 'Consumer Ethnocentrism;' Zambuni, 'Developing Brands across Borders.'

57.   Holt, Quelch, and Taylor, 'How Global Brands Compete.'

58.   Verlegh and Steenkamp, 'A Review and Meta-Analysis,' 522.

59.   See Pappu, Quester, and Cooksey, 'Country Image,' 727–728.

60.   Toncar and Fetscherin, 'The Effects of the Country,' 166.

61.   Dichter, 'The World Customer,' 116.

62.   Schooler, 'Product Bias.'

63.   Pharr, 'Synthesizing,' 34–35; Peterson and Jolibert, 'A Meta-Analysis,' 886.

64.   Peterson and Jolibert, 'A Meta-Analysis,' 894–895. In the mid-1990s, Robert Peterson and Alain Jolibert undertook the most important attempt to synthetise the literature on the CoO effect. Despite showing that CoO has a strong influence on product evaluation, they confessed that the phenomenon was not well understood at that time.

65.   Obermiller, 'Comments of Evolving Country.'

66.   The advantages of CoO indications primarily appear when it comes to products that are more dependent on the brand image, such as the more expensive wines or perfumes. In these cases, the origin, price, and brand name to a greater extent serve as a guarantee of quality. Toncar and Fetscherin, 'The Effects of the Country,' 165–166; Agrawal and Kamakura, 'Country of Origin.'

67.   Yasin, Noor, and Mohamad, 'Does Image of Country-of-Origin Matter to Brand Equity?'

68.   Samiee, Shimp, and Sharma, 'Brand Origin Recognition Accuracy.'

69.   Verlegh and Steenkamp, 'A Review and Meta-Analysis.'

70.   Fournier, 'Consumers and Their Brands.'

71.   Anholt, 'Nation-Brands of the Twenty-First Century;' 'Beyond the Nation Brand.' Anholt has created an index that measures the power and appeal of the brand image of different countries. For the United States, for example, see Anholt, 'Nation Brands Index.'

72.   Olins, 'Branding the Nation;' Anholt, *Brand New Justice*.

73.   Varga, 'The Politics of Nation Branding,' 828.

74.   Hansen, 'The Narrative Nature of Place Branding.'

75.   Varga, 'The Politics of Nation Branding,' 828. See also Kaneva, 'Nation Branding.'

76.   Schroeder, 'Cultural Codes,' 124.

77.   Church, 'New Perspectives,' 428.

78.   Wilkins, 'The Neglected Intangible Asset.'

79.   Corley, 'Consumer Marketing;' Hollander and Rassuli, *Marketing*, XV; Tedlow and Jones, *The Rise and Fall*.

80.   Jones and Morgan, *Adding Value*, Chapters 2–5.

81.   Casson, 'Brands: Economic Ideology.'

82.   Balasubramanyam and Salisu, 'Brands and the Alcoholic.'

83.   For a European vision, see Segreto et al., *European Business*.

84.   Koehn, 'Henry Heinz,' 362.

85.   She also identifies other successful entrepreneurs who lived and worked during periods of widespread change: Henry Heinz, Marshall Field, Estee Lauder, Howard Schultz (of Starbucks), and Michael Dell. See Koehn, *Brand New*.

86.   Lopes and Casson, 'Entrepreneurship and the Development,' 678.

87.   Lonier, 'Alchemy in Eden,' 697, 701.

88.   Jones, 'Brand Building,' 87.

89.   Marchand, *Creating the Corporate Soul*; Bird, *Better Living*.

90.   Heller, 'Corporate Brand Building.'

91.   Barjot, 'Michelin's Corporate Image.'

92.   George, 'The Sun's Only Rival,' 62, 70.

93.   Heller, 'Corporate Brand Building,' 194.

94. See the section 'Key concepts in the study of reputation, brands and trademarks' in Casson and Wadeson, 'Export Performance and Reputation,' 32–36.
95. Akerlof, 'The Market for 'Lemons.''
96. Casson and Wadeson, 'Export Performance and Reputation,' 33.
97. Duguid, 'Brands in Chain.'
98. For the toothpaste industry, see Miskell, 'Cavity Protection,' 31–32. For Unilever, see Miskell, 'Unilever's (Other) Brand Wars,' and Miskell, 'Unilever and Its Brands.'
99. Lopes, 'Building Brand Reputation,' 482.
100. Lopes, *Global Brands*, 149.
101. Fernández, 'Unsuccessful Responses.'
102. Casson and Wadeson, 'Export Performance and Reputation,' 45.
103. Olins, 'Branding the Nation,' 245.
104. Head, *Made in Germany*.
105. Casson and Wadeson, 'Export Performance and Reputation.'
106. For embedded institutional structures, see Mordhorst, 'Arla.' For the importance of a state's intervention, see Higgins and Mordhorst, 'Bringing Home,' 179; Higgins and Mordhorst, 'Reputation and Export Performance,' 199. On the negative effects of state intervention, see Câmara, 'Madeira Embroidery.'
107. Higgins, *Brands, Geographical Origin*, especially Chapters 3, 4, and 9.
108. Hansen, 'Co-branding Product,' 77, 83.
109. Rius-Ulldemolins, 'Barcelona and SEAT,' 837–838.
110. Goñi-Mendizabal, 'Brands in the Basque Gun Making Industry,' 11.
111. Miranda, 'Expansion of Spanish Fashion Companies.'
112. Mercer, 'A Mark of Distinction,' 32, 35; Schwarzkopf, 'Turning Trademarks into Brands.'
113. Schwarzkopf, 'Turning Trademarks into Brands,' 166, 173, 188.
114. Heller and Kelly, 'Throwaway History.'
115. Colli and Merlo, 'Family Business.' In the same line, see Merlo, 'The Ascendance.'
116. Pouillard, 'Design Piracy.'
117. Pouillard, 'Fashion for All?'
118. Pouillard, 'Keeping Designs and Brands.'
119. Pouillard, 'Managing Fashion Creativity.'
120. Bonin, 'A Reassessment.'
121. Manera and Garau-Taberner, 'The Invention of the Camper Brand;' Carmona, 'Corporate Growth.'
122. Capalbo, 'Creativty and Innovation.'
123. Belfanti and Merlo, 'Patenting Fashion.'
124. Amerian, 'Fashioning and Selling.'
125. Blaszczyk and Pouillard, *European Fashion*.
126. Other issues are the visions of charismatic designers, notions of luxury, icons of attraction, and concepts of consumer taste, appearance, and identity. See Zhiyan, Borgerson, and Schroeder, *Chinese Brand Culture*, 46.
127. Jones, 'Brands and Marketing,' 2.
128. Lopes and Casson, 'Entrepreneurship and the Development,' 678.
129. Hansen, 'Co-branding Product.'
130. Jastrząb, 'Operation Abundance.'
131. 'It's the Real Thing – Schumpeter,' *The Economist*, 14 November 2015.
132. Kathman, 'Brand Identity Development,' 24.
133. Simonson and Rosen, *Absolute Value*.
134. http://ibcnetwork.org/gestion/uploads/news_events/document_23.pdf.
135. Goldsmith et al., 'Consumer Attitudes,' 340.
136. Rossi, Borges, and Bakpayev, 'Private Labels versus National Brands,' 74.
137. Several firms adopted a PLBs strategy. First A&P (1859), followed by Penney (1914), Sears (1926), and Marks and Spencer (1928). Montgomery, 'Marks and Spencer Ltd. (A);' Spector, 'The Evolution.'

138. https://www.nytimes.com/2018/10/14/business/sears-bankruptcy-filing-chapter-11.html.
139. OECD, *Trade in Counterfeit*, 11.

Disclosure statement

No potential conflict of interest was reported by the authors.

References

Aaker, David A. *Building Strong Brands*. New York: Simon and Schuster, 1995.
Aaker, David A. *Managing Brand Equity: Capitalizing on the Value of a Brand Name*. New York: Free Press, 1991.
Aaker, Jennifer, Susan Fournier, and S. Adam Brasel. "When Good Brands Do Bad." *Journal of Consumer Research* 31, no. 1 (2004): 1–16. doi:10.1086/383419
Aaker, Jennifer, Verónica Benet-Martínez, and Jordi Garolera. "Consumption Symbols as Carriers of Culture: A Study of Japanese and Spanish Brand Personality Constructs." *Journal of Personality and Social Psychology* 81, no. 3 (2001): 492–508. doi:10.1037//0022-3514.81.3.492
Aggarwal, Pankaj, and Ann L. Mcgill. "When Brands Seem Human, Do Humans Act Like Brands? Automatic Behavioral Priming Effects of Brand Anthropomorphism." *Journal of Consumer Research* 39, no. 2 (2012): 307–323. doi:10.1086/662614
Agrawal, Jagdish, and Wagner A. Kamakura. "Country of Origin: A Competitive Advantage?" *International Journal of Research in Marketing* 16, no. 4 (1999): 255–267. doi:10.1016/S0167-8116(99)00017-8
Akerlof, George A. "The Market for 'Lemons': Quality Uncertainty and the Market Mechanism." *The Quarterly Journal of Economics* 84, no. 3 (1970): 488–500. doi:10.2307/1879431
Amerian, Stephanie M. "Fashioning and Selling the American Look: Dorothy Shaver and Modern Art." *Investigaciones de Historia Económica–Economic History Research* 12, no. 2 (2016): 100–108. doi:10.1016/j.ihe.2015.05.001
American Marketing Association. "Dictionary." Accessed October 13, 2018. https://www.ama.org/resources/Pages/Dictionary.aspx?dLetter=B
Anholt, Simon. "Anholt Nation Brands Index: How Does the World See America?" *Journal of Advertising Research* 45, no. 3 (2005): 296–304. doi:10.1017/S0021849905050336
Anholt, Simon. "Beyond the Nation Brand: The Role of Image and Identity in International Relations." In *Brands and Branding Geographies*, edited by Andy Pike, 289–304. London: Edward Elgar, 2011.
Anholt, Simon. *Brand New Justice: The Upside of Global Branding*. Burlington, MA: Butterworth-Heinemann, 2003.
Anholt, Simon. "Nation-Brands of the Twenty-First Century." *Journal of Brand Management* 5, no. 6 (1998): 395–406.
Arnould, Eric J., and Craig J. Thompson. "Consumer Culture Theory (CCT): Twenty Years of Research." *Journal of Consumer Research* 31, no. 4 (2005): 868–882. doi:10.1086/426626
Babutsidze, Zakaria. "How Do Consumers Make Choices? A Survey of Evidence." *Journal of Economic Surveys* 26, no. 4 (2012): 752–762. doi:10.1111/j.1467-6419.2011.00693.x
Balasubramanyam, Vudayagiri, and Mohammed A. Salisu. "Brands and the Alcoholic Drinks Industry." In *Adding Value: Brands and Marketing in Food and Drink*, edited by Geoffrey G. Jones and Nicholas Morgan, 59–75. Cambridge, UK: Routledge, 1994.
Barjot, Dominique. "The Building of Michelin's Corporate Image and Brand." In *European Business and Brand Building*, edited by Francesca Tesi, Hubert Bonin, Andrzej K. Kozminski, and Carles Manera, 51–75. Bern, Switzerland: P.I.E. Peter Lang, 2012.
Bastos, William, and Sidney J. Levy. "A History of the Concept of Branding: Practice and Theory." *Journal of Historical Research in Marketing* 4, no. 3 (2012): 347–368. doi:10.1108/17557501211252934
Belfanti, Carlo Marco. "Branding before the Brand: Marks, Imitations and Counterfeits in Pre-Modern Europe." *Business History* 60, no. 8 (2017): 1127–1146. doi:10.1080/00076791.2017.1282946

Belfanti, Carlo Marco, and Elisabetta Merlo. "Patenting Fashion: Salvatore Ferragamo between Craftmanship and Industry." *Investigaciones de Historia Económica–Economic History Research* 12, no. 2 (2016): 109–119. doi:10.1016/j.ihe.2015.07.010

Belk, Russell W. "Possessions and the Extended Self." *Journal of Consumer Research* 15, no. 2 (1988): 139–168. doi:10.1086/209154

Berkman, Harold W., and Christopher C. Gilson. *Consumer Behavior: Concepts and Strategies.* Kent: Kent Publishing Company, 1986.

Bird, William L. *"Better Living": Advertising, Media and the New Vocabulary of Business Leadership, 1935–1955.* Evanston, Illinois: Northwestern University Press, 1999.

Blaszczyk, Regina Lee, and Véronique Pouillard, eds. *European Fashion: The Creation of a Global Industry.* Manchester: Manchester University Press, 2018.

Bonin, Hubert. "A Reassessment of the Business History of the French Luxury Sector. The Emergence of a New Business Model and a Renewed Corporate Image (from the 1970s)." In *European Business and Brand Building,* edited by Luciano Segreto, Hubert Bonin, Andrzej K. Kozminski, and Carles Manera, 113–136. Bern, Switzerland: P.I.E. Peter Lang, 2012. https://www.peterlang.com/view/978 3035261424/9783035261424.00009.xml.

Brodie, Roderick J., Mark S. Glynn, and Joel van Durme. "Towards a Theory of Marketplace Equity: Integrating Branding and Relationship Thinking with Financial Thinking." *Marketing Theory* 2, no. 1 (2002): 5–28. doi:10.1177/147059310200200101

Câmara, Benedita. "Madeira Embroidery: A Failed Collective Brand (1935–59)." *Business History* 53, no. 4 (2011): 583–599. doi:10.1080/00076791.2011.574693

Capalbo, Cinzia. "Creativity and Innovation of the Italian Fashion System in the Inter-War Period (1919–1943)." *Investigaciones de Historia Económica–Economic History Research* 12, no. 2 (2016): 90–99. doi:10.1016/j.ihe.2015.08.002

Carmona, Xoan. "Corporate Growth and Changes in Brand Identity. The Case of the Zara Group." In *European Business and Brand Building,* edited by Luciano Segreto, Hubert Bonin, Andrzej K. Kozminski, and Carles Manera, 187–208. Bern, Switzerland: P.I.E. Peter Lang, 2012.

Carter, Martin, Mark Casson, and Vivek Suneja. "Introduction." In *The Economics of Marketing,* edited by Martin Carter, Mark Casson, and Vivek Suneja, 13–24. Cheltenham, UK: Edward Elgar, 1998.

Casson, Mark. "Brands: Economic Ideology and Consumer Society." In *Adding Value: Brands and Marketing in Food and Drink,* edited by Geoffrey G. Jones and Nicholas Morgan, 41–58. Cambridge, UK: Routledge, 1994.

Casson, Mark, and Nigel Wadeson. "Export Performance and Reputation." In *Trademarks, Brands, and Competitiveness,* edited by Teresa da Silva Lopes and Paul Duguid, 31–55. New York: Routledge, 2010.

Chaudhuri, Arjun, and Morris B. Holbrook. "The Chain of Effects from Brand Trust and Brand Affect to Brand Performance: The Role of Brand Loyalty." *Journal of Marketing* 65, no. 2 (2001): 81–93. doi:10.1509/jmkg.65.2.81.18255

Chernatony, Leslie de, and Francesca Dall'Olmo Riley. "Defining a 'Brand': Beyond the Literature with Experts' Interpretations." *Journal of Marketing Management* 14, no. 5 (1998): 417–443. doi:10.1362/026725798784867798.

Christodoulides, George, and Leslie de Chernatony. "Consumer-Based Brand Equity Conceptualisation and Measurement: A Literature Review." *International Journal of Market Research* 52, no. 1 (2010): 43–66.

Church, Roy. "New Perspectives on the History of Products, Firms, Marketing, and Consumers in Britain and the United States since the Mid-Nineteenth Century." *Economic History Review* 52, no. 3 (1999): 405–435. doi:10.1111/1468-0289.00131

Colli, Andrea, and Elisabetta Merlo. "Family business and luxury business in Italy (1950-2000)." *Entreprises et Histoire* 46, no. 1 (2007): 113–124. doi:10.3917/eh.046.0113

Corley, T. A. B. "Consumer Marketing in Britain 1914–60." *Business History* 29, no. 4 (1987): 65–83. doi:10.1080/00076798700000081

Costa, Daniel Fonseca, Francisval de Melo Carvalho, and Bruno César de Melo Moreira. "Behavioral Economics and Behavioral Finance: A Bibliometric Analysis of the Scientific Fields." *Journal of Economic Surveys* 33, no. 1 (2018): 3–24. doi:10.1111/joes.12262.

Cunningham, Ross M. "Brand Loyalty, What, Where, How Much?" *Harvard Business Review* 34, no. 1 (1956): 116–128.

Dichter, Ernest. "The World Customer." *Harvard Business Review* 40, no. 4 (1962): 113–122. doi:10.1002/tie.5060040415

Dong, Lily, and Kelly Tian. "The Use of Western Brands in Asserting Chinese National Identity." *Journal of Consumer Research* 36, no. 3 (2009): 504–523. doi:10.1086/598970

Duguid, Paul. "Brands in Chain." In *Trademarks, Brands, and Competitiveness*, edited by Teresa da Silva Lopes and Paul Duguid, 138–164. Cambridge, UK: Routledge, 2008.

Fernández, Eva. "Unsuccessful Responses to Quality Uncertainty: Brands in Spain's Sherry Industry, 1920–1990." *Business History* 52, no. 1 (2010): 100–119. doi:10.1080/00076790903469638

Fournier, Susan. "Consumers and Their Brands: Developing Relationship Theory in Consumer Research." *Journal of Consumer Research* 24, no. 4 (1998): 343–353. doi:10.1086/209515

Foxall, Gordon R., Jorge M. Oliveira-Castro, and Teresa C. Schrezenmaier. "The Behavioral Economics of Consumer Brand Choice: Patterns of Reinforcement and Utility Maximization." *Behavioural Processes* 66, no. 3 (2004): 235–260. doi:10.1016/j.beproc.2004.03.007

Foxall, Gordon R., Jorge M. Olivera-Castro, Victoria K. James, and Teresa C Schrezenmaier. *The Behavioral Economics of Brand Choice*. New York: Springer, 2007.

Foxall, Gordon R., and Teresa C. Schrezenmaier. "The Behavioral Economics of Consumer Brand Choice: Establishing a Methodology." *Journal of Economic Psychology* 24, no. 5 (2003): 675–695. doi:10.1016/S0167-4870(03)00008-4

Gardner, Burleigh B., and Sidney J. Levy. "The Product and the Brand." *Harvard Business Review* 33, no. 2 (1955): 33–39.

George, Leigh. "'The Sun's Only Rival:' General Electric's Mazda Trademark and the Marketing of Electric Light." *Design Issues* 19, no. 1 (2003): 62–71. doi:10.1162/074793603762667719

Goldsmith, Ronald E., Leisa R. Flynn, Elizabeth Goldsmith, and E. Craig Stacey. "Consumer Attitudes and Loyalty towards Private Brands." *International Journal of Consumer Studies* 34, no. 3 (2010): 339–348. doi:10.1111/j.1470-6431.2009.00863.x

Goñi-Mendizabal, Igor. "Brands in the Basque Gun Making Industry: The Case of ASTRA-Unceta y Cía." *Business History* 60, no. 8 (2018): 1196–1226. doi:10.1080/00076791.2017.1282947

Goyat, Sulekha. "The Basis of Market Segmentation: A Critical Review of Literature." *European Journal of Business and Management* 3, no. 9 (2011): 45–54.

Hampf, Anders, and Kirsti Lindberg-Repo. "Branding: The Past, Present, and Future: A Study of the Evolution and Future Branding." Svenska Handelshögskolan, 2011. http://econpapers.repec.org/paper/hhbhanken/0556.htm.

Han, Young Jee, Joseph C. Nunes, and Xavier Drèze. "Signaling Status with Luxury Goods: The Role of Brand Prominence." *Journal of Marketing* 74, no. 4 (2010): 15–30. doi:10.1509/jmkg.74.4.15

Hansen, Per H. "Co-Branding Product and Nation: Danish Modern Furniture and Denmark in the United States, 1940–1970." In *Trademarks, Brands, and Competitiveness*, edited by Teresa da Silva Lopes and Paul Duguid, 77–101. New York: Routledge, 2010.

Hansen, Rebecca Hjortegaard. "The Narrative Nature of Place Branding." *Place Branding and Public Diplomacy* 6, no. 4 (2010): 268–279. doi:10.1057/pb.2010.27

Hardie, Bruce G. S., Eric J. Johnson, and Peter S. Fader. "Modeling Loss Aversion and Reference Dependence Effects on Brand Choice." *Marketing Science* 12, no. 4 (1993): 378–394. doi:10.1287/mksc.12.4.378

Hattwick, Richard E. "Behavioral Economics: An Overview." *Journal of Business and Psychology* 4, no. 2 (1989): 141–154. doi:10.1007/BF01016437

Head, David. *"Made in Germany": The Corporate Identity of a Nation*. London: Hodder & Stoughton, 1992.

Heller, Michael. "Corporate Brand Building Shell-Mex Ltd. in the Interwar Period." In *Trademarks, Brands, and Competitiveness*, edited by Teresa da Silva Lopes and Paul Duguid, 194–214. New York: Routledge, 2010.

Heller, Michael, and Aidan Kelly. "Throwaway History: Brand Ephemera and Consumer Culture." *Journal of Macromarketing* 35, no. 3 (2014): 397–406. doi:10.1177/0276146714555134

Higgins, David M. *Brands, Geographical Origin, and the Global Economy: A History from the Nineteenth Century to the Present*. Cambridge: Cambridge University Press, 2018.

Higgins, David M., and Mads Mordhorst. "Bringing Home the 'Danish' Bacon: Food Chains, National Branding and Danish Supremacy over the British Bacon Market, c. 1900–1938." *Enterprise & Society* 16, no. 1 (2015): 141–185. doi:10.1017/eso.2014.14

Higgins, David M., and Mads Mordhorst. "Reputation and Export Performance: Danish Butter Exports and the British Market, c.1880–c.1914." *Business History* 50, no. 2 (2008): 185–204. doi:10.1080/00076790701868601

Hofstede, Geert. "The Cultural Relativity of Organizational Practices and Theories." *Journal of International Business Studies* 14, no. 2 (1983): 75–89. doi:10.1057/palgrave.jibs.8490867

Hollander, Stanley C., and Kathleen M. Rassuli, eds. *Marketing*. Hants, UK: Edward Elgar, 1993.

Holt, Douglas B. "How Consumers Consume: A Typology of Consumption Practices." *Journal of Consumer Research* 22, no. 1 (1995): 1–16. doi:10.1086/209431

Holt, Douglas, John Quelch, and Earl L. Taylor. "How Global Brands Compete." *Harvard Business Review*, 82, no. 9 (2004): 68–75. https://hbr.org/2004/09/how-global-brands-compete.

Jastrząb, Marius. "Operation Abundance. Brands and Polish Consumers after WWII." In *European Business and Brand Building*, edited by Hubert Bonin, Andrzej K. Kozminski, and Carles Manera, 209–234. Bern, Switzerland: P.I.E. Peter Lang, 2012.

Jones, Geoffrey G. "Brands and Marketing." In *Adding Value: Brands and Marketing in Food and Drink*, edited by Geoffrey G. Jones and Nicholas Morgan, 1–14. Cambridge, UK: Routledge, 1994.

Jones, Geoffrey G., and Nicholas Morgan, eds. *Adding Value: Brands and Marketing in Food and Drink*. Cambridge, UK: Routledge, 1994.

Jones, S. R. H. "Brand Building and Structural Change in the Scotch Whisky Industry since 1975." *Business History* 45, no. 3 (2003): 72–89. doi:10.1080/713999319

Kahneman, Daniel, and Amos Tversky. "Choices, Values, and Frames." *American Psychologist* 39, no. 4 (1984): 341–350. doi:10.1037//0003-066X.39.4.341

Kaneva, Nadia. "Nation Branding: Toward an Agenda for Critical Research." *International Journal of Communication* 5 (2011): 25.

Kapferer, Jean-Noël. *Strategic Brand Management: Creating and Sustaining Brand Equity Long Term*. Dover, NH: Kogan Page, 1997.

Kapferer, Jean-Noël. *The New Strategic Brand Management: Creating and Sustaining Brand Equity Long Term*. London: Kogan Page, 2008.

Kathman, Jerry. "Brand Identity Development in the New Economy." *Design Issues* 18, no. 1 (2002): 24–35. doi:10.1162/07479360252756269

Keller, Kevin Lane. "Conceptualizing, Measuring, and Managing Customer-Based Brand Equity." *Journal of Marketing* 57, no. 1 (1993): 1–22. doi:10.2307/1252054

Keller, Kevin Lane. *Strategic Brand Management: Building, Measuring, and Managing Brand Equity*. Upper Saddle River, NJ: Prentice-Hall, 1998.

Keller, Kevin Lane, and Donald R. Lehmann. "Brands and Branding: Research Findings and Future Priorities." *Marketing Science* 25, no. 6 (2006): 740–759. doi:10.1287/mksc.1050.0153

Koehn, Nancy F. *Brand New: How Entrepreneurs Earned Consumers' Trust from Wedgwood to Dell*. Cambridge, MA: Harvard Business School Press, 2001.

Koehn, Nancy F. "Henry Heinz and Brand Creation in the Late Nineteenth Century: Making Markets for Processed Food." *The Business History Review* 73, no. 3 (1999): 349–393. doi:10.2307/3116181

Kornberger, Martin. *Brand Society: How Brands Transform Management and Lifestyle*. New York: Cambridge University Press, 2010.

Landes, William M., and Richard A. Posner. "Trademark Law: An Economic Perspective." *The Journal of Law & Economics* 30, no. 2 (1987): 265–309. doi:10.1086/467138

Lazer, William. "Symbolism and Life Style." In *Toward Scientific Marketing: Proceedings of the Winter Conference, December 27-28, 1963*, edited by Stephen A. Greyser, 140–149. Chicago: American Marketing Association, 1963.

Leone, Robert P., Vithala R. Rao, Kevin Lane Keller, Anita Man Luo, Leigh McAlister, and Rajendra Srivastava. "Linking Brand Equity to Customer Equity." *Journal of Service Research* 9, no. 2 (2006): 125–138. doi:10.1177/1094670506293563

Levitt, Theodore. "The Globalization of Markets." *Harvard Business Review* 61, no. 3 (1983): 92–102.

Lonier, Terri. "Alchemy in Eden: Entrepreneurialism, Branding, and Food Marketing in the United States, 1880–1920." *Enterprise & Society* 11, no. 4 (2010): 695–708. doi:10.1017/S1467222700009502

Lopes, Teresa da Silva. "Building Brand Reputation through Third-Party Endorsement: Fair Trade in British Chocolate." *Business History Review* 90, no. 3 (2016): 457–482. doi:10.1017/S0007680516000738

Lopes, Teresa da Silva. *Global Brands: The Evolution of Multinationals in Alcoholic Beverages*. Cambridge: Cambridge University Press, 2007.

Lopes, Teresa da Silva, and Mark Casson. "Entrepreneurship and the Development of Global Brands." *Business History Review* 81, no. 4 (2007): 651–680. doi:10.2307/25097419

Manera, Carles, and Jaume Garau-Taberner. "The Invention of the Camper Brand. Brand Building of Mallorca Shoe-Manufacturing." In *European Business and Brand Building*, edited by Luciano Segreto, Hubert Bonin, Andrzej K. Kozminski, and Carles Manera, 155–186. Bern, Switzerland: P.I.E. Peter Lang, 2012.

Marchand, Roland. *Creating the Corporate Soul: The Rise of Public Relations and Corporate Imagery in American Big Business*. Berkeley: University of California Press, 2001.

Martineau, Pierre. "The Personality of the Retail Store." *Harvard Business Review* 36, no. 1 (1958): 47–55.

Mercer, John. "A Mark of Distinction: Branding and Trade Mark Law in the UK from the 1860s." *Business History* 52, no. 1 (2010): 17–42. doi:10.1080/00076790903281033

Merlo, Elisabetta. "The Ascendance of the Italian Fashion Brands (1970–2000)." In *European Business and Brand Building*, edited by Luciano Segreto, Hubert Bonin, Andrzej K. Kozminski, and Carles Manera, 137–154. Bern, Switzerland: P.I.E. Peter Lang, 2012.

Miranda, José Antonio. "The Country-of-Origin Effect and the International Expansion of Spanish Fashion Companies, 1975–2015." *Business History* (2017). doi:10.1080/00076791.2017.1374370

Miskell, Peter. "Cavity Protection or Cosmetic Perfection? Innovation and Marketing of Toothpaste Brands in the United States and Western Europe, 1955–1985." *The Business History Review* 78, no. 1 (2004): 29–60. doi:10.2307/25096828

Miskell, Peter. "Unilever and Its Brands since the 1950s. Competitive Threats and Strategic Responses." In *European Business and Brand Building*, edited by Luciano Segreto, Hubert Bonin, Andrzej K. Kozminski, and Carles Manera, 29–50. Bern, Switzerland: P.I.E. Peter Lang, 2012.

Miskell, Peter. "Unilever's (Other) Brand Wars Retailers, Private Labels, and Struggles for Supremacy within Product Supply Chains." In *Trademarks, Brands, and Competitiveness*, edited by Teresa da Silva Lopes and Paul Duguid, 215–233. New York: Routledge, 2010.

Mohaidin, Zurina. "Behavioural Economics Approach on Consumer Brand Choice—An Individual Analysis." *Procedia–Social and Behavioral Sciences* 65 (2012): 410–418. doi:10.1016/j.sbspro.2012.11.142

Montgomery, Cynthia A. "Marks and Spencer Ltd. (A)." *Harvard Business School* Case 391-089 (revised in 1994 1991). https://www.hbs.edu/faculty/Pages/item.aspx?num=11946.

Mooij, Marieke de, and Geert Hofstede. "The Hofstede Model." *International Journal of Advertising* 29, no. 1 (2010): 85–110. doi:10.2501/S026504870920104X

Moore, Kark, and Susan Reid. "The Birth of Brand: 4000 Years of Branding." *Business History* 50, no. 4 (2008): 419–432. doi:10.1080/00076790802106299

Mordhorst, Mads. "Arla and Danish National Identity—Business History as Cultural History." *Business History* 56, no. 1 (2014): 116–133. doi:10.1080/00076791.2013.818422

Obermiller, Carl. "Comments of Evolving Country of Origin Research." *Advances in Consumer Research* 20 (1993): 690–691.

OECD. *Trade in Counterfeit and Pirated Goods: Mapping the Economic Impact*. Paris: OECD Publishing, 2016.

Olins, Wally. "Branding the Nation—The Historical Context." *Journal of Brand Management* 9, no. 4 (2002): 241–248. doi:10.1057/palgrave.bm.2540075

Oliveira-Castro, Jorge M., Gordon R. Foxall, and Teresa C. Schrezenmaier. "Consumer Brand Choice: Individual and Group Analyses of Demand Elasticity." *Journal of the Experimental Analysis of Behavior* 85, no. 2 (2006): 147–166. doi:10.1901/jeab.2006.51-04

Pappu, Ravi, Pascale G. Quester, and Ray W. Cooksey. "Country Image and Consumer-Based Brand Equity: Relationships and Implications for International Marketing." *Journal of International Business Studies* 38, no. 5 (2007): 726–745. doi:10.1057/palgrave.jibs.8400293

Peterson, Robert A., and Alain J. P. Jolibert. "A Meta-Analysis of Country-of-Origin Effects." *Journal of International Business Studies* 26, no. 4 (1995): 883–900. doi:10.1057/palgrave.jibs.8490824

Pharr, Julie M. "Synthesizing Country-of-Origin Research from the Last Decade: Is the Concept Still Salient in an Era of Global Brands?" *Journal of Marketing Theory and Practice* 13, no. 4 (2005): 34–45. doi:10.1080/10696679.2005.11658557

Pine, B. Joseph, and James H. Gilmore. *The Experience Economy: Work Is Theatre & Every Business a Stage*. Boston, MA: Harvard Business Press, 1999.

Pouillard, Véronique. "Design Piracy in the Fashion Industries of Paris and New York in the Interwar Years." *The Business History Review* 85, no. 2 (2011): 319–344. doi:10.1017/S0007680511000407

Pouillard, Véronique. "Fashion for All?" *Journalism Studies* 14, no. 5 (2013): 716–729. doi:10.1080/1461670X.2013.810907

Pouillard, Veronique. "Keeping Designs and Brands Authentic: The Resurgence of the Post-War French Fashion Business under the Challenge of US Mass Production." *European Review of History: Revue Européenne D'histoire* 20, no. 5 (2013): 815–835. doi:10.1080/13507486.2013.833720

Pouillard, Véronique. "Managing Fashion Creativity. The History of the Chambre Syndicale de La Couture Parisienne during the Interwar Period." *Investigaciones de Historia Económica–Economic History Research* 12, no. 2 (2016): 76–89. doi:10.1016/j.ihe.2015.05.002

Ramello, Giovanni B., and Francesco Silva. "Appropriating Signs and Meaning: The Elusive Economics of Trademark." *Industrial and Corporate Change* 15, no. 6 (2006): 937–963. doi:10.1093/icc/dtl027

Ries, Al, and Jack Trout. *Positioning: The Battle for Your Mind*. New York: McGraw-Hill, 1981.

Rius-Ulldemolins, Joaquim. "Barcelona and SEAT, a History of Lost Opportunity: Corporate Marketing, Nation Branding, and Consumer Nationalism in the Automotive Industry." *Enterprise & Society* 16, no. 4 (2015): 811–846. doi:10.1017/eso.2015.24

Roper, Stuart, and Cathy Parker. "Evolution of Branding Theory and Its Relevance to the Independent Retail Sector." *The Marketing Review* 6, no. 1 (2008): 55–71. doi:10.1362/146934706776861555

Rossi, Patricia, Adilson Borges, and Marat Bakpayev. "Private Labels versus National Brands: The Effects of Branding on Sensory Perceptions and Purchase Intentions." *Journal of Retailing and Consumer Services* 27 (2015): 74–79. doi:10.1016/j.jretconser.2015.07.006

Roth, Martin S. "Effects of Global Market Conditions on Brand Image Customization and Brand Performance." *Journal of Advertising* 24, no. 4 (1995): 55–75. doi:10.1080/00913367.1995.10673489

Roth, Martin S. "The Effects of Culture and Socioeconomics on the Performance of Global Brand Image Strategies." *Journal of Marketing Research* 32, no. 2 (1995): 163–175. https://doi.org/10.2307/3152045.

Sáiz, Patricio, and Rafael Castro. "Trademarks in Branding: Legal Issues and Commercial Practices." *Business History* 60, no. 8 (2018): 1105–1126. doi:10.1080/00076791.2018.1497765

Samiee, Saeed, Terence A. Shimp, and Subhash Sharma. "Brand Origin Recognition Accuracy: Its Antecedents and Consumers' Cognitive Limitations." *Journal of International Business Studies* 36, no. 4 (2005): 379–397. doi:10.1057/palgrave.jibs.8400145

Schooler, Robert D. "Product Bias in the Central American Common Market." *Journal of Marketing Research* 2, no. 4 (1965): 394–397. doi:10.2307/3149486

Schroeder, Jonathan E. "The Cultural Codes of Branding." *Marketing Theory* 9, no. 1 (2009): 123–126. doi:10.1177/1470593108100067

Schwarzkopf, Stefan. "Turning Trade Marks into Brands: How Advertising Agencies Created Brands in the Global Market Place, 1900–1930." In *Trademarks, Brands, and Competitiveness*, edited by Teresa da Silva Lopes and Paul Duguid, 165–193. Cambridge, UK: Routledge, 2008.

Segreto, Luciano, Hubert Bonin, Andrzej K. Kozminski, and Carles Manera, eds. *European Business and Brand Building*. Bern, Switzerland: P.I.E. Peter Lang, 2012.

Shimp, Terence A., and Subhash Sharma. "Consumer Ethnocentrism: Construction and Validation of the CETSCALE." *Journal of Marketing Research* 24, no. 3 (1987): 280–289. doi:10.2307/3151638

Shin, Sangwoo, Sanjog Misra, and Dan Horsky. "Disentangling Preferences and Learning in Brand Choice Models." *Marketing Science* 31, no. 1 (2012): 115–137. doi:10.1287/mksc.1110.0680

Simon, Carol J., and Mary W. Sullivan. "The Measurement and Determinants of Brand Equity: A Financial Approach." *Marketing Science* 12, no. 1 (1993): 28–52. doi:10.1287/mksc.12.1.28

Simon, Herbert A. "Rational Decision Making in Business Organizations." *The American Economic Review* 69, no. 4 (1979): 493–513.

Simonson, Itamar, and Emanuel Rosen. *Absolute Value: What Really Influences Customers in the Age of (Nearly) Perfect Information*. New York: Harper Collins, 2014.

Smith, Wendell R. "Product Differentiation and Market Segmentation as Alternative Marketing Strategies." *Journal of Marketing* 21, no. 1 (1956): 3–8. doi:10.2307/1247695

Spector, Bert. "The Evolution of a Private-Label Brand Strategy at J.C. Penney, 1902–33." *Management & Organizational History* 8, no. 4 (2013): 387–399. doi:10.1080/17449359.2013.831736

Steenkamp, Jan-Benedict E. M., Rajeev Batra, and Dana L. Alden. "How Perceived Brand Globalness Creates Brand Value." *Journal of International Business Studies* 34, no. 1 (2003): 53–65. doi:10.1057/palgrave.jibs.8400002

Swaminathan, Vanitha, Karen M. Stilley, and Rohini Ahluwalia. "When Brand Personality Matters: The Moderating Role of Attachment Styles." *Journal of Consumer Research* 35, no. 6 (2009): 985–1002. doi:10.1086/593948

Tedlow, Richard S., and Geoffrey G. Jones, eds. *The Rise and Fall of Mass Marketing*. Cambridge, UK: Routledge, 1993.

Toncar, Mark, and Marc Fetscherin. "The Effects of the Country of Brand and the Country of Manufacturing of Automobiles: An Experimental Study of Consumers' Brand Personality Perceptions." *International Marketing Review* 27, no. 2 (2010): 164–178. doi:10.1108/02651331021037494

Varga, Somogy. "The Politics of Nation Branding: Collective Identity and Public Sphere in the Neoliberal State." *Philosophy & Social Criticism* 39, no. 5 (2013): 825–845. doi:10.1177/0191453713494969

Veblen, Thorstein. *The Theory of Leisure Class. An Economic Study of Institutions*. London: McMillan, 1899.

Verlegh, Peeter W. J., and Jan-Benedict E. M. Steenkamp. "A Review and Meta-Analysis of Country-of-Origin Research." *Journal of Economic Psychology* 20, no. 5 (1999): 521–546. doi:10.1016/S0167-4870(99)00023-9

Wells, Victoria K. "Behavioural Psychology, Marketing and Consumer Behaviour: A Literature Review and Future Research Agenda." *Journal of Marketing Management* 30, no. 11–12 (2014): 1119–1158. doi:10.1080/0267257X.2014.929161

Wilkins, Mira. "The Neglected Intangible Asset: The Influence of the Trade Mark on the Rise of the Modern Corporation." *Business History* 34, no. 1 (1992): 66–95. doi:10.1080/00076799200000004

Yasin, Norjaya M., Mohd N. Noor, and Osman Mohamad. "Does Image of Country-of-Origin Matter to Brand Equity?" *Journal of Product & Brand Management* 16, no. 1 (2007): 38–48. doi:10.1108/10610420710731142

Yuran, Noam. "Meaningful Objects or Costly Symbols? A Veblenian Approach to Brands." *Theory, Culture & Society* 33, no. 6 (2016): 25–49. doi:10.1177/0263276416656410

Zambuni, Richard. "Developing Brands across Borders." *Journal of Brand Management* 1, no. 1 (1993): 22–29. doi:10.1057/bm.1993.4

Zangger, Andreas P. "Chops and Trademarks: Asian Trading Ports and Textile Cranding, 1840–1920." *Enterprise & Society* 15, no. 4 (2014): 759–790. doi:10.1017/S1467222700016104

Zhiyan, Wu, Janet Borgerson, and Jonathan E. Schroeder, eds. *From Chinese Brand Culture to Global Brands: Insights from Aesthetics, Fashion, and History*. Basingstoke, UK: Palgrave Macmillan, 2013.

The transformation of global luxury brands: The case of the Swiss watch company Longines, 1880–2010

Pierre-Yves Donzé

ABSTRACT
This article discusses the transformation of global brands between the 1880s and the early twenty-first century, through the example of the Swiss watch company Longines. It shows that the concept of 'global brand' changed over time and was related to the nature of the product. Until the 1970s, luxury was linked to precision. Manufacturers focused on the production of movements and adapted the design of end products to each market. Yet the paradigm shift brought about by electronics led to a new definition of luxury during the 1990s, a change which led to a new generation of global brands.

1. Introduction

Nowadays, the luxury industry is a sector in which the presence of global brands is the strongest.[1] According to the purist approach defended by French marketing gurus Bastien and Kapferer, luxury brands must not adapt to customers and to local markets. Producers must develop and manufacture the goods they can and are able to, according to their know-how and heritage, without thinking to enlarge sales and adjust to new markets: 'the brand must always dominate its client.'[2] Hence, luxury brands' identity is the same throughout the world. They are global brands. Yet this idealistic view is rarely followed by Western contemporary luxury companies for which the growth of sales and profits are key challenges, related to the expansion of markets, especially in culturally different environments like Asia.[3] For some scholars, luxury goods are targeted at social elites around the world, especially the newly rich in emerging countries. As these customers are looking for status symbols and Western goods, adaptation is not required.[4] But this question is still debated by scholars in management studies, the issue being the scope of standardisation rather than its existence.[5]

However, despite the huge amount of literature in management about luxury brands, scholars have not addressed the issue of the construction and transformation of global brands, as if they had always been globalised. The lack of a long-run perspective in these works led management scholars to consider luxury as an unchanging industry and to minimise the dynamics of the brand identity of luxury goods over time. Hence, this article offers a business history approach which stresses how luxury brands were built, evolved, and finally globalised. Notwithstanding, literature on the historical evolution of brands is not very developed. In her seminal work on global brands in alcoholic beverages, Teresa da Silva Lopes acknowledged the small number of works in business history on brands, despite the fact that brand management is a key component of modern enterprises.[6] For most researchers in this field, brand is an outcome of mass production and mass distribution. Alfred Chandler argues that companies began to adopt brand management in the late-nineteenth century when their markets expanded geographically.[7] The transformation of the distribution system, with the emergence of chain stores and supermarkets, and the enlargement of consumption led to a need to identify products, especially in the consumer goods industry (processed food, beverages, tobacco, etc.). Yet, despite the fact that packaged consumer goods manufacturers (Heinz, Kellogg, Nestlé, etc.) spread worldwide and built up global organisations during the years 1880–1914, this did not lead to the appearance of global brands. Geoffrey Jones emphasises that 'most multinationals owned numerous local or regional brands in different markets.'[8] He also showed that for Western cosmetic companies which grew in a different cultural environment, such as Asia, in the interwar years, 'the extent of local adaptation of brands […] was a major marketing challenge.'[9] Stefan Schwarzkopf developed a slightly different point of view, arguing that advertising agencies played a major role in conceptualising branding for manufacturing firms as early as the years 1890–1930, and that they developed in particular 'the idea of the global brand'.[10] However, he gives little evidence to support such an argument.

The major shift occurred after WWII with the appearance of global brands, usually launched and developed by American multinational enterprises (MNEs) such as Coca-Cola or McDonald's. However, this was not a unidirectional trend and other MNEs, such as Unilever and Procter & Gamble, continued to manage large portfolios of regional brands.[11] The idea of the emergence of a globalised and homogenised world market was popular in the US in the early 1980s, as embodied by the iconic paper published by Ted Levitt, professor of marketing at Harvard Business School, entitled *The Globalization of Markets*.[12] In most industries, however, adaptation to regional markets is far more important than standardisation.[13] Moreover, even when a company is building a global brand, brand image and content can vary from one market to another – sometimes considerably – so that one must discuss what the basis of global brands is, what makes them global. In the case of the cosmetic industry, Geoffrey Jones maintains that, on the one hand, there appeared 'a major homogenization of beauty ideals which the beauty companies helped diffuse'[14] that gave birth to some global brands, while on the other hand 'the persistence of distinctive local consumer preferences' is important even for companies whose organisation is global, like L'Oréal or Procter & Gamble.[15] Using the example of the beverage industry, Teresa da Silva Lopes shows that the construction of real global brands is a relatively recent phenomenon, which accelerated in the 1990s, in relation to cross-border mergers and acquisitions (M&A).[16]

This article builds on Lopes' work, maintaining that the globalisation of today's luxury brands is a consequence of the industrial reorganisation which occurred in this sector during the 1980s and 1990s. The foundation of large enterprises through M&A led to a new marketing strategy in which brand management played a key role. However, the existence of global brands is not a new phenomenon in the luxury business. This article argues that the identity of brands shifted from their intrinsic material characteristics to design and immaterial values within the context of industrial transformation. As a case study for exploring this process of building and transforming global brands, this article focuses on the Swiss watch company Longines, founded in 1832, which was one of the largest enterprises in the industry during the twentieth century until it was merged into Swatch Group (SG) (1983). Among hundreds of companies and brands, Longines holds the particular position, together with Omega and Rolex, of already being established as a luxury brand in the late-nineteenth century thanks to its ability to manufacture high-precision watches; the company has maintained this status to this day, despite the merger with SG. Longines thus provides an excellent example for discussing the creation and transformation of global brands in the luxury business. In the 10-year stretch between 1975 and 1985, the Swiss watch industry was hit hard by competition from Japanese watch manufacturers, which caused employment to decline by around two-thirds.[17] However, it staged a comeback on the world market in the late 1980s via the rationalisation of the production system and a move up to luxury, and has been the uncontested leader of the industry ever since. Previous studies have shown that the paradigm shift experienced by this industry in the 1980s led to the implementation of a new brand strategy, as characterised by brand globalisation.[18] Yet this article adopts a different perspective. It aims at discussing more deeply the issue of the nature of global brands by going back to the late-nineteenth century and analysing the development of Longines' brand strategy. Of course, Longines, like other Swiss watch companies, benefitted from an institutional environment that kept production capabilities in Switzerland (the cartel policy in effect between 1934 and the early 1960s and then the Swiss Made law in place since 1971) and consequently contributed to the consistently high reputation of Swiss watches.[19] This context, common to all the watch companies, is not, however, part of the scope of this article, which concentrates on brand management by a particular company. The main questions this article addresses are: What are global brands? How can worldwide customers identify a brand as similar throughout the world? Which elements relies on brand identity to globalise?

The article is divided into three parts. The first briefly introduces brand management in the Swiss watch industry before the transition to luxury then tackles the change in this industry and the move to the upmarket sector. Next, section II takes a close look at brand management by Longines – one of the largest Swiss watch manufacturers – until the 1980s. Finally, section III focuses on the adoption of a new brand strategy by SG, the world's largest watch manufacturer, within the context of its repositioning to luxury, emphasising the changes in Longines.

2. Brand management in the Swiss watch industry before the 1980s

Until the late-nineteenth century, Swiss watchmakers used to sign their watches with their own name. The first brands appeared as a consequence of industrialisation and the emergence of modern industrial enterprises, as emphasised in the Chandler model. The shift from family name to brand embodied a new commercial concept and the first watch companies to adopt a brand were the largest and most modern enterprises at the time, such as Longines (1889), Omega (1894), Zenith (1897) and Rolex (1908).[20] The mass production and worldwide mass distribution of watches gave way to the adoption of a new marketing strategy, especially a desire to differentiate products on the world market and to ensure that consumers can identify them easily, through advertisement and branding. This led watchmakers to give their products specific names and to lobby the Swiss Parliament for a law to protect trademarks and brands (1880). This legal instrument was soon followed by the signature of the

Paris Convention for the Protection of Industrial Property (1883), which allowed Swiss watch-makers to effectively protect their brands in foreign markets.[21]

However, the appearance of brands in the Swiss watch industry did not lead to the stand-ardisation of products, as was the case in most other manufacturing sectors. Watch compa-nies used the same brand to sell products whose design sometimes differed substantially from one market to another, depending on the needs and tastes of local customers. Hence, in 1912, the Association of Watchmakers of La Chaux-de-Fonds, a professional body which grouped together 190 members, explained in a leaflet that the objective of Swiss watch-makers was to 'respond to the needs of all countries, all demands, all tastes and all purses.'[22] In this context, adapting products was a major issue.

Yet competition from American watches at the end of the nineteenth century, then from Japan after the interwar years, underlined the need to rationalise the production system. Consequently, in order to reconcile the apparently contradictory goals of cutting production costs and maintaining a wide range of end products, the main Swiss watch companies adopted a specific strategy, characterised by the production and export of movements, which were then assembled and cased in the countries in which they were sold. This practice was primarily used for the largest markets (US, Japan, Germany, Italy, Hong Kong, etc.), where independent importers of movements sourced cases and straps from local manufacturers.

Consequently, from the interwar years onwards, there was no worldwide consistency between brand and product specificities. For a given brand, such as Omega or Longines, watch design, price and style differed considerably from one country to another. Yet this was not a contradiction in terms of brand management. Until the advent of electronic watches in the 1970s, the competitiveness of firms in this business relied on the precision and durability of products, not their design. Whatever its design, a watch's brand name referred directly to its precision, i.e. movement quality. In this sense, Omega and Longines can be understood as global luxury brands, because they embodied high precision, which made them top-of-the-range goods. Customers throughout the world admired – and pur-chased – these watches because their names were synonymous with quality. This was their competitive advantage.

Using Swiss foreign trade statistics, we can pinpoint the proportion of movements among the volume of watch exports since 1890 (see Figure 1). Despite fluctuations, the period 1890–2013 can be divided into four major phases. At first, the years 1890–1940 were a period of expansion and crisis characterised by a rise in the share of movements, which soared from 5.9% in 1890 to 40.2% in 1940. Custom protectionism, a worldwide phenomenon during these years, was the primary factor driving this trend. Subsequently, the proportion fell for three decades, until 1972 (26.4%), primarily owing to increased production of cheap, low-quality mechanical watches (*pin-lever watches*). These were mass produced without brand value or identity, and competed solely on their low price. Hence, the growing share of movements during the third phase (1972–1983), which peaked at 48.2% in 1983, was mainly due to the collapse of the production of pin-lever watches, which could no longer compete with electronic watches.[23] Consequently, there were no significant changes in brand management from the 1890s to the 1970s.

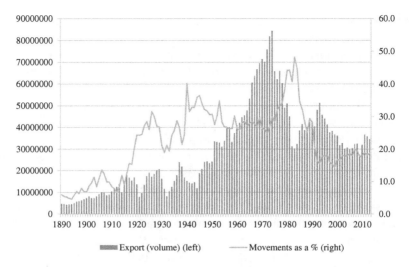

Figure 1. Swiss watch export, volume and share of movements, 1890–2013. Source: Swiss foreign trade statistics.

3. The example of Longines

The Compagnie des Montres Longines Francillon SA (Longines) is a good illustration of the changes in brand management and the emergence of global brands in the Swiss watch industry.[24] This company, whose roots go back to 1832, established itself at the end of the nineteenth century as one of the major Swiss watch *manufactures*, thanks to the early modernisation of production systems and a worldwide presence through a wide network of agents and importers.

During the 1880s and 1890s, Longines was a pioneer in adopting a strategy of focusing on the production and the export of movements, the idea being to have enough finished goods to meet the needs of all customers throughout the world. In March 1915, Alfred Pfister, technical director of the firm, wrote in his annual report that:

> 'the strength of the Longines brand consists of the wide variety of products it offers customers: all kinds of styles in various sizes and thicknesses, simple and complicated, go out of Longines workshops; they can satisfy all of the public's tastes.'[25]

Longines archives do not contain any documents that could be used to calculate the importance of movement production from a long-term perspective, but it was a widespread phenomenon. In 1938, the share of complete watches amounted to only 48.8% of sales.[26] The US provides a clear illustration of this strategy. It was one of Longines' major outlets in 1900–1930, with 15% of sales. Its representative in the country was a firm with Swiss origins, Wittnauer & Co., which purchased several American companies in the early-twentieth century so as to finish and assemble Longines watches for the country. In 1929, it possessed a company for case-making, Brighton Watch Case Co., and a parts maker, Majestic Watch Co.[27] The proportion of movements out of sales to Wittnauer was only 11.6% in 1880. It reached 44.7% in 1900 and averaged 81.9% in the 1920s.[28] Wittnauer was in charge of selecting cases, straps and dials to make complete watches that would suit US customers. This production system, which was reproduced in most markets, had a major impact on brand management. The brand Longines was linked to the high quality of watches, that is, movement precision. The company generally used this argument for communication from the late nineteenth century. For example, it started participating in chronometry contests at the observatories of Neuchâtel (Switzerland) and Kew (UK) in 1889 and showcased its prize-winning achievements in advertisements. During the interwar years, the company also began supporting explorers and aviators and engaged in timing sport events.[29] While this style of communication emphasising product quality had a global span and formed the basis of the Longines brand's distinctiveness, the style of watches changed with the country.

At the beginning of the 1950s, Longines adopted a new strategy for product development and marketing: the creation of complete watches to be sold throughout the world with a similar sub-brand and design. The competition with other Swiss high-quality watch companies, especially Omega and Rolex, became strong after WWII, particularly on the US market. All these companies needed to differentiate their image and strengthen their brand identity, leading to the construction of a new kind of global brand that did not rely only on technical characteristics. At first, this strategy was implemented for the highest segment of each company, on cost grounds. Thus, in 1954 Longines marketed its first self-winding watch under the sub-brand Conquest. This new choice reflected a desire to differentiate the product on the world market. Longines' commercial directors selected 'a name with a pleasant sound, easy to pronounce in all languages,'[30] and appropriate for a product positioned as a luxury good, for which the company launched for the first time a 'worldwide advertisement',[31] that is an advertising campaign which did not differ between countries.

As the Conquest watch was an immediate hit throughout the world, other sub-brands were launched in the second half of the 1950s, like Silver Arrow (1955) for 'a watch for young people, for the modern generation,'[32] or Flagship (1957), for 'absolutely sensational goods.'[33] These different models marked a major innovation in terms of product development and brand strategy. From this point onward, agents and importers were no longer all-powerful agents who conferred the design and style they wanted on Longines watches. The new marketing strategy led to a strengthening of vertical integration. Headquarters began to decide directly and to control brand identity and management. This change also reflected a desire to reduce dependency on the American market and extend business to other markets around the world.

Longines conducted the first modern marketing surveys during this period, which covered, inter alia, product development, sub-brand choice and a global advertising campaign. Since 1955, advertising on world markets has been characterised by the standardisation of logo and slogan (*'the privilege of elites'*). The name Longines was accompanied in adverts by words like 'accuracy', 'quality', and 'style'. Then, in November 1956, the Board of Directors declared that due to 'the need to give a special name to a larger number of products, we have registered a set of names.'[34] At the time, however, it was not limited to the registration of the first global brands, but also covered the protection of Longines' brand name against copies. During the 1950s, the brands registered by Longines included counterfeited names (Sangines 1952; Longer 1952; Lorgir 1952) with a view to prosecuting the manufacturers, a strategy which dates back to 1949 with the registration of Lonjin (see Figure 2).

Consequently, complete watches' share of sales grew steadily, accompanied by an increase in overall production. Between 1946 and 1957, the share of movements dropped from 75.6% to 58%.[35] However, these were large shares, and the strategy of launching global sub-brands was limited to the luxury segment. At the same time, Longines kept on exporting movements, a practice widespread in the Swiss watch industry at the time. In addition, the

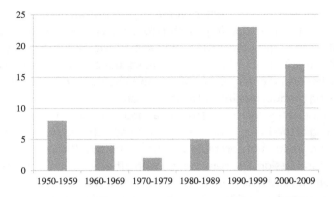

Figure 2. Number of brands registered by Longines, 1950–2009. Source: WIPO, Romarin database.

following decades were characterised by a decline in brand registrations and the develop-ment of contracts with foreign partners for licensed production. Longines registered a scant four brands in the 1960s and two in the 1970s. As for licensing contracts, these were primarily signed with American and South Korean firms. In the US, the multinational company Westinghouse Electric took over the distribution company Longines-Wittnauer in 1970 and signed a contract in 1975 for 'the right to use Longines brand for American solid state watches [electronic watches], against the payment of royalties.'[36] Since then, most of the Longines watches sold on the American market have been assembled in a workshop in Puerto Rico.

The situation was very similar in South Korea, a country subject to strict limits on watch exports. Longines signed a licensing agreement with Samsung Watch Co., a joint venture co-founded in 1983 by the Korean industrial group Samsung and the Japanese watch maker Seiko. This company assembled Longines watches with movements imported from Switzerland as well as other watches with Seiko movements, sold under the brand name Kappa.[37] This cooperation with Swiss and Japanese watch companies enabled Samsung to establish itself as a leader on the Korean watch market in the 1990s.

The Longines experience in brand management from the 1880s through the 1980s reflects the change in the meaning of global brand identity over time. Since the late nineteenth century, Longines watches had been recognised worldwide as high-quality goods and their competitive advantage relied on their accuracy, not their design, image or price. Hence, Longines was a global luxury brand which signified precision. However, if only this aspect is emphasised, the brand cannot be distinguished from other high-quality products made by its direct competitors (Omega, Rolex, and Zenith). Consequently, the manufacturers of precision watches needed to differentiate themselves through a stronger brand identity, which included design and name. During the 1950s, Longines launched new models of luxury watches which can be considered as a new kind of global product. They had the same sub-brand, design, price and image throughout the world. Yet, it was not so much Longines itself which was rebranded and globalised, but rather specific luxury products made by this company and sold with special sub-brands. At the same time, Longines continued to localise products as late as the 1970s and 1980s. The major changes occurred in the 1990s, in relation to the new industrial organisation of the Swiss watch industry and its overall shift towards luxury. Longines became part of SG at its foundation in 1983 and adopted a new brand management in this context.

4. The shift of the Swiss watch industry to luxury

The shift to luxury of the overall Swiss watch industry in the early 1990s was an answer to the advent of electronic watches and lost competitiveness in relation to companies based in Japan and in Hong Kong. High accuracy was not no longer a competitive advantage; rather, it had become the norm. Hence, watch manufacturers like Longines had to readapt their strategy and transform their brand in order to regain their competitiveness. This move occurred within the context of a new industrial organisation, so that we must first understand this changing environment.

Swiss foreign trade statistics provide an excellent macroeconomic overview of the shift towards luxury. First, Figure 1 clearly shows that the decline in the share of movements during the 1980s and 1990s, which remained under 20% from 1992 onwards and averaged 18.2% in 2000–2013, was driven by the industry's repositioning towards luxury and its adoption of a new marketing strategy. Second, Figure 3 reflects the process of this move towards luxury. After the crisis of 1975–1984, the Swiss watch industry has experienced a new period of growth up until the present moment, marked by two different phases. First, until 1992, the comeback of the Swiss watchmakers on world markets went hand in hand with steady growth in watch exports, with the Swatch, launched in 1983, playing a key role in this process.[38] Second, since 1992, the growing increase in export value has been accompanied by a decline, followed by a stagnation, in volume, reflecting the sharp increase in the average value of watches – that is, their transformation into luxury goods. The new marketing strategy adopted by SG in the early 1990s has been emblematic of this change.

SG was created in 1983 by the merger of the two largest Swiss watchmaking conglomerates, with the goal of undertaking a thorough restructuring to restore the ability to compete with Japanese rivals.[39] Hence, the Group brought together some 15 watch companies and brands when it was founded. The strategy implemented by Nicolas G. Hayek, long-standing Group CEO (1986–2003), consisted of two major pillars. The first, not tackled in this article, was the rationalisation of production (concentration in Switzerland; relocation of parts supply in Asia; reduction of model ranges). It was implemented from Day 1 onwards and was a focal point for management until the mid-1990s.[40] The second pillar was a new marketing strategy

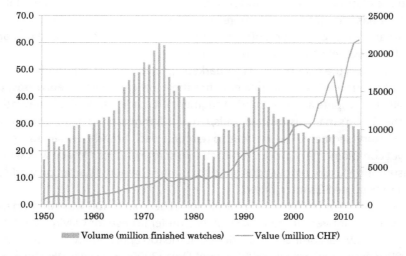

Figure 3. Swiss watch exports, volume and value, 1950–2013. Source: Swiss foreign trade statistics.

where brand management featured prominently. It appeared later, starting in the late 1980s, and was characterised by both brand portfolio rationalisation and individual brand globalisation. However, before we look at these changes, it is useful to recall the story of the Swatch, which had a major impact on the entire Group in terms of brand management.

This world-famous plastic watch, launched in 1983, played a key role in the growth of SG, as it generated large profit margins that gave the company part of the capital it needed for restructuring. Beyond this financial aspect, one of the Swatch's real innovations was that it was sold as a global brand, that is, a product that is not adapted to local markets but is marketed throughout the world in exactly the same way – a completely new feature in the watch industry. This novel marketing strategy was implemented by a new breed of managers, some of whom came from other industrial sectors, especially multinationals dealing in consumer goods (e.g. Colgate, Nestlé, and Procter & Gamble). This new generation of managers brought with them new marketing concepts, which were instrumental in renewing brand image. One of the major innovations borrowed from the fashion industry was the concept of mono-brand stores. They feature a uniform design and atmosphere throughout the world and are generally located on the main shopping streets of the planet's major metropolises. In the case of SG, these flagship stores were first introduced with the Swatch brand, with a first Megastore opening in 1996 in New York. The following year, SG opened some 60 Swatch Stores all over the world, doubling the number of brand outlets in one fell swoop.

4.1 Managing a brand portfolio

In the 1980s, SG's management focused on restructuring production and distribution and on developing the Swatch. The Group had no real brand policy as such, and did not manage the brand portfolio as a whole. Differentiation between brand images was not very pronounced. A new marketing strategy was implemented at the beginning of the following decade. In 1990, N.G. Hayek reorganised operational management at SG in order to introduce brand management Group-wide, characterised by brand differentiation and market segmentation. Accordingly, the Executive Group Management Board, the body tasked with overseeing the merger and streamlining the company during the 1980s, was restructured, becoming the platform for inter-brand coordination and the adoption of a global strategy. Since 1990, it has brought together representatives of the Group's main brands, the sales subsidiaries and a few production officers, with a view to coordinating and managing the brand portfolio. SG held a total of 11 brands at the time (see Table 1).

Consequently, in the mid-1990s, SG embarked upon a policy of differentiating and repositioning its various brands, in order to enhance their complementarity and boost the company's ability to compete across all market segments. It made a special differentiation effort between the Group's main historical brands, Omega, Longines and Rado with the so-called 'affordable luxury' segment. The aim was to reinforce each brand's own image, generating different yet complementary products targeting discrete publics. Omega was selected as a mass consumption luxury product designed to counter Rolex and Cartier on world markets. It went on to become SG's main brand.

This process of brand differentiation and market segmentation was strengthened after the creation of a joint venture to make watches under license for Calvin Klein (1997), and the purchase of several companies positioned at the top end, namely Breguet (1999), Léon Hatot (1999), Glashütte Original (2000), Jaquet Droz (2000) and Harry Winston (2013). The

Table 1. Consolidated turnover for the various Swatch Group brands, estimates, 2014.

Name	Date of acquisition	Sales in 2014 (CHF millions)	As a % of the total	Price range (in CHF)
Breguet	1999	700	8.8	>15,000
Harry Winston	2013	520	6.6	>12,000
Blancpain	1992	275	3.5	>10,000
Glashütte Original	2000	90	1.1	>6000
Jaquet Droz	2000	35	0.4	>6000
Omega	1983	2,150	27.2	>4000
Rado	1983	480	6.1	2000–12,000
Union Glashütte	2000	15	0.2	2000–12,000
Longines	1983	1,240	15.7	800–5000
Tissot	1983	1,100	13.9	<2000
CK Watch	1997	140	1.8	<1000
Balmain	1987	20	0.3	<1000
Certina	1983	90	1.1	<1000
Mido	1983	210	2.7	<1000
Hamilton	1983	70	0.9	<1000
Swatch	1983	760	9.6	50–200
Flik Flak	1987	15	0.2	35–55
Endura	1983	5	0.1	30–100

Source: *Watch Industry*, Zurich: Vontobel, 2015, 17.

same strategy was used for all these companies. SG picked up prestigious brands whose main weaknesses were of a marketing-related nature: weak retail networks and the absence of a distinctive graphic line. SG defined designs particular to each brand, incorporated them into its international retail network and turned them into global brands. As for CK and Harry Winston watches, they of course benefited from the brand strategies and sales networks of their partners, which were already strongly established.

Yet this marketing strategy was not limited to building and rationalising a brand portfolio. Each watch subsidiary adopted a very active policy of making its brand global, that is, unifying and controlling designs, styles, advertising, communication, distribution, and prices from Swiss headquarters, with the goal of shaping a worldwide brand image. There were many tools for implementing such a strategy. One was to redesign all models and to launch new collections with a strong identity, as Omega did with Speedmaster (1994) and Constellation (1995).[41] These collections and sub-brands became a key brand management component for the watch subsidiaries, as reflected by the figures for brands registered by SG. Figure 4 shows a clear change in the 1990s: the number of brands registered by SG shot up from 33 in 1985–1989 to 111 in 1995–1999, then stabilised after 2000. The company experienced a paradigm shift characterised by the emergence of brand management as a key point for global competitiveness and the transformation of watches into luxury goods.

Another prime example of this transformation and the twofold shift towards luxury and global brands is provided by the distribution system and the spread of flagship stores. The idea was to improve the quality of distribution rather than increase the number of sales outlets as much as possible. Accordingly, the Omega distribution network was restructured in 2005/6 on the German, British and Japanese markets, where the number of sales outlets was reduced by 20% to 25%. Distribution is an effective tool for reinforcing the exclusive image particular to luxury goods. In 2000, Omega had 178 flagship stores around the world, Tissot had 79, and Longines 20.[42] Moreover, SG founded a global network of luxury shops, Tourbillon Boutique, in 2001, which numbered a total of 19 shops by 2014. These shops stock

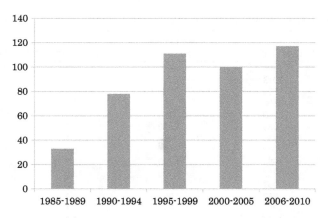

Figure 4. Number of watch brands registered by Swatch Group and its subsidiaries, 1985–2010. Source: WIPO, romarin database.
Note: this data include brands registered by Longines.

a full range of exclusive luxury brands as well as Omega and Swatch, which benefit from the image boost.

4.2 New luxury brand management by Longines

Longines was merged into SG when the latter was established in 1983. The restructuring policy implemented within this Group led to the closure of Longines' production workshop in 1988 and its transfer to ETA SA, the subsidiary in charge of movement production for all watch companies of the group. That year, the head of the sales and marketing department, Walter von Kaenel, was appointed CEO of Longines. From that time on, Longines focused on marketing activities, especially brand management. The aim was to transform the brand, to focus its identity on a few key elements taken from the company's history (classical elegance, technical quality, contribution to sport), and to use it throughout the world with very few adaptations.

Hence, the transformation of the brand occurred in the early 1990s, within the context set out above. It was repositioned in a less expensive segment, which corresponds to what scholars in management call 'accessible luxury,'[43] and graphically redesigned as an object of elegance and classicism, which did not compete head on with the SG's other products situated in the same product range, namely, Rado (high technology and modern design) and Glasshütte Original (technical tradition and classicism), while Tissot was used for modern sports and new technology. For example, since the 1990s Longines has refocused on sponsoring activities consistent with this image of classic elegance (riding, gymnastics, skiing and tennis), abandoning such former areas as Formula 1 racing (1992). Unlike Blancpain, a company acquired in 1992 which emphasises the traditional know-how of its watchmaking craftsmen, Longines is part of the historical tradition of a manufacture which played a pioneering role in modernising and industrialising watch production, an image which is better suited to its 'affordable luxury' products.[44]

This repositioning undertaken in the 1990s featured three main characteristics. First, SG negotiated an end to licensing contracts, managing to have them cancelled in South Korea (1993) and in the US (1994).[45] From this point on, headquarters controlled the design and style of all Longines watches sold worldwide. Second, Longines strengthened its historical roots via the launch of anniversary models, for example the sub-brands Charleston (1986) and Grande Classique (1992). Moreover, in 1992, the 160th anniversary of the company's founding provided an occasion for opening a brand museum and publishing a corporate history. Third, in 1996, Longines opted for *elegance* as the key concept of the brand and the company. More specifically, the management referred to the classical elegance of the inter-war years, a period during which Longines used the slogan 'Precise and elegant' for its adver-tising campaigns, and which became the source of inspiration for designers in the 1990s and from 2000 onwards. The sub-brand and collection Dolce Vita was launched in 1997 with models inspired by a watch produced in 1925. This strategy was developed in the following years, for example with the sub-brands Les Elégantes (2002) and Evidenza (2003). This was a strategy close to the first sub-brands launched in the 1950s, and brand registration took off after 1990 (see Figure 2). Since the 1990s, however, the globalisation of the brand Longines and its sub-brands has been used for all watches marketed by Longines, not only for the most exclusive segment.

5. Conclusion

The main objective of this article was to discuss the nature of a global brand in the luxury watch industry from a long-term perspective. The case study of Longines, one of the most important Swiss watch companies, shows that the definition of the global brand changed over time, together with the evolution of technology and industrial organisation. Until elec-tronic watches appeared in the 1970s, precision drove competitiveness on the world market. Brand image was associated with a watch's technical quality, not its design or style, so that luxury was attached to high precision. The first generation of global brands relied on tech-nique, not image. They embodied high-precision goods, regardless of their design. This enabled companies like Longines or Omega to focus on the production of high-precision movements and to export them to agents who assembled and finished them with external parts (cases, dials, straps) that suited the tastes of local customers. The variety of designs for a given brand was not seen as a lack of identity, as brand image was linked to movement precision and durability. Customers identified luxury watches like Longines by their technical elements; one could then argue that these brands were global, even with their varying designs and prices.

Electronic watches had a considerable impact and led to a paradigm shift, whereby the precision of watches stopped being a competitive argument and became the norm. Consequently, in order to restore their ability to compete with Japanese and Hong Kong companies, Swiss watchmakers had no choice but to reposition to luxury and to turn their watches into fashion objects and goods of social distinction. Since then, as far as consumers are concerned, rather than merely offering a guarantee of precision, Swiss brands embody new values (tradition and years of know-how, crafts, heritage, etc.) which make them luxury goods. Hence, brand identity no longer depends on objective elements such as precision but rather on a set of subjective images whose control by headquarters has become a major issue. As with most other luxury goods, brand identity in the watch industry has been stand-ardised and globalised, a process supported by the transformation of watch groups – espe-cially SG – into multinational enterprises with wide, global distribution networks. A new generation of global brands emerged from this process, but it was not the starting point of their existence.

Beyond the case of the watch industry, this article makes a contribution by highlighting the fact that both brand management and the degree of brand adaptation or standardisation are consistent with the nature of goods. When the intrinsic qualities of goods are only distantly related to their attraction for consumers, as in the luxury industry, this facilitates their adaptability to various cultural areas, hence brand globalisation. However, when goods are consumed for their intrinsic qualities and when these qualities have a strong cultural dimension, as with food, cosmetics or fast fashion, brand adaptability and regionalisation are important.

Another implication of this article is the contribution to a better understanding of the process involved in building and transforming global brands in the luxury industry. The case of Longines shows that the emergence of the new generation of global brands occurred within the context of industrial reorganisation and the creation of a large enterprise (SG), which manages a portfolio of brands and holds a worldwide distribution network. The need to position each brand precisely and to control brand identity throughout the world led SG to globalise its brands. This article therefore opens up new avenues of research for other sectors of luxury. For example, in the French luxury fashion industry, companies like Christian Dior started their foreign expansion after WWII through licensing contracts with US and Japanese partners.[46] This led to a dispersal of brand identity around the world. Yet following their acquisition by new luxury groups like Moët Hennessy Louis Vuitton (LVMH) or Richemont, Christian Dior and other luxury fashion manufacturers stopped licensing and switched to a strategy of building global brands and exercising control from European headquarters.[47] A comparative study of the process of building global brands in the luxury industry, stressing similarities and differences between companies and products, would undoubtedly contribute greatly to our understanding of brand globalisation in the late twentieth century.

Notes

1. Jain, "State of the Art"; Jackson, "A Contemporary Analysis"; De Pelsmacker, Geuens, and Van den Bergh, *Marketing Communications.*
2. Kapferer and Bastien, *The Luxury Strategy*, 70.
3. Donzé and Fujioka, "European Luxury Big Business."
4. Zhou and Belk, "Chinese Consumer Readings.,"
5. See for example, Roper, Caruana, Medway and Murphy, "Constructing Luxury Brands"; Attal and Bryson, *Luxury Brands.*
6. Da Silva Lopes, Global Brands, 2.
7. Chandler, *Scale and Scope*, 63–65, 168–170.
8. Jones, *Multinationals and Global Capitalism*, 87.
9. Jones, *Beauty Imagined*, 130.
10. Schwartzkopf, "Turning Trademarks into Brands," 168.
11. Jones, *Multinationals and Global Capitalism*, 197–198.
12. Levitt, "The Globalization of Markets."
13. Kapferer, "The Post-global Brand."
14. Jones, *Beauty Imagined*, 360.
15. Jones, *Beauty Imagined*, 361.
16. Da Silva Lopes, *Global Brands.*
17. Donzé, *History of the Swiss Watch Industry.*
18. Donzé, *A Business History of the Swatch Group.*

19. Donzé, *History of the Swiss Watch Industry*, 75–104, 119–120 ; Pasquier, La «Recherche et développement» en horlogerie.
20. Linder, *Histoire, enjeux, construction d'une marque*.
21. Linder, *Histoire, enjeux, construction d'une marque*, 33; Borloz, *100 ans Office fédéral de la Propriété Intellectuelle*.
22. Bubloz, *La Chaux-de-Fonds*, 12.
23. Blanc, *Suisse-Hong Kong*.
24. Henry Bédat, *Une région, une passion*.
25. Archives of the Compagnie des Montres Longines (AL), Saint-Imier, annual report of the Technical Director, unfiled document, March 1915.
26. AL, « Rapport Pfister, » 1938.
27. Erastus, *The Sesqui-Centennial International Exposition*, 353.
28. AL, H512.1–2, registers of invoices by client, 1880–1935.
29. Donzé, *Longines*, 128–132.
30. AL, B32.5, minutes of the Board meeting, 30 November 1956.
31. Ibidem.
32. Ibidem.
33. Ibidem.
34. Ibidem.
35. AL, annual report of the technical manager, 1946–1957.
36. AL, B32.5, Board minutes, 11 September 1975.
37. *Seiko*, 291–293.
38. Donzé, *A Business History of the Swatch Group*, 25–37.
39. Ibidem.
40. Ibidem.
41. Richon, *Omega Saga*.
42. Brands' Internet sites (7 July 2010).
43. Allérès, « Spécificités et stratégies marketing. »
44. Henry Bédat, *Une région, une passion*.
45. Trueb, *World of Watches*, 424.
46. Jones and Pouillard, *Christian Dior*; Fujioka, "Hyakkaten no Kakushinsei."
47. Okawa, "Licensing Practices," 106–107.

Disclosure statement

No potential conflict of interest was reported by the author.

References

Allérès, D. "Spécificités et stratégies marketing des différents univers du luxe [Specificities and Marketing Strategies of the Various Universes of Luxury]." *Revue française du marketing* [French Review of Marketing] 132 no. 8 (1991): 71-96.
Attal, G., and D. Bryson (eds.). *Luxury Brands in Emerging Markets*. Basingstoke: Palgrave Macmillan, 2014.

Blanc, J.-F. *Suisse-Hong Kong: le défi horloger. Innovation technologique et division internationale du travail* [Switzerland-Hong Kong: The Watchmaking Challenge. Technological Innovation and International Division of Labour]. Lausanne : Ed. d'en bas, 1988.

Borloz, J.. *100 ans Office fédéral de la Propriété Intellectuelle* [100 years of the Federal Office of Intellectual Property]. Bern: Bundesamt für Geistiges Eigentum, 1988.

Bubloz, G. La. *Chaux-de-Fonds, métropole de l'industrie horlogère suisse* [La Chaux-de-Fonds, Metropolis of the Swiss Watch Industry]. La Chaux-de-Fonds: Société des fabricants d'horlogerie de La Chaux-de-Fonds, 1912.

Chandler, A. *Scale and Scope: The Dynamics of Industrial Capitalism.* Cambridge: Harvard University Press, 1994.

Da Silva Lopes, T. *Global Brands.* New York, NY: Cambridge University Press, 2007.

De Pelsmacker, P., M. Geuens, and J. Van den Bergh. *Marketing Communications. A European Perspective.* 3rd ed. Harlow: Pearson Education Ltd., 2007.

Donzé, P. -Y. *History of the Swiss watch industry from Jacques David to Nicolas Hayek.* Berne: Peter Lang, 2011.

Donzé, P. -Y. *A Business History of the Swatch Group.* Basingstoke: Palgrave Macmillan, 2014.

Donzé, P. -Y. *Longines: From a Family Business to a Global Brand, 1832-2012.* Saint-Imier: Edition des Longines, 2012.

Donzé, P. -Y., and R. Fujioka. "European Luxury Big Business and Emerging Asian Markets, 1960–2010." *Business History* 57, no. 6 (2015): 822–840.

Erastus, L. A. *The Sesqui-Centennial International Exposition.* 2nd ed. Philadelphia: Current Publications Ltd., 1929.

Fujioka, R. "Hyakkaten no Kakushinsei to sono Henyo [Innovation and transformation of Japanese department stores]." In *Kourigyou no Gyotai Kakushin [Innovation of the Japanese Retailers]*, edited by J Ishii and M Mukoyama, 125–145. Tokyo: Chuokeizaisha, 2009.

Henry Bédat, J. *Une région, une passion: l'horlogerie* [A Region, a Passion: Watchmaking]. Saint-Imier: Compagnie des Montres Longines Francillon SA, 1992.

Jackson, T. "A Contemporary Analysis of Global Luxury Brands." In *International Retail Marketing: A case study approach*, edited by M Bruce, C Moore, and G Birtwistle, 155–169. London: Routledge, 2004.

Jain, S. C. "State of the Art of International Marketing Research: Directions for the Future." *Journal for Global Business Advancement* 1, no. 1 (2007): 4–19.

Jones, G. *Multinationals and Global Capitalism: From the Nineteenth to the Twenty-First Century.* Oxford: Oxford University Press, 2005.

Jones, G. *Beauty Imagined: A History of the Global Beauty Industry.* Oxford: Oxford University Press, 2010.

Jones, G., and V. Pouillard. *Christian Dior: A New Look for Haute Couture.* Cambridge: Harvard Business School (HBS case no. 9-809-159), 2013.

Kapferer, J. -N. "The Post-Global Brand." *Journal of Brand Management* 12, no. 5 (2005): 319–324.

Kapferer, K. -N., and V. Bastien. *The Luxury Strategy: Break the Rules of Marketing to Build Luxury Brands.* London: Kogen Page, 2009.

Levitt, T. "The Globalization of Markets." *Harvard Business Review*, May-June 1983, 92-102.

Linder, P. *Histoire, enjeux, construction d'une marque: Longines, un sablier et des ailes* [History, Challenges, and the Construction of a Brand: Longines, a Hourglass and Wings]. Saint-Imier: Edition des Longines, 2009.

Okawa, T. "Licensing Practices at Maison Christian Dior." In *Producing Fashion: Commerce, Culture, and Consumers*, edited by R Lee Blaszczyk, 82–107. Philadelphia, PA: University of Pennsylvania Press, 2008.

Pasquier, H. La. *"Recherche et Développement" en horlogerie: Acteurs, stratégies et choix technologiques dans l'Arc jurassien suisse (1900–1970)* [Research and Development in the Watch Industry: Actors, Strategies and Technological Choices in the Swiss Jura Region, 1900–1970]. Neuchâtel: Alphil, 2008.

Richon, M. *Omega Saga.* Bienne: Fondation Adrien Brandt en faveur du patrimoine Omega, 1998.

Roper, S., R. Caruana, D. Medway, and P. Murphy. "Constructing Luxury Brands: Exploring the Role of Consumer Discourse." *European Journal of Marketing* 47, no. 3/4 (2008): 375–400.

Schwartzkopf, S. "Turning Trademarks into Brands: How Advertising Agencies Practiced and Conceptualized Branding, 1890-1930." In *Trademarks, Brands, and Competitiveness*, edited by T da Silva Lopes and P Duguid, 165–193. New York, NY: Routledge, 2010.

Trueb, L. F. *World of Watches: History - Technology - Industry*. New York, NY: Ebner, 2005.

Vontobel. *Watch Industry*. Zurich: Vontobel, 2015.

Seiko tokei no sengoshi [Postwar History of Seiko Watches]. Tokyo: Seiko, 1996.

Zhou, N., and R. W. Belk. "Chinese Consumer Readings of Global and Local Advertising Appeals." *Journal of Advertising* 33, no. 3 (2004): 63–76.

Making Italian fashion global: Brand building and management at Gruppo Finanziario Tessile (1950s–1990s)

Elisabetta Merlo and Mario Perugini

ABSTRACT
This paper deals with the role of brands in the emergence of the Italian fashion business. Starting from the mid-1950s, the main Italian clothing manufacturer Gruppo Finanziario Tessile (GFT) managed brands to build a domestic market for mass-produced clothing. In the 1970s increasing competition and changing consumption patterns pushed GFT towards partnerships with leading fashion designers for building new brands and entering international markets. The emergence of strong designers' brands determined major organisational challenges that resulted in opposite outcomes: the demise of GFT, which failed in its attempt to control the entire value chain, and designers' achievement of an international standing in the fashion industry thanks to improved brand management capabilities.

1. Introduction

According to Edith Penrose's seminal work on the theory of the growth of the firm,

> a firm is more than an administrative unit; it is also a collection of productive resources the disposal of which between different users and over time is determined by administrative decision. When we regard the function of the private business firm from this point of view, the size of the firm is best gauged by some measure of the productive resources it employs.[1]

Following Penrose, resource-based theorists adopted the idea that the firm could be viewed as a collection of 'resources': tangible and intangible assets that are idiosyncratic to the firm.[2] These are not only the bases upon which a firm can establish its identity and frame its strategy, but also the primary sources of the firm's profitability. Thus, the resource-based theory of strategy sought to explain firm performance differences by understanding the relationships between resources, capabilities, competitive advantage, and profitability.[3]

The emergence of the resource-based view has provided the conceptual foundations for linking brands and brand management to the development of sustained competitive advantage.[4] Indeed, strong brands conform to the criteria proposed by Jay Barney for identifying rent-generating resources and capabilities. In particular strong brands are (1) valuable, to the extent that they enable firms to explore opportunities (e.g. brand extension) and neutralise environmental threats; (2) rare among an organisation's current and potential competitors; (3) costly to imitate; and (4) without close strategic substitutes.[5] Within this perspective, brands retain a significant potential to enable the achievement and sustenance of superior performance.[6]

Since M. Wilkins underlined the role of brands in the evolution of modern corporations,[7] business historians have also paid increasing attention to issues like the evolution of trade-marks and brands in the marketplace,[8] their legal protection,[9] and their role in explaining the competitiveness of firms, industries, and even countries.[10] In contrast, brand building and brand management as resource-based strategies are topics still under-investigated in business history literature. In an effort to fill this gap, this article aims to analyse the complex relationship developed between Italian fashion designers and clothing manufacturers during the second half of the twentieth century.

The practice of branding fashion items dates back to the second half of the nineteenth century. Charles Frédérick Worth (1825–1895), who is attributed with being the originator of the concept of *haute couture*, was the first to put labels onto the clothing he manufactured. The innovation of labels, based on the idea of intertwining the couturier's identity with his own products to gain faithful customers within the European and American elite,[11] played a significant role in establishing French leadership in fashion. The primacy of French fashion designers remained unchallenged until the mid-1970s, when Italian designers emerged as influential representatives of the new ready-to-wear fashion.[12] In contrast to *haute couture*, which is synonymous with uniqueness, ready-to-wear fashion is meant to be reproduced on an industrial scale for the general market. As a result, the birth of Italian ready-to-wear fashion ushered in a paradigm shift in fashion brand management and, consequently, in the history of fashion business itself.[13] To understand the scope of that change, one must bear in mind that Italian ready-to-wear fashion was born in an international context shaken by deep and irreversible transformations in supply and demand trends.

On the supply side, French ready-to-wear fashion was just one of Italian fashion's great competitors, and not even the most formidable one when compared to emerging American designers. By the mid-1970s, the brands of stylists such as Calvin Klein, Donna Karan, and Ralph Lauren became synonymous with contemporary, casual yet elegant American style. Soon they all recognised the commercial potential of producing fashionable collections that were more accessible than *haute couture*. As a result, they rapidly evolved from being indi-vidual designers to establishing and managing huge fashion companies with an international reach.[14] However, competition was not only a matter of new fashion counterparts. Highly cost-competitive apparel items produced by less developed countries were about to invade the international markets.[15] Consequently, the main advantage traditionally boasted by the Italian clothing industry – i.e. low wages – was seriously threatened.

On the demand side, the prevailing models of consumption became outdated at a fast pace with the emergence of young people as new consumers with high expectations. These new consumers conceived of mass-produced clothing as a symbol of passé adult conformity. Their demand for more choices in the marketplace gave the first push towards increasing market segmentation and differentiation that still characterises the fashion supply.[16]

Italian clothing companies reorganised themselves in different ways in response to market turbulence. In order to improve flexibility, restructuring was mainly aimed at closely adhering to Marshallian notions of external economies, whereby small firms reap benefits from the clustering of activities. In an effort to exploit market niches, manufacturers focused on value-added activities such as product development, brand building, and advertising. Gruppo Finanziario Tessile (GFT), the main Italian clothing manufacturer, was among those few large firms that had previously exploited economies of scale. GFT's strategy for innovation involved the investment in a new kind of human capital: the fashion designers.[17] In the 1980s, as a result, the Italian clothing companies operated according to two main business models. The first one included those industrial companies, such as Zegna and Ferragamo, headed towards the establishment of powerful brands. As a general rule, these companies had a decades-long history, possessed a strong know-how that was deeply rooted in the industrial sector (where the founder had started his career), and entered the clothing business at a very early stage by investing in retailing and distribution in an effort to get closer to the final consumer. The second business model concerned industrial brands growing as licensees for today's well-known fashion designers (Giorgio Armani, Valentino Garavani, Franco Moschino, and Gianni Versace, to name a few) whose success stories originated in the ready-to-wear segment of the market. Before founding their own companies, they all initially benefited from the support of industrial companies that produced their fashion collections and marketed them in fast-growing European, American, and Japanese markets. The two business models differ in many respects, particularly with regard to brand management. In the first business model, the brand name coincides with the founder's and producer's name. In the second, the name of the industrial company that produces the fashion collections remains in the background, or is even eclipsed by the fashion designer's name.

This paper deals with the latter business model and focuses on GFT, whose growth has been closely linked to the international success of contemporary well-known Italian fashion designers. This case study will allow us to deepen the knowledge of how some of the most famous Italian fashion brands have been built and to understand who – GFT or fashion designers — really improved brand management. This will also allow us to find out what consequences such relationship in branding had both for the company and for the designers. The paper is structured as follows. Section two traces the company's inception by contrasting the adverse economic conditions in which Italian clothing firms operated in the 1930s with the economic potential of the post-war domestic market for ready-to-wear clothing. Section three outlines the main characteristics of the collaboration established in 1957 between GFT and the *couturiere* Elvira Leonardi Bouyeure, known as Biki (1906–1999), which can be considered as the precursor of the partnerships that GFT negotiated with Giorgio Armani and with Valentino Garavani in the 1970s. In section four, the analysis of these partnerships will allow us to show to what extent the management of brands related to emerging fashion designers affected the company's organisational structure. Section five explains the reasons why the business model based on industrial companies producing as licensees for promising fashion designers eventually declined, thus paving the way for the emergence of the major Italian fashion companies.

2. 'Run to wear it, it is a FACIS suit'

At the end of the 1930s the Ente Nazionale della Moda (National Fashion Body), established by Mussolini with the aim of coordinating all aspects of fashion production and consumption, planned a 'Congresso Nazionale Abbigliamento e Autarchia' (National Congress on Clothing and Autarchia) to be held in Turin in 1940. The numerous papers and reports sent in advance

Figure 1. Archivio Centrale dello Stato, Trademark Tre Nani, registered by Lanifici Rivetti in 1951.

Figure 2. Archivio Centrale dello Stato, Trademark Golden Set, registered by Lanifici Rivetti in 1961.

by the attendants were published as proceedings, thus providing us with a historical source of great value to have an idea of the conditions of the Italian clothing industry at the time.[18]

Figure 3. Archivio Centrale dello Stato, Trademark FACIS, registered by Gruppo Finanziario Tessile in 1954.

Figure 4. Archivio di Stato di Torino, Archivio Gruppo Finanziario Tessile, box 2744. Poster FACIS, (1954).

In its propagandist agenda, the regime conceived of clothing as one of the most influential means to convey the message that Fascism was synonymous with political order, discipline, and widespread wellbeing.[19] Thus, Fascism called for a uniform civil dress – e.g. the black

Figure 5. Archivio di Stato di Torino, Archivio Gruppo Finanziario Tessile, box 2776. Poster FACIS, (1960).

Figure 6. Archivio Centrale dello Stato, Trademark Cori, registered by Gruppo Finanziario Tessile in 1959.

shirt for men – to be worn in parades, in public offices, and even in private life, and propa-gandised it as a way to prompt the development of the domestic clothing industry. Indeed, in the regime's expectations, the demand for clothing arising from the new, strongly stand-ardised way of dressing would have allowed Italy to overcome the technical and organisa-tional backwardness that still prevented the ready-to-wear garment from being a feasible alternative to the bespoke one. With a few exceptions, the authors of the papers were quite sceptical about the effectiveness of such a mechanism of cause and effect. They were con-scious that, albeit strongly authoritarian, even the Fascist attempt at homogenisation would not easily prevail over the different traditions in clothing manufacture and the different consumption habits that were deeply rooted in the Italian culture. They were also fully aware that the Italian population still lacked a strong national identity and unfavourably considered clothing that was not custom-made. The participants to the congress thus suggested intro-ducing the neologism *confezione pronta* (ready-to-wear suit) in the Italian clothing glossary in order to stress that the garments produced on an industrial scale were far from being standardised.[20] The Italian consumers, accustomed to choosing among a large variety of fabrics, colours, sizes, and shapes, would have otherwise rejected the ready-made clothing, thus preventing manufacturers from relying on a domestic demand large enough to enable the development of firms on an industrial scale.

Admittedly, at the end of the 1930s the domestic demand for clothing was not encour-aging to the Italian manufacturers. The few existing big Italian companies looked at the foreign markets, but all their efforts to augment exports systematically failed due to the adverse international political climate. Among these producers was Alessandro Rivetti, the owner of the largest Italian clothing firm – the FACIS Company based in Turin – producing men's and boys' suits. In his congress paper, Rivetti complained that the sanctions the League of Nations had imposed on Italy in the mid-1930s had frustrated any attempt to export clothing and had discouraged manufacturers from experimenting with solutions to over-come the technical problems they encountered in the production of ready-to-wear clothing.

Not surprisingly, the National Congress on Clothing and Autarchy never took place. The outbreak of World War II silenced the debate and postponed the search for innovations in the Italian clothing industry until peacetime. As a result, in the mid-twentieth century, ready-to-wear garments were still rare in Italy. In 1944, the National Statistical Institute (ISTAT) ascertained that the clothing of most of the Italian population was obsolete and in poor condition.[21] Ten years later, a survey on the consumption of textiles in Italian families showed that a large part of Italians still prevalently wore custom-made, home-made, and sec-ond-hand garments.[22] According to the same source, consumption habits differed depend-ing on a mix of factors. Predictably, ready-to-wear garments were preferred by male consumers (while women still considered tailoring as the best way to keep themselves up-to-date with fashion) and by consumers living in the (few) large Italian cities, where the presence of a number of shops made these items more easily available. Also, the inhabitants of the southern regions were largely accustomed to the ready-to-wear clothing. In the poorest areas ready-made clothing existed alongside a broad category including any kind of dress except for the never used one.

To sum up, at the beginning of the 1950s a market for ready-made, mass-produced cloth-ing had still to be built in Italy. As the industrialists had pointed out in 1940, different tradi-tions in clothing manufacturing and contrasting consumption habits had kept the Italian consumers little acquainted with the uniformities necessary to the industrial product. Furthermore, Fascism had exploited clothing as one of the most effective means of the bombastic rhetoric of the autarchic campaign. As a result, in the 1950s the main concern was how to make ready-to-wear an industrial product endowed with an attractive, completely renewed cultural identity. Within the Rivetti family, the youngest generation represented by Franco (1919–1986), Silvio (1921–1961), and Pier Giorgio (1927–1983) accepted such a challenge.

In 1946, Franco, Silvio, and Pier Giorgio inherited from their father, Adolfo (1890–1946), 30% shares each of both Lanifici Rivetti and GFT companies. With 5000 employees, the former was among the biggest Italian wool textile businesses. In comparison, the latter was a small company, employing only a few hundred workers.[23]

The three brothers soon became impatient with any restriction imposed by the elder family members on their ambitions in ready-made clothing production. In 1952, they eventually sold their shares of Lanifici Rivetti to the family and took over GFT. Their decision was not at all a 'leap in the dark'. At the time, GFT was a very solid company, whose activities were prudently diversified in textile commercialisation (accounting for about 60–70% of the whole business) and in production and distribution of the off-the-peg garments. Considering the features of the Italian market, however, it certainly took a lot of entrepreneurial intuition and boldness to bet on attaining popularity and profits by producing ready-made clothing.

The beginning of the new entrepreneurial adventure coincided with a radical restyling of the GFT's FACIS trademark that had been introduced in the 1930s. Twenty years later the acronym FACIS (Fabbrica Abbigliamento Confezionato in Serie – Manufacture of Mass-Produced Garments) had achieved permanent recognition as a reliable trademark by the means of long-lasting use. Thus, the restyling led to the removal from the trademark of any allusion to the Fascist rhetoric. A red circle around the acronym focused the consumer's attention on the company's name. Yet the most appealing novelty relied on the picture of a running man wearing a formal outfit – black suit, white shirt, black hat and shoes, blue socks, and a red and blue striped tie – and under his left arm a blue, perfectly tailored man's suit with a white, neatly folded pocket-handkerchief (Figure 3). The picture had the twofold aim of disclosing the meaning of the acronym to the consumer and transforming it into the label proper to every man who aims at keeping pace with a modern, dynamic society. In this way, GFT definitively distanced itself from the image and history of Lanifici Rivetti as wool textile producer (Figure 1 and 2).

In 1954 the new trademark – a well balanced mix of restyled lettering and appealing iconography, enforced by the slogan 'Di corsa ad indossarlo, è un abito FACIS' (Run to wear it, it is a FACIS suit; Figure 4) – was eventually registered, thus indicating the emergence of a new business culture. The three brothers were fully aware that the long-established FACIS trademark boasted intrinsic, trustworthy attributes that could be successfully exploited. At the same time, they were conscious that those habits, traditions, and conventions that had previously contributed to making FACIS a reliable trademark belonged to the past and were rapidly changing. The thriving Italian economy of the 1950s prompted them to adopt a new approach to the trademark. The FACIS name turned from being a sign that had achieved permanent recognition by the means of long-lasting use into a strategic asset that needed to be carefully managed. Such an innovative business culture affected the company's business strategy as well as its organisational structure and corporate identity.

In the 1930s, GFT still considered traditional values – firm longevity and tangible product attributes such as the durability and thickness of the fabric – as key resources to preserve and strengthen the company's role as top player in the wool industry. In the 1950s, GFT focused its strategy on gaining the status of first mover in the market of mass-produced clothing. This goal should be achieved both by solving technical problems, such as how to refine fabrics and how to size clothing,[24] and by exploiting the FACIS trademark as a means, if not *the* means, to dominate the menswear market.[25] The organisational structure, which in the 1930s comprised two main autonomous divisions for production and distribution, adapted to such a major change in the way of approaching the market. In the mid-1950s, GFT introduced the marketing and communication division as a final, albeit essential part of a vertically integrated pipeline that started from the selection of fabrics and ended with delivery of the off-the-peg garment.[26] In an attempt to establish a direct relationship with the retail customer, distribution was entrusted to the chain of MARUS (Magazzino Abbigliamento Ragazzo Uomo Signora) shops, owned by GFT itself and located in the most important Italian towns, as well as to authorised sales outlets.[27] To the same purpose, a programme of joint advertising with the retail sales outlet started in 1958 and retail prices of products appeared standardised in all media until the end of the 1960s.

The new marketing and communication division was responsible for developing advertising campaigns aimed at conveying the values inherent in the FACIS trademark through all means of communication – posters, magazines, and television, but also cigarette packets, boxes of matches, football pool cards, and tickets for horse-race lotteries – suitable for reaching the masses. To this end, selecting the right consultants for advertising was of paramount importance and the choice of GFT was Armando Testa, the illustrator who had designed the FACIS trademark. Testa not only combined the taste of Italian and European poster artists with the newest strategies of communication; his open-mindedness also enabled him to consider the relationship between the corporation and the advertising agency as a matter of organisational culture. Not by chance, *L'Ufficio Moderno* – the first Italian journal in the field of organisational studies – published an article in 1958 about the connections between the strategies of GFT and the advertising agency established by Testa.[28]

Unlike posters, which mainly emphasised graphics (see Figures 4 and 5), press advertising campaigns normally made use of photographs representing persons of various sizes and shapes. Italian sports celebrities, such as the mighty pugilist Primo Carnera and the lanky soccer player Cesare Maldini, were placed side by side next to the slogan 'FACIS ha le misure per tutti, incluse le tue' ('FACIS has everybody's size, including yours'). Another campaign presented the stocky body of sport journalist Gianni Brera along with the slender figure of the filmmaker and writer Mario Soldati, who at the time – in coincidence with the hundredth anniversary of Italian unification – was strongly committed to making the population aware of national history, culture, and traditions. Fascinating and well-known actors, such as Giulio Bosetti and Alberto Lupo, played the role of gallant charmer in GFT's commercials thus enforcing the message that FACIS provided men (as well as women) with *the* model of fine gentleman acquainted with style and fashion in dress and appearance.

Thanks to its innovative advertising campaigns, GFT got rid of any heritage that the consumer could perceive as anachronistic. Results were impressive. The revenues arising from ready-made men's clothing grew from roughly 1.5 billion lire in 1955 to more than 6 billion lire in 1960 (at constant prices).[29] In the mid-1960s, when profits reached almost 10 billion lire,[30] the FACIS trademark became synonymous with Italian men's ready-to-wear.

To sum up, the FACIS trademark allowed GFT to gain a hegemonic position in the domestic menswear market. As shown above, this result was achieved by adopting a corporate strategy in which the organisation of work within the productive plants, the network of retailers, the advertising campaigns, and even the choice of the advertising agencies showed the Rivettis' fascination with American organisational culture. Their aim was to transform GFT into an innovative firm while at the same time preserving its distinctive industrial genetic code. Hence, the brand focused on the technical, functional, and economic properties of mass-produced clothing when it emphasised that the FACIS suit had all possible sizes and was affordable to the majority of male Italian consumers.

Such a strategy inflicted a shock on the Italian traditional consumer society, which was still unfamiliar with industrial and urban civilisation. The FACIS name evoked more than a newly acquired well-being. It symbolised the technological progress applied to clothing production.

A similar strategy was used to capture the attention of female consumers. The attempt, however, was less successful than expected. Exploring the reasons for this failure will allow us to ascertain how GFT reassessed its approach towards management of intangible assets, and how such a change affected the company's development.

3. 'CORI, elegance on the wings of a butterfly'

The available historical sources do not make clear exactly when GFT started to produce ready-wear clothing for women. However, we know that it methodically collected measurements of women's bodies in 1957,[31] the year the Rivettis asked Biki to try a one-season collaboration with GFT.

An established member of the Milanese fashion community, in the 1950s Biki enjoyed increasing success thanks to the wide appeal of the celebrities – primarily Maria Callas – who were her loyal customers. Far from making any contribution to the renewal of the stylistic codes, she considered herself the custodian of tradition in fashion. Her adherence to the French fashion had never failed, not even in the face of the autarchic restrictions imposed by Fascism. In accordance with the severity and sobriety that distinguished Milanese fashion from the seductive and glamorous costumes designed for the Roman aristocracy or inspired by the Renaissance past, she looked at French ateliers such as those of Paquin and Piguet, internationally renowned for the elegance of their creations.[32]

Biki's reputation as a conservative *couturiere* of feminine elegance and her close familiarity with some of the most renowned exponents of the French *haute couture* could not pass unnoticed by a clothing company – like GFT – in search of a way to make ready-wear garments enticing to any woman.[33] With this aim, in 1957 the Rivettis asked Biki to draw a certain number of suits for the GFT's upcoming Autumn/Winter collection. They would have selected those suitable for industrial production and then produced a specimen of each of them. In this way, they obtained prototypes to be submitted to Biki, who tailored a copy of them using GFT's fabrics. The copies served as models to be reproduced by GFT on an industrial scale.[34] In the case that Biki discarded some prototypes, the use of them as models would be at the discretion of GFT.

Hoping for a continued collaboration, Biki offered the Rivettis what she deemed to be extremely favourable economic conditions: 40,000 lire for each drawing selected, 75,000 lire for each prototype, 150,000 lire for each model she tailored, and a minimum economic obligation equal to 2,000,000 lire.[35] The first 'experiment' earned Biki 2,020,000 lire.[36] On this occasion, she drew 40 suits, of which GFT selected 28. Biki tailored only a dozen models that GFT reproduced on an industrial scale, along with five prototypes among those that Biki had discarded. Apparently, she was not interested in tailoring models that others would have reproduced on an industrial scale. To the Rivettis, Biki's proposal appeared to be too onerous and they invited her to accept a compromise that would allow them to collaborate until the end of 1959. In that two-year period, Biki designed five collections that earned her an overall reward of 11,000,000 lire.[37]

In 1960, Biki and GFT negotiated a new deal. While the previous agreement concerned the typical outputs of the designer's creativity – drawings and models – the new one also included immaterial assets such as the designer's name, style, and look. More precisely, the Rivettis guaranteed to buy 12 models from Biki for 200,000 lire each. In exchange, the women's clothing produced by taking inspiration from Biki's creations had to bear a label stating 'model designed by Biki for CORI'. The same notice had to be used in advertising campaigns that would be approved by Biki herself.[38]

The CORI (Confezioni Rivetti) advertising campaigns stressed the concept of elegance, which recurred both in press campaigns and in commercials. The slogan 'CORI, l'eleganza sulle ali di una farfalla' ('CORI, elegance on the wings of a butterfly') echoed the trademark – a butterfly-woman with spread wings (Figure 6) – and accompanied icons both of French stylishness, such as Capucine and Catherine Spaak, and of Italian beauty, such as Sofia Loren and Eleonora Rossi Drago.

The agreement secured Biki against business uncertainty but, between the two partners, GFT surely got the main advantage from it. The Rivettis agreed to more than double the payment due for the purchase of a fixed number of models. In exchange, they obtained the exclusive right to use Biki's name.

Not surprisingly, the couturiere withdrew from the agreement in 1961, just one year after the signing. In her opinion, the diffusion of CORI collections had largely benefited from the increasing national and international notoriety she had gained in the meantime, but the agreement with GFT had not taken it sufficiently into account. Thus, a major revision of their reciprocal obligations was necessary.[39]

Mainly, Biki rejected the idea that fashion designers were not involved in the management of the manufacturing process and proposed her son-in-law, Alain Reynaud, as a supervisor. A designer trained at Jacques Fath's school, Reynaud had collaborated with Biki since 1952 and had spent some time working in the US clothing industry. Thanks to him, GFT could have a right-hand man in managing the manufacture of women's clothing. As for Biki herself, she would supervise the fabric samples and attend the French fashion shows twice a year with the aim of keeping GFT updated to the latest novelties and buying models to be produced according to Reynaud's suggestions.

The Rivettis offered to buy a minimum of 27 models for each collection and to pay 250,000 lire for each one of them. The annual minimum economic obligation was increased to 24,000,000 lire for a three-year period (from the Autumn/Winter collection of 1962–1963 to the Spring/Summer collection of 1965). In addition, they acknowledged that royalties had to be paid for the use of Biki's name and assessed the amount at 3% of CORI-Biki's revenues. In exchange, Biki was prevented from establishing any other kind of industrial partnership.[40] Once again, the Rivettis had made their economic proposal without changing the essence of the collaboration between creativity and industry.[41]

In 1965, when the agreement was coming to an end, Biki wrote to Franco Rivetti that she had admired him 'for having embarked on CORI-Biki partnership'. She considered GFT 'a big company ahead of its time and aimed at giving a completely new contribution to the clothing business'. This ambitious task allowed it to become 'the first mover in the Italian market of ready-wear women's clothing'.[42] Yet, despite such a promising beginning, GFT had disappointed her. Instead of being regarded as a skilled and talented *couturiere*, she had been treated as a fashion icon. Moreover, her trusted Reynaud had been excluded from supervising the manufacturing process. As a result, GFT had produced CORI-Biki collections that poorly resembled *haute couture* creations, rather than taking inspiration from them in order to produce fashionable ready-made clothing endowed with an autonomous style.

In the second half of the 1960s, the collaboration between Biki and GFT was regulated by two different agreements. The first was a private deed that still dealt with models and prototypes.[43] The second was a licensing contract concerning the reciprocal obligations related to the use of the newly registered Biki trademark.[44] Both deals lasted until the end of the 1960s. Since then – as Biki wrote in 1972 – 'clouds cast a shadow over our path'.[45]

There was a storm of protest when GFT proved that Biki had infringed the clause that prevented her from collaborating with other clothing manufacturers. As reported by the fashion press, she had entered into business with Marie d'Arc – Stellina (clothing for babies), Fenicia (men's shirts), and Lanerossi (fabrics).[46] At the same time, GFT was accused of having labelled women's clothing with the Biki trademark after the contract had come to an end.[47] Despite a profusion of letters with declarations of reciprocal allegiance and everlasting friendship, Biki's dossier migrated from GFT's sales management offices to the legal unit. A lawyer skilled in matters of intellectual property rights, whose counsel was requested, alerted GFT to the dangers of suing the *couturiere*. Firstly, the lawsuit's outcome was uncertain given that Italian jurisprudence in the matter of intellectual property was still sketchy with regard to the commercial use of fashion designers' names by a third party. Secondly, and even worse, GFT could have to cope with the regrettable contingency of being compelled to admit that it had trademarked non-Biki garments with the Biki name. To some extent, GFT had misled consumers by making them believe that CORI-Biki collections were the result of a close collaboration between the designer and the manufacturer. GFT's house counsel argued that the private deed signed in 1965 clearly stated the terms of partnership. Furthermore, in the case that GFT had produced and marketed garments labelled with the Biki trademark but not in line with her style, the *couturiere* would have been the first to notice. Undoubtedly, the feedback sent by MARUS shops to GFT headquarters confirmed that the style of CORI-Biki collections was not fully in accordance with the taste of Italian women.[48]

The available sources allow us to draw only partial and provisional conclusions about how CORI-Biki collections performed. The business accounting registers show that sales almost halved between 1963 and 1965, in terms both of number of items sold and of revenues.[49] We do not know how much each collection effectively cost GFT. However, if we consider the fixed costs of each collection, their variable costs (namely, royalties assessed at 3% of revenues), and the costs related to manufacturing, marketing, and advertising, we must conclude that CORI-Biki collections were not a very profitable business, or were operating at a loss.

In 1972, the partnership between Biki and GFT came to end and the Rivettis excluded a renewal. In exchange for avoiding any controversy, Biki received several million lire as final compensation.[50]

GFT failed in its attempt to secure the market for women's ready-to-wear garments by using the joint CORI-Biki trademark as a flagship brand. As the company's house counsel retrospectively stated, 'the Biki-GFT partnership was a collaboration aimed at making the mass produced clothing for women commercially appealing through the exploitation of the *couturiere*'s creativity and fame'.[51] Yet the evolution of the GFT–Biki partnerships shows that the Rivettis were much more interested in exploiting the designer's name than her creativity. Biki's name, which GFT amplified by sponsoring a massive advertising campaign, was used as a weapon to discourage domestic competitors of GFT from entering the women's wear business. Along with the system of sizes specifically developed by GFT to produce clothing that fit the majority of Italian women, Biki's name was expected to give the industrial partner an additional advantage over European competitors' imports. Not by chance, Silvio Rivetti approached Biki in 1957, on the eve of the advent of the newly established European Common Market. Thus, the name of the *couturiere* should have merely made the industrial product more attractive. The main prerogatives of the product did not change: they still relied on technical, functional, and economic properties.

Accordingly, the business strategy and organisation designed for the FACIS brand prevented GFT from being flexible enough to manage the female division. Not surprisingly, the Rivettis never considered the possibility of involving the *couturiere* in the manufacturing process. On the contrary, they increasingly distanced designing from manufacturing, sartorial models from industrial prototypes, creativity from trademark, to the point that two different kinds of legal agreement – a private deed and a licensing contract – eventually regulated the partnership from the mid-1960s.

In 1976, significantly, GFT launched a remarkable new advertising campaign. It was in black and white, and it did not show the product. It used posters and a press campaign enforced by an editorial mention in order to make up for the absence of the product in the institutional campaign. It was centred on the provocative sentence 'Né strega né madonna, solo donna' ('Neither witch nor virgin, just woman')[52], which definitely put an end to the old-fashioned concept of elegance and called into question GFT's model of business as well as its organisational structure.

4. The birth of the 'Italian look'

At the beginning of the 1970s, the company's position as a low-cost producer was becoming increasingly difficult to sustain. The massive labour unrest that spread throughout Italy in the late 1960s led to new, more restrictive labour laws, such as the government's decision to index workers' wages to the inflation rate (1975). In this new context, the internal rigid cost structure eroded the competitive advantage – namely, low wages – traditionally enjoyed by Italian apparel manufacturers. Furthermore, the advent of the boomer generation in Western societies radically changed clothing consumption. From the end of the 1960s, young people emerged as a new kind of consumer demanding a more casual and less classic clothing style. As a result, from the 1970s, clothing for young people became an autonomous and rapidly increasing market calling for greater segmentation in supply and for the development of different styles.[53] Adults' consumption patterns were also evolving in those years and the United States was at the forefront of the trend. Middle and upper middle class American customers with rising buying power were increasingly rejecting mass-produced garments, looking for signs of 'distinction', and asking for more personalised and refined garments.[54]

The changes that occurred in consumption, along with increasing international competition, pushed GFT to drastically change its business model. The company resorted to a new alliance with fashion designers in order to broaden the company's product line by entering niches at the high end of the clothing industry rather than meet the demands of the emerging mass market.[55] The origins of the new course of action date back to 1972, when GFT signed an agreement with Emanuel Ungaro.[56]

Ungaro was the first fashion designer who collaborated in implementing the new strategy. The son of an Italian tailor, Ungaro trained at Cristobal Balenciaga's atelier before launching his own fashion house in 1965. Along with Pierre Cardin and André Courrèges (himself nurtured by Balenciaga studio in the 1950s), Ungaro played an important role in the rejuvenation of Paris fashion. When the Rivettis engaged him, he was already well-known as a fashion designer who created feminine looks that were not only elegant, but also audacious and provocative.[57] GFT was not directly involved in the partnership with Emanuel Ungaro. The Rivettis established a new society – CIDAT (Compagnia Italiana di Abbigliamento Torino) – specifically aimed at managing the relationship with the fashion designer. As a consequence, the labels resulting from the partnership – Ungaro Parallèle (luxury ready-to-wear suit for women), Ungaro Solodonna (ready-to-wear suit for women), Ungaro Ter (a women's knitwear line, produced from 1988 to 1991), and Ungaro Uomo (men's clothing) – did not mention the manufacturer's name. This change in strategy also required a new approach in advertising and marketing. It is interesting to note that the company's archives started collecting advertising concerning Ungaro from the mid-1960s, almost 10 years before the agreement with the designer.[58] Those published by Vogue since 1966, the year Condé Nast began to publish the Italian edition of the American fashion magazine, formed a separate dossier. The American publisher had gained his first foothold in Italy a few years before – in 1962 – by acquiring Novità, a magazine founded in 1950 by Emilia Kuster Rosselli. She came from the circle of prominent Italian architects who collaborated with Domus publishing house and with the Triennale, the international exhibition of decorative arts held in Milan since 1933. Novità reflected the founder's cultural background, dealing with fashion, as well as with furnishings, as a matter of industrial design. Such an approach made it an absolute novelty compared to the contemporary Italian fashion magazines, which still considered fashion just a matter of women's appearance.[59] Not surprisingly, Condé Nast targeted Novità as the best candidate for Vogue to enter the Italian market as a 'class' fashion magazine, that is a magazine 'designed to have a small but selected affluent readership which would appeal to the advertisers of luxury manufacturers and their retailers'.[60] The entry of Vogue into the Italian market strongly influenced the local fashion magazines and pushed GFT to drastically reorient its advertising strategy. In 1967, the magazine L'abito FACIS SIDI CORI, that GFT itself published and distributed through the retail chains MARUS, ceased to be printed. Even more interestingly, GFT reduced those advertising means addressed to the mass market which it had intensively exploited in previous years. At the same time, GFT undertook a long-lasting partnership with Vogue as advertiser of collections branded by fashion designers.

The second and most important phase of GFT's evolution started with the establishment of a partnership with two well-known Italian fashion designers, Giorgio Armani[61] and Valentino Garavani,[62] who signed agreements with GFT in 1978 and 1979 respectively. In the case of Armani, the licensing agreement concerned both the Giorgio Armani 'white label' diffusion (or bridge) line – a secondary line intended to reach customers with lower price points – and the more exclusive Giorgio Armani 'black label' collection. In 1979, GFT and Armani created a joint venture – the Giorgio Armani Men's Wear Corporation – in the United States. The new corporation would serve to introduce Armani's labels to a broader North American audience and would be responsible for the manufacture and distribution of the new label *Giorgio Armani Le Collezioni*.

GFT's goal was to create fashionable ready-to-wear garments by combining the advantages of industrial production in terms of scale with those deriving from the creative control of an iconic fashion designer, which granted a sense of independence, uniqueness, and an authentic identity to the brand.[63] In her extensive research on the Italian design revolution, Silvia Giacomoni observed that, in the second half of the 1970s, Italians 'lost their accent'. The renowned capabilities in manufacturing high-quality textiles and fashion goods – along with the outstanding talents of a new generation of fashion designers – led to the emergence of a new 'Italian look'.[64]

The partnerships allowed both GFT and designers to grasp the opportunities offered by the growing interest in Italian fashion in the American market. As highlighted by the art historian John Potvin, it was not until the deal with GFT that the Armani brand became a cultural and economic force to be reckoned with outside of Italy. Since his debut under his own name in 1975, the designer had received high praise, but his access to American customers was still rather limited. The huge commercial success of the new diffusion line allowed him to expand his influence within the highly lucrative American market. Thanks to the industrial partnership with GFT, Armani's diffusion line retained many distinctive features of the designer's style – that 'very classic, elegant, relaxed and truly Italian' style – in spite of being sold at half the price of the 'black label' couture collection.[65]

In 1982 Giorgio Armani became the first Italian fashion designer to be featured on the cover of *Time* magazine.[66] A year later, he modified his contract with GFT to produce Mani, a second diffusion line of menswear for Canada and the United States and of womenswear for the European market. By 1984 GFT exports rose to a staggering 23.4%. Such a growth was due almost entirely to the increase in sales of the Armani and Valentino lines in the United States, which comprised 25% of the company's exports. By the same year the United States imported more than $551 million worth of Italian clothing. In 1986, that number rose to a stunning $851 million.[67]

The partnerships with the designers changed GFT in different ways. Primarily, the group had to implement a tighter integration between manufacturing and marketing by reducing the gaps between the consumers' taste, the fickle trends of fashion, and the commercial side of the business. Furthermore, and most importantly, after many years spent manufacturing standardised products in high volumes and at a low cost, the company's traditional focus on efficiency had to combine with a new emphasis on flexibility and extremely high quality.[68] Yet this momentous change occurred without developing a coherent business strategy, to the point that three different production systems worked in parallel within GFT's plants.[69] The first one resembled the original FACIS mass production system, as it consisted of large plants with long cutting tables and hundreds of sewing machines arranged in long lines. This system was extraordinarily flexible in that it allowed for rapid changes of style and the use of a wide variety of fabrics, but it depended upon the costly equipment of production, planning, and controlling. The second system, in contrast, was the modern version of a tailor's shop, as it focused on the sartorial production of luxury ready-to-wear for women, to be sold through exclusive boutiques. The annual production ranged from 20 to 200 prototypes to be reproduced using expensive materials that were specifically designed for each model. The productive process began with a designer's free-hand drawing, which was intelligible only to his closest collaborators, the *modelliste*. Highly skilled seamstresses, the *modelliste* assembled fabrics according to the fashion designer's sketch. Then teams of skilled tailors and dressmakers reproduced the models. At first glance, this production system featured a high degree of flexibility. In truth, the characteristics of the sartorial expertise and the consequent extreme specialisation of the workforce make difficult any adjustment to broad changes in working rates and methods.

A hybrid of the two mentioned above, the third type of productive system concerned mass production of diffusion lines that GFT commercialised both under its own labels and using the labels of the fashion designers. The plurality of labels entailed a high degree of product differentiation. The production process consisted of many relatively small operations carried out by workers who were more skilled than those employed in mass production. However, a close collaboration among *modelliste*, tailors, and industrial engineers was essential in order to turn the fashion designers' drawings into prototypes to be reproduced on an industrial scale.

Much of GFT's success in the early 1980s relied on mass-production of luxury ready-to-wear garments. Yet the business strategy based on the involvement of fashion designers in product development, brand communications, and distribution led the company to suffer from loss of control over the entire value chain. In the end, clothing was marketed using the designers' brands exclusively, and production was strictly regulated by licensing agreements that greatly differed from those signed with Biki in the 1960s. These obliged GFT to accept the stylist's decisions in matters of design and to pay royalties for the licence to use his brand. Moreover, the manufacturing process was under the exclusive control of designers who also autonomously administered the budget, paid entirely by GFT, for the promotion of the fashion collections. Just to give an example, the 1979 agreement between GFT and Valentino granted the designer an astounding 10% royalty on net sales plus 2% for the advertising budget. In addition, the designer benefited from a 'golden parachute' clause that protected him from fluctuations in sales. At his discretion, Valentino could stop production if the output did not comply with the prototypes. All advertising and promotional campaigns had to be approved by him in advance. As for the commercial side, Valentino reserved the right to manage his own boutiques and to open additional ones; to sell any Valentino merchandise in such boutiques; and to sell *haute couture* to American department stores.[70]

On top of all this, the collaboration with the designers soon brought out a fundamental contradiction. Repositioning from the traditional mass market to the high end market for clothing was extremely profitable to GFT, but it also created a misalignment between the company's strategy and image. Traditional organisational strengths – such as productivity and industrial efficiency – were now negatively perceived by consumers as factors that somehow deprived the product of exclusivity and distinctiveness. Furthermore, licensing agreements required huge investments in promoting the designers' labels while preventing GFT from promoting its own brand. The role of GFT in making the product (and the designer's label) successful was thus overshadowed. In the mid-1980s, top management attempted to reorganise GFT's strategic communications by establishing a dedicated department and creating a 'GFT Group' brand, to be used as a communication tool in order to strengthen the corporate image. The initiative, however, had poor results.[71] In the case of Armani, as under-lined by John Potvin:

> throughout the 1970s, 1980s and 1990s Armani advertisements in … Italian magazines also listed the names of the textiles mills and manufacturers he collaborated with in the creation of the collection. The same could not be said when he used identical advertisements in foreign magazines.[72]

As for Valentino, from the late 1980s GFT's marketing managers started to complain to the stylist's collaborators about the frequent absences of the GFT Group brand in advertise-ments and other promotional materials (e.g. window signs).[73]

5. The fall of GFT

Around the middle of the 1980s, GFT had become the world's largest manufacturer of fashion clothing. At the beginning of 1985, the GFT Group owned 12 factories (10 in Italy, one in the United States and one in Mexico) and employed over 7000 people. The consolidated accounts closed with a turnover of $372 million, 52.3% of which was from sales in Italy, 12.2% in EC countries, 23% in the US and Canada, and 6.2% in Mexico. The following year, the turnover increased to $560 million, reaching $694 million in 1987. In those years, among the Italian clothing groups, only Benetton managed to equal and exceed GFT's economic results. In 1988, GFT owned 15 Italian subsidiaries and 15 foreign subsidiaries in Europe, Canada, the United States, Mexico, and Australia; in the same year it became the first producer of luxury goods to create a joint venture to operate in China with direct participation from the Chinese government. Its retailing network involved 70 countries and marketed a widely diversified clothing supply that included ready-to-wear branded by Valentino,[74] Armani,[75] Ungaro,[76] sportswear under the C.P. Company and Taverniti brands, more classical clothing by FACIS, CORI, Profilo, Max Honorati, and fashion collections by Chiara Boni, Christian Dior, and Louis Feraud. Among the group's companies responsible for this impressive growth was the GFT USA subsidiary, which marketed clothing branded *Giorgio Armani Le Collezioni* and *Mani*, and whose turnover increased from $7 million in 1980 to $304 million by 1989.[77]

Yet in the late 1980s GFT's profitability began to decline rapidly. While in 1986 net profit as a percentage of sales came to 4.5% with an income of 40.17 billion lire on sales of 900.4 billion, in 1988 the profits of 40.4 billion lire amounted to 3.4% of 1.19 trillion lire in sales. In these years, the market for designer clothing had become a lot tougher. The recession that affected the United States in the late 1980s dampened the demand in a key market and depressed GFT's earnings. Further difficulties came from increasing global competition. Just to give an example, in the same period German apparel manufacturers like Hugo Boss and Escada developed new production technologies and better logistic systems that enabled them to capture part of GFT's market share by providing slightly inferior products but in a more timely and reliable fashion.[78]

GFT's top management observed that, paradoxically, the market slowdown should also be ascribed to their own success in educating consumers. As stated by Marco Rivetti, President of GFT,

> We taught people how to get dressed, how to have a taste for clothing. And once people learn, they become free to make choices of their own. It's like having a baby girl: you tell her how to dress when she's young and she accepts it. But once she grows up, she starts saying 'I know what I want. I'm not going to buy everything from you anymore.'… It took the consumer 10 years, but

now she has arrived. ... Once the consumer has evolved, her tastes are mature and designer X can't sell the same product all over the world the same way.[79]

The mere fact of seeing a designer label or the 'Made in Italy' label was no longer enough. Customers still wanted high quality, but they wanted it at a lower price. The emphasis was now on 'value' and on a much tighter trade-off between quality and cost. Every item of a particular designer collection had to be competitive in price or retailers would not carry them in the stores. This pushed GFT to simplify its production by selecting designers on the basis of their ability to meet the market demands.[80]

The conditions that had previously led to the phenomenal growth of the company were now regarded as a historical anomaly. In 1991 Marco Rivetti warned that 'the extraordinary growth granted by the partnership between Italian design and Italian industry [was] over. Periods like 1983 to 1986 [would] never be repeated, and in a certain sense that [was] good'.[81] He also spoke of the need to 'turn a label into a brand', a commercial and symbolic strategy crucial for secondary, diffusion, or bridge lines.

> Couture works equally well from Switzerland to South Africa. Ready-to-wear is always more difficult. Bridge lines must be one way in Italy and another in France and Germany, both in men's and women's, and this is transforming the label into a brand.

Rivetti cited the GFT–Armani collaboration as an example of a product designed expressly for the American market while maintaining the aura of the designer – a brand in itself rather than simply a label.[82]

In the late 1980s, in response to the pressures for increased product differentiation and responsiveness as well as greater price competitiveness, GFT initiated a strategy aimed at becoming an 'insider' in some of its most important markets. This meant giving GFT's subsidiaries around the world enough autonomy to adapt themselves to the specific features of the markets in which they operated. Marco Rivetti put it this way: 'traditionally, we delegated the creativity to the designers and the relationship with the customer to the retailer. Now, we have to do both. We have to reinvent everything from scratch'.[83]

The goal of getting closer to local markets pushed GFT to create a new, more decentralised organisational structure. In 1989, GFT became a financial holding company made up of six autonomous operating divisions. Two of them were based on geographical markets: North America (the United States, Canada, and Mexico) and the Far East. The remaining four operating divisions were based on GFT's main product lines – menswear, womenswear, and sportswear – and on the company's long-established, albeit decreasingly important fabric business. While the four product divisions coordinated most of GFT's traditional businesses in Europe, the two geographic divisions were designed to give greater autonomy to its subsidiaries in these two key markets. The key elements of this new structure concerned the decentralisation of various functions – including operations, marketing, personnel, accounting, and strategy – to each division. Finance, corporate relations, legal services, and training remained centralised at corporate headquarters. Relations with designers were also decentralised, so that each division could sign contracts directly with them.[84]

GFT USA became the flagship company of the North American division and began to develop relationships with local fashion designers whose work captured the style or customer wants of a particular country. In the United States, it signed agreements with Andrew Fezza and Joseph Abboud, American designers with a distinctive American style that nevertheless fit into GFT's global image of high quality and good design. The bulk of the Fezza and Abboud menswear collections were not 'Made in Italy' but at GFT group's manufacturing plants in Mexico and the United States. The partnership with Fezza and Abboud represented an organisational as well as a product innovation. Different from the traditional licensing arrangement, both agreements were actual joint ventures and subsidiaries of GFT USA, in which GFT held the majority interest. This was yet another way to link designers more closely to the market and to make sure their offerings were responsive to the business environment.[85]

However, it soon became clear that the strategy was incomplete. Firstly, becoming an insider in the American market would have required a more decisive redistribution of power within the company. Secondarily, the implementation of this strategy would have entailed not only a more flexible production system, but also a major overhaul of the company's relations with designers and retailers. GFT USA is a good case in point to understand such limitations. After a couple of highly successful fashion seasons, the flagship company of the North American division started to lose ground, partly because of tensions between the American subsidiary and the parent company. One of the main problems was the cost of importing garments from Italy. The GFT's hybrid production system, which combined the original FACIS mass production system with semi-artisanal techniques and processes, had never been particularly cost-efficient. According to a manager of the American subsidiary, the overhead costs alone amounted to 55% of the cost of producing a suit in the GFT's Italian factories. By 1988, the prices of Armani's collections marketed in the United States increased between 12% and 15% on average while in Valentino's case increases were between 20% and 24%.[86] Additionally, labour cost in Italian factories registered an increase of 10% as exchange rates became unfavourable. If in the early 1980s the strong dollar had helped GFT to conquer the American market despite the company's high production costs, these favourable conditions changed drastically in 1987, when the huge real exchange rate depreciation of the dollar against the Italian lira threatened to push GFT's products out of the market. A second object of dispute concerned the relationship with designers. Prominent European designers did not care about the characteristics of the American market when creating their collections. At the same time, transforming the labels of the emerging American designers into fully fledged brands soon proved to be arduous. The fashion stage had become too crowded: launching an *haute couture* collection – a pivotal moment for a designer who aimed at being positioned as a 'creator' – as well as marketing new ready-to-wear collections required increasingly high investments in advertising. Thus, financial resources became an actual barrier to the establishment of new fashion brands as never before.[87]

After several quarters of declining profits, GFT plunged into the red in 1991 for the first time in its history. The world's largest manufacturer of fashion apparel lost $11.8 million, with sales decreasing by 1.2%. This was in part a consequence of the slowdown experienced by Western economies in that period, but was primarily due to the expensive restructuring plan that GFT had initiated in previous years. Despite its decline in sales and profit losses, the company maintained its course by 'creating separate operating companies for its various sectors, rationalising its product range, redefining relationships with designers for closer cooperation on commercial lines, cutting expenditures, and decreasing structural costs.'[88] However, with reported net losses of about $32 million (40 billion Italian lire) in 1991 and about $56 million (70 billion lire) in the following year, the crisis proved to be irreparable. After a failed attempt to sell a majority stake of GFT to Miroglio Spa, the Rivetti family was forced to relinquish control of the company to a powerful Milanese merchant bank,

Mediobanca, and to a consortium of creditor banks in exchange for a financial restructuring plan for the company's $300 million debt.[89]

In the following years, the void left by GFT was filled by those companies that had developed from small *maisons* into integrated groups. A 'combination of coherent brand management with high-quality manufacturing, subcontracted to a tight network of regular partners',[90] Armani's fashion company represents the most successful example of the business model that the Italian fashion companies adopted in the 1990s. The licensing agreements with GFT, along with the even more profitable ones signed by Armani himself in 1980 with L'Oréal for the production and distribution of the first fragrances for women and for men (launched in 1982 and 1984 respectively), generated a constant flux of financial resources that Armani mostly invested in retailing. In 1981, he opened the first of a chain of shops called *Emporio Armani* – branded with the logo representing an imperial eagle with Armani's initials – for the sale of a full line of clothing spanning from evening dress to jeans; whose prices, however, were significantly lower than those of his ready-to-wear collections – *Giorgio Armani Le Collezioni* and *Mani* – distributed by GFT. New collections – *Armani Jeans, Emporio Armani Underwear*, and *Emporio Armani Swimwear* – followed while the range of products branded with his name extended to accessories such as socks, ties, shoes, bags, belts, and eyewear. This strategy allowed Armani to achieve impressive economic results. In 1990 Armani fashion group's revenues were $306 million. Retail stores provided $160 million, while royalties and fees accounted for $130 million. Total retail sales, including those of licensed products, amounted to $1.6 billion. Net income after taxes was $54.2 million.[91] The following year Armani opened in New York the first of a new chain of stores in the USA, known as A/X, that featured a lower-priced, basic casual and denim collection.[92]

Thanks to the resources arising from sales and royalties, Giorgio Armani began to build a vertically integrated business by taking direct control over all aspects of design, manufacturing, distribution, and retail.[93] In 1990 he acquired a 20% equity stake in Società Manufatti SpA (SIM). SIM manufactured the men's and women's Armani Jeans collections for Europe and abroad and it also held the distribution licences for jeans and children's collections for Moschino, Krizia, and Versace. With this investment Armani moved beyond design and marketing into the spheres of production and distribution. In 1993 Armani purchased an additional stake in Simint Spa (formerly SIM) for $20 million, becoming the single largest shareholder with a 39.5% stake. The following year Simint started to manufacture part of the *Emporio Armani* and *Giorgio Armani* collections, in addition to producing all the jeans and some of the knitwear for *Emporio Armani*. Between 1996 and 2001 Armani purchased another 53.2% shares in Simint (raising his total to a 92.7% stake) and acquired a controlling share of the knitwear manufacturing company Deanna and of the shoe manufacturing company Guardi.

At the end of 2000 Armani finally severed the relationship with GFT and took the *Giorgio Armani Le Collezioni* and *Mani* labels in-house. In the process, Armani acquired two GFT menswear-manufacturing factories in Settimo Torinese outside Turin and one in Matelica in the Marche region. In addition, the house acquired the GFT America Fashion Group, formerly owned and controlled by GFT and responsible for the sale and distribution of the Armani lines in the United States.

Conclusion

In his seminal work on the social significance of brands, the business historian Mark Casson warned about how theoretical analysis should be complemented with empirical, historical, cultural, and even ideological studies on trademarks and branding in order to correctly assess their actual role in economic growth and the problems of their management over time.[94] The resource-based view of the firm provides a satisfactory account of how firms go about sustaining their existing competitive advantages, but it is less successful in accounting for how firms create such advantages.[95] Following the conceptual framework established by Robert Grant, strategy formulation should comprise five stages that link strategy, competitive advantage, resources, and capabilities. The last of these five stages refers to 'identifying the resource gaps which need to be filled and invest in replenishing, augmenting and upgrading the firm's resource base'.[96] To fill such gaps might require complementary resources to be acquired externally. In this case the firm must be able to appropriate the rents generated by those strategic resources in order to develop a competitive advantage.

Business historians in their turn can provide useful insights on how firms create, acquire, and exploit resources. In these pages, through the lens of GFT's history, we have dealt with brand as a means to build up a national market for mass-produced clothing in the 1950s and we deemed such a result as the first step toward the achievement of the leadership in the foreign markets. The early success of the FACIS brand was the result of some decisive factors: the acquisition and adaptation to the Italian market of American mass production manufacturing techniques; the adoption of a modern sizing system; investments in retailing; and innovative advertising campaigns. In those years, brand management at GFT pivoted on the technical, functional, and economic properties of mass-produced clothing. The brand image built in this period emphasised that the FACIS suit came in all possible sizes and was affordable enough to be bought by the majority of male Italian consumers. The limits of this product-oriented strategy clearly emerged from the unsuccessful attempt to enter the market for women's ready-to-wear. Despite the potential commercial appeal of the CORI-Biki trademark, the absence of structural bonds between designing and manufacturing hindered the efforts of the firm to transform a well-known designer's label into a new, successful brand.

In the 1970s, the fast-growing demand for more personalised and refined garments forced GFT to radically change its business model. This change included involvement of resources acquired externally – the fashion designers – at the product planning stage, greater attention to consumers' tastes and preferences, flexibility in response to fickle trends of fashion, and increased engagement in the commercial side of the business.[97] Through the partnership with fashion designers, GFT built a unique competitive advantage, based upon the alliance between creativity and manufacturing capabilities. Designers' imaginative ideas were transformed into fashionable commodities produced on an industrial scale. Huge investments in advertising and distribution allowed fashion brands to be turned into powerful strategic assets.

Although strongly differentiated, both the strategies shared a common feature: they were designed for adapting to specific market conditions. In the first era (1950s–1960s) of fashion brand management at GFT, the market was the domestic one. After that, GFT targeted the European and the American markets by leveraging Valentino's and Armani's labels respectively.

Paradoxically, the alliance with the designers also sowed the seeds of the 1990s GFT crisis, as it provided fashion designers with the means – such as royalties, business expertise, and entrepreneurial apprenticeship – to become independent from their industrial partner. Yet the partnerships with fashion designers were unbalanced. GFT relied on revenues generated by licensing agreements which granted fashion designers, along with royalties, almost full discretion in matter of production, advertising, and distribution. Thus, one must conclude that lack of ownership and control of designers' brands prevented GFT from fully appropriating the rents generated by their exploitation and progressively eroded its competitive advantage. This conclusion, however, does not explain why fashion designers eventually overcame their mentor.

Drawing once again from the resource-based theory we can answer this question and provide a final critical insight. As mentioned in the introduction, the resource-based theory argues that rent-generating resources are valuable, rare, and imperfectly imitable. However, for a firm, controlling and exploiting these resources is a necessary but not sufficient condition to achieve a sustained competitive advantage. A further and final condition pertains to the organisation. Even if a resource is valuable, rare, and imperfectly imitable, a firm must be 'organized to exploit the full competitive potential of its resources and capabilities'.[98] That is, poor organisational processes, policies, and procedures may undermine a resource's potential competitive advantage. Thus, the organisation acts as an 'adjustment factor' that either enables or prevents a firm from fully realising the benefits embodied in its valuable, rare, and costly-to-imitate resources.[99]

GFT and fashion designers: in the end, who really improved brand management? If one contrasts the decline experienced by GFT with the success of fashion designers, the answer, of course, is fashion designers. However, it is important to correctly assess the organisational factors associated with GFT's decline and what fashion designers learned from it. In the 1980s Italian fashion brands competing in the ready-to-wear business grew rapidly following the designers' vision and supported by the manufacturing skills of licensee companies. Since the 1990s an ever more competitive and globalised market has instead required a new organisational approach that presupposes a greater flexibility and responsiveness to customer expectations maintained throughout the entire supply chain, from production to distribution to retail stores. Over the same period the critical success factors for fashion companies shifted from the product and manufacturing technologies to brand and retail management. In today's fashion industry the brand more than the product plays a fundamental role because it represents a tool capable of creating a long-term relationship between the company – or one of its product lines – and specific consumer segments. Italian fashion designers learned from the demise of GFT, decoupling their brands from the product and the production process.[100] They thus pay close attention to brand management (marketing, advertising, promotion) in itself, distinct from the monitoring of product, creation, or distribution. They have subcontracted a large share of their manufacturing activities, keeping in-house only a few key product lines. In this way, Italian designers' companies have kept the advantages of small size and flexibility: creativity, adaptability, and speed of reaction to market changes. By limiting, and in many cases completely avoiding, the licensing strategy, they have been able to keep stricter control over product and brands.

Notes

1. Penrose, *The Theory*, 24.
2. Barney, "Firm Resources"; Peteraf, "The Cornerstones"; Wernerfelt, "A Resource Based."
3. Conner, "A Historical Comparison"; Dierickx and Cool, "Asset Stock"; Grant, "Prospering."
4. Runyan and Huddleston, "Getting Customers."
5. Barney, "Firm Resources."
6. Hall, "A Framework."
7. Wilkins, "The Neglected Intangible Asset."
8. Higgins, "Forgotten Heroes and Forgotten Issues"; Mercer, "A Mark of Distinction"; McKendrick, Brewer, and Plumb, *The Birth*.
9. Da Silva Lopes and Casson, "Brand Protection"; Dahlén, "Copy or Copyright."
10. Da Silva Lopes, "The Growth and Survival"; Da Silva Lopes and Duguid, *Trademarks, Brands and Competitiveness*; Da Silva Lopes and Guimaraes, "Trademarks and British Dominance"; Duguid, "Developing the Brand"; Jones and Morgan, *Adding Value*; Sáiz and Fernández, "Catalonian Trademarks."
11. Vergani, *Fashion Dictionary*, ad vocem.
12. Merlo, "Italian Fashion."
13. Patsiaouras and Fitchett, "The Evolution of Conspicuous Consumption."
14. Djelic and Ainamo, "The Coevolution."
15. OECD, *Textile and Clothing Industries*.
16. Breward, *Fashion*.
17. Merlo, *Moda italiana*.
18. Ente Nazionale Della Moda, *Congresso Nazionale Abbigliamento e Autarchia*.
19. Paulicelli, *Fashion Under Fascism*; Lupano and Vaccari, *Una giornata moderna*.
20. Rosso, "Lo sviluppo della confezione maschile."
21. ISTAT, *Censimenti ed indagini*.
22. Doxa, *Il consumo di prodotti tessili*.
23. Caccia and Micheletto, *Gruppo Finanziario Tessile*, 7.
24. Merlo, "Size Revolution."
25. Abruzzese and Aimone, *FACIS SIDI CORI*.
26. Rivetti, "La struttura organizzativa," 3.
27. Lisiani, "Efficacia dei marchi," 10.
28. Abruzzese and Aimone, *FACIS SIDI CORI*, 48.
29. AsTo (Archivio di Stato, Torino), GFT, box 1671, Profit and loss account 1955; box 1693, Profit and loss account 1960.
30. AsTo, GFT, box 1717, Profit and loss account 1965.
31. AsTo, GFT, box 2732, booklet "Confezione pronta – Istruzioni per prendere le misure," 1958, and box 2733, IRIS (Istituto Ricerche Statistiche), "Misurazione della popolazione femminile italiana," Turin, 1957.
32. Olivari Binaghi, "La moda"; Blignaut, *La scala di vetro*; Boneschi, "Le sarte milanesi."
33. Another example of partnership between a famous *couturière*, Madeleine Vionnet, and a mass-market manufacturer, the leading Parisian department store Galeries Lafayette, is described in Brachet Champsaur, *Madeleine Vionnet*.
34. AsTo, GFT, box 2127, Typescript, June 1957.
35. AsTo, GFT, box 2127, Letter sent by Biki to Silvio Rivetti, June 26, 1957.
36. AsTo, GFT, box 2127, Letter sent by Silvio Rivetti to Biki, September 17, 1957.
37. AsTo, GFT, box 2127, Payment mandates issued by GFT, 1957–1959.
38. AsTo, GFT, box 2127, Private deed, August 31, 1960.
39. AsTo, GFT, box 2127, "Partnership Biki/GFT," Minutes of the meeting held in Biki's atelier, December 14, 1961.
40. Evidence of GFT's commercial proposal and of the subsequent negotiation can be found in detailed correspondence between Biki and Franco Rivetti, preserved in AsTo, GFT, box 2127.
41. AsTo, GFT, box 2127, Private deed, November 20, 1962.

42. AsTo, GFT, box 2127, Letter sent by Biki to Franco Rivetti, March 26, 1965.

43. AsTo, GFT, box 2142, Private deed, January 24, 1966.

44. AsTo, GFT, box 2142, Licensing agreement, Notarial deed, January 24, 1966, notary Ugo Gancia, file number (repertorio) 43735. As a trademark licensing agreement, it was also registered at the Italian Trademark and Patent Office, Registration act no. 7378, March 10, 1966. Biki had registered her trademark at the beginning of 1966 as found in the Central State Archives, Trademark and Patent Office, Registration act no. 178838, January 18, 1966. In June 1966, she also registered the same trademark at the French Trademark and Patent Office, Registration act no. 315,720.

45. AsTo, GFT, box 2142, Letter sent by Biki to Franco Rivetti, November 29, 1972.

46. AsTo, GFT, box 2142, Dossier 'Biki' containing newspaper advertising about Lanerossi, Fenicia, and Stellina – Marie d'Arc.

47. AsTo, GFT, box 2142, Letter sent by Biki to Franco Rivetti, July 24, 1971, and letters sent by Biki's lawyer Corso Bovio to GFT's house counsel Alberto Ugona, March 12, 1972 and May 12, 1972.

48. AsTo, GFT, box 2892.

49. AsTo, GFT, box 2127, Biki collections, Revenues summary chart. Figures concern the Autumn/Winter collections 1963/64, 1964/65, and 1965/66. The number of items sold is equal, respectively, to 6963, 5418, and 3514, corresponding to revenues amounting to 165, 135, and 86 million lire. As far as the Spring/Summer collections are concerned, available data refer to 1964 and 1965. The number of items sold decreased from 10,340 to 4534 and the revenues from 10,340 to 4534 million lire.

50. AsTo GFT, box 2606, *Fatture Biki*.

51. AsTo, GFT, box 3321, Ugona, A., "L'esperienza del gruppo GFT nel campo della griffe e della proprietà industriale," speech of GFT's house counsel Alberto Ugona at the meeting "Griffe, marchi e brevetti europei alla vigilia del 1992."

52. Abruzzese and Golzio Aimone, *FACIS SIDI CORI*.

53. Mendes and de la Haye, *Twentieth Century Fashion*, 220–223.

54. Bourdieau, *Distinction*; Macchion, Fornasiero, and Vinelli, "Supply Chain Configurations."

55. Significantly, at the same time, the formal outfit that the running man tucked under his arm in the FACIS trademark was replaced by the acronym itself, thus signalling that in GFT's history the time of ready-made, mass-produced dress was over.

56. AsTo, GFT, box 2238, "Riflessioni sul rapporto tra la produzione industriale del GFT e gli stilisti" (1989).

57. Mendes and de la Haye, *Twentieth Century Fashion*, 167.

58. AsTo, GFT, box 2463, 1.

59. Carrarini, "La stampa di moda."

60. Cox and Mowatt, "*Vogue* in Britain," 74.

61. In 1957 Armani worked at La Rinascente, the largest Italian department store in Italy at the time. He then joined the staff of Cerruti, one of the biggest Italian firms producing men's clothing, as a designer. With the encouragement of his friend Sergio Galeotti, Armani started to collaborate as a freelance designer with other companies as well. Armani and Galeotti became business partners in July 1975, when they founded Giorgio Armani Spa. The company's first collection – a men's clothing line – debuted that year. A year later, Armani launched a women's collection, which received a warm reception. Since 1976, Armani's collections have been included among the foreign luxury commodities sold by Barneys New York department store. See White, *Giorgio Armani*.

62. After studying in Paris and working as an apprentice for Jean Dessès and Guy Laroche, Valentino established his atelier in Rome in 1959. Throughout the 1960s and 1970s, his glamorous, sophisticated designs attracted high-profile customers such as Jacqueline Onassis, Elizabeth Taylor, and the Empress of Iran, Farah Diba. In 1969, he opened his first ready-to-wear boutique and introduced the 'V' logo. Valentino's emblem owed much of its initial success to American customers, who especially appreciated his soft tailoring and lavish evening gowns. See Mendes and de la Haye, *Twentieth Century Fashion*, 204.

63. Potvin, *Giorgio Armani*, 85.

64. Giacomoni, *The Italian Look Reflected*, 9.
65. Potvin, *Giorgio Armani*, 284.
66. Among others, the cover of *Time* featured Claire Mc Cardell in 1955, Christian Dior in 1957, Rudi Gernreich in 1967, and Gianni Versace in 1995.
67. Potvin, *Giorgio Armani*, 85.
68. Howard, "The Designer Organisation."
69. Locke, "Unity in Diversity"; Locke and Antonelli, "International Competitiveness."
70. AsTo, GFT, box 1583, Agreement between Valentino Couture and Gruppo Finanziario Tessile Spa, October 5, 1979.
71. AsTo, GFT, box 2283, GFT Group Corporate Communications and Image. International Policies and Corporate Image; AsTo, GFT, box 2276, "Studi per la promozione del marchio GFT."
72. Potvin, "Giorgio Armani," 85.
73. AsTo, GFT, box 2238, "Riflessioni sul rapporto tra la produzione industriale del GFT e gli stilisti" (1989); AsTo, GFT, box 2283, Strategic Plan, GFT USA, February 1992.
74. Valentino's labels licensed to GFT included: *Valentino Boutique, Valentino Night, Valentino Miss V, Valentino Studio,* and *Valentino Carisma* for womenswear; *Valentino Uomo, Valentino Beachwear,* and *Valentino Couture* for menswear.
75. Armani's labels licensed to GFT included: *Giorgio Armani, Giorgio Armani Le Collezioni, Mani* (Canada and USA), and *Emporio Armani* for menswear; and *Mani* (Europe) for womenswear.
76. Ungaro's labels licensed to GFT included: *Ungaro Parallèle, Ungaro Solo Donna, Ungaro Ter* for womenswear; and *Ungaro Uomo* for menswear.
77. Merlo, "Italian Fashion," 351.
78. Stielau, "Competitive Strategy."
79. *Women's Wear Daily*, May 1, 1990.
80. Howard, "The Designer Organisation."
81. Quotation from Marco Rivetti in *Women's Wear Daily*, June 11, 1991.
82. Quotation from Marco Rivetti in *Women's Wear Daily*, May 1, 1990. See also Potvin, "Giorgio Armani," 92.
83. Quotation from Marco Rivetti in Howard, "The Designer Organisation."
84. AsTo, GFT, box 2276, "Studi per la promozione del marchio GFT."
85. AsTo, GFT, box 2276, GFT in North America.
86. Potvin, "Giorgio Armani," 90.
87. *Women's Wear Daily*, May 1, 1990.
88. *Women's Wear Daily*, October 10, 1991.
89. *Women's Wear Daily*, August 8, 1994.
90. Djelic and Ainamo, "The Coevolution," 632.
91. Ingram, "Giorgio Armani S.p.A."
92. Potvin, *Giorgio Armani*, 106.
93. Potvin, *Giorgio Armani*, 103–109; Merlo, "Italian Fashion," 352.
94. Casson, "Brands."
95. Bowman and Collier, "A Contingency Approach."
96. Grant, "The Resource-Based Theory," 115.
97. Macchion, Fornasiero, and Vinelli, "Supply Chain Configurations."
98. Barney and Hesterly, *Strategic Management*, 94.
99. Barney and Clark, *Resource-based Theory*.
100. Djelic and Ainamo, "The Coevolution."

Acknowledgements

The authors wish to thank the anonymous referees for their useful comments and Catia Brilli for translation revision. All errors and omissions are ours. The article represents a joint effort. Elisabetta Merlo wrote the introduction and sections 2 and 3, Mario Perugini wrote sections 4 and 5 and the conclusion.

Disclosure statement

No potential conflict of interest was reported by the authors.

References

Abruzzese, A., and E. Golzio Aimone. *FACIS SIDI CORI. Un'Analisi condotta sui fondi dell'Archivio Storico sulla Grafica e la Pubblicità dal 1954 al 1979* [*FACIS SIDI CORI*: Graphics and Advertising in the Historical Archive, 1954–1979]. Torino: Gruppo GFT, 1989.

Barney, J. "Firm Resources and Sustained Competitive Advantage." *Journal of Management* 17 (1991): 99–120.

Barney, J., and D. Clark. *Resource-Based Theory: Creating and Sustaining Competitive Advantage*. New York: Oxford University Press, 2007.

Barney, J., and W. Hesterly. *Strategic Management and Competitive Advantage: Concepts and Cases*. New Jersey: Pearson, 2012.

Blignaut, H. La. *La scala di vetro, il romanzo della vita di Biki* [The Glass Ladder, Biki's Life Novel]. Milano: Rusconi, 1995.

Boneschi, M. "Le sarte milanesi del 'miracolo' tra moda, industria e cultura [The Milanese Seamstresses at the Time of the 'Economic Miracle' between Fashion, Industry and Culture]." *Annali di storia dell'impresa* 18, no. 1 (2007): 75–103.

Bourdieu, P. *Distinction: A Social Critique of Judgement of Taste*. Cambridge, MA: Harvard University Press, 1979.

Bowman, C., and N. Collier. "A Contingency Approach to Resource-Creation Processes." *International Journal of Management Reviews* 8, no. 4 (2006): 191–211.

Breward, C. *Fashion*. Oxford: Oxford University Press, 2003.

Caccia, G., and S. Micheletto. *Gruppo Finanziario Tessile. Inventario* [Inventory]. Torino: Archivio di Stato, 2014.

Carrarini, R. "La stampa di moda dall'unità ad oggi [Fashion Press Since the Unification Until Today]." In *La Moda* [Fashion], edited by C. Belfanti and F. Giusberti, 797–834. Turin: Einaudi, 2003.

Casson, M. "Brands: Economic Ideology and Consumer Society." In *Adding Value: Brands and Marketing in Food and Drink*, edited by G. Jones and N. Morgan, 41–58. London: Routledge, 1994.

Conner, K. "A Historical Comparison of Resource-Based Theory and Five Schools of Thought within Industrial Organisation Economics: Do We Have a New Theory of the Firm?" *Journal of Management* 17 (1991): 121–154.

Cox, H., and S. Mowatt. "Vogue in Britain: Authenticity and the Creation of Competitive Advantage in the UK Magazine Industry." *Business History* 54 (2012): 67–87.

Da Silva Lopes, T. "The Growth and Survival of Multinationals in the Global Alcoholic Beverages Industry." *Enterprise and Society* 4 (1993): 592–598.

Da Silva Lopes, T., and M. Casson. "Brand Protection and the Globalization of the British Business." *Business History Review* 86 (2012): 287–310.

Da Silva Lopes, T., and P. Duguid, eds. *Trademarks, Brands and Competitiveness*. New York and London: Routledge, 2010.

Da Silva Lopes, T., and P. Guimares. "Trademarks and British Dominance in Consumer Goods, 1876–1914." *Economic History Review* 67 (2014): 793–817.

Dahlén, M. "Copy or Copyright Fashion? Swedish Design Protection Law in Historical and Comparative Perspective." *Business History* 54 (2012): 88–107.

Dierickx, I., and K. Cool. "Asset Stock Accumulation and Sustainability of Competitive Advantage." *Management Science* 35 (1989): 1504–1511.

Djelic, M. L., and A. Ainamo. "The Coevolution of New Organisational Forms in the Fashion Industry: A Historical and Comparative Study of France, Italy, and the United States." *Organisation Science* (1999): 622–637. doi: 10.1287/orsc.10.5.622.

Duguid, P. "Developing the Brand: The Case of Alcohol, 1800-1880." *Enterprise and Society 4*, no. 3 (2003): 405–441.

Ente nazionale della moda. *Congresso nazionale abbigliamento e autarchia: relazioni e riassunti di comunicazioni* [National Congress Clothing and Autarchy: Reports and Summaries of Speeches]. Torino: Ente nazionale della moda, 1940.

Fernie, J., C. Moore, A. Lawrie, and A. Hallsworth. "The Internationalisation of the High Fashion Brand: The Case of Central London." *Journal of Product and Brand Management* (1997): 151–162. doi: 10.1108/09590551011085984.

Florence Brachet Champsaur. "Madeleine Vionnet and Galeries Lafayette: The Unlikely Marriage of a Parisian Couture House and a French Department Store, 1922–40." *Business History* 54 (2012): 48–66.

Giacomoni, S. *The Italian Look Reflected*. Milan: Mazzotta, 1984.

Grant, R. M. "The Resource-Based Theory of Competitive Advantage: Implications for Strategy Formulation." *California Management Review* 33 (1991): 114–135.

Grant, R. M. "Prospering in Dynamically-Competitive Environments: Organisational Capability as Knowledge Creation." *Organisation Science* 7 (1996): 375–387.

Hall, R. "A Framework Linking Intangible Resources and Capabilities to Sustainable Competitive Advantage." *Strategic Management Journal* 14 (1993): 607–619.

Higgins, D., and T. Geoffrey. "Asset or Liability? Trade Marks in the Sheffield Cutlery and Tool Trades." *Business History* 37 (1995): 1–27.

Howard, R. "The Designer Organisation. Italy's GFT Goes Global." *Harvard Business Review* September–October 69, no. 5 (1991): 28–44.

Ingram, F. C. "Giorgio Armani S.P.a." In *International Directory of Company Histories*, edited by J. P. Pederson, Vol. 45, 180–183. Chicago, IL: St. James Press.

ISTAT. *Censimenti ed indagini per la ricostruzione nazionale eseguiti nel settembre 1944* [Censuses and Surveys for National Reconstruction, September 1944]. Roma: ISTAT, 1945.

Jones, G., and N. Morgan, eds. *Adding Value: Brands and Marketing in Food and Drink*. London: Routledge, 1994.

Lisiani, V. "Efficacia dei marchi [The Effectiveness of Brands]." *L'Abito FACIS SIDI CORI* 1, no. 2 (1963): 10–14.

Locke, R. M. "Unity in Diversity: Strategy and Structure of the Italian Apparel Industry in the 1980s." Paper presented at the Conference on "Ready Made Fashion; Research and problems in the History of Mass-Produced Clothing", Milan, Italy, February 26-28, 1990.

Locke, R. M., and C. Antonelli. "International Competitiveness, Technological Change and Organisational Innovation: Strategy and Structure of the Italian Apparel Industry in the 1980s." In *Managing the Globalisation of Business*, edited by D. Lessard and C. Antonelli, 151–172. Naples: Editoriale Scientifica, 1990.

Lupano, M., and A. Vaccari, eds. *Una giornata moderna. Moda e stili nell'Italia fascista* [A Modern Day. Fashion and Styles in Fascist Italy]. Bologna: Damiani Editore, 2009.

Luzzatto-Fegiz, P. "Il consumo di prodotti tessili nelle famiglie italiane [Consumption of Textiles in the Italian Families]." In *Il consumo di prodotti tessili nelle famiglie italiane, 1953–195. Indagine campionaria eseguita per incarico del Comitato nazionale della produttività (Gruppo di lavoro industria tessile)* [Consumption of Textiles in the Italian Families, 1953–1956. Survey Carried Out by the National Committee of Productivity (Textile Industry Working Group)], Vol. 2, 150–168. Milano: Doxa, 1955.

Macchion, L., R. Fornasiero, and A. Vinelli. "Supply Chain Configurations: A Model to Evaluate Performance in Customised Productions." *International Journal of Production Research* 55, no. 5 (2017): 1386–1399.

McKendrick, N., J. Brewer, and J. H. Plumb. *The Birth of a Consumer Society. The Commercialization of Eighteenth-century England*. London: Europa Publications, 1982.

Mendes, V., and A. de la Haye. *20th Century Fashion*. London: Thames and Hudson, 1999.

Mercer, John. "A Mark of Distinction: Branding and Trade Mark La in the UK from the 1860s." *Business History* 52 (2010): 17–42.

Merlo, E. *Moda italiana. Storia di una industria* [Italian Fashion. The History of an Industry]. Venezia: Marsilio, 2003.

Merlo, E. "Italian Fashion Business: Achievements and Challenges (1970s–2000s)." *Business History* 53, no. 3 (2011): 344–362.

Merlo, E. "'Size Revolution': The Industrial Foundations of the Italian Clothing Business." *Business History* 57, no. 6 (2015): 919–941. doi: 10.1080/00076791.2014.992336.

OECD. *Textile and Clothing Industries. Structural Problems and Policies in OECD Countries*. Paris: OECD, 1983.

Olivari Binaghi, M. T. "La moda: le tendenze [Fashion: Trends]." In *Storia di Milano. Il Novecento* [History of Milan. The Twentieth Century], edited by Istituto della Enciclopedia Italiana, 496–563. Roma: Istituto della Enciclopedia Italiana, 1996.

Patsiaouras, G., and J. A. Fitchett. "The Evolution of Conspicuous Consumption." *Journal of Historical Research in Marketing* 4, no. 1 (2012): 154–176. doi: 10.1108/17557501211195109.

Paulicelli, E. *Fashion under Fascism: Beyond the Black Shirt*. Oxford – New York: Berg, 2004.

Penrose, E. T. *The Theory of the Growth of the Firm*. New York: John Wiley, 1959.

Peteraf, M. "The Cornerstones of Competitive Advantage: A Resource Based View." *Strategic Management Journal* 14 (1993): 179–191.

Potvin, J. *Giorgio Armani: Empire of the Senses*. Aldershot: Ashgate, 2012.

Rivetti, F. "La struttura organizzativa del Gruppo Finanziario Tessile [The Organizational Structure of Gruppo Finanziario Tessile]." *L'Abito FACIS SIDI CORI* 2, no. 3 (1964): 3–4.

Rosso, F. "Lo sviluppo della confezione maschile in serie in Italia [Development of the Production of Standardized Clothing for Men in Italy]." In *Congresso nazionale abbigliamento e autarchia: relazioni e riassunti di comunicazioni* [National Congress Clothing and Autarchy: Reports and Summaries of Speeches], edited by Ente nazionale della moda, 120–128. Torino: Ente Nazionale della Moda, 1940.

Runyan, R. C., and P. Huddleston. "Getting Customers Downtown: The Role of Branding in Achieving Success for Central Business Districts." *Journal of Product & Brand Management* 15, no. 1 (2006): 48–61.

Sáiz, P., and P. Fernández. "Catalonian Trademarks and the Development of Marketing Knowledge in Spain, 1850–1946." *Business History Review* 82, no. 2 (2012): 239–260.

Stielau, A. *Competitive Strategy and Business Performance. A Case in the German Clothing Industry*. Munich: GrinVerlag, 1999.

Vergani, G., ed. *Fashion Dictionary*. Milan: Baldini Castoldi Dalai, 2006.

Wernerfelt, B. "A Resource Based View of the Firm." *Strategic Management Journal* 5 (1984): 171–180.

White, N. *Giorgio Armani*. London: Carlton, 2000.

Wilkins, M. "The Neglected Intangible Asset: The Influence of the Trade Mark on the Rise of the Modern Corporation." *Business History* 34 (1992): 66–99.

Brand image, cultural association and marketing: 'New Zealand' butter and lamb exports to Britain, c. 1920–1938

Felicity Barnes and David M. Higgins

ABSTRACT
This article examines the branding and marketing strategies of New Zealand Producers Boards which were established in the early 1920s to coordinate the export of butter and lamb to Britain. The brand 'New Zealand' featured prominently in the promotion of lamb exports to Britain, whereas much more emphasis was placed on the 'Anchor' brand for butter. Because the 'Mother Country' was by far the biggest single export market for New Zealand butter and lamb, the branding and marketing activities of the Boards emphasised the strong cultural affinity that existed between Britain and New Zealand. Drawing on the relevant branding and marketing literature, the Boards' annual reports, and reports by the Ministry of Agriculture and Fisheries, we show that 'New Zealand' and 'Anchor' conveyed the fundamental message of a shared British identity.

Introduction

'Anchor' and 'New Zealand' are synonymous with butter and lamb. They are amongst the most famous and recognisable brands in the supermarket, and the former is the UK's oldest butter brand, with an estimated valuation, in 2016, of £95 m.[1] 'Anchor' was ranked amongst the top 10 leading supermarket brands in Britain, and according to Mike Walker, its senior brand manager, 'Its simple, proud, iconic design stands out … People know they are buying proper butter and a brand they can trust.'[2] Turning to lamb, in 2012, 73 per cent of the UK's sheep meat imports originated from New Zealand. Recent advertising campaigns for lamb have used the 'Meat New Zealand' logo to emphasise that the country possesses, 'a gentle climate, lush grass, unpolluted air and clean water, and television adverts showing prepared lamb being served with the New Zealand lamb rosette and the accompanying legend "It doesn't get any more free range than this."' Moreover, the concentration on exports was often at the expense of the domestic market: 'The country that was gaining an international reputation for high-quality lamb was not offering a similar level of quality in its domestic market.'[3]

This article examines the interconnections between brands, country of origin and advertising using a case study of New Zealand's exports of butter and lamb to Britain during the

Figure 1. Point of sale material for butcher-shop windows. New Zealand Meat Producers Board Annual Report and Statement of Accounts, 1930, Wellington, 1930, n.p.

Figure 2. Meat marketing in the New Zealand High Commission Window of the Strand, London. New Zealand Meat Producers Board Annual Report and Statement of Accounts, 1930, Wellington, 1939, n.p.

interwar period. Butter and lamb were branded and marketed as 'New Zealand', although the most successful butter brand was 'Anchor'(see Figures 1–3). These brands were created before 1914 and were at the forefront of advertising campaigns launched by the New Zealand Dairy Produce Control Board (NZDPCB), and the New Zealand Meat Produce Board (NZMP), formed in 1924 and 1922 respectively, and the New Zealand Co-operative Dairy Company (NZCDC). We argue that the brands 'New Zealand' and 'Anchor' had strong cultural foundations which made them particularly appealing to British consumers. This article demonstrates that it is possible to build a major brand, based on country of origin, without trade mark

Figure 3. Anchor advertisement for wrapped, patted, butter. New Zealand Dairy Exporter, 1 October 1932, p. 54.

protection. Moreover, we extend historical analyses of brand development by showing that during the interwar period, New Zealand was a pioneer in the use of mass-marketing campaigns to promote country of origin. This final contribution is particularly pertinent because it casts doubt on some of the more recent perspectives on the development of New Zealand food exports. Thus, the evidence presented in this article, which deals specifically with butter and lamb, suggests that some qualification needs to be made to the assertion of Eric Pawson and Tom Brooking that, 'Prior to 1973 … New Zealand faced no pressing need to add value through branding food … according to consumer preference', and, most recently, the claim by Geoffrey Jones and Simon Mowatt, that by the mid-1920s, the 'commodity-driven approach' of New Zealand was in '*marked contrast*' to Danish dairy exports which, 'were attempting to compete by differentiation through the creation of strong brands, such as Lurbrand, which were gradually extended to other products … as a strategy to create a long-term national quality image in export markets'.[4]

Making 'New Zealand' attractive to consumers in the 'Mother country' was important because Britain was by far New Zealand's biggest export market. A defining feature of the evolution of the nineteenth-century international economy was the growth of a global supply-chain for foodstuffs and primary products centred on the British market. One consequence of this trend was that many countries became heavily dependent on Britain for their economic survival and modified their production to 'suit the British food market'.[5] Of these 'Anglo-adapted' producers, perhaps the best-known examples are Danish and New Zealand exports of bacon and butter, and butter and lamb, respectively.[6] For example, between 1880 and 1914, Britain accounted for over 80 per cent of Danish butter exports; over a similar period Britain absorbed an average of 96.3 per cent, by value, of all meat exports from New Zealand.[7] This dependence on Britain continued during the interwar period: between 1923 and 1938, Britain absorbed, on average, 93 per cent (by weight) and between 1923–1936 over 50 per cent (by weight) of New Zealand butter and lamb exports respectively.[8] In other words, the viability of the New Zealand butter and lamb industries and, therefore, the agriculture sector as a whole, were critically reliant on maintaining their share of the UK market.

Studies of branding are becoming more prominent in business history and this provides one of the reasons for this special issue. Much of the previous work on brands focused on individual firms, especially those in the alcoholic beverages industry, in which international supply chains and multinational companies were paramount.[9] Subsequently, this scholarship was complemented by articles on country of origin, with particular reference to Danish exports of butter and bacon in the pre-1914 period and during the interwar years respectively. Additionally, business-history studies utilising the country of origin effect have been extended to include US, Australian and New Zealand exports of beef, lamb and mutton prior to 1914.[10] This article develops the nascent business history literature on country of origin by discussing the promotion of New Zealand butter and lamb in Britain during the interwar period. In contrast to recent work on Denmark's domination of the British bacon market during the same period,[11] we argue that New Zealand was able to appeal to the strong cultural and economic ties that existed between it and the 'mother country'. This relationship was communicated by the iconic brands 'Anchor, and 'New Zealand' for butter and lamb respectively.

There exist significant differences between private brands and country of origin indicia. Perhaps the most important difference is that the latter can be used by all producers within a nation state. Often, such indicia were developed and then marketed by cooperatives: the 'Lur Brand' as applied to Danish butter exports, being an especially strong example. A further difference between private brands and country of origin is that the economic importance of the latter extends beyond individual firms to entire regions and, indeed, nations. This observation is especially relevant to the case study of this article, given New Zealand's reliance on Britain.

Our discussion of New Zealand butter and lamb exports raises a number of fundamental questions. First, to what extent was New Zealand able to overcome the first-mover advantage that Denmark enjoyed in the British butter market? By 1914, Denmark was by far the single biggest supplier of butter to Britain, accounting for 40 per cent of total imports (by weight). Second, in the case of lamb, how successful was New Zealand in preserving its market share from growing competition from Latin America? On average, between 1909 and 1913, imports of mutton and lamb into Britain from Empire sources (principally New Zealand), were 61.8 per cent, compared to 38.2 per cent for foreign countries (Latin America). However, the disruption caused by World War I eroded this difference: by 1924, the respective figures were 55.4 and 44.6 per cent.[12]

A further question to be considered is how successfully did major food exporters over-come British initiatives to increase domestic supplies? A recent study showed that Danish bacon reigned supreme during the interwar period, despite efforts to improve the sup-ply-side response of British farmers.[13] In this article we argue that the Danish experience is generalisable: New Zealand butter and lamb were also immune to British efforts to increase self-sufficiency. Part of the explanation for this immunity is that the NZDPCB and the NZMPB were able to launch extensive advertising campaigns using 'New Zealand', 'Fernleaf' and 'Anchor' because British consumers were confident that these brands guaranteed consist-ently high and uniform levels of quality. The contrast with the British response was stark. In the case of mutton and lamb, for example, an official investigation noted significant variation in the grading of carcasses, little (if any) standardisation and concluded: 'Up to the present, the home product has received virtually no advertising.'[14] Further, as detailed later, campaigns to promote British-grown produce were always compromised by Empire. The 'Buy British' campaign of 1931, for example, not only promoted local products but also classified Empire-grown produce such as 'New Zealand' butter and lamb as 'British'.[15]

This imperial connection created two important differences from the Danish and Latin American experience. First, New Zealand's status as a dominion of the British Empire meant there were strong cultural, economic and political ties with Britain. Thus, between 1870 and 1914, British foreign investment in the Dominions (principally, Australia, Canada and New Zealand) increased rapidly from 12 to 37 per cent.[16] James Belich has argued that these tightened ties created a 'recolonial' effect, bringing Britain and New Zealand into a closer cultural as well as economic relationship. The impact of this is explored below, which con-siders the development of a 'British' New Zealand identity.[17] On a priori grounds, therefore, there is reason to believe that New Zealand capitalised on 'British sentiment' to increase rapidly its share of the British market for butter and lamb, especially when these ties were further strengthened by the First World War and the participation of ANZAC forces in this conflict. According to Lord Jellicoe, consumption of New Zealand butter was a patriotic requirement for British consumers and, 'Anybody who ate Danish instead of New Zealand butter should be shot'.[18] Second, as discussed later, by 1932 these imperial ties would provide a material advantage, being called upon to help exclude 'foreign' produce from Denmark and Latin America and bolster Empire sales through imperial preference agreements signed at Ottawa.

This article is organised as follows. In the next section, we discuss country of origin in the branding and marketing literature and explain why its effects are potentially powerful in the case of foodstuffs. We then examine differences in the legal protection afforded country of origin compared to private trade marks and brands and explain why this difference is not important for our case study. The following section examines the development of the 'New Zealand brand' through the formation of the New Zealand Meat Producers Board (NZMPB) and the New Zealand Dairy Producers Control Board (NZDPCB). These Boards were estab-lished to provide national control of the export of meat (principally lamb), and butter and dairy produce respectively. The NZMPB initiated a marketing strategy in which the brand 'New Zealand' was a central feature. For butter, we argue that 'Anchor', a brand developed by the New Zealand Cooperative Dairy Company, eventually superseded the NZDPCB's pre-ferred brand – the Fernleaf – to become de facto the principal brand applied to butter exports. The marketing strategies of both Boards, which emphasised the cultural links between Britain (the Mother Country) and New Zealand, are examined and assessed in

Section five. We assess the effectiveness of the New Zealand branding and marketing campaign in the penultimate section, before presenting conclusions.

Brands, trade marks and country of origin

There is general agreement that brands and trade marks are closely connected. Trade marks denote the trade or commercial origin of a product. Statutory and common law definitions of this term indicate that it is, 'a mark used or proposed to be used upon or in connection with goods for the purpose of indicating that they are the goods of the proprietor of such trade mark by virtue of manufacture, selection, certification … or offering for sale'.[19] Brands are similar to trade marks in that they, too, help producers differentiate their products from rivals. However, there can exist important differences between these indicia. The first is that *registered* trade marks give property rights to the proprietor who can take action for infringement. Only registered marks benefit from this protection – which prevents others from copying the mark. But brands need not be registered. In this case, there exists a different class of legal remedies, usually relating to unfair competition, which can be employed to prevent others imitating the brand. Most famous brands are registered in order to secure the stronger protection afforded trade marks.[20]

A further distinction between trade marks and brands is the different messages they convey. Registered trade marks are no more than the 'legal scaffolding' on which brands are built.[21] Protection against infringement ensures that the products sold by one producer cannot be represented as those of another. Brands go far beyond trade origin per se. It has been argued, for example, that the owner of a trade mark is not the owner of the brand: the brand image resides in the mind of the consumer, not the factory where the products are made.[22] Other scholars have argued that a brand is the sum of the product, the emotions it generates and its socio-cultural significance.[23] At a broader level, it has been suggested that cultural principles – the ideas or values according to which cultural phenomena are evaluated and construed – are substantiated by consumer products, such that 'goods are both the creations and the creators of the culturally constituted world'.[24]

Advertising plays a crucial role in the communication of the meanings and associations attached to brands. Advertising is more than simply a 'mediator between supply and demand' because it 'embeds products, services and organisations in cultural contexts that are meaningful for consumers. It creates brands by linking culture and commerce … Advertising has become inextricably meshed with culture'.[25] The transfer of cultural meaning effected by advertising involves assessment of many factors, including which cultural principles the manufacturer seeks for the product and which cultural meaning is to be portrayed in the advertisement. Effective brand advertising encourages:

> a metaphoric identification of 'sameness' by the would-be consumer. World and good must be seen to enjoy a special harmony. They must be seen to 'go together.' When this sameness is glimpsed … the process of transfer has taken place. Meaning has shifted from the culturally constituted world to the consumer good.[26]

It may appear ahistorical to discuss country of origin as a brand in the context of this article: the earliest study in this field, conducted by Robert Schooler, was published in 1965.[27] Nonetheless, for contemporaries, clear indications of the country of origin effect were known by the First World War. Perhaps the most famous example of this was the 'Made in Germany' legend which became a *cause célèbre* in late nineteenth century Britain.[28] Subsequently,

Gabriele Morello has shown that the 'Made in Germany' label was imposed by the victors to help consumers identify and avoid products from the former enemy. But even this initiative backfired: Germany's reputation for good engineering enabled consumers to identify and purchase German products![29] Turning to foodstuffs, contemporaries were well-informed about the merits of 'Danish' bacon and butter, as well as 'US' beef, 'Canadian' cheese, and 'New Zealand' butter and lamb.[30]

Since Schooler's pioneering work, the volume of literature devoted to the country of origin effect has increased substantially.[31] Much of this later scholarship was critical of 'single-cue' studies because they tended to exaggerate the importance of origin per se. Subsequently, a number of themes have emerged which have particular relevance to this article. First, consumers pervasively use country of origin, sometimes denoted as 'Made in', when it is an indicator of quality.[32] This relationship is strengthened by recognition that certain countries are renowned for particular products: France for perfume and haute couture; Germany for precision engineering; Italy for fashion. In the same vein, New Zealand has been described as 'Butterland'.[33] The relationship between product *and* country moved the marketing debate on from 'Made in' to 'product–country–image' and its emphasis on 'what origin information is available to consumers'. Of particular relevance to our study is the observation that country of origin can be promoted as a significant part of a brand's unique selling proposition. In this regard, as we detail below, the marketing campaigns of the NZDPCB and the NZMPB made extensive use of country image and representative symbols of origin (e.g. 'Fernleaf'). Sometimes the country of origin may be communicated through the names of companies: in the same way that Lamborghini is understood to be 'Italian' and Toyota denotes 'Japan', so 'Anchor' became synonymous with New Zealand.[34]

In other words, substantial consonance existed between the brands and country of origin indicia used by New Zealand: brand names such as 'Anchor' evoked beliefs for consumers about the brand itself and triggered recall of the country associated with it – its country of origin. This is a phenomenon with a long history, and a growing literature especially in relation to Empire: trade cards depicting American Indians or Chinese workers helped eighteenth-century British consumers connect tobacco with America and tea with China, while recent work on the 'cultural economy' of the nineteenth-century British Empire argues that 'Britishness' was an important factor in facilitating trade between metropolis and colonies.[35] Later work by the Empire Marketing Board sought to create, and capitalise on, a shared sense of 'British' identity to promote sales of products from the dominions in particular.[36] Moreover, while consumers form overall images of a country's ability to produce particular products, at the time of making the decision to purchase, this overall perception is mitigated by a corresponding identification of the country as a source of a *particular* product line.[37] Just as eighteenth-century America was aligned with tobacco through the image of the 'Indian', so 'New Zealand' and 'Anchor' were perfectly aligned with New Zealand's reputation for lamb and butter and became synonymous with this produce.

Marketing scholars have devised conceptual frameworks which differentiate between consumer perceptions of the country with which a product/brand is identified and the country of manufacture. For example, 'Honda' is identified as a Japanese product, but the country of manufacture may be the US or Britain.[38] Increasingly, the literature on country of origin recognises that the development of global supply chains means that 'country of origin' may differ from 'Made in'; that 'Made in' may refer to country of assembly, country of design or country of manufacture.[39] However, while such considerations are particularly relevant to manufactures, there are two reasons why such issues have no bearing on this article. First, during the interwar period, 'Anchor' was owned by the NZCDC which was based in New Zealand and which applied the 'Anchor' brand to butter produced in New Zealand.[40] Second, it is tautological that when the name of a country is used to promote *produce* exports, the country of origin is an indication of geographical origin. Consequently, 'The cultural aspect of national image is irreplaceable and uncopiable because it is uniquely linked to the country itself'.[41] In other words, country of origin cannot be delocalised. In contrast, *private* brands do not indicate geographical origin: the US company Coca Cola licenses the production of its beverages in the UK.[42]

Within the marketing literature there is also growing awareness of the operational requirements for successful advertising of country of origin. As noted, particular countries are renowned for certain products. Consequently, an effective campaign extolling country of origin needs to focus on the products for which a country is most famous. To achieve success, it is imperative that the country of origin brand generates collective meaning, which is obtained in two stages. First, the various stakeholder interests (in our case, farmers, government inspectors, shippers and UK retailers) need to be coordinated by an industry marketing association which represents the industry. Second, once this coordination is achieved, emphasis switches to developing country of origin branding which facilitates an interactive process: collective meaning and identity is developed and enhanced by farmers, the industry as a whole and, importantly, the final consumer.[43] Such a perspective reinforces our central argument that the brands 'New Zealand' and 'Anchor' had strong cultural foundations which made them particularly appealing to British consumers.

Differences in legal protection

The 'New Zealand' brand possess a number of features which differentiate it from privately owned brands: it could be used by all producers based in New Zealand provided their butter reached a minimum, officially defined standard.[44] Viewed from this perspective, 'New Zealand' functioned as a certification mark.[45]

A further feature of the brand 'New Zealand' is that it was not registered as a trade mark during the interwar period.[46] In fact, online examination of the UK Patent Office suggests that 'New Zealand Lamb' was not registered until 1976. In the case of butter, 'Fernleaf' was registered as a trade mark in 1925, but the mark 'Fernleaf' accompanied by the words 'New Zealand butter' was not registered until 1950. In other words, during the interwar period the marketing campaigns of the NZDPCB and the NZMPB developed the brand 'New Zealand', even though it was not eligible for registration as a trade mark.[47] It might appear odd that a famous brand has developed without trade mark registration. Providing an explanation for this observation further helps to differentiate country of origin indicia from private trade marks.[48]

In Britain, a series of Trade Mark Acts established the 'essential particulars' that a trade mark had to possess:[49] the name of an individual or firm 'printed, impressed, or woven in some particular and distinctive manner'; and 'a distinctive device, mark, brand, heading, label or ticket'.[50] The 1875 Act, and its successors, ensured that the proprietor of a registered trade mark had exclusive rights to use this mark. Consequently, those who sought to copy or imitate a registered mark could be subject to an action for infringement. What, then, of geographical marks? Before the Trade Mark Acts, some geographical names functioned as trade marks. This occurred when the geographical term had acquired 'secondary meaning' and indicated the goods of a particular trader.[51] However, the Patents, Designs and Trade Marks Act, 1888, specifically excluded geographical names as trade marks.[52] This stipulation caused problems because certain geographical names were being used when their *primary* signification, to the 'ordinary' observer, was not geographical. One of the leading cases which clarified this issue involved the Magnolia Metal Co (1897). In this case, the company's name, Magnolia, was also the name of numerous small towns in the US. The key question to be decided was: did the term 'Magnolia' indicate that the company's metal was produced in a location with that name? If the answer to this question was positive, then 'Magnolia' could not be registered. According to Lewis Sebastian, a leading counsel on these matters, 'Magnolia' was registered because its geographical allusion was not generally understood in Britain and 'The effect of this decision appears to be that a word is not to be regarded as geographical unless its primary signification is geographical, or unless it has become recognised in this country as a geographical word'.[53]

Because 'New Zealand' was ineligible for registration in Britain, it did not benefit from the higher protection afforded trade marks. But this did not mean that the brand was totally defenceless against misuse. Indeed, it is significant that Britain was a pioneer among common-law countries in the prevention of unfair competition, which includes: 'Conduct of every kind, which is calculated to pass off the goods of the defendant as those of the plaintiff ... [and includes] the imitation of the general appearance or "get up" of his goods as they appear in the market; or of the imitation of the name under which he trades'.[54] In 1887, Britain introduced the Merchandise Marks Act which prohibited the use of false trade descriptions, including 'the place or country in which any goods were made or produced'.[55] As a result of this Act, the misuse of geographical indicia was made illegal and punishable under criminal law. The 1887 Act remained the principal Act governing misrepresentation throughout the interwar period.

In contrast, 'Anchor' was registered in Britain in 1905 by the New Zealand Dairy Association (later the New Zealand Co-operative Dairy Company) – the largest butter cooperative in New Zealand. Initially, this brand was used within trade circles, but during the interwar period it became, de facto, the export brand for New Zealand butter. As explained below, by the late 1920s it had superseded the 'Fernleaf', which had been established by the NZDPCB in 1925.

Producer boards and the development of the 'New Zealand' brand

The development of the 'New Zealand' brand followed the establishment of producer boards. As noted in the introduction, by 1914, and during the interwar period, New Zealand butter and lamb exports were heavily dependent on the British market. In this respect, New Zealand was comparable to Denmark, whose butter and bacon exports were also concentrated on Britain. Other similarities between these two countries can also be observed by 1914. For example, the cooperative system was firmly established in both countries (though less so in the case of New Zealand meat production.)[56] Additionally, both countries had introduced rigorous grading standards for their exports.[57] However, unlike Denmark, New Zealand did not possess a country of origin brand comparable to 'Lurbrand' or 'Danish', and nor did it benefit from the same degree of centralised control over exports. Instead, New Zealand meat and dairy producers developed a multitude of brands, shipping and grading marks.

One shipment of 150,000 carcases had 917 different identifying marks,[58] while dairy produce was sent under 600 or more different brands.[59]

This situation changed radically after World War I when, prompted by volatile market conditions, both the meat and dairy industries turned away from free marketing and developed the world's first producer boards. The meat industry was the first to act, lobbying a sympathetic government to pass the Meat Export Control Act in 1922, with a similar export control act passed for the dairy industry in 1923. Initially, the newly constituted meat and dairy boards had very similar mandates: power to control all exports; negotiate shipping and insurance rates; charge levies; institute and enforce grading regimes; and carry out marketing and promotional activities. The meat industry's transition to board control was relatively straightforward, for whilst the industry was centralised, meat continued to be sold on the open market at Smithfield. However, a disastrous attempt by the NZDPCB in 1926 to institute compulsory pooling of produce, combined with fixed-price selling, led to a farmer revolt when returns failed to meet expectations. Consequently, some of the Board's powers, including full control of selling, were rolled back. Dairy companies were once again free to choose how they marketed their produce, and, as we will see, this would have consequences for the success of the Board's branding campaigns.

It may seem self-evident that these newly formed producer boards would adopt a country of origin branding strategy when marketing 'New Zealand lamb' and 'New Zealand butter'. Yet, as we will see, the issue was more complex. Certainly, the Boards' operational goals of reducing costs and raising prices came, by default, to reinforce country of origin identity. Hundreds of brands and marks increased handling costs, and created opportunities for lower quality commodities from other countries to be passed off as 'New Zealand' produce, potentially dampening prices.[60] For these reasons, both Boards introduced standardised grading systems to ensure quality, reducing those hundreds of marks to just two export grades each. These quality marks were then linked with the brand 'New Zealand'. For example, from 1926, the Dairy Board's new 'Fernleaf' brand, 'designed to be a hall mark of quality' replaced 'all existing brands on butter boxes and cheese crates containing superfine or first grade quality.'[61] Meanwhile, the NZMPB congratulated its members for their 'united desire to uphold the good name of the Dominion in our meat trade by maintaining a proper and strict standard of grading.'[62]

Advertising campaigns then worked to reinforce the connection developed between 'New Zealand' and 'quality' in grading systems. Starting in 1927, the Meat Board's campaigns proclaimed 'New Zealand lamb: the best in the world' in posters, streamers, van signs and shop windows; it then invested in 1000 prime carcases for display purposes to prove it.[63] Demonstrators cooked up lamb samples for shoppers to reduce any lingering stigma around frozen meat, while a million copies of a booklet 'stressing the high quality of lambs, the freedom from disease, cleanliness in handling etc' were distributed.[64] By 1932, the Board claimed 'it is impossible to visit any town or village in Great Britain without being reminded that 'NEW ZEALAND LAMB IS THE BEST IN THE WORLD'".[65] The link between New Zealand and quality was further reinforced in 1935, when the British government introduced a Meat Branding Order requiring all imported meat be marked as either 'foreign', 'Empire' or with the country of origin. In response, the Board developed a new semi-circular 'New Zealand' brand, aimed not just at the trade, but at shoppers as well. To familiarise the trade with this new brand, the Board ran a competition showing 'how, where and why New Zealand meat is branded'. The new design was 'considered very much more legible when the meat is on sale at retail shops, and dissimilar to any brand used by other countries'.[66] New point of sale material quickly followed, and 'all of this material pointedly stresses the fact that all New Zealand mutton and lamb is branded NZ and invited the consumer to 'look for the mark "NZ"'.[67] Should those shoppers have had any difficulty, a million copies of an educational booklet were printed to show where on the joint the brand could be found. As a further quality safeguard, retailers were only eligible to receive new point of sale material if certified by a wholesaler that 'he is a regular stockist of New Zealand lamb'.[68]

Dairy advertising also sought to link New Zealand with quality. The Board believed 'the central point in all our advertising propaganda must be to get New Zealand in the minds of the people', and from 1927, they began to undertake the same sorts of promotional activities as the Meat Board, with shopping weeks, posters and general newspaper advertising.[69] But there were two important differences between the meat and Dairy Boards. First, the Dairy Board's attachment to the 'Fernleaf' brand did not last long. Just three years later, in 1930, the Board had begun joint marketing 'Empire butter' with Australia, hoping to cash in on a more general campaign, developed by Britain's Empire Marketing Board, to encourage consumers to buy more Empire produce. However, as a report issued in 1934 concluded, this may have 'helped New Zealand by encouraging consumers to buy Empire goods, but ... New Zealand had recently tended to lose by merger of its identity'.[70] Second, they struggled to connect the Fernleaf brand with consumers. In the 1920s, butter, traditionally sold by the scoop, started to be sold in pats or packets. These wrapped pounds and half pounds were a growing part of trade, but the Board failed to take advantage of the new marketing opportunity they provided. By 1932, they concluded that 'the sale of New Zealand butter in pats under the existing Fern Leaf Brand or any similar brand ... is not a proposition that can be put across on this country'.[71] In 1934, they worried that 'it would be unwise to push the sale of New Zealand butter in packets in opposition to the existing packet butters ... it is safer to leave it to the importers and wholesaler to meet the demand for New Zealand butter in packets'.[72] Board butter continued to be sold in scoops, the only consumer marking being an impression of a fern stamped into 56 lb bulk blocks, and the possibility that butter might be wrapped by a conscientious grocer in branded butter paper. Consequently, some considered the Fernleaf moribund, having become 'a quality mark ... [with] no sales value as far as the public is concerned'.[73] As late as 1938, the Dairy Board was still providing branded wrappers for bulk butter, not pre-packaged and ready-branded butter packets.[74]

The space left for a major dairy brand was quickly taken by the NZCDC's 'Anchor' brand. New Zealand's largest dairy company, the NZCDC controlled around one-third of national dairy exports. Formed by a series of mergers in 1919, the cooperative owned the 'Anchor' brand, which had been registered as a trade mark in 1905. By 1925 'Anchor' was regarded as 'the superfine N.Z.' butter'.[75] When the powers of the producer board were rolled back in 1926, the co-operative developed its own marketing and distribution organisations. Already a de facto quality standard for the wholesale trade, the NZCDC was quick to capitalise on opportunities to promote 'Anchor' to consumers. Though the Dairy Board could not envisage how to promote pre-packed butter, 811 tons of 'Anchor' brand patted butter was sold in London in 1926. By 1932, the NZCDC had its own packaging plant in London.[76] Trade was bolstered by the NZCDC's marketing agency, Empire Dairies, which undertook extensive consumer advertising. They even developed an 'Anchor club' for children, complete with a monthly magazine, badges, and 'Uncle Anchor', who wrote letters, organised outings and sent birthday cards.[77] Empire Dairies was so successful it was later bought by the Dairy Board to market all New Zealand butter and cheese.[78]

The development of 'Anchor' as the de facto national brand suggests we should not be too quick to conclude that the institution of national producer boards automatically led to the promotion of country of origin. Indeed, there was also a brand battle for meat, but in this case the NZMPB's 'New Zealand' was the winner. Before their campaigns began in the 1920s, the best-known brand for New Zealand mutton and lamb was 'Canterbury', reflecting both the region's long history of exporting frozen meat and its high quality. Nor did it hurt that British consumers sometimes confused New Zealand's Canterbury with the British version, increasing its appeal. These factors had a compounding effect. Farmers preferred their stock to be marketed by businesses with a 'Canterbury' brand, like the Christchurch Meat Company (CMC). Indeed, it was alleged as early as 1902 that some Canterbury processors bought up sheep elsewhere in the country and sold the end product as Canterbury lamb.[79] Smaller meat processors also hoped to export their product through such companies. In 1928, the Ocean Beach Freezing Company, which was based some distance from the Canterbury region in the southern town of Bluff, suggested the CMC might sell its meat so they would 'receive the premium paid for 'Canterbury mutton and lamb on the United Kingdom markets'.[80] Losing that brand could likewise spell disaster, as a North Otago farmers' cooperative discovered when they took over their local freezing works in 1920. Suddenly, meat which 'had commanded the "prime Canterbury premium" when marketed under the Christchurch Meat Company mark sold at a discount under the [new] brand'. Farmers switched freezing works and by 1924 the company was 'in serious difficulty'.[81]

These factors helped establish 'Canterbury' for consumers and trade alike.[82] Yet, despite the brand's premium price and quality associations, when the NZMPB began to promote its meat to British consumers, it chose to market it as 'New Zealand' lamb or mutton. 'Canterbury' was retained as a quality mark only.[83] It is tempting to see this as a rational reaction to the growing proportion of frozen meat sourced from other parts of New Zealand by the 1920s, especially the North Island. But the reasons are more complex. As the earlier examples show, the Canterbury brand could be used for meat produced elsewhere in the country. Bluff farmers, far from Canterbury at the end of the South Island, would have happily sent their lamb to London under the Canterbury mark. But not all New Zealand farmers felt the same. When the Christchurch Meat Company founded a freezing works in the North Island town of Wanganui, they changed their name to the New Zealand Refrigerating Company as a 'diplomatic move'.[84] Nor was internal farmer rivalry the only cultural consideration for the Board. It seems 'Canterbury' was not necessarily always associated with quality for British consumers. Instead, it had begun to be used as a generic term for all imported frozen meat.[85] A butcher prosecuted for passing off a South American leg of lamb as 'Canterbury' in 1930 claimed, as his defence, that 'in general usage by the public "Canterbury" lamb covered frozen lamb'. Another argued that in 'South Shields, people called frozen meat "Canterbury" whatever it was'.[86] Though the judges in these cases remained unconvinced, it seems the Meat Board did recognise the problem. In 1931, they ran advertisements in Wales to inform housewives that 'all imported lamb is not New Zealand but the finest lamb sent to Britain comes from New Zealand'.[87]

Whether for butter or lamb, then, the development of producer boards, with their emphasis on quality, played a key role in the establishment of a 'New Zealand' brand. But even more interesting is the nature of that brand. New Zealand producers were not simply 'Anglo adapted': in their advertising, they became 'British'.

Constructing a 'New Zealand' brand identity

The interwar invention of 'British' New Zealand was shared by both butter and lamb advertising, which sought to excise the 12,000 miles separating New Zealand from its metropolis by reimagining the former colonial frontier as a neighbouring, British, farming hinterland. In shop windows and on billboards, geographical borders were deliberately blurred as New Zealand sheep were advertised as 'British', while New Zealand butter was made in the 'British Empire Dairy Factory'.[88] Nor was 'British' New Zealand just a figment of a copywriter's imagination. The Meat Board, for example, saw Britishness as integral to the success of their product, noting that

> the New Zealand producer is out to follow the traditions of British quality in the produce he exports to his homeland and, secure in the goodwill of his countrymen at home, he looks with confidence to an ever–expanding trade for increasing qualities of his prime New Zealand produce.[89]

The development of a strong 'British' identity was an essential component of the 'New Zealand brand'. In contradistinction to the 'New Zealand' brand today, which emphasises an almost otherworldly, pristine natural environment, imaginatively distanced from the consumers' daily grind, the interwar version of the brand preferred to create a sense of cultural closeness. Such an approach was of course made possible by New Zealand's almost complete reliance on the British market. With nearly all New Zealand's exports sent to Britain, the brand 'New Zealand' could be closely contoured to suit this one marketplace. But British New Zealand was also enabled by Empire. The 'New Zealand' brand not only mobilised a 'metaphoric identification of "sameness" by the would-be consumer',[90] that 'sameness' was underwritten by the dense cultural, social and political ties woven by imperialism. The brand 'New Zealand' both reflected and reinforced the idea of a wider British world.

Actual ties of kinship notwithstanding, a sense of cultural affinity was carefully constructed in advertising, which sought to emphasise the familiar and marginalise any 'foreign' elements. This was made easier by the nature of New Zealand's commodities. Butter and lamb were the familiar products of British farms, not the exotic produce of colonial plantations. Indeed, it was claimed that Cornwall and Devon were two of New Zealand's best butter customers, possibly because Cornish and New Zealand butter possessed similar flavour.[91] Advertising reinforced their 'Home-like' nature, constructing images of New Zealand farms that owed as much to English rural idylls as they did to the actual New Zealand landscape. Though milking in New Zealand was both increasingly mechanised and male-dominated, the Dairy Board hearkened back to a nostalgic 'merry old England', with cheery milkmaids in long aprons appearing in posters and in exhibition space. In deference to the 'Fernleaf' brand, their aprons sported a few silver ferns, which was more than some of the promotional farming landscapes did.[92] In these images, sheep and cows grazed on verdant, rolling hills, with any strange native flora carefully relegated to the margins. Tree stumps and remnants of bush burns, signatures of New Zealand's newly cleared pastoral areas, but not features of 'Home' farms, were also notably absent.

It was not only native flora that was marginalised on the 'British' New Zealand farm. Just as in real life, there also seemed to be little room for the country's indigenous inhabitants.

Maori motifs, along with Maoris themselves, were almost non-existent in national branding campaigns. When they did appear, their role was carefully managed. Like the fernleaf, indigeneity could be used, sparingly, to add a dash of distinctiveness; it could also be used as a contrast, to highlight the country's progress from colonial frontier to British farm. A Meat Board display in the New Zealand High Commission's window on the Strand in 1935 illustrates this process in action. Designed to promote the new 'New Zealand' brand, the window's centrepiece was a rather romantic-looking New Zealand farmhouse, nestled in a sylvan glade, surrounded by gently grazing sheep. A native cabbage tree was allowed to flourish in one corner, whilst at the edges of the display, safely corralled in small boxes, were a few distinctive New Zealand symbols: geysers; caves; and a couple of Maori figures, their traditional dress reminders of a now vanquished colonial past.

Co-option of Britishness was not limited to subtle shifts in New Zealand's appearance. In 1930, when the Meat Board debuted its 'British New Zealand lamb', New Zealand became 'British' too, in an acutely transnational array of display material that included a map of New Zealand labelled 'British!' By 1931, the 'British!' New Zealand map was incorporated into window friezes, included in window streamers up to six feet long, printed on window discs and even hung around the necks of cut-out cardboard lambs. Should consumers have somehow missed the message, a later campaign assured them New Zealand meat was 'British to the backbone'. Even the Dairy Board, which had chosen to promote Empire, rather than New Zealand, butter still adopted a British tone. In 1930, in a ceremony complete with trumpeters and the ubiquitous dairymaids, the Lord Mayor of London specially welcomed the first shipment of Australian and New Zealand butter. A similar welcome would be extended to Empire cheese the following year.[93]

However, as we have noted, it was the NZCDC's 'Anchor' brand, not the Dairy Board's 'Fernleaf', that had taken the lead in dairy advertising, and this too drew on explicitly British imagery. The fouled anchor symbol seems to have been inspired by a tattoo on a factory worker's arm. Yet, as one historian has noted, 'Britain has been the single largest external influence on New Zealand's trademarks … presumably to act as reminders of home'.[94] New Zealand's isolation meant naval symbols were also welcome reminders of British naval superiority.[95] The 'Anchor' brand was particularly reassuring, for the fouled anchor was the top ranking naval symbol, adorning the Admiralty flag from 1856. The naval theme continued in the advertising of 'Anchor' which, from around the 1930s, featured a sailor boy. The sailor boy worked in two ways. Along with being a recognisably British symbol, the sailor helped to elide the distance between Britain and New Zealand. In one extant poster, he is seen not on a ship, but striding over farmland, carrying a package of 'Anchor' butter 'Direct From New Zealand'. Blurring geographical boundaries further, an airy image of St Pauls floated, cloud-like, over the farm.[96] Even 'Uncle Anchor' worked to blur those boundaries. Children's letters were sent, not to far-off New Zealand, but to the Birmingham branch office.[97]

The 'Anchor' brand also worked to encourage a feeling of propinquity, in both its senses of physical proximity and kinship, through its Christmas gift schemes. New Zealanders were encouraged to 'send a gift of Anchor' to 'friends at "Home"'. Orders and messages could be placed at any NZCDC factory or office 'for delivery in Great Britain or on the Continent'.[98] The producer boards offered similar schemes. In another strategy to reduce the stigma around frozen meat, the Meat Board introduced a 'Lamb Presentation Scheme', which encouraged New Zealanders to gift legs of lamb to their family and friends at 'Home'.[99] Butter could be sent through the Dairy Board's 'gift butter' programme, with two thousand four-pound cartons being sent in its second year of operation.[100] For the Board, these were two thousand attempts at 'vitalising connecting links between the two countries.'[101]

The British nature of all three organisations was also supported by the work of the Empire Marketing Board.[102] The EMB's key message was to 'buy Empire', but its campaigns clearly differentiated between the white dominions and other types of colonies, in part by stressing the dominions' familiar British qualities in the same way that the producer boards did.[103] In EMB posters, produced by British artists, New Zealand butter and lamb were posed in front of 'Home-like' rural scenes, devoid of indigenous symbols,[104] while distance was diminished in straplines like 'New Zealand serves our Table' and 'Direct from New Zealand'.[105] Like the producer board gift schemes, EMB newspaper advertisements also imagined commodities as 'vitalising connecting links'. A 1926 Christmas campaign imagined friends discussing their children farming overseas: 'For all I know,' mused one, 'I may actually be eating stuff from their own farms or if not, it comes from their friends or from sons of my friends. Anyway, it's all in the family as it were. I always like dealing with my own people. Everybody ought to do the same.'[106]

The assertion of New Zealand's familial 'British' identity may have helped producers cosy up to British consumers, but it also had competitive implications. New Zealand's most important competitor in butter was Denmark, so claims to Britishness also meant Danish butter, despite its Anglo-adapted nature, could be positioned as 'foreign'. The same advantage obviously did not apply in the case of Australian competition, but their butter presented less of a market threat. Indeed, from time to time Australia and New Zealand would join forces, marketing 'Empire' butter, which again bolstered both over their 'foreign' Danish rival. Likewise, New Zealand's 'British' lamb offered a familiar edge over 'foreign' Latin American meat. In both cases, branding New Zealand as British was a reminder that Denmark, Latin America and other producers, such as Estonia, or the Netherlands, were not.

Evaluating success

New Zealand's butter and lamb marketing, whether undertaken by producer boards, the NZCDC or the EMB, relied heavily on the construction of a shared British identity, enhancing similarities and carefully managing any differences. The co-option of 'Home' and Empire aimed to both increase the acceptability of New Zealand's produce and differentiate it from 'foreign' non-Empire competitors like Denmark and Latin America. But the question remains: how successful were these campaigns? Did that shared identity translate into greater sales, increased market share or premium prices? Of course, data for this period are limited, and some have been sceptical of advertising's ability to effect change. Assessing the EMB's contribution, for example, Ian Drummond found it 'hard not to laugh' at the Board's efforts to promote Empire buying, allowing only that 'one could see why politicians might think [advertising] could make the British housewife prefer Australian butter to Danish'.[107] Yet, a study of the Buy British campaign of 1931, organised by the EMB in the depths of the depression to help stimulate consumer demand for 'Home' and Empire produce, is more positive. Whilst noting the limits of contemporary market research, Stephen Constantine argued that the campaign did have an effect on consumers, based on the Board's own surveys of retailers and reports from dominions like New Zealand, which claimed a noticeable increase in sales of meat and dairy produce.[108] It appears sentiment could be effective in guiding consumer choice. Contemporary Australian marketing made even bolder claims: the head of Australia's trade publicity organisation claimed shops stocking Australian produce had risen from 12–14,000 in 1926 to 36,000 by 1933 thanks to their sales efforts.[109]

However, Constantine also draws attention to the difficulties of attributing success or, for that matter, failure to the campaigns alone, given the multitude of external factors that might contribute to increased sales, including falling prices or changes in wages and employment levels throughout the period. In the case of New Zealand produce, we must also take account of the effects of the Ottawa agreements from 1932. Following the Ottawa Conference of 1932, Britain introduced imperial preference: differential rates of duty and quotas were applied to products according to whether they were imported from the Empire or non-Empire (foreign) countries. According to Tim Rooth:

> imperial preferences, confirmed and extended at Ottawa, were effective in increasing the Empire's share of the British market ... Where foreign countries lost in the British market the prime cause was imperial competition ... in general, foreign trading partners with a heavy dependence on agricultural exports tended to suffer lower export values and shares.[110]

These factors make it difficult to be precise about the impact of such campaigns. Still, in broad terms, there are two ways in which their success may be measured. First, we may consider changes in the origin of British imports. Such a metric indicates changes in the *relative* competitiveness or attractiveness, of imports from various countries. A second, and related, benchmark is to assess changes in the *total* volume of imports of butter and lamb into the British market. This latter variable reveals how successful British farmers were in responding to government initiatives that Britain needed to be more self-sufficient. Each is considered in turn.

The first metric, major changes in British butter imports, is shown in Table 1, from which a number of observations can be made.[111] Over the period 1923–1938, Empire exports gained at the expense of foreign countries. Such an observation accords with Rooth's comments, reported above. The performance of the Empire countries is particularly noteworthy because total British imports over the same period almost doubled. However, the distinction between Empire and foreign obscures performance differences at the country level. A second observation is that among the Empire countries, the Australian share grew faster than New Zealand's (though it starts from a much lower base); in any event, throughout the period New Zealand's total market share was comfortably in excess of Australia's.[112] A further

Table 1. Total volume[a] of imports of butter into the UK, 1923–1938 (Selected dates).

	1923	1925	1928	1931	1933	1935	1938	Percentage change, 1923–1938[b]
UK total imports	5096	5853	6113	8060	8832	9608	9509	87.0
Total Empire	2201	2989	2654	3865	4654	5435	4803	118.0
Total foreign	2894	2864	3459	4195	4178	4173	4706	63.0
New Zealand	1131	1255	1222	1926	2512	2638	2582	128.0
Australia	533	1161	873	1558	1692	2113	1798	237.0
Denmark	1838	1658	2016	2466	2519	2186	2365	29.9
Netherlands	175	76	129	96	146	464	712	307.0
Baltic Countries[c]	95	47	1	204	334	493	751	691

[a]In 000's of cwts.
[b]Figures rounded-up.
[c]Estonia, Latvia and Lithuania. No data are recorded for Lithuania between 1923 and 1925, inclusive, or Latvia and Estonia in 1928.
Sources: 1923–1925 from Imperial Economic Committee, *Marketing and Preparing for Market of Foodstuffs Produced Within the Empire*, 1926, p.103; 1928 and 1931, from Rooth, *British Protectionism*, p.121; 1933–1938, from Imperial Economic Committee, *Dairy Produce Supplies*, 1938, p.16.

observation is the comparatively poor performance of Denmark: its market share grows much slower than that of other Empire countries (though it starts from a much larger base). In fact, during the 1920s, New Zealand's share of the British butter market converged on Denmark's, and in 1934 New Zealand overtook the latter to become the UK's biggest butter supplier.[113] Finally, it is apparent that the rates of growth achieved by the Netherlands and the Baltic countries exceeded those of all other major exporters, though again they start from a low base.

With the exception of Britain, all of the countries referred to in Table 1 had a common characteristic: their butter exports were branded with country of origin indicia, often accompanied by a quality grade. For example, 'Nederlandsche Botercontrole', 'Esthonian Brand butter' and 'New Zealand Produce: Pure Creamery Butter' accompanied by a fern leaf on which 'New Zealand' was embossed. Such country of origin indicia were valuable in the marketing campaigns because they also communicated quality. From the late nineteenth century, all the major butter exporting nations had systems for the inspection, grading and certification of butter.[114]

We indicated above that in broad terms, Empire producers gained at the expense of foreign countries. One feature of this trend which deserves further commentary was the emergence of New Zealand as Britain's principal butter supplier. Although New Zealand acquired market share at the expense of Denmark, this was not uniform. The majority of New Zealand butter was imported via London, whereas Danish butter was imported via east-coast ports, principally Grimsby and Newcastle. One consequence was that a marked geographical bifurcation existed: Danish butter was overwhelmingly consumed in the northern cities and areas of Birmingham, Manchester, Liverpool, Yorkshire and Scotland. In contrast, New Zealand butter was more prominent in London, Bristol, the South-west and Wales.[115]

This geographical division has a bearing on our discussion of price differences between butter according to its country of origin. In broad terms, taking the interwar period as a whole, the price of foreign butter can be ranked in descending order as: Danish; Irish; New Zealand; and Australian. The most expensive butter was, in fact, home-produced butter.[116] Such comparisons need to be treated with caution. First, Australasian butter supplies exhibited greater seasonality compared to Danish.[117] Second, investigations conducted in the 1930s indicated that Danish butter was always considerably more expensive than New Zealand butter in the North of England, and slightly more expensive in Liverpool and Birmingham. Conversely, Danish butter was cheaper than New Zealand butter in London, Bristol and the South-west.[118]

Competition in the British market for mutton and lamb is shown in Table 2. The main trends may be summarised as follows: British dependence on imports increased by 18 per cent – a figure which is almost identical to the difference in the relative shares of Empire and foreign supplies. Throughout this period, Australia and New Zealand continued to be the principal Empire suppliers to Britain, though on average during our period New Zealand was about three times as important as Australia.[119] Finally, and in contrast to butter, Table 2 also indicates that the Empire gained at the direct expense of foreign suppliers. Argentina, was particularly badly hit by the provisions of the Ottawa Conference of 1932. Following this Conference, Britain's imports of foreign (non-Empire) beef, lamb and mutton were progressively reduced, and by the mid-1930s they were 65 per cent of their 1932 level. Because Argentina was heavily reliant on the British market, the Ottawa agreement meant it had few

Table 2. Total volume[a] of imports of lamb and mutton into the UK and the relative shares of New Zealand, Australia and Argentina (selected dates).

	1923	1925	1928	1931	1933	1935	1938	Percentage change, 1923–1938[b]
UK total imports	5862	5465	5643	7132	6696	6752	6913	18.0
Total Empire	3559	3030	3363	5024	5087	5471	5608	59.0
Total foreign[c]	2303	2435	2280	2108	1609	1281	1305	−43.0
New Zealand	2287	2502	2795	3470	3734	3634	3676	61.0
Australia	1272	527	547	1529	1306	1784	1898	49.0
Argentina	1744	1841	1511	1553	1146	906	894	−49.0

[a]In 000's of cwts.
[b]Figures rounded-up.
[c]Argentina was by far the biggest foreign exporter of mutton and lamb to the UK throughout this period.
Sources: 1923, 1925 and 1938, from *Annual Statement of Trade of the United Kingdom with Foreign Countries and British Countries*, Vol. II, various issues. Data for 1928–1935, inclusive, obtained from Imperial Economic Committee, *Meat: A Summary of Figures of Production and Trade*, 1935, p.40; Imperial Economic Committee, *Meat: A Summary of Figures of Production and Trade*, 1938, pp. 48–49.

alternative outlets, and during the 1930s the number of sheep in Argentina declined by 11.5 per cent.[120]

Turning to the ruling prices obtained for mutton and lamb, the picture is comparable to that noted for butter. Generally, British lamb commanded a significant premium over imports from the Empire and Argentina. However, this observation only applies to the very best qualities of English lamb: by the 1930s, it was apparent that the best New Zealand lamb was selling at a higher price compared to the lowest-quality English. It was also the case that English and New Zealand lamb command a premium over Australian and Argentine lamb.[121] This last observation is particularly important: supplies from Empire and foreign countries were frozen. In other words, it is remarkable that New Zealand lamb was beginning to command a premium over fresh English lamb.

Tables 1 and 2 demonstrate that throughout the interwar period, Britain's dependence on butter, mutton and lamb imports increased. The corollary of this was that British farmers were unable to satisfy the demands of the domestic population. For example, over the periods 1929–32 and 1936–39, British consumption of mutton and lamb increased by 7.9 per cent, whereas over the period 1930 and 1937, domestic supply increased by just 2.9 per cent.[122] Why, then, were British farmers unable to keep pace with rising domestic demand?

Structural weaknesses in British agriculture were formally identified by the Linlithgow Committee, appointed in 1922. In its final report, the Committee emphasised the need for British farmers to develop a 'marketing sense'. Particular emphasis was placed on the need for grading and standardisation of produce by which foreign countries had secured an increasing share of the British market. In this regard, the practices of the Danish bacon industry were highlighted as exemplary. The committee also recommended that cooperative structures be developed because they were integral to the standardisation and production of high-quality produce.[123]

From the late 1920s, legislation was enacted to improve the competitiveness of British farming. Such Acts permitted: the application of 'grade designations' to indicate that produce had reached a particular standard; the establishment of schemes regulating the marketing of produce; they empowered (producer and marketing) boards to determine the grading, marking and packing of the produce of registered producers. Such boards were also authorised to encourage agricultural cooperation, research and education. Additionally, the Acts regulated the importation and sale of agricultural products (without which schemes for reorganisation could not succeed), and approved the power of boards to make loans and grants.[124]

Investigations by the Ministry of Agriculture and Fisheries (MAF), recognised the considerable benefits that Empire and foreign countries derived from indications of country of origin, but were highly doubtful of whether such schemes would be successfully adopted by British butter and mutton and lamb producers. For butter, the MAF thought adoption of a national mark was potentially dangerous: the extreme variation in quality and grading of British butter meant that adoption of such a mark might backfire and become a mark of disrepute and encourage consumers to seek out Empire and foreign butters.[125] To the best of our knowledge, a national mark scheme for butter was only adopted in 1934, for a trial period of one year.[126] Turning to mutton and lamb, a similar MAF report lamented the absence of a uniform system of grading.[127] Again, to the best of our knowledge, British mutton and lamb producers never adopted the national mark during our period.

Conclusions

This article has examined the branding and advertising of 'New Zealand' lamb and the related brands of 'Anchor' and 'Fernleaf' on butter during the interwar period. Our discussion focused on Britain which was, by far, New Zealand's biggest export market for this produce. A central argument of this article is that the marketing campaigns of the NZMPB and the NZDPCB emphasised the cultural links that existed between New Zealand and Britain. In the pre-1914 period, which was characterised by rapidly growing exports, the coordinated and centralised production and marketing of these outputs was absent. In contrast, the highly volatile interwar period marked the beginning of a concentrated export campaign promoting 'New Zealand' in Britain. Put bluntly, by the interwar period, agricultural exports were vital to the national economy, and it was therefore inevitable that the state became heavily involved in regulating and coordinating the activities of the NZDPCB and the NZMPB.

As indicated in the previous section, structural weaknesses meant Britain continued to be heavily dependent on imported supplies of butter and lamb. Moreover, import restrictions necessarily placed limits on the ability of Denmark and Argentina to supply more butter and lamb, respectively to the British market. Nonetheless, it cannot be assumed that the emergence of New Zealand as Britain's principal butter supplier was a fait accompli: Australian exports and those from the Baltic ountries increased rapidly during the interwar period (though from a much lower base). A similar comment can be made in relation to lamb, for which Australian exports grew rapidly.

One of the principal themes which has emerged from our discussion is the way in which a variety of different indicia were initially used to promote New Zealand butter and lamb. In the former, we have shown how the 'Anchor' brand gained ascendancy over the 'Fernleaf'. For the latter, we have discussed the battles that ensured 'New Zealand', not Canterbury Meat Company (CMC), became the dominant export brand. It appears from our analysis that the structural characteristics of the dairy and meat industries had a role to play in these conflicts. For example, the dairy industry was substantially more cooperative in organisation and benefitted from higher levels of concentration. A survey in 1933 indicated that of 478 dairy factories, 91 per cent were cooperative. One of these companies, the New Zealand Cooperative Dairy Company, resulted from the amalgamation in 1920 of the New Zealand

Diary Association, Thames Valley Dairy Co. and Waikato Dairy Co. As a result of this combination, the parent company not only owned the 'Anchor' brand, but was reckoned in the 1930s to be 'one of the largest (if not the largest) cooperative dairy companies in the world.[128] In contrast, the lower levels of cooperation and concentration in the meat industry meant that, 'no individual company held the combination of resources and market share to create an individual brand that could displace consumer recognition of New Zealand lamb in international markets'.[129]

In a similar vein, it is instructive to consider the extent to which images previously used to promote country of origin can fall into abeyance and then be resurrected as part of a broader – and more appealing – marketing campaign. For example, we argued that the Fernleaf became moribund as a New Zealand butter brand by the early 1930s. However, as a national icon, the silver fern persists and thrives today. This brand has been jealously guarded by the All Blacks and it was adopted by the country's leading trade and development agency, New Zealand Trade and Enterprise, to promote coherence and consistency:

> The potential benefits of implementing a country trademark as an embodiment of a country brand include the creation of a coherent country image, protection of national symbols, and value enhancement. These opportunities were recognized by NZ government authorities who undertook various activities as part of a coherent country trademark program.[130]

A further conclusion which results from this article is that, like private brands, country of origin indicia can benefit from considerable longevity. The investments made by the NZDPCB and the NZMPB to improve quality and uniformity in butter and meat instilled confidence among British consumers and helped dispel any remaining myths about the quality of frozen or chilled produce exported from New Zealand. It was claimed that in the 1900s the export of New Zealand butter represented a 'triumph of human ingenuity', but by the 1920s 'the freshness, as well as the quality, of the article is now taken as a matter of course'.[131] The goodwill that was created for New Zealand produce by the heavy advertising campaigns of the dairy and meat produce export boards resonates today: the hygiene standards adopted in the meat industry, for example, exceed the specifications of any exporting country, and a survey conducted in 2004 indicated that '80 per cent of British consumers mention New Zealand when asked what countries produce lamb … and British consumers prefer New Zealand lamb more than lamb from any other country'.[132]

Our final conclusion is that during the interwar period, the branding and advertising campaigns of the NZDPCB and the NZMPB established 'Anchor' as the major butter brand in Southern England, and entrenched 'New Zealand' as the premier country of origin brand for lamb in Britain. The marketing campaign of both cooperatives was based on their cultural appeal to citizens of the 'Mother country' and were in stark contrast to insipid British initiatives to reclaim a larger share of the domestic market.

Notes

1. We are grateful to Nicola Hedge (Arla Foods) for supplying this figure.
2. http://2012.effectivedesign.org.uk/pdf/2012/gold/4.1.9.pdf.
3. Clemens and Babcock, 'Country of Origin': 5; 7.
4. Emphasis added. Pawson and Brooking, 'Empires': 108; Jones and Mowatt, 'National image': 1266. Ironically, the latter are correct to argue that New Zealand's well-established 'green' reputation undermined attempts to foster a country of origin for organic foodstuffs after the 1970s. We are grateful to a referee for this observation.
5. Belich, Replenishing the Earth, p. 447.

6. Ibid.
7. Higgins and Mordhorst, 'Reputation': 187–188.
8. Calculated from *Annual Reports* of the NZMPB and NZDPCB. The figures quoted for lamb are based on carcasses. After 1936, the lamb export data are reported in tons, so it is not possible to construct a meaningful series for the entire period 1923–1938.
9. Lopes, Global Brands; Duguid, 'The emergence'; Simpson, 'Selling to reluctant'; Bower, 'Scotch whisky'; Jones, 'Brand building'.
10. See, for example, Higgins, 'Mutton dressed as lamb?'; Higgins and Mordhorst, 'Reputation'; Liebcap, 'The Rise'.
11. Higgins and Mordhorst, 'Bringing Home'.
12. *Report of the Imperial Economic Committee on the Marketing and Preparing for Market of Foodstuffs Produced in the Overseas parts of the Empire. Second Report, Meat*: 7.
13. Higgins and Mordhorst, 'Bringing home'.
14. Ministry of Agriculture and Fisheries, *Report on the marketing of Sheep, Mutton and Lamb in England and Wales*. Economic Series No.29, London: HMSO, 1931: 91.
15. Constantine, "The Buy British Campaign": 44.
16. Kenwood and Lougheed, *The Growth*: Table 4, p.30.
17. For New Zealand see Belich, *Paradise Reforged: A History of the New Zealanders*; for recolonisation, or 'export rescue' as a phenomenon in the Anglosphere generally, see Belich, *Replenishing the Earth*.
18. Times, 13 January, 1928:7. Jellicoe was appointed Governor-General to New Zealand in 1920.
19. Blanco-White, *Kerly's Law of Trade Marks*: 18.
20. In Britain, 'brands' originally referred to the practice of producing a mark by burning. The word 'brand' was introduced by the Patents, Designs and Trade Marks Act, 1883. Blanco-White, *Kerly's Law of Trade Marks*: 21.
21. George, 'Brand Rules': 217.
22. Anholt, *Competitive identity*: 5.
23. Olins, quoted in Schultz, Antorini and Csaba, *Corporate Branding*: 28.
24. McCracken, *Culture and Consumption*: 76–77.
25. Kornberger, *Brand Society*: 60; 64.
26. McCracken, *Culture and Consumption*: 79.
27. Schooler, 'Product Bias'.
28. Williams, *Made in Germany*.
29. Morello, 'International product': 287.
30. Ministry of Agriculture and Fisheries, *Report on the Marketing of Sheep, Mutton and Lamb in England and Wales*; Ministry of Agriculture and Fisheries, *Report on the Marketing of Dairy Produce, part II Butter and Cream*.
31. Pharr, 'Synthesising': p. 34. By 2002, over 700 papers had been published on this subject; a recent search of Google Scholar using 'country of origin' appearing in article titles only yielded 3460 publications.
32. Kotler and Gertner, 'Country as brand': 252.
33. Steele, 'New Zealand is Butterland'.
34. Papadopoulos, 'What product and country images'.
35. Bickham, 'Eating the Empire'; Thompson and McGee, *Empire and globalisation;* Regan-Lefebvre, 'John Bull's Other Vineyard';.
36. Allen-Moore, 'Selling empire'; Barnes, 'Bringing Another Empire'.
37. Jaffe and Nebenzahl, National Image: 55; 93.
38. Jaffe and Nebenzahl, *National Image*: 25–26.
39. Jaffe and Nebenzahl, National Image: 26–30; Diamantopoulos, Schlegelmilch and Palihawadana, 'The relationship'; Usunier, 'Relevance'.
40. Ironically, the 'Anchor' brand is now owned by Arla Foods (previously Arla Foods Fonterra, AFF). AFF had imported 'Anchor' butter from New Zealand. But, in 2009, Fonterra sold its share in AFF. Subsequently, Arla switched the production of 'Anchor' butter from New Zealand to Britain. Prior to this restructuring, 'Anchor' butter was always produced in New Zealand. In contrast,

'Lurpak' is only produced in Denmark. We are grateful to a referee for this observation. http://www.nzherald.co.nz/business/news/article.cfm?c_id=3&objectid=11173058.

41. Anholt, 'Foreword': 236.

42. Other brands do indicate geograhical origin – e.g. wine appellations such as Champagne, Cognac, but these appellations are owned by all producers within that region.

43. Brodie and Rea. Country of origin.

44. These are discussed in the next section.

45. 'Certification marks are principally indicia of conformity of goods or services to particular standards stipulated by the proprietor of the mark … Certification may be in respect of geographical origin, material, mode of manufacture … The mark signifies that its proprietor vouches for the conformity of the goods ... to approved and often quantitative standards. To the extent that the standard goes to quality, the certification mark attests to attainment of an absolute level of quality'. Belson, *Certification Marks*: 20.

46. It should be emphasised that although 'New Zealand' indicates country of origin, it is not a geographical indication (GI). The latter indicates that produce derives its reputation, quality or characteristics from a specific geographical location. For example, 'Champagne' can only be lawfully produced in the Champagne region in France. GI's were not defined as such until the TRIPS Agreement, 1995, although terms such as 'appellation' and 'appellation of origin' were well-established by the interwar period. Raustiala and Munzer, 'The global struggle': 342. We are grateful to a referee for this comment.

47. International registration of the name of a country as an appellation was not possible until the Lisbon Agreement, 1958. Registration of 'New Zealand Lamb', surrounded by a rosette, would have constituted a composite or figurative mark, not a purely word mark. Additionally, this mark would have acquired distinctiveness to indicate a trade source. We are grateful to Dev Gangjee for this explanation.

48. This observation does not conflict with the Danish butter industry because 'Lurbrand', *not* 'Denmark', was registered as a trade mark. Higgins and Mordhorst, 'Reputation': 196.

49. For a discussion of the legal and business issues involved in the campaign which led to the Trade Marks Act, 1875, see Bently, 'The Making of Modern': 3–41.

50. Trade Marks Registration Act, 1875, 38 & 39 Vict., Ch.91: s.10; Patents, Designs and Trade Marks Act, 1883, 46 & 47 Vict., Ch.57: s. 64.

51. The key point here is 'secondary meaning', which indicates that a geographical name is associated with the products of a particular firm and is not descriptive of the place. Kerly's *Law of Trade Marks*: 253; 758–59.

52. Patents, Designs and Trade Marks Act, 1888, 51 & 52 Vict., Ch.50: s.64 (1) (e).

53. Sebastian, *The Law of Trade Marks*: 60. Subsequently, an act in 1905 permitted the registration of geographical terms which, in their 'ordinary signification', were not understood as denoting geographic places. Trade Marks Act, 1905, 5 EDW. 7. Ch.15, s.9 (4).

54. Blanco-White, Kerly's, *Law of Trade Marks*: 4.

55. Merchandise Marks Act, 1887, 50 & 51 Vict., Ch.28: s.3 (1) (b). This Act repealed the more limited Merchandise Marks Act of 1862, and became the principal means by which governments could protect their national marks against misuse.

56. It has been argued that in the New Zealand meat industry, greater emphasis was placed on 'collaborative links' between entrepreneurs and the formation of networks whereas in dairy, the cooperative organisation became more important. Hunter, 'Commodity chains': 287; 300. We are grateful to a referee for this observation.

57. See, for example, Faber, *Cooperation*; Jensen, *Danish Agriculture*; Ministry of Agriculture and Fisheries, *Report on the Marketing of Dairy Produce, part II Butter and Cream*.

58. Ibid: 48.

59. Barnes, *New Zealand's London*: 171.

60. See, Higgins, 'Mutton Dressed As Lamb?'

61. New Zealand Dairy Produce Control Board, *First Annual Report and Statement of Accounts*, 31 January 1924– 31 July 1925: 10.

62. New Zealand Meat Producers Board, *Sixth Annual Report and Statement of Accounts, Year ended 30th June 1928*: 10.

63. Barnes, *New Zealand's London*: 159.
64. New Zealand Meat Producers Board, *Sixth Annual Report and Statement of Accounts, Year ended 30th June 1928*: 23.
65. New Zealand Meat Producers Board, *Tenth Annual Report and Statement of Accounts, Year ended 30th June 1932*: 8. This intensive marketing campaign simultaneously addressed two questions which have featured in the country of origin literature: do consumers notice origin information? And, what origin information is available to consumers? Papadopoulos and Heslop, Product Country Images: 14.
66. Ibid: 6.
67. New Zealand Meat Producers Board, *Tenth Annual Report and Statement of Accounts, Year ended 30th June 1932*: 8.
68. Ibid.
69. Ward, *A Command:* 57.
70. New Zealand Dairy Industry Commission, *1934 New Zealand Dairy Industry Commission*, New Zealand, 1934, p.34, quoted in Barnes, *New Zealand's London*: 173.
71. *NZ Dairy Produce Exporter*, 30 January 1932: 18.
72. *Appendix to the Journals of the House of Representatives*, 1934 Session I, H-30 Dairy Industry Commission, p.36.
73. *NZ Dairy Produce Exporter*, 30 January 1932: 18.
74. Though Messrs Joseph Nathan & Co., operating in New Zealand and Britain, maintained a packing factory in England for the use of factories that wished to sell their butter in pats. Stephens, 'The processing': fn.35: 676.
75. Ward, *A Command:* 56.
76. Barnes, *New Zealands' London*, 173.
77. Webber, The Anchor Story: 4.
78. Evans, *A History*: 193.
79. *Appendix to the Journals of the House of Representatives*, 1902 Session I, I-10, Frozen-meat Committee: Report, together with minutes of evidence and appendix, p.42.
80. Loach, A History: 93.
81. Ibid, p82.
82. NZ Meat Producers Board *Annual Report and Statement of Accounts, Year Ending 30th June 1925*: 6.
83. 'Canterbury' continued to be used by meat retailers like W and R Fletchers in their independent advertising e.g. *Lincolnshire Echo*, 16 July 1931: 5.
84. Ibid: 80.
85. Hayward, *Golden Jubilee*: 28.
86. *Press*, 5 November 1930: 16.
87. *Press*, 4 December, 1931: 12.
88. Barnes, *New Zealand's London*: 162; 183.
89. NZ Meat Producers Board Eighth *Annual Report and Statement of Accounts, Year Ending 30th June:* 16.
90. McCracken, *Culture and Consumption*: 79.
91. *Times*, 27 February, 1930: 11.
92. Barnes, *New Zealand's London*: 172.
93. Ibid: 168–172.
94. Wolfe, *Well Made:* 8.
95. Ibid: 45.
96. The New Zealand Co-operative Dairy Company, *New Zealand Dairy Group, 1919–2001.*
97. Webber, *The Anchor Story*: 4.
98. *New Zealand Dairy Exporter*, 1 October 1932: .54.
99. Barnes, *New Zealand's London*: 160.
100. Ibid: 171.
101. New Zealand Dairy Produce Control Board, *Third Annual Report and Statement of Accounts*, Wellington, 1927: 9.

102. There is a substantial literature explaining the formation of the EMB and assessing its impact. See, for example, Constantine, *Buy and Build*; Constantine, 'Bringing the Empire'; Self, 'Treasury Control'; Trentmann, *Free Trade Nation*.
103. Barnes, 'Bringing Another Empire?'.
104. Ibid: 68–69.
105. 'British Cloth in NZ', H.S. Williamson, CO 956/145, PRO; 'NZ Serves Our Tables', H.S. Williamson, CO 956/147, PRO.
106. *The Times*, 22 December 1926: 9.
107. Drummond, *British Economic* Policy: 67.
108. Constantine, 'Buy British': 57.
109. Publicity – Australian Trade Publicity reports, A2910/430/1/98 PT 5, Monthly Report No. 48, August, 1933, p.9, National Archives Australia.
110. Rooth, *British Protectionism*: p.238. The exercise of imperial preference complicates an assessment of the effectiveness of the advertising boards. We return to this later in the article.
111. UK imports almost double over the period 1923–1938, and we return to this point later.
112. Between 1931 and 1938, New Zealand accounted for 27.5 and 53.6 per cent of total UK butter imports and UK butter imports from the Empire respectively. The corresponding figures for Australia are 19.5 and 36 per cent.
113. Obtained from comparing Denmark and New Zealand shares of British imports during the 1920s and 1930s. Calculated from sources in Table 1.
114. Ministry of Agriculture and Fisheries, *Report on the Marketing of Dairy Produce, part II Butter and Cream*: 47–62. In the pre-1914 period, there was no general requirement that imported products be marked with the country of origin. The major exceptions to this were if an imported article bore a trade mark which was identical with or similar to British trade mark, or if the imported product was embossed with an indication of geographic origin which was similar to a British locality. Irrespective of origin, British legislation (the 'Butter' and 'Margarine' Acts) stipulated that the term 'butter' could only be lawfully applied if it met certain standards of composition regarding water content and butter fat. This latter legislation was a response to concerns about misrepresentation of the composition of foodstuffs, not their origin. See, for example, French and Philips, Cheated not Poisoned'. We are grateful to a referee for this comment.
115. Empire Marketing Board, The Demand for Empire Butter: 14.
116. Ministry of Agriculture and Fisheries, *Report on the Marketing of Dairy Produce, part II Butter and Cream*: 33. However, the same report noted that high-quality home-produced butter was found 'only rarely'.
117. See, for example, Henriksen and 'O'Rourke, 'The transition'.
118. Empire Marketing Board, *The Demand for Empire Butter*: 28. A detailed discussion of price differentials in the butter trade during this period is provided in Higgins, *Brands, Geographic Origin*.
119. Imports from Eire were either infinitesimally small or not recorded.
120. Rooth, *British Protectionism*: 213; 232; Perren, *Taste, Trade*: Table 4.7: 108.
121. This ranking of prices is confirmed by examination of Ministry of Agriculture, *Agricultural Statistics: Report on the Prices and Supplies of Agricultural Produce and Requirements in England and Wales*. Various issues.
122. Calculated from Perren, *Tastes, Trade*: Table 5.2: 124; Imperial Economic Committee, *Meat*: Table 31: 48.
123. Ministry of Agriculture and Fisheries. Departmental Committee on the Distribution and Prices of Agricultural Produce: *Final Report*: 12–14; 27–29; 31; 39.
124. Agricultural Produce (Grading and Marketing) Act, 1928 (18 & 19 Geo.5. Ch.19); Agricultural Marketing Act, 1931 (21 & 22 Geo.V.c.42); Agricultural Marketing Act, 1933 (23 & 24 Geo.V.c.31); Agricultural Marketing (No.2) Act, 1933 (24 Geo.V.c.1).
125. Ministry of Agriculture and Fisheries, *Report on the Marketing of Dairy Produce, part II Butter and Cream*: 62–63.
126. *Times*, 17 December, 1934: 7.

127. Ministry of Agriculture and Fisheries, *Report on the Marketing of Sheep, Mutton and Lamb in England and Wales*: 105.
128. Stephens, 'The Processing and Marketing': 653.
129. Clemens and Babcock, 'Country of origin': 6.
130. Florek and Insch, 'The trademark protection': 297.
131. *Times*, 12 November, 1923: 18. Similar sentiments applied to New Zealand lamb. *Times*, 9 January, 1925:8.
132. Clemens and Babcock, 'Country of origin': 10.

Acknowledgement

We have benefitted from many useful comments made by referees. Dev Gangjee provided incomparable advice on the broader legal framework. The usual disclaimer applies.

Disclosure statement

No potential conflict of interest was reported by the authors.

Funding

Some of the research for this article was funded by the Nuffield Foundation, Grant: SGS/33846.

References

Original Sources

New Zealand Meat Producers Board *Annual Report and Statement of Accounts*, Wellington, National Library of New Zealand, Wellington.
New Zealand Dairy Produce Control Board, *Annual Report and Statement of Accounts*, Wellington, National Library of New Zealand, Wellington.

Official Sources

Report and Proceedings of Conference to Consider the Position of the Frozen-Meat Industry. Wellington: New Zealand Government, 1896.
Empire Marketing Board. The Demand for Empire Butter. London: HMSO, 1930

Ministry of Agriculture and Fisheries. Departmental Committee on the Distribution and Prices of Agricultural Produce: *Final Report*. Cmd.2008. London: HMSO, 1924.

Ministry of Agriculture and Fisheries. *Report on the Marketing of Sheep*. Mutton and Lamb in England and Wales. London: HMSO, 1931.

Ministry of Agriculture and Fisheries. *Report on the Marketing of Dairy Produce in England and Wales: Part II Butter and Cream*. London: HMSO, 1932.™™

Secondary Sources

Anholt, Simon. *Competitive Identity*. Basingstoke: Palgrave Macmillan, 2007.

Barnes, Felicity. *New Zealand's London: A Colony and its Metropolis*. Auckland: Auckland University Press, 2012.

Barnes, Felicity. "'Bringing Another Empire Alive?' The Empire Marketing Board and the Construction of Dominion Identity, 1926–33." *Journal of Imperial and Commonwealth History* 42, no. 1 (2014): 61–85.

Belson, Jeffrey. *Certification Marks*. London: Sweet & Maxwell, 2002.

Bently, Lionel. "The Making of Modern Trade Mark Law: The Construction of the Legal Concept of Trade Mark (1860–1880)." In *Trade Marks and Brands*, edited by Lionel Bentley, Jennifer Davies, and Jane Ginsburg, 3–41. Cambridge: Cambridge University Press, 2008.

Belich, James. *Replenishing the Earth: The Settler Revolution and the Rise of the Anglo-World, 1783–1939*. Oxford: Oxford University Press, 2009.

Bickham, Troy. "Eating the Empire: Intersections of Food, Cookery and Imperialism in Eighteenth-Century Britain." *Past and Present* 198, February (2008): 88–94.

Brodie, Roderick, and Maureen Benson-Rea. "Country of Origin Branding: an Integrative Perspective." *Journal of Product & Brand Management* 25, no. 4 (2016): 322–336.

Clemens, Roxanne, and Bruce Babcock. *Country of Origin as a Brand: The Case of New Zealand Lamb*. MATRIC Briefing Paper 04-MBP 9, November, Iowa State University, 2004.

Constantine, Stephen. *Buy and Build*. London: HMSO, 1986.

Constantine, Stephen. "Bringing the Empire Alive: The Empire Marketing Board and Imperial Propoganda, 1926-33." In *Imperialism and Popular Culture*, edited by John Mackenzie, 192–231. Manchester, NH: Manchester University Press, 1986.

Diamantopoulos, Adamantios, Bodo Schlegelmilch, and Dayananda Palihawadana. "The Relationship Between Country-of-Origin Image and Brand Image as Drivers of Purchase Intentions." *International Marketing Review* 28, no. 5 (2011): 508–524.

Drummond, Ian. *British Economic Policy and Empire, 1919–1939*. London: Allen and Unwin, 1972.

Duguid, Paul. "Developing the Brand: The Case of Alcohol." *Enterprise & Society* 4 (September 2003): 405–441.

Duguid, Paul. "Networks and Knowledge: The Beginning and End of the Port Commodity Chain, 1703–1860." *Business History Review* 79 (Autumn 2005): 493 –926.

Evans, Benjamin Lindsay. *A History of Agricultural Production and Marketing in New Zealand*. Palmerston North: Keeling and Mundy, 1969.

Faber, Harald. *Cooperation in Danish Agriculture*. London: Longmans, Green & Co, 1931.

French, Michael, and Jim Phillips. *Cheated not Poisoned?*. Manchester, NH: Manchester University Press, 2000.

George, Alexandra. "Brand Rules: When Branding Law Meets Trade Mark Law." *Brand Management* 13, no. 3 (2006): 215–232.

Hansen, Per. "Co-Branding Product and Nation: Danish Modern Furniture and Denmark in the United States, 1940–1970." In *Trademarks, Brands and Competitiveness*, edited by Teresa da Silva Lopes and Paul Duguid, 77–101. New York: Routledge, 2010.

Hayward, Dai. *Golden Jubilee: The Story of the First Fifty years of the New Zealand Meat Producers Board, 1922–1972*. Wellington: Universal Printers, 1972.

Henriksen, Ingrid, and Kevin O'Rourke. "Incentives, Technology, and the Shift to Year-round Dairying in Late Nineteenth Century Denmark." *Economic History Review* LVIII, no.3 (2005): 520–554.

Higgins, David. "Mutton Dressed as Lamb? The Misrepresentation of Australian and New Zealand Meat in the British Market, c. 1890–1914." *Australian Economic History Review* 44, no. 2 (2004): 161–184.

Higgins, David Michael. *Brands, Geographic Origin, and the Global Economy: A History from the Nineteenth Century to the Present*. Cambridge: Cambridge University Press, forthcoming.

Higgins, David, and Mads Mordhorst. "Reputation and Export Performance: Danish Butter Exports and the British Market, c. 1880–1914." *Business History* 50, no. 2 (2008): 185–204.

Higgins, David, and Mads Mordhorst. "'Bringing Home the Danish Bacon': Food Chains, national Branding and Danish Supremacy Over the British Bacon Market, c. 1900–1938." *Enterprise & Society* 16, no. 1 (2015): 141–185.

Hoffman, Andrew. *From Heresy to Dogma. An Institutional History of Corporate Environmentalism*. Stanford, CA: Stanford University Press, 2001.

Hunter, Ian. "Commodity Chains and Networks in Emerging Markets: New Zealand, 1880–1910." *Business History Review* 79, no. 2 (2005): 275–304.

Jaffe, Eugene, and Israel Nebenzahl. *National Image and Competitive Advantage*. Copenhagen: Copenhagen Business School, 2001.

Jensen, Einar. *Danish Agriculture: Its Economic Development*. Copenhagen: J. H. Schultz Forlag, 1937.

Jones, Geoffrey, and Simon Mowatt. "National Image as a Competitive Disadvantage: The Case of the New Zealand Organic Food Industry." *Business History* 58, no. 8 (2016): 1262–1288.

Jones, Stephen. "Brand Building and Structural Change in the Scotch Whisky Industry." *Business History* 45, no. 3 (2002): 72–89.

Kotler, Philip, and David Gertner. "Country as Brand, Product and Beyond: A Place Marketing and Brand Management Perspective." *Brand Management* 9, no. 4–5 (2002): 249–261.

Kornberger, Martin. *Brand Society*. New York: Cambridge University Press, 2010.

Regan-Lefebvre, Jennifer. "John Bull's Other Vineyard: Selling Australian Wine in Nineteenth-Century Britain." *Journal of Imperial and Commonwealth History* published online 1 March (2017): 1–25

Libecap, Gary. "The Rise of the Chicago Packers and the Origins of Meat Inspection and Antitrust." *Economic Inquiry* XXX, April (1992): 242–262.

Loach, Albert Cyril. *A History of the New Zealand Refrigerating Company*. Christchurch: Caxton, 1969.

Lopes, Teresa da Silva. *Global Brands: The Evolution of Multinationals in Alcoholic Beverages*. New York: Cambridge University Press, 2007.

McGee, Gary, and Andrew Thompson. *Empire and Globalisation : Networks of People, Goods and Capital in the British World, c.1850–1914*. New York: Cambridge University Press, 2010.

McCracken, Grant. *Culture and Consumption*. Bloomington: Indiana University Press, 1988.

Moore, Jonathan Allen. "Selling empire: a historical perspective on selling foreign products in domestic markets." *Journal of Historical Research in Marketing* 8, no. 2 (2016): 263–283.

Morello, Gabriele. "International product Competitiveness and the 'Made in' Concept." In *Product Country Images*, edited by Nicolas Papadopoulos and Louise Heslop, 285–309. New York: International Business Press, 1993.

Papadopoulos, Nicolas, and Louise Heslop. *Product Country Images*. New York: International Business Press, 1993.

Pawson, Eric, and Tom Brooking. "Empires of Grass: Towards an Environmental History of New Zealand Agriculture." *British Review of New Zealand Studies* 17 (2008): 95–114.

Perren, Richard. *Taste, Trade and Technology*. Aldershot: Gower, 2006.

Pharr, Julie. "Synthesizing Country-of –Origin Research from the Last Decade: Is the Concept still Salient in an Era of Global Brands?" *Journal of Marketing Theory and Practice* 13, no. 4 (2005): 520–554.

Philpott, Harold. *A History of the New Zealand Dairy Industry*. Wellington: New Zealand Government Printer, 1937.

Raustiala, Kal, and Stephen Munzer. "The Global Struggle Over Geographic Indications." *The European Journal of International Law* 18, no. 2 (2007): 337–365.

Routh, T. *British Protectionism and the International Economy*. Cambridge: Cambridge University Press, 1993.

Schooler, Robert. "Product Bias in Central American Common Market." *Journal of Marketing Research* 2, no. 4 (1965): 394–397.

Schultz, Majken, Yun Antorini, and Fabian Csaba. *Corporate Branding*. Copenhagen: Copenhagen Business School, 2005.

Self, Robert. "Treasury Control and the Empire Marketing Board." *Twentieth Century British History* 5, no. 2 (1994): 153–182.

Sebastian, Lewis. *The Law of Trade Marks*. London: Stevens & Sons, 1911.

Simpson, James. "Selling to Reluctant Drinkers: The British Wine Market, 1860–1914." *Economic History Review* 57, no. 1 (2004): 80–108.

Steele, Frances. "New Zealand is Butterland": Interpreting the Historical Significance of a Daily Spread." *New Zealand Journal of History* 39, no. 2 (2005): 475–479.

Stephens, F. "The Processing and Marketing of New Zealand Foodstuffs." In *Agricultural Organisation in New Zealand*, edited by Belshaw Horace, 648–678. Melbourne: Melbourne University Press, 1936.

Stringleman, Hugh, and Frank Scrimgeour. "Dairying and dairy products - Cooperatives and centralisation." *Te Ara - the Encyclopedia of New Zealand*. Accessed 13 July, 2012. http://www.TeAra.govt.nz/en/dairying-and-dairy-products/

Trentmann, Frank. *Free Trade Nation*. Oxford: Oxford University Press, 2009 (paperback edition).

Usunier, Jean-Claude. "Relevance in Business Research: The Case of Country-of-Origin Research in Marketing." *European Management Review* 3 (2006): 60–73.

Ward, Arthur. *A Command of Co-operatives*. Wellington: New Zealand Dairy Board, 1975.

Webber, Grahame. *The Anchor Story*. n.p., Canterbury: Lincoln University. 1988.

Blanco White, Thomas. *Kerly's Law of Trade Marks and Trade Names*. London: Sweet & Maxwell, 1966.

Williams, Ernest. *Made in Germany*. London: William Heinemann, 1897.

Wolfe, Richard. *Well Made New Zealand*. Auckland: Reed Methuen, 1987.

The expansion of branding in international marketing: The case of olive oil, 1870s–1930s

Ramon Ramon-Muñoz

ABSTRACT

Drawing on a variety of sources, this article investigates the emergence and expansion of branding in the international olive oil markets prior to World War II. It documents the rapid growth of the world trade in packaged olive oil from the 1870s onwards and shows that the main destinations of this consumer-ready product were in the Americas. In this respect, it complements previous findings based on the use of trademark registration figures. The article then argues that the expansion of canned and branded olive oil exports to the New World was the result of three interconnected factors: the mass migration of southern Europeans in the late nineteenth century and the formation of a new market on the other side of the Atlantic; significant transformations in the commodity chain of the product in the Americas during the first third of the twentieth century; and the problems of quality uncertainty and fraud in the emerging New World markets for olive oil. By analysing these factors, this study also provides evidence to further the debate on the purpose of branding and modern marketing.

1. Introduction

Packaging, product design, branding, pricing, market research and advertising are concepts generally identified with today's modern marketing. However, historical research in the field has conclusively shown that many of these practices are less novel than they may seem.[1] Although the chronology differs according to country and sector, an increasing number of scholars have argued that in the advanced world, practices of modern marketing,[2] particularly branding, were already expanding rapidly in the first decades of the nineteenth century.[3] Food and drink industries pioneered this expansion in western economies such as France, the UK and the US.[4]

The olive oil industry – an important economic activity in countries in the Mediterranean basin – was no exception to this general rule. Like other food industries, it increasingly implemented packaging, branding and advertising both in the domestic market and abroad in the second half of the nineteenth century,[5] in the form of labelled and branded bottles and cans. The importance of package and label design was well understood by exporters in the early years of the twentieth century who made extensive use of sales promotion methods and segmented their product according to quality and taste.

This article extends the current scholarship on selling and marketing food products to foreign markets. The focus is on the expansion of branding in the international olive oil market between the late nineteenth and early twentieth centuries. For some business historians, the first globalisation was a period of fundamental changes in marketing,[6] one that also saw major transformations in the international olive oil market.[7]

This article aims to answer three interconnected questions: where, why and in what quantities did olive oil firms export packaged and branded olive oil? The list of possible answers is very long, and in spite of the burgeoning research on modern marketing, none of them appear to be conclusive. Drawing on the foreign trade statistics of a large sample of countries, this article shows that between 1870 and 1938, the world trade in bottled and canned olive oil – a proxy for branded olive oil – grew more rapidly than the total world olive oil trade. The article also documents the existence of well-differentiated patterns of export marketing across foreign markets; olive oil traders made only limited use of branding and modern marketing methods in Europe and focused their attention on the Americas, which soon emerged as the world's leading importer of bottled, canned and branded olive oil.

In the new and emerging markets of the New World, the commodity chain of the product underwent notable modifications. Importers, food processors and distributors developed new marketing strategies for olive oil: for example, importing the product in bulk to be canned and branded in the consuming markets. This strategy made its mark, especially in the US, although in the late 1920s, exporters' own brands were still present on the other side of the Atlantic, and more than 70% of the olive oil imported into the Americas had been packaged and branded in the Mediterranean basin.

Consular information, trade data, government reports, trademark registrations, business journals and company records suggest that the continued flow of canned, bottled and branded olive oil from the Old to the New World was the result of at least three interconnected factors. First, mass migration from southern Europe in the late nineteenth century created the American market for olive oil and boosted the expansion of modern marketing. Second, transformations in the commodity chain and retailers' own-branding strategies in the Americas during the first third of the twentieth century fostered a growing demand for variety and, perhaps unexpectedly, provided some advantages to the firms that were closest to the sources of supply in the Mediterranean basin. Third, quality uncertainty and the problem of fraud in the American markets caused branding to expand and, to some extent, engendered a reputation premium for the olive oil packaged and branded in southern Europe. Ultimately, these three factors contributed to explaining the expansion of branding and modern marketing in the international market for olive oil prior to World War II.

While this study examines marketing in the context of an important and relatively unexplored industry, it sheds light on several general issues on historical marketing as well. The reasons for the emergence of techniques and practices associated with modern marketing in a particular location and on a particular scale have also been widely discussed in research on branding and marketing history and marketing history and remain relevant to the business sector today.[8] In analysing export marketing, this study helps to explain the origin of some of the most salient features in the modern-day international marketing of olive oil.

The article is organised as follows. Section 2 provides quantitative estimates on the evolution of international trade for packaged and branded olive oil since the 1870s. It also quantitatively assesses patterns of export marketing across continents and shows that in this case its rapid expansion paralleled the growth of American markets for (Mediterranean) olive oil. The remainder of the article explores the reasons why modern export marketing boomed in the Americas. Section 3 associates mass migration and market formation with the expansion of export branding. Section 4 explores cross-continent differences in packaging, blending and storing in a context of changes in the commodity chain and growing demand for variety. In this section, the case of the US – together with Argentina, the most dynamic export market for canned and branded olive oil – receives particular attention. Section 5 deals with quality uncertainty, fraud and the responses of authorities to these challenges in the US as well as in other American markets. Section 6 concludes.

2. Expansion of branding and modern marketing in olive oil prior to World War II

Marketing techniques underwent dramatic transformations in the nineteenth and early twentieth centuries. In food and drink, branding and other components of modern marketing expanded in both domestic and foreign markets. The olive oil industry was no exception to this general rule. However, prior to World War II, it is extraordinarily difficult to determine exactly the extent of the use of new marketing techniques in the product's international markets, simply because statistical information is not available. Trademark agencies provide data on trademark registration, but hardly anything is known about the total number of olive oil brands operating in foreign markets. The data available on sales abroad according to firm and brand are incomplete, and the advertising expenditures of exporting firms dealing in olive oil have not been reported.

Surprisingly, the only light in the darkness comes from the foreign trade statistics of the largest importing and exporting countries. Of course, they do not offer any indications about the practice of branding, to say nothing of advertising. However, they progressively detail the weight and size of the packages that were used to trade olive oil in international markets, which appears to be a good (though imperfect) proxy for the extent of the use of modern marketing techniques in international markets.

Indeed, prior to 1938, contemporaries argued that the use of cans, bottles and other small packages was generally an indication that the product was branded, while the use of barrels, casks and other large containers was associated with trading olive oil in bulk. More recently, Alfred Chandler identified packaging with branded products, especially after the 1880s when the first automatic-line canning factory was built in the US. So, too, did Richard Tedlow, who argued that the beginning of mass brand marketing in the US was closely linked to the fact that the new machinery allowed manufacturers of consumer goods to put their own name on a large volume of small packages. And, finally, Mira Wilkins pointed out that packaged, canned and bottled foods and beverages were almost always branded in the developed world, especially between 1914 and 1938.[9]

Using import data, Figure 1 presents estimates of the quantity of olive oil traded in cans, bottles and other small packages in the international markets for the period 1870–1938.[10] Although rough and provisional, these estimates show that international trade in canned and bottled olive oil increased at a very rapid pace from the 1870s onwards. They also

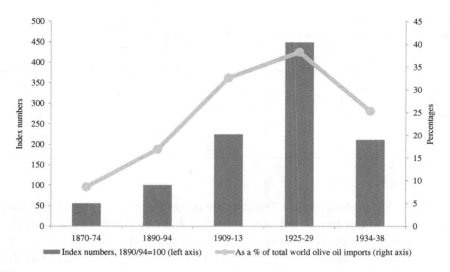

Figure 1. Estimates of total world imports of olive oil in cans, bottles and other small packages, 1870–1938: Index numbers and percentages (five-year averages, original data in quantities).
Notes and Sources: These estimates are based on import data compiled from the foreign trade statistics of a large sample of countries. Total world imports include only Europe and the Americas, by far the world's largest importers of olive oil prior to 1938. See also text and footnotes.

coincide with most of the existing evidence on trademark registrations in several countries in the Atlantic economy.[11] Rates of growth of canned and bottled olive oil were very high, much higher than those recorded in olive oil traded in large packages. While imports (and exports) of canned and bottled olive oil approximately doubled every 20 years between 1870 and 1929, olive oil traded in large packages performed worse over the same period, particularly prior to 1913. As a result, canned and bottled olive oil increased its share in international markets: in the early 1870s, for example, it accounted for less than 10% of total world olive oil imports, but by the early 1890s, this proportion had risen above 15%. By the second half of the 1920s, around 40% of all the olive oil put on the international markets was traded in cans and bottles of different weights, sizes and shapes. After 1929, this international trade fell dramatically, as did trademark registrations in Argentina, France, the UK and the US, but this was because of the exceptional circumstances in the wake of the Wall Street crisis. Indeed, following the 1929 crash, tariffs on canned and bottled olive oil were generally higher than those on oil traded in bulk, and therefore had a greater impact on the former's sales.

Taking the period 1870–1938 as a whole, there is no doubt that there was a boom in the international trade in branded olive oil and a rapid expansion in the use of modern marketing in olive oil exports. However, this expansion had its limits. The estimates presented in Figure 1 show that the quantity of olive oil traded in cans and bottles through the international markets never surpassed the amount commercialised in bulk. A non-negligible share of this bulk olive oil was bottled, canned and branded on arrival in its destination and reached the final consumer in the form of salad or table oil, an issue that will receive further attention below.

Export patterns differed across markets. Table 1 provides evidence on imports of bottled and canned olive oil by distinguishing between Europe and the Americas, the world's two

Table 1. Estimates of olive oil imported in cans, bottles and other small packages in Europe and the Americas, 1870–1938 (five-year averages, original data in quantities).

Periods	As a percentage of total olive oil imports in cans, bottles and other small packages			As a percentage of total olive oil imports in		
	Europe	America	Total	Europe	America	Total
1870–1874	8.2	91.8	100.0	0.8	87.5	8.6
1890–1894	10.8	89.2	100.0	2.3	88.6	17.7
1909–1913	10.9	89.1	100.0	5.7	74.5	32.1
1925–1929	9.3	90.7	100.0	6.8	73.2	38.3
1934–1938	11.1	88.9	100.0	4.7	56.5	25.3

Notes and Sources: See Figure 1.

largest olive-oil-importing regions. The data are presented in percentages, and speak for themselves: the largest foreign markets for bottled and canned olive oil were in the New World, where the product arrived mainly in cans and other small packages. It is also clear that the olive oil trade differed enormously on the two sides of the Atlantic, at least in terms of packaging. Certainly, the period 1870–1938 saw a certain convergence in trading patterns, as the percentage of olive oil imports in cans, bottles and other small packages relative to total olive oil imports increased in Europe and tended to decrease in the Americas; even so, in the late 1920s the Americas were still the destination of more than 90% of all the canned and bottled olive oil exported from the Mediterranean basin. Similarly, American markets continued to import bottled and canned olive oil, which, on average, accounted for around three-quarters of the total olive oil introduced into the continent. By contrast, in the late 1920s, Europe still accounted for more than 75% of the total world olive oil trade in barrels or casks and, in addition, continued to import olive oil in bulk, since only 7% of the total quantity of oil imported was in cans and bottles.

This evidence suggests that export marketing clearly differed on the two sides of the Atlantic. Extensively used in American markets, branding and other modern marketing techniques appear to have been applied far less by exporters trading olive oil towards Europe.

Of course, Europe and the Americas were not the only regions where olive oil was marketed. In Asia and Oceania, some olive oil was imported as well, and, in Asia at least, it mostly arrived in cans and bottles.[12] Cans and bottles were also mainly used to export olive oil to some African countries. For example, prior to World War I, most of the olive oil exported to Egypt consisted of bulk olive oil, of which a certain amount was used in the domestic soap industry. Exports to Tunisia, an important olive oil producer in its own right, comprised a combination of branded and bulk olive oil, though bulk olive oil appears to have predominated.[13] Nonetheless, Africa, Asia and Oceania were minor destinations for olive oil; in 1909–1911, they accounted for tiny proportions of world olive oil imports, namely 2.5, 0.3 and 0.2% respectively compared with figures of 54% for Europe and 43% for the Americas.[14]

Why did the patterns of export marketing differ so markedly in America and Europe? One obvious reason is to do with demand. In Europe, olive oil was mainly traded outside the producing countries as a raw material. For example, in France and Italy, the two leading importers as well as two important producers, the bulk of olive oil was imported for refining, blending, packaging and, finally, re-exporting. In northern Europe, the low demand for table and kitchen olive oils, together with the characteristics of the distribution systems and a discriminatory tariff policy on canned and bottled olive oil, significantly limited the use of modern packaging, branding and advertising techniques.[15]

The American pattern of demand was different. From the late nineteenth century onwards, a growing amount of olive oil crossed the Atlantic to be consumed as salad oil and for other cooking purposes. It still remains unclear why, for the most part, exporting firms decided to package and brand their product before dispatching it; they could have sent it from the Mediterranean basin to the Americas in bulk and then packaged, branded and sold it to the final consumer. While a certain amount of the product did arrive in bulk, about three-quarters of the total imports were already packaged and branded. The remainder of this article is devoted to explaining the reasons for this pattern of export marketing.

3. Mass migration and modern marketing in the Americas

Until the last decades of the nineteenth century, the consumption of olive oil remained at very low levels in the Americas. This situation changed after the 1870s with the arrival of a mass movement of migrants from southern Europe crossing the Atlantic. Clearly, the three decades prior to 1913 represented a period of rapid growth for olive oil trade in the Americas (Figure 2), while the opposite was true for northern Europe.

Perhaps not surprisingly, the mass migration from southern Europe to the New World in the late nineteenth century paralleled the emergence of modern marketing in the Americas. Although in the 1880s (and even before) several brands were already well established in the largest American markets, it seems obvious that this new mass migration represented a new challenge for the competitive strategies and the marketing techniques of exporting firms.

Between 1880 and 1913, more than 10 million people left southern Europe to settle either permanently or temporarily in the New World.[16] As olive oil was a key element in the diet of Italians, Spaniards, Portuguese and Greeks, exporting firms suddenly saw that this far-off but rapidly growing market represented a huge opportunity.[17] Persuading potential consumers to buy their products rather than those of their competitors became an essential task for exporters who strove to highlight the quality of their oil. Consumers had to be able to distinguish the olive oil supplied by a particular firm, and branding, together with

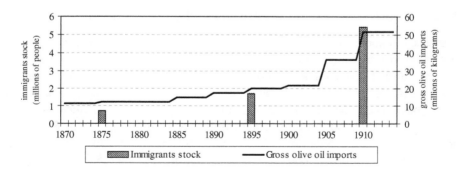

Figure 2. Aggregate Southern European immigrants' stock and gross olive oil imports in the Americas, 1870–1914 (five-year averages).

Notes and Sources: Gross olive oil imports are estimates based on trade data collected from the foreign trade statistics of the largest olive oil importing countries in America, namely Argentina, Brazil, Chile, Cuba, Mexico, the US and Uruguay. When necessary, these import data have been complemented with trade data from the foreign trade statistics of France, Greece, Italy, Portugal and Spain as well as the *International Yearbook*. The figures for the stock of immigrants have been taken directly from the Population Censuses of the American countries mentioned above. In the case of Brazil, the stock of immigrants has been estimated on the basis of gross immigration data. A complete and detailed list of the sources used in the estimation of these figures can be found in Ramon-Muñoz 'Patterns of export', appendix; and Ramon-Muñoz 'Migration and trade', appendix.

packaging, labelling and advertising, was a means to achieve this.[18] It also allowed exporters to attempt to establish a sort of link with the migrants' country of origin; appealing to their loyalty, or at least to their familiarity with the product, might persuade consumers to purchase a particular brand and thus increase the firm's market share.

Unfortunately, the evidence available at firm level is very fragmentary, but it suggests that several exporting firms rapidly understood the potential benefits of promoting a cultural identification between olive oil and the home country of the new immigrants. Brands therefore promoted both tangible and intangible characteristics of the product[19]; brand names, symbols and label designs would often evoke famous areas of olive oil production in the Mediterranean.[20] This practice might even be manipulated: in Brazil, for example, with its very large Portuguese community, both the Portuguese Chamber of Commerce and Industry in Rio de Janeiro (in 1916) and the Spanish attaché (in 1925) reported that olive oil that had been canned, labelled and branded in Spain and exported to Brazil was being marketed under Portuguese-sounding brand names.[21]

To sum up, the mass migration from southern Europe in the late nineteenth century encouraged olive-oil-exporting firms to make more intensive use of packaging, branding and advertising.[22] These and other marketing techniques served firms both to inform consumers and to earn their loyalty. Thus, information and persuasion were not contradictory goals, although in their efforts to win over consumers, some firms were quite liberal with the truth regarding the origin of the products.[23] The fact is that, through branding and other modern marketing techniques, Mediterranean olive oil firms were able to differentiate their products from those of their competitors. Of course, the mass migration from southern Europe also caused the American market for olive oil to expand; this attracted new Mediterranean firms, increased competition and, in turn, intensified the use of modern marketing techniques as a competitive strategy. Not surprisingly, one outcome of applying branding and modern marketing was that barriers to entry increased; by 1930–1934, entry barriers were on average higher in the New World than in the Old World and were mainly influenced by product differentiation.[24]

4. Transformation of the commodity chain: the case of the US

Mediterranean exporters were not alone in using modern marketing techniques. As the market grew, an increasing number of importers, wholesalers and retailers began to create their own brands of olive oil, even though the product continued to be packaged and labelled in the Mediterranean basin by exporting firms. There are many instances of this practice, which, in addition, covers a large number of importing countries, including Uruguay, Peru, Argentina, Brazil and the US.[25] Other merchants went a step further. By the time of World War I, importers, canners and other food producers and distributors had built their own plants in the consuming countries to carry out filtering, blending, repackaging and labelling operations with olive oil imported from abroad.[26] As will be shown later, other food merchants acted in a similar way, but this time building plants in the olive oil-producing countries and from there exporting a ready-packaged product to the final market, either under their own brands or packaging for brands owned by retailers in the Americas. Clearly, the commodity chain for canned and branded olive oil was changing.

This transformation is well documented in the US. It was a partial result of more general changes in markets and technology including the introduction of automatic-line canning technology in the food industry. In a context of population growth, increasing per capita income, transport improvements and technological change,[27] the production of canned and branded products expanded and new sources and forms of demand for olive oil emerged. The rapid growth of canned products such as fish, mayonnaise, salad dressings and sauces increased demand for vegetable oils, including, if only modestly, (bulk) olive oil.[28]

The packaging and canning industry also required olive oil of different qualities and grades for sale as a salad oil. A share of this new demand came from processors and distributors of a large variety of food products, among them the well-known H. J. Heinz & Co. For these companies, which had integrated canning and distribution into their operations, packaging and selling olive oil represented an opportunity to capture a share of the growing olive oil demand and probably also to exploit economies of scale and scope in production and distribution, since the integration of new product lines helped to ensure the continuing throughput of the canning plants.

Alongside the large can-making companies and food processors, American olive oil importers also began to participate in packaging operations. Indeed, from the beginning of the twentieth century, and boosted by a discriminatory tariff against bottled and canned olive oil imports, some olive oil importers reinvented themselves as olive oil processors, taking over functions that had been previously carried out by exporters in the countries where the oil was produced. However, prior to 1914, these functions were limited to a few firms that had commenced the packaging of olive oil in cans and bottles in the US and not in the countries of origin. With the outbreak of World War I, a larger number of importers found it necessary to set up plants in the US and to install machinery for filtering and packaging foreign olive oil in cans and glass bottles of different sizes and shapes.[29] These new plants were situated near the North Atlantic seaboard cities of Baltimore, Boston, Philadelphia and, above all, New York – that is, close to the main areas of olive oil consumption and trade.

Heavily dependent on continuous supplies of foreign olive oil and a certain degree of tariff protection, the US olive oil packaging industry operated throughout the interwar period. It is true that the quantity of olive oil imported for packaging remained relatively stagnant during the 1920s, as will be shown later. Nonetheless, an estimate from the US Tariff Commission suggested that in 1928–1930, about 60% of the bulk olive oil imported into the US was consumed by the olive oil packaging industry; the remainder was bulk olive oil for fish-canning and other food industries or for blending with other vegetable oils, and a very small part was given over to technical uses.[30]

Notable as they were, one might have expected importers and canners' strategies of packaging olive oil in the Americas to have extended even further over the course of the twentieth century. Importing bulk olive oil was less expensive than importing packaged olive oil, partly because transport costs were lower for bulk olive oil and also partly because specific tariff duties tended to favour it. In spite of this, in the late 1920s most of the American brand-owners still preferred to import olive oil in small packages ready for final distribution and consumption rather than filter, blend and package the product in the consuming market, and the same could be said for most American food producers, importers and retailers working with olive oil. By 1925–1929, the volume of edible olive oil imported in bulk in the US accounted for 40% of total edible olive oil imports, while olive oil imported in cans, bottles and other small packages represented 60%. In the American continent as a whole, these proportions were around 25% and 75% respectively (Table 1).

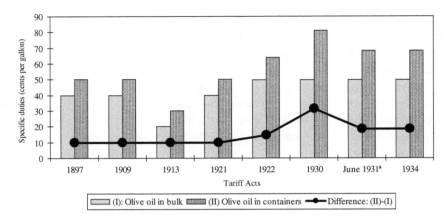

Figure 3. US tariff duties on olive oil by packages under the tariff acts of 1897–1934 (specific duties).
Notes and Sources: ᵃ1931 corresponds to a Proclamation by the President regarding the US's decreasing rate of duty on olive oil weighing less than forty pounds with the immediate container, Washington 24 June 1931. Calculated from US Tariff Commission, *Report to the President*, 5, 19–20; and *The Foreign*, various issues.

The simple, obvious reason why olive oil continued to be mostly imported from Europe in cans and bottles for consumption in the Americas was that the cost of packaging was lower in Europe. This is at least what the US packagers of olive oil argued after World War I; according to them, in the 1920s lower labour costs and lower costs of packaging materials gave European olive oil exporters the opportunity to undersell the American-packaged product.

Although perhaps correct, the US packagers' view has to be considered with some care. In the hearings before the Tariff Act of 1929, the American packagers called for an increase in the tariff duties imposed on olive oil imported in small packages. In fact, the American packaging industry already enjoyed a certain protection; since the Tariff Act of 1897, olive oil imported in small packages had been taxed at 10 cents per gallon more than olive oil imported in bulk. This difference was maintained in the subsequent tariff acts of 1909 to 1921 and was increased to 14.5 cents per gallon in the 1922 act (Figure 3). Nevertheless, in 1929, R.U. Delapenha, who represented the US olive oil packagers working with containers weighing less than forty pounds, concluded that: 'the differential at present existing is not sufficient to protect the American packer' since packaging abroad, even including American duties, was cheaper than packaging in the US.[31]

Of course, American importers of olive oil in small packages offered a very different view. They argued that while the labour costs in the US were higher, this factor was negligible owing to the better machinery used by the US packaging industry and also owing to the fact that only non-skilled manual labour was required. As a result, costs of cans and wooden cases in the US were slightly lower than abroad or, at the most, about the same.[32] However, if the existing duty was taken into account, 'domestic [packagers would] have enjoyed for the last six years a protection superior to the real difference existing [between] the cost of packaging abroad and the United States of America [which would explain why domestically packaged] olive oil [was] being sold at 10 to 20 cents per gallon cheaper' than foreign packaged olive oil.[33]

Were American importers of canned olive oil correct? Fortunately, a detailed (and apparently independent) investigation carried out by the US Tariff Commission for the period of

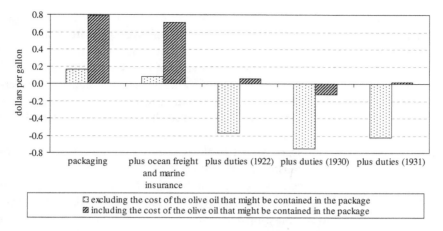

Figure 4. Cost differences in packaging olive oil in the US and abroad, 1928–1930 (amount by which the US costs exceeded foreign costs).
Notes and Sources: See Figure 3.

1928–1930 helps to throw some light on the issue. According to the figures provided by the Commission, the average costs of packaging in the US exceeded foreign costs by around 15 cents per gallon (Figure 4). This difference increased if the cost of the olive oil to be contained in the package was included in the calculations, because the olive oil was imported in bulk from southern Europe and represented around 80% of the total costs of the US olive oil packaging industry. Of course, the differences in cost begin to decrease if ocean freight and marine insurance are added to the calculation of the oil packaged abroad.

However, the decrease in the differences only becomes significant when, in addition to ocean freight and marine insurance, US tariff duties are included. For example, according to the duties fixed in the Tariff Act of 1922, the difference between olive oil packaged in the US and abroad (including the oil contained in the package) was minimal, around 0.6 cents per gallon; but if the oil was not included, the American packaging industry had an advantage of 6 cents per gallon. To some extent, the aim of the US tariff policy seems to have been the equalisation of foreign and domestic costs of packaged olive oil, at least in the interwar period. Thus, occasional cost advantages for domestic packagers deriving from excess protection tended to be corrected by reducing specific duties in order to equalise domestic and foreign costs, as was the case with the Tariff Act of 1930 and the subsequent reduction of duties in the Presidential proclamation of June 1931 (Figure 4).

Consequently, the evidence suggests that although the cost of packaging was lower in Europe than in the Americas, tariff duties tended to reduce these differences, at least in the US. If the cost of packaging (plus tariffs) was about the same, other factors should obviously be taken into account to explain why firms continued to export olive oil from Europe in small packages and under brand names instead of trading bulk olive oil to be repackaged in the Americas.

One of these factors was probably the quality of blending and storage in Europe, and another the growing demand for variety in the US over the first third of the twentieth century. Why did demand for variety emerge? Together with income growth (which is generally considered to boost demand for variety), mass migration from southern Europe in the late nineteenth century created marked differences in tastes and income in the New World and among potential consumers of olive oil, most of them of Italian origin or from other countries bordering on the Mediterranean basin. Though these factors were undoubtedly important, a final aspect needs to be stressed: the transformation of the commodity chain, described above in this section, and importers' and retailers' brand-owning strategies which increased demand for variety and caused product differentiation to rise. Suppliers soon faced the challenge of producing several different varieties of olive oil, which, in addition, had to remain constant over time – no easy task, considering the characteristics of the product.

Like other agricultural goods, olive oil has always been a product with a wide quality range. There are a number of reasons for this: there are a large number of fruit varieties, which, in the period that interests us, were grown in areas that differed widely in terms of climate, soil and other natural conditions. The methods used in harvesting olives, the technology used in the crushing and pressing and, last but not least, the storage of both the fruit and the final product all differed from one region to another. All these factors influenced the product's taste, colour and acidity level, which, in addition, might vary from one year to another owing to the vagaries of the climate and (on occasion) the presence of disease. As a result, harvest fluctuation was another characteristic of olive and olive oil production, which might lead to shortages in the supply of particular varieties of olive oil.

The use of appropriate blending practices and easy access to sources of supply was essential in order to guarantee variety among the different commercial products, but also at the same time a degree of uniformity. Expert blenders were needed both to create a homogeneous product and to produce a larger number of commercial varieties of olive oil.[34]

Of course, the location of skilled labour does not necessarily determine the location of a processing or exporting industry. In olive oil, as in many other sectors, skilled labour was a mobile factor; in addition, American workers could learn blending techniques. Finally, the diffusion of olive oil industrial refineries from the first decade of the twentieth century onwards made the production of unobjectionable olive oils possible and allowed better adjustment of the oil to the specific tastes of the consumer markets. Nevertheless, it is also true that if a great variety of different products were required, proximity to the source of supply made blending operations easier. The words of Charles A. Tossi, vice-president of P. Pastene & Co, during the hearings of the US tariff act of 1929, are highly illustrative in this respect:

> '[olive oil]…varies in its characteristics from year to year, and as a uniform type is demanded by the consumer, it is necessary to blend oil from different sections in order to maintain the uniform type packed in small containers in which it is sold direct to the consumers. It was because of that fact (….) that we shifted our packing operations abroad and closed our plant in New York. With supplies available at any time and in any quantity, packing in Italy avoided the necessity of carrying tremendous stocks and the risk of running short of certain types of oil required in our blends. In this connection, it might be interesting to state that our experience of many years has taught us that it requires a minimum of three and as many as seven different types of oil to maintain our blends uniform from year to year. As we pack possibly 200 brands for customers in the United States alone, and the tastes of these customers vary, requiring different blends of oil, the logical place for a factory is at the source of the supply, rather than at 4,000 miles distance'.[35]

On the eve of World War I, this firm had olive oil and packaging plants in Italy. With the outbreak of war, it brought its packaging plant to New York, partly because of the war itself and partly because of the embargoes placed on exports by the Italian government. The end of the war and the removal of these embargoes provoked a new change in the marketing strategy of the firm. The managers decided to close the plant in New York and to return the packaging operations to Italy – not because packaging was more economical in Italy than in the US, but because the firm had to have large and varied supplies of olive oil at its disposal in order to meet its varied demand. Consequently, for some American firms, it might have been more useful to be next to the sources of supply (and to carry out packaging there) rather than close to the consumption markets.

Tossi's statement helps to explain why canned and branded olive oil was exported from the Mediterranean basin to the US markets. It also illustrates two of the issues raised above: the emerging role of American merchants and retailers in the commodity chain, and the rapid expansion of brands owned by non-Mediterranean firms. These important transformations represented a serious threat to the market share of Mediterranean exporters' brands and one might hypothesise that, in the end, merchants' and retailers' own brands sold more packaged olive oil than the brands owned by Mediterranean exporters.[36] While this might have been the case in some years after 1914, the truth is that most of the brands registered (and perhaps most of the brands operating) in the US belonged to American firms.

Figure 5 displays data on trademark registration for olive oil in the US in 1905, 1915, 1925 and 1935, that is, from the year in which a new trademark federal law was enacted until after the New York stock market crash of 1929.[37] Although the figures are approximate, they make it clear that trademark registration grew rapidly between 1905 and 1915, peaked in the 1920s and collapsed in the 1930s, confirming the trend outlined in previous sections. These data also clearly illustrate that American firms and citizens, especially of Italian origin, owned most of the trademarks for olive oil registered in the first third of the twentieth century and accounted for more than three-quarters of the total registrations approved in the years under consideration.

So, did the brand become a valuable asset that had to be legally defended, as Mira Wilkins and other scholars have argued?[38] The evidence suggests an affirmative answer to this question, at least as far as the leading Mediterranean exporters are concerned. Indeed, by the

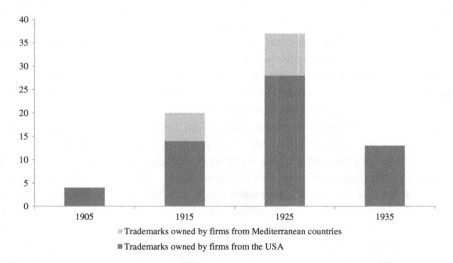

Figure 5. Number of trademarks for olive oil registered in the US by origin of the brand-owner in selected years, 1905–1935.
Notes and Sources: See text and footnotes.

turn of the twentieth century, some Italian firms had already brought legal action against other firms accused of misbranding practices,[39] and the same was true in the interwar period. In early 1932, the well-known Italian firm F. Bertolli & Co. accused Stefano Crisafulli and associates of having sold olive oil in packages imitating the name and, above all, the design of the Bertolli brand, and the Supreme Court of New York found in its favour. A few months later, the United Cicchetti Stores, Inc., P. Cicchetti & Co. and Nazareno Pichione & John of New York were also found guilty and fined after another suit brought by Francesco Bertolli. According to the injunction granted by the Supreme Court, the defendants were selling Bertolli's original cans which they had punctured and refilled with inferior oils.[40]

5. Problems of quality uncertainty and fraud

This evidence of firms protecting their brands through court actions brings us to a more general issue, which, in addition, helps to explain why olive oil for cooking and dressing continued, in the main, to be exported from southern Europe to the Americas in cans and bottles as a consumer-ready product. This issue is quality uncertainty and fraud. Though not always successful, bottling, canning and branding were in fact strategies designed to overcome the major problems of quality and fraud.[41]

In the US, as well as in other countries in America with a large olive oil consumption, fraud became a major concern for those in the olive oil business. Indeed, there is abundant evidence of this from the end of the nineteenth century onwards, when adulterated olive oil was being packaged inside the country and sold as pure olive oil – a practice strongly condemned by the Italian Chamber of Commerce in New York.[42]

Of course, olive oil was not the only product that suffered from adulterations.[43] To prevent this and other fraudulent practices, the US authorities passed the Pure Food and Drug Act on 30 June 1906.[44] This Act permitted blends of olive oil with other vegetable oils but stated that this fact had to be clearly labelled on the package, and also punished illegal mixtures of olive oil as well as misbranding, short sizing and other fraudulent practices. Finally, it established that foods and drugs offered for sale in the US, including olive oil arriving from foreign countries must undergo examination by the Bureau of Chemistry of the Department of Agriculture, or under the direction and supervision of this Bureau, for the purpose of determining whether these articles were adulterated or misbranded.

Nonetheless, fraudulent practices in olive oil seem to have continued, especially among (small) local packagers and dealers. During the second annual meeting of the Olive Oil Association of America, held in New York on 4 April 1922, the president of the Association's fraud committee announced that the committee had uncovered a large number of fraudulent practices in packaging and trading. These practices took two main forms: attaching place symbols on containers to suggest that they contained pure olive oil, when in fact they only contained other cheaper vegetable oils, and placing adulterated olive oil in real olive oil barrels, which in a number of cases were purchased from second-hand dealers. Seven years later, the former chief of the New York branch of the Bureau of Chemistry of the US Department of Agriculture stated that between 1924 and 1928 an enormous number of violations had been committed by dishonest domestic packers and mixers, of which only 175 were brought to the Federal courts.[45] In 1932, Charles A. Tossi, president of the Olive Oil Association of America, called attention to this problem; he reported several recent cases and insisted that the economic crisis was leading consumers to prioritise the price of products rather than their quality, a situation which played into the hands of dishonest packagers and dealers.[46]

By contrast, olive oil imported either in tins or in bulk from producing countries does not appear to have been adulterated or misbranded. This was not only because exporting firms were interested in protecting their brands in the US market, but also because of the stricter controls carried out by US customs officers, who from 1906 onwards were able to apply the rules of the Pure Food and Drug Act. The evidence is conclusive in this respect, although it is true that the opposite was occasionally claimed.[47]

In 1905, detailed investigations made by the Bureau of Chemistry of the US Department of Agriculture concluded that the adulteration of foreign olive oil imported into the US was of little importance. The Bureau found that in the first inspection only five of the 61 samples obtained from the customs officers contained oils other than olive oil, while a second inspection showed that only nine samples out of 250 contained cottonseed oil. On the other hand, oils bought on the market and bearing labels indicating a foreign origin were found to be quite extensively adulterated with cottonseed oil. According to the Bureau of Chemistry, these adulterated oils bearing foreign labels appeared to have been labelled and adulterated after leaving the port of entry and were probably produced by domestic packagers or dealers rather than by foreign exporters or producers.[48]

In 1929, the Director of Regulatory Work in the Food, Drug and Insecticide Administration of the US Department of Agriculture, who was in charge of examining the olive oil entering the US, reached a similar conclusion. According to him, foreign olive oil, whether imported in tins or in bulk, rarely, if ever, arrived adulterated with foreign vegetable oils. Of all the records of the Administration for the period 1924–1928, only three showed olive oil adulteration at the time of importation; this probably represented around 1% of the total olive oil imported from abroad.[49] And in 1932, during a meeting with olive oil importers, the representative of the Federal Administration made it clear that the 1931 customs statistics had recorded only 992 boxes of foreign olive oil imported in tins presenting misbranding and short sizing, that is, around 1% of total olive oil imports. Interestingly, the representative reported that these violations were generally associated with tins addressed to small, local distributors and that none of them involved either well-known brands or larger importers.[50]

In the light of the available evidence, it seems fair to conclude that olive oil packaged, branded and shipped from Europe, mostly by Mediterranean exporting firms, offered consumers a certain guarantee in terms of quality and, therefore, a sort of quality premium. In all likelihood, this could not always be said of the olive oil packaged and labelled in the US. Branding and strict customs controls seem to have been successful responses to the problems of quality uncertainty and fraud. In the words of a leading member of the Olive Oil Association of America, in 1929 the American

> consumer knows that every shipment of olive oil imported in the containers in which it is sold, is protected by careful and stringent examinations by the Department of Agriculture. The buyer knows that he has an assurance that the oil [which] these tins contain, is pure olive oil; that the volume of the contents is as specified on the tins; that it is full in measure; that it is absolutely free from illegal mixtures; that the possibility of fraud is minimised to the point of zero.[51]

Although probably a slight exaggeration, the statement appears to be correct in general terms. One would expect consumption of olive oil packaged and labelled abroad to grow and to gain a share in the US market. This is precisely what the available foreign trade data

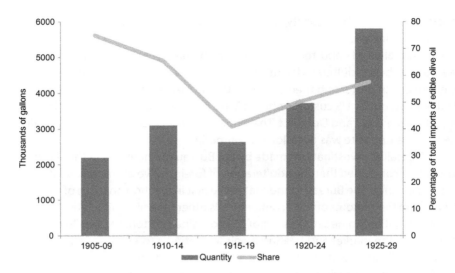

Figure 6. Imports of olive oil in cans, bottles and packages of less than 5 gallons for domestic consumption into the US, 1905–1929 (five-year averages).
Notes and Sources: *The Foreign*, various issues.

suggest during the 'roaring twenties' (Figure 6). Indeed, after the exceptional years of World War I, the aggregate consumption of the olive oil that was canned and branded in the Mediterranean basin increased more rapidly than total consumption of edible olive oil: whereas between 1920–24 and 1925–29 it rose by almost 60%, bulk imports increased by only around 15%.

Of course, this does not mean that the reputation of imported bulk olive oil suffered. To start with, as already mentioned, customs controls contributed to reducing fraud in this segment of the market. Moreover, because of the characteristics of the product, the quality of bulk olive oil could vary from one year to another and from one region to another, and so consumers were in need of information on current standards. The exporter provided this information and, to some extent, the exporter's name usually became a guarantee for product quality, as illustrated by the commercial correspondence of Hijos de J. Sabater, a firm based in an area of Spain which produced high-quality olive oils.[52] If the exporter's name was an indication of product quality, the geographical origin of the oil provided further information in this respect as well as with regard to the product's potential uses.[53]

In short, the cause of the problem of fraud and adulteration was not the olive oil arriving in bulk from the Mediterranean basin, but the practices of dishonest domestic packers and mixers. This situation was highlighted by several Spanish reports on the current state and future prospects of the US olive oil market in the mid-1930s.[54]

Was the US the only importing country where adulteration and other fraudulent practices could be found? The answer is clearly no, and many examples could be given to show this. Perhaps the most important thing to note is that, as in the US, chemical analyses and controls on imported olive oil became the rule rather than the exception during the first third of the twentieth century. This was so in many European countries as well as in the largest Latin American markets for olive oil. Nevertheless, it was only during World War I and, especially, from the early 1920s onwards, that more protective legislation against misbranding and illegal blending was passed in the countries of Latin America.

The Uruguayan authorities, for example, passed laws in 1914 (the Law of 2 December 1914 and the Regulations of 14 June 1915) pertaining to olive oil imports. According to article three of these Regulations, blends of olive oil with other vegetable oils were allowed, but this fact had to be clearly labelled on the package in which they were sold. In addition to the weight, cans containing blends of olive oil and other edible oils also had to specify the proportion of vegetable oils in blends.[55] In 1917, the Argentinian Ministry of Finance passed two laws (26 February 1917 and 16 August 1917) making chemical analysis mandatory for foreign olive oil before entering the country. In addition, in 1919 the local authorities of Buenos Aires established a new Decree (26 November 1919) regulating olive oil production and trade in the city, which also insisted on chemical analysis before the oil could be sold in Buenos Aires. Both producers and traders were also required to label and brand the cans properly, by including the type of product, its brand name, the names of the importer and the exporter, the weight of the can, the place of production as well as the kinds of oils used if the product was blended. The right to include the words 'olive oil' on the cans was reserved to pure olive oil.[56] Finally, a new Decree passed by the Federal authorities on 25 October 1926 maintained part of the former legislation on the olive oil trade but authorised a controversial practice: edible vegetable oils could be sold in the domestic market without having to specify the composition of the product, and their containers could use the words 'Pure edible oil'. Not surprisingly, this legislation was widely criticised by both importers and exporters.[57] As in Argentina, the Chilean government established a new legal framework in 1918 with the Law of 9 October, which not only strengthened the control of foreign olive oil by means of chemical analysis, but also reserved the words 'olive oil' and 'edible oil' for pure olive oil. [58]

Unfortunately, it is difficult to establish how far fraud and irregular practices in olive oil trade decreased as a consequence of this legislation. Whatever the case, the legislation represented an important step forward for both consumer protection and the exporting firms' reputation, since stricter controls and regulations offered a higher guarantee of the quality of the olive oil produced, labelled and traded in small tins directly from the main producing and exporting areas. This was the conclusion of the Spanish commercial attaché in South America in 1925. After drawing attention to the large-scale fraud and adulteration in Brazil, he proposed a partial solution to the problem: the passing of legislation for olive oil and other foodstuffs similar to that existing in Argentina and Uruguay.[59]

6. Conclusions

This article has provided new evidence of the use of branding and modern marketing in the international markets for food products between the 1870s and the 1930s. Using olive oil as a case study, it quantifies the expansion of export branding, shows the geographical patterns of this expansion and discusses its determinants. In particular, this research has demonstrated that the world trade of packaged olive oil – a proxy for branded olive oil – increased more rapidly than the total world olive oil trade from the 1870s onwards. It has shown that, in contrast to the Old World, most of the olive oil exported to the Americas consisted of packaged (and, therefore, branded) olive oil. Finally, it has been argued that the extensive application of modern marketing techniques when the product was exported to the other side of the Atlantic was the result of three interconnected factors: the mass migration from southern Europe in the late nineteenth century and the formation of a new market in the Americas; transformations in the commodity chain, the emergence of own-branding strategies, and the growing demand for variety; and lastly the problems of product uncertainty and fraud, and how both authorities and firms responded to them.

A number of more general conclusions can also be drawn from this research. First, the use of foreign trade data for assessing the growth of branding in export trade offers new insights into marketing – complementing, and probably extending, previous findings based on the use of trademark registration figures. Thus, while the estimates presented in this article reflect an enormous increase in export branding since the 1870s, they also allow an assessment of the participation of canned and branded olive oil in the total world olive oil trade. The use of foreign trade data also sheds new light on patterns of export marketing in the different continents. This is another interesting finding; in his analysis of the world wine industry, James Simpson stressed the existence of important differences in the production and marketing of wines between the Old and New World. [60] Our research has demonstrated that these differences across continents are also found in other industries and other fields, in this case the export marketing of olive oil.

Second, this study provides further evidence regarding the debate on the purpose of branding and modern marketing. This important topic has generated a considerable volume of research. A first area of debate is the informative or persuasive nature of branding.[61] A second area of discussion is the role of modern marketing in the competitive strategy of firms and industries, either as an entry barrier or, in the case of branding, as part of the innovative process.[62] While information, persuasion and competitiveness all played a role in the expansion of olive oil export branding, the results presented in this article expand on some of these issues, showing that mass migration fostered the transformation of selling and marketing methods. In creating a new market for olive oil, migration challenged the competitive strategies of exporting firms which now found themselves obliged to inform, persuade and compete for consumers who were far away from the areas of production. Later, migrants also appear to have become active actors in the transformation of the commodity chain in response to the demand for variety and the changing costs of packaging, storing and blending. Like many other studies, this article has also found that export branding went hand in hand with the problem of quality uncertainty and fraud. Nevertheless, and in contrast to the conclusions reached for other Mediterranean products,[63] in the case of olive oil the strategy of packaging and branding in its areas of production rather than in the consuming markets appears to have been relatively effective in maintaining and increasing the flows of packaged and branded olive oil from the Old World to the Americas. This strategy was boosted by the emergence of new food regulations and strict customs controls on the other side of the Atlantic.

Third, the findings of this study illustrate the enduring nature of international marketing patterns and how historical analysis can aid the understanding of current situations. In the early 2010s, the US consumed about 300,000 metric tonnes of olive oil, far more than any other non-Mediterranean country. More than nine-tenths of this consumption consisted of imported olive oil, of which about two-thirds arrived in consumer-ready bottles and the rest of imports were shipped in bulk. As a bulk product, olive oil is consumed by bottling plants, which 'package the products for sale to retail businesses, under brand names or private labels (…), or to the food service segment'. The marketing characteristics of the US market are considered by some experts to be unique 'among countries that import significant quantities of olive oil'.[64] This article has documented the historical roots of this 'marketing uniqueness'.

Notes

1. For modern marketing, see, for example, Fullerton's general rejection of the belief that 'sophisticated marketing is a recent phenomenon'. Fullerton, 'How', 108. For the particular case of branding, Moore and Reid 'The birth', 419 argued that 'brands and branding are as old as known civilisation'. For modern retailing, Alexander and Akehurst, 'Introduction', 5 proposed 'the emergence of modern retail systems during the period 1750–1950' as the theme that connected the essays they were editing; and for modern advertising, Church 'Advertising', 641, concluded by suggesting that in Britain 'modern advertising originated during the late seventeenth century'. On the periodisation of marketing history, see also Berghoff, Scranton and Spiekermann, 'The Origins'.
2. On the concept of modern marketing applied to historical research, see, among others, Church and Godley, 'The emergence', 1 and Church 'New', 407.
3. There are, certainly, dissenting views regarding the chronology, as well as the typology, of firms in the genesis of modern marketing. For the particular case of branding, see Wilkins, 'The neglected', Wilkins 'When', and Duguid, 'Developing'.
4. Duguid, da Silva Lopes and Mercer, 'Reading'.
5. Ramon-Muñoz, 'Product'.
6. See, for example, Chandler, *The visible*; Tedlow, *New*; Wilkins, 'The neglected'.
7. Ramon-Muñoz, 'Specialization'.
8. For references, see below.
9. Chandler, *Scale*, 63–65, 147–49; Tedlow, 'The fourth', 12; and Wilkins, 'When', 30. If packaging can be considered a proxy for branding, one is tempted to say that it can also be considered a proxy for advertising, since branding and advertising progressively became two sides of the same coin. This is, however, more difficult to prove. Advertising is related to many factors that differ from firm to firm as well as from country to country, although it is true that a larger use of branding techniques would be expected to correspond with a higher intensity in advertising.
10. The foreign trade statistics of the largest trading countries progressively detailed both the use and quality of the product (edible and inedible olive oil) and the weight and size of the package used to trade it. On the basis of these sources, as well as other qualitative and quantitative information obtained from a large variety of sources, the data shown in Figure 1 and Table 1 have been estimated. These data report estimates on international olive oil imports for the period from 1870–74 to 1934–38 distinguishing by packages (large and small) and continents (Europe and the Americas, which accounted for more than 90 per cent of total world olive oil imports). The sample countries for Europe are Austria-Hungary (only up to 1914), Belgium, Bulgaria (excluding 1870–1874), Czechoslovakia (only after 1919), France, Germany, Hungary (only after 1919), Italy, Norway, Portugal, Romania (excluding 1870–1874), Russia (only up to 1913), Switzerland and the United Kingdom. For the Americas, the sample includes Argentina, Brazil, Chile (excluding 1870–1874), Cuba, Mexico (excluding 1870–1874), Peru (excluding 1870–1874), Uruguay (excluding 1870–1874), the US and Venezuela (excluding 1870–1874 and 1890–1894). When necessary, data from the foreign trade statistics of Spain as well as of other exporting countries have also been considered in the estimates. As a rule, and in accordance with the information available, it has been assumed that olive oil imported for industrial uses was traded in large packages. For more details on methods and sources, see Ramon-Muñoz, 'Patterns'.
11. Da Silva Lopes and Guimaraes, 'Trademarks', Duguid, da Silva Lopes and Mercer, 'Reading'; Higgins, 'The making'; Lluch 'Marca'; Mercer, 'A mark'; Sáiz and Fernández, 'Catalonian'.
12. Ministero di Agricoltura, Industria e Commercio (hereafter MAIC), 'Il commercio', 3–38.
13. MAIC, 'Il commercio', 44–101.
14. Author's own estimates from *International Yearbook*, various issues.

15. Ramon-Muñoz, 'Patterns'.
16. Ferenczi and Willcox, *International*. See, among others, Hatton and Williamson, 'The issues', on the nineteenth century European mass migration.
17. See Ramon-Muñoz, 'Migration', and Fernández, *Un 'mercado étnico'*, for the particular case of Argentina.
18. Wilkins, 'When'.
19. On this issue, see, for example, the summary by da Silva Lopes *Global*, 5–7.
20. Tolman and Munson, 'Olive oil', 56–59.
21. Câmara Portuguesa de Comércio e Indústria do Rio de Janeiro, *Inquérito*, 301–2 and Consejo de Economía Nacional, *El aceite de oliva*, 11.
22. This process might also be expected in colonial territories. Late-nineteenth century colonialism also encouraged European settlement abroad; when the new settlers came from olive oil-producing countries such as France or Italy, the demand for southern European oil in the newly colonised territories might have been expected to increase, contributing both to the creation of new markets for olive oil and the expansion of branding and other modern marketing techniques. More research into this issue is needed, but at present there is no clear evidence to support this hypothesis; in fact, French olive oil exports to its colonial possessions declined between the periods of 1897–1899 and 1909–1913. The only colonial territory where the consumption of French olive oil appears to have significantly increased was Tunisia, a French protectorate since 1881 as well as an emerging producer and exporter of olive oil. In this respect, and for the case of the wine industry, James Simpson has argued that 'the vine followed European settlement in the New World and North Africa' (Simpson, 'The Emergence', 267). For the case of the olive oil industry, the picture is slightly different: the European settlers certainly promoted the olive oil industry in northern Africa, but the New World remained highly dependent on the supply of Mediterranean olive oil.
23. Casson, 'Brands', 42.
24. Ramon-Muñoz, 'Product'.
25. For Uruguay, see for example, *Mercurio. Revista Comercial Ibero-Americana*, No. 167 (January), 1913 and *El Aceite de Oliva de España* (hereafter AOE), No. 49 (December), 1932, 347. For Argentina and Peru, see MAIC, *Il commercio*, 186–87, 384. According to an Italian consul in Argentina, once a firm had established its own brand '[retailers and importers] can enhance their sales and obtain major profits, which would be more difficult to achieve if consumers bought the same brand of olive oil from other retailers, [In addition,] 'the same type and quality of olive oil [is] sold under different names'. MAIC, *Il Commercio*, 186–87. The translation is mine. For Brazil, *Hijos de J. Sabater*, a Spanish exporting firm, acknowledged in the mid-1920s that they were both producing and exporting seven different brands of olive oil for Brazil; two of them belonged to the firm itself but the other five were property of different Brazilian importers. Sabater was not alone in applying this strategy. According to his agent in Rio de Janeiro, this was an extended practice for many Spanish firms exporting olive oil to Brazil (Arxiu Comarcal del Baix Camp. Fons Sabater (hereafter ACBC. FS). Letter from Rio de Janeiro dated 8 July 1926). For the US, see, among others, Tolman and Munson, 'Olive oil', 53–59 and Espuny, *De Gallur*, 51, who refers to the case of the firm Giacomo Costa fu Andrea, from Genoa, one of the largest exporters of canned olive oil to the US in the late 1920s. According to T. Espuny, a Spanish businessman, in 1929 Costa exported 35,000 boxes to the US, of which 5,000 contained a high-quality olive oil sold under the brand Costa and 15,000 consisted of olive oil of lower quality sold under the brand Dante, which was also owned by this Italian company. The other boxes (15,000) contained olive oil packaged and exported by Costa under brands owned by several importers.
26. The strategy of establishing warehouses in the largest producing areas seems to have been followed by a number of US firms. Musher & Co, for example, which opened for business in New York in 1907, imported about 1,300,000 gallons of olive oil in bulk in 1919, around 14% of all bulk olive oil imports. In 1921, the company president Nathan Musher stated that 'Musher & Co. maintain very expensive warehouses throughout Spain and Italy, where the oil is brought in by local farmers and immediately placed in tiled tanks and kept at an even temperature, away

from the light and air, which are detrimental to olive oil' (US Congress, *Tariff information*, 240. Heinz (H.J.) & Company, the well-known US food processing firm, also invested in the olive oil business abroad. In the early 1930s, the Spanish attaché in Texas noted that 'Spanish olive oil imports to the South of the United States are almost totally made by means of Heinz (…), who (…) has its own house in Spain'. AOE, No. 73 (November), 1934, 377.

27. Chandler, *The visible*; Chandler, *Scale*; Tedlow, *New*.
28. In 1931, for example, information concerning the result of operation of 27 plants packaging Maine sardine (herring) shows that sardines in olive oil only accounted for 0.2% of the total product value, whereas in the case of sardines in cottonseed oil the figure was 45%. *Olive oil. Official organ of the olive oil industry published monthly by the Olive oil Association of America* (hereafter OAA), 5, No. 9 (September, 1932), 9.
29. US Congress, *Tariff Information*, 240–41.
30. US Tariff Commission, *Report*, 8.
31. US Congress, *Tariff Readjustment*, 706. In 1913, however, the representative of the Pompeian Corporation, from Baltimore M.D., argued that 'the 10 cents per gallon differential not only protects the manufacturers of packages and labels used in packaging olive oil, but gives the American packager a chance to spend a little more on packaging the olive oil under better conditions'. US Congress, *Tariff Schedules*, 121.
32. US Congress, *Tariff Act*, 241–43, 248–49, 259–61; US Congress, *Tariff Readjustment*, 712–29.
33. US Congress, *Tariff Readjustment*, 714.
34. US Congress, *Tariff Act*, 259–61.
35. US Congress, *Tariff Readjustment*, 721. P. Pastene and Co. was a company established in Boston in 1874. By the late 1920s, it had become one of the largest distributors of imported groceries in the US and Canada.
36. For the role of retailers' own brands, see, for example, Wilkins, 'When', and Williams, 'Multiple'.
37. The numbers included in this figure must be considered approximate. The *Annual report*, the *Index of trademarks* and the database of the US Patent and Trademark Office, the sources used to create this figure, do not always allow proper identification of the trademarks that were registered to brand a large variety of food products under the same trademark. For example, the firms that were classified in the official reports under the trademark title of canned food might have branded canned olive oil, among many other products, although this is not always stated in the sources.
38. Wilkins, 'The neglected'. For a dissenting view, Higgins and Tweedal, 'Asset'. For the protection of firms' brand through court actions see, among others, Duguid, 'Developing', Duguid, 'French', Higgins and Mordhorst 'Reputation', and for the legal use of the word 'sherry', Fernández, 'Unsuccessful'. On the responses of British multinationals in roder to protect the global reputation of their brands between 1870 and 1929, see da Silva Lopes and Casson, 'Brand'.
39. Camera di Commercio Italiana in New York (hereafter CCINY), *Nel cinquentenario*, 129.
40. OAA, 5, No. 3 (March, 1932), 8. Other examples include actions brought by P. Sasso & Figli and Filippo Berio & Co., two other well-known Italian exporters from Oneglia (Liguria) and Lucca (Tuscany) respectively. In the case of Sasso, the defendants were again the United Cicchetti Stores, Inc., P. Cicchetti & Co. and Nazareno Pichione & John in New York, who were accused of both filling Sasso's cans with inferior olive oils and selling a blend consisting mainly of cottonseed oil in cans which – Sasso claimed – were deceptively coloured and labelled to imitate his brand. The lawsuit brought by Filippo Berio was against A. Ferrara & Bros, who ran a grocery store. This time the defendant admitted, first, packing mixtures of sesame oil with olive oil and selling these mixtures in cans supplied by the Superior Can Co., and, second, attaching labels with the word 'Tiberio' and 'Luca & Co.', in an attempt, according to the plaintiffs, to imitate the brand name of Berio from Lucca.
41. These strategies have been well documented for the wine industry. See for exemple Duguid, 'Developing'; Duguid, 'Networks'; Fernández, 'Unsuccessful'; Simpson, 'Selling', and Simpson, 'Too little'.
42. CCINY, *Nel cinquentenario*, 160.

43. See, among others, Dupré, 'If it's yellow' for the case of butter in north America between the 1880s and the 1940s, and Stanziani, 'Negotiating' for wine, butter, and milk adulteration in France between 1870 and 1914.
44. Wood, 'The Strategic'. For a more general approach to pure food regulation, see, for example, Law, 'The Origins' and Stanziani, 'Negotiating'.
45. US Congress, *Tariff Act*, 243.
46. Tossi, 'Protect Sales'. As in the early 1920s, many cases of fraud still consisted in repackaging mixtures of olive oil with other cheaper vegetable oils, which were sold in cans labelled with foreign names and symbols in an attempt to mislead the buyer. Together with this 'traditional' fraud, another more simple violation was becoming common: the short-filling of the containers. The most sophisticated fraud, however, consisted of blending olive oil with tea oil, a mixture that was difficult to detect by traditional chemical analysis, something which only became possible in 1936. CCINY, *Nel cinquentenario*, 129. Finally, misbranding practices were not uncommon either. See, for example, OAA, 5, No. 3 (March), 1932, 5, 9 and Servicio Informativo de la Federación de Exportadores de Aceite de Oliva de España (hereafter SIFE), Reports No. 1,494 (1932), 1,546 (1932) and 1,547 (1932).
47. For example, in 1926, Italian olive oil exporters (and importers) were accused of introducing adulterated olive oil to the US. These accusations mobilised both those involved in the business and the Italian Chamber of Commerce in New York. They probably also led Tossi to call the matter to the attention of the members of his association and to recommend that the product, either in cans or in bulk, should be imported directly from well-known and credited exporting firms even if this proved more expensive. See CCINY, *Nel cinquentenario*, 149 and SIFE, Supplement to the Report No. 199 (1927), copied from a letter sent by Tossi to the members of the Olive Oil Association of America on 2 September 1927.
48. Tolman and Munson, 'Olive oil'. 62.
49. US Congress, *Tariff Act*, 245–46.
50. SIFE, Reports No. 1,494 (1932) and 1,495 (1932), originally published in OAA, volume V, 1932.
51. US Congress, *Tariff Readjustment*, 716.
52. In 1929, A. E. Rittwagen, Sabater's agent in New York, reported that in the US the (Catalan) name of Gasull, the owner of the firm Establecimientos Félix Gasull, S.A., was associated with a very high-quality olive oil. Rittwagen regretted that the same could not be said of Sabater, suggesting the existence of a connection between the exporter's name and product quality. Letter dated 19 March 1928. ACBC. FS. Letters to and from A. E. Rittwagen, New York (1923–1933), boxes 4 and 165 M respectively.
53. In 1921, the representative of the Pompeian Sea Food Co. claimed that the packagers of sardines and tuna fish in California used almost three-quarters of a million gallons of olive oil a year (around 2.6 thousand metric tons), but that all of it had to be imported because the oil produced in California contained a high percentage of free fatty acid. US Congress, *Tariff Information*, 241. While this statement probably requires some qualification, what is clear is that packagers of fish required a high-standard product, although they did not always make use of the same grades of olive oil. In fact, fish-canners' demands for olive oil tended to differ, not only because of the particular variety of olive oil used in canning but also because of the quantity of refined olive oil introduced in the can and the amount of vegetable oils other than olive oil that they used.
54. AOE, 6, No. 70 (September 1934), 310; AOE, 7, No. 74 (January, 1935), 455; AOE, 7, No. 81 (September, 1935), 716.
55. Ministerio de Estado (hereafter ME), *Estudio comercial*, 8–9.
56. ME (1920), pp. 21–29, for a detailed review of the Argentinian legislation between 1913 and 1920.
57. The Spanish Chamber of Commerce in Buenos Aires opposed this new legislation forcefully; the law was confusing, since it not only failed to protect olive oil against adulterations but also showed that the Argentinian authorities were exclusively interested in protecting the interests of the national industry of vegetable oil rather than the domestic consumers. The main arguments of the Spanish Chamber of Commerce are summarised in SIFE, Reports No. 45 (1927), No. 137 (1927), No. 244 (1928), No. 605 (1929), No. 845 (1930) and Supplement to

the Report, No. 1,028 (1930). For an opposing view in SIFE, Supplement to the Report No. 193 (1927), Supplement to the Report No. 358 (1928) and Supplement to the Report No. 352 (1928).
58. ME, *El aceite español*, 21–23.
59. Consejo de Economía Nacional, *El aceite de oliva*, 10–12.
60. Simpson, 'The emergence'.
61. In the particular case of branding, see, for example, Wilkins, 'When' and Cason, 'Brands'.
62. A short review of the literature on product differentiation and entry barriers can be found in Ramon-Muñoz, 'Product'.
63. See, for example, Simpson, 'Selling', for fortified wines in Britain in the nineteenth century, and Fernández, 'Unsuccessful', for the case of the sherry industry in the twentieth century.
64. US International Trade Commission, 'Olive oil', 4.3.

Acknowledgements

Previous versions of this article were presented and discussed at the 16th Annual Conference of the European Business History Association (Paris, 2012), the 14th International Conference on Agricultural History (Badajoz, 2013), the International Seminar 'Brand and its History: Economic, Business and Social Value' (Madrid 2014) and the 11th International Conference of the Spanish Economic History Association (Madrid, 2014). I would like to thank the participants at these meetings, as well as Jaime Reis, the editors of this special issue and the anonymous referees of this journal for their useful comments. The usual disclaimer applies.

Disclosure statement

No potential conflict of interest was reported by the author.

Funding

This work was supported by Spanish Ministry of Economy (MINECO) and European Regional Development Fund (ERDF) [grant number HAR2015-64769-P].

References

Alexander, Nicholas, and Gary Akehurst. "Introduction: The Emergence of Modern Retailing, 1750–1950." *Business History* 40, no. 4 (1998): 1–15. doi:10.1080/00076799800000335.

Berghoff, Hartmut, Philip Scranton, and Uwe Spiekermann. "The Origins of Marketing and Market Research: Information, Institutions, and Markets." In *The Rise of Marketing and Market Research*, edited by Hartmut Berghoff, Philip Scranton, and Uwe Spiekermann, 1–26. New York: Palgrave Macmillan, 2012.

Câmara Portuguesa de Comércio e Indústria do Rio di Janeiro. *Inquérito para a expansão do comércio português no Brasil* [Inquiry into the expansion of the Portuguese trade in Brazil]. Porto: Imprensa Portuguesa, 1916.

Camera di Commercio Italiana in New York. *Nel cinquentenario della Camera di Commercio Italiana in New York* [On the fiftieth anniversary of the Italian Chamber of Commerce in New York]. New York: Camera di Commercio Italiana, 1937.

Casson, Mark. "Brands. Economic Ideology and Consumer Society." In *Adding value: brands and marketing in food and drink*, edited by Geoffrey Jones and Nicholas Morgan, 41–58. London: Routledge, 1994.

Chandler, Alfred D. *The Visible Hand. The Managerial Revolution in American Business*. Cambridge, MA: Harvard University Press, 1977.

Chandler, Alfred D. *Scale and Scope. The Dynamics of Industrial Capitalism*. Cambridge, MA, and London: Harvard University Press, 1990.

Church, Roy. "New Perspectives on the History of Products, Firms, Marketing, and Consumers in Britain and the United States since the Mid-Nineteenth Century." *The Economic History Review* 52, no. 3 (1999): 405–435. doi:10.1111/1468-0289.00131.

Church, Roy. "Advertising Consumer Goods in Nineteenth-Century Britain: Reinterpretations." *The Economic History Review* 53, no. 4 (2000): 621–645. doi:10.1111/1468-0289.00172.

Church, Roy, and Andrew Godley. "The Emergence of Modern Marketing: International Dimension." *Business History* 45, no. 1 (2003): 1–5. doi:10.1080/713999301.

Consejo de Economía Nacional. *El aceite de oliva en el mercado del Brasil. Por Emilio Boix*. Madrid: Imprenta del Ministerio de Estado, 1925.

Duguid, Paul. "Developing the Brand: The Case of Alcohol, 1800-1880." *Enterprise and Society* 4, no. 3 (2003): 488–500. doi:10.1017/S1467222700012660.

Duguid, Paul. "Networks and Knowledge: The beginning and End of the Port Commodity Chain, 1703–1860." *Business History Review* 79, no. 3 (2005): 453–466. doi:10.1017/S0007680500081423.

Duguid, Paul. "French Connections: The International Propagation of Trademarks in the Nineteenth Century." *Enterprise and Society* 10, no. 1 (2009): 3–37. doi:10.1093/es/khn104.

Duguid, Paul, Teresa da Silva Lopes, and John Mercer. "Reading Registrations: An Overview of 100 Years of Trade Mark Registrations in France, the United Kingdom, and the United States." In *Trademarks, Brands and Competitiveness*, edited by Teresa Da Silva Lopes and Paul Duguid, 9–30. London: Routledge, 2010.

Dupré, Ruth. "If It's Yellow, It Must Be Butter?: Margarine Regulation in North America Since 1886." *The Journal of Economic History* 59, no. 2 (1999): 353–371. doi:10.1017/S0022050700022865.

El Aceite de Oliva de España. Órgano de la Federación de Exportadores de Aceite de Oliva de España [Spanish Olive Oil. Organ of the Spanish Olive Oil Exporters Federation]. Madrid, 1929–36, various issues.

Espuny, Tomás. *De Gallur a Nueva York. Diario de viaje (1929)* [From Gallur to New York. Travel Diary (1929)]. Zaragoza: Ayuntamiento de Gallur, 2002.

Ferenczi, Imre, and Walter F. Willcox. *International Migrations, Volume I: Statistics*. New York: National Bureau of Economic Research, 1929.

Fernández, Alejandro E. *Un "mercado étnico" en el plata. Emigración y exportaciones españolas a la Argentina, 1880–1935* [An "ethnic market" in the Plata. Emigration and Spanish exports to Argentina, 1880–1935]. Madrid: Consejo Superior de Investigaciones Científicas, 2004.

Fernández, Eva. "Unsuccessful Responses to Quality Uncertainty: Brands in Spain's Sherry Industry, 1920–1990." *Business History* 52, no. 1 (2010): 100–119. doi:10.1080/00076790903469638.

Fullerton, Ronald A. "How Modern is Modern Marketing? Marketing's Evolution and the Myth of the 'Production Era'." *Journal of Marketing* 52, no. 1 (1988): 108–125. doi:10.2307/1251689.

Hatton, Timothy J., and Jeffrey G. Williamson. "The Issues." In *The Age of Mass Migration. Causes and Economic Impact*, edited by Timothy J. Hatton and Jeffrey G. Williamson, 7–31. New York and Oxford: Oxford University Press, 1998.

Higgins, David M., and Mads Mordhorst. "Reputation and Export Performance: Danish Butter Exports and the British Market, c.1880–c.1914." *Business History* 50, no. 2 (2008): 185–204. doi:10.1080/00076790701868601.

Higgins, David, and Geoffrey Tweedale. "Asset or Liability? Trade Marks in the Sheffield Cutlery and Tool Trades." *Business History* 37, no. 3 (1995): 1–27. doi:10.1080/00076799500000088.

Higgins, David M. "The Making of Modern Trade Mark Law: The UK, 1860–1914. A Business History Perspective." In *Trade Marks and Brands. An Interdisciplinary Critique*, edited by Lionel Bently, Jennifer Davis, and Jane C. Ginsburg, 42–62. Cambridge: Cambridge University Press, 2008.

International Institute of Agriculture. *International Yearbook of Agricultural Statistics*. Rome: International Institut of Agriculture, 1909–39.

Law, Marc T. "The Origins of State Pure Food Regulation." *Journal of Economic History* 63, no. 4 (2003): 1103–1130. doi:10.1017/S0022050703002547.

Lluch, Andrea. "Marca registrada: Reflexiones sobre el uso de las marcas comerciales, el consumo y la comercialización de bienes en el mundo rural argentino (1900-1930)." *Mundo Agrario* 13, no. 26 (2013). http://www.memoria.fahce.unlp.edu.ar/art_revistas/pr.5691/pr.5691.pdf.

Mercer, John. "A Mark of Distinction: Branding and Trade Mark Law in the UK from the 1860s." *Business History* 52, no. 1 (2010): 17–42. doi:10.1080/00076790903281033.

Mercurio. Revista Comercial Ibero-Americana [Mercurio. Ibero-American Trade Journal]. Barcelona, 1913, various issues.

Ministerio de Estado. *Estudio comercial sobre la República Oriental del Uruguay. Por Emilio Boix* [Trade Report on the Oriental Republic of Uruguay. By Emilio Boix]. Madrid: Imprenta del Ministerio de Estado, 1919.

Ministerio de Estado. *Los aceites en la República Argentina. Por Emilio Boix* [Oils in the Argentine Republic. By Emilio Boix]. Madrid: Imprenta del Ministerio de Estado, 1920.

Ministerio de Estado. *El aceite español en Chile. Por Cayetano Rosich* [The Spanish olive oil in Chile. By Cayetano Rosich]. Madrid: Imprenta del Ministerio de Estado, 1922.

Ministero di Agricoltura, Industria e Commercio. *Il commercio dell'olio d'oliva all'estero. Parte II* [The olive oil trade abroad. Part II]. Roma: Tipografia Nazionale di G. Bertero e C., 1913.

Olive Oil. Official Organ of the Olive Oil Industry Published Monthly by the Olive oil Association of America/Olive Oil and Imported Foods. New York: Official Organ of the Olive Oil Association of America, 1929–1935.

Ramon-Muñoz, Ramon. "Migration and Trade: The Case of Southern European Immigration and Olive Oil Imports in the Americas (1875–1930)." Paper presented at the 8th Conference of the European Historical Economics Society (EHES), Geneva, Graduate Institute of International and Development Studies, September 4–5, 2009.

Ramon-Muñoz, Ramon. "Product Differentiation and Entry Barriers: Mediterranean Export Firms in the American Markets for Olive Oil Prior to World War II." *Business History* 52, no. 3 (2010): 390–416. doi:10.1080/00076791003721613.

Ramon-Muñoz, Ramon. *Patterns of Export Marketing in the International Market for Olive Oil, 1870s–1930s.* Mimeo, Barcelona, 2016.

Ramon-Muñoz, Ramon. "Specialization in the International Market for Olive Oil before World War II." In *The Mediterranean Response to Globalization before 1950*, edited by Sevket Pamuk and Jeffrey G Williamson, 159–198. London and New York: Routledge, 2000.

Sáiz, J. Patricio, and Paloma Fernández Pérez. "Catalonian Trademarks and the Development of Marketing Knowledge in Spain, 1850–1946." *Business History Review* 86, no. 2 (2012): 239–260. doi: 10.1017/S0007680512000396.

Servicio Informativo de la Federación de Exportadores de Aceite de Oliva de España [Information Service of the Spanish Olive Oil Exporters Federation]. Reports and Supplements to the Reports for the Years. Madrid, 1927–35, various issues.

da Silva Lopes, Teresa. *Global Brands: The Evolution of Multinationals in Alcoholic Beverages.* New York: Cambridge University Press, 2007.

da Silva Lopes, Teresa, and Mark Casson. "Brand Protection and the Globalization of British Business." *Business History Review* 86, no. 02 (2012): 287–310. doi:10.1017/S0007680512000414.

da Silva Lopes, Teresa, and Paulo Guimaraes. "Trademarks and British Dominance in Consumer Goods, 1876–1914." *Economic History Review* 67, no. 3 (2014): 793–817. doi:10.1111/1468-0289.12039.

Simpson, James. "Selling to Reluctant Drinkers: The British Wine Market, 1860–1914." *The Economic History Review* 57, no. 1 (2004): 80–108. doi:10.1111/j.0013-0017.2004.00273.x.

Simpson, James. "Too Little Regulation? The British Market for Sherry, 1840–90." *Business History* 47, no. 3 (2005): 367–382. doi:10.1080/00076790500055988.

Simpson, James. *Creating Wine. The Emergence of a World Industry, 1840–1914.* Princeton: Princeton University Press, 2011.

Stanziani, Alessandro. "Negotiating Innovation in a Market Economy: Foodstuffs and Beverages Adulteration in Nineteenth-Century France." *Enterprise and Society* 8, no. 02 (2007): 375–412. doi:10.1017/S1467222700005899.

Tedlow, Richard S. *New and Improved: The Story of Mass Marketing in America.* New York: Basic Books, 1990.

Tedlow, Richard S. "The Fourth Phases of Marketing: Marketing History and the Business World Today." In *The Rise and Fall of Mass Marketing*, edited by Richard S. Tedlow and Geoffrey Jones, 8–35. London and New York: Roudledge, 1993.

Tolman, L. M., and L. S. Munson. "Olive oil and its substitutes." *Bureau of Chemistry Bulletin*, no. 77 (1905): 1–62.

Tosi, Charles A. "Protect Sales of Pure Olive oil." *Olive Oil and Imported Foods. Official organ of the Olive Oil Association of America* V, no. 8 (1932): 1–3.

US Congress. *Tariff Schedules.* Vol. I. Washington: Government Printing Office, 1913.

US Congress. *Tariff Information, 1921. Part I.* Washington: Government Printing Office, 1921.

US Congress. *Tariff Act of 1929.* Vol. I. Washington: Government Printing Office, 1929.

US Congress. *Tariff Readjustment, 1929.* Vol. I. Washington: Government Printing Office, 1929.

US Department of Commerce and Labor. *The Foreign Commerce and Navigation of the United States for the Year Ending.* Washington: Government Printing Office, 1904/1905–1910/1911.

US Department of Commerce. *The Foreign Commerce and Navigation of the United States for the Year Ending.* Washington: Government Printing Office, 1911/1912–1929.

US International Trade Commission. "Olive Oil: Conditions of Competition between U.S. and Major Foreign Supplier Industries." Investigation No. 332–537, USITC Publication 4419, August 2013.

US Patent Office. *Annual Report of the Commissioner of Patents for the Year...* Washington: Government Printing Office, 1905–25.

US Patent Office. *Index of Trademarks Issued from the United States Patent Office, 1935.* Washington: Government Printing Office, 1935.

US Tariff Commission. *Report to the President on Olive Oil.* Washington: Government Printing Office, 1931.

Wilkins, Mira. "The Negleted Intangible Asset: The Influence of the Trade Mark on the Rise of the Modern Corporation." *Business History* 34, no. 1 (1992): 66–95. doi:10.1080/00076799200000004.

Wilkins, Mira. "When and Why Brand Names in Food and Drink." In *Adding Value: Brands and Marketing in Food and Drink*, edited by Geoffrey Jones and Nicholas Morgan, 15–40. London: Routledge, 1994.

Williams, Bridget. "Multiple Retailing and Brand Image: An Anglo-American Comparison, 1860–1914." In *Adding Value: Brands and Marketing in Food and Drink*, edited by Geoffrey Jones and Nicholas Morgan, 291–309. London: Routledge, 1994.

Wood, Donna J. "The Strategic Use of Public Policy: Business Support for the 1906 Food and Drug Act." *Business History Review* 59, no. 3 (1985): 403–432. doi:https://doi-org.sire.ub.edu/10.2307/3114005.

The making of Labatt 'Blue': The quest for a national lager brand, 1959–1971

Matthew J. Bellamy

ABSTRACT

This article examines the creation of a national beer brand in Canada. It analyses the challenges faced by the marketing managers at John Labatt Limited – one of Canada's oldest and most successful brewers – in solving the 'national lager problem' (i.e. the inability of Labatt's 'Pilsener' to capture a significant share of the Canadian market). It examines how executives use marketing knowledge to recreate brand identities. It argues that the rebranding of 'Pilsener' as 'Blue' was successful because Labatt's managers fashioned a new brand identity that downplayed the 'ethnic' heritage of the brand by appealing to a new 'Canadian' cosmopolitan modernity.

Introduction

Developing popular brands is essential for success in the alcoholic beverage industry.[1] Brands add value to a firm by sustaining a constant revenue stream as a consequence of the consumer's propensity for long-term brand loyalty.[2] For the consumer, brands simplify the decision-making process and 'enable consumers to associate certain values and rewards with particular products'.[3] Brands also provide security to consumers when it comes to the quality and consistency of the product.[4] Successful brands – i.e. those that have become leaders in their product categories in the national or international market[5] – have emotional characteristics that appeal to the self-image of the consumer and his/her aspirations and fantasies.[6] In regard to alcoholic beverages, such 'intangible' elements are especially important in establishing the 'identity' of a brand.[7] And while a brand's 'identity' is developed over time, it is usually embedded in a particular culture and a specific set of values.[8] The 'identity' of a brand is particularly important in the alcoholic beverages industry where products tend to have long life cycles and have very strong associations with tradition, heritage, craftsmanship, naturalness and the place of origin.[9] These elements give a brand its 'authenticity', which according to a number of recent studies constitutes a cornerstone of modern marketing.[10]

In many countries, national beer brands existed well before the 1960s. In the United States, for example, a handful of large brewers with highly mechanised factories and merchandising chains extending beyond their hometowns developed a national market for their brands in the late nineteenth and early twentieth century. These modern, vertically integrated firms were usually based in medium-sized cities (e.g. Pabst, Schlitz, Miller and Blatz in Milwaukee, Anheuser-Busch in St Louis and Stroh in Detroit) and utilised railroads, refrigeration, advertising and, above all, economies of scale.[11] The entrepreneurs that founded these firms or their descendants used their 'sticky' knowledge – i.e. that type of marketing knowledge that is path dependent, 'tacit' and accumulated within the firm over time.[12] Many of these 'shipping brewers' – as they came to be called – appropriated the markers of the national identity to promote their brands. For example, in 1872, Anheuser-Busch began using an image of the American eagle on its beer labels. Five years later the 'A and eagle' became a registered trademark with the US Patent Office. In a similar effort to tap into the national enthusiasm of the late nineteenth and early twentieth century, in 1902 Pabst introduced 'Red, White and Blue' beer.[13] In the United Kingdom, national beer brands had also emerged well before the 1960s. During the nineteenth century, enterprising brewers invested in capital intensive brewing technologies in order to achieve scale economies and utilised the railroad to branch out into distant regions of the nation. The fact that the brewers' major markets were public houses that were limited in number by law inspired some brewers to buy or lease these retail outlets.[14] A small number of brewers, however, managed to develop a national market for their brands without investing heavily in 'tied houses'. For example, Bass did not invest substantially in public houses prior to 1914. Instead, its success was based on having access to a good water supply; the growing national preference for lighter pale ale; a central location in the railway network that facilitated distribution; and an easily recognisable trademark.[15] Likewise, Guinness was heavily dependent on free trade and brand recognition.[16] In 1862, Guinness began using the harp – the national symbol of Ireland – to brand its beer. Due to the fact that Guinness and Bass did not control the entire supply chain, the two breweries were prone to infractions of their trademarks. But they both proved indefatigable when it came to defending their brands.[17] Unsurprisingly, therefore, they were among the first brewers to register their brands after the passing of the Trade Marks Registration Act of 1875. Thus due to the institutional and cultural environment, national beer brands developed relatively early in the US and the UK.

But in Canada it has often been difficult for firms to create successful national brands. The nature of the nation is such that regional, religious, linguistic and ethnic diversity has frequently prevented a brand from easily gaining national popularity.[18] The period under review was particularly difficult for those brand managers who were seeking to standardise their message due to the large number of immigrants arriving from Europe. Between 1951 and 1971 the foreign-born in Canada increased twentyfold. This phenomenon triggered a debate over what was, and what was not, 'Canadian'.[19] Given the diversity of the nation, some companies appealed to history and their role in 'helping Canada grow' to build their brands.[20] For instance, the Bank of Nova Scotia ran a series of advertisements during the 1950s, celebrating the accomplishments of various prominent Canadians who were 'responsible' for Canada's development. The ads then reminded the reader that such triumphs were only possible due to the financial backing of Canada's banks, specifically the Bank of Nova Scotia.[21] As Ire Wagman has recently written, this approach to branding reveals a 'certain conservatism about Canadian cultural life; one which appreciates various kinds of difference, but not with some need to reassert a past in which such differences were less prominent than they are today'.[22] Others firms have appropriated the symbolic markers of the national identity to promote their brands.[23] As Paul Rutherford points out, a variety of companies, including Molson Breweries, the Bank of Montreal and Red Rose Tea, used Canadian patriotism to sell their products in the 1970s.[24] Similarly, the Canadian retailer, Roots, used Canadian symbols – beavers, canoes and the maple leaf – in the 1980s and 1990s to allow Canadians 'to purchase identity and proudly display their country's cool image to the rest of the world'.[25]

Other companies, however, have taken a more nuanced approach to branding. As James Opp notes in the case of the Hudson's Bay Company's corporate rebranding exercise during the 1960s, the firm found itself navigating the historical attachments of its western base, the nationalist aspirations of Quebec – Canada's French-speaking province – and the indifference of metropolitan Ontario. The rebranding of the Hudson's Bay Company as *The Bay/la Baie* was ultimately successful because the company managed to bridge multiple identities and align its 'image worlds' to meet the demands of language and place.[26] Such was not always the case. For instance, when Dow Breweries – which was a subsidiary of Ontario-based Canadian Breweries Limited (CBL) – launched *Kebec* ale, in an effort to capitalise on the rising tide of French Canadian nationalism that was fuelling the Quiet Revolution during the 1960s, it met with resistance and a consumer backlash. What raised the ire of nationalists was the fact that the blue and white label looked suspiciously like the Quebec flag. [27] What made the nationalists in Quebec even angrier was that it appeared that English capitalists were exploiting Quebec's sacred symbols to market beer and line their pockets. Unlike such patriotically named brands as Molson's *Laurentide* Ale and a cigarette called *La Quebecquoise*, the *Kebec* brand failed because it 'linked a symbol considered sacred with the profane aim of selling beer'.[28] In the parlance of modern-day marketing experts, the brand was 'inauthentic' because it lacked a concrete relationship to place and was seen by consumers as being tied to commercial motives.[29] Thus, creating national brands has been difficult due to the diversity of the nation.

For those Canadian firms in the alcoholic beverage industry, the task of developing successful national brands has been made doubly difficult because of the nature of the regulatory environment. Under the terms of the nation-forming British North America Act of 1867, the provinces had the constitutional power to prohibit the retail sale and importation of intoxicating drinks. Eager to protect local manufacturers and increase tax revenue, provincial governments implemented tariffs on out-of-province spirits, beer and wine. These restrictions and the onset of prohibition in the United States led some firms in the alcoholic beverage industry, like Seagram Company, to become international concerns before becoming national in scope.[30] After the 'noble experiment' came to an end in Canada,[31] provincial governments imposed new restrictions on the importation, distribution and marketing of intoxicating beverages. These post-prohibition provincial regulations delayed the emergence of truly national brewing companies. Prior to the rise of national breweries in the 1950s there was little incentive to develop national brands. Only after a small number of breweries gained a physical presence in each of the provinces and secured the means of distribution did Canadian brewers attempt to create and promote national brands. But even then the process was not without its challenges, as this article seeks to make clear.

While there has been a significant increase in the number of studies on brands/trademarks and their histories over the last 20 years,[32] there have been very few case studies on the role of the modern, organisation-centred manager in the development of successful national brands. This article seeks to add to our understanding of this neglected aspect of the brand and its history. Drawing on documentation in the Labatt Collection,[33] the article analyses the development of one of Canada's most successful beer brands, Labatt 'Blue'.[34] The first section of the article examines the post-war geographic expansion of John Labatt Limited – one of Canada's oldest brewers – in order to provide the institutional context for the development of national beer brands in Canada. The second section examines the formation of the 'decision problem' – i.e. the 'national lager problem' – and the inability of Labatt's 'Pilsener' to capture the imaginations of a large number of Canadians. The third and final section analyses how the marketing managers at one of Canada's most venerable manufacturing companies attempted to solve the 'national lager problem' by negotiating the sentimentalities of diverse drinking communities in order to create a 'Canadian' beer brand. By placing Labatt's flagship lager in its particular historical context, this article explores how the use of market knowledge contributed to the development of a successful brand in a consumer good industry. By historicising how Labatt's executives came to know the minds of consumers, and by analysing how 'image worlds' were aligned to meet the demands of the marketplace, the article adds to our understanding of the business principles of product rebranding. The article argues that Labatt marketing managers used their market knowledge of brands and cultural trends to create a successful national brand. By abandoning the imagery and moniker of 'Pilsener', and developing a new aesthetic that appealed to 'Canadian' cosmopolitan modernity, the marketing managers at Labatt helped elevate the brand and the firm to the top spot in the Canadian brewing industry.

Becoming a 'truly national brewing company'

In 1954, Jake Moore, Labatt's director of finance and a rising star at John Labatt Limited, addressed a group of securities analysts. While the subject of his talk was the 'outlook for the brewing industry', Moore could not resist reflecting on past developments. The most obvious change that had taken place in the industry since the end of the Second World War was that there were fewer independent breweries in operation. Many of the smaller region-ally oriented breweries that had been in existence at the end of the war were now in the hands of the nation's biggest breweries. Indeed, in 1954 Labatt along with CBL and Molson dominated the domestic market, producing over 80% of all beer sold in Canada. These breweries constituted a national brewing oligopoly and collectively were known as the 'big three'. The breweries that had disappeared, Moore stated, striking a Darwinian chord, were those of a weaker nature that were unable to adapt to the changes taking place in the insti-tutional environment. The nature of the post-prohibition Canadian beer market was such that price competition was virtually non-existent because the price of beer was 'fixed' by the various provincial liquor control boards. This had the effect of putting greater emphasis on non-price competition, especially branding and advertising expenditures. As with their counterparts south of the border, Canadian brewers considered it necessary to create national brands in order to obtain scale economies. As the empirical works of Pels, Tremblay, Ackoff and Emshoff show, advertising expenditures per barrel and marginal benefits of advertising are greater for national than for regional or local brewers.[35] The advent of tele-vision in the late 1940s further elevated the marginal benefits of advertising for firms which were able to market and advertise national brands. The enormous outlay necessary to market national brands was an important factor in the consolidation of the Canadian brewing indus-try after the Second World War.[36] And while Moore lamented the disappearance of the nation's smaller breweries because 'they provided us all with a basic popular support for the industry that the larger breweries find difficult to duplicate', he was quick to note 'the portents are for a continuation of the process of concentration or amalgamation'.[37]

Recent developments elsewhere in the world of brewing influenced Moore's prediction. In the United States and Great Britain, for example, smaller brewers were also finding it increasingly difficult, if not impossible, to compete with their larger counterparts. In Britain, the practice of tying outlets to brewers, the legal restrictions on opening retail outlets and the high proportion of consumption of draft beer at the pub, together with a permissive policy towards mergers, made acquisition of small and medium-sized firms the main route towards market consolidation (rather than internal growth and liquidation of inefficient firms).[38] In the United States, on the other hand, an increase in minimum efficient scale due to technological innovation, combined with competition in advertising outlays, led to the emergence of a national brewing oligopoly during the period 1933 to 1958.[39] To fully realise the benefits of national advertising and to retain parity in transportation costs, the biggest American brewers invested in geographically dispersed processing facilities.[40] After their triumph, the national brewers in the US proved to be largely invulnerable to competition from new entrants because of their large 'sunk' investments in television advertising. [41] For Moore this all suggested that the process of amalgamation would continue with the big brewers getting bigger by devouring the small. 'It is not inevitable that all the small brewers will disappear', he stated, 'but it does seem increasingly difficult for them to survive.'[42] What Moore failed to state that day was that Labatt had played a critical role in accelerating the pace of 'concentration' in Canada.

Labatt had been making beer in London, Ontario since 1847, when John Kinder Labatt – an Irish immigrant of Huguenot stock – joined Samuel Eccles in the business of brewing. During the brewery's formative years, the partners exploited the region's rich supply of natural resources to produce quality British-styled ales and stouts, which were copiously consumed by the military and civilian population in London – most of whom could trace their ancestry to the great beer-drinking nations of England, Scotland and Ireland.[43] Labatt prospered enough to be able to buy Eccles' interest when he retired in 1853. In the years that followed, John Kinder Labatt was among the first Canadian brewers to seize the opportunities of the new age of steam, steel and rail, by using the railroad to ship his beer to various outlets across the colony/province. When his third eldest son, John Labatt, took over the business in 1866, he followed the strategy established by his father, ploughing the profits back into the business in order to expand the scale and scope of his production.[44] He rarely borrowed from outside sources and promoted his products with missionary zeal. By using the railway to ship his products to agents in distant regional markets, John Labatt helped initiate a sharp turn towards market integration and essentially set the course for the rise of large industrial breweries and the gradual decline of small locally oriented ones at the end of the nineteenth century.[45] During the first half of the twentieth century, Labatt continued to grow in large part by making what Alfred Chandler describes as a 'three-pronged investment' in production, distribution and retailing networks, and managerial organisation.[46]

By the final months of the Second World War, Labatt was one of the largest brewers in the nation. Eager to maintain the firm's standing in the industry, executives reflected on what was needed to succeed in the post-war world. They concluded that in order to survive, it was – as one executive put it – necessary to 'go ahead to become truly national'.[47] In 1945, the Canadian brewing industry was made up of 61 breweries – 28 in Western Canada (i.e. in the provinces of British Columbia, Alberta, Saskatchewan and Manitoba), 29 in Central Canada (i.e. in Ontario and Quebec) and 4 in the Maritimes (i.e. in Prince Edward Island, Nova Scotia and New Brunswick), and together they brewed 159 brands.[48] Central Canada was home to the nation's largest breweries – CBL, Labatt, Molson and National Breweries. This region was the heartland of the Canadian brewing industry and the Canadian economy more generally, and its captains of industry had long looked to the 'hinterland' for opportunities for growth.[49] Nevertheless, in 1945 not a single brewery or beer brand was 'truly national'. But that changed after the war as Labatt and the rest of the 'big three' gained a physical presence in each of the major regions of the nation.

Having begun construction on a modern brewery in Quebec in 1952, Labatt turned its attention to gaining a foothold in the west. The western economy was booming, especially after the discovery of large reserves of oil beneath the wheat fields of Leduc, Alberta. And although sales in Manitoba, Saskatchewan, Alberta and British Columbia combined to total only a quarter of the domestic beer market, executives at Labatt were convinced that the west would soon experience 'a growing population' and with it an increasing appetite for beer.[50] In theory, Labatt could have produced its beer in a central Canadian location and shipped it westward, as had been done south of the border. The American 'shipping brewers' had gained a national presence for their brands at the end of the nineteenth century by utilising the railroads, refrigeration, advertising and, above all, economies of scale.[51] But such an approach was practically impossible in Canada for three reasons.

The first reason related to the system of distribution. In the west, brewers were allowed to own hotels, which gave them a private channel to funnel their brands to consumers. For example, in Manitoba virtually all the hotels were 'tied' to either CBL or Shea's Winnipeg Brewery – a large western concern, whose origins lay in the Old Winnipeg Brewery, which was built in the brothel district of Colony Creek by Celestin Thomas in 1873, before Winnipeg won its City Charter. CBL had acquired its hotels during its own post-war geographic expansion when, in 1953, it had purchased Western Canada Breweries Limited, a regional holding company that owned Vancouver Breweries and Drewry's breweries in Manitoba and Saskatchewan. The following year, CBL purchased Grant's Brewery in Manitoba and the year after that it acquired the Red Deer Brewing Company in Alberta. In Manitoba, almost 90% of the draft beer and approximately 57% of the bottled beer was sold in the hotels that Shea's and CBL owned. Various provincial governments in the west passed laws in the 1950s requiring the brewers to sell their hotel holdings. But the brewers often found ways around these laws. For example, when the outspoken founder and president of CBL, Edward Plunkett Taylor, heard about the government's plans to cut the ties between the brewers and the hotels, he decided to sell the company that held CBL's hotels, Reliance Securities Ltd., to a friendly buyer. 'If we have to get out of the hotel business', Taylor stated, 'we must have Reliance in friendly hands in order to retain the gallonage of these hotels'. As a consequence, Reliance was sold to Alex Campbell, the former vice president of finance and treasurer of Taylor's Western Breweries Ltd. Campbell agreed not to transfer his shares in the company to anyone deemed by Taylor to be 'unfriendly'.[52] The move allowed CBL to sidestep the government's legislation and maintain its market share in Manitoba.

The second reason was the tariff on out-of-the-province beer.[53] In 1928, as part of the everlasting oscillation in federal and provincial jurisdiction, the federal government of William Lyon Mackenzie King gave the provinces the right to regulate the local trade in liquor. In the period that followed, provincial governments instituted tariffs and imposed import quotas that limited out-of-province beer or stopped it altogether. The tariffs were often substantial. In Manitoba and Alberta, for example, a charge of five cents per bottle was imposed on out-of-province beer. For those large central Canadian brewers, like Labatt, who were seeking to expand their market share after the war, this served to increase the price of their brands by approximately 30% above the price of local brands.[54] In Saskatchewan and British Columbia imported brands were priced at a premium and exclusively available in government-owned and -controlled liquor stores.[55]

The third reason that explains why the large central Canadian brewers did not 'ship' their beer to distant markets was because of the system of sales quotas that was in existence in the western province. Following prohibition, production became concentrated in the hands of a few relatively large western breweries (e.g. Sick's, Lucky Lager, Drewry's and Shea's). Having cornered their regional markets, the large brewers often agreed not to compete with one another for market share. In Manitoba, such an agreement split the market more or less down the middle, with 60% of sales going to Shea's and the other 40% allocated to Drewry's. The quota agreements were attached to the firm. Thus when CBL acquired Drewry's in 1953, it instantly gained 40% of the Manitoba market.

Due to these factors, executives at Labatt determined that the proper course of action was to expand across the nation by purchasing a few prosperous western concerns. In 1953, Labatt made its first move by purchasing one of Western Canada's largest independent brewers, Shea's Winnipeg Brewery. A change in the company's capital structure in 1926 placed a percentage of voting stock in public hands, and by 1946 more than 50% of the shares were owned by two Winnipeg hospitals. In 1952, the hospital boards indicated their intention to sell their shares in Shea's in order to expand their healthcare facilities. In 1953, Labatt purchased Shea's Winnipeg Brewery for $9 million.[56] The acquisitions continued thereafter and before the decade was out, Labatt had purchased Lucky Lager in British Columbia as well as the Saskatoon Brewing Company in Saskatchewan. At the same time plans were underway to build a state-of-the-art brewery in Edmonton, Alberta. When Labatt purchased the Bavarian Brewery Limited in St John's, Newfoundland in 1962, Jake Moore, who in 1958 had become the first non-family president of Labatt, stated: 'the acquisition gives the Company production facilities from the Atlantic to the Pacific and puts us in a position to compete in the total Canadian market'.[57]

Labatt and CBL were not the only brewers 'going national' during the 1950s and 1960s. Long a 'fast follower', Molson undertook its own national expansion. Like Labatt, it employed both a brownfield and greenfield approach, acquiring existing breweries as well as building new ones. Molson's first move came in 1955 when it struck back at the Ontario brewers that had invaded its home territory by building a 300,000-barrel brewery on Fleet Street, right in CBL's backyard. In 1958, Molson went west, purchasing the prairie powerhouse Sick's Brewery. Sick was the maker of such popular prairie brands as 'Bohemian' and 'Old Style Pilsner'. Molson would continue to manufacture these brands alongside a few of its own. In 1962, Molson again quickly followed the actions of Labatt and CBL by purchasing Newfoundland Brewery Ltd, an established brewery in St. John's, Newfoundland.

By 1962, the 'big three' produced almost 95% of the beer sold in Canada. Nearly all of the 61 breweries that were in operation in 1945 were still producing beer, but now most of them were owned by the 'big three'. The 'big three' had a physical presence in every region across the land, except for the Maritimes and Northern Ontario.[58] The market structure of the Canadian brewing industry was thus transformed during the post-war period from one made up of a relatively large group of regional brewers catering to local drinking preferences, into a stable national oligopoly.

In Canada the nature of the institutional environment was such that it prevented the development of national beer brands prior to the 1960s. The tariff on out-of-the-province brands, the tightly held system of distribution and the quota agreements between brewers all stood in the way of the emergence of a national beer market. Until a truly national beer market existed, there was little incentive for brewers to develop national brands. Only when brewers had established a physical presence across the country did they attempt to promote a few 'national' brands in order to realise scale economies in advertising. Labatt 'Pilsener' was one of those brands. But unfortunately, for reasons discussed in the following section, it failed to capture the imagination of significant number of Canadian beer drinkers.

The 'national lager problem'

In 1959, Labatt's marketing managers met at Oakwood, Ontario to discuss the subject of national brands. Those at the conference had the foresight to realise that in the future 'national brands' would dominate the marketplace and that huge savings could be achieved by promoting a single brand with a cohesive identity and advertising theme across the nation.[59] At the time, a truly national lager brand did not exist. The closest thing to one was CBL's 'Carling Black Label'. Since the 1930s, CBL had promoted 'Black Label' as its flagship lager. But the brand lacked popularity in many parts of Canada. While 'Black Label' was highly favoured in Ontario and had some strength in Manitoba and British Columbia, the brand was not — as one up-and-coming Labatt executive, Peter Widdrington, noted — 'a serious contender in any other market'.[60] In 1959, CBL controlled 48.2% of the national market (see Table 1), by producing and promoting a number of popular regional brands — many of which were acquired during the firm's post-war geographic expansion. It was a similar story at Molson Breweries, which controlled 25.3% of the national market. Molson's dominant position in Saskatchewan and Alberta was the result of its acquisition, in 1958, of Sick's Breweries Ltd., and the continued production and promotion of its brands. In 1959, Molson launched two new brands, Golden Ale and Canadian Lager, but neither brand had a significant share of the national market until the 1970s.[61]

Labatt's own line of beers consisted of five brands: Crystal Lager, Labatt's IPA, Labatt's '50', Extra Stock Ale and Labatt's 'Pilsener'. Labatt produced these brands along with those regional brands (e.g. Lucky Lager) which it had gained ownership of during its post-war acquisition phase. Given the trend towards milder tasting beer, the executives attending the Oakwood Conference chose 'Pilsener' to promote as its national lager. But 'Pilsener' had a difficult time gaining significant market share outside of Western Canada. 'Pilsener's' lack of appeal constituted what the marketing men at Labatt termed a 'national lager problem'. The challenge, as Widdrington put it, was 'to broaden the brand image to appeal to the mass lager market'.[62]

The 'national lager problem' proved to be a difficult one to solve, in part because of the regional character of the Canadian beer market. In the west there was a well-established tradition of brewing and drinking Pilsener. A pale, golden lager, Pilsener (or Pilsner) was first brewed in Pilsen, a city in Western Bohemia in the Czech Republic. Pilsener revolutionised the brewing world when it first appeared due to its seductive glow and its crisp, mild and refreshing flavour. The custom of brewing Pilsener was first brought to Western Canada by German and American immigrants during the last half of the nineteenth century. One such brewer, Fritz Sick, had emigrated from Freiburg, Germany to Trail, British Columbia in the

Table 1. Percentage sales by province of the leading breweries in Canada, 1959.

Brewingfirm	Nova Scotia	NB	PEI	Nfld.	Quebec	Ontario	Manitoba	Sask.	Alberta	BC	Canada
CBL	14.9	5.7	0.0	0.0	51.8	60.9	41.0	34.2	7.9	36.0	48.2
Molson	6.2	3.7	0.0	0.0	43.3	13.7	0.4	50.9	40.6	16.3	25.3
Labatt	6.5	1.3	0.0	0.0	4.7	20.7	50.2	0.4	0.3	35.1	15.9
CB&M*	0.0	0.0	0.0	0.0	0.0	0.0	0.0	3.0	51.2	5.3	4.1
Olands	67.7	15.2	n.a	n.a	0.2	0.0	0.0	0.0	0.0	0.0	1.8
Moosehead	4.7	74.1	n.a	n.a	0.0	0.0	0.0	0.0	0.0	0.0	1.2
Others	0.0	0.0	n.a.	n.a.	0.0	4.7	8.4	11.5	0.0	7.1	3.5
Total	2.2	1.5	0.6	1.2	29.9	40.0	5.2	3.9	7.0	8.5	100.0

*Calgary Brewing and Malting Co.; Source: Jones, "Competition in the Canadian Beer Industry," 116; Brewer's Association of Canada, *Brewing in Canada*, 111–27.

1890s. After a couple of short-lived business ventures, Sick moved his family to Alberta and opened the Lethbridge Brewing and Malting Company. Soon after he began making 'Old Style Pilsner Beer'. The brew was an overnight success and over the next few decades it gained so much in popularity that when Labatt began construction of its state-of-the-art brewery in Edmonton in 1964, 'Old Style Pilsner' had a tight grip on the Alberta market. In addition to dominating the Alberta market, Sick's Old Style Pilsner shared a top spot with Carling Pilsener and Lucky Lager in British Columbia.[63] In the province of Saskatchewan, where lager sales constituted 97% of the beer market, Sick's 'Bohemian' pilsner was the best-selling beer. In 1962, Labatt's 'Pilsener' only had 8% of the Saskatchewan market, making it the fifth best-selling beer in the province, behind 'Old Vienna' (with 9% market share), Black Label (with 10%), Molson 'Pilsener' (with 22%) and Sick's 'Bohemian' (with 46%).[64] In Manitoba, where there was also a vibrant tradition of brewing and drinking pilsner, Labatt's 'Pilsener' was the best-selling brand, with a 35% market share.

Unlike in the west, in Ontario, Quebec and the Maritimes the brewing industry had been controlled by a group of brewers who were, for the most part, of British descent. Men like John Molson, John Labatt, Thomas Carling, Eugene O'Keefe, John Sleeman, William Dow and Alexander Keith had established breweries to produce British-styled ales, porters and stouts. As a result, the western thirst for pilsner/lager did not exist to the same extent in the east. That is not to say that lager drinking did not take place. It did, and in some places – as Labatt's market research showed[65] – lager's popularity was rapidly growing. While only 5% of Quebecers and 20% of Maritimers stated that they drank lager on a regular basis in 1965, in Ontario the number of regular lager drinkers was close to 35%.[66]

Relative to elsewhere in Canada, the Ontario beer market was huge. In 1962, per capita consumption in Ontario was 69.14 litres. That same year, those in the four western provinces drank, on average, about 30% less than their Ontario counterparts. On the east coast, per capita beer consumption was even lower. For instance, in 1962, each New Brunswicker drank on average just 28.73 litres of beer. In part, the lower level of beer consumption was a result of the lingering shadow of prohibition. Before the 1960s, the Maritime Provinces had the most restrictive liquor laws in the country.[67] But it was not just that each Ontarian was drinking more, it was also that there were more of them. As a consequence, total beer consumption in Ontario in 1962 equalled 43.6 million litres of beer. Ontarians were consuming more beer than all of the other provinces (excluding Quebec) and territories combined.[68] To put it in slightly different terms, Ontario beer consumption represented 62% of total Canadian

Table 2. Labatt's Blue market share (%).

	Ontario	Manitoba	Sask.	Alberta	BC	Canada
1960	6.90	n/a	n/a	n/a	n/a	n/a
1965	10.20	37.15	10.40	12.10	7.00	6.55
1968	11.48	37.42	n/a	14.97	10.00	6.57
1970	16.75	42.50	29.00	23.35	14.00	13.11
1975	15.50	38.25	22.18	n/a	32.25	15.12
1980	23.64	25.68	14.50	18.37	34.18	16.06
1985	25.73	18.62	12.55	11.25	21.00	15.23

Sources: "Labatt's Blue 1988 Marketing Plan," Box A08–053-711, *Labatt Collection*; "Labatt's Prairie Region 1988 Marketing Plan," Box A08–053-711, ibid.; C. A. Stock to E. G. Bradley, August 15, 1975, Box A08–039-228, ibid.; "Saskatchewan Benchmark Study," November 1, 1970, Box A08–053-603, ibid.; "Ontario Lager Benchmark Study," July 17, 1970, Box A08–053-603, ibid.; "British Columbia Benchmark Study," December 1, 1970, Box A08–053-603, ibid.; "Quebec Benchmark Study," November 24, 1970, Box A08–053-603, ibid.; "1983 Spring Tracking Study – Summary of Brands by Province," Box A08–053-318, ibid.; "Pilsener Share of Market Trends – 1959–1967," Box A08–058-713, ibid.; Brand Designation Committee, "A Working Paper – Problem Definition" (March 1970), Box A08–053-603, *Labatt Collection*; *Minutes*, September 5, 1975; "Marketing Priorities F81 and Beyond," Box A08–053-598, *Labatt Collection*.

consumption. Having a significant slice of the Ontario beer market was therefore critical to the growth and survival of Canadian brewers in the post-war period.

The problem for Labatt was that its flagship lager, 'Pilsener', had never captured the imagination of beer drinkers in Ontario, where a third of the nation's lager drinkers lived in 1962. Since 'Pilsener's' earliest days it had held only a small share of the Ontario market, accounting for between 6% and 12% of lager sales during the 1960s (see Table 2). Carling 'Black Label' and 'Old Vienna' had maintained a strong grip on the Ontario lager market until 1963 when Molson 'Canadian' challenged the duopoly through aggressive direct sales and a stepped up advertising campaign, which included sponsoring of the National Hockey League.[69] To the extent that Labatt 'Pilsener' was being consumed at all, Labatt's market research showed, it was downed by a relatively small group of people outside the beer-drinking mainstream.[70] Labatt 'Pilsener' drinkers were typically better-educated men and women. 'There is clear cut evidence', Labatt's Director of Marketing, Paul J. Henderson wrote in the winter of 1964, 'that Pilsener does much better among certain socio-economic groups – i.e. white collar consumers, in better districts; and not as well among blue collar groups'.[71] The brand was also more popular with recent immigrants, particularly with those of European descent. On 29 October 1964, P.J. Henderson wrote to his colleague, B.G. Elliot, lamenting the fact that 'Pilsener seems to have got itself into a rather restricted area – i.e. new Canadians and Europeans, not unqualified good things in other studies'.[72] Henderson could not hold back his disappointment. 'Obviously, this is not a satisfactory state of affairs', he stated. 'A main lager brand should have a broad appeal', he continued, 'especially to the big volume drinker'.[73]

So what was the cause of the problem? Why was Labatt 'Pilsener' having such a difficult time capturing a significant share of the national lager market? When the problem was first identified in 1962, more than one Labatt executive thought that perhaps the product itself was to blame. Under the heading, 'hypothesis which may account for the problem', P.J. Henderson wrote that, 'the product itself is not sufficiently acceptable to consumer tastes in the problem markets'.[74] The proposition was disturbing, but, as Henderson himself insisted, it had to be explored. Immediately blind taste tests were performed to compare Labatt 'Pilsener' to its key competitors. What the taste tests revealed was that there was little difference between Labatt 'Pilsener' and the other lagers on the market.[75] Since the mid-1950s, the 'big three' had been producing blander beers in an effort to appeal to as many beer drinkers as possible. As a result, there was very little in the way of substance to distinguish the brands of the 'big three'. 'In brewing today all brands of any one type are fairly close', stated Labatt's Quality Control Manager John Compton in 1963, 'and it is the finer points we are working on'.[76] Public opinion surveys, which had been undertaken by Labatt's marketing managers, further confirmed the extent of the homogenisation. In 1964, over 80% of those Canadians polled stated that, 'the mass of brands are much alike'.[77] When it came to Labatt's flagship lager, blind taste tests showed 'no significant difference in preference between Pilsener, on the one hand, and Canadian, Black Label, and Old Vienna, on the other'.[78] As a result, when P.J. Henderson, N.E. Hardy, J. Burke-Gaffney, C.A. Stock, D.G. McGill and T.M. Kirkwood met in Toronto on 5 July 1965 to further discuss the 'national larger problem' they took some comfort in the fact that the evidence showed that the product itself was not the problem. 'Any marketing failures of the brand', Labatt's marketing managers declared, 'can not be charged to the product'.[79] Rather, they concluded, 'Pilsener has an image problem'.[80]

But what was wrong with 'Pilsener's' image? Senior management struggled to come up with an answer to this question for a number of years. Ultimately they determined that part of the problem was that the brand was considered too European and therefore 'not basically Canadian'.[81] At a time when the government, the popular media and the public at large was preoccupied with protecting the 'Canadian way of life' from the threat of newcomers,[82] 'Pilsenser's' popularity was being undermined by the brand's association with a number of countries in Central Europe. In 1964, Labatt's marketing men conduct a survey of beer drinkers in the Welland-Windsor region of Ontario. This study, and a subsequent one undertaken in Canada's largest city, Toronto, in 1965, concluded that 'users and non-users very heavily associate Pilsener with Europe'.[83] In May 1967, C.A. Stock summarised the finding of the market research that had been done at Labatt over the previous four year by stating: 'Its name [i.e. "Pilsener"] has strong European connotations, especially with Germany, Austria and Czechoslovakia'.[84]

Labatt's marketing managers had emphasised 'Pilsener's' Central European heritage since the brand's introduction in 1951. In its ads, Labatt had played up the fact that the beer was based on a Central European recipe, which had been brought back to Canada after the Second World War by Hugh Labatt, the grandson of the brewery's founder, John Kinder Labatt. 'Only Labatt's Pilsener Lager Beer has the exciting flavour', one ad proclaimed, 'because only Labatt's possess the secret of the original lager recipe from Pilsen, birthplace of lager beer'. The company also emphasised that 'Pilsener' was made from European yeast and hops imported from the Pils region of Czechoslovakia. Early promotional pictures showed Hugh Labatt and his wife consulting with Czech brewers in Prague. In 1961, the label of the Labatt 'Pilsener' was changed to include the arms of the city of Pilsen (see Figure 1). At the same time, Labatt began using a foil label for the first time, in part because 'women are particularly attracted by the gay, colourful sparkle and charm of foil labels'.[85] The ads for 'Pilsener' featured middle-class couples in formal attire (and certainly not jeans and T-shirts), enjoying their lager in a cocktail lounge rather than a working-class beer parlour (see Figure 2).[86] Until the end of the 1960s, the people pictured in Labatt's lager ads were middle-aged or older. The government's regulations on beer advertisements kept the scenes being depicted in the tradition of romance and glamour.[87]

In a further attempt to appeal to recent immigrants, Labatt began running a few ads in German. The ads declared that Labatt 'Pilsener' was 'good in taste' and 'should be your beer'.

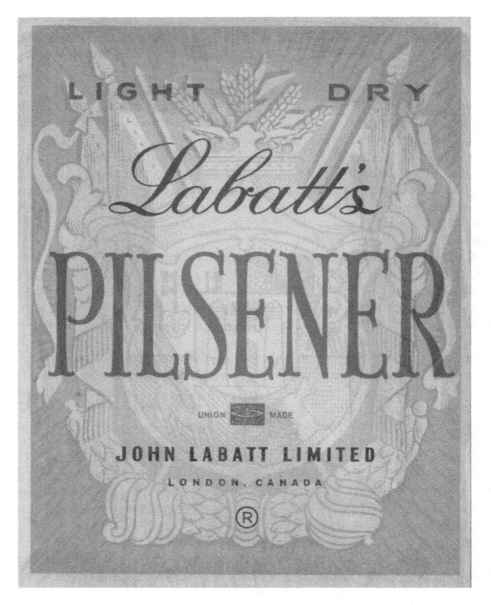

Figure 1. Labatt 'Pilsener' beer bottle label with the city of Pilsen's coat-of-arms (1962), Box A08-053-1242, *Labatt Collection*.

'Gut Im Geschmack', one advertisement in a Toronto newspaper read, 'Labatt Pilsener, Soll Dein Bier Sein'.[88] The European bond was further forged by Labatt's use in its ads of 'Mr. Pilsener', a jovial, white haired, Alpine figure, who was often decked out in lederhosen and a Tyrolean hat. Mr. Pilsener started to appear in ads during the 1950s. The diminutive European character also appeared on beer serving trays, bottle openers, postcards and, for a period in the early 1960s, on every cap, bottle and case of Labatt's 'Pilsener' (see Figure 3). The marketing managers at Labatt concluded that it all added up to a derivative and

Figure 2. Labatt 'Pilsener' ad (1966), Box A08-053-1296, *Labatt Collection*.

decidedly European brand identity at a time when the symbols of national identity were being reformulated and modernised.[89]

Creating a 'Canadian' brand

In the mid-1960s, marketing executives at Labatt began making changes to the firm's flagship lager brand in an effort make it appear less 'ethnic' and more 'Canadian'. One of the first changes the company made was to remove the city of Pilsen's coat-of-arms from the label

Figure 3. A postcard featuring Mr. Pilsener overseeing the bottling and packaging at Labatt (@1963), Box A10-039-415, *Labatt Collection*.

and replace it with a coat-of-arms featuring a maple leaf (see Figure 4). The maple leaf had long been a symbolic marker of the national identity. Since Confederation, the maple leaf had appeared on coins, flags and military adornments. In 1867, Alexander Muir had composed 'The Maple Leaf Forever', which in the years that followed became English Canada's de facto national anthem. At the same time, the name 'Labatt's' became more prominent on the label and the word 'Pilsener' — which 87% of those surveyed in Toronto associated with a country other than Canada[90] — became less so. In an effort to remind consumers of Labatt's continued commitment to quality and tradition — elements that modern marketing experts assert are central to a brand's authenticity[91] — the label also featured an image of the four gold medallions that the company had won at international brewing competitions since the 1870s. 'The new label', one internal report noted, 'gives the impression of a Canadian beer, and expresses the vigor and energy of people on the move'.[92] Finally, Mr. Pilsener vanished once-and-for-all from the company's merchandise and promotional campaigns.

At the same time, Labatt's marketing managers decided to emphasise the colour blue more fully on the label. Internal research showed that blue projected 'relaxation', 'smoothness', 'coolness', 'balance of product' and 'quality'.[93] In addition, the image makers at Labatt were in possession of Louis Cheskin's groundbreaking 1951 study, *Colour for Profit*, which suggested that blue was the 'preferred colour of men'.[94] But beyond its universal psychological appeal, the utilisation of blue would allow Labatt to avoid the politics of 'red and white' in Canada. During the 1960s, 'Britishness' versus 'Canadian' symbolism was highly contested. This was particularly the case in Ontario. The adoption in 1965 of the new Canadian flag, which consisted of a red field with a white square and a maple leaf at its centre, led to Ontario's adoption of a modified Red Ensign as its provincial flag. Labatt's use of the colour blue sidestepped both forms of 'nationalism'.

Other aesthetic aspects of the brand took much more time to change. Senior management struggled for years with what to do about the brand's name. In April 1963, B.G. Elliot, Labatt's executive assistant to the vice president and general manager, stated that the name 'Pilsener' should be abandoned because it was not resonating with beer drinkers in Ontario.

Figure 4. Labatt's flagship lager, 'Blue', and Labatt's flagship ale, '50' (1971), Box A08-053-349, *Labatt Collection*.

Elliot's report, 'Recommendations for a Brand Name', contained a long list of possible appellations to replace 'Pilsener'. Some of the names were quickly struck off the list because they were antagonistic to certain segments of the population. For example, the brand name 'Friar's' was rejected because it might offend Roman Catholics, who were 'an important part of our market'.[95] Likewise, the name 'Mohawk' was crossed off the list because it had 'bad connotations' and 'only a very tenuous association with beer'.[96] On the other hand, 'North Star' was thought to be a good moniker because it was a 'Canadian term' that was 'well known' and 'nationally popular'.[97] The name 'Viking' was also in the running because it 'was strong in masculinity and adventurous quality'. Finally, the appellation 'Grand National' was seriously being considered because it 'expresses high quality with reference to achievement ... and extremely well suited for bilingual use'.[98]

None of these brand names were adopted at the time, however, due to an internal dispute over the appropriate approach to marketing and which market(s) should be privileged. Some executives felt that a regional approach to marketing beer was best. For example, Tom Cadham, the head of Labatt's Saskatchewan Division, thought that Labatt might best be served by a regionally oriented advertising campaign. 'Where there has been tremendous success in several provinces for the product [i.e. "Pilsener"]', Cadham asked, 'should any change from the present proven successful approach be made?'[99] As a result, when P.J. Henderson asked the heads of the various operating divisions to suggest a new name for 'Pilsener', Cadham refused to participate. This infuriated Henderson. 'I am mystified by the form of your division's response to our solicitation', Henderson angrily wrote to Cadham in December 1966.

> We have on a number of occasions attempted to explain that we are undertaking the explo-
> ration only of a beer brand designation other than Pilsener ... If your division chooses not to
> play a part by throwing the names you like into the pot, Tom, I guess this is your prerogative.[100]

Unlike Cadham, Henderson was confident that the 'national lager problem' could only be solved by a 'national approach' to marketing. He was not alone. He had the support of all of those at Labatt's Head Office in London, none of whom went on the record as advocating a different approach. Seemingly everyone in London agreed with Labatt's vice president, J.R. Robertson, who had previously stated that the trend in Canada was 'towards larger marketing areas, not smaller'.[101] This kind of language around standardising the image of brands reflected the trend of corporate mass advertising more generally during the period. There was a constant tension between regional managers who thought they 'knew their markets' and the centralised professional public relations technocrats, like Robertson, who were perturbed by the messiness/untidiness of mixed messages/brands.[102] Robertson was not even willing to concede that Quebec, which was in the midst of the Quiet Revolution, represented a special case. 'If any region warranted regional brands because it is a different cultural area with a different language', Robertson stated, 'that region is Quebec. But even here, brewers have seen fit to promote brands that are national in the context in which Ale is national'. Thus, in regard to the 'national lager problem', Robertson recommended that, 'every effort should be made to achieve the same image and to direct the same appeal to different parts of the country'.[103]

Robertson was not naïve, however. He was the first to admit that 'no brand can be all things to all people – so some penalty must be paid in certain areas'.[104] The question was which areas should be privileged and which should pay the penalty when it came to rebranding Labatt's lager. Increasingly Labatt's executives were of the opinion that the Ontario market should be privileged. To be sure, it would be nice to maintain, or even better, increase, market share in the west. But the litmus test was now Ontario. Any changes would be judged, first and foremost, based on their effects on market share in Canada's most populated province. 'This Pilsener matter', Labatt's executive vice president, N.E. Hardy, wrote to P.J. Henderson, 'must be primarily the responsibility of the Ontario division. But since there are national considerations and because head office research facilities are probably involved', he continued, 'I am asking you to give the utmost assistance to the Ontario division by coordinating this important project and assigning to it your department's top priority'.[105]

In the west, however, beer drinkers had started to refer to 'Pilsener' as 'Blue' because of the predominance of the colour on the label.[106] But executives at Labatt's head office did not have enough faith in their western base to label the brand with that name – at least, initially. Instead, Labatt's marketing managers decided that perhaps the new brand name should contain the word 'Blue'. Shortly therefore senior executives were sent a list of 160 names and asked to 'circle those which they believed to have good potential as brand names for Labatt's lager beer'. The long list included such monikers as: Blue Grade, Blue Bonnet, Blue Twin, Blue Wave, National Blue, Blue Star, Blue 'n Gold, Blue Extra, Blue Eagle, Northern Blue, Blue #1, London Blue, Blue North, Blue Keg, Blue Shield, Cool Blue and Happy Blue. The name that emerged as a possible replacement for Labatt's 'Pilsener' was 'Blue Star'. In the months that followed the consultants, Ben Crow & Associates, conducted a market survey for Labatt to measure the acceptability of 'Blue Star' as a possible replacement name for Labatt's 'Pilsener'. The firm found that the appellation fared rather badly against 'Pilsener' in key Ontario markets. In addition, some senior executives thought the name change might bewilder regular beer drinkers. 'By changing across the country to Blue Star, those who know the brand as Labatt's Pilsener will be confused', N.E. Hardy stated, 'and those who know it as Labatt's Blue will be confused, and everyone will be confused as to the logical nickname, Blue, Star, B.S. etc.'[107] And thus it was rejected.

On 1 June 1967, N.E. Hardy wrote to P.J. Henderson stating that it was important that 'faster progress be made' in resolving the national lager problem. Henderson stated,

> For a long time we have all been aware that Ontario's progress, dependent largely on the per-formance of '50' Ale, cannot be secure or soundly based until we have a stronger national lager brand in that market and one that is able to compete effectively in the key lager markets which Pilsener does not do.[108]

In late 1967, it finally dawned on executives at Labatt that perhaps the answer had been staring them in the face for some time. 'Is it not possible', P.J. Henderson wrote, 'that the solution to our national lager problem lies solely in the word Blue'. Part of the attraction of the name 'Blue' was that – in the words of one senior executive – 'by itself, it is bilingual'.[109] While the Quebec lager market was small, executives at Labatt were still determined to create a brand that would appeal to beer drinkers in both English and French Canada. In the months that followed, Labatt began testing the brand name 'Blue' in smaller Ontario markets. The tests went well and as a result, in July 1968, the wording 'Call for a Labatt Blue' was added to the Ontario label and a 'Blue' advertising theme was launched across the province.[110] At the same time, the phrase 'the great beer Westerners call Blue' was added to the label in the west.[111]

In 1968, Arthur Lenox, a long-time Labatt executive and former editor of the company's magazine, *The Spearhead*, contacted the advertising firm J. Walter Thompson to see if it could produce an attention-grabbing television commercial for 'Blue'. Colour television had only recently hit the Canadian scene and executives at Labatt believed that 'Blue' would be a natural attention-getter on the screen if it were associated with the right jingle and moving images.[112] J. Walter Thompson promised that it would come up with something interesting and assigned the task to one of its young executives, Bob Byron. Having taken a short retreat to reflect on the challenge, Byron returned with an idea for an ad campaign with three key elements: a blue balloon – as a symbol of escape – light music and the refrain, 'When you're smiling, the whole world smiles with you'.

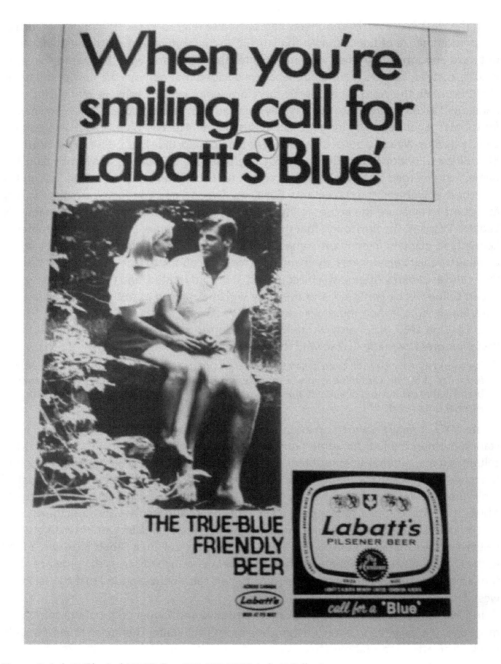

Figure 5. Labatt 'Blue' ad (1969), Box A08-053-1255, *Labatt Collection.*

By the late 1960s those in the automobile, tobacco and alcoholic beverage industries were marketing to what the *Wall Street Journal* in 1967 termed the 'Mustang generation'– i.e. 'young, educated men and women who supposedly lived in pads (apartments) and spent much of their money on socialising and consumer goods'.[113] At a time when popular culture was very youth-oriented, the people in Labatt's 'Blue' ads were visibly younger than they were in previous advertisements for 'Pilsener'. These youthful people were also situated in

Figure 6. Labatt 'Blue' ad (1972), Box A08-053-1296, *Labatt Collection.*

more casual settings (see Figure 5). The 'Blue' ads of the late 1960s and early 1970s displayed relaxed, mixed-gendered socialising, with hints of the 'swinging' singles lifestyles (Figure 6). The focus on youth would pay dividends when the minimum drinking age was lowered from 21 to 18 or 19 in all of the provinces and territories between 1970 and 1972.

The rebranding of 'Pilsener' as 'Blue' and the subsequent ad campaigns had positive results. Due to the fact that Labatt slowly phased out 'Pilsener' in markets where the brand was strong, and phased in 'Blue' where 'Pilsener' was weak, market dislocations were kept to a minimum. Beer drinkers in the west still recognised 'Blue' as the lager that they had come to prefer. In each of the western provinces, Blue's market share increased significantly after the rebranding. In Alberta, Blue's share of the market increased from 14.97% to 23.35% between 1968 and 1970 (see Table 2). In British Columbia, Blue's market share doubled between 1968 and 1972, from 10% to 20%. Gains were also experienced in Manitoba, where Blue's popularity increased by 5% between 1968 and 1970. By the summer of 1971, Blue was the best-selling beer brand in the west.

In Ontario, beer drinkers saw 'Blue' as a new, modern, Canadian-made lager, that was 'brewed for people born in Canada'.[114] By February 1970, Labatt Blue's share of the all-important Ontario market increased to 16.75%, which was up from 11.48% just two years earlier.[115] Labatt's gains had come at the expense of its competitors, with 17% of Molson 'Canadian' drinkers, 13% of 'Old Vienna' drinkers and 12% of 'Black Label' drinkers switching to 'Blue'.[116] What was even more encouraging for those at Labatt was the fact that younger drinkers were starting to swap their regular brands for 'Blue'. In November of 1971, 30% of those between 21 and 24 years of age stated that they drank 'Blue' on a regular basis.[117] As the baby boomers came of drinking age and per capita consumption continued to increase during the early 1970s, Labatt 'Blue' benefited from having a modern brand image and a catchy, bilingual name that resonated with the young adults of the nation.

By 1975, 'Blue' was the best-selling lager brand in the nation. Five years later it had the distinction of being Canada's most popular beer and – as a Labatt report noted – was 'the single largest marginal profit contributor that this company has'.[118] But what pleased executives at Labatt the most was the fact that the rebranding of 'Pilsener' as 'Blue' had helped propel Labatt to the top spot in the Canadian brewing industry. In 1975, Labatt controlled 38.2% of the national market.[119] The rise from third place, which Labatt had held in 1959, to first place was due in large part to the rising popularity of 'Blue' and the applied marketing knowledge and innovative strategies of the managers at Labatt.

Conclusion

This case study demonstrates that in non-science industries with a high level of competition and concentration, as Canadian brewing was after 1959, brands and marketing knowledge are central to explaining the growth and survival of firms. A basic function of a brand is to segment a market, and a 'brand' is valueless unless it communicates with potential purchasers. Successful brands in the beer industry rest on quality products, supported by effective channels of distribution and a brand identity that appeals to drinkers. Brand identities are often created by the entrepreneurial founders of firms and/or their family members, but sometimes, as was the case at Labatt during the period under review, they are made by corporate marketing managers. Labatt was fortunate to have strong marketing executives who possessed a keen sense of consumer needs, market conditions and cultural trends. Without any objective criteria to guide them, Labatt's managers imaginatively used their marketing knowledge to refashion the firm's flagship lager as 'Blue'.

This case study also demonstrates that branding is an on-going process. To be successful, a brand's identity needs to be refashioned from time to time to meet the evolving demands of the marketplace. During the 1950s, Labatt's marketing managers attempted to imbue its flagship lager with authenticity by linking it to the city of Pilsen, the birthplace of Pilsner beer. While the brand's identity resonated with recent immigrants and those of European descent, it failed to capture the imagination of a significant number of Canadians. During the 1960s, with the debate over who was and who was not 'Canadian' raging, and with Europeans viewed by many Canadians as 'foreign', the brand came to be seen as unsuitably 'ethnic'. 'British' Ontario was particularly hostile to anything that sounded Central European. As a result, Labatt's marketing managers decided to embark upon a rebranding exercise in order to make its flagship lager seem more 'Canadian'. Having defined the national lager problem, the decision-makers at Labatt spent years generating and analysing data in order to make a decision about the rebranding of 'Pilsener'. Due to the diversity of the Canadian nation, the reimaging of 'Pilsener' as 'Blue' took a good deal of time.

In the end, the marketing managers at Labatt decided on the moniker 'Blue' because it was able to transcend region by downplaying the Czech heritage of the brand. But due to the fact that Labatt was picking up on a Western Canadian colloquialism, the brewery was able to maintain its constituency of beer drinkers in the West. In addition, the appellation and imagery of 'Blue' avoided the divisive politics of 'red and white' and appealed to beer drinkers of various socio-economic backgrounds in both English and French Canada. By rebranding its flagship lager 'Blue', the decision-makers at Labatt managed to avoid taking a stand on the various types of 'nationalism' that were occupying the body politic. Branding in the 1960s in Canada was about wrestling with regional identities, standardising the image/message, and laying claim to 'national' status. By appealing to a new 'Canadian' cosmopolitan modernity, Labatt 'Blue' was able to bridge multiple histories and multiple identities. The refashioned brand transmitted cultural characteristics that resonated with a large number of Canadians, particularly, and most importantly, those of the baby boom generation. The rebranding of 'Pilsener' as 'Blue' and the advertising campaign that followed was an important part of the Labatt's business strategy and a critical factor in the firm's ability to gain a competitive advantage in the Canadian brewing industry.

Finally, this case study suggests that building and managing brands is a complex exercise, requiring a deep knowledge on the part of marketing managers of market tastes, consumer fantasies and needs, and societal and cultural trends. It requires extensive market research and the exchange of innovative knowledge among employees, consultants, clients and distributors. Building a brand is an analytical process that depends on data-driven decision-making. Looking in from the outside, branding/rebranding exercises and advertising campaigns often appear to be coherent and straightforward. But in reality these exercises and campaigns are frequently characterised by trepidation, anxiety, uncertainty, inconsistency, contestation and debate. This was certainly the case during the making of Labatt 'Blue'.

Notes

1. Lopes, *Global Brands*, 1–66, 129–79; Duguid, "Developing the Brand," 405–41; Merrett and Whitwell, "The Empire Strikes Back," 162–90; Wilson, "Selling Beer in Victorian Britain," 103–25; Johansen, "Marketing and Competition in Danish Brewing," 126–38; Weir, "Managing Decline," 139–62.
2. Barwise and Robertson, "Brand Portfolios," 277–85.
3. Sáiz and Pérez, "Catalonian Trademarks," 255.
4. Aaker, *Building Strong Brands*; Doyle, "Building Successful Brands," 18; Barwise and Robertson, "Brand Portfolios," 277–85; Casson, "Brands," 41–58; Wilkins, "When and Why: Brand Names," 19–20; Jones, "Brands and Marketing," 1–12.
5. Lopes and Casson, "Entrepreneurship and the Development of Global Brands," 661–80.
6. Lopes, "Brands and the Evolution of Multinationals," 1–30; Chernatony and Riley, "Defining "Brand,'" 417–44; King, *Developing New Brands*.
7. For more on the differences between the tangible and intangible elements of brands see Chernatony and Riley, 'Modeling the Components of the Brand," 1077–90.
8. Lopes, *Global Brands*, 148–79; Casson, "Brands," 41–58.
9. Lopes, *Global Brands*, 6 and 153; Bilkey and Nes, "Country-of-Origin Effects," 89–99; Guy, *When Champagne Became French*, 2; Beverland, "The 'Real Thing,'" 251–8; O'Neill, Houtman, and Aupers, "Advertising Real Beer," 5–15.
10. Peñaloza, "The Commodification of the American West," 82–109; Grayson and Martinec, "Consumer Perceptions of Iconicity and Indexicality," 296–312; Beverland, Lindgreen, and Vink, "Projecting Authenticity Through Advertising," 5–15.
11. Cochran, *Pabst*, 129–59; Baron, *Brewed in America*, 257–64; Plavchan, *A History of Anheuser-Busch*, 91–2.
12. For more on the notion of sticky knowledge see: Lopes, *Global Brands*, 7–9.
13. Cochran, *Pabst*, 216.
14. Chandler, *Scale and Scope*, 267; Deconinck and Swinnen, "Tied Houses," 231–6.
15. Hawkins, *A History of Bass Charrington*; Owen. *The Greatest Brewery in the World*.

16. Gourvish and Wilson, *The British Brewing Industry*, 92, 94, 98, 146–7, 273, 438–9; Hannah, *The Rise of the Corporate Economy*, 190; Owen. *The Greatest Brewery in the World*, 5, 164; Gourvish and Wilson, *The British Brewing Industry*, 438–49.

17. Higgins and Verma, "The Business of Protection," 1–19; Duguid, "Developing the Brand," 405–41.

18. Penfold, *The Donut*, 176. For an analysis of some of the regional and international hurdles faced by early twentieth-century 'universal' branding efforts, see Strasser, *Satisfaction Guaranteed*, 139–44.

19. Iacovetta, *Gatekeepers*, 1–19.

20. Murton, "The Normandy of the New World"; Wagman, "Peace, Order, and Good Banking"; Hammerschmidt, "Images of Canadian Advertising."

21. Wagman, "Peace, Order, and Good Banking," 548–56.

22. Ibid., 560.

23. Penfold, "'Eddie Shack,'" 48–66.

24. Rutherford, *The New Icons*, 91–5.

25. Carstairs, "Roots Nationalism," 235–55.

26. Opp, "Branding the Bay/la Baie," 223–56; for more on 'image worlds', see Nye, *Image Worlds*.

27. *Globe and Mail*, November 14, 1963, 1.

28. Frederick, *Rebels and Colleagues*, 186.

29. Beverland, "The 'Real Thing,'" 251–8. For more on 'inauthentic' brands see Brown, Kozinets, and Sherry, "Teaching Old Brands New Tricks," 19–33.

30. Taylor, "The Whiskey Kings," 187–96.

31. Due to the division of powers between the federal and provincial governments, prohibition lasted longer in some provinces than in others. Prohibition was first implemented in Canada's smallest province, Prince Edward Island – where prohibition lasted the longest (1901 to 1948). Nova Scotia was the next Canadian province to jump aboard the wagon (1916 to 1930), then came Ontario (1916 to 1927), Alberta (1916 to 1924), Manitoba (1916 to 1923), Saskatchewan (1917 to 1925), New Brunswick (1917 to 1927), British Columbia (1917 to 1921) and the Yukon Territory (1918 to 1921). Newfoundland, which was not part of Canada at that time, imposed prohibition in 1917 and repealed it in 1924. Quebec's experiment with banning the sale of all alcoholic drinks, in 1919, lasted only a few months. For more on prohibition in Canada see Heron, *Booze*, 235–71.

32. For example, see Sáiz and Fernández Pérez, "Catalonian Trademarks"; Lopes, *Global Brands*; Church and Clark, "Origins of Competitive Advantage"; Fielden, *A Drink Dynasty*; Jones, *Renewing Unilever*; Koehn, *Brand New*; Wilkins, "The Neglected Intangible Asset"; Lonier, "Alchemy in Eden"; Zangger, "Chops and Trademarks"; Eeckhout and Scholliers, "The Proliferation of Brands"; Higgins and Mordhorst, "Bringing Home the 'Danish' Bacon"; Weir, "Managing Decline"; Mercer, "A Mark of Distinction"; Fernández, "Unsuccessful Responses to Quality Uncertainty"; De Munck, "The Agency of Branding.".

33. The Labatt Collection was recently donated to the University of Western Ontario Archives in London, Ontario. The collection is one of the largest corporate archives in Canada. Contained in over 2600 boxes and spanning the period 1832 to 2009, it comprises some 450 linear metres of textual documents, more than 45,000 photographs and illustrations, and almost 15,000 audio-visual items. Of particular interest to this study is the textual and graphic material in 'Series 16' on 'Brand Identity'. Included in this series are project files, working papers, market research, brand benchmark studies, selling sheets, packaging specifications, graphics manuals, as well as the correspondence of Labatt's marketing managers.

34. For most of the period from 1970 to 2000, Labatt 'Blue' was Canada's best-selling beer. But this is no longer the case. Today, Labatt 'Blue's' share of the national market is less than 5%. When AB Inbev purchased Labatt in 1995, it began throwing its weight behind Budweiser and let Labatt's former flagship brand fade away. Today Budweiser is the best-selling beer in Canada. For more on the decline of Labatt and the rest of the 'big three' see Bellamy, "I Was Canadian," 206–30.

35. Peles, "Economies of Scale," 32–7; Ackoff and Emshoff, "Advertising Research at Anheuser-Busch," 1–15; Tremblay, "Strategic Groups and the Demand for Beer," 183–98.

36. Roseman, "The Canadian Brewing Industry," 239–54; Jones, "Competition in the Canadian Beer Industry," 142–55.
37. J. H. Moore, "The Outlook for the Brewing Industry," Box A08–053-1077, *Labatt Collection*, University of Western Ontario Archives (hereafter *Labatt Collection*).
38. Lopes, "Brands and the Evolution of Multinationals," 1–30; Esteve-Pérez, "Consolidation by Merger," 209–12; Sutton, *Sunk Costs*; Gourvish and Wilson, *The British Brewing Industry*, 447–97.
39. McGahan, "The Emergence of the National Brewing Oligopoly," 229–84.
40. Ibid.
41. Greer, "The Causes of Concentration," 100; Sutton, *Sunk Costs and Market Structure*, 287–95; Tremblay and Tremblay, *The U.S. Brewing Industry*, 41–66; George, "The Growth of Television," 213–27.
42. J. H. Moore, "The Outlook for the Brewing Industry," Box A08–053-1077, *Labatt Collection*.
43. Phillips, *On Tap*, 58–61; Tucker, "Labatt's: A History," 10–39; Sneath, *Brewed in Canada*, 40–41.
44. Tucker, "Labatt's: A History," 53–129.
45. Gilmour, *Spatial Evolution of Manufacturing*, 154–8.
46. Tucker, "Labatt's: A History," 130–275; Chandler, *Scale and Scope*, 8.
47. John Labatt Limited, *Minutes*, August 26, 1957, 61.
48. The province of Newfoundland is on Canada's east coast. It did not join the Confederation until 1949.
49. Dominion Brewers' Association, *Facts on the Brewing Industry in Canada*, 32, 38.
50. *Globe and Mail*, November 17, 1953, 22.
51. Cochran, *The Pabst Brewing Company*, 72–8; McGahan, "The Emergence of the National Brewing Oligopoly," 229–84.
52. Jones, "Competition in the Canadian Beer Industry," 72.
53. E. P. Taylor, October 26, 1942, quoted in Sneath, *Brewed in Canada*, 169.
54. Roseman, "The Canadian Brewing Industry," 229.
55. Ibid., 230.
56. Ibid., 227.
57. Jake Moore, "Know Your Company," October 29, 1962, Box LATXT0039, *Labatt Collection*, 5.
58. The Northern Ontario market was protected by a Wartime Prices and Trade Board order that prohibited brewers south of the 46th parallel from selling their products in the north. See Ontario, Department of Provincial Secretary and Citizenship, *Report of the Inquiry into the Brewing Industry of Northern Ontario* (1972), 2–3.
59. For more on economies of scale in advertising see Peles, "Economies of Scale in Advertising," 32–7.
60. Peter Widdrington to D. G. McGill and N. E. Hardy, June 30, 1965, Box A08–053-603, *Labatt Collection*.
61. Heron, *Booze*, 305–6.
62. Ibid.
63. "An Awareness and Attitude Study of Alberta Breweries and Brands, vol. 2 – Analysis and Summary," Box A08–053-594, *Labatt Collection*, 7.
64. "A Review of Labatt's Position in the Saskatchewan Market" (August 1977), Box A08–057-566, *Labatt Collection*.
65. "Report of a March Research Project – Summer 1960," Box A08–053-603, *Labatt Collection*.
66. Brewer's Association of Canada, *Brewing in Canada*, 38.
67. Even after prohibition had come to an end, it was more difficult to get a 'drink' on the east coast than in any other region of Canada. Indeed, public drinking was not allowed until 1948 in Nova Scotia and not until the early 1960s in New Brunswick and Prince Edward Island. For more see Heron, *Booze*, 269–71 and Marquis, "A Reluctant Concession to Modernity," 44.
68. In 1962, total beer consumption in all the provinces and territories excluding Ontario and Quebec totalled 36.4 million litres. Brewer's Association of Canada, *Brewing in Canada*, Appendix III.
69. P. J. Henderson to B. G. Elliot, October 29, 1964, Box A08–053-603, *Labatt Collection*.
70. "Report of a March Research Project – Summer 1960," Box A08–053-603, *Labatt Collection*.

71. P. J. Henderson to N. E. Hardy, December 31, 1964, Box A08–053-603, *Labatt Collection*.
72. P. J. Henderson to B. G. Elliot, October 29, 1964, Box A08–053-603, *Labatt Collection*.
73. P. J. Henderson to N. E. Hardy, December 31, 1964, Box A08–053-603, *Labatt Collection*.
74. P. J. Henderson, "Working Document – Ontario Lager Study," October 28, 1964, Box A08–053-603, *Labatt Collection*.
75. "Highlights of Research of Significance of Alberta Marketing," Box A08–053-595, *Labatt Collection*.
76. John Compton, "Quality Control," February 19, 1963, Box LATXT0039, *Labatt Collection*.
77. "An Awareness and Attitude Study of Alberta Breweries and Brands," Box A08–053-595, *Labatt Collection*, 42.
78. "Ontario Lager Inquiry," November 5, 1964, Box A08–053-603, *Labatt Collection*.
79. "Notes on a meeting held in Toronto," July 5, 1965, Box A08–053-603, *Labatt Collection*.
80. Ibid.
81. "Research Objectives – Ontario Lager Problems – June/67," Box A08–053-603, *Labatt Collection*.
82. Iacovetta, *Gatekeepers*, 203–32.
83. "Pilsener Survey – Windsor-Welland – December 1964," Box A08–053-603, *Labatt Collection*, 2; "Pilsener Survey – Toronto – March 1965," Box A08–053-603, *Labatt Collection*, 4.
84. C. A. Stock, "What Research to Date Tells us about Pilsner," Box A08–053-603, *Labatt Collection*.
85. "Generalized Summary of Consumer Research on New Pilsener Label," May 9, 1961, Box A08-053-1252, *Labatt Collection*.
86. For more on the difference between cocktail lounges and beer parlours see Heron, *Booze*, 322–32.
87. Warsh and Marquis, "Gender, Spirits and Beer," 213–15.
88. *Toronto Courier*, January 4, 1962.
89. "Pilsener Survey – Toronto – March 1965," Box A08–053-603, *Labatt Collection*, pp. 40–41.
90. Ibid.
91. Beverland, "The 'Real Thing,'" 251–8.
92. "Pilsener Survey – Toronto – March 1965", Box A08–053-603, *Labatt Collection*, 40–41.
93. "B. W. Crow, Letter of April 7, re 'Blue' and Colour in General," Box A08–053-603, *Labatt Collection*.
94. R. C. Dill to C. A. Stock and P. J. Henderson, April, 23 1970, Box A08–053-603, *Labatt Collection*.
95. "Recommendation for a Brand Name," April 18, 1963, Box A08–053-603, *Labatt Collection*.
96. Ibid.
97. Ibid.
98. Ibid.
99. T. O. Cadham to P. J. Henderson, December 14, 1966, Box A08–053-603, *Labatt Collection*.
100. P. J. Henderson to T. O. Cadham, December 16, 1966, Box A08–053-603, *Labatt Collection*.
101. J. R. Robertson to J. W. Howell, November 9, 1964, Box A08–053-603, *Labatt Collection*.
102. At the Hudson's Bay Company, for example, the tension between regional managers and modernist corporate elites was clearly evident in the early 1960s, since traditionally the stores themselves individually controlled their advertising copy for local newspapers. See Opp, "Branding the Bay/la Baie." For a discussion of this trend in America see Jackall and Hirota, *The Image Makers*; Frank, *The Conquest of Cool*; Warlaumont, *Advertising in the 60s*. On the British scene, see Fletcher, *Powers of Persuasion*.
103. J. R. Robertson to J. W. Howell, November 9, 1964, Box A08–053-603, *Labatt Collection*.
104. Ibid.
105. N. E. Hardy to P. J. Henderson, June 1, 1967, Box A08–053-603, *Labatt Collection*.
106. "Notes on a Meeting Held in Toronto," July 5, 1965, Box A08–053-603, *Labatt Collection*.
107. M.D. Hurst, "Pros/Cons Labatt Labatt Blue (?) Brand Designation Committee Meeting," June 11, 1970, Box A08–053-603, *Labatt Collection*.
108. N. E. Hardy to P. J. Henderson, June 1, 1967, Box A08–053-603, *Labatt Collection*.
109. T. C. Fleming to P. J. Henderson, February 26, 1969, Box A08–053-603, *Labatt Collection*.
110. Brand Designation Committee, "A Working Paper – Problem Definition" (March 1970), Box A08–053-603, *Labatt Collection*.
111. Ibid.
112. Tucker, 'Labatt's: A History," 394.

113. *Wall Street Journal*, February 23, 1967, 1. Warsh and Marquis, "Gender, Spirits and Beer," 219–20.
114. "Ontario Lager Benchmark Analysis," November 29, 1971, Box A08–053-602, *Labatt Collection*, Table 47.
115. Brand Designation Committee, "Minutes of Meeting Held on 24 July 1970," Box A08–053-603, *Labatt Collection*.
116. Ibid. In Quebec, Labatt's Blue's share of the packaged lager market increased from 14% in 1965 to 52.81% in 1973.
117. "Ontario Lager Benchmark Analysis," November 29, 1971, Box A08–053-602, *Labatt Collection*, 2.
118. John Labatt Limited, "Marketing Priorities F81 and Beyond," Box A08–053-598, *Labatt Collection*.
119. John Labatt Limited, "Director's Report," June 11, 1976, Box AFC101–30, *Labatt Collection*.

Acknowledgment

I would like to thank Amanda Oliver and Bev Brereton at the Western Archives in London, Ontario for helping me locate much of the primary material for this article. I would also like to thank the editors and the anonymous readers for their insights and advice. Finally, I would like to thank Teresa da Silva Lopes, Andrew Smith and James Opp for commenting on earlier versions of this article.

Disclosure statement

No potential conflict of interest was reported by the author.

References

Aaker, D. *Building Strong Brands*. London: Simon & Schuster, 2010.
Ackoff, R., and J. Emshoff. "Advertising Research at Anheuser-Busch Inc. (1963-1968)." *Sloan Management Review* 16, no. 2 (1975): 1–15.
Balasubramanyan M. N., and M. A. Salisu. "Brands and the Alcoholic Drinks Industry." In *Adding Value: Brands and Marketing in Food and Drink*, edited by Jones and Morgan, 59–75. London: Routledge, 1994.
Barwise, P., and T. Robertson. "Brand Portfolios." *European Management Journal* 10, no. 3 (1992): 277–285.
Belasco, W., and P. Scranton. *Food Nations: Selling Taste in Consumer Societies*. New York: Routledge, 2002.
Bellamy, M. "I Was Canadian: The Globalization of the Canadian Brewing Industry." In *Smart Globalization: The Canadian Business and Economic Experience*, edited by Smith and Anastakis, 206–30. Toronto: University of Toronto Press, 2014.
Beverland, M. "The 'Real Thing': Branding Authenticity in the Luxury Wine Trade." *Journal of Business Research* 59, no. 2 (February 2006): 251–258.
Beverland, M., A. Lindgreen, and M. W. Vink. "Projecting Authenticity through Advertising: Consumer Judgments of Advertisers' Claims." *Journal of Advertising* 37, no. 1 (Spring 2008): 5–15.
Bilkey, W. J., and E. Nes. "Country-of-Origin Effects on Products Evaluations." *Journal of International Business Studies* 13, no. 1 (1982): 89–100.
Borg, E. A., and K. Gratzer. "Theories of Brands and Entrepreneurship: Conceptualizing Brand Strategies." *Annual International Conference on Business Strategy & Organizational Behaviour* (2013): 58–64.

Brewer's Association of Canada. *Brewing in Canada*. Montreal: Ronalds-Federated Ltd, 1965.

Brown, S., R. V. Kozinets, and J. F. Sherry, Jr. "Teaching Old Brands New Tricks: Retro Branding and the Revival of Brand Meaning." *Journal of Marketing* 67 (July, 2003): 19–33.

Carstairs, C. "'Roots Nationalism: Branding English Canada Cool in the 1980s and 1990s", Histoire Sociale/Social." *History* 39, no. 77 (2006): 235–255.

Casson, M. C. "Brands: Economic Ideology and Consumer Society." In *Adding Value: Brands and Marketing in Food and Drink*, edited by Jones and Morgan, 41–58. London: Routledge, 1994.

Chandler, A. *Scale and Scope: The Dynamics of Industrial Capitalism*. Cambridge, MA: Harvard University Press, 1990.

Chematony, L., and F. D. Riley. "Defining 'Brand.' *Beyond the Literature with Experts' Interpretations, Journal of Marketing Management* 14, no. 5 (1998): 417–443.

Chernatony, L., and F. D. Riley. "Modelling the Components of the Brand." *European Journal of Marketing* 32, no. 11/12 (1998): 1077–1090.

Church, R., and C. Clark. "Origins of Competitive Advantage in the Marketing of Branded Package Consumer Goods: Coleman's and Reckitt's in Early Victorian Britain." *Journal of Industrial History* 3, no. 2 (2000): 621–645.

Cochran, T. C. *The Pabst Brewing Company: History of an American Business, Westport*. CT: Greenwood Press, 1975.

De Munck, B. "The Agency of Branding and the Location of Value. Hallmarks and Monograms in Early Modern Tableware Industries." *Business History* 54, no. 7 (2012): 1055–1076.

Dominion Brewers' Association. *Facts on the Brewing Industry in Canada*. Montreal: Federated Press, 1948.

Doyle, P. "Building Successful Brands: The Strategic Options." *Journal of Marketing Management* 5, no. 1 (1989): 77–95.

Duguid, P. "Developing the Brand: The Case of Alcohol, 1800-1880." *Enterprise & Society* 4, no. 3 (2003): 405–441.

Eeckhout, P., and P. Scholliers. "The Proliferation of Brands: The Case of Food in Belgium, 1890–1940." *Enterprise & Society* 13, no. 1 (2012): 53–84.

Esteve-Pérez, S. "Consolidation by Merger: The U.K. Beer Market." *Small Business Economics* 39, no. 1 (July 2012): 209–212.

Fernández, E. "Unsuccessful Responses to Quality Uncertainty: Brands in Spain's Sherry Industry, 1920–1990." *Business History* 52, no. 1 (2010): 100–119.

Fielden, C. *A Drink Dynasty: The Suntory Story*. Throwbride: Wine Source, 1996.

Fletcher, W. *Powers of Persuasion: The inside Story of British Advertising: 1951–2000*. Oxford: Oxford University Press, 2008.

Frank, T. *The Conquest of Cool: Business Culture, Counterculture, and the Rise of Hip Consumerism*. Chicago, IL: University of Chicago Press, 1998.

Frederick, E. *Rebels and Colleagues: Advertising and Social Change in French Canada*. Montreal and Kingston: McGill-Queen's University Press, 1973.

George, L. M. "The Growth of Television and the Decline of Local Beer." In *The Economics of Beer*, edited by Johna Swinnen, 213–226. Oxford: Oxford University Press, 2011.

Gourvish, T. R., and R. G. Wilson. *The British Brewing Industry, 1830–1980*. Cambridge: Cambridge University Press, 2009.

Grayson, K., and R. Martinec. "Consumer Perceptions of Iconicity and Indexicality and Their Influence on Assessments of Authentic Market Offerings." *Journal of Consumer Research* 31 (September 2004): 296–312.

Greer, D. F. "The Causes of Concentration in the U.S. Brewing Industry." *Quarterly Review of Economics and Business* 21, no. 4 (Winter 1981): 87–106.

Guy, K. M. *When Champagne Became French: Wine and the Making of a National Identity*, Baltimore. MD: John Hopkins University Press, Baltimore, 2002.

Higgins, D. M., and M. Mordhorst. "Bringing Home the 'Danish' Bacon: Food Chains, National Branding and Danish Supremacy over the British Bacon Market, C. 1900–1938." *Enterprise & Society* 16, no. 1 (2015): 141–185.

Iacovetta, F. *Gatekeepers: Reshaping Immigrant Lives in Cold War Canada*. Toronto: Between the Lines, 2006.

Jackall, R., and J. M. Hirota. *The Image Makers: Advertising, Public Relations, and the Ethos of Advocacy.* Chicago, IL: University of Chicago Press, 2000.

Johansen, H. C. "Marketing and Competition in Danish Brewing." In *Adding Value: Brands and Marketing in Food and Drink*, edited by G. Jones and N. J. Morgan, 126–138. London, Routledge, 1994.

Jones J. C. H. "Competition in the Canadian Beer Industry." Ph.D. Dissertation, Queen's University, Canada, 1965.

Jones, G. *Renewing Unilever – Transformation and Tradition.* Oxford: Oxford University Press, 2005.

Jones, G., and N. J. Morgan, eds. *Adding Value: Brands and Marketing in Food and Drink.* London: Routledge, 1994.

Jones. G. "Brands and Marketing." In *Adding Value: Brands and Marketing in Food and Drink*, edited by G. Jones and N. J. Morgan, 1–12. London, Routledge, 1994.

King, S. H. *Developing New Brands.* Bath, UK: John Wiley and Sons, 1973.

Kohern, N. *Brand New: How Entrepreneurs Earned Consumer from Wedgewood to Dell.* Boston, Mass: Harvard University Press, 2001.

Landstörm, H., and F. T. Lohrke. *Historical Foundations of Entrepreneurship Research.* Cheltenham: Edward Elgar Publishing, 2010.

Lonier, T. "Alchemy in Eden: Entrepreneurialism, Branding, and Food Marketing in the United States, 1880–1920." *Enterprise & Society* 11, no. 4 (2010): 695–708.

Lopes, T. da Silva. *Global Brands: The Evolution of Multinationals in Alcoholic Beverage.* Cambridge: Cambridge University Press, 2007.

Lopes, T. da Silva. "Brands and the Evolution of Multinationals in Alcoholic Beverages." *Business History* 44, no. 3 (July 2002): 1–30.

Marquis, G. "'A Reluctant Concession to Modernity': Alcohol and Modernization in the Maritimes, 1945-1980." *Acadiensis* XXXII, no. 2 (Spring 2013): 31–59.

McGahan, A. M. "The Emergence of the National Brewing Oligopoly: Competition in the American Market, 1933-1958." *Business History Review* 65, no. 2 (Summer, 1991): 229–284.

Mercer, J. "A Mark of Distinction: Branding and Trade Mark Law in the UK from the 1860s." *Business History* 52, no. 1 (2010): 17–42.

Merrett D., and G. Whitwell. "The Empire Strikes Back: Marketing Australian Beer and Wine in the United Kingdom." In *Adding Value: Brands and Marketing in Food and Drink*, edited by G. Jones and N. J. Morgan, 162–190. London, Routledge, 1994.

Neatby, N., and P. Hodgins, eds. *Settling and Unsettling Memories: Essays in Canadian Public History.* Toronto: University of Toronto Press, 2012.

Nye, D. *Image Worlds: Corporate Identities at General Electric.* Cambridge, MA: MIT Press, 1985.

O'Neill, C., D. Houtman, and S. Aupers. "Advertising Real Beer: Authenticity Claims beyond Truth and Falsity." *European Journal of Cultural Studies* 17, no. 5 (October, 2014): 5–15.

Opp, J. "Branding 'The Bay/La Baie': Corporate Identity, the Hudson's Bay Company, and the Burden of History in the 1960s." *Canadian Historical Review* 96, no. 2 (June 2015): 223–256.

Peles, Y. "Economies of Scale in Advertising Beer and Cigarettes." *The Journal of Business* 44, no. 1 (January 1971): 32–37.

Peñaloza, L. "The Commodification of the American West: Marketers' Production of Cultural Meanings at the Trade Show." *Journal of Marketing* 64, no. 4 (October 2000): 82–109.

Penfold, S. *The Donut: A Canadian History.* Toronto: University of Toronto Press, 2008.

Penfold, S. "'Eddie Shack Was No Tim Horton': Donuts and the Folklore of Mass Culture in Canada." In *Food Nations: Selling Taste in Consumer Societies*, edited by W. Belasco and P. Scranton, 48–66. New York: Routledge, 2002.

Roseman, F. "The Canadian Brewing Industry: The Effect of Mergers and Provincial Regulation on Economic Conduct and Performance." Ph.D. Dissertation, Northwestern University, 1968.

Rutherford, P. *The New Icons: The Art of Television Advertising.* Toronto: University of Toronto Press, 1994.

Sáiz, P., and P. Fernández Pérez. "Catalonian Trademarks and the Development of Marketing Knowledge in Spain, 1850–1946." *Business History Review* 86 (Summer 2012): 239–260.

da Silva Lopes T., and M. Carson. "Entrepreneurship and the Development of Global Brands." *Business History Review* 81, no. 4 (Winter, 2007): 661–680.

Strasser, S. *Satisfaction Guaranteed: The Making of the American Mass Market*. Washington, DC: Smithsonian Institution Press, 1989.

Sutton, J. *Sunk Costs and Market Structure: Price Competition, Advertising, and the Evolution of Concentration*. Cambridge, MA: MIT Press, 1991.

Tremblay, V. J. "Strategic Groups and the Demand for Beer." *The Journal of Industrial Economics* 34, no. 2 (1985): 183–198.

Tremblay V. J., and C. H. Tremblay, *The U.S. Brewing Industry: Data and Economic Analysis*, Cambridge, MA: MIT Press, 2005.

Tucker, A. "Labatt's: A History – From Immigrant Family to Canadian Corporation." Unpublished manuscript in author's possession.

Wagman, I. "Peace, Order, and Good Banking: Packaging History and Memory in Canadian Commercial Advertising." In *Settling and Unsettling Memories: Essays in Canadian Public History*, edited by N. Neatby and P. Hodgins, 538–565. Toronto: University of Toronto Press, 2012.

Warlaumont, H. *Advertising in the 60s: Turncoats, Traditionalists, and Waste Makers in America's Turbulent Decade*. Westport, CT: Praeger, 2001.

Warsh, Cheryl Krasnick, and Greg Marquis. "Gender, Spirits and Beer: Representing Female and Male Bodies in Canadian Alcohol Ads, 1930s-1970s." In *Contests and Contestations: Bodies and Nations in Canadian History*, edited by J. Nichols and P. Gentile, 203–225. Toronto: University of Toronto Press, 2013.

Weir, R. B. "Managing Decline: Brands and Marketing in Two Mergers, 'The Big Amalgamation' 1925 and Guinness-DCL 1986." In *Adding Value: Brands and Marketing in Food and Drink*, edited by G. Jones and N. J. Morgan, 139–162. London: Routledge, 1994.

Wilkins, M. "The Neglected Intangible Asset: The Influence of the Trademark on the Rise of the Modern Corporation." *Business History* 34, no. 1 (1992): 66–95.

Wilson, R. "Selling Beer in Victorian Britain." In *Adding Value: Brands and Marketing in Food and Drink*, edited by G. Jones and N. J. Morgan, 103–125. London: Routledge, 1994.

Zangger, A. "Chops and Trademarks: Asian Trading Ports and Textile Branding, 1840–1920." *Enterprise & Society* 15, no. 4 (2015): 759–790.

The emergence of Italy as a fashion country: Nation branding and collective meaning creation at Florence's fashion shows (1951–1965)

Valeria Pinchera and Diego Rinallo

ABSTRACT

We analyse the emergence of Italy as a fashion country with a reconstruction of the history and impact of the collective fashion shows that Giovanni Battista Giorgini organised in Florence in 1951–1965. Our cultural analysis highlights the role events play in the mobilisation of local actors and the creation of nation brands, which we conceive as ongoing narrations built on a country's material and symbolic resources that differentiate its image in valuable ways for export markets. Despite their decline, the Florentine shows created an intangible asset that facilitated the ascent of Milan as Italy's fashion capital in the 1970s.

Introduction

'Just like the Chianti. Italy's fashions are becoming as well-known as its table wine'. That was the headline of an April 1952 article in the US magazine *Life*.[1] 'Paris has a rival', read the caption of an article in a UK magazine during the same period.[2] How could a country like Italy, so shortly after the Second World War, come to challenge Paris's (and France's) long-established fashion hegemony? Historical analyses on the emergence of Italy as a fashion country have highlighted the important role that Giovanni Battista Giorgini's collective fashion shows in Florence played in the development of a distinctly Italian fashion that provided North American department stores and consumers with an alternative to French fashion for the first time.[3] This paper extends studies on this crucial period by means of an in-depth analysis of the Giorgini archive and other data sources, which we interpret by using a conceptual framework to link together cultural views on collective marketing events and their role in nation branding.

More specifically, our study is theoretically informed by the cultural approach that has provided a theoretical basis for studies of markets for more than 30 years, and has recently also been advocated in the field of business history.[4] Our goal is to critically examine Giorgini's nation branding strategy, based on the use of the Florentine shows he organised as a promotional platform aimed at the North American market. Studies based on a cultural approach focus on the meanings and narratives key actors use to make sense of events, phenomena, organisations and their broader context. Nation branding is based on the diffusion of meanings resulting from coding and encoding processes that use selective readings of the past and which other actors often contest and contrast.[5]

In particular, in this period of Italian fashion history, the key actors were the US fashion press,[6] which supported Giorgini strongly, acting as an important source of legitimacy for his fashion shows, and the other Italian fashion organisations which, to a great extent, contrasted with Giorgini's activities. Each of these organisations, localised in different cities and representing the interests of local governments and entrepreneurial associations, engaged in concurrent nation branding initiatives and lobbied to obtain Italy's central government support. As we show in our empirical analysis and discuss in our conclusions, these concurrent efforts were detrimental to Giorgini's initiatives and fragmented the emerging Italian fashion field that could have possibly achieved more had it presented to export markets a united front. Based on these premises, our research questions are:[7] (i) What meanings did Giorgini attribute to the emerging Italian fashion? (ii) How did the US media interpret the emerging Italian fashion? And (iii) how did contemporaneous Italian fashion organisations react to Giorgini's initiatives? Beyond the specificities of the empirical context and the historical period investigated, our underlying research question is: what role do collective events play in the mobilisation of local actors and the creation of nation brands?

From a methodological point of view, our study is mostly based on data from the Giorgini Archive of Italian Fashion, which contains over 12,000 records, including press clippings (mostly from US and Italian newspapers and magazines), press releases, promotional materials, letters, pictures and other miscellaneous sources covering 29 editions of the collective fashion shows that Giorgini organised and supervised between 1951 and 1965. We combined data from the Giorgini archive with additional material collected from the Archive of the Florence Chamber of Commerce, the Archive of 1900s Fashion (Archivi della Moda del '900), the Pitti Immagine Archive and relevant audio-visual documents from the Istituto Luce and the Rai Teche. While our account emerges from our data gathering and analysis activities, we selectively integrated findings from other published accounts of fashion history in the period under investigation. This enabled us to better reconstruct the context in which the emergence of Italian fashion occurred and to enrich our findings with data from different sources.

Our research findings show that, for the first time, Giorgini's nation branding strategies created a widespread perception of Italy as a country of fashion creators. By promoting frequent interaction with foreign buyers and media, driving innovation efforts, adapting the latter to evolving market conditions and manifesting the intangible meanings that were associated with emergent Italian fashion in a tangible form, the fashion shows Giorgini organised provided a focal point for the collective action of Italian couturiers and other sectors of the Italian fashion system (e.g. leather, textiles, shoes and millinery). As Belfanti also highlights, a key theme in Giorgini's nation branding strategy was the (historically inaccurate) narrative that Italian fashion was the direct heir of the Renaissance craftsmanship tradition.[8] This narrative played a major role in defining and legitimising Italian fashion in foreign markets (notably, the US), but it only had limited effects on bringing Italian couturiers together in a unitary export-promotion project. As we demonstrate in this article, tensions rose among groups of couturiers based in different parts of Italy and eventually contributed to the demise of the Florentine fashion shows.

The rest of this article is structured as follows. First, we propose a conceptual framework that links place branding with meaning creation and the uses of history in the context of collective events such as Giorgini's fashion shows. We continue with a contextual analysis of Italy before the 1950s, in which we compare Italy's attempts to create a national fashion during the Fascist regime against the backdrop of French haute couture and its key organisation, the *Chambre Syndicale de la Couture Française*. Subsequently, to better set the background of our analysis, we describe the Turin, Milan and Rome-based organisations that acted as rivals of Giorgini's nation branding activities and, to some extent, undermined these activities' results. Having described the context, we provide an in-depth analysis of Giorgini's promotional strategies and an account of these strategies' reception in the US press and by internal stakeholders. We conclude with a discussion of our findings, which offers a more nuanced view of the decline of Florence as Italy's fashion capital and subsequent developments.

Our theory-informed analyses allow our study to contribute to previous accounts of this crucial period in Italian fashion history by linking together Giorgini's promotional strategies and uses of the past, their external reception by foreign media, and domestic competition with other Italian fashion organisations. To the best of our knowledge, ours is the first attempt to examine the emergence of Italian history by means of a theoretical framework linking nation branding with the creation of a 'made in Italy' intangible asset (a collective nation brand) that, long after the demise of Giorgini's Florentine shows, contributed to the international affirmation of Italian pret-à-porter in the late 1970s and 1980s.[9] Moving beyond our empirical context, our longitudinal study contributes to the literature on nation branding by shedding light on the features and dynamics of promotional strategies based on collective marketing events.

Nation branding, narration, and collective marketing events

Most studies of fashion, including traditional business history analyses, have examined the socio-cultural and economic contexts that provided the conditions for the emergence – and subsequent development – of national fashion industries characterised by a distinct style.[10] Khaire, however, recently noted that studies on fashion history have not sufficiently examined how the actions of key actors contribute to creating an identity for the industry.[11] In this article, following the lead of Khaire and others who have contributed to highlighting the role of key actors in fashion history,[12] we focus on Giovanni Battista Giorgini. We examine how the collective fashion shows that he organised in the 1951–1965 period strengthened the outside recognition of Italy as a fashion country. Beyond Giorgini, our analysis also follows two other important actors in the period under investigation: the foreign media and the other Italian fashion organisations that competed with Giorgini, eventually contributing to the end of the Florentine fashion shows.

Nation branding activities such as those developed by Giorgini are typically carried out by trade associations, export-promotion agencies and other collective actors with the goal of developing a positive nation image and successfully transferring it to its export.[13] Consumers often consider country of origin as an indicator of product quality and they might even pay a premium price for products from countries that have a good reputation in a specific product category.[14] By building or reinforcing country-of-origin effects, nation brand-ing initiatives support the development of intangible assets that all firms from a given coun-try can exploit.

Most nation branding approaches are built on already-existing national stereotypes, which can be an advantage in international markets; for example, France's long-established association with taste and luxury, Germany's superior technology and Italy's recognised product aesthetics. However, in her critique of these approaches, Hansen suggests that place branding is best understood as the construction of powerful narratives that create resonant cultural meanings about a country and its products.[15] In other words, meaning is not inherent in a place, but rather culturally produced by carefully selecting (from among countless alter-natives) those narratives that have the potential to be more persuasive for foreign target markets. Thus, nation branding is about telling stories about a country by using a self-ro-manticizing mix of fact and fiction that is both credible and effective in generating favourable symbolic meanings. Narratives constructed around the past can therefore serve as strategic resources that frame the way relevant audiences view the country.[16]

There are various strategies that can be used to promote a country's image. In this paper, we focus on collective marketing events that bring together, albeit for a limited period of time, numerous suppliers who present their offer to buyers, the media, and other purchase influencers. Trade shows are the most studied among such collective marketing events. Economists consider these events as transaction cost-saving institutions, because by locating those actors representing the supply and demand in the same time and space, they can significantly reduce the costs that buyers incur when searching for suitable suppliers.[17] Most marketing literature on these events focuses on individual suppliers ('exhibitors' in the con-text of trade shows) and provides insight on how to maximise their returns on investments.[18]

More recently, a new generation of studies has looked at the broader effects of these events on their underlying industries. In marketing, scholars have looked at the ritual nature of these events, which are meeting places for professional communities and key sites for meaning generation and public memory.[19] In organisation studies, a stream of research on 'field-configuring events' suggests that these events can affect the innovation trajectories of underlying industries.[20] Building on a knowledge-based view of the firm and of territorial agglomeration, economic geography has reinterpreted trade fairs and other events as tem-porary clusters where forms of organised proximity between suppliers and buyers provide platforms for observation and interaction that accelerate learning and innovation.[21] Research on temporary clusters also highlights various functions of these events, two of which are particularly important in the context of our study.[22] First, by highlighting the history of the national industry and educating the market about the key functional and/or symbolic dif-ferences in product quality, trade shows and other collective events can be utilised as stra-tegic tools to generate meaning. Secondly, local trade show organisers, supported by local governments and industry actors, often compete against each other; this leads to smaller events that are ill-suited to attracting foreign buyers and generate confusion in the market.

In this paper, we build on these conceptual developments with respect to the culture-producing function of collective events and their role in nation branding. We suggest that the Giorgini organised fashion shows were instrumental in creating an internationally recog-nised Italian fashion. Fashion shows are promotional events specific to the fashion field, originating from the practices adopted by French couturiers, who employed 'mannequins' (in-house models) to show clients their latest creations.[23] By 1910, these practices had evolved into 'fashion parades' – scheduled events, repeated every day over the course of a few weeks, where mannequins modelled the new couture collection sequentially. By 1918, fashion houses started organising their fashion shows on fixed dates to facilitate the travels of foreign buyers, which was the start of organised collection presentations, known today as fashion weeks.

Contrary to trade shows, which are collective exhibitions based on the display of products that clients can physically examine, fashion shows are spectacular events that, since their origins, have been inspired by the world of performing arts.[24] Both fashion weeks and trade shows, however, are collective promotional events where suppliers meet buyers. The organisers of these events coordinate the promotional initiatives of the participating suppliers by providing their product presentations with temporal or spatial order: spatially, in the case of trade shows, by arranging the exhibitors in the exhibition layout; temporally, in the case of fashion weeks, by arranging fashion shows according to the calendar, that is, at a specific day and time. Literature on these events can therefore be aptly employed to make sense of the role that the Giorgini organised fashion shows played in the emergence of Italy as a fashion country.

Antecedents: The supremacy of Paris and Italy's fascist-era emancipatory attempts

For most of French fashion history, dressmakers were skilled artisans who did not create original styles, but instead fashioned garments based on their client's specifications.[25] New styles, originating from elite women who, due to their exquisite taste and social status, served as opinion leaders, were diffused by means of the French and international fashion press.[26] The first couturier (in the modern sense of the term) was an Englishman residing in Paris, Charles Frederick Worth (1825–1895), who opened his highly successful *maison de couture* in 1858.[27] Self-portraying as artists and arbiters of taste, Worth and the other couturiers, who soon established their fashion houses in Paris, became the ultimate fashion authorities, imposing their views on how women should be dressed.[28]

Only ten years later, couturiers funded the *Chambre Syndicale de la Couture Française*, whose goal was to promote individual couture houses and Parisian couturiers as a collective. The members earned the right to label themselves a *maison de couture* by adhering to strict quality requirements. The *Chambre Syndicale* played a key role in the organisation of haute couture, educating the workforce, protecting its members against mutual threats, lobbying public authorities, organising the fashion show calendar, and jointly promoting the sector in the domestic and international market.[29] French haute couture, located in Paris, was therefore internationally recognised, well-organised and cast its cumbersome shadow over foreign emancipatory attempts.

The idea of creating recognisably Italian fashion had circulated since the country's unification in the 1860s, but it was only in the 1920s and 1930s, with the advent of Fascism, that serious attempts started to be made in this direction. With its political project of developing an independent cultural identity, the Fascist regime tried to persuade Italians to avoid French fashion in favour of dresses and accessories based on traditional regional clothing. In 1932, the Ente Autonomo per la Mostra Nazionale Permanente della Moda (EAMNPM, Authority for the Permanent National Fashion Exhibition) was established in Turin with the goal of nationalising Italian fashion production by means of a biannual national fashion show and exhibition taking place in spring and autumn.[30] Given the institution's limited impact regarding changing Italian consumers' and dressmakers' reliance on Parisian couture, a new law modified the constitution of the Ente Autonomo in the second half of 1935. The institution was renamed Ente Nazionale Moda (ENM, National Fashion Authority) and given broad powers to grant an Italian 'guarantee label' (marca di garanzia) to dressmakers. Nevertheless, the extremely bureaucratic process, the focus on the internal market and the lack of business logic compromised its operations severely.[31]

Under the new regime, dressmakers had to declare their activities to the Authority and mark at least 25% of their models with a label attesting to the design and production's 'Italianness'. To do so, they needed to send the Authority, at their expense, a photo and fabric sample of each model, as well as pay a fee for each item granted the label. Tradespeople considered the entire top-down process questionable. How could the Authority staff judge fashion items by merely looking at photos? Indeed, the Authority granted most of the products requesting one, including low quality ones, a *marca* (label). In 1939, a new law determined that the *marca d'oro* (golden label) would only be granted to Italian haute couture houses. Despite these attempts, most dressmakers continued to take inspirations from French collections. In a first phase, even women's magazines kept reporting on Paris fashions, lamenting the unavailability of photos of Italian fashion products, which the Authority – required to protect dressmakers' intellectual property – was unwilling to provide.

In sum, the Authority, backed by the Italian government, adopted a top-down approach to rid Italian fashion of French influences. They left creative decisions in the hands of Italian dressmakers and tailors who, working in small ateliers and producing handmade items, worked in isolation, never engaging in the kind of cooperative efforts that would have made a recognisable unitary Italian fashion possible.[32] In addition, the Authority made no significant effort to promote Italian fashion internationally. Nonetheless, the Authority's import-discouraging activities stimulated the development of 'autarchic' textiles and materials, which would later play a role in the development of Italian fashion.

The lack of a commonly recognised Italian style did not mean that Italian dressmakers were not internationally acknowledged, in the pre-Giorgini era. The Roman dressmaker and artist Maria Monaci Gallenga received the Grand Prix in 1925 at the International Exposition of Decorative and Industrial Arts in 1925, eventually opening an atelier in the centre of Paris.[33] International markets also appreciated Italian (especially Florentine) artisanal leather accessories and footwear, which was mostly due to the achievements of Salvatore Ferragamo and Guccio Gucci. Ferragamo, after a long and successful period in Hollywood, where he had established himself as the shoemaker to the stars, returned to Italy in 1927. He opened a workshop in Florence for the artisanal production of high-quality women's shoes, which rapidly attracted a noteworthy international clientele, including royals and actresses.[34] In 1937, the American fashion magazine *Vogue* honoured Ferragamo's ability and creative genius by calling him 'the wonderful little shoemaker of Florence'.[35] Gucci started in 1921 as a producer of equestrian-inspired leather luggage. By the mid-1930s, he had extended his business to bags, wallets and belts. Owing to the word-of-mouth of foreign tourists visiting Florence and Rome, where the company opened its second shop in 1938, he soon had an international reputation.[36]

In the immediate aftermath of the Second World War, American consumers had more chances to notice and appreciate Italian products. Several factors facilitated this exposure, including the economic recovery of Italy stimulated by the American financial support (initially by the United Nations Relief and Rehabilitation Administration [UNRRA] and then, from 1948, by the European Recovery Program [Marshall Plan]).[37] The re-opening of the international trade and the development of tourism also contributed to the exposure. The supply of wool and cotton yarns obtained in the context of the UNRRA aid programme, meant that the production of Italian knitwear had recovered, as early as in 1947. Firms such as Luisa Spagnoli and, from 1949 Laura Aponte, Marisa Arditi and Mirsa by Olga di Grésy exported their knitwear (to the US, but also to UK).[38] Clothes designed by Simonetta (nobly born as Simonetta Visconti di Cesarò) in Rome were featured in a two-page fashion spread in the US edition of *Vogue* in 1947. The same year, Neiman Marcus, the US luxury department store, bestowed its prestigious award on Ferragamo. The following year, the winter edition of *Harper's Bazaar* fashion magazine published an article with four pictures of the women's ski outfits that marquis Emilio Pucci had created.[39] The presence of US movie stars in Rome, whose Cinecittà studios made it 'the Hollywood on the Tiber', also provided the city's tailors and dressmakers with an opportunity to gain international fame.

During this time, however, the popularity of the limited number of Italian couturiers and accessory producers did not play a particularly strong role in spreading the idea of Italy as a country of fashion creations. While there were established fashion houses with solid technical skills and a local reputation, they were still dependent on Parisian models, which they adapted to Italian consumers' tastes by simplifying the cuts and decorations that Italian women would have considered excessive or even ridiculous.[40] Pucci, Ferragamo, and Simonetta were therefore outliers – exceptions to the rule that fashion was French. Their international notoriety was the result of their individual promotional efforts, rather than an organised collective action. The media treated them as individuals, rather than as specific manifestations of an Italian style characterised by common characteristics. A recognised 'made in Italy' collective brand, while building on these antecedents, had yet to be created.

Creating Italian fashion: Many contenders fighting each other

After the end of the Second World War, in Italy, various local organisations attempted concurrently to organize and promote Italian fashion internationally. These organisations were located in different cities, all of which had the ambition to become Italy's fashion capital. This resulted in conditions quite different from those that, 90 years before, had facilitated the collective organisation of haute couture in France: the co-localisation of all haute couture houses in the same city and the establishment of a single organisation representing the interest of the entire couture field. To better understand the background of our analysis of Giorgini's activities, we describe the Italian fashion organisations active in the period 1945–1951.

The Ente Italiano Moda (EIM, Italian Fashion Authority), building on the heritage of the almost homonymous Fascism-era Ente Nazionale Moda, was established in Turin in 1945, soon after the end of the Second World War. The city of Turin and the local industry actors strongly supported the re-foundation of the Ente, albeit for different reasons.[41] The Chamber of Commerce and the Industrial Union sustained the Ente financially and felt its activities would benefit the textile industry, which was important for Piedmont's economy. Count Dino Lora Totino of Cervinia (1900–1980), from an old family of wool manufacturers in Biella (an important wool processing district in Piedmont), was the first President of the Ente.[42] The general manager was Vladimiro Rossini, who had fulfilled the same function at the previous Fascist-era fashion authority and remained in office until November 1970, playing a key role in the Ente's direction as well as in Italian fashion. In October 1946, the Ente organised its first National Exhibition of Fashion Art in Turin's Royal Palace. A total of 75 Italian fashion houses (and a few French ones), including some of the most important Italian dressmakers from Rome (Fontana and Antonelli) and Milan (Biki, Fiorani and Vanna) participated in the Exhibition.

In 1949, a second fashion organisation appeared in Milan, the Centro Italiano Moda (Italian Fashion Centre). This organisation, 'the Lombard response to the Turin's authority'[43] was aimed at coordinating all Italian fashion activities, whose 'dispersion' was 'without any doubt the greatest obstacle to its expansion in Italy and outside Italy.'[44] Franco Marinotti (1891–1966), headed the Centre as well as being the President of SNIA Viscosa (Società Nazionale Industria e Applicazioni Viscosa, the National Rayon Manufacturing and Application Company).[45] Milan was regarded 'as the city of commerce, of industries, of international exchanges, of practical sense, of speed,'[46] which motivated the choice of this Lombard city as the Centre's headquarters. The city was thought to provide the best context to facilitate achieving the new organisation's goals. Through its interlocking directorate with SNIA Viscosa, the organisation also guaranteed the link to Italy's textile industry.

Despite being located in Milan, the Centre organised promotional activities in other cities, which served as effective commercial showcases for Italy's fashion. In April 1949, the Centre organised a show in Rome, during which 15 high fashion houses from Milan, Rome and Florence presented their models to the public at the Opera Theatre.[47] In September 1949 and 1950, the Centre also organised a Fashion Festival in Venice, to benefit from the international attendance and media visibility of the city's International Film Festival. In the years that followed, the Centro Internazionale delle Arti e del Costume (CIAC, International Centre for the Arts and Costume) – a separate organisation, but with strong links to the Milanese' Centre, continued to organise Venice's Fashion Festival. Franco Marinotti founded the Venetian Centre in 1951 and his son, Paolo Marinotti directed it. The Milanese Centre also organised commercial missions abroad, the first of which was in Zurich (April 1950) with the presentation of the collections of some of Italy's most important creators (including Antonelli, the Fontana sisters, Marucelli, Simonetta Visconti and Veneziani).

In 1949, the founding in Rome of a new organisation further complicated the map of the emerging Italian fashion field. Earlier in the year, on 27 January, the Roman wedding of the American stars Tyrone Power and Linda Christian had cast an international spotlight on Rome's haute couture:[48] the bride's wedding gown was a creation of the Fontana sisters, while the Roman tailors Brioni and Caraceni had dressed the groom. In May 1949, Rome's Chamber of Commerce organised the First Fashion National Congress, which paved the way for the constitution of the Comitato della Moda (CM, Fashion Committee), on 5 November. The Committee's goal was to 'strengthen and increase the productive activities to the maximum' and 'maintain constant and active relationships with all national and foreign fashion centres for the technical, artistic and professional development of the national production.'[49] Despite its ambitious goals, the CM had appeared on an already crowded and conflictual scene, with constrained margins for manoeuvring, thus limiting its activity.

To sum up, in the years following the Second World War, various Italian organisations attempted to concurrently coordinate Italian fashion, based on different constituencies, interests and resources. Located in different cities, these organisations engaged in collective promotional activities requiring the support of fashion houses in other parts of the country. On 17 February 1951, the Italian Government recognised Turin's Authority and granted it 'specific responsibility regarding the subject of fashion and clothing' under the supervision of the Minister of Trade and Industry,[50] thus acquiring a position of supremacy over the other organisations. This was the context that the marquis Giovanni Battista Giorgini (1898–1971) faced when his activities added Florence to the Italian fashion map.

Giorgini's nation branding strategy

Claims that the day that Giorgini organised his first collective Italian fashion shows in Florence (12 February 1951) marks the birth of Italian fashion might be exaggerated given the various promotional initiatives that had already occurred after the end of Second World War. However, this event did represent a turning point in the emancipation of Italy from French inspirations, in the stabilisation of relationships with North American buyers and media, and in the diffusion of a coherent symbolism that could be superimposed on the material elements of the collections presented on Italy's catwalks. Having been an independent resident buyer of Italian (especially Tuscan) craftsmanship for some prominent US department stores since 1923, Giorgini had extensive first-hand knowledge of the North American market. Between 1944 and 1946 he managed a gift shop for the Allied troops in the centre of Florence.[51] It was during this time that he started thinking about promoting Italian production on the international market. The first step toward this goal was an exhibition that he conceived and arranged, entitled 'Italy at work. Her Renaissance in Design Today'. It opened in November 1950 at the Brooklyn Museum in New York City and represented a first, positive test of the idea of promoting Italy's contemporary productions by linking them to the Italian Renaissance.[52]

Giorgini identified clothing as the most suitable Italian product for export to the United States. In November 1950, Giorgini, using his wide-ranging knowledge of the North American market and extensive network, sent out formal invitations to some of the most important North American buyers (including Bergdorf Goodman of New York, I. Magnin of San Francisco and Henry Morgan of Montreal) to attend the 'First Italian High Fashion Show' in Florence. The invitation consisted of a card decorated with a reproduction of Raphael's 'Portrait of Maddalena Strozzi' and the lily symbol of Florence, along with an English-language brochure on the history of Italian fashion and its artistic tradition.[53] Having secured an audience, Giorgini convinced a group of Italian dressmakers to take part in the initiative, with the recommendation that they present only Italian-inspired creations in order to prove the 'original excellence of the Italian fashion tradition':

> In the interest of the houses themselves, it is a categorical condition that the designs that will be presented be of pure and exclusive Italian inspiration. In this first show next February, it will not be easy to have many American buyers attending, as they are convinced that Italian fashion is derived from Paris [...] It is therefore up to us to demonstrate that Italy, which through the centuries has always been an authority in the field of fashion, has retained its genius and can still create with genuine spirit.[54]

The first Italian collective fashion show took place in Giorgini's palatial residence, Villa Torrigiani, immediately after the Parisian shows. In the presence of six of the important American buyers and five fashion reporters, a group of 13 Italian couturiers from Milan, Rome and Florence displayed their creations, for a total of 180 different models.[55] Despite the limited audience, the event found enormous resonance, principally due to well-known journalists' flattering accounts in the most important international (especially US) newspapers and fashion magazines. The second edition of the Florentine fashion show in July 1951 marked the definitive consecration, as the number of Italian couturiers in attendance increased from 13 to 15 and the number of models shown grew from 180 to 700. More importantly, the participation of buyers rose sharply: from six to more than 300, which required moving the show to a larger venue, Florence's Grand Hotel.[56] Given the city of Florence's support, Giorgini was able to relocate the shows to the White Hall (Sala Bianca) of the Palazzo Pitti, a (mainly) Renaissance palace previously owned by the Medici family and the former residence of the grand dukes of Tuscany, in July 1952.

Giorgini's nation branding strategy was multifaceted and remarkably innovative in comparison with those adopted by the other Italian fashion promotion organisations. First, in terms of product mix, he successfully differentiated Italy's fashion offer from that of France. As previously noted, Giorgini required the participating fashion houses to present original models without a trace of French influence. Conversely, the other Italian fashion organisations did not constrain the creativity of the houses participating in their promotional initiatives. Furthermore, Giorgini not only included producers of haute couture in his shows, but also houses specialising in the so-called boutique fashion – high-quality artisanal ready-to-wear clothing characterised by being casual and sporty, for example knitwear, blouses, pants and jumpsuits.[57] Boutique fashion had attracted the attention of American department stores since the late 1940s, and was an original element of the emerging Italian offer.[58] Finally, Giorgini invited producers of complementary items, including accessories (bags, hats, gloves, shoes, bijouterie). Presented as such, Italian fashion was intended to be more wearable and suited to American consumers than its French counterpart.

Secondly, the fashion shows' format was designed to facilitate the audience's selection of models to buy or write about. The Florentine catwalks were collective in kind, as they adopted a 'unique runway' system. In other words, instead of having buyers and journalists move from one atelier to the next in a stressful and exhausting tour de force as they did in Paris, fashion creators would present their collections one after another on the same runway and in front of a seated (and more relaxed) audience. As a result of this innovation format, the fashion show programme was arranged according to product categories (e.g. haute couture, boutique fashion, etc.). Giorgini also limited the number of designs each house could present (60 models for high fashion, 20 for boutique collections). The reason for this limit was time management, but it also compelled fashion houses to showcase only their best proposals and prevented the long, repetitive and, to some extent, boring presentations that were the norm in Paris.[59] Buyers and the media, tired of the opulence and mannerism of French couturiers, immediately took to the new formula.[60]

Finally, at the symbolic level, Giorgini insisted on presenting Italy's fashion as one founded on the Renaissance tradition. Such was the strength of France's long-held association with fashion that a powerful origin myth was required to legitimise Italy as a country of fashion creators. Florence's historical, artistic and architectural heritage provided the material and symbolic bases to infuse the collections showcased at the Pitti Palace with resonant cultural meanings.[61] First, the physical environment of the city of Florence, as well as the venues for the fashion shows and ancillary events, contributed to making the link between Italian fashion and the Renaissance tangible and credible. After the shows, buyers would go to the

Palazzo Strozzi for negotiations with the fashion houses. In the evenings, they would attend receptions, balls and parades that often had a historical theme and were organised in suggestive venues. For example, in January 1953 Giorgini organised a re-enactment of the wedding of Eleonora de' Medici and Vincenzo Gonzaga in the Palazzo Vecchio in January 1953, with actors chosen from Florence's aristocratic families.[62] Fashion models were often photographed inside or against the backdrop of the palaces and gardens of Florence's nobles. Many of the fashion creators belonged to the Italian aristocracy, including Emilio Pucci (a marquis), Tessitrice dell'Isola (the baroness Clarette Gallotti) and Mirsa (the marquise Olga di Grésy).[63] Giorgini's public relations with the media and buyers, based on extensive personal correspondence and missions abroad, often leveraged the links Italian fashion had with the Renaissance and aristocracy. For example, in February 1956 he organised a two-week journey to New York City on the cruise ship Cristoforo Colombo to present the latest Italian fashion creation with eight mannequins from noble families – an initiative that was really successful with the American media.[64]

Having ensured that Florence would be a stop on buyers' grand tour in Europe, Giorgini tried to stabilise the initiative. First, to obtain institutional and financial support, he built relationships with the EIM and the leading Italian textile companies of the period (Italviscosa, Cotonificio Val di Susa and Lanificio Rivetti). In 1953 and 1954 these companies co-sponsored the Pitti fashion shows, providing financial support, respectively, of $8,000 and $12,800 for each of them.[65] When these actors failed to renew their sponsorship, Giorgini secured the financial support of the local stakeholders – the Municipality of Florence, the local Chamber of Commerce and Industrial Association, and the Tourist Board – providing varying contributions of between $24,000 and $32,000 per year.[66] In 1954, these actors also helped Giorgini create the Centre of Florence for Italian Fashion (Centro di Firenze per la Moda Italiana), which assumed the responsibility for organising the Florentine fashion shows and promoting Italian fashion.

During these years, Giorgini continued to broaden and adapt the content of the fashion shows to follow evolving market needs and emerging opportunities. From July 1954 onwards, he brought in new artisanal businesses by setting up an Accessory Exhibition at the Grand Hotel. In later years, he introduced new fashion categories, such as the earliest models of prêt-à-porter (1956), teenager fashion (1962) and lingerie (1964), as well as securing the presence of new designers such as Lancetti (1961) and Valentino (1962) for haute couture, and Ken Scott (1962), Krizia and Mila Schön (both 1965) for boutique fashion.[67] As the market evolved, Giorgini gradually shifted the focus of the Pitti presentations to boutique and sportswear fashion and ended up changing their name from 'High Italian Fashion Show' to 'Italian Fashion Show' in January 1961. Finally, in January 1963, he admitted Italian buyers that had previously been excluded, as the models presented in Florence were expressly designed for international markets.[68]

In the second half of the 1950s, the number of buyers and press at the Pitti fashion shows increased considerably, reaching 600 people from 13 countries in 1959, although the figure mainly comprised German and US buyers.[69] Between the end of the 1950s and the beginning of the 1960s, the number of fashion houses participating in the Pitti fashion shows rose significantly, as did the clothing designs presented to 2,000–3,000 models. Nevertheless, the other Italian fashion organisations' competitive moves, which resulted in the withdrawal of some well-known haute couture and boutique fashion designers, undermined the prominence and the image of the Pitti fashion shows. Before turning to these difficulties, we analyse the external reception of Italian fashion and the way in which the media interpreted Giorgini's nation branding.

External reception: Foreign media interpretations of Italian fashion

The press are important gatekeepers whose role in fashion history has been at the centre of various analyses.[70] In this section, we highlight how the foreign press contributed to Giorgini's nation branding by reinforcing his narratives and linking them to some of the more favourable of Italy's established national stereotypes (e.g. Italy's creativity and *joie de vivre* – instead of, say, laziness and organised crime).[71] Our analysis also highlights that not only were the fashion media instrumental in promoting the emerging Italian fashion to North American retailers and consumers, but they also provided – for Giorgini and individual couturiers – important feedback on what the North American market appreciated. In line with findings from literature on field-configuring events and temporary clusters,[72] the Florentine shows provided opportunities to learn from the market and, through this mechanism, influence the innovation trajectories of the emerging Italian fashion field.

The North American press, confronted with the task of reporting on emerging Italian fashion, engaged in extensive descriptions and evaluations, often in comparative terms: that is, by showing the key points that distinguished it from French fashion, which was more familiar to them and their readers. What follows is the result of a qualitative content analysis highlighting the most frequently recurring elements employed to qualify Italian fashion. Most observers focused on the products themselves and their material attributes: the superior fabrics, considered 'among the best in the world', the excellent craftsmanship ('the fine Italian hand'), the new combination of colours, the innovative designs of boutique garments and the beautiful accessories. The US press also noted that the prices of Italian fashion products were significantly lower than those of their French counterparts:

> Why do buyers and private customers flock to Italy? The prosaic fact is that Italian fabrics are of the most tempting quality. Also a frock in Italy costs about a third of the French price. Also the perfection of main d'oeuvre allows great variety in trimming and most especially embroidery.[73]

To better understand the impact of Italian's fashion quality/price ratio, one has to consider how the luxury and exclusiveness meanings associated with French fashion were attributed to a wide range of market offerings in North America. Christian Dior, which had the most extended product portfolio in the US, is a case in point.[74] American buyers could choose between an 'original' Dior dress made in France; a Dior dress made in the US by Dior-New York, specifically designed to appeal to American women; licensed copies by luxury retailers (such as Ohrbach's, Macy's and Gimbels), reproduced in original materials but often adapted for practical reasons and to suit American consumers' tastes; and unauthorised imitations from local manufacturers sold for a few dollars, which specific Dior models nevertheless inspired.[75] This situation was confusing for the market and specifically for elite women, who risked ending up wearing dresses remarkably similar to those their husbands' secretaries wore.

While the average price of a Parisian haute couture daytime dress was about $500, the Italian prices ranged from $90 to $150 for haute couture dresses and from $12 to $48 for boutique garments.[76] The licensed reproductions that department stores sold, which could be easily confused with unauthorised knock-offs, could not compete with the prices of the 'original' boutique products that came directly from Italy. Examples of such products were the sweaters and cardigans by Mirsa, which the American department store I. Magnin sold for between $12.95 and $18.95; the 'puffy playsuit' by Simonetta, which was available at Bergdorf Goodman for $40 and the stripped cotton shirt by Cosetta Innocenti, which was priced as little as $3.[77] The affordable prices of Italian fashion, along with a favourable lira–dollar exchange rate (625 lira for a US dollar) allowed US buyers to buy the original models, especially the boutique collections, thus eliminating (at least at the outset) the need for copies or adaptations of French haute couture creations.[78] Furthermore, direct imports of Italian fashion products allowed American consumers to experience the purchase of original garments in the 'easy casual' Italian style and appreciate their high quality stitching and fabrics.[79]

On a broader front, the US press realised that Italian fashion was different from its French counterpart because the collections' overall wearability was simpler, more modern and characterised by a more casual and innovative style (especially regarding sportswear). The collections also served different functions, which were more in line with US women's needs.

> Italian style [is] less extreme than those of French designers, more adapted to requirements of American women – Italians design for individuals [...] they look at woman herself and attempt to dress her, rather than put her into a creation dreamed up for art's sake only.[80]

To boost sales, some of the most important US department stores, including I. Magnin, Gimbels and Bergdorf Goodman, promoted their newly introduced boutique fashion collections through fashion shows and large advertising campaigns directed at the press. These promotions helped spread the image of Italy as a fashion country as much as France, as well as making the made in Italy label a legitimate alternative to the made in France label.[81]

Beyond product attributes and their functional benefits, the media characterised these fashion proposals at the symbolic level as 'completely Italian',[82] that is, as stemming from specific elements of Italy's pre-existing image:

> Italy is a country where good wine, and warm hearts abound, has given the world its art inspiration for centuries [...] Like the Italian sun rich things are plentiful here, Palatial rooms, servants, flowers, wine, carriages and rich silks are as abundant as the grape, and the opulence of Italian living is manifest in the magnificent clothes that we along the visiting world press have seen [...] Italy's clothes, like the country itself, are most 'bellissima'. Since this is only the second time this country has shown its great soul to the world, it makes one anticipate all that is to come from this land of art.[83]

At the same time, negative stereotypes about Italy were rarely remembered in this early phase, and if they were recalled they were debunked as pre-conceived ideas that did not fit with the image emerging from Italy's fashions:

> Everything that Italy had to offer converged in Florence [...] Let's hope that the myth of Italian laziness will at last be added to the dustheap of bromidic fallacies! For this marvellous taste is accompanied by great industry as is apparent in the beauty of the materials shown.[84]

Overall, the Giorgini promotional activities supported the idea of continuity between the past glories of Italy's fashions:

> Centuries of elegance and good taste distinguish Italian fashion. Fourteenth-century Tuscan elegance, the Italian Renaissance, seventeenth-century pomp and luxury, eighteenth-century Venetian refinement spread all over Europe and it was then reputed fashionable and smart to dress in the Italian way.[85]

Following Giorgini's storytelling, observers kept on remarking that the country's historical heritage inspired Italian fashion. By linking the products' characteristics with the presence of a 'genius loci' (that is, the spirit of the place) these cultural intermediaries were forging a cognitive link between the emerging Italian fashion and desirable benefits such as elegance and good taste, in their audience:

> Italy is a country of skilled artisans and the encouragement of native crafts was the surest way of attracting foreign visitors to buy from an inexhaustible market of fine goods […] But, after all, there is another very simple explanation for this tremendous vitality and inventiveness. They may well be due to the fact that the Italian people have such a rich heritage of visual beauty. What goes to make up the life of this lovely land seems to have been handed down from generation to generation and the habit of living in beautiful surroundings tends to give every Italian an instinctive talent for harmonious design.[86]

More generally, the availability of an alternative to Paris at a significantly lower price raised doubts regarding to whether the high prices of French fashion were justified, which led to the polarisation of trades people's opinions:

> There are two schools of thought on the high prices of the models. One group is of the opinion that Paris is pricing itself out of the market. This contingent also points to the fact that many of the couturiers have tieups with American manufacturers to produce a special line. They say this has the tendency to take away some of the value of their purchases. The second group feels that Paris is the inspirational center for the fashion business and that the creator is worth the price he is getting. They accent the ingenuity of the couturier and the cost of making the creation as justifying the asking price. It is noted that the prices of the Italian […] creations are quite a bit lower but purchasers say that it is as yet a secondary high-style market compared to Paris.[87]

Put another way, and keeping literature on country-of-origin effects in mind, Paris was still the top of the ideal world fashion capitals' hierarchy. It commanded higher premium prices than non-French products, but no longer had a monopoly and the presence of Italian alternatives was weakening some buyers' willingness to pay. The foreign media not only described and evaluated Italian fashion for their readership (women as well as department stores), but were also acting as surrogate consumers. These media provided Giorgini and Italian couturiers with significant feedback on adapting their collections to the needs of the US market. Specifically, the most influential journalists proscribed imitations of French styles and supported the development of a specific Italian creativity built on the country's strengths. For example, Vogue wrote in 1952 that 'the Italians need to be encouraged […] to develop their native specialties and urgently discouraged from French adaptations'.[88]

Similarly to export-oriented trade fairs,[89] the Florentine fashion shows not only provided Italian couturiers with an opportunity to promote themselves to foreign markets, but also to learn about market needs. This occurred through countless informal interactions with buyers and journalists. The Sala Bianca's shared catwalk was one opportunity for such inter-actions: it not only produced visible audience reactions, but also led to buyers' orders, whose total amounts quantified the market's appreciation for whole collections and individual products, as well as to media reports, which made couturiers visible and highlighted news-worthy trends and products. Such learning fed back into the collection development, helping couturiers develop their individual style, and Italian fashion as a whole become sufficiently different from the French (without becoming extravagant) and sufficiently suited to the needs of the American market (without losing its creativity).

After the early years, with Florence having firmly established itself as one of Europe's fashion capitals and retaining the occasional reference to its heritage, the foreign press kept on reporting on Italian fashion.[90] Beyond the descriptions and assessments of individual collections, the press kept on comparing Italy with France and frowned upon unfavourable similarities. For example, one journalist 'was left with the unhappy feeling that much of what was shown belonged to six months ago in Paris, rather than to new interpretations of a silhouette'.[91] On other occasions, reporters criticised the lack of novelty: 'The Italian couture this season [...] has produced very few brand new ideas. It appears that there is an inverse proportion at Italian showings each season between commercial success and original talent. The greater, the one, the less the other', Women's Wear Daily wrote in 1961 in reference to the ongoing conflict between artistic creativity and commercial sensitivity that has been a leitmotif of fashion reporting ever since.[92]

As the Florentine shows established themselves, exports of Italian fashion skyrocketed. Between 1950 and 1957 the exports of Italian readymade women's clothes rose from approximately $72,000 to $2.88 million, and those of knitwear from $332,800 to $30.4 million – with a growth rate significantly greater than that of the overall Italian exports.[93] Between 1953 and 1963, clothing was one of Italy's most dynamic sectors, increasing its weight from 3.5% to 6.2% of total manufacturing exports.[94] Within a decade, Italian clothing and accessory exports to the United States surpassed those of France: more than $35 million, with the total fashion exports as much as $745 million, compared with France's approximate $20 million.[95] In the meantime, especially German and English buyers and press increasingly attended the Florentine shows. By 1957 their numbers exceeded those of the Americans.[96] Paradoxically, this huge achievement triggered feuds not only between couturiers, but especially between the different Italian fashion organisations.

Italy's fashion civil wars

Despite the gratifying feedback obtained from the international press and market, the fashion shows in Florence faced numerous difficulties from the outset. The literature on trade shows as temporary clusters shows that collective events – and the industry actors supporting them – often compete against each other, resulting in a proliferation of activities. Likewise, centrifugal forces and delegitimising moves from the existing fashion organisations, which reacted negatively to the presence of yet another contender, thwarted Giorgini's attempts to unify the country's fashion producers under one (prestigious) roof – that of the city's Pitti Palace. To further complicate matters, minor bodies were also created in other cities after 1951, including in Naples and Palermo, bringing the total number of Italian organisations promoting fashion to 13.[97]

This confusing situation led to uncertain alliances. Immediately after the first edition of the International Italian Fashion Show, Giorgini sought the patronage of the EIM. However, the Turin-based organisation's initial reaction to Giorgini's initiative was far from positive. In July 1951, EIM's general manager Rossini sent a letter to the member fashion houses that had not attended the Florentine presentation. In this letter he remarked that it was a 'private enterprise', 'organised outside any EIM intervention', while acknowledging the festival's success.[98] The organisation also announced that it would manage contact with the foreign press and buyers in the future. Rossini later officially presented Italy's government agencies with a schedule of fashion presentations, first in Rome and then in Florence at the fashion houses' own ateliers, without any reference to Giorgini's collective event.[99] In November 1951, in partnership with Milan's Centro Italiano Moda, the EIM established the 'Italian Fashion Service', whose mission was to organise and regulate fashion events in Italy. At the end of December of the same year, the new agency sent a newsletter to the foreign press,

communicating the presentations of Italian fashion in Milan, Rome and Florence the following January, without specifying the dates.

While covering the 'battle for fashion supremacy', the Italian and foreign press often drew
on Italian history to make sense of a situation that, to external eyes, was difficult to understand. Again, the period of reference was the Renaissance, but instead of focusing on the
artistic achievements of the period, journalists remembered the political turmoil and the
frequent wars between Italian city-states. The unstable alliances and the attempts to dele-
gitimise Florence were seen as conspiracies against Florence and Giorgini.[100] Reporting on
the feud between Rome and Florence, the foreign press reminded its readers that until
80 years earlier, Italy had been a collection of rival city states and that Giorgini's 'labor of love
and patriotism' was even more admirable given the difficulties ('conflicting temperaments
and jealously guarded local interest') he had to face.[101] An account by journalist Vera Vaerini,
which appeared in the newspaper *Il Popolo di Roma* in February 1952, clearly outlined these
domestic struggles and blamed not so much the centres in Turin and Milan but above all
the textile industrial groups SNIA Viscosa and Marzotto, the real sponsors of the Italian
Fashion Service with the blessing of the Minister of Trade and Industry[102]:

> At the beginning of December a new institution, the 'Italian Fashion Service', a parent–child
> relationship of the reconciliation between the Turin Fashion Centre and the Milan Fashion Entity
> appeared. The representative of the two institutions had contact with adv. Cingolani Guidi under-
> secretary of the Ministry of Industry and Trade [...] and [...] succeeded in obtaining a subsidy,
> some say of 30 million lire, others say 100 million lire. Marinotti and [Gaetano] Marzotto, who
> were contacted, also responded with generosity [...] The Italian Fashion Service [...] first of all
> attempted to agitate the dressmakers belonging to the Giorgini group to leave Florence; having
> failed in that, it formed a group of dissidents led by a Roman dressmaker [...] As a result, nobody
> understands anything any longer.[103]

Common enemies sometimes led to unlikely alliances. In 1953, Giorgini obtained the
support of the EIM, Milan's Centro Italiano Moda, and the textile industry for his fashion
shows. This common front formed by Turin, Florence and Milan, resulted in a Roman defection. That same year, eight important Roman couturiers (including Fabiani, Simonetta,
Schuberth, the Fontana sisters, Ferdinandi and Carnet) founded the Sindacato Italiano Alta
Moda (Italian High Fashion Syndicate). They began showing their collections in their own
ateliers in Rome, two days before the Florentine presentations, with the endorsement of the
local institutions and part of the press.[104] One element of dissatisfaction was Giorgini's focus
on boutique fashion and accessories, which would distract buyer and press attention from
haute couture proposals. There was also the 'unique runway' formula, much appreciated by
the foreign buyers, which clashed with the couturiers' need for 'protagonism', because it
reduced the number of models that could be shown. More importantly, this formula, made
the audience's occasional lack of appreciation for some proposals and rivals' successes visible.[105] Finally, Italy's capital had better international access and accommodation than
Florence. The press, reporting on the rivalry, often took sides with one or the other of the
contenders:

> The inconvenience most often mentioned [by the Americans] is that there is not a 'fashion
> centre', a geographical centre, over here. In France there's Paris, in Italy there's Rome, Florence,
> Milan, Turin and sometimes Venice. The Americans who come to Italy to buy or describe and
> praise the models don't like going back and forth between one city and the other and would
> rather concentrate all their activity in one city only [...] Buyers and journalist come to Italy before
> going to seeing Paris's collections and would like to complete to their business in 10 days or so

[...] the Americans would like to see Rome also become the capital of fashion, because Rome is beautiful, pleasant, offers perfect hotel accommodation and is a stopover for all airlines. Florence didn't leave them with good memories, due to the lack of convenient accommodation and, last summer, although the exhibition that a private citizen organised was a triumph, foreign guests didn't always find the welcome they had expected.[106]

The Italian situation was unstable, and year after year there were new twists, to the extent that foreign observers suggested the battle between Rome and Milan came 'complete with style espionage, midnight meetings, and unscheduled showings'.[107] In 1955, after two years of continued backing, the EIM ceased its support of the Florentine shows. Season after season, Roman couturiers kept on going back and forth, alternating between individual Roman and collective Florentine presentations to follow the business.[108] Even the partnership with the textile industry ceased in July 1955, as textile producers needed to take part in two new and more strategic EIM-sponsored trade shows: SAMIA (International Market Exhibition of Apparel, in Turin, first held in November 1955) and MITAM (International Market of Textile for Clothing and Furniture, in Milan, first held in July 1957), both under the direction of EIM's Vladimiro Rossini.[109] The fate of the Palazzo Pitti's shows therefore lay with the revenue generated by the fees, the security deposits paid by buyers, and the Municipality of Florence's public funding, which respectively amounted to about 50–60% and 30% of the operating costs.[110] In contrast, the subvention paid by the Minister of Trade and Industry to Giorgini's organisation, despite increasing from $800 in 1952 to $4,800 in 1954, covered just 10% of the total costs.

The situation remained unsettled and chaotic during the following years. In 1961, the Italian Prime Minister's Office sent a note to Giorgini highlighting the need for the high fashion shows be moved to Rome.[111] This city was 'from many quarters' supposedly considered to be the most appropriate location for such a presentation. In particular, the memorandum highlighted the disordered state in which the sectors of haute couture, boutique fashion and accessory production found themselves. Nevertheless, the memorandum also noted that the situation was not due to 'objective and serious economic troubles', but rather to the 'peculiar natures' of the fashion houses, which were 'managed with egotistic standards'.[112] The note pointed out that the overlapping missions and lack of coordination between the various Italian fashion centres made it impossible for Giorgini to unite Italian fashion under one roof – an unfair accusation, given that the Italian government had contributed to the situation.[113] In 1962, a few well-known Roman designers (Capucci, Fabiani and Simonetta) deserted all the Italian catwalks to present their collections at the fashion shows in Paris. Italian fashion houses had not only divided themselves between fashion cities, some of them had now even left the country. This renewed the debate on the problematic state of Italian fashion. The press hinted at the possibility of a French conspiracy, supposedly supported by the prestigious US magazine *Women's Wear Daily*, which aimed to weaken Italian fashion by taking away some of its leading elements. Echoes of these suspicions even reached the Italian Parliament.[114] In a letter to the journalist Irene Brin, Giorgini bitterly noted that stronger support for the shows he had organised since 1951 could have prevented the crisis:

> It is needless to close the stable door after the horse has bolted and cry crocodile's tears. If, during these years, everyone had understood my problem and all the forces had tightened their grip around the Florentine initiative, this would have become an unassailable stronghold. Do all critics realise that I created this huge movement without a penny's help from the government? [...] An initiative that gave Italy tens of billions of liras in advertising and hundreds of billions

in exports, but no minister or director or president of the ICE [Istituto per il Commercio Estero, Institute for Foreign Trade] ever realised what the Pitti Palace was! [...] Capucci says its unique runway was Florence's mistake. Is it possible that he doesn't realise that it was precisely the unique runway that made his fortune?[115]

In September 1962, in order to increase collaboration between the Italian fashion houses, a new body (created in 1958, but idle until then) was tasked by the most important fashion bodies (Turin's EIM, and the fashion centres of Florence, Milan, Rome and Naples) to coordinate the chaotic Italian fashion show calendar. The Camera Nazionale della Moda (CNM, National Chamber of Fashion), modelled after the French *Chambre Syndicale de la Couture Française*, had Giorgini as its first president. Nevertheless, the establishment of the CNM contributed to the demise of Florence as the capital of Italian fashion, because the new body granted Rome a more central role.[116] In October 1964, Giorgini's suggestion that the Pitti fashion shows gradually open to the emerging ready-to-wear sector offered Roman houses the opportunity to definitely abandon Florence for good.

> You have probably heard that Galitzine, Forquet, Valentino, Lancetti and maybe De Barentzen have decided that they will not join the Palazzo Pitti showings next January but they will show in Rome in their own premises. The first one to take this decision was Irene Galitzine: she said that to make a collection for the Sala Bianca is too engaging and expensive (personally I think she was too jealous of the success of the others). Tired of all this, I had almost decided to close Palazzo Pitti.[117]

The coup de grace came in January 1965, with the defections of some Milanese couturiers, including Jole Veneziani and Olga di Grésy (Mirsa), who had presented their collections in Florence from the start and were long-time friends of Giorginis.[118] The mediocre outcome of this edition led an embittered Giorgini to give up the organisation of his fashion shows in April of the same year.[119] With Giorgini's departure, the direction of the Palazzo Pitti showings was initially taken over by Emilio Pucci (1965–1967), followed by others.[120] By the spring of 1965, the fashion calendar coordinated by the CNM became operational, sanctioning a division of promotional labour built on each city's vocation. Florence would start with boutique fashion, knitwear and, until 1973, ready-made high fashion shows (that is, serial industrial reproductions of haute couture dresses, with lower quality fabrics and simpler cuts). Rome would conclude Italy's presentations with haute couture shows (women's, men's and children's collections).[121] In between, there would be the trade shows in Turin and Milan dedicated to manufactured clothing and textiles (SAMIA and MITAM). Overall, the number of buyers increased during this period – mostly due to of Italian and other European boutiques and retailers, which reduced Italian fashion's dependence on North American department stores.[122]

Despite the difficulties caused by the economic crises of the 1970s, the Pitti showings continued until 1982. During this period, Florence's portfolio of fashion events expanded further with new specialised initiatives (Pitti Uomo, for men's clothing and accessories from 1972; Pitti Bimbo, dedicated to children's wear from 1975; Pitti Filati, focused on yearns for knitwear in 1977 and Pitti Casual, for casual wear, in 1978). In this phase, however, the key contender was no longer Rome but Milan, which with the advent of prêt-à-porter and designer–manufacturer collaborations became Italy's new fashion capital.[123] Nevertheless the legend of Florence's Sala Bianca as the birthplace of Italian fashion is so well-established that it eclipses all other narratives.[124]

Discussion and conclusion

In this paper, building on the literature on collective marketing events and their role in nation branding, we analysed the emergence of Italy as a fashion country. In particular, we focused on the promotional activities of Giovanni Battista Giorgini and on the collective shows he organised in Florence in the period from 1951 until 1965. Specifically, our study shows how Giorgini strategically differentiated the emerging 'made in Italy' fashion from French haute couture, by keeping the needs of the North American market clearly in mind and building on existing material and cultural resources. As a result, the idea of an Italian fashion built on the Renaissance tradition and which could be an alternative to French fashion, was firmly established in the discourse and practices of foreign buyers and journalists. Giorgini's success, however, triggered various tensions and rivalries between Italy's many potential fashion capitals. Competing organisations, which leveraged other sources of legitimacy (including Turin's state support; Rome's image produced by Cinecittà and American movie stars and Milan's preferential relationships with textiles and, later, clothing manufacturers), attempted to counter-organise Italian fashion. This created a hard-to-understand situation that reminded foreign observers of the centuries-old struggles between Italian city-states before the country's unification. Nonetheless, Giorgini's initiative acted as a catalyst that accelerated the coalescence of the emerging Italian fashion field and its interaction with strategic export markets. Consequently, Italian fashion creators did not only benefit from a highly visible and prestigious promotional window, but they also learned from and adapted their offerings to evolving market needs.

Despite being negatively affected – and to some extent, marginalised – by the prominence of Rome on the Italian fashion calendar during the 1960s, Pitti's Florentine fashion shows left an intangible legacy that would benefit the Italian fashion system in years to come. While the connection with Renaissance art was lost with the demise of Florence, the 'made in Italy' country-of-origin effect had been created and lingered on, giving US media and consumers an established term of reference to make sense of the subsequent market offering originating in the Belpaese. American journalists had already familiarised their readers with 'made in Italy fashions' in 1951 as they already had 'with spaghetti, olive oil and grand opera'.[125] Italy's new reputation for fashion also tied in with other sectors of Italian exports. The general media, while reporting about Giorgini's initiative, noted that 'made in Italy' had become a brand of excellence that extended to numerous other products, including sewing machines, calculators and films. By the time of the advent of prêt-à-porter in the late 1970s, the idea that Italy was a country of fashion creators had already been circulating in international markets for more than two decades. This was, as a matter of fact, an intangible asset that the new generation of fashion designers could easily exploit. As a case in point, a special issue of *Women's Wear Daily* dedicated to the 25th year of 'Italian ready to wear' in 1976, found similarities between the style of the new prêt-à-porter brands being shown in Milan (such as Basile, Callaghan and Genny) and some of their haute couture predecessors from Pitti's Sala Bianca (Capucci, Mirsa and Pucci).[126]

Our historical reconstruction of the emergence of Italy as a fashion country sheds light on some features of nation branding that previous literature has neglected. First, successful nation branding initiatives lead to the creation or reinforcement of favourable country-of-origin effects, whose content is based on product imagery built on the country's material and symbolic resources as well as on selective, strategic readings of its history. Second, nation branding is a territorial form of collective branding that is built over time and requires the orchestration of firms and other stakeholders (in our case, local governments, the State, and various trade associations) with regard to joint promotional efforts. Third as Giorgini's strategies show, effective nation branding should be based on differentiating the country's image in ways that the export markets will find valuable; that is, which results in retailers and consumers from import markets showing willingness to pay a premium price. Fourth, nation branding relies on firms (that is, individual brands) and their products that provide the basic material resources upon which national brand storytelling can be built. In other words, not only does a nation's image connote the products of local firms, but local brands also connote their nation's image, through their products and their brand image. Finally, the contributions to – and benefits from – nation branding initiatives are unevenly distributed across the participating actors. Smaller or younger firms with limited brand awareness and access to international market benefit the most from joint promotional initiatives, but their presence contributes only marginally to the nation brand. Conversely, firms with stronger brand image and access to international markets can legitimise collective branding initiatives with their presence, but receive little from the co-presence of other, rival firms. Their incentives to participate in joint promotional projects are therefore more limited.

By highlighting the dynamics of event-based nation branding initiatives, our study also contributes to the literature on marketing, economic history and organisation studies that examines promotional events and their impact on underlying organisational fields. First, as firms grow bigger, better known and internationalised, dependence on collective promotional projects decreases, which potentially leads them to abandon these initiatives. In our case, this is best exemplified by the Roman couturiers who, at a moment when they were fairly well-established, resented the excessive cost of participating in the Florentine shows (implicitly, in respect of the benefits they could obtain). Event-based brand nation projects are therefore inherently unstable, and those who organise them need to manage their lifecycle carefully by maintaining a dynamic balance between known brands and emerging ones. Second, with its comparatively recent national unity and many fashion capitals, Italy highlights that federating a country's actors under the banner of a common project is no easy task. Utilising different sources of legitimacy, these actors may compete against each other not only for the attention of external audiences, but also for the support of local firms and other domestic stakeholders. In other words, the scale of place branding initiatives is not necessarily the nation. In this sense, French couturiers were in an ideal, but not necessarily typical situation. They were all located in the same city, Paris and just one organisation, the *Chambre Syndicale de la Couture Française* represented all of their interests. Many countries do not have an undisputed fashion capital, for example, Madrid vs. Barcelona in Spain and Montreal vs. Toronto in Canada; as a result, these countries' nation branding dynamics might resemble the Italian case more than the French one. When internal competition occurs and too many incompatible narrations are diffused at the same time, a clear nation brand positioning is unlikely to emerge, which creates a situation that will mostly benefit foreign rivals. As is often the case, when two dogs fight for a bone, a third runs away with it.

Notes

1. 'Italian imports. Just like the Chianti.' *Life*, 14 April 1952, 89–92: ASF, AMIGBG, Album 5, n. 102.
2. J. Nicholson. 1952 'Florence declares fashion war. Paris has a rival.' *Picture Post*, 1 March: ASF, AMIGBG, Album 1, n. 340–342.

3. Merlo and Polese, 'Turning Fashion'; Paris, 'Fashion as System' and *Oggetti Cuciti*; Pinchera, *Moda in Italia*; White, *Reconstructing Italian Fashion*.
4. For business history: Hansen, 'Networks, Narrative'; Mordhors, 'Arla and Danish'. For marketing and consumer research: Arnould and Thompson, 'CCT' and 'Consumer Culture Theory'; McCracken, 'Culture and Consumption'.
5. Thompson and Tian, 'Counter-memories'.
6. In the post-war period, the US were the only possible market for luxury products such as European fashion. See White, *Reconstructing Italian Fashion*; Merlo and Polese, 'Turning Fashion'.
7. Our focus on Giorgini does not imply that we subscribe to the so-called 'great man theory of history'. However, both journalistic accounts of the period and other works investigating the emergence of Italian fashion tend to focus on Giorgini. We also follow this convention, because, at the beginning of our observation period (1951–1954), Giorgini's initiatives were frequently criticised for being one man's private initiatives; it was only with the creation of the Centro di Firenze per la Moda Italiana (Florence Center for Italian fashion, 1954) that he gave the Florentine fashion shows a more formal organisational structure.
8. Belfanti, 'History as Intangible' and 'Renaissance'.
9. Merlo and Polese, 'Turning Fashion', 430–438; Segre Reinach, 'Italian Fashion Revolution', 65–70.
10. See, among others, Djelic and Ainamo, 'Coevolution'; Kawamura, *Japanese Revolution*; Rantisi, 'Ascendance'; Steele, *Paris Fashion* and *Fashion Italian Style*.
11. Khaire, 'Indian Fashion Industry', 345–347; Khaire and Hall, 'Medium and Message', 846–847.
12. Merlo and Polese, 'Turning Fashion'; Paris, *Oggetti Cuciti*; Pouillard, 'Keeping designs'.
13. Kaneva, 'Nation branding'.
14. Al-Sulaiti and Baker, 'Country'; Verlegh and Steenkamp, 'Country-of-origin'; Dinnie, 'Country-of-origin 1965–2004'.
15. Hansen, 'Narrative nature'.
16. See also literature in organisation studies on the strategic uses of the past. For a review of the relevance of this literature for business history, see Foster et al. 'Strategic use'.
17. Florio, 'Fairs Trades'.
18. Gopalakrishna and Lilien, 'Three Stage Model'; Smith, Gopalakrishna and Smith, 'Complementary Effect'.
19. Borghini, Golfetto and Rinallo, 'Ongoing Search'; Rinallo, Borghini and Golfetto 'Exploring Visitor'; Peñaloza, 'Commodification'.
20. Lampel and Meyer, 'Field-configuring'.
21. Bathelt, Golfetto and Rinallo, *Trade Shows*; Bathelt and Schuldt, 'Luminaries and Meat'; Maskell, Bathelt and Malmberg, 'Temporary Clusters'; Rinallo, Bathelt and Golfetto, 'Economic Geography'.
22. Rinallo and Golfetto, 'Exploring the Knowledge-based'; Bathelt, Golfetto and Rinallo, *Trade Shows*.
23. Kawamura, *Fashion-ology*, 83–84.
24. Duggan, 'Greatest Show' and Troy, *Couture Culture*.
25. Kawamura, *Fashion-ology*, 93.
26. Kawamura, *Fashion-ology*, 73–76; Steele, *Paris Fashion*, 104–105 and 115–118.
27. Kawamura, *Fashion-ology*, 64–66; Steele, *Paris Fashion*.
28. Troy, *Couture Culture*.
29. Pouillard, 'Managing fashion creativity'.
30. The Duce himself was behind the creation of the Ente, whose initial capital was predominantly constituted by the City of Turin together with various other Turinese or Piedmontes organisations representing industrial and commercial interests. Its first president was Silvio Ferraccini, followed in Paolo Ignazio Maria Thaon de Revel, who was at the time Podestà (mayor) of Turin. Vladimiro Rossini, who played an important role in Italian fashion until 1970, was appointed general director of the Ente. Pinchera, *Moda in Italia*, 17–20; Gnoli, *Donna*, 89–90; Discussione e approvazione del disegno di legge: Costituzione dell'Ente autonomo per la Mostra permanente nazionale della moda in Torino (Discussion and approval of the draft law: Establishment of the Authority for the Permanent National Fashion Exhibition in Turin), Atti Parlamentari. Camera dei Deputati, 6 December 1932, 7502–7509.

31. Gnoli, *Donna*, 91. The first President of the Ente Nazionale Moda was Giovanni Vianino, who had previously been appointed vice-president of the EAMNPM and, after Thaol de Revel's resignation, had substituted him as President. Vladimiro Rossini kept hold of the post of general manager for the new Ente.
32. Paris, *Oggetti Cuciti*, 269.
33. Capalbo, *Storia della moda*, 82–86.
34. Ricci, 'Salvatore Ferragamo', 13–15.
35. 'Fine Italian Hand for Shoes.' *Vogue*, 15 July 1937.
36. Pinchera, *Moda in Italia*, 98–99.
37. White, *Reconstructing Italian Fashion*, 12–17; Pinchera, 'Provvedimenti economici', 487–489; on the general impact on the Italian economy: Fauri, *Piano Marshall e l'Italia*.
38. White, *Reconstructing Italian Fashion*, 39–41; Pinchera, *Moda in Italia*, 28.
39. Capalbo, *Storia della moda*, 130; Mannucci, *Marchese rampante*, 187–188; White, *Reconstructing Italian Fashion*, 75–83.
40. Paris, *Oggetti Cuciti*, 184–185.
41. Ibid., 241–243.
42. After Lora Totino of Cervinia, the Ente was presided over by Filippo Alberto Giordano delle Lanze (1875–1952) and Furio Cicogna (1891–1975), both coming from an industrial background. In 1953, the Ente, which was under the control of the Ministry of Trade and Industry, was put under the administration of an external commissioner: Pinchera, *Moda in Italia*, 75; Paris, *Oggetti Cuciti*, 249.
43. Paris, *Oggetti Cuciti*, 187.
44. Ibid., 189.
45. SNIA Viscosa, founded in 1917, in the 1930s was already a global leader in the artificial and synthetic textile fibre industry. Franco Marinotti became the director and president of SNIA Viscosa in 1939. Paris, *Oggetti Cuciti*, 188; Spadoni, *Gruppo SNIA*.
46. Paris, *Oggetti Cuciti*, 188–189.
47. Ibid.
48. Capalbo, *Storia della moda*, 131; White, *Reconstructing Italian Fashion*, 136–149.
49. Capalbo, *Storia della moda*, 142.
50. Paris, *Oggetti Cuciti*, 241–243.
51. Pinchera, *Moda in Italia*, 32–33.
52. Pinchera, *Moda in Italia*, 33–34; Belfanti, 'History as Intangible', 74–76.
53. Pinchera, *Moda in Italia*, 29–30.
54. ASF, AMIGBG, Album 3, n. 20, Letter 28 December 1950. Originally in Italian, our translation.
55. Vergani, 'Sala Bianca', 44–47.
56. Pinchera, *Moda in Italia*, 31.
57. Caratozzolo, 'Reorienting Fashion', 51–52; Paris, *Oggetti Cuciti*, 218–231.
58. Paris, 'Fashion as system', 534–535.
59. The runway show of Christian Dior's Autumn/Winter collection 1950–1951 had more than 250 models and lasted about 3 h: 'Prèmiere de la mode d'automne *chez* Dior.' *Paris Match*, 12 August 1950; Erti. 1951. 'La moda italiana alla conquista dell'America.' *Grazia*, 10 November: ASF, AMIGBG, Album 1, n. 175.
60. ASF, AMIGBG, Album 3, n. 150; B. Griggs. 1960. 'Italian fashions on the right lines,' *The Star*, 18 January: GCPP, AG, CD-Rom 9, n. 84; N. Salvalaggio. 1961. 'La moda italiana si impone a Londra.' *Il Giornale d'Italia*, 16 January: ASF, AMIGBG, Album 44, n. 161.
61. McCracken, 'Culture and Consumption'.
62. Among numerous others: C. Snow. 1953. 'Italian fashion have a real meaning.' *New York Journal*, 15 February; C. Snow. 1953. 'Italian coats and suits feature colorful design.' *New York Journal*, 16 February: ASF, AMIGBG, Album 9, n. 9 and 14.
63. Belfanti, 'History as Intangible', 84–85.
64. ASF, AMIGBG, Album 20 and GCPP, AG, CD-Rom 6, n. 386–478, in particular n. 471–473 'Italy Four Roman beauties, in dresses for the new Italian Collections.' *Vogue*, 15 March 1956.
65. ASF, AMIGBG, Ente Italiano Moda 1953–1962, File 1.

66. ASF, AMIGBG, Ente Italiano Moda 1953–1962, File 2; I. Brin. 1955. 'Il giudizio dei buyers'. *Settimana Incom*, 6 August 44: GCPP, AG, CD-Rom 5, n. 360–362; and see the section Italy's fashion civil war below.

67. ASCCF, Enti di Iniziativa 1933–1962, Box 19 Centro di Firenze per la Moda Italiana 1952–1962, File 3; programmes and reports on the Pitti fashion shows.

68. ASF, AMIGBG, Album 44, n. 61, Report on XXI Presentation and n. 42, Program XXI Italian Fashion Show, 14–20 January 1961; Album 51 n. 62, Report on XXV Presentation, 19–24 January 1963.

69. ASF, AMIGBG, Album 28, n. 62, table on buyer firms' attendance 1954–1959.

70. Kawamura, *Fashion-ology*, 89; Khaire and Hall, 'Medium and Message'; Pouillard, 'Fashion for All'; White, 'Italy: Fashion'.

71. Ortoleva, 'Buying Italian'; Steele, 'Italian fashion'.

72. Lampel and Meyer, 'Field-configuring'; Bathelt, Golfetto and Rinallo, *Trade Shows*; Bathelt and Schuldt, 'Luminaries and Meat'; Maskell, Bathelt and Malmberg, 'Temporary Clusters'; Rinallo, Bathelt and Golfetto 'Economic Geography'.

73. C. Snow. 1953. 'Italian fashions have a real meaning'. *New York Journal*, 15 February: ASF, AMIGBG, Album 9, n. 9.

74. In the 1950s Christian Dior couture house represented more than 50% of the overall French haute couture export, and the overseas sales of Dior products accounted for about two-thirds of his entire business: Okawa, 'Licensing Practices', 91.

75. Jones and Pouillard, 'Christian Dior', 10–11; Palmer, *Dior*, 58–61 and 78–82.

76. B.J. Perkins. 1953. 'Collections opens today in Florence. Boutique, Millinery, Fabric and Accessories lines will be shown at Giorgini's event'. *Women's Wear Daily*, 22 July; 'Masters of Fashion From France and Italy'. *The Milwaukee Journal*, 8 January 1952, ASF, AMIGBG, Album 4, n. 160; Album 9, n. 109; Palmer, *Couture*, 176–178.

77. Palmer, *Dior*, 78–83; 'Paris, Italian Import Copies Dominate N.Y. Sunday Ads'. *Women's Wear Daily*, 30 September 1954; 'Italian imports. Just like the Chianti'. *Life*, 14 April 1952, 90; 'Resort Fashions from Italy'. *Women's Wear Daily*, 18 September 1956: ASF, AMIGBG, Album 12, n. 5 and Album 20, n. 101.

78. Italian imports. Just like the Chianti." *Life*, 14 April 1952; M. Hall. 1952. 'N.Y. Rome: our new fashion capital?'. *Post*, 12 January; L. Averill. 1952. 'Originals from the Italian couture seen at luncheon show'. *Los Angeles Times*, 19 March 1952: ASF, AMIGBG, Album 4, n. 160 and 170. By the mid-1950s the increasing success of Italian fashion in the American market pushed the low price department stores to reproduce Italian models.

79. C. Snow. 1951. 'Italy gets dressed up, A big hectic fashion show attracts U.S. style leaders, poses a challenge to Paris'. *Life*, 20 August, 104–112; C. Snow. 1951. 'Italian Designers' Grand Entrance. The Smart Set'. *New York Journal*, 26 August; 'Italian imports. Just like the Chianti'. *Life*, 14 April 1952: ASF, AMIGBG, Album 1, n. 49 and 50.

80. H. Gaggiottini. 1952. 'Italians accent simplicity in bid for fashion lead'. *Chicago Daily Tribune*, 15 October, and also F. de Santis. 1952. 'Fashion of Italy today'. *The Hartford Bulletin*, 14 December: ASF, AMIGBG, Album 5, n. 160 and Album 1, n. 28.

81. Among others: Babette. 1952. 'I. Magnin's presents Italian originals'. *The Examiner*, 18 March; L. Averill. 1952. 'Originals from the Italian couture seen at luncheon show'. *Los Angeles Times*, 19 March; D. O'Neill. 1954. 'Foreign fashions and American copies defy identification at showing in store'. *Times*, 17 March; J. Worth. 1954. 'Low cost copies of chic imports'. *The New York Daily Mirror*, 30 March: ASF, AMIGBG, Album 1, n. 297 and 283 and Album 9, n. 290 and 295.

82. C. Snow. 1952. 'Hand painted fabrics in spotlight at Italy shows'. *San Francisco Examiner*, 15 August: ASF, AMIGBG, Album 1, n. 453.

83. Spadea. 1952. 'Fashion jottings from fabulous Italy'. *Times Union*, 15 February: ASF, AMIGBG, Album 1, n. 338, and on the American stereotypes about Italy: Steele, 'Italian fashion', 496.

84. C. Snow. 1951. 'Italian Designers' Grand Entrance. The Smart Set'. *New York Journal*, 26 August.

85. Interview by G.B. Giorgini, 'Fashion is a wonderful thing'. *St. Louis Dispatch*, 6 December 1957: ASF, AMIGBG, Album 22, n. 162; Belfanti, 'History as Intangible'.

86. C. Snow. 1951. 'Italy's artistry lends enchantment to fashion world'. *New York Journal*, 27 August: ASF, AMIGBG, Album 1, n. 51.

87. F. Engle. 1953. 'Record U.S. turnout seen for Paris openings the fashion markets of Europe will attract a near if not record crowd for the fall couture showings.' *Women's Wear Daily*, 15 July: ASF, AMIGBG, Album 9, n. 106.

88. 'Italian Collection Notebook.' *Vogue*, 15 September 1952: ASF, AMIGBG, Album 5, n. 154.

89. Bathelt, Golfetto and Rinallo, *Trade Shows*; Rinallo and Golfetto, 'Exploring the Knowledge-based'.

90. 'Italy's fashion industry-still young but challenging Paris.' *Business Week*, 15 August 1959; J.W. Cohn. 1960. 'Italy couture gathers strong buyer support.' *Women's Wear Daily*, 21 January; C. Donovan. 1961. 'Designer's fancy turns to thoughts of Romance.' *The New York Times*, 16 January: ASF, AMIGBG, Album 28, n. 65; Album 44, n. 67 and GCPP, AG, CD-Rom 9, n. 92.

91. 'The eye of the beholder.' *The Times*, 27 January 1958: GCPP, AG, CD-Rom 7, n. 20.

92. E. Massai. 1961. 'Italian couture.' *Women's Wear Daily*, 20 January: ASF, AMIGBG, Album 44, n. 63.

93. L. Olivetti. 1958. 'La moda in cifre.' *La Nazione*, 30 December; E. Ferro. 1958. 'Le cifre delle esportazioni provano lo sviluppo della moda italiana.' *L'Avvenire*, 7 January: ASF, AMIGBG, Album 27, n. 181 and 182.

94. Between 1958 and 1963 the average annual growth rate of the Italian leather and clothing sectors was more than 23% (the average annual growth rate of the Italian manufacturing industry was nearing 16%): Gomellini and Pianta, 'Commercio', 408 and 412–413.

95. Data reported in J. Troxell Stark. 1960. 'The Italian *influence*.' *Look*, 5 January, 35; 'Italy's fashion industry-still young but challenging Paris.' *Business Week*, 15 August 1959: ASF, AMIGBG, Album 30, n. 63.

96. ASF, AMIGBG, Album 28, n. 62, Table of buyer firms' attendance 1954–1959.

97. I. Brin. 1955. 'Conservare il posto e il prestigio della moda italiana.' *Bellezza*, Marzo: GCPP, AG, CD-Rom 5, n. 253.

98. G.B. Giorgini, typewritten memorandum: ASF, AMIGBG, Ente Italiano Moda 1951–1963.

99. Pinchera, *Moda in Italia*, 62–68.

100. Among others, V. Vaerini. 1953. 'La moda italiana respinge l'aiuto del Governo.' *La Patria*, 2 March; I. Brin. 1953. 'La moda a Firenze. Una polemica che deve finire.' *Il Giornale d'Italia*, 29 July; F. Hammond. 1953. 'Rome, Florence Battle for Fashion Supremacy.' *Los Angeles Times*, 2 August: GCPP, AG, CD-Rom 2, n. 213 and CD-Rom 3, n. 52 and 59.

101. M.J. Harlepp. 1957. 'Florence: two cities bury the hatchet.' *The Times*, 22 July: ASF, AMIGBG, Album 22, n. 94.

102. Marzotto was one of the most important and large Italian wool textile company, with 15,000 employees in 1948. During the early 1950s, the company integrated downstream in the production of ready to wear clothing for men and women. In the 1960s, both Marzotto and SNIA Viscosa were important financial supporters of the Camera Nazionale della Moda: Paris, *Oggetti Cuciti*, 188–195; idem, 'Fashion as system', 528–529; Roverato, *Casa industriale*.

103. V. Vaerini. 1952. 'Un mondo illusorio e scintillante di cui si misconosce la vita.' *Il Popolo di Roma*, 24 February: ASF, AMIGBG, Album 5, n. 170.

104. Capalbo, *Storia della moda*, 145.

105. Capalbo, *Storia della moda*, 143–144; V. Lucci. 1953. 'Le dannose concorrenze di un inutile campanilismo.' *Il Giornale d'Italia*, 1 March: ASF, AIMGBG, Ente Italiano Moda 1953–1962.

106. E. della Giovanna. 1953. 'Il pericoloso successo della moda italiana negli Stati Uniti.' *Il Giornale d'Italia*, 18 April: ASF, AMIGBG, Album 9, n. 105.

107. B. Bruce. 1957. 'A fashionable rivalry.' *The Journal American*, 23 July: ASF, AMIGBG, Album 22, n. 103.

108. A. Rizzotti Veronese. 1956. 'Roma non vuole che Firenze voglia.' *Le Ore*, 15 December: GCPP, AG, CD-Rom 6, n. 373–377.

109. Paris, *Oggetti Cuciti*, 272 and 294; E. Nasi and F. Ducry Giordano. 1969. 'Impegno di Torino per la moda italiana.' *Torino*, January/February, no 1, 50–55.

110. ASCCF, Enti di iniziativa 1933–1962, Box 19 Centro di Firenze per la moda italiana 1952–1962, Files 2-3-4.

111. Ibid., File 5.

112. Ibid.

113. On the debate about the numerous fashion centres in Italy: M. Gobessi. 1956. 'La pianificazione della moda.' *Cronaca Italiana*, 28 July: GCPP, AG, CD-Rom 6, n. 225; E. Robiola. 1960. 'Troppi centri di moda in Italia?.' *Bellezza*, September: ASF, AIMGBG, Ente Italiano Moda 1953–1962.

114. Speech by E. Savio to the Minister of Industry and Trade E. Colombo, Atti Parlamentari. Camera dei Deputati, 27 October 1961, 25,713–25,714.

115. Letter from G.B. Giorgini to Irene Brin, 18 April 1962: ASF, AMIGBG, Album 48, n. 228.

116. Paris, *Oggetti Cuciti*, 231–240 and 459–463.

117. Letter from G.B. Giorgini to Fay Hammond, 1 December 1964: ASF, AMIGBG, Correspondence 13 1962–1969, Correspondence designers' defection 1964–1968; E. Robiola. 1965. 'Nuvole nere su una moda rosa.' *Il Tempo*, 10 February; I. Brin. 1965. 'Moda braccio di ferro.' *Il Giornale d'Italia*, 10 June: Album 57, n. 92 and Album 58, n. 219.

118. Letters from Jole Veneziani to G.B. Giorgini, 24 April 1965, and from Olga di Grésy to G.B. Giorgini, 11 May 1965: ASF, AMIGBG Correspondence 13 1962–1969, Correspondence designers' defection 1964–1968.

119. Letter from G.B. Giorgini to Olga di Grésy, 18 May 1965: ASF, AMIGBG Correspondence 13 1962–1969, Correspondence designers' defection 1964–1968; L. Griffo. 1965. 'Roma contro Firenze. Inasprita la polemica sulla moda.' *La Nazione*, 24 April; 'Riunione al Centro della Moda.' *La Nazione*, 23 April 1965: Album 58, n. 95 and 96.

120. Pinchera, *Moda in Italia*, 42–43.

121. ASF, AMIGBG, Camera Nazionale della Moda 1963–1970; Paris, *Oggetti Cuciti*, 240.

122. Pinchera, *Moda in Italia*, 315–319 and 328–336.

123. Paris, *Oggetti Cuciti*, 484–494; Merlo and Polese, 'Turning Fashion', 431–434; Segre Reinach, 'Italian Fashion Revolution', 65–70.

124. Stanfill, 'Introduction', 15.

125. H. Carlton. 1951. 'Designers flock to Florence for three day fashion show.' *New York Herald Tribune*, 21 July: ASF, AMIGBG, Album 1, n. 31.

126. 'Italian ready-to-wear in its 25th year,' *Women's Wear Daily*, 1 October 1976: 19–20; Merlo and Polese, 'Turning Fashion', 415–416.

Acknowledgements

We would like to thank the guest editors, Patricio Sàiz and Rafael Castro, for their support, and two anonymous referees for their constructive criticism. We are also grateful to the staff of the Florence State Archive and the Costume Gallery Pitti Palace, Florence, for the documental support. A preliminary version of this paper was presented in 2015 during research seminars at the Cass Business School, London, and the Skema Business School, Lille. We are indebted to Professors Fleura Bardhi, Daniel Kjeldgaard, Nil Özçağlar-Toulouse, Davide Ravasi and many others colleagues for the helpful suggestions received on those occasions.

Disclosure statement

The study upon which the article is based was not financially supported by any institution or corporation. The authors declare that they have no conflicts of interest related to the research described in the paper.

References

Archival sources

ASF, AMIGBG (Florence State Archive, Archive of Italian Fashion Giovanni Battista Giorgini), Florence: Albums 1, 3, 4, 5, 9, 11, 12, 20, 22, 27, 28, 30, 44, 48, 51, 57 and 58; Camera Nazionale della Moda 1963–1970; Ente Italiano Moda 1953–1962, Correspondence 13 1962–1969, Correspondence designers' defection 1964–1968.

ASCCF (Historical Archive of the Florence Chamber of Commerce), Florence: Enti di Iniziativa 1933–1962, Box 19 Centro di Firenze per la Moda Italiana 1952–1962, files 1-2-3-4-5.

GCPP, AG (Costume Gallery Pitti Palace, Archive Giorgini), Florence: CD-Roms 1, 2, 3, 5, 6, 7 and 9.

Bibliography

Al-Sulaiti, K. I., and M. J. Baker. "Country of Origin Effects: A Literature Review." *Marketing Intelligence & Planning* 16, no. 3 (1998): 150–199.

Arnould, E. J., and C. Thompson. "Consumer Culture Theory (CCT): Twenty Years of Research." *Journal of Consumer Research* 31, no. 4 (2015): 868–882.

Arnould, E. J., and C. Thompson. "Consumer Culture Theory: Ten Years Gone (and beyond)." In *Research in Consumer Behavior. Consumer Culture Theory*, Vol. 17, edited by A. E. Thyroff, J. B. Murray, and R. W. Belk, 1–21. Bigley: Emerald, 2015.

Bathelt, H., F. Golfetto, and D. Rinallo. *Trade Shows in the Globalizing Knowledge Economy.* Oxford: Oxford University Press, 2014.

Bathelt, H., and N. Schuldt. "Between Luminaries and Meat Grinders: International Trade Fairs as Temporary Clusters." *Regional Studies* 42, no. 6 (2008): 853–868.

Belfanti, C. M. "History as an Intangible Asset for the Italian Fashion Business (1950–1954)." *Journal of Historical Research in Marketing* 7, no. 1 (2015): 74–90.

Belfanti, C. M. "Renaissance and 'Made in Italy': Marketing Italian Fashion through History (1949–1952)." *Journal of Modern Italian Studies* 20, no. 1 (2015): 53–66.

Borghini, S., F. Golfetto, and D. Rinallo. "Ongoing Search among Industrial Buyers." *Journal of Business Research* 59, no. 10–11 (2006): 1151–1159.

Capalbo, C. *Storia della Moda a Roma. Sarti, Culture e Stili di una Capitale dal 1871 a Oggi* [History of Fashion in Rome. A Capital's Dressmakers, Cultures and Styles from 1871 to Today]. Roma: Donzelli, 2012.

Corattozolo, V. C. "Reorienting Fashion: Italy's Wayfinding." In *The Glamour of Italian Fashion Since 1945*, edited by S. Stanfill, 46–57. London: V&A Publishing, 2014.

Dinnie, K. "Country-of-Origin 1965–2004: A Literature Review." *Journal of Customer Behavior* 4, no. 2 (2004): 165–213.

Djelic, M. L., and A. Ainamo. "The Coevolution of New Organizational Forms in the Fashion Industry: A Historical and Comparative Study of France, Italy, and the United States." *Organization Science* 10, no. 5 (1999): 622–637.

Duggan, G. G. "The Greatest Show on Earth: A Look at Contemporary Fashion Shows and Their Relationship to Performance Art." *Fashion Theory* 5, no. 3: 243–270.

Fauri, F. *Il Piano Marshall e l'Italia* [The Marshall Plan and Italy]. Bologna: Il Mulino, 2010.

Florio, M. "Fair Trades by Trade Fairs: Information Providing Institutions under Monopolistic Competition." *Small Business Economics* 6, no. 4 (1994): 267–281.

Foster, W. M., D. M. Coraiola, R. Suddaby, J. Kroezen, and D. Chandler. "The Strategic Use of Historical Narratives. A Theoretical Framework." *Business History* (Forthcoming). doi:10.1080/00076791.2016.1224234.

Gnoli, S. *La Donna, l'eleganza, il fascismo: la moda italiana dalle origini all'Ente nazionale della moda* [Woman, Elegance, Fascism: Italian Fashion from the Origins to the National Fashion Authority]. Catania: Edizioni del Prisma, 2000.

Gomellini, M., and M. Pianta. "Commercio con l'Estero e Tecnologia in Italia negli Anni Cinquanta e Sessanta [Foreign Trade and Technology in Italy in the 1950s and 1960s]." In *Innovazione Tecnologica e Sviluppo Industriale nel Secondo Dopoguerra* [Technological Innovation and Industrial Development in the Second Post-War Period], edited by C. Antonelli, F. Barbiellini Amidei, R. Giannetti, M. Gomellini, S. Pastorelli, and M. Pianta, 359–594. Roma: Laterza, 2007.

Gopalakrishna, S., and G. L. Lilien. "A Three Stage Model of Industrial Trade Show Performance." *Marketing Science* 14, no. 1 (1995): 22–42.

Hansen, H. R. "The Narrative Nature of Place Branding." *Place Branding and Public Diplomacy* 6, no. 4 (2010): 268–279.

Hansen, P. "Networks, Narratives, and New Markets: The Rise and Decline of Danish Modern Furniture Design, 1930–1970." *Business History Review* 80, no. 3 (2006): 449–483.

Jones, G., and V. Pouillard. *Christian Dior: A New Look for Haute Couture.* Cambridge, MA: Harvard Business School (HBS case no. 9-809-159), 2013.

Kaneva, N. "Nation Branding: Toward an Agenda for Critical Research." *International Journal of Communication* 5 (2011): 117–141.

Kawamura, Y. *Fashion-ology. An Introduction to Fashion Studies.* Oxford: Berg, 2005.

Kawamura, Y. *The Japanese Revolution in Paris fashion.* Oxford: Berg, 2004.

Khaire, M. "The Indian Fashion Industry and Traditional Indian Crafts." *Business History Review* 85, no. 2 (2011): 345–366.

Khaire, M., and E. V. Hall. "Medium and Message: Globalization and Innovation in the Production Field of Indian Fashion." *Organization Studies* 37, no. 6 (2016): 845–865.

Lampel, J., and A. D. Meyer. "Field-configuring Events as Structuring Mechanisms: How Conferences, Ceremonies, and Trade Shows Constitute New Technologies, Industries, and Markets." *Journal of Management Studies* 45, no. 6 (2008): 1025–1035.

Mannucci, E. *Il marchese rampante. Emilio Pucci: Avventure, Illusioni, Successi di un Inventore della Moda Italiana* [The Marquis Rampant. Emilio Pucci: Adventures, Illusions, Successes of One of Italian Fashion's Inventors]. Milano: Baldini & Castoldi, 1998.

Maskell, P., H. Bathelt, and A. Malmberg. "Building Global Knowledge Pipelines: The Role of Temporary Clusters." *European Planning Studies* 14, no. 8 (2006): 997–1013.

McCracken, G. "Culture and Consumption: A Theoretical Account of the Structure and Movement of the Cultural Meaning of Consumer Goods." *Journal of Consumer Research* 13, no. 1 (1986): 71–84.

Merlo, E., and F. Polese. "Turning Fashion into Business: the Emergence of Milan as an International Fashion Hub." *Business History Review* 80, no. 3 (2006): 415–447.

Mordhorst, M. "Arla and Danish National Identity: Business History as Cultural History." *Business History* 56, no. 1 (2014): 116–133.

Okawa, T. "Licensing Practices at Maison Christian Dior." In *Producing Fashion. Commerce, Culture, and Consumers,* edited by R. L. Blaszczyk, 82–107. Philadelphia, PA: University of Pennsylvania Press, 2008.

Ortoleva, P. "Buying Italian: Fashion, Identities, Stereotypes." In *Volare: The Icon of Italy in Global Pop Culture,* edited by G. Malossi, 46–54. Florence: The Monacelli Press, 1999.

Palmer, A. *Couture & Commerce. The Transatlantic Fashion Trade in the 1950s.* Vancouver: UBC Press, 2001.

Palmer, A. *Dior.* London: V&A Publishing, 2009.

Paris, I. "Fashion as a System: Changes in Demand as the Basis for the Establishment of the Italian Fashion System." *Enterprise & Society* 11, no. 3 (2010): 121–155.

Paris, I. *Oggetti Cuciti. L'Abbigliamento Pronto in Italia dal Primo Dopoguerra agli Settanta* [Sewn Objects: Ready Made Apparel in Italy from the First Post-War Period to the 1970s]. Milano: Franco Angeli, 2006.

Peñaloza, L. "The Commodification of the American West: Marketers' Production of Cultural Meanings at the Trade Show." *Journal of Marketing* 64, no. 4 (2000): 82–109.

Pinchera, V. "I Provvedimenti Economici per la Ripresa del Secondo Dopoguerra: Strategie e Settori d'Intervento. Promozione e Sostegno della Moda Italiana 1945–1970 [Economic Measures for the Recovery in the Second Post-War period: Strategies and Sectors of Intervention. Promotion and Support of Italian Fashion]." In *L'Intervento dello Stato nell'Economia Italiana* [State Intervention in the Italian Economy], edited by A. Cova and G. Fumi, 485–513, Milano: FrancoAngeli, 2011.

Pinchera, V. *La Moda in Italia e in Toscana. Dalle Origini alla Globalizzazione* [Fashion in Italy and in Tuscany. From the Origins to Globalisation]. Venezia: Marsilio, 2009.

Pouillard, V. "Fashion for All? The Transatlantic Fashion Business and The Development of a Popular Press Culture During the Interwar Period." *Journalism Studies* 14, no. 5 (2013): 716–729.

Pouillard, V. "Keeping Designs and Brands Authentic: The Resurgence of The Post-War French Fashion Business Under the Challenge of US Mass Production." *European Review of History* 20, no. 5 (2013): 815–835.

Pouillard, V. "Managing Fashion Creativity. The History of the Chambre Syndicale de la Couture Parisienne during the Interwar Period." *Investigationes de Historia Económica* 12 (2016): 76–89.

Rantisi, N. "The Ascendance of New York Fashion." *International Journal of Urban and Regional Research* 28, no. 1 (2004): 86–106.

Ricci, S. "Salvatore Ferragamo: An Evolving Legend." In *Salvatore Ferragamo: Evolving Legend 1928–2008*, edited by S. Ricci, 13–26. Milano: Skira, 2008.

Rinallo, D., H. Bathelt, and F. Golfetto. "Economic Geography and Industrial Marketing Views on Trade Shows: Collective Marketing and Knowledge Circulation." *Industrial Marketing Management* 61, February (2017): 93–103.

Rinallo, D., S. Borghini, and F. Golfetto. "Exploring Visitor Experiences at Trade Shows." *Journal of Business and Industrial Marketing* 25, no. 4 (2010): 249–258.

Rinallo, D., and F. Golfetto. "Exploring the Knowledge-based Strategies of Temporary Cluster Organizers: A Longitudinal Study of the EU Fabric Industry Trade Shows (1986–2006)." *Economic Geography* 87, no. 4 (2011): 453–476.

Roverato, G. *Una casa industriale. I Marzotto* [An Industrial House: The Marzotto Family]. Milano: Franco Angeli, 1986.

Segre Reinach, S. "The Italian Fashion Revolution in Milan." In *The Glamour of Italian Fashion Since 1945*, edited by S. Stanfill, 58–73. London: V&A Publishing, 2014.

Smith, T. M., S. Gopalakrishna, and P. M. Smith. "The Complementary Effect of Trade Shows on Personal Selling." *International Journal of Research in Marketing* 21, no. 1 (2004): 61–76.

Spadoni, M. *Il Gruppo SNIA dal 1917 al 1951* [The SNIA Group from 1917 to 1951]. Torino: Giappichelli, 2003.

Stanfill, S. "Introduction." In *The Glamour of Italian Fashion Since 1945*, edited by S. Stanfill, 8–31. London: V&A Publishing, 2014.

Steele, V. *Fashion Italian Style*. New Haven, CT: Yale University Press, 2003.

Steele, V. "Italian Fashion and America." In *The Italian Metamorphosis, 1943–1968*, edited by G. Celant, 494–505. New York: Guggenheim Museum, 1994.

Steele, V. *Paris Fashion: A Cultural History*. Oxford: Berg, 1998.

Thompson, C., and K. Tian. "Reconstructing the South: How Commercial Myths Compete for Identity Value through the Ideological Shaping of Popular Memories and Counter-memories." *Journal of Consumer Research* 34, no. 5 (2008): 595–613.

Troy, N. J. *Couture Culture. A Study in Modern Art and Fashion*. Cambridge, MA: MIT Press, 2003.

Vergani, G. "La Sala Bianca: Nascita della Moda Italiana [The White Hall: The Birth of Italian Fashion]." In *La Sala Bianca. Nascita della moda italiana* [The White Hall: The Birth of Italian Fashion], edited by G. Malossi, 23–86. Milano: Electa, 1992.

Verlegh, P. W. J., and J.-B. E. M. Steenkamp. "A Review and Meta-analysis of Country-of-origin Research." *Journal of Economic Psychology* 20, no. 5 (1999): 521–546.

White, N. "Italy: Fashion, Style and National Identity 1945-1965." In *The Fashion Business. Theory, Practice, Image*, edited by N. White and I. Griffiths, 183–204. Oxford: Berg, 2000.

White, N. *Reconstructing Italian Fashion. America and the Development of the Italian Fashion Industry*. Oxford: Berg, 2000.

Dreaming of the West: The power of the brand in Soviet Lithuania, 1960s–1980s

Brigita Tranavičiūtė

ABSTRACT
The article reveals the interest in foreign trademarks observed in Lithuanian society from the 1960s through the 1980s, when the demand for brand names spread after Western culture reached the Soviet Union. The consumption of Western cultural products, or imitations thereof, became one of the key symbolic expressions of freedom in Soviet society. In Lithuania, the most popular clothes were those bearing fake trademarks, even though Soviet authorities attempted to prevent the desire for and the wearing of these garments through the use of ideological tools.

Introduction

Starting in 1944, the Soviet reoccupation of Lithuania brought totalitarian political control and delineated the economic structure – that is, state monopoly – that lasted almost half a century. Within the socialist economic structure, some businesses run by private individuals were allowed.[1] Approved private entrepreneurial activities included fine household items, clothing, and other items stipulated under the Registration Rules of Non-Cooperated Homeworkers and Craftsmen, adopted by the Council of Ministers of the USSR on 30 June 1949.[2] Those engaged in state-approved private production and trade were classified as *homeworkers*, thereby constituting the only allowable form of private economic activity in the Soviet Union. Their activities were highly restricted by Soviet legal regulations; any *other* private production and trade was illegal under Soviet criminal law and classified as forbidden businesses and speculation.[3] In reality, approved craft businesses were closely related to selling and were often interlaced with forbidden businesses; consequently, in many cases, even allowed private activities shifted into the shadow economy.

Despite the narrow permitted activities for homeworkers, opportunities continuously expanded, which Soviet authorities could not eliminate. This expansion was because there were few goods, and especially few high-quality ones, in the planned economy. These shortages stimulated consumers to find alternative ways of shopping, and the items produced by homeworkers became key sources of such goods. Starting in the 1960s, there was an increased demand from the Soviet population in search of a better life, which they expected to be satisfied through greater consumption possibilities and a higher supply of products.

This belief was enhanced when the Soviet Union entered into the Cold War, creating competition with Western states; one fundamental ideological element was not to equate Soviet society to the standards of the West but to surpass them. Nevertheless, Western culture and fashion significantly influenced the perceived needs and style of the Soviet Union population, eventually becoming serious factors for the Soviet authorities to battle. As a matter of fact, Soviet society started to consider owning Western products to be a sign of material wealth. If a Soviet was rich, he or she owned Western music records, owned imported music equipment, or owned blue jeans. In Soviet Lithuania, lifestyles were influenced by Western cultural trends and expressed through buying expensive items or clothes manufactured by foreign companies … or, at least, by making an impression they were produced abroad. The deficit in fashionable and high-quality clothes in the official state market forced shoppers to look for alternative, usually informal, ways to buy garments. Across Lithuania, the possible ways to buy fashionable clothing varied. In this regard, a few Lithuanian cities and towns should be mentioned, in which large-scale shadow markets were created that specialised in the production of clothing imitations or fake Western brands.[4]

This shadow economy is missing in comprehensive historiographical studies. This article aims to fill the gap by analysing the Soviet shadow economy in Lithuania from the 1960s through the 1980s, covering production and sales of garments with fake foreign trademarks and lettering. Discussed in the first part of this article are the reasons behind the material consumption by Soviet society that started in the 1960s, when items with (false) foreign logos or lettering became symbolic of an individual's social status and prestige. The second part of the article introduces the legal and ideological aspects of falsification of foreign trademarks and explores why such garments were observed in Lithuania in the time period covered. The third part focuses on the employment forms and social status of manufacturers and distributors of such garments in Lithuania through the 1980s.

Assumptions of Material Consumption in Soviet Society, 1960s–1980s

The post-Stalinist period was followed by Soviet authorities wanting to prove that the Soviet management model could develop a successful, educated, and fully satisfied society, with an increased number of available flats; a greater focus on health, education, and culture; and increased consumption.[5]

Authors who explore consumption in Soviet society under Khrushchev focus significantly on the problematic issues related to Soviet authorities' efforts to form a modern consumer culture. For example, Susan Reid looks at the tendencies observed among Soviet citizens in acquiring flats, revealing that new furniture and innovative technologies adapted for home and household became must-haves for the modern Soviet lifestyle. Reid shows the change when an item was replaced because it was uninteresting rather than worn out. In addition, a new relationship with 'things' transformed Soviet consumption because items were acquired not out of necessity but because they offered a higher social status.[6] As Reid states, improvement in living conditions and the increased consumption of household items in Soviet society in the 1960s contributed to the processes of modernisation and development of the consumer society.[7] However, an increase in housing and household goods was only one of many goals in Khrushchev's policy.

Another goal was the so-called 'Turn to the West', emphasised as far back as in the 20th Congress of the Communist Party of the Soviet Union in 1956.[8] Along with the improvement in material living conditions, reducing the consequences of cultural isolationism was declared. The latter occurred when Soviet authorities periodically allowed in certain Western products, for example, literature, films, music, and fashion.

However, attempts to reduce this cultural isolation was mostly declarative, with Soviet authorities focusing on developing a distinctive, socialist culture and demonstrating its advantage by comparing itself to the West rather than by actually sharing intercultural experiences. In fact, cultural and economic goals were often interlaced after the Soviet Union's pursuit for superiority increased. The World Festival of Youth & Students, hosted by Moscow in 1957, was declared as an opportunity for Soviet youth to experience the cultures of young people of other countries, with the Soviet press writing glowing articles that praised Soviet culture and the Soviet system.[9] One article described the impressions of an Italian student:

> Sympathy and warmth showed to us by the Soviet people having welcomed us in Moscow, at the stadium, all over the Soviet territory we moved within: Brotherhood having burst suddenly at all meetings demonstrates the real friendship feelings ... All this was above reproach, i.e. both organisation and realisation matters. The same applies to the festival, hotels, communication means, canteens and public order ... I have walked much through Moscow and I would like to know it even better. Moscow is big and nice, with convenient and wide streets, old and new buildings surprising by grandiosity. In the suburbs, I've noticed old houses, but also saw rapid development of construction and I'm sure that in a few years the last old buildings will be removed and replaced by new and nice houses that will be more comfortable, modern, beautiful.[10]

Despite Soviet propaganda, the appearance of foreigners in the Soviet Union had a certain influence on how Soviet youth perceived cultural self-expression. This influence was not in accord with the principles of the proposed Soviet culture. According to Larisa Zakharova, the World Festival of Youth & Students encouraged two ways for the spread of fashion in the Soviet Union. One was the trade that started between Soviet Union citizens and foreign students who were selling the clothes they brought to Moscow. The other was from the Italian neorealism films approved by the Communist Party of the USSR. These films become major sources of Western high fashion in the Soviet Union.[11] Nevertheless, the World Festival of Youth & Students and foreign films were not the only ways Soviet society came into contact with Western fashion.

In 1959 the Christian Dior Collection was shown in Moscow. Although it was too extravagant and complex for Soviet society of that time, it created an impulse for fashion in everyday life. Shortly after the show, Gorky Street in Moscow was full of women dressed in simplified Dior imitations.[12] Along with Soviet economics and other achievements, fashion was considered a competitive subject with the United States. According to Stephanie Amerian, both US and Soviet politicians expressed the ideological values of their own political and economic systems through the use of fashion. The gap between US and Soviet consumers was significant because Americans were already enjoying American-made fashionable garments, while the Soviets were still tackling problems with both the development and production of fashionable goods.[13]

The introduction of high Western fashion to the Soviet audience was not an accident. In the 1950s, after the Stalin era, Soviet authorities made efforts to develop clothing production with higher fashion and better-quality garments.[14] In the context of tension between these two political systems, the Soviet authorities set goals to study the best examples of Western fashion, to criticise Western designers, and then to outdo them. Soviet designers were sent to the most famous Western fashion houses to gain experience. However, transferring models into practice failed due to issues with long-term planning and the excessively slow techno-logical development of Soviet industrial companies.[15]

By analysing the process of creating Soviet fashion authorities, Gronov and Zhuravlev discovered that the modernisation process had a twofold purpose. Modernisation 'from above' helped shape and develop Soviet fashion as well as serving as a tool to educate the public's aesthetic taste. The authors note that the large and well-developed Soviet fashion network of the late 1970s and early 1980s led to an increase in clothing variety that did not result in decreased quality. Additionally, consumer demands pushed Soviet designers to adapt new and trendy clothing options. The ideologically driven Soviet fashion industry was expected to maintain a balance among promoting the values of socialism, the state's expectations on 'rational' economic needs, and what the state considered 'irrational' individual desires.[16]

Stephan Merl explores the Brezhnev era through the prism of reforms, when the pro-grammes to overtake and surpass the West set by Khrushchev and the idea of Socialist Modernity were both unsuccessful. As Merl states, essential economic reforms focused on enabling increases in the efficiency of the command economy, whereas public management focused on developing the communist society and on forming consumerism based on rational and scientific standards.[17] Consumer opportunities in Soviet society during the period under discussion improved significantly both from an increased variety in goods and amended social conditions. However, the start of the shadow market offered even greater opportunities for buying goods.

In the Brezhnev era, Soviet society could be characterised as having a better education system, greater career opportunities, and improved living conditions, but also lower loyalty to the regime and with being nonconformist. This generation's main concern was achieving the lifestyle and level of consumerism of Western society.[18] The analysis conducted by Natalya Chernyshova of different aspects of Soviet consumption shows that consumers under Brezhnev were more independent, more discerning, and more affected by global processes. Increasing the number of higher-quality goods, including foreign ones, encouraged new expectations. Actually, imports fostered comparisons between socialist and capitalist life-styles, the latter of which was, of course, unfavourable to Soviet authorities.[19] Unsatisfied Soviet consumers, especially younger ones, regularly turned to shopping in the shadow market. Soviet consumers were also affected when Western consumerism and cultural prac-tices periodically reached the Soviet Union. The imitation of Western culture and clothing styles by Soviet society occurred when Western goods entered the Soviet Union, both through official and unofficial channels. For example, youth purchased Western products, such as music, as the dominant form of expressing cultural consumption within a closed society. This galvanized the process of Westernisation and contributed to the formation of identify – but it also challenged the authorities' ideological control.[20]

According to Sergei Zhuk, youth in the Soviet Union had growing access to Western music, especially in the 1970s, from concerts of foreign groups broadcast via Moscow radio. Zhuk, in referring to the Ukrainian example, points out that such intense Westernisation through imitation of Western fashion and music became a source of worry for Soviet authorities.[21] Zhuk also identifies informal cultural channels in the Ukraine through music, from Beatlemania, starting in the early 1960s, to fascist punk and heavy metal hysteria, reaching the Ukraine in the 1980s.[22]

The influence of Western cultural trends was felt throughout all regions of the Soviet Union. Cultural consumption was observed in the lifestyle and clothing of youth; and society generally accepted that clothes affected how a person looked and that material goods should be guaranteed in everyday life. As occurred in the Ukraine at the end of the 1960s, youth propagated hippie ideas in Lithuania, which deviated from the Soviet regime's image of Komsomol youth.[23] Under politically unfavourable conditions, after mandatory dogmas of the Soviet culture were directed at them, youth developed a particular music underground by independently composing music that copied groups such as the Beatles and the Rolling Stones.[24] The youth also used other cultural alternatives found at that time via broadcasts of the BBC, Voice of America, and French and Swedish radio stations. Eventually, the regime's ideological and cultural confrontations with youth weakened a little in 1972, but only after the self-immolation of Romas Kalanta, a student from Kaunas, Lithuania, after the KGB and other authorities disbanded groups of young followers of Western ideas.[25]

Products or goods representing Western culture continued to enter Lithuania through various channels, and this was sufficient for on-going consumer practices incompatible with official Soviet goals. Citizens started wanting household goods and garments with the spirit of the West. It should be pointed out that cultural isolation was also (slightly) reduced by correspondence with relatives living abroad and by the parcels sent from them that contained foreign magazines, clothing, music records, and other items that successfully slipped past the filter of the Soviet regime. According to reports of the KGB in the 1960s, the second largest city in Lithuania, Kaunas, had a population of some 330,000, including 50,000 who corresponded with relatives living abroad. Even so, the first tourists from capitalist countries were only allowed to visit this city in 1970.[26]

Being allowed to visit Socialist Bloc countries or Western countries was possible only for a small, usually exceptional, group of persons. Opportunities for average Lithuanian residents with respect to mobility and communication with the outer world were strictly limited. Trips to Socialist Bloc countries were mostly available for representatives of the nomenclature, cultural collectives, or athletes, whereas ordinary people had to overcome a range of bureaucratic obstacles, and even after doing so there was no guarantee that they would be allowed to travel. As Anne Gorsuch points out, citizens going to capitalist countries were expected to definitively demonstrate that they represented the reputation of the Soviet Union. The trips allowed to Eastern Europe were aimed at making less-developed countries support the dominion of the Soviet Union.[27] Along with limited opportunities for ordinary Lithuanians to visit the West, all applicants were thoroughly selected and KGB agents supervised nearly all trips. It should be highlighted that in the 1960s, the main tourist flow into and out of Lithuania was by crossing its capital, Vilnius. Even in the 1980s, tourism was still only a minor reason for Lithuanian residents to be allowed to go abroad. Documents by the Prosecutor of the Lithuanian Soviet Socialist Republic provide the following information: in 1985 the number of citizens allowed to visit Socialist Bloc countries and capitalist countries was 10,134 and 1,443, respectively.[28] Of those allowed to visit Socialist Bloc countries, the greatest number (310 persons) went to the German Democratic Republic, 240 persons went to Poland, and 200 went to Czechoslovakia. Of those allowed to travel to capitalist countries, the greatest number visited the United States, followed by the Federal Republic of Germany, and Canada.[29] Despite limited tourism, trips became one way to spread intercultural knowledge, which raised questions on the principles imposed by Soviet ideology. According to Zhuk, travelling to foreign countries allowed contact with foreigners. Moreover, the trips brought partial satisfaction for the growing demand for Western music, pop culture, and goods.[30] However, tourism was not the only way Lithuanians could buy certain items. Trafficking also served as a rather significant channel for exchanging goods with citizens of foreign countries. In Klaipėda, the third largest city of Lithuania, the fishing and commercial seaport allowed for a thick trafficking network developed by both inbound foreign sailors and outbound local seamen. This network saw goods enter Lithuania from seaports cities such as Bremen and Hamburg (Germany), Antwerp (Belgium), Santa Cruz and Las Palmas (Spain), and Helsinki and Malmo (Scandinavia). Informal relations were created between the seamen and traders operating at the seaports; these traders were called *maklakai* – after the German *Makler*, which translates as broker. Lithuanian sailors had access to goods that allowed them to look wealthy in comparison with ordinary citizens: they wore Western clothes and smoked Western cigarettes. They also enjoyed Japanese or other foreign audio and video equipment.[31] For citizens without opportunities to travel and buy goods, Klaipėda seamen were key carriers and sellers of foreign products in Lithuania. With average citizens having no other sources to purchase Western goods, Klaipėda seamen carried out an important function of the shadow market. Importantly, the garments brought from abroad by the seamen, such as jeans and jackets, with their sewing technology, style, or trademarks, served as examples for homeworkers who later produced Western-style clothing.

The spread of foreign trademarks was considered an especially unfavourable cultural and social development, and it contradicted the ideology imposed by the Soviet authorities. Regardless of the efforts made by the authorities to stop the plagiarism of foreign trademarks, it was obvious that they failed to persuade the population to observe its principles. The socialist system failed to satisfy the social needs of the people, and the planned economy failed to meet their growing consumerism.

Legal and Ideological Aspects of False Foreign Trademarks

This failure was not related to the amount of goods in general but to the limited number of certain items and certain quality that underlined social status. Efforts were made by authorities to persuade consumers that the Soviet industry produced good quality items, and that this quality was ensured by active government control of legal tools, such as the use of Soviet-approved trademarks.

The first two pieces of legislation to specify legal protection for trademarks was the Decree Regarding the Taxes for Trademarks[32] and the Resolution Regarding the Trademarks, adopted by the Council of People's Commissars on 15 August 1918 and 10 November 1922, respectively.[33] During the Cold War, that latter resolution was also adopted by the Council of Ministers of the USSR on 15 May 1962, to regulate the legal framework applicable to trademarks.[34] It offered the possibility of registering foreign trademarks in the Soviet Union on condition that the Soviet Union was also able to register its own trademarks in the applicant's country. Additionally, the Regulations Applicable for Trademarks was approved on 8 January 1974 by the State Committee for Inventions and Discoveries of the Council of Ministers of the USSR.[35] This legislative act was adopted after the Soviet Union signed international agreements that regulated the protection of industrial property and trademarks.[36] It stipulated the conditions under which a trademark was registerable in the Soviet Union; it also specified, in a laconic manner, that foreign citizens and legal entities with a permanent residence abroad were entitled to use the regulations to register trademarks with the

Chamber of Commerce of the USSR. Thus, natural persons and legal entities that did not register their trademarks were not protected by the legislation.[37]

Foreign legal entities wishing to register their trademarks in the Soviet Union usually encountered a range of obstacles, and their applications were often refused by Soviet institutions as being misleading, contradicting socialist morals, and for other reasons.[38] The ability for foreign entities to employ effective legal tools in the fight against mass falsification of their trademarks within the Soviet Union and its former satellites appeared only after the collapse of the Soviet Union.[39]

According to the Soviet law theory, the main purpose of a trademark is to individualise goods produced by a certain enterprise or firm and to help the buyer find the goods of the company from among other goods supplied to retail networks by other enterprises. Companies with registered trademarks care for the quality of their trademarked goods and the reputation of the company[40] – which for buyers means buying brand names ensures high quality. Hence, trademarks also perform a certain function in advertising the quality of goods.[41] In the Soviet Union, trademarks were more significant for exported articles, which were usually of considerably higher quality as compared to items made for local markets. For example, the same article intended for export might have been produced with higher-quality raw materials and placed in a nicer, more colourful package, whereas the goods supplied to a local market were usually produced with lower-quality raw materials and sold without packaging.

The State Quality Mark was created to approve especially high-quality goods and to ensure that they represented the latest trends in fashion, and was one way to persuade consumers that the Soviet industry produced quality products.[42] Each factory or plant was obligated to produce a certain per cent of items that met the standards of the State Quality Mark. Each year, every Soviet Republic ministry had to submit to the State Committee of Standards, under the Council of Ministers of the USSR, samples of goods that might be approved for the State Quality Mark. The committee issued certificates for approved goods that were then labelled with the quality mark. Later, manufacturers placed this mark on packaging and labels, too.

Usually, the goods with the State Quality Mark served as showpieces at local and international exhibitions. In the daily life of consumers, however, they were rarely purchased. The goods had no obvious defects, but they were also unattractive to consumers. This situation can be explained in very simple terms: the process from new product design to new product introduction lasted a very long time, leaving no chance to keep up with the latest trends in fashion. A trader at that time stated, 'We hear nothing but talk of how differently a showpiece and a mass-production item look: fabric, colour and finish of the latter changed very often. … What concerns us, however, we would be happy to offer new, practical and nice goods for the joy of our buyers.'[43] There were not enough goods attractive to consumers while there was plenty of low-quality, unattractive clothing and footwear buyers did not want. No one wanted to buy a coarse wool overcoat or shoes in which the soles fell off after only a few wearings. Problems related to quality and aesthetics were usually caused by violations in production technology or by the failure of companies to replace out-dated production technologies with new ones. For these reasons, some goods remained the same for many years.

Consumers disappointed with the low-quality products from the Soviet industry helped homeworkers prosper both legally and on the shadow market. Large-scale private production of goods was encouraged both because there was an opening up of allowed craft businesses and an eventual liberalisation in craft businesses in the 1970s and 1980s.[44] In some republics, especially those focused on light industrial goods, conditions developed for private mass-production of clothes. Fake foreign trademarks became a key component of this business.

Over time, foreign brands became symbols of personal freedom, image, and choice in Soviet society, all criticised by Soviet propaganda:

> Without jeans and music equipment – nowhere, as even those who contribute to development of art values (artistic directors, painters) wear jeans … Jeans represent the latest trends in fashion. If some boy gets into a conversation with us, he looks, 'Do you wear jeans or not?' If you do, he talks with you. If you don't, he takes no notice of you, and it doesn't matter how nice a person you could be.[45]

Moralising Soviet propaganda, explaining the damage done by fashion, or threatening possible sanctions against those engaged in production, selling, or trafficking of goods with fake trademarks could stop this phenomenon. On the contrary, growing demand meant an increased need for such goods and clothing.

The authorities tried to stop imitations of foreign brands because letterings in foreign languages, especially English, were not in line with the Soviet ideology; authorities also denied the advantages of foreign articles as compared to Soviet industrial ones. State cooperatives as well as public enterprises in the Soviet Union were obligated to mark their goods with trademarks. Authorities also emphasised the fact that only legally registered trademarks were protected, and those who violated regulations faced possible criminal charges. In Soviet Lithuania, criminality was established in 1961 with Clause 166 of the Criminal Code of the Lithuanian Soviet Socialist Republic (hereafter, the CC of the LSSR); it stipulated legal responsibility of persons who used illegal trademarks. It should be noted that Clause 166 implied protection only for *trademarks* registered within the Soviet Union, while *natural persons* could be classified as the subject of a crime.[46] Therefore, homeworkers could formally become the subject of a crime. The clause included a special qualification which stipulated additional charges for fraud or deception in selling low-quality goods as high-quality goods to get higher prices;[47] after all, high-quality items in Soviet society were associated with imported goods and with real foreign brands.

While the CC of the LSSR did not specify legal responsibility for using fake foreign trademarks, central Soviet Union institutions nevertheless tried to scare homeworkers from marking goods with them. Measures were taken in Lithuania in 1987, when the Ministry of Finance and the Ministry of the Interior of the LSSR instructed local financial institutions and the Prosecutor of the LSSR to punish natural persons pursuant to Clause 166. The regulation stated:

> After establishing that self-employed persons engaged in individual activities sell their products marked with foreign trademarks, the report on the violation of the procedure of individual work activity shall be drawn and delivered to the local prosecutor's office according to the place of residence of an offender. Referring to the reports and other material, the question of bringing the offender to criminal responsibility shall be considered.[48]

However, the Prosecutor's Office refused to pursue these measures because criminal cases could not be opened for such violations; that is, there was an absence of criminal activities in the actions of the persons under discussion.[49]

Authorities had no control over the supply of goods with fake foreign trademarks due both to legal gaps and a well-organised process of production. If caught by the *militsiia* (militia; Soviet police) or officers of Soviet institutions, homeworkers and resellers denied any relations with other shadow market workers, refused to divulge their names, or stated that the goods with fake trademarks were accidently obtained from strangers. A critical issue in potential criminal charges against homeworkers was that the purchase of raw materials was illegal; that is, buying sufficient raw materials on the official market was impossible due to limited quantities. Also, the raw materials offered for official sale were smaller items such as threads more suitable for handicrafts or, in the best-case scenario, for simple knitting or sewing machines, whereas the raw materials required for wide-scale production with large sewing or knitting machines were procured by stealing them from factories.

Because of the foregoing, the *militsiia* was impeded in initiating criminal proceedings against persons engaged in the widespread sale of goods with fake trademarks. When selling on the street, resellers would have just one or two articles, because being caught with such low quantities usually meant only administrative fines. Selling garments with fake foreign trademarks, however, was the final point in the process, and reducing the number of garments was hopeless due to the high numbers of sellers. The production of garments with fake trademarks was mostly done outside the knowledge of the authorities, so active punishment was not significant. The inability of Soviet institutions to identify manufacturers of goods with false foreign trademarks was captured by the Soviet press:

> Especially live sale of 'branded' shirts and jeans is observed ... It is interesting, however, that nobody cares (I have in mind *militsiia*) where these 'branded' masterpieces are born and through what channels they enter the hands of resellers. In what way is 'Montana' and 'Puma' from the outskirts of Lithuania found in the marketplace of the capital?[50]

Cooperation between homeworkers and resellers extended the Soviet shadow market through forbidden businesses and other economic crimes. Homeworkers and shadow business representatives worked together very closely, although their legal boundaries were rather different: in contrast to selling, private economic activities were rarely considered the subject of criminal law, excluding when evidence of the illegal procurement of raw materials was found.

Soviet propaganda was used not only to try to stop the manufacture and selling of items with fake trademarks but also to moralise buyers. Soviet civilians' desire to emphasise their own individuality through clothing was incompatible with Soviet garments. Meanwhile, authorities considered these actions to be signs of philistinism and materialism: the desire to look extraordinary was related to moral decline manifested by greed and consumerism. In the Soviet press, two correspondents offered impressions after their supposed visits to where they were born:

> How nice is a pedestrian boulevard and how gorgeous are people this sunny day! 'The real town of "Montana"', says Valdas. And we are happy, as nobody notices us as if we were somewhere else. 'Montana' sees only 'Montana'. Their eyes catch only the branded clothing or footwear. And you may feel the growing dissatisfaction in the eyes of the gorgeous; the things they wear have been obtained by great efforts, you may look richer than another, but there are always ones looking richer than you. Thus, an internal engine switches on again: 'To get!' To get something that nobody has yet. Or – to get and look like 'everyone else'.[51]

This quote illustrates the attempts of the Soviet press to relate those who hunt for brand names both to material greed and the unoriginality of many people wearing the same clothing with the same trademark.

Materialism and unoriginality were part of the moralising. Persons wearing such clothing could be misidentified with abusers, alcoholics, thieves, cheats, or even prostitutes. Individuals wearing garments marked with fake foreign trademarks were often criticised by journalists:

> At first, the sale of shirts printed with any foreign lettering was allowed. Then a verbal instruction was given forbidding the names of non-existing firms. It is surprising, however, that garments are printed with anything that comes to mind. What if our fair maidens start wearing shirts and pullovers declaring: 'Five dollars per hour, fifteen dollars per night?'[52]

Wearing clothing with foreign lettering or false foreign trademarks was also often related to poor education. Efforts were made to stop the spread of foreign trademarks and lettering by emphasising the lack of English knowledge of manufacturers:

> After taking the pullover into my hands, I'm reading an English lettering printed on the chest: 'University of North Carolina'. I ask the knitter why especially this university of the USA is advertised and not, for instance, Vilnius University or Kaunas Polytechnic Institute? Maybe she is sentimental about the University of North Carolina? R. T. was told she did not speak English and was not interested in the content of the lettering at all. Such patterns for printing pullovers are used not by her, but by another woman who also takes pullovers brought by other knitters. A rate per pattern print is rather inexpensive at this woman's place, i.e. a half rouble. Therefore, by courtesy of such 'printers', we have streets full of 'Montana', 'Wrangler', 'Marlboro' and other cheap attributes of Western life.[53]

Actually, certain letterings in English met neither the rules of grammar nor the rules of logic. Among buyers, popular clothing with lettering consisted of as many words or word combinations as possible, and not necessarily with any meaning.

Social Consequences of Fake Foreign Brands in Lithuania at the End of the 1980s

The 1980s was the peak of popularity for clothing with fake foreign brands and foreign letterings; by the end of the decade, nearly every item produced by homeworkers included these. Most of these activities were considered criminal acts in the Soviet Union (that is, stealing of state property, reselling, etc.), and was underground. The concern of the authorities was that private production often surpassed the limits of state-allowed activities based on reselling rather than in response to liberalisation of the state economic system. Even after the reorganisation started by Mikhail Gorbachev in 1985 and passage of the new USSR law, Regarding Individual Work Activity, adopted on 19 November 1986 and put into force on 1 May 1987,[54] a considerable share of underground private production continued.

Homeworkers decided to keep their activities in the shadows because of their immense profitability and cooperation with resellers from the outermost places of the Soviet Union coming to Lithuania for garments. Reports of the Ministry of the Interior of the LSSR pointed out that jumpers and pullovers produced with knitting machines by homeworkers were bought on a massive scale by resellers from Latvia, Estonia, and from Moscow, Leningrad, Novosibirsk, and other Soviet Union cities. Their buyers were especially fascinated by, and demanded, fake foreign brands or foreign lettering, even though these were more expensive garments.

Documentation of the Executive Committees of cities and towns included statements such as, 'in other cities and towns, dissatisfaction is caused by marking of all the garments with foreign brands or letterings in English'.[55] This fact was supported by constant reports from state institutions of other republics of the USSR to institutions of finance and the interior of Soviet Lithuania of having detained a significant number of Lithuanian homeworkers and resellers. One example was from the Department of Finance of the Executive Committee of the Council of People's Deputies of Brest City,[56] in Soviet Belarus, which sent a report to the Ministry of Finance of the LSSR with respect to the reselling of goods with fake foreign brands by three citizens of Kaunas. The report stated that the Department of Finance of Brest City was not competent to decide whether the design and lettering of foreign labels complied with the ideological, aesthetical requirements, and applicable legislation; therefore, Lithuanian authorities should make the decision with respect to the activity of the home-workers and resellers from Kaunas. Soviet ideology attitudes were emphasised. As the report stated: '[L]ocal residents are indignant at the sale of such garments, it would be much better if they propagate the Soviet culture and ideology'.[57]

Nevertheless, the institutions of some cities and towns made decisions themselves on such illegal activities. For instance, after detaining a group of Lithuanian citizens selling items with foreign brands, the Department of Finance of Krasnodar, Soviet Russia, drew up its report pursuant to Clause 155 of the Criminal Code of Soviet Russia. The report, and other collected material on the acts carried out by these detainees, was forwarded to the financial institutions of Lithuania with instructions that Krasnodar officials would inform them on further results of the investigation and on the decisions made.[58]

In other cases, official documents identified what articles with brands were sold. For example, on 29 November 1987, in the town of Baranovichi, Belarus, five residents of Kaunas were detained while selling from their cars articles marked with foreign trademarks, including 'Baron' and 'Montana'.[59] Some reports illustrated that neither sellers nor buyers took care of correct grammar or meaning of English lettering. On 22 November 1987, in the marketplace of Maladzyechna, in Belarus, articles were marked with English lettering: 'Fun stailing' (fun sailing) and 'Super style' (a nonexistent trademark). In Soviet ideology, English wording on clothing was not allowed.[60] At the prosecutor's office in Maladzyechna, the seller explained that the plastic and metal fittings to mark clothes were bought by her at one marketplace in a Lithuanian town, and that trousers were decorated with leather pieces covered with stickers containing English letterings or placed on the articles following patterns of clothing also bought at the marketplace. On 25 January 1988, the officers of the Lithuanian Department of Finance inspected this seller's home. During the inspection, the following were found: 14 pieces of sports suits for children with lettering 'Benjamin Blumen'; 7 pullovers with lettering, 'Fun sailing greater-lake master fights'; and 17 pullovers with lettering 'Super style'.[61] It should be noted that goods produced in Lithuania spread rapidly to other Soviet republics.

In the 1980s, production of garments with false brands acquired new forms, that is, the production process became fragmented. While one group stole the raw materials needed to produce garments, a second group sewed or knitted, a third group created false brands, and a fourth group sold the goods. The Soviet press described this fragmentation:

> Most knitters working under registration certificates have long been participating in the so-called 'cooperation of businessmen': let's say, one knits only chest parts, second knits only pockets, third just sews individual pieces together to make a pullover and so on ... Not only have knitters specialised but they follow other chains of the business as well. One group carries out threads from the factories, another group rewinds them into hanks, the third group delivers them to knitters. Many knitters have already refused the sale of readymade articles, therefore ... the knitters sell their articles by wholesale to various businessmen, usually strangers, who take the products to places with stable demand.[62]

As far back as the Soviet era, a significant number of people working for the official state sector became involved in the private production of goods. Many of these official workers were drawn to private production or selling of garments. The job in a plant or a factory was necessary as a source of raw materials at best, while their main source of income was generated by their entrepreneurial activity. Improvement in the material condition of these workers was stimulated by legislation that liberalised craft businesses, especially knitting and sewing, although prosperity was determined both by the demand of the local market and consumer interest in these goods across the Soviet Union. The change in craft workers' social status was also supported by the changed behaviour of the stratum of the society; by the end of the 1980s, compulsory (or assumed) modesty of lifestyles and material conditions was replaced by luxurious houses being constructed in the suburbs, and the ability to purchase cars and other property.[63]

Also by the end of the 1980s, some in the stratum who flaunted wealth started forming the first criminal gangs, and private production and selling of goods became one of their most profitable activities. Generally, gangs hired tailors for cheap sewing of garments or just to attach fake brands and labels. In some cities and towns, these underground plants produced articles taken to Soviet Russia or other republics belonging to the former Soviet Union. These organised crime gangs accumulated a considerable amount of property and often used violence against others engaged in the same private production and selling.[64]

A protection racket – protecting traders selling counterfeit garments – also turned into a rather profitable sphere that attracted an increasing number of youth (known as the lost generation) who wanted to get rich fast. In the last years of the planned economy, those in the shadow production and trade started to suffer from organised crime gangs operating within the same market, as they became an unavoidable factor in doing business. The Soviet press described the reality of the protection racket at the end of the 1980s:

> More than ten fashionably dressed guys step through the market gates. It's not a secret that the market is also controlled by racketeers, and visually they look especially like them. Without any ceremony, in broad daylight, they surround the fellow selling sneakers, grip him by his hands and a pair of sneakers flops down on the ground. Flops down next to the tourist bag containing even more shoes brought for sale.[65]

The shadow economy determined significant social outcomes and employment forms of residents after the collapse of the Soviet Union. In the period of transition from the planned economy to the market economy, the business of fake brands attracted people having nothing to do with this field before, because the transition to a free market economy meant rising prices of goods and services that were absolutely incompatible with the income levels.

In 1991, for instance, the price of a pair of shoes in a commercial shop sold for 600 to 1,500 roubles, whereas a worker's wage was 150 to 200 roubles per month.[66] Therefore, in order to avoid poverty, even people such as librarians, artists, or employers of enterprises close to bankruptcy or who could not pay wages started to undertake sewing activities. The first private limited liability companies also sold counterfeit garments; that is, instead of legally produced clothes with attached logos, labels, and so on of foreign firms. For some time even after the economy opened, and there was an increased flow of imported goods and the possibility of a free market, the practices developed over the previous decades did not stop. Buyers were still charmed by labels such as 'Baumwolle', 'Made in Turkey', 'Mohair', and garments marked with 'Adidas' or 'Lacoste' logos. Sometimes, however, the fake Lacoste crocodile on Lithuanian counterfeits was far from the original: it faced in the opposite direction or even two crocodiles could be depicted. The obsession with the goods marked with 'Adidas' was the main clothing of criminal gangs at the end of the 1980s. The 'Adidas' trademark, along with the 'Made in Turkey' label, served as a warranty of originality and enhanced demand for the article.[67]

In Soviet Lithuania, fake foreign brands formed a rather broad niche shared both by workers in the shadow economy and legally operating homeworkers. Developed in the context of the Soviet shadow economy, entrepreneurial activity was significant for the formation of the first business entities during the transition from a planned economy to a market economy, when the skills acquired through business development were applied under conditions of a free market.

Conclusions

Starting in the 1960s, the influence of Western cultural trends stimulated the consumption of Western products by Soviet society, which later contributed to the development of a shadow economy for such goods. In Soviet Lithuania, people's choice of clothing contradicted the Soviet ideology of modesty, good taste, and advantages of Soviet culture. Starting in the 1980s, counterfeit foreign trademarks or letterings, especially in English, symbolised the possibility of cultural freedom, personal image, and better financial situations. Falsification of foreign trademarks was not classified as a formal crime in Lithuanian legislation; therefore, ideological tools were applied to prevent the popularity of these trademarks. The greatest criticism of people wearing clothing with fake trademarks came from the Soviet press, which focused on negative behaviours and materialistic attitudes, as well as a lack of morals. The practice of counterfeit trademarks, inspired by the Western cultural trends, reached Lithuania in the 1960s. By the 1980s, it had significant outcomes in the employment forms and social status of Lithuanian society. The increased demand for garments that met the needs of buyers led to the prosperous activity of homeworkers and sellers in the shadow economy, both in Lithuania and throughout the Soviet Union. The expanded market for selling goods with fake trademarks allowed those engaged in this activity to forego compulsory work in the state sector, secure a good financial standing, and, eventually, apply acquired skills at the beginning of the development of the market economy.

Notes

1. Constitution of the Lithuanian Soviet (1940), 657.
2. Registration Rules of Non-Cooperated Homeworkers and Craftsmen (1949), 35–41.
3. The term 'speculation' in the Soviet context means reselling goods. Speculation in the USSR was considered illegal income and was a criminal offense.
4. Tranavičiūtė, 'Formation and Transformation'.
5. Zubok, *Failed Empire*, 164.
6. Reid, 'Cold War Binaries and the Culture'.
7. Reid, 'This is Tomorrow!' 32–35.
8. The 20th Congress of the Communist Party of the USSR (1956).
9. 'The Youth of the World Marching On'.
10. De Benedeti, 'We Met in the Country of Peace'.
11. Zakharova, 'How and What to Consume', 105.
12. Salisbury, 'To Moscow and Beyond', 238.
13. Amerian, *Fashion Gap*, 65.

14. Smorodinskaya, Romaine-Evarts, and Goscilo, *Encyclopedia of Contemporary Russian Culture*, 184.
15. Zakharova, 'Dior in Moscow', 100.
16. Gronow and Zhuravlev, *Fashion Meets Socialism*, 12, 249–252.
17. Merl, 'Soviet Economy', 35, 62.
18. Lane, *Soviet Society under Perestroika*, 273.
19. Chernyshova, *Soviet Consumer Culture in the Brezhnev Era*, 160.
20. Zhuk, *Rock and Roll in the Rocket City*.
21. Zhuk, 'Détente and Western Cultural Products', 123.
22. Zhuk, 'Closed Soviet Society and the West'.
23. Komsomol was an organization for communist youth in the former Soviet Union.
24. Kuklytė, 'Variety Art and Music Amateur Art', 129.
25. Anušauskas et al. *Lithuania in 1940–1990*, 531–533.
26. Letter by the KGB of the LSSR (1971), LYA, f. K-18, ap. 1, b. 154, l.56.
27. Gorsuch, *All This is Your World*, 79.
28. Report by the Prosecutor of the LSSR (1986), LYA, f. K-6, ap. 2, b. 234, l. 20, 21–22.
29. Ibid.
30. Zhuk, 'Closing and Opening Soviet Society', 133, 137.
31. Tranavičiūtė, 'Economic Activities of Klaipėda Seamen', 59–68.
32. Decree, Regarding the Taxes for Trademarks (1918), 791–792.
33. Resolution, Regarding the Trademarks (1922), Sec. 939.
34. Resolution, Regarding the Trademarks (1962).
35. Regulations Applicable for Trademarks (1974).
36. Grzybowski. *Soviet International Law*, 54.
37. Regulations Applicable for Trademarks (1974).
38. Hober, 'Protection of Foreign Trademarks', 373–376.
39. Cohen and Bauer, 'The New Trademark Law', 397–407.
40. Kučinskas, 'Legal Protection of Industrial Samples', 32.
41. Kudžmienė, 'The Brand'.
42. State Quality Mark was assigned to the Articles of Higher Quality.
43. Bartusevičienė, 'Art of Selling'. 67.
44. Resolution No. 283, Regarding the Approval of Regulations Applicable for Craft and Amateur (1976); USSR Law 'Regarding Individual Work Activity' (1986), 3–15.
45. Razmislevičiūtė, 'What Clothing Is Worn by Evil?'.
46. The Criminal Code of the Lithuanian SSR (1970), Clause 166.
47. Ibid.
48. Notification by the Ministry of Finance (1987). LCVA, f. R-164, ap. 3, b. 739, l. 41–42.
49. Ibid.
50. 'The Market As It Is'.
51. Vainauskienė, and Valiukevičius, 'We and 'Montana'.
52. Sakavičius, 'Wild Power of Things'.
53. Bukinas, 'How to Shut the Genie in the Bottle?'.
54. Regulations Applicable for Trademarks (1974).
55. Notification by the Department of Finance (1987), KAA, f. R-375, ap. 1, b. 1691, l. 71.
56. This was more of a 'tax office'.
57. Notification by the Council of People's Deputies (1988). LCVA, f. R-164, ap. 3, b. 749, l. 9.
58. Reports by the Department of Finance (1988). KAA, f. R-375, ap. 1, b. 1728, l. 181–183.
59. Notification by the Executive Committee (1987). LCVA, f. R-164, ap. 3, b. 739, l. 122.
60. Complaint by O. S. to the Head of the Department of Finance (1988). KAA, f. R-375, ap. 1, b. 1729, l. 44.
61. Ibid.
62. Bukinas, 'How to Shut the Genie in the Bottle?'.
63. Bogušienė, 'Roots of the Crime'.
64. Letter by Kaunas City Branch of the KGB (1989), LYA, f. K-1, ap. b. /n-1, b. 153, l. 52.

65. Tarvydas and Beleckas, 'Chronicles of the Market'.
66. Brazaitienė, 'Barefoot Residents of Kaunas'.
67. Liauškienė, 'A Bludgeon to the Offendee'.

Disclosure statement

No potential conflict of interest was reported by the author.

Primary and secondary sources

The greatest number of archival references is from the Ministry of Finance of the LSSR (R-164), at the Lithuanian Central State Archives (hereafter, LCVA) and from the Department of Finance under the Council of People's Deputies of Kaunas (R-375), at Kaunas County Archives (hereafter, KAA). This represents the activities of self-employed persons engaged in individual work or craft business, violations, etc. These references make a significant contribution to the study of the problematic issues with respect to fake foreign trademarks. The article also refers to documents of the KGB (State Security Committee) Investigation Department (f. K-6), under the Prosecutor's Office of the Lithuanian SSR, at the Lithuanian Special Archives (hereafter, LYA). These files contain information on tourism of citizens of Soviet Lithuania. A range of the Soviet law references, including legislation regulating the individual work activity of persons, issues of trademarks, and so on, has been reviewed. The Soviet press has been cited to illustrate the Soviet ideological tools targeted at those who propagated the principles of consumption (as incompatible with Soviet ideology). These include, among others, the publications *Komunistas* (Communist), *Komjaunimo tiesa* (Truth of Komsomol), *Vakarinės naujienos* (Evening News), *Švyturys* (Lighthouse), and *Jaunimo gretos* (Ranks of Youth).

References

Amerian, S. M. "The Fashion Gap: The Cold War Politics of American and Soviet Fashion, 1945-1959." *Journal of Historical Research in Marketing* 8, no. 1 (2016): 65–82. doi:10.1108/JHRM-07-2015-0025.
Anušauskas, A., J. Banionis, Č. Bauža, V. Brandišauskas, A. Bubnys, A. Jakubčionis, L. Jonušauskas, et al. *Lithuania in 1940–1990: The History of Occupied Lithuania*. Vilnius: Genocide and Resistance Research Centre of Lithuania, 2005.
Bartusevičienė, B. 1983. "The Art of Selling." *Komunistas*, no. 8.
Bogušienė, V. 1986. "The Roots of the Crime: Greed and Disorder." *Tiesa*, June 11.
Brazaitienė, R. 1991. "Barefoot Residents of Kaunas. Daily." *Kauno tiesa*, March 6.
Bukinas, E. 1982. "How to Shut the Genie in the Bottle?" *Švyturys'*, no. 12.
Chernyshova, N. *Soviet Consumer Culture in the Brezhnev Era*. London: Routledge, 2013.
Cohen, Johnathan, and Serge Bauer. "The New Trademark Law in the Soviet Union." *Trademark Reporter* 81, no. 4 (1991): 397–407.
Complaint by O. S. to the Head of the Department of Finance of the Executive Committee of the Council of People's Deputies. 23 March 1988, f. R-375, ap. 1, b. 1729, l. 44. KAA, Kaunas.
"Constitution of the Lithuanian Soviet Socialist Republic (Basic Law) as of 25 August 1940." *Vyriausybės žinios* (Official Gazette), 10 September 1940, no. 730, 657.
De Benedeti, A. 1957. "We Met in the Country of Peace: I Think This Way!" *Jaunimo gretos'*, no. 10.
Decree, Regarding the Taxes for Trademarks, adopted by the Council of People's Commissars of the RSFSR on 15 August 1918. Digest of the Resolutions of the Government of 1917–1918. Management Board of the Council of People's Commissars of the USSR, 1942.
Gorsuch, E. A. *All this is your WorldSoviet Tourism at Home and Abroad after Stalin*. New York: Oxford University Press, 2011.
Gronow, J., and S. Zhuravlev. *Fashion Meets Socialism: Fashion Industry in the Soviet Union after the Second World War*. Helsinki: Finnish Literature Society, 2015.

Grzybowski, K. *Soviet International Law and the World Economic Order*. Durham: Duke University Press, 1987.

Hober, C. "Protection of Foreign Trademark in the Soviet Union." *Texas International Law Journal* 14 (1979): 367–388.

Kučinskas, L. "Legal Protection of Industrial Samples and Trademarks." *Socialistinė teisė* 4 (1977): 29–34.

Kudžmienė, A. 1974. "The Brand." *Mokslas ir technika*, no. 9.

Kuklytė. "Variety Art and Music Amateur Art in Soviet Lithuania at the Joint of the 1970s and 1980s: Development of Alternative Forms and the Last Dictate." *Lietuvos istorijos studijos* 29 (2012): 127–141. doi:10.15388/LIS.2012.0.7447.

Lane, D. *Soviet Society under Perestroika*. London: Routledge, 2002.

Letter by Kaunas City Branch of the KGB of the LSSR to the Head of the Board No. 2 with Respect to the Situation of Criminal Crimes. 3 August 1989, f. K-1, ap. b. /n-1, b. 153, l. 52. LYA, Vilnius.

Letter by the KGB of the LSSR on the Activity of the Kaunas City Branch of the KGB in 1961–1971. 15 November 1971, f. K-18, ap. 1, b. 154, l.56. LYA, Vilnius.

Liauškienė, A. 1993. "A Bludgeon to the Offendee or a Few Thoughts about the Trademarks of Famous Firms on Lithuanian Stuff." *Veidas*, no. 19.

Merl, S. "The Soviet Economy in the 1970s: Reflections on the Relationship between Socialist Modernity, Crisis and the Administrative Command Economy." In *The Crisis of Socialist Modernity: The Soviet Union and Yugoslavia in the 1970s*, edited by Marie-Janine Calic, Dietmar Neutatz, and Julia Obertreis, 28–65. Göttingen: Vandenhoeck & Ruprecht GmbH & Co, 2011.

Notification by the Council of People's Deputies of Brest City, Regarding Individual Work Activity, to the Ministry of Finance of the LSSR. 19 January 1988, f. R-164, ap. 3, b. 749, l. 9. LCVA, Vilnius.

Notification by the Department of Finance of the Executive Committee of the Council of People's Deputies of Kaunas City, Regarding the Violations of the Procedure of Individual Work Activity, to Financial Departments of Executive Committees of Leninas, Požėla and Panemunė Districts of Kaunas City. 10 October 1987, f. R-375, ap. 1, b. 1691, l. 71. KAA, Kaunas.

Notification by the Executive Committee of the Council of People's Deputies of Baranovichi Town to the Ministry of Finance of the LSSR. 7 December 1987, f. R-164, ap. 3, b. 739, l. 122. LCVA, Vilnius.

Notification by the Ministry of Finance, Ministry of the Interior and Prosecutor's Office of the LSSR to the Departments of Finance and of the Interior of the Executive Committees of Cities, Towns and Districts and to the Prosecutors of Cities, Towns and Districts. 3 November 1987. LCVA, f. R-164, ap. 3, b. 739, l. 41–42.

Razmislevičiūtė, R. 1983. "What Clothing Is Worn by Evil?" *Komjaunimo tiesa*, January 4.

Regulations Applicable for Trademarks. State Committee for Inventions and Discoveries of the Council of Ministers of the USSR. Accessed January 8, 1974. https://docs.cntd.ru/document/600299

Registration Rules of Non-Cooperated Homeworkers and Craftsmen as of 30 June 1949, No. 2883, f. R-164, ap. 20, b. 39, l. 35-41. LCVA, Vilnius.

Reid, E. S. "Cold War Binaries and The Culture of Consumption in The Late Soviet Home." *Journal of Historical Research in Marketing* 8, no. 1 (2016): 17–43. doi:10.1108/JHRM-09-2015-0038.

Reid, E. S. "This is Tomorrow! Becoming a Consumer in the Soviet Sixties." In *The Socialist Sixties: Crossing Borders in the Second World*, edited by Anne E. Gorsuch and Diane P. Koenker, 25–65. Bloomington: Indiana University Press, 2013.

Resolution No. 283, Regarding the Approval of Regulations Applicable for Craft and Amateur Businesses of Citizens, adopted by the Council of Ministers of the USSR. Lietuvos TSR Aukščiausiosios Tarybos ir Vyriausybės žinios (Official Gazette), as of 3 May 1976, No. 18–158. See also USSR Law No. XI-6050, Regarding Individual Work Activity. Individual Work Activity and Operation of Cooperatives: Digest of Laws as of 19 November 1986. Vilnius, 1988, 3–15.

Resolution, Regarding the Trademarks, adopted by the Council of Ministers of the USSR. Classified Compilation of the Laws Applicable in the Lithuanian SSR No. 11, as of 15 May 1962. Vilnius: Mintis, 1977.

Reports by the Department of Finance of the Council of People's Deputies of Krasnodar City. 16 February 1988, f. R-375, ap. 1, b. 1728, l. 181–183. KAA, Kaunas.

Report by the Prosecutor of the LSSR, State Counsellor of Justice of Class 2. 30 September 1986, f. K-6, ap. 2, b. 234, l. 20, 21–22. LYA, Vilnius.

Resolution, Regarding the Trademarks, adopted by the Council of People's Commissars of the RSFSR on 10 November 1922. SU RSFSR, 1922, No. 75, Section 939.

Sakavičius, M. 1987. "The Wild Power of Things." *Komjaunimo tiesa*, September 11.

Salisbury, E. H. "To Moscow and Beyond." In *Cold War in the Kitchen: Gender and the de-Stalinization of Consumer Taste in the Soviet Union under Khrushchev*, edited by E. S. Reid, special issue, Slavic Review 61, no. 2, 211–252, 2002.

Smorodinskaya, T., K. Romaine-Evarts, and H. Goscilo, eds. *Encyclopedia of Contemporary Russian Culture*. London: Routledge, 2007.

Tarvydas, R., and S. Beleckas. 1989. "Chronicles of the Market." *Jaunimo gretos*, no. 12.

The 20th Congress of the Communist Party of the USSR. 14–15 February 1956. Stenographic Report, vol 2. Moscow, 1956.

The Criminal Code of the Lithuanian SSR. *Clause 166*. Vilnius: Mintis, 1970.

Tranavičiūtė, B. "Economic Activities of Klaipėda Seamen in the Context of Soviet Entrepreneurship in the 1970s–1980s." *History: A Collection of Lithuanian Universities Research Papers* 92, no. 4 (2013): 59–68.

Tranavičiūtė, B. "Formation and Transformation of Entrepreneurship and Entrepreneurial Society in Kaunas in 1960–1990." PhD diss., Vytautas Magnus University, 2015.

USSR Law No. XI-6050, Regarding Individual Work Activity'. Individual Work Activity and Operation of Cooperatives: Digest of Laws as of 19 November 1986. Vilnius, 1988, 3–15.

Vainauskienė, B., and V. Valiukevičius. "We and 'Montana.'" *Komjaunimo tiesa*, May 14, 1988.

Zakharova, L. "Dior in Moscow: A Taste for Luxury in Soviet Fashion under Khrushchev." In *Pleasures in Socialism: Leisure and Luxury in the Eastern Bloc*, edited by David Crowley and Susan E. Reid, 95–120. Evanston, IL: Northwestern University Press, 2010.

Zakharova, L. "How and What to Consume: Patterns of Soviet Clothing Consumption in the 1950s and 1960s." In *Communism and Consumerism*. 7 vols., edited by Timo Vihavainen and Elena Bogdanova, 85–112. Leiden: Brill, 2015.

Zhuk, I. S. *Rock and Roll in the Rocket City: The West, Identity, and Ideology in Soviet Dniepropetrovsk, 1960–1985*. Baltimore, MD: Johns Hopkins University Press, 2010.

Zhuk, I. S. "'Closing and Opening Soviet Society'. Introduction to the Symposium: Closed City, Closed Economy, Closed Society: The Utopian Normalization of Autarky." *Ab Imperio* 2 (2011): 123–158.

Zhuk, I. S. "Détente and Western Cultural Products in Soviet Ukraine during the 1970s." In *Youth and Rock in the Soviet Bloc: Youth Cultures, Music, and the State in Russia and Eastern Europe*, edited by William J Risch, 117–151. Lanham, MD: Lexington Books, 2014.

Zhuk, I. S. "The Closed Soviet Society and the West: Consumption of the Western Cultural Products, Youth and Identity in Soviet Ukraine during the 1970s." In *In The Crisis of Socialist Modernity: The Soviet Union and Yugoslavia in the 1970s*, edited by Marie-Janine Calic, Dietmar Neutatz, and Julia Obertreis, 87–117. Göttingen: Vandenhoeck & Ruprecht GmbH & Co., 2011.

Zubok, V. M. *A Failed Empire: The Soviet Union in the Cold War from Stalin to Gorbachev*. Chapel Hill: University of North Carolina Press, 2007.

Index

Note: Figures are indicated by *italics*. Tables are indicated by **bold**. Endnotes are indicated by the page number followed by 'n' and the footnote number e.g., 20n1 refers to footnote 1 on page 20.

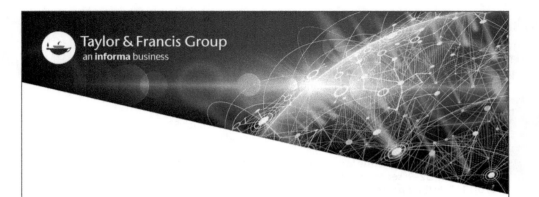

Taylor & Francis eBooks

www.taylorfrancis.com

A single destination for eBooks from Taylor & Francis
with increased functionality and an improved user
experience to meet the needs of our customers.

90,000+ eBooks of award-winning academic content in
Humanities, Social Science, Science, Technology, Engineering,
and Medical written by a global network of editors and authors.

TAYLOR & FRANCIS EBOOKS OFFERS:

A streamlined
experience for
our library
customers

A single point
of discovery
for all of our
eBook content

Improved
search and
discovery of
content at both
book and
chapter level

REQUEST A FREE TRIAL
support@taylorfrancis.com

Printed in the USA
CPSIA information can be obtained
at www.ICGtesting.com
LVHW081535150324
774517LV00042B/1815